Dictionary of Developmental Disabilities Terminology

Dictionary of Developmental Disabilities Terminology

by

Pasquale J. Accardo, M.D.

Barbara Y. Whitman, M.S.W., Ph.D.

with

Carla Laszewski, M.S.W., L.C.S.W.

Carol A. Haake, Ed.D.

Jill D. Morrow, M.D.

Illustrations by Tony Stubblefield

·P·A·U·L·H·
BROOKES
PUBLISHING CO.

Baltimore • London • Toronto • Sydney

Paul H. Brookes Publishing Co.
Post Office Box 10624
Baltimore, Maryland 21285-0624

Typeset by Brushwood Graphics, Inc., Baltimore, Maryland.
Manufactured in the United States of America by
The Maple Press Co., York, Pennsylvania.

Library of Congress Cataloging-in-Publication Data
Accardo, Pasquale J.
    Dictionary of developmental disabilities terminology / by Pasquale J. Accardo and
Barbara Y. Whitman ; with Carla Laszewski, Carol Haake, and Jill Morrow ; illustrated
by Tony Stubblefield.
        p.   cm.
    Includes bibliographical references.
    ISBN 1-55766-245-2 (hc). — ISBN 1-55766-112-X (pc)
    1. Child development deviations—Dictionaries.   2. Developmental disabilities—
Dictionaries.   3. Developmentally disabled children—Dictionaries.   I. Whitman,
Barbara Y.   II. Title.
RJ135.A26   1996
618.92'85889003—dc20
                                                                                        95-47373
                                                                                        CIP

British Library Cataloguing-in-Publication data are available from the British Library.

This book is dedicated to those families
in which we learned our first words.

Preface

"I am not the sort of precisian who prefers conveying correctly what he doesn't mean, rather than conveying incorrectly what he does. I am totally indifferent to the term as compared to the meaning."

G. K. Chesterton
The Outline of Sanity (1926)

"Ignorance of the mechanics of definition has encouraged too much defining."

Bernard Dupriez

"The dictionary is nothing but a lot of words."

Samuel Goldwyn
(1884–1974)

"All donkeys love big words."

L. Frank Baum
The Road to Oz

"There is, in fact, no formal difference between inability to define and stupidity."

Robert Pirsig
Zen and the Art of Motorcycle Maintenance

This work is intended to be of use to professionals and students involved directly or indirectly in the transdisciplinary diagnosis and management of people with developmental disorders. The authors have attempted to define the terms in this volume in English as plain as is compatible with retaining the meaning of the more commonly used technical terms peculiar to the wide variety of professions associated with developmental disabilities. The developmental disorders that are the subject of this book include mental retardation, cerebral palsy, neurologically based specific learning disabilities, autistic spectrum disorders, attention-deficit/ hyperactivity disorder, language and communication disorders, genetic disorders and malformation syndromes, neurosurgical problems, and the associated disorders of epilepsy and of vision and hearing. Chronic diseases not of a neurodevelopmental nature have not been routinely included.

Terminology addressed herein has been taken from the fields of pediatrics, anatomy, genetics, orthopedics, neurology, neurosurgery, pathology, pharmacology, physiology, psychiatry, psychology, education, social work, family therapy, law, speech-language pathology, linguistics, audiology, physical therapy, occupational therapy, and nutrition. These terms represent signs, symptoms, syndromes, diagnoses, intervention modalities, theories, medications, eponyms, acronyms, organizations, tests, instruments, and even lay descriptors. The most common form (noun/adjective, acronym/eponym) that is likely to be encountered provides the primary entry; (near) synonymous terms are cross-referenced.

To undergird the transdisciplinary base on which this volume was conceptualized, authors were not simply assigned terms from their area of professional expertise; instead each author defined a selection of terms that crossed disciplinary boundaries. The criteria for inclusion of items have been the subject of continued discussion among the authors, although the two senior authors assume responsibility for the final revision of the text.

A standard medical dictionary typically contains 2,000 double-column pages, and all of its entries might be used to describe some aspect of the health status of a person with a developmental disability. The authors of this volume have restricted their selection to terms with more direct relevance to neurodevelopmental disorders, but they have also tried to explicate the implications of using the terms with regard to developmental disabilities. In addition, some unrelated technical terms that might be easily confused with those having a developmental implication have been included for the purpose of clarification.

Medical terms have been allocated a larger percentage of the total number of entries. This is a reflection of the much longer history that lies behind medical terminology and the evolution of medicine into the numerous strands of high-technology subspecialization. Western scientific medicine has its deepest roots in the Greco-Roman world in which the classic texts for almost 2 millennia were written in Latin and discussed with Greek terminology. In contrast, many terms in nonmedical fields have their origins later than the Romance languages and employ words with a nontechnical or common-sense denotation. This historical contrast should receive neither a positive nor a negative connotation.

Because of their cumulative impact on our understanding of developmental disabilities, terms relating to the pediatric age group have been given greater representation than those for other age ranges. The lengths of the entries bear some relation either to their importance or to the difficulty of defining the specific term; if some lengths appear unduly short, the authors welcome suggestions from readers for helpful expansions.

The brief descriptions of medical syndromes give only key findings; the differential diagnoses of specific signs and symptoms are not intended to be exhaustive but only suggestive. It should be noted that for many items described as "syndromes" nothing approaching the cohesive data available on an entity such as Down syndrome is possible; many such "syndromes" are little more than loose collections of signs or symptoms. No attempt has been made in this work to correct this rather informal approach to the usage of the word "syndrome"; such flexibility has contributed in the past to the growth of medical knowledge. Included with entries that are recognized syndromes, medical and other types of treatment have not been covered in detail. A focus on such intervention really must be considered as beyond the scope of a dictionary. It is impossible to address treatment to the extent that it deserves in a book of this type; a dictionary is of its nature oriented to definitional issues and not to discursive questions. The occasional references to therapeutic modalities should not be taken as anything more than anecdotal. Improved techniques of prenatal diagnoses and the daily identification of specific gene loci are both proceeding at such an accelerated pace that all suggestions of their absence should be interpreted as possibly dated by the time of publication. When an incidence rate is not reported, the syndrome can be considered to be extremely rare.

With regard to tests, selection and abbreviation were necessary if this volume were not to grow beyond all reasonable boundaries. Tests that are used most frequently by clinicians working with children and adults with developmental disabilities have been given somewhat more extensive coverage. Questions of test standardization, reliability, and validity must unfortunately be considered as beyond the scope of a dictionary. Many tests that have excellent quantitative statistics for their reliability and validity have nevertheless never been adequately standardized on either the general population or on the subpopulation of people with disabilities for whom the specific instruments might be recommended or under consideration for usage. There are, however, tests in common usage with relatively incomplete or poor standardization that with appropriate clinical judgment can be quite helpful in specific assessment situations. A generic statement that information on standardization, validity, and reliability can be found in the test manual would convey little additional meaning; any attempt to critically summarize the more complex statistics on the psychometric properties of tests seems inappropriate for a dictionary. The entries on tests in this dictionary should not be taken as supporting any claims by test publishers and users that the specific instruments actually measure definable traits in certain individuals. Similarly, addresses of instrument distributors are also inappropriate; readers interested in further information on tests referred to in this volume should consult the standard textbooks on test psychology. What this dictionary is expected to provide such readers includes the nature of the test and what it purports to measure.

The brevity of several of the test entries reflects a variety of contributing factors that include very little objective material available either as published for general information or available to this volume's authors in particular. The authors have taken the liberty to include brief references to many instruments that they have never seen and would most probably never consider using. The purpose of such entries is to give the reader at least minimal data for the interpretation of references to such instruments in either case reports or the literature. Again, it should be parenthetically noted that the term "test" in its medical usage exhibits a wide variety of meaning, ranging from laboratory procedures that have a scientific accuracy beyond any obtainable by behavioral measures to the looser usage that places "test" in the same word family as "sign."

A few professional and family-oriented disability associations have been included, but this has not been an area of primary focus in this first edition. Consideration will be given to expanding this category of entries in the next edition. Similarly, biographical references have been restricted to people whose names have become synonymous with an approach to treatment, a sign or syndrome, a developmental theory, an operation, a test, or other procedure. Entries of purely historical interest have been severely limited, although somewhat antiquated technical terms have been included for the simple reason that professionals working with older children and adults with disabilities may have access to and need to review and interpret records that still employ such terms. Alternatively, older terms that are not in current usage but that might readily be found in the past records of living patients have been included.

This volume was first conceived as a glossary to *Developmental Disabilities in Infancy and Childhood*, edited by Arnold J. Capute and Pasquale J. Accardo, but both works quickly outgrew any possibility of combination. This volume was also in preparation at the same time as the manual *The Infant Neurodevelopmental Assessment* was being coauthored by Arnold J. Capute and Pasquale J. Accardo. It is for this reason that a number of the illustrations by Tony Stubblefield (Department of Design and Illustration of St. Louis University Health Sciences Center) appear in both volumes. The radiographs printed in this volume were supplied by Dr. E. Richard Graviss (Department of Diagnostic Imaging, Professor of Pediatrics, Professor of Radiology, St. Louis University School of Medicine), and the chromosomal plates shown herein were provided by Dr. Jacqueline R. Batanian (Assistant Professor of Pediatrics and Pathology, St. Louis University School of Medicine, and Director of Molecular Cytogenetics Laboratory, Cardinal Glennon Children's Hospital); the authors extend their gratitude to Dr. Graviss and Dr. Batanian. During the 5 years of circulating definition cards for comments and criticism, the contributions of the five coauthors have evolved. The two senior authors assume full responsibility for the final text, while expressing their gratitude to the tireless efforts of Kathy L. Boyd and the editorial staff at Paul H. Brookes Publishing Co. for their constant flow of ideas and supportive criticism. As with previous books that have evolved at the Knights of Columbus Developmental Center since the 1980s, the preparation of this volume was supported by Columbian Charities of Missouri and the Knights of Columbus of Missouri and Illinois.

With no small degree of irony it has been suggested that all professions are conspiracies against the laity. Technical jargon is the linchpin for many of these pseudoconspiracies. The highly specialized vocabulary that provides many useful shortcuts for the trained professional in a given discipline becomes an insurmountable barrier to communication for the beginning student, for the professional in an unrelated discipline, and, of course, for the parent of a child with a developmental disability. Over the past half century, the field of developmental disabilities has evolved from unidisciplinary through multidisciplinary and interdisciplinary to transdisciplinary. The present volume is a first attempt at a transdisciplinary dictionary. There has been no attempt to be encyclopedic. The references appended were of assistance in at least several of our definitions. They should be of help in further clarifying relevant terms. Many other sources were used for individual items. The authors welcome suggestions for the improvement of future editions.

Pasquale J. Accardo

Contents

About the Authors

Pasquale J. Accardo, M.D., Professor of Pediatrics, St. Louis University School of Medicine, Medical Director, Knights of Columbus Developmental Center, Cardinal Glennon Children's Hospital, St. Louis, Missouri 63104

Dr. Accardo is Professor of Pediatrics at the St. Louis University School of Medicine and, since 1980, has directed the Knights of Columbus Developmental Center at Cardinal Glennon Children's Hospital in St. Louis, Missouri. Dr. Accardo attended medical school at the State University of New York, Downstate Medical Center in Brooklyn, New York. He obtained his training in pediatrics at Riley Children's Hospital in Indianapolis, Indiana, and his neurodevelopmental disabilities training at the John F. Kennedy Institute of The Johns Hopkins Medical Institutions in Baltimore, Maryland. His more than 200 publications cover the entire spectrum of developmental disabilities as well as his interests in Sherlock Holmes and G.K. Chesterton.

Barbara Y. Whitman, M.S.W., Ph.D., Associate Professor of Pediatrics, St. Louis University School of Medicine, Director of Family Services, Knights of Columbus Developmental Center, Cardinal Glennon Children's Hospital, St. Louis, Missouri 63104

Dr. Whitman is Associate Professor of Pediatrics at St. Louis University School of Medicine and Assistant Director of the Knights of Columbus Developmental Center at Cardinal Glennon Children's Hospital. Dr. Whitman obtained her master of social work and doctoral degrees at Washington University in St. Louis, and completed a postdoctoral fellowship in psychiatric epidemiology at Washington University School of Medicine. She completed additional postdoctoral training in family therapy at the Menninger Clinic. Dr. Whitman has published extensively in the areas of parents with mental retardation, Prader-Willi syndrome, and attention deficit disorders.

Carla Laszewski, M.S.W., L.C.S.W., Medical Social Consultant, Cardinal Glennon Children's Hospital, St. Louis, Missouri 63104

Ms. Laszewski joined the staff of the Knights of Columbus Developmental Center at Cardinal Glennon Children's Hospital in 1987, and from 1988 to 1993 evaluated and counseled children with learning and behavioral difficulties and their families. She is providing evaluative and therapeutic services to children and adolescents with emotional and behavioral problems at Cardinal Glennon Children's Hospital, Department of Child and Adolescent Psychiatry.

Carol A. Haake, Ed.D., Assistant Professor of Pediatrics, St. Louis University School of Medicine, Director of Special Education, Knights of Columbus Developmental Center, Cardinal Glennon Children's Hospital, St. Louis, Missouri 63104

Dr. Haake is Director of Special Education at the Knights of Columbus Developmental Center of the Cardinal Glennon Children's Hospital and is Assistant Professor of Pediatrics at St. Louis University School of Medicine. She has been a member of the speakers' bureau for the hospital and has been active in the Learning Disabilities Association. She is President of the St. Louis affiliate of the Learning Disabilities Association.

Jill D. Morrow, M.D., Director of Developmental Pediatrics, Polyclinic Medical Center, Harrisburg, Pennsylvania 17110

Dr. Morrow is Director of Developmental Pediatrics at Polyclinic Medical Center in Harrisburg, Pennsylvania. She provides subspecialty care for children with a variety of developmental and physical disabilities, directs multidisciplinary teams treating attention and learning disabilities and providing neonatal follow-up, and is a developmental consultant to the regional lead poisoning program. She acts as medical adviser to a number of early intervention programs and provides consultative services at the county level. Dr. Morrow represents the Pennsylvania chapter of the American Academy of Pediatrics on the State Interagency Coordinating Council. Dr. Morrow completed her fellowship in developmental pediatrics at the Knights of Columbus Developmental Center at St. Louis University School of Medicine. Her research interests include behavioral and cognitive development in children with lead poisoning and language development in young children.

Guide to
the Dictionary

The following sample entries from this volume are provided to highlight the various features of the *Dictionary of Developmental Disabilities Terminology*; many of these features are elaborated upon in the pages that follow.

acronym as headword

cross-reference to full name of acronym

AAC   *See* Augmentative and alternative communication; *see also* augmentative communication.

head-words

athetosis   Literally, "without position"; in motor disabilities, a pattern of movement disorder characterized by involuntary, slow, writhing, and undulating movements of flexion, extension, pronation, and supination—more peripheral than central, sometimes called vermicular or wormlike. When the associated motor delay is serious, the type of extrapyramidal cerebral palsy present is usually described as choreoathetoid. More purely athetoid movements are slower and more sustained than choreiform (involuntary twitching) movements. *See also* choreoathetosis.

specific cross-reference

parenthetical clarification

life dates (given for deceased)

auxology   The study or science of (human) growth. The term was introduced by Paul Godin (1860–1935) in 1919 and was popularized by J.M. Tanner in the 1970s to refer to the whole subject of physical and physiological growth and development.

no life dates (not given for living)

PL   *See specific* Public Law *entries.*——nonspecific cross-reference

port-wine stain   Purple, sometimes raised, and irregular skin lesion; can be a component of Sturge-Weber syndrome. Also known as *nevus flammeus.*

synonym

xv

ENTRY SELECTION

The first, and the major, criterion for the selection of an entry in this volume was the likely occurrence of the term in a discipline evaluation or multidisciplinary team report on a person with a developmental disability. The second criterion for entry selection was the probability that the term might not make immediate sense to a reader of such a report whose training was in a different discipline from that of the author of a given section of the report. The goal in defining the selected entries was to provide sufficient information for the term to be intelligible in context. Exactly how much information would then be needed was the subject of continuing discussion among all of the authors of the dictionary. Unlike most dictionaries, this volume does not attempt to define exhaustively all terms in the field of developmental disabilities; those that would be considered obvious to everyone (even if they are the subject of much debate [e.g., **intelligence**]) have received less attention. Textbooks remain the major source for the student or novice to locate extensive information. Expanding on these original selection criteria, other terms were added to the volume that might not readily appear in a patient/client report but that would help in the understanding of terms that do. Thus, this volume is not intended to be a combined glossary for a variety of disciplines; rather it is a working clinical tool.

MULTIPLE DEFINITIONS

When a single term has different connotations, it may be described continuously, as part of the same entry (e.g., **embryo**). When, however, meanings or uses of a term are sufficiently distinct and originate from different disciplines with little or no relationship, two separate contiguous definition entries are provided (e.g., **accommodation, discipline, information processing**).

EPONYMS

Eponymous terms ending in syndrome, disease, or sign are presented without the possessive's (e.g., **Down syndrome, Hirschsprung disease, Macewen sign**).

ACRONYMS

Entries are provided for the most commonly used acronyms. Such acronyms are especially likely to appear in professional reports. This alphabet soup includes both formally recognized acronyms (e.g., **WISC–III, NIH**) as well as ones that could be considered jargon (e.g., **BK, KUB**).

ALPHABETICAL ORDER

The entries are alphabetized in telephone-book style: word by word, including spaces and hyphens.

day care   Education of the Handicapped Act Amendments of 1990
day hospital   (PL 101-476)
daydream   educational sign systems

The alphabetization is alphanumeric: Numbers are positioned as if they were spelled-out numerals. Compound headwords are given in their most common usage form; this is indicated by cross-references, when appropriate. Terms with multiple entries are alphabetized in dictionary style with the first word of the definition acting as the headword.

CROSS-REFERENCING

Throughout this volume, cross-referencing has been used minimally. Its primary purposes are to assist readers in locating the full name of a word or term that has come to be known by its acronym (e.g., **IEP** to **individualized education program**), in identifying the full and correct name of a public law (e.g., **PL 94-142** to **Education for All Handicapped Children Act of 1975**), and in finding entries that provide significantly fuller information in a place where the reader might be unlikely to look for it (e.g., under **emotion**, *see also* **affect**).

TYPES OF ENTRIES

Although not all synonyms are cross-referenced and defined, an attempt has been made to include with entries every possible synonym or related usage.

Medical syndrome and disease entries give synonyms, major diagnostic findings, associated findings, incidence, and genetics or other etiology (if known). Medical syndromes were selected as entries specifically because of the presence of associated neurodevelopmental findings, such as mental retardation, learning disabilities, autism, communication disorders, and impairments of vision and hearing. Occasionally, a syndrome without any associated neurodevelopmental association is included because the condition is frequently mistaken to have such an associated disability. An entry's length generally otherwise tends to vary in direct proportion with its frequency and importance. Also included occasionally are very rare conditions about which it is difficult to find information in standard general textbooks; these conditions have been given more detailed consideration herein.

Information provided with test entries includes the type of test (e.g., group or individual, oral or written) and the purpose of the test (e.g., to assess cognitive, language, or writing skills). For the more widely used instruments, details on scoring, subscore breakdown, and interpretation are given. Administration format is sometimes noted. For less widely used tests, less information is provided.

Individual people are listed as entries when their names are synonymous with a theory, an approach, or other major development in the field of neurodevelopmental disabilities. The rule of thumb here has been to be quite restrictive. Life dates are given for people who are deceased but not for living people.

MENTAL RETARDATION TERMINOLOGY

This work utilizes the 1983 system for classification of mental retardation (Grossman, 1983) rather than the newer one (Luckasson et al., 1992). The decision to use the older system was based on the fact that the bulk of the scientific literature in print and the majority of patient/client records extant utilize the 1983 terminology. A dictionary's purpose is to explain the meaning of words that may be unfamiliar to a person encountering them. If one were to review the records of an adult client with mental retardation and to read a report that characterized this person as being moderately mentally retarded in childhood, it would be helpful to know what was meant by "moderately mentally retarded" even if one used a different classification schema. Many older (antiquated and sometimes even objectionable) terms for developmental disabilities have been included for a similar reason. One does not change history by rewriting the past à la George Orwell but by writing the future.

PARENTHETICAL CLARIFICATION

Brief parenthetical definitions are provided within entries as short reminders for the reader. For most of the terms so parenthetically defined, fuller and more technically accurate definitions are provided under the entry corresponding to that term.

Dictionary of
Developmental Disabilities
Terminology

A

AAC *See* achievement ability comparison.

AAC *See* Augmentative and alternative communication; *see also* augmentative communication.

AACPDM *See* American Academy for Cerebral Palsy and Developmental Medicine.

AAMFT *See* American Association of Marital and Family Therapy.

AAMR *See* American Association on Mental Retardation.

AAMR Adaptive Behavior Scales–School, Second Edition (ABS–S:2) A behavior rating scale that evaluates the adaptive potential of children with behavior disorders; ABS–S:2 evaluates coping skills in nine behavioral domains and examines social maladaptations in seven domains to help differentiate and diagnose children manifesting adaptive behavior problems, those requiring special educational assistance, and those who can manage in a general classroom.

AAP *See* American Academy of Pediatrics.

AAPEP *See* Adolescent and Adult Psychoeducational Profile.

Aarskog-Scott syndrome A rare genetic syndrome in males that combines ocular hypertelorism (widely spaced eyes), a widow's peak, brachydactyly (short fingers), shawl scrotum (scrotum forms a fold around the dorsum, or top, of the penis), cryptorchidism (undescended testes), and later growth retardation. Most of these children have normal intelligence, but mild mental retardation and learning disabilities occur more often than in the general population. Inheritance is believed to be X-linked semidominant in males, with partial expression in carrier females. Treatment includes symptomatic treatment of the growth parameters and cryptorchidism, and genetic counseling.

AAUAP *See* American Association of University Affiliated Programs for Persons with Developmental Disabilities.

abasia An inability to walk despite the presence of normal motor strength and coordination. This neurological finding can be observed in typically developing infants from 7 to 8 months of age. Prior to that time, the infant may go through the motions of (supported) walking on a reflex basis; after that time, independent walking begins to emerge. Physiologically, abasia follows astasia (inability to stand due to lack of motor coordination).

ABC inventory A brief screening test (approximately 15-minute administration time) for children between 3½ and 6½ years of age; it assesses fine motor, academic, and language areas.

abducent nerve The sixth cranial nerve; cranial nerve VI innervates the muscle that abducts the eye (turns it outward); damage to this nerve causes diplopia (double vision) and strabismus (squint) with a tendency for the eye to deviate nasally.

abducent palsy Paralysis of the sixth cranial nerve leading to an internal strabismus (esotropia) that occurs with fever, increased pressure within the skull, or brain-stem tumors.

abduction Sideways movement of an extremity (arm or leg) away from the midline of the body.

Abecedarian Project A model North Carolina preschool and school-age educational program to minimize school failure among rural African-American children of parents with borderline intelligence.

aberrant behavior Behavior that deviates markedly from what is considered typical.

Aberrant Behavior Checklist A 58-item behavioral scale to measure the effect of drugs and other therapeutic interventions on individuals with moderate to profound mental retardation. Its five subscales are irritability, lethargy/withdrawal, stereotypic behavior, hyperactivity/noncompliance, and inappropriate speech.

abetalipoproteinemia Bassen-Kornzweig disease; a genetic disorder that combines intestinal malabsorption, progressive ataxia (unsteady gait), mental retardation, acanthocytes (burr-shaped red blood cells) in the blood, and retinitis pigmentosa (night blindness and progressively restricted visual field). High doses of vitamin E stop the progression of the neurological syndrome. Inheritance is autosomal recessive.

ability A quality that enables an individual to perform an act, solve a problem, or make an adjustment. Ability refers to potential performance or whether an individual can act in a specified manner or demonstrate certain skills or knowledge at a given time. This can originate from inherited traits, previous learning, or a combination of both. Intelligence tests are assumed to be tests of ability.

ablation Removal; eradication.

able Competent; sometimes used to refer to gifted children.

above elbow (AE) An anatomical term used to describe the location of an amputation, either congenital or acquired.

above knee (AK) An anatomical term used to describe the location of an amputation, either congenital or acquired.

ABR Auditory brain-stem response; *see* brain-stem auditory-evoked response.

abruptio placenta The premature detachment (abruption, tearing away) of the placenta (which, among its other functions, acts as the baby's lungs for its oxygen supply) before the baby is born and can breathe independently. Abruption is accompanied by severe bleeding and represents a significant risk to both the mother and baby. In the normal delivery process, after the baby has been born, the placenta separates spontaneously and a hormonally mediated process prevents severe maternal hemorrhage (bleeding).

absence seizure Transient loss of consciousness lasting up to 30 seconds and a diagnostic electroencephalogram (EEG) pattern of a 3-per-second spike wave. Such seizures are most common after the age of 5 years and often disappear at puberty. Absence seizures are more common in girls. Children with such staring spells rarely have impairment of intellectual function. Daydreaming in children with attention-deficit/hyperactivity disorder (ADHD) may be misinterpreted as absence seizures.

ABS–S:2 *See* AAMR Adaptive Behavior Scales–School, Second Edition.

Academy of Certified Social Workers (A.C.S.W.) A recognition of practice competence conferred by the National Association of Social Workers (NASW) to social workers who meet several academic and practice standards. These include a Master of Social Work degree or better, 2 or more years of supervised practice, and successful completion of a competency examination. According to the professional standards of the NASW, a social worker cannot practice independently prior to reaching this level of certification. Evidence of this attainment should be readily visible to anyone seeking services.

acataleptic Antiquated term for an individual with mental retardation.

accent Relative stress or prominence assigned to a particular syllable of a word or group of words. This emphasis is demonstrated through greater intensity (stress accent) or by variation or modulation of pitch or tone (pitch accent). Placement of accent on a word or group of words can be determined by the regional, social, or developmental background of the speaker. Individuals with congenital hearing loss typically have difficulty with standard or expected placement of accent in spoken language and tend to speak in a monotone (with no stress or pitch accent).

accessibility Modification of buildings, curbs, and other physical structures to allow unrestricted movement and unlimited admittance to people whose mobility may be limited by motor or sensory impairment and who may or may not use a wheelchair. Accessibility of all public and private facilities is now mandated by PL 101-336, the Americans with Disabilities Act of 1990. This might include special ramps and additional elevators for those with motor impairments, and special braille and sound adaptations for those with visual impairments. Accessibility also requires modification of services for persons who speak another language, who have hearing impairment, and who have other cognitive or learning problems.

accident-prone An unusually high susceptibility to unintentional injury, often assumed to have an emotional basis. Although accident-proneness can be an emotional symptom in children, it more likely reflects the inattention and impulsivity of attention-deficit/hyperactivity disorder (ADHD), the cognitive impairment of mental retardation, or the motor impairment of clumsy child syndrome or developmental dyspraxia.

accommodation A learning process that applies a general cognitive structure to understanding a particular situation, which then changes the cognitive structure. Accommodation focuses on the adaptation or change in the learning organism.

accommodation The ability of the eye to change the shape of its lens to produce a clear image. Problems with accommodation can produce fatigue, visual discomfort, eye strain, headaches, and blurred vision. Ophthalmologists do not treat mild accommodative disorders to improve reading; optometrists frequently prescribe lenses and orthoptics (eye exercises) to treat mild accommodative and convergence disorders associated with reading

disorders. This therapy is controversial and unproven.

acetabulum The cup-shaped cavity in the hip bone that holds the head of the femur (thigh bone); abnormalities of the acetabulum contribute to hip pain, instability at the hip joint, dislocation of the hip, and limping.

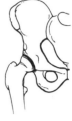

acetabulum

acetaminophen Trade name Tylenol; a drug used to reduce fever and pain. Acetaminophen has replaced the use of aspirin for pain because of the latter's suspected contribution to the onset of Reye syndrome; acetaminophen does not, however, have the same anti-inflammatory effect as aspirin.

achievement ability comparison (AAC) A rating that describes a student's achievement in relation to the achievement of other students with the same measured ability.

achievement battery A group of tests that measure the amount and degree of attainment of information, knowledge, and skills in specified areas.

achievement test A test designed to document what a person has learned, usually in specific academic areas such as reading or mathematics. This is in contrast to intelligence tests, which are designed to reflect the individual's intellectual potential (what could be learned). In practice, this distinction is less clear, because intelligence tests reflect past educational achievement (e.g., vocabulary), whereas achievement tests sometimes examine factors (e.g., abstract reasoning, logic) typically associated with intelligence.

Achilles tendon The heel cord. This tendon is named for Achilles, a

Achilles tendon

hero in Greek mythology whose only weakness was his heel. Shortening or tightening of the Achilles tendon gives rise to toe walking (an equinus [an involuntary foot extension] gait).

achondroplasia A genetic syndrome that combines short stature with short limbs, bowed legs, and megalocephaly (large head) usually without hydrocephalus (excess fluid in the brain) or accompanying developmental disorders. Obstructive apnea (temporary cessation of breathing) and neurological complications secondary to bone or disc compression are major medical concerns. Intelligence in people with achondroplasia is usually normal. Inheritance follows an autosomal dominant pattern with a recurrence risk of 50%. Incidence is estimated at 1/25,000, with 90% of cases representing new mutations. Treatment is generally symptomatic for orthopedic or neurological complications.

ACLC *See* Assessment of Children's Language Comprehension.

ACLD Association for Children and Adults with Learning Disabilities; *see* Learning Disabilities Association.

acoupedic An approach to learning speech by children with hearing impairments that relies on hearing alone.

acoustic Pertaining to sound, the sense of hearing, and the science of sounds.

acoustic impedance The measurement of sound reflected by the tympanic membrane (ear drum) after the introduction of a test tone into the external ear canal. The amount of sound reflected depends on the mass, stiffness, and the acoustic resistance of the air surrounding the tympanic membrane. This measurement requires no participation by the individual. Static acoustic impedance (relative flexibility of the ear drum), the point of maximum comparable acoustic reflex (relative contraction of middle-ear muscles), and tympanometry (the resistance to the flow of acoustical energy at the tympanic membrane during various pressure changes) are three aspects of acoustic impedance.

acoustic impedance audiometry A measurement of the sound reflected by the ear drum, performed by emitting a test tone into the ear and measuring three components of ear function: static acoustic impedance, acoustic reflex, and tympanometry. Static acoustic impedance relates to the compliancy or flexibility of the ear drum. Acoustic reflex measures the contraction of the muscles in the middle ear. Tympanometry measures the movement of the tympanic membrane during various pressure changes. These three components measure middle-ear functioning in relation to turning sound waves into electrical activity in the cochlea and eighth nerve.

acquired Postnatal; the absence of significant innate, genetic, or prenatal factors. When describing the etiology of developmental disabilities, an acquired condition is contrasted with a *congenital* one, the implication in the former being that the person was neurodevelopmentally normal until something happened (e.g., a head injury or brain infection). Acquired blindness and acquired deafness, however, are termed *adventitious*.

acquired immunodeficiency syndrome (AIDS) A chronic and ultimately fatal disease process resulting from infection with a retrovirus (HIV-1). The most severe manifestation is suppression or deficiency of the cellular immune system. In addition, HIV infects other white blood cells, the brain, the bowel, the skin, and other body organs. Suppression of the immune response system predisposes the infected person to opportunistic infections and malignancies. Transmission to children is by body fluid (blood or semen); many cases in children result from in utero contact, with an infected mother transmitting the virus across the placental barrier to her fetus or infant. Current prevalence figures suggest that pediatric AIDS cases represent less than 2% of all AIDS cases. The course is typically prolonged, with neurodevelopmental complications in 90% of affected children. These include a spectrum ranging from mild delays in attaining developmental milestones to frank developmental regressions. Treatment is two-pronged: treatment of the opportunistic infections and malignancies coupled with drugs specifically targeted to delay the progression of the HIV infection. Many of the risk factors for a child being placed in foster care in infancy overlap with risk factors in their mothers, who may also be HIV positive. Thus, HIV testing should be considered for children who were placed in foster care in infancy and who present with developmental problems in early childhood.

acrocephaly A "tower-shaped" skull secondary to craniosynostosis (premature fusion of skull sutures). Acrocephaly is found in a number of genetic syndromes, including turribrachycephaly (an odd-shaped skull), turricephaly, hypsicephaly, and oxycephaly.

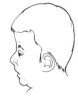
acrocephaly

acrodysostosis A genetic syndrome characterized by prenatal onset growth failure, mental retardation, a strikingly small nose, short hands with stubby fingers, and involvement of other bone structures.

acrolect Any dialect that closely resembles the accepted standard usage of a language. For example, in Black English, "he be saying" is the equivalent of "he is saying."

acromelic Affecting the distal segment of a limb (the hand or foot).

acronym The naming of a syndrome or other condition by a word, each of the letters or syllables of which is the first letter or syllable of one of the components of the syndrome; the acronym serves as a mnemonic (memory) device. Examples include the LEOPARD and TORCH syndromes. Acronyms are also used loosely to refer to the abbreviated names of organizations and tests (e.g., AMA, American Medical Association).

A.C.S.W. *See* Academy of Certified Social Workers.

ACTH *See* adrenocorticotropic hormone.

acting out A behavioral, rather than a verbal, expression of feelings, unconscious drives, or impulses. The behavioral acting out of feelings is usually expressed in annoying, disruptive, or antisocial ways. A child exhibiting acting-out behavior is difficult to manage, has trouble adhering to structural limits, and resists timely redirection. Acting-out behaviors are similar to conduct disorders but are typically not so severe in nature nor so fixed in the personality; however, when diagnosing conduct disorders, acting-out behavior is one in a list of criterion symptoms. Although acting-out behaviors occur frequently and are of significant duration, they do not include daily misbehaviors of little consequence. When a behavior is considered to be an indicator of acting out, it is most often operationally defined, observed, and recorded in formal settings such as the classroom, residence, or hospital. Some of the behaviors typically considered as acting out include fighting, stealing, crying, pouting, hyperactivity, temper tantrums, and verbal threats. Children often act out their feelings (termed *externalizing*), although some may demonstrate emotional conflict in a more introspective or internalizing manner, thus presenting as depressed, lethargic, self-injurious, and withdrawn.

activities of daily living (ADL) Self-help activities such as bathing, toileting, eating, cooking, mobility, simple health care procedures, and housekeeping. ADL are a major goal of habilitation and rehabilitation.

actometer A mechanical device to measure children's activity levels; examples include pedometers (instruments that record the number of steps taken) and accelerometers (devices that measure change in velocity). All such instruments are of questionable reliability and validity.

acuity The degree of clarity. The sharpness, clearness, and distinctness of stimuli with respect to the reception of sensory data. Visual acuity is measured against a standard of 20/20 (measuring the accuracy with which people with impairments can visually discriminate objects/shapes/

letters at 20 feet against that demonstrated by a person without impairments at 20 feet). (In the metric system 6/6 is the standard.) A visual acuity of 20/40 indicates that the individual with an impairment discriminates at 20 feet what the individual without impairments can discriminate at 40 feet. Visual acuities better than 20/40 are not typically disabling, whereas those worse than 20/40 suggest a problem with far vision. Auditory acuity refers to the sensitivity of the ear to sound.

acuity The degree of urgency or significance. An illness is acute when it comes on suddenly and unexpectedly; if the illness persists for a long time (usually defined as greater than 3 months or hospitalization exceeding 30 days), it is chronic.

acute Sharp or sudden; of short duration (the opposite of chronic).

acute dystonic reaction Uncontrolled muscle activity with stiffness or twisting of extremities and other body parts (including facial grimacing, torticollis (stiff neck), oculogyric crisis, opisthotonos [an arching of the back]). This side effect of antipsychotic drugs can occur with the onset of treatment.

acute infantile spinal muscular atrophy (AISMA) A type of Werdnig-Hoffmann disease.

ADA *See* Americans with Disabilities Act of 1990 (PL 101-336).

adaptation An equilibration between assimilation and accommodation. In Piagetian theory, a heavily biological process.

adapted physical education A component of the educational curriculum in which physical, recreational, and other therapists work with children who exhibit delays in motor development and perceptual motor skills in the absence of a motor diagnosis; the program of games, sports, and other activities typically comes under the heading of recreation or play.

Adapted Sequence Inventory of Communication Development for Adolescents and Adults with Severe Handicaps (A–SICD) An extension of the Sequences Inventory of Communication Development–Revised (SICD–R) to adolescents and adults, including those with severe hearing loss, legal blindness, epilepsy, spastic quadriplegia, and nonambulation.

adaptive behavior 1. Ability to function in nonacademic skill areas such as self-help, social abilities, and mobility. 2. Activities the individual uses to cope with the natural and social demands of the environment, including feeding, dressing, toileting, and higher-level social interaction skills. Significant limitations in adaptive behavior are necessary components of mental retardation diagnoses.

adaptive education A general term referring to modifications in instructional methods, materials, or expectations to address students' individual differences.

adaptive equipment A wide array of devices that provide proper positioning to facilitate motor performance and independence; adaptive equipment includes seating inserts and positioning devices, such as sidelying and prone standers.

Adaptive Learning Environment Model (ALEM) A mainstream program for integrating students with mild disabilities into the general classroom on a full-time basis. The goals of this model are to modify conditions in the general classroom to accommodate the instructional and special service needs of a range of individuals and to promote students' social and personal development by having them plan and manage their own classroom learning behaviors. The ALEM includes 12 program dimensions, 9 related to providing adaptive instruction and 3 related to supportive implementation of adaptive instruction in the classroom. General classroom teachers, working individually and in teams, are the primary instructors for general and special education students. The services of special education range from consultation with general educators to direct instruction for special education students in the general classroom.

ADD *See* Administration on Developmental Disabilities.

ADD Attention deficit disorder; *see* attention-deficit/hyperactivity disorder.

addiction A term widely used by the lay public to indicate a habit of compulsive drug use and drug-seeking behavior that is associated with physical and/or psychological dependence. The term *addiction* has been replaced in medical literature and professional practice by the more restrictive terms *substance tolerance, substance dependence,* and *substance abuse.*

additivity principle If two events are mutually exclusive, then the probability of finding one of the events is the sum of their individual probabilities.

adduction Sideways movement of an extremity (arm or leg) toward the midline of the body.

adductor tenotomy An orthopedic surgery procedure in which the tendons of several of the hip adductor muscles are cut; this procedure is used to treat severe adduction (scissoring), hip dislocation/dysplasia, and related problems in spastic cerebral palsy. It is frequently performed in conjunction with obturator neurectomy in people with severe cases.

adenoid facies A clinical presentation with the mouth hanging open, mouth breathing, and a generally dull and apathetic expression; there is usually a history of snoring. This is frequently secondary to hypertrophied (enlarged) adenoids and may accompany recurrent tonsillitis and otitis (inflammation in the ear). Hearing loss is possible, and a more detailed inquiry about allergy symptoms should be made.

adenoid facies

adenoidectomy The surgical removal of the adenoids; often performed simultaneously with tonsillectomy and ear tube (pressure equalizing [PE] or ventilation) placement.

adenoids Hypertrophied (enlarged) pharyngeal tonsils that often give rise to snoring and mouth breathing and contribute to recurrent ear infections with intermittent hearing impairment.

adenoma sebaceum A skin lesion found in tuberous sclerosis.

adenovirus A DNA (deoxyribonucleic acid) virus that can be associated with respiratory infections and diarrhea.

ADHD *See* attention-deficit/hyperactivity disorder.

adjudication A court decision rendered as a result of a hearing or trial. Many adults with developmental disabilities are adjudicated for the purpose of determining the need for a guardian.

adjustment disorder A maladaptive reaction to an identifiable stressful event. The hallmarks of this response include onset within 3 months of the stressor, duration of less than 6 months, and an impairment in school, social, or interpersonal functioning not due to a previously diagnosed psychiatric disorder. Adjustment disorders may take one of two forms: 1) marked deterioration of normal functioning or 2) excessive and continued overreaction to the stressor.

ADL *See* activities of daily living.

Administration on Developmental Disabilities (ADD) The federal agency mandated to carry out and monitor programs for persons with developmental disabilities. This administrative office was authorized under PL 101-457 and is housed in the U.S. Department of Health and Human Services.

adolescence Transition period between latency (late childhood) and young adulthood. It is characterized by physical changes such as the adolescent growth spurt, puberty, and, in girls, thelarche and menarche. Complex psychosocial changes also occur. The development of abstract logical thinking (Piaget's formal operational thinking) during this period comprises both deduction and induction.

Adolescent and Adult Psychoeducational Profile (AAPEP) A criterion-referenced task performance test that is a sequel to the Psychoeducational Profile (PEP) and assesses learning styles and strengths of adolescents and adults with autism and other communication disorders. Test results constitute a profile that is translated into individualized goals and objectives to serve as a foundation for instructional planning and community placement. The time required to administer the test varies. The test is not intended for group use.

Adolescent Language Screening Test (ALST) A screening test of speech and language for 11- to 17-year-old students. Includes seven subtests: pragmatics, receptive vocabulary, concepts, expressive vocabulary, sentence formulation, morphology, and phonology.

adrenergic Mediated by adrenalin, as in the sympathetic nervous system.

adrenocorticotropic hormone (ACTH) A compound secreted by the pituitary gland that stimulates the adrenal gland's cortex (outer part) to make cortisol (a steroid hormone). Excess amounts of cortisol can be found in pituitary tumors called *adenomas*. The side effects of large amounts of cortisol include truncal obesity, striae (stretch marks), stomach ulcers, osteoporosis (thinning of the bones), and an increased susceptibility to infection. ACTH is used therapeutically in infantile spasms. It is given in the muscle (IM) and used until the spasms and hypsarhythmia (a continuous pattern of high-voltage slow waves and spikes) disappear. The dose is then decreased until the minimal amount for seizure control is reached, at which point it may be discontinued. Although ACTH does not alter the generally poor outcome in infantile spasms, it can improve both the seizures and the electroencephalogram (EEG) pattern.

adrenoleukodystrophy A syndrome that combines a disorder of brain white matter with atrophy (wasting) of the adrenal glands. It is one of several hereditary degenerative disorders—under the general term *sudanophilic cerebral sclerosis*—that are characterized by progressive intellectual and visual deterioration, spasticity (increased muscle tone), and seizures. Adrenoleukodystrophy, one of the best described disorders, includes an insufficiency of the adrenal cortex, which makes cortisol (a steroid hormone). The clinical course is variable, with onset generally between 5 and 8 years of age. The progression begins with disturbances in walking and mild intellectual deterioration, followed by seizures, screaming attacks, spasticity, and ataxia (unsteady gait). This progressive neurodegenerative disease is genetic in origin and is inherited as an X-linked recessive trait.

adult day care A continuum of service including sheltered work, day hospital, socialization groups, or custodial services provided to adults who are unable to care for themselves. Often these adults have developmental disabilities from birth, but they may also be older adults who are no longer able to care for themselves when left alone, but who do not need a full-time caregiving placement such as a nursing home.

adult foster care Placement in the home of a nonrelated family for adults who are unable to care for themselves because of disabilities or health problems and whose biological families are unable to provide the care they need.

adult protective services The provision of or monitoring of social, medical, legal, residential, or custodial services to adults who are unable to provide such services for themselves. These adults may have developmental disabilities or aging or disease processes that have rendered them incapable of caring for themselves. In the event there is no guardian or significant other, or in cases of a guardian or significant other being abusive to the adult with a disability, a public or private agency may provide adult protective and service coordination services.

adventitious Acquired; blindness and deafness are divided by origin into two types: congenital (existing at or dating from birth) and adventitious (acquired).

adverse reaction Harmful side effect.

AE *See* above elbow.

AE scores *See* age-equivalent scores.

aerophagia Air swallowing that can lead to abdominal distension and discomfort; in many infants aerophagia reflects a mild feeding disorder, but children with developmental disabilities may engage in aerophagia as a self-stimulatory behavior; aerophagia may predispose these children to aspiration.

AFB *See* American Foundation for the Blind.

affect A term that until recently referred to both subjectively experienced inner feeling states and their external manifestations. Recent usage separates these two phenomena into 1) mood, to signify inner feeling states; and 2) affect, to refer to the external manifestation of feeling states. Thus, what were affective disorders have become mood disorders. Although mood and affect are both considered psychological phenomena, each has physiological components that are usually expressed through somatic manifestations such as blushing, crying, excessive heart rate, sweating, or shaking. Changes in facial expression, voice tone, activity level, posture, and gait may occur as well. Disorders of affect and mood occur when the intensity, duration, appropriateness, or ability to cope with one's own inner feeling state becomes impaired. Until children learn to express their feelings verbally, they frequently do so through their behavior. An interpersonal process in which the caregiver interprets the child's behavior as a feeling state and offers the appropriate label to the child allows the child to associate this label with the inner feeling state. Children with developmental disabilities frequently have difficulty acquiring this skill and even as adults may continue to act out their feelings. Thus, caregivers must learn to read external manifestations of affect in order to sensitively interact with persons with developmental disabilities.

affective disorder *See* mood disorder.

affordance The complementarity of the organism and the environment that is part of an ecological approach to developmental psychology.

AFO Ankle-foot orthosis; *see* orthosis.

AFP *See* alpha-fetoprotein.

aftercare Continued treatment and support services to formerly hospitalized or institutionalized persons after transition into the community.

AGA *See* appropriate for gestational age.

age-equivalent (AE) scores Ratings derived by determining the average score obtained on a test taken by children of various ages. For example, if the average score for 8-year-old children on a test is 15 correct out of 25, any child obtaining a score of 15 receives an age-equivalent score of 8. These scores should be interpreted with care. The differences between scores may not represent equal units at all ages. Furthermore, at upper levels, they have little meaning for school subjects not taught at that age.

age ratio The chronological age of a child at one testing divided by the child's chronological age at a later testing date. This ratio can be used as a crude measure of a test's predictive power, which depends on the age at which the test is given and the length of time between administrations. The younger the child, the poorer the predictive power of the test. The longer the interval between tests, the poorer the prediction from one testing to the next. Thus, prediction would most likely be better from ages 7 to 8 (7/8) than from ages 5 to 6 (5/6).

agenesis Not born: failure of a structure to develop; a specific etiology for the absence of the structure as opposed to later removal or destruction. This may occur because of genetic factors or because of a vascular accident during fetal development.

Aggregate Neurobehavioral Student Health and Educational Review (ANSER) A series of questionnaires for parents, teachers, and students to assess all aspects of a child's behavior. The ANSER system is not a standardized test; rather, it is a method of systematically collecting information from parent(s), school personnel, and the child.

aggression A poorly defined set of human behaviors interpreted from physical or verbal behavior directed at others. Intention differentiates true aggression from pseudo-aggression; the impulsive actions (both verbal and physical) of the child with attention-deficit/hyperactivity disorder can easily be mistaken for aggression and can instigate physical fights. Aggression can be part of the behavior disorder and conduct disorder outcomes of inadequately treated attention-deficit/hyperactivity disorder and learning disabilities.

agitation Extreme motor restlessness and increased activity level associated with anxiety and tension; a sign of mental distress.

agnosia Not knowing, with particular reference to sensory stimuli such as visual agnosia, auditory agnosia, color agnosia, and finger agnosia.

agonist A muscle that while contracting to move a body part is opposed by another muscle, which is termed the antagonist. Every muscle in the body is both an agonist and an antagonist to its opposite number that is needed to reverse its movement.

agrammatism An inability to produce words in their correct sequence; a marked difficulty with grammar and syntax; speech that is nonfluent, oddly inflected or not inflected at all, slow, and hesitant, with initial words stressed and frequent omission of important connectives. The individual is able to produce words but is unable to arrange them into coherent and coordinated phrases. Agrammatism can be a component of Broca's or syntactical aphasia when a previously established ability to create and adhere to grammatical structure is lost.

agraphia An acquired condition (usually as a result of brain damage such as fol-lows a stroke in adults) of impaired or absent ability to write or draw (graphomotor skill); the typically milder congenital form seen in children is usually referred to as dysgraphia and may be part of a learning disability syndrome.

Aicardi syndrome The combination of generalized seizures, severe mental retardation, agenesis (absence of formation) of the corpus callosum (growth failure of part of the brain that is one of the major connections between the two hemispheres), and retinal and vertebral defects. Although not genetically caused, the first trimester intrauterine insult that produces this syndrome occurs only in girls. The clinical seizure type and the EEG pattern suggest that this syndrome may be a variant or subtype of infantile spasms. It must be distinguished clinically from members of the TORCH group of infections, which it may resemble.

Aid to the Permanently and Totally Disabled (APTD) A 1950 amendment to the Social Security Act, providing financial assistance to those with permanent physical or mental disabilities. This amendment and its provisions were incorporated into the Supplemental Security Income (SSI) program in 1972.

AIDS *See* acquired immunodeficiency syndrome.

AISMA *See* acute infantile spinal muscular atrophy.

AK *See* above knee.

akathisia 1. A disorder with objective motor restlessness accompanied by subjective anxiety; not usually described in children but considered in the differential diagnosis of hyperactivity in adults. 2. One of the motor complications of antipsychotic drugs often used to treat severe maladaptive behavior in people with developmental disorders.

akinesia A state of diminished or absent motor activity.

akinetic seizure A type of seizure with head-nodding spells and loss of movement without atonia (loss of tone). *Akinetic seizure* refers inconsistently to the seizure type associated with Lennox-Gastaut syndrome. These seizures are also known as *astatic* or *atonic* seizures.

Albers-Schönberg disease　Marble bone disease; a genetic disease with increased density of all bones or mild osteopetrosis, facial palsy, visual impairment, and conductive (involving the middle and outer ear) hearing loss. The severe variant is lethal by adolescence. Inheritance follows an autosomal recessive pattern.

Albert Einstein Scales of Sensorimotor Development　An early attempt at a formal application of Piagetian principles to infant assessment in the following areas: 1) spatial relationships (a 21-item measure of successive stages in the capacity to adapt to the objective properties of physical space as defined by Piaget), 2) object permanence (an 18-item measure of Piagetian object permanence for children ages 5–24 months), and 3) prehension (a 15-item measure of Piagetian developmental advances involving the grasping of objects and their apprehension by the senses for infants ages 2–8 months). There are no "failures" because performance is determined to be at one stage or another; items within a stage represent alternate and often equivalent opportunities to obtain the same developmental level. Scores are based on the pattern of response to stimuli rather than actual achievement of the task. Mean ages for entry and completion of each stage are provided. Named for the College of Medicine in New York City at which the scales were developed.

albinism　The genetic absence of pigment of the skin, hair, and eyes, or eyes only. Visual impairment, nystagmus (involuntary eye movements), and photosensitivity are common.

alcohol (ETOH)　A chemical compound composed of varying parts of carbon, hydrogen, and water. The number of parts of each of these chemical elements determines the type of alcohol. Drinking (ethyl) alcohol consists of C_2H_5OH. All alcohols are, in varying degrees, toxic (poisonous) to humans. Alcohol challenges the body to see how quickly it can be broken down into its nontoxic elements of carbon, hydrogen, and oxygen. The slower the body's ability to break it down (in the presence, for example, of liver damage), the more toxic the effect of the alcohol. Alcohol is also teratogenic (causing malformations in the developing fetus): a child with fetal alcohol syndrome (FAS) may have multiple organ system defects that can include blindness, deafness, and severe mental retardation.

alcoholic family　A characteristic set of family dynamics first identified in families in which one spouse was an alcohol abuser. Similar dynamic patterns have since been identified in families with other types of substance abuse. The dynamic interaction between the "dependent" spouse and the "codependent" spouse in maintaining the substance abuse has been reported, along with the characteristic roles assumed by each child according to his or her birth order in the family. The long-term emotional consequences to the children and the characteristic behaviors they exhibit as they move into their own adult intimate relationships are described. Typical behavioral and emotional interventions are prescribed.

alcoholism　The excessive use of alcoholic beverages motivated by either a psychological or a physiological dependence on the chemical effect and mood impact produced by such beverages. Diagnostic criteria assume this underlying dependence and include 1) quantity of usage; 2) failed efforts to stop usage; 3) impaired life functioning in social areas such as family, occupation, and legal difficulties; 4) inability to stop usage despite knowledge of having a persistent problem in one of these life areas due to excess use; 5) increased and driven efforts to obtain alcohol; and 6) increased tolerance for alcohol leading to greater intake before achieving the desired effect.

ALEM　*See* Adaptive Learning Environment Model.

alexia　An acquired condition, usually as a result of brain damage (such as follows strokes in adults), of impaired or absent ability to read; the typically milder congenital form seen in children is usually referred to as dyslexia.

algorithm A rule to solve a certain class of problems, especially a formula that automatically generates a solution; loosely, a rule of thumb.

Alice in Wonderland syndrome A symptom complex characterized by metamorphopsia (hyper- and hyposchematia [visual distortions of size, shape, and spatial relations]). This symptom can occur with migraine, seizure disorders, drug-induced hallucinations, and infectious mononucleosis.

alimentation Feeding.

ALL *See* Analysis of the Language of Learning.

Allen Kindergarten Picture Cards A preschool vision screening test for children as young as 2½ years of age; the child identifies pictures of common items at a distance of 20 feet. The test is used until children are ready to convert to a letter-based screening chart.

allergen Any substance—food, chemical, drug, or inhalant (pollen, mold, dust)—that, upon repeat exposure, can produce allergic symptoms in a person.

allergic tension fatigue syndrome Also known as "cerebral allergy." The dual symptoms of tension and fatigue are seen in persons with classically defined allergic disorders. The hypothesis that unsuspected (subclinical or otherwise asymptomatic) food allergies can produce central nervous system irritability and fatigability and thus mimic or cause attention-deficit/hyperactivity disorder (ADHD) and learning disabilities remains unproven.

allergy "Altered reactivity." The production of symptoms in a person by substances (allergens) that do not produce symptoms in most other persons. The presence of a family history of atopy (allergy) can help in the interpretation of many nonspecific signs of allergy in chil-

dren: nasal speech, adenoidal facies, allergic salute (rubbing the nose upward with the heel of the palm), fatigue, nasal polyps, allergic (transverse nasal) crease, allergic shiners (dark circles under the eyes), and a variety of skin conditions (e.g., hives, eczema). Despite extremely high prevalence rates for allergy, the role of allergies in developmental disabilities is often exaggerated. Poor medical management of allergic disease exacerbates but does not cause developmental problems. The contribution of poorly defined subclinical allergies (e.g., to food or yeast via such entities as the allergic tension fatigue syndrome) to the etiology of developmental disabilities remains unproven and controversial.

allied health professional A person with special training who works under the supervision of a health professional in the provision of direct patient care; a member of the same discipline may function as an allied health professional in a medical setting and as an independent professional in another setting.

alopecia Hair loss; frequently patchy in children (alopecia areata). This condition is secondary to a variety of conditions including trauma, drugs, endocrine disorders, and ringworm.

Alpern-Boll *See* Developmental Profile II.

ALPHA (Assessment Link between Phonology and Articulation) Test of Phonology A 15-minute test designed to relate articulation assessment results to phonological analysis.

alphabet The letters or symbols of a given language arranged sequentially in the order determined by custom.

alpha-fetoprotein (AFP) A normal protein found in the serum (liquid part of blood) that is present in large amounts in a developing fetus. Measurements of maternal blood levels of AFP are used as a screening test for potential problems with the developing fetus. An elevated AFP is found with anencephaly (no brain or absent top of skull) and open neural tube defects (spina bifida). The open defect leaks AFP into the amniotic fluid, which then passes it into the maternal bloodstream, thus elevating the maternal AFP level. Levels that are two or more times normal detect 79% of open neural tube defects. Amniotic fluid AFP levels are more accurate, detecting 98% of these defects. The neural tube defect can be confirmed by ultrasound. Low levels of AFP are thought to be associated with trisomy 21 (Down syndrome) in the fetus.

Alport syndrome A genetic syndrome with progressive bilateral sensorineural (involving the inner ear or the auditory nerve) hearing loss (starting by about age 10) and progressive chronic nephritis (kidney disease starting by age 6). Of those affected, 10% also have ocular/visual abnormalities. Although the syndrome is autosomal dominant, males are more severely affected than females; an X-linked pattern has been described in some families.

ALST *See* Adolescent Language Screening Test.

Alström syndrome A genetic syndrome with progressive central and peripheral impairment of vision, retinitis pigmentosa (night blindness and progressively restricted visual field), progressive sensorineural deafness, early transient truncal obesity, and juvenile onset diabetes mellitus. The syndrome is extremely rare, with all known cases being of Swedish extraction. Inheritance is autosomal recessive.

alternative communication Any procedure or device that substitutes a nonspeech mode of communication for spoken language. Such alternative communication may be aided (e.g., communication board) or unaided (e.g., sign language).

alternative medicine Nontraditional or unproven approaches to the treatment of disease; treatment modalities outside the mainstream of medical practice; other descriptive synonyms include unorthodox, irrational, controversial, sectarian, questionable, and fringe therapies. The use of

mystical or *metaphysical* in this context should be discouraged, since these terms have valid references in other contexts. New age and holistic treatments, as well as most diet and many allergy therapies for developmental disabilities, fall into this category. *See also* optometric training.

Alzheimer disease A late-onset, degenerative disease of brain tissue that results in amnesia (impaired memory), apraxia (inability to perform purposeful movements), agnosia (inability to recognize objects or familiar people so that many people with Alzheimer disease fail to recognize their spouses), aphasia (loss of language skills), impaired thinking and judgment, disorientation, marked personality and behavioral deterioration, and loss of adaptive abilities. The disease affects an estimated 11% of the general population under age 65 and 47% of those over age 85; etiology remains unclear. Among people with developmental disabilities, people with Down syndrome have incidence rates of Alzheimer disease greater than that of the general population (33%–40% of people with Down syndrome over age 50 are affected), and the disease manifests itself at a much younger age. The disorder is named after German neuropathologist Alois Alzheimer (1864–1915).

amaurosis Blindness; specifically, blindness due to disease of the optic nerve, with the rest of the eye remaining intact; a component of a number of hereditary neurodegenerative diseases.

ambidextrous Equally skilled with both hands; not yet exhibiting handedness or hand preference. Ambidexterity can be familial or can reflect global or specific cognitive delay or dysfunction.

amblyopia Decreased vision or visual acuity in one eye. There are two major causes of amblyopia: 1) obstructive amblyopia, and 2) amblyopia ex anopsia. Obstructive amblyopia is the loss of vision resulting from blockage of the retinal path so that images cannot reach the retina (e.g., cataracts, ptosis [drooping so that the eyelid cannot be raised], corneal opacity [clouding]). Amblyopia ex anopsia is caused by either a refractive error (correctable by glasses) or strabismus (a crossed eye secondary to a weak eye muscle that can be surgically treated). In amblyopia without intervention, the image from the weaker eye is suppressed by the brain, and that eye gradually loses its vision; thus, monocular vision results. If diagnosed and treated early, many of the causes of amblyopia can be treated or managed in such a way that vision is preserved. Treatment can involve patching, glasses, or surgery.

ambulation Walking (a gross motor skill). A delay in ambulation is often upsetting and worrisome to parents out of proportion to its developmental significance. The parental preconscious equation of an erect mobility at 1 year of age with being fully human appears to be stronger than the association of connected speech at 2 years of age with normal intelligence. Most children walk independently between 12 and 13 months of age. Caucasian children tend to walk later than African American children. The range for normal walking is 7–24 months. In persons with motor disorders, ambulation is classified according to the degree of assistive support (braces, canes, and wheelchairs) needed and the distance that can be covered; such categories include community walker, household walker, physiological walker, and nonwalker. Delayed walking is most often noted first in spastic diplegia (paralysis of both sides of the body); other types of cerebral palsy are suspected from earlier delays in rolling over and sitting.

amenorrhea Absence of menstrual periods; this can occur because of pregnancy, endocrine dysfunction, general debilitation associated with poor diet or health, or as part of a genetic syndrome.

amentia An obsolete term for mental retardation.

American Academy for Cerebral Palsy and Developmental Medicine (AACPDM) A professional medical organization of physicians and other professionals in the fields of cerebral palsy, mental retardation, and learning and language disorders. Members include orthopedic surgeons, developmental pediatricians, neurologists, physiatrists, and professionals from associated disciplines. Founded in 1947, the AACPDM annually sponsors a national meeting, as well as several regional courses; it publishes a newsletter; and, along with the British Paediatric Neurology Association, its official journal is *Developmental Medicine and Child Neurology.*

American Academy of Pediatrics (AAP) A professional organization of physicians with board-certified specialty training in the diseases of childhood. Founded in 1891, the first meeting of the new AAP section on children with disabilities was in 1991.

American Association of Marital and Family Therapy (AAMFT) A professional organization for certifying and regulating the practice of marital and family therapists. Membership is achieved through demonstrated competence and acceptance of the code of ethics.

American Association of Speech-Language Pathology and Audiology *See* American Speech-Language-Hearing Association (ASHA).

American Association of University Affiliated Programs for Persons with Developmental Disabilities (AAUAP) A network of federally funded programs that fosters graduate training in 10 core disciplines serving people with developmental disabilities. Formerly, UAPs were termed UAFs, for University Affiliated Facilities.

American Association on Mental Retardation (AAMR) An interdisciplinary association of professionals, parents, consumers, and others interested in mental retardation. Originally the American Association for the Study of the Feebleminded (1876–1940); followed by the American Association on Mental Deficiency (AAMD, 1940–1988). The AAMR publishes the *American Journal on Mental Retardation (AJMR)*, *Mental Retardation (MR)*, and *AAMR News and Notes.* The AAMR is active in advocacy and conducts both national and state-level professional meetings.

American Foundation for the Blind (AFB) An independent nonprofit organization founded in 1921 to function as the national association of local services for people who are blind and have visual impairments. Helen Keller (1880–1968) was closely connected with the AFB from its inception until her death. The AFB has national consultants in many areas, including education, employment, and rehabilitation; it provides direct consumer resources and services and conducts research. Several regional offices serve as liaisons to public and private agencies and institutions serving people with visual impairments in the United States.

American Manual Alphabet Specific positioning of the hands and fingers to symbolize the various letters of the alphabet. When communicating with individuals who have profound hearing loss, the manual alphabet supplements the use of sign language by spelling out words.

American Occupational Therapy Foundation (AOTF) The philanthropic sister organization of the American Occupational Therapy Association (AOTA). Founded in 1965, the foundation raises funds and distributes resources across three program areas: scholarships, publication, and research associated with the profession and practice of occupational therapy. Scholarships are offered to provide study in the field. The AOTF publishes the *American Journal of Occupational Therapy* and offers an interlibrary loan program. Professional research is supported through grant and fellowship awards.

American Orthopsychiatric Association (AOA) A multidisciplinary organization of mental health professionals founded in 1924 to support knowledge development and professional practice and to advocate for appropriate public policy in areas of mental health and human development. The organization is unique in that it was one of the first to seek multiprofessional and interprofessional cooperation in all areas of human development and mental health. It publishes two quarterly journals, the *American Journal of Orthopsychiatry* and *Readings.*

American Physical Therapy Association (APTA) A professional organization for physical therapists, the APTA accredits academic programs in physical therapy, assists in designing certification examinations, and offers continuing education courses. The association publishes a newsletter and a journal and distributes a variety of pamphlets on injury prevention and chronic conditions. It also provides a referral service for individuals needing physical therapy.

American Psychiatric Association (APA) An organization founded in 1844 under the name, the Association of Medical Superintendents of American Institutions for the Insane; the current name was adopted in 1921. The APA's objectives include improving the treatment and rehabilitation of people with mental illness, mental retardation, and emotional disturbances. The organization promotes professional research and education, provides information to the public, and fosters cooperation among professionals concerned with mental health. Its membership includes psychiatrists, other physicians, mental health professionals, lawyers, and members of various other professions. The APA's official journal is the *American Journal of Psychiatry.* In addition, the APA publishes *Hospital and Community Psychiatry, Psychiatric News,* and the *Psychiatric Residents' Newsletter.* Workshops, continuing education, and library services are available to members.

American Psychological Association (APA) A professional organization with the following goals: to promote psychology as a science, as a profession, and as a means of promoting human welfare; to set standards for education and training; to disseminate knowledge through professional and lay publications; to ensure the quality of professional and ethical practice; to conduct public and professional advocacy; and to hold an annual convention. The APA publishes *The American Psy-*

chologist and the *APA Monitor* as well as more focused professional literature. The 47 different divisions in the APA reflect the diverse nature of psychological practice.

American Sign Language (ASL, sign, Ameslan)　A formal method of communication used by people with hearing impairments, in which manual sign symbols function as words. Each sign consists of four basic parameters: hand shape, location or place of articulation, movement in a particular direction, and palm orientation occurring with various hand shapes. Recognized as a "natural language," American Sign Language has its own structure, semantics (the meaning of words), and syntax (grammar). Manual aspects of ASL include sign formation and placement, whereas nonmanual aspects include facial expression, movements, postures, and other nonmanual signs that enhance and emphasize the meaning of signs.

American Speech-Language-Hearing Association (ASHA)　Formerly the American Speech and Hearing Association. ASHA is the national professional, scientific, and credentialing organization for speech-language pathologists and audiologists. Its mission is for all people with speech, language, and hearing disorders to have access to quality services to help them communicate more effectively. Its activities include setting academic standards and accrediting educational training programs; public and professional advocacy; certifying professional competence; providing continuing education; dissemination of knowledge; and ensuring quality clinical and ethical practice. ASHA publishes *Asha*, the *Journal of Speech and Hearing Research*, the *Journal of Speech-Language Pathology: A Journal of Clinical Practice*, and other specialty practice journals. As of January 1, 1997, ASHA's full name will be the American Association of Speech-Language Pathology and Audiology.

Americans with Disabilities Act (ADA) of 1990 (PL 101–336)　A joint antidiscrimination and affirmative action federal legislative mandate enacted to 1) protect people with disabilities against further discrimination, while 2) jointly expanding social role valorization and inclusion for such people in all aspects of society. Disability is broadly defined as a physical or mental impairment that substantially limits one or more major life activities. Titles I–V of the act systematically address employment, public and private services, public and private architectural accommodations, transportation, and telecommunications. A multistage implementation strategy provides time lines for compliance. This law is considered the most significant legislation for people with developmental disabilities since the 1975 enactment of PL 94–142, the Education for All Handicapped Children Act.

Ameslan　*See* American Sign Language.

amitriptyline　Trade name Elavil; a tricyclic antidepressant.

Ammons Quick Test　*See* Quick Test (QT).

amnesia　Loss of memory; amnesia after a head injury can be retrograde (before the injury) or anterograde (after the injury).

amniocentesis　A procedure that introduces a needle into a pregnant uterus to withdraw amniotic fluid. The fluid contains fetal cells that are used for prenatal diagnosis of chromosomal abnormalities. It is also used to measure the amount of alpha-fetoprotein (AFP; a protein), which may be increased in myelomeningocele (protuberance of both the spinal cord and its lining) or decreased in Down syndrome.

amphetamine　A central nervous system stimulant drug; street names include "speed" and "upper." Because of their abuse potential (including addiction), drugs in this group have been placed in the Class II (non-narcotic) schedule by the U.S. Drug Enforcement Administration and can be prescribed only by a licensed physician under federal and state regulations. In the past, amphetamines were used for weight reduction because of their marked appetite suppression effect.

amplification　The process of increasing the magnitude of an impulse or signal.

For example, an amplifier that increases the strength of electrical impulses is a component of hearing aids.

anaclitic depression A behavioral syndrome of weepiness, apprehension, withdrawal, refusal to eat, sleep disturbances, and eventually stupor, all secondary to a lack of nurturance or mothering in an infant late in the first year of life. Originally thought to be an infantile depression, it is now interpreted as the behavioral correlate of the more severe degrees of failure to thrive or reactive attachment disorder of infancy. When the primary caregiver is suddenly lost, the infant turns inward and becomes extremely passive. *See also* hospitalism, institutionalism.

anal wink Stimulation of the rectum produces anal contraction. This reflex may be absent when either sensory or motor pathways to the anal area are interrupted, as occurs in spina bifida or myelomeningocele (protuberance of both the spinal cord and its lining).

Analysis of the Language of Learning (ALL) A standardized test of metalinguistic knowledge of words, syllables, and sentences, and understanding of directions. ALL is appropriate for 5- to 9-year-old children, even when nonreaders.

anamnesis Patient history.

anarithmetria A problem in carrying out arithmetical operations; also known as *anarithmia*.

anarithmia *See* anarithmetria.

anemia "Low blood." Reflected in decreases in red blood cell number, size (MCV), or hemoglobin content (MCH). Tiredness is one of the primary findings in mild anemia.

anencephaly A birth defect in neural tube closure during the first 28 days of embryogenesis, leading to an absent forebrain, an incompletely developed skull, and a variety of facial abnormalities. It is incompatible with survival. The recurrence risk is 4%. Alpha-fetoprotein,

sonography, and X rays allow prenatal detection.

angel dust *See* phencyclidine.

Angelman syndrome "Happy puppet" syndrome. A syndrome of severe mental retardation with paroxysmal laughter, an ataxic "puppetlike" gait, and a characteristic facies (large mouth, protruding jaw, and midface hypoplasia [atypical tissue development]). Angelman results from a deletion on the proximal arm of the maternal contribution to the chromosome 15 pair. Transmission and incidence patterns are as yet undetermined.

anhedonia A state of being unable to experience pleasure.

animism The belief that all things in nature, both animate and inanimate, are alive.

Aniridia-Wilms tumor association A rare chromosomal disorder that can include mental retardation, a peculiar facies, aniridia (absent irises), and Wilms' tumor (a malignancy of the kidney). This association is frequently caused by a deletion of part of the short arm of chromosome 11.

aniseikonia An optometric disorder in which the visual images from the two eyes arrive at the brain with different sizes or shapes. This rare condition is diagnosed with an instrument called an eikonometer and is treated with eiseikonic lenses. The theory that aniseikonia contributes to reading disorders is controversial.

anisometropia An optometric disorder in which the visual acuity in one eye is significantly different from the visual acuity in the other eye.

ankle-foot orthosis (AFO) *See* orthosis.

ankylo A prefix relating to abnormal fusion, usually of a joint.

ankyloglossia *See* tongue-tie.

anlage An initial or elementary structure that embryologically develops into a more complex structure; used analogously for any primordium (early stage).

anomalad *See* sequence anomalad.

anomia An acquired condition (usually on the basis of brain damage such as follows a stroke in adults) of impaired or absent ability to name objects or find the correct words; the typically milder congenital form seen in children is usually referred to as *dysnomia* and may be part of a learning or language disorder pattern.

anorexia Loss of appetite; a common side effect of certain drugs (amphetamines), a symptom of psychiatric disorders (e.g., depression, eating disorders), and a nonspecific sign of acute or chronic illness.

A not B error Searching for a hidden object where it was last found, rather than in its demonstrated new hiding place; this perseveration is normal in infants 8–12 months of age.

anoxia A lack of oxygen delivered to tissue; prolonged anoxia leads to cell death. Anoxia is relatively more dangerous to brain tissue because the surviving brain cells cannot replace lost neurons.

ANSER *See* Aggregate Neurobehavioral Student Health and Educational Review.

antagonist A muscle that opposes or resists the action of another muscle (the agonist).

anteroposterior view (AP) An X ray taken so that the beam goes from front to back.

anteversion Turning or tipping forward.

anthropometry The science and study of comparative measurement of the human body.

antianxiety drug Minor tranquilizer.

anticipation A characteristic of certain genetic disorders in which the age of onset is earlier with each generation.

anticipatory guidance Parent education about child development that is included as part of the well-child visit to the primary health care provider. Parents are taught how to recognize, respond to, and facilitate age-appropriate behaviors; discipline and developmental stimulation are major concerns. Medical problems that are stage related (e.g., bow legs in the toddler) and variations in development in the presence of chronic disease are also covered.

anticonvulsant Any of a broad class of drugs used to reduce the frequency or severity of seizures (convulsions). The drug chosen is based on the type of seizures. Dosage is based on a milligram per kilogram of body weight until therapeutic blood levels are reached. The most common side effects of anticonvulsant medications include blood and liver problems, rashes, and drowsiness. Many of these drugs have subtle effects on attention and cognition, and several are known to be teratogenic (causing malformations). Seizure medication must be taken every day and continued for a time period adequate to treat the type of seizure. The goal is to control seizures without inducing debilitating side effects. The major anticonvulsants include phenobarbital, primidone, phenytoins, ethosuximide, valproic acid, benzodiazepines, trimethadione, and paramethadione.

anticonvulsant embryopathy *See* fetal Dilantin (phenytoin) syndrome.

antidepressant *See* heterocyclic antidepressants.

antiepileptic *See* anticonvulsant.

antihistamine A broad group of drugs used to treat allergic symptoms by blocking the effects of histamine (a chemical that produces allergic symptoms such as pruritus [itching] and urticaria [hives]). The most commonly used antihistamine is Benadryl (diphenhydramine hydrochloride). A common side effect of most drugs in this class is drowsiness; however, children with attention disorders may become more hyperactive when given such drugs.

antimongoloid slant A term for downslanting (going from the nose laterally) palpebral fissures. This feature is a component of the facies in a variety of genetic syndromes and, potentially, an isolated finding of no clinical significance. The name derives by contrast with the mongoloid slant in Down syndrome. The anti-mongoloid slant may be more common in syndromes with mid-facial hypoplasia (atypical tissue development).

antisocial personality (ASP) disorder A chronic pattern of irresponsible behavior with poor social relationships and non-conformity with accepted social standards; the person must be at least 18 years of age with a diagnosis of conduct disorder prior to age 15. Failure to parent, pay bills, hold a job, and plan ahead, as well as criminal antisocial actions, are common features, along with substance abuse, spouse and child abuse, and sexual promiscuity. Antisocial personality disorder is more common in males with a family history of similar disorders. It represents a possible outcome of poorly treated attention-deficit/hyperactivity disorder (ADHD) and conduct disorder. Many qualitative features, such as a tendency to seek immediate gratification, an inability to discern consequences, and a failure to learn from mistakes, suggest an underlying immaturity such as that found in ADHD.

anxiety An internal state of fear in response to external or a perceived danger. Anxiety may be distinguished from fear, however, in that fear is a response to a real and present external threat or danger, whereas anxiety often exists in anticipation of a danger with an unknown and unspecifiable source. An exception to this distinction occurs when anxiety attaches to a real danger, precipitates an emotional overreaction, and reduces the person's capacity to respond realistically to life events. Anxiety may be mild (in the form of apprehension) or severe and functionally debilitating (in the form of panic attacks or phobias). It may occur in discrete periods of sudden onset or may become constant and unfocused (termed *free-floating*). Anxiety is an unpleasant emotional state accompanied by physiological arousal and the cognitive elements of apprehension, guilt, and a sense of impending disaster.

anxiety disorder A generic term for a group of disorders characterized by 1) an internal state of extreme, disabling anxiety; and 2) an avoidance behavior pattern. Some anxiety disorders are episodic in nature, such as the panic disorders, while others are more chronic, such as a generalized anxiety disorder. The person is affected by both the internal state itself, a subsequent recursive fear of experiencing this internal state in response to certain external stimuli, and a progressive limiting of life experiences due to the need to avoid those stimuli that provoke the anxiety.

anxiolytic A medication for modifying the intensity or impact of mental tension and anxiety without interfering with normal mental activity.

AOA *See* American Orthopsychiatric Association.

AOTF *See* American Occupational Therapy Foundation.

AP *See* anteroposterior view.

APA *See* American Psychiatric Association.

APA *See* American Psychological Association.

Apert syndrome Acrocephalosyndactyly type I; a genetic syndrome characterized by craniosynostosis (premature fusion of skull sutures) and turribrachycephaly (an odd-shaped skull) and syndactyly (webbing of the fingers or toes). Conductive hearing loss and speech problems secondary to oropalatal structural defects are common. Because all people with Apert syndrome have cognitive impairments (regardless of early craniectomy), it is important to distinguish mental retardation from hearing impairments, speech and language disorders, and other learning disabilities. The true prevalence of mental retardation in Apert syndrome is unknown; incidence is estimated at 1 in 160,000, with the majority of cases representing fresh mutations, although an autosomal dominant pattern has also been demonstrated. When the latter is true, the recurrence risk is 50%. The disorder is named after French pediatrician Eugene Apert (1868–1940).

Apgar Family Version　A five-item self-report questionnaire to elicit a family member's perception of the current state of his or her family's functioning. Patterned after the pediatric Apgar, the family Apgar acronym denotes Adaptation, Partnership, Growth, Affection, and Resolve, the elements of functioning tapped by the instrument. The reliability and validity of this instrument are adequate for use as a screening instrument for troubled families. An average Apgar score, however, should not rule out family-level difficulties.

Apgar score　A technique to assess the status of a newborn baby at 1 and 5 minutes of age by assigning scores of 0 to 2 for each of five descriptors: A—appearance (color); P—pulse (heart rate); G—grimace (response to stimulation); A—activity (muscle tone); R—respiration (breathing effort). Named after Virginia Apgar (1909–74), the Apgar score is an acceptable measure of the acute status of the infant; however, it is a poor predictor of later developmental outcome. The best possible score is 10; however, because most babies have blue extremities (arms or legs) for several hours after birth, a score of 9 is usually the highest obtained.

aphakia　Absence of the lens from the eye.

aphasia　Diminished ability to correctly use and comprehend language. In developmental pediatrics, aphasia is usually limited to a profound lack of language. Children with a less severe disorder are diagnosed with a language disorder. Aphasia may be due to damage to the cortex (outer part) of the left hemisphere of the brain.

aphemia　Obsolete and vague term for aphasia.

APIB　*See* Assessment of Preterm Infant Behavior.

apnea　"No breathing"; respiratory arrest, either transient or prolonged, which can lead to cyanosis (blue color), decreased heart rate, hypotonia (decreased muscle tone), and, eventually, brain damage and death. True apnea is defined as a period of at least 15 seconds without breathing. Origin can be obstructive (mechanical) or central (physiological central nervous system response). Apnea is common in premature infants as a result of the developmental immaturity of the regulatory mechanisms of the respiratory system. An apnea monitor is a device that sounds an alarm when an infant stops breathing; home apnea monitors are used for some infants at high risk.

apoplexy　An antiquated term for stroke.

appendicular　Relating to an appendage; with regard to the body, reference is to the peripheral arms and legs, rather than to the central head and trunk.

apperception　The perception of stimuli combined with additional mental abilities, including interpretation, classification, and recognition. The process of understanding how newly observed qualities of an object, picture, or situation are related to past experience. Apperception is assessed through projective techniques in psychological testing. *See* Children's Apperception Test, Thematic Apperception Test (TAT).

APP–R　*See* Assessment of Phonological Processes–Revised.

appropriate for gestational age (AGA)　A birth weight and length compatible with length of pregnancy.

apraxia　An inability to perform familiar purposeful movements in the absence of motor (paralysis) or sensory loss.

aprosody　Loss or absence of prosody (melody of speech), leading to a monotone delivery. Aprosody can be a component of a communication disorder; milder versions are referred to as dysprosody.

APTA　*See* American Physical Therapy Association.

APTD　*See* Aid to the Permanently and Totally Disabled.

aptitude An individual's potential for learning a certain skill or developing a particular type of knowledge. Aptitude differs from ability in that the latter is generally used in a more restrictive sense to refer to a specific skill or area of knowledge. Ideally, aptitude is measured prior to any specific training. Aptitude may result from environmental influences that provide appropriate attitudes or related knowledge and skills or to a combination of hereditary and environmental factors. Aptitudes are usually measured by specifically devised tests; for example, the Scholastic Aptitude Test (SAT) is designed to measure success in postsecondary education.

aptitude test A test that attempts to measure specific types of mental competence, often aimed at predicting achievement in certain areas. For example, aptitudes may be described as language (verbal), nonverbal, reasoning, or motoric. In practice, descriptions of these tests often use the terms *aptitude, ability,* and *intelligence* interchangeably. For example, the Detroit Test of Learning Aptitude–Revised (DTLA–2) is described as measuring abilities in linguistic, cognitive, attention, and motor domains. The Peabody Picture Vocabulary Test–Revised (PPVT–R) is described as estimating verbal ability. The Test of Nonverbal Intelligence–2 (TONI–2) is described as a language-free measure of intelligence, aptitude, and reasoning. Subtests of the Woodcock-Johnson Psycho-Educational Battery–Revised (WJ–R) are described as measuring various cognitive abilities. The subtests measuring these abilities are then regrouped to measure scholastic aptitude in order to provide information regarding a subject's expected achievement in reading, mathematics, written language, and general knowledge. Aptitude tests do not measure the effects of a standard curriculum or set of experiences; they do include the effects of learning through daily living in combination with innate predispositions.

arachnodactyly "Spider fingers"; long and slender fingers and toes; can

arachnodactyly

be part of a syndrome such as Marfan syndrome.

arbovirus A group of RNA (ribonucleic) viruses that includes the rubella virus and that is the most common cause of epidemic encephalitis (brain inflammation).

ARC AIDS-related complex, the prodrome to acquired immunodeficiency syndrome (AIDS).

ARC–US *See* The Arc.

arching The tendency of a baby to bend the head, neck, and back in a concave curve backward as if withdrawing or pulling away from a frontal stimulus. Arching can be a manifestation of an exaggerated tonic labyrinthine reflex and may then suggest an underlying motor diagnosis. It may also be a behavioral pattern observed in children with autism, pervasive developmental disorder, and other atypical patterns of development.

arching

arginase deficiency A metabolic disorder of the urea cycle; because the associated hyperammonemia is mild, acute presentation in infancy does not occur. Toe walking (an equinus [involuntary foot extension] gait) and progressive spastic diplegia (paralysis on both sides of the body) may accompany mental retardation and recurrent episodes of vomiting, headache, and irritability. Dietary restriction can prevent the progression of symptoms.

argininosuccinicaciduria One of the urea cycle defects caused by a block in the enzyme argininosuccinate lyase, the gene for which is found on chromosome 9. The condition is characterized by mental retardation and poor hair formation. It is diagnosed by an elevation in argininosuccinic acid on amino acid screens. Often protein-loading (giving a protein meal) is required to identify affected people and carriers.

arithmetic A Wechsler verbal subtest comprising 18 mathematical problems that the child is required to compute mentally and answer orally, thus forbidding the use of paper and pencil. The subtest is timed and requires that the child process verbal information, store components of the problem in auditory memory, manipulate the numbers, and arrive at a solution. The test assesses abstract thinking ability and concentration in addition to auditory memory and arithmetic ability, which makes it difficult to accurately interpret the test in isolation. Success is also influenced by fluctuations of attention and is highly susceptible to anxiety. The subtest is discontinued after three consecutive failures. Adapted sample item: "If I cut a pear in half, how many pieces will I have?"

Arnold-Chiari malformation A malformation of the brain in which the base (cerebellum, medulla, pons) is elongated and protrudes into the foramen magnum (the opening in the skull where the spinal cord exits). There are four types of malformation numbered I–IV and indicating increasing severity. Hydrocephalus (excess fluid in the brain) is common with a Chiari malformation and generally occurs earlier in life with the more severe types. The most common variant is Type II, which is often found in association with a lumbar or sacral myelomeningocele (protuberance of both the spinal cord and its lining). Type III is more commonly associated with a cervical myelomeningocele. Diagnosis is made by either computed tomography (CT scan) or magnetic resonance imaging (MRI). Treatment generally involves a shunting procedure for the hydrocephalus. Sometimes the pressure within the cervical spinal canal causes neurological dysfunction, and the tops of the cervical vertebrae must be removed in a procedure called a cervical laminectomy.

arousal State of alertness.

arthritis Inflammation of a joint; symptoms can include pain, limitation of motion, warmth, redness, and swelling.

arthro A prefix relating to the joint.

arthrodesis An orthopedic surgical procedure that immobilizes or fixes a joint by fusion.

arthrogryposis multiplex congenita A syndrome of multiple congenital joint contractures with a usual pattern of symmetrical involvement of all four limbs. There are no associated neurodevelopmental deficits. This is a pure motor impairment syndrome to be treated by physical therapy, casting, and orthopedic surgery. Etiology and incidence are unknown, although oligohydramnios (too little amniotic fluid) is suspected to contribute to causation. There is no recurrence risk within a family. There is a higher than expected incidence in identical twins; however, only one twin is affected.

Arthur Adaptation of the Leiter International Performance Scale A nonverbal intelligence test for children between 2 and 12 years of age.

articulation The way speech sounds are formed. Proper formation requires correct placement, timing, direction, pressure, speed, and integration of the movement of the lips, tongue, palate, and pharynx.

articulation disorder Developmental articulation disorder, phonological disorder, speech defect; difficulty with pronunciation. This disorder is characterized by consistent failure to use developmentally expected speech sounds.

ash leaf spot A hypopigmented skin lesion found in tuberous sclerosis.

ASHA *See* American Speech-Language-Hearing Association.

Ashworth scale A grading scale for degree of spasticity (increased muscle tone) with resistance to passive range of motion, scored 1 for no tone, 2 for marked increase in tone but limb easily flexed, 3 for considerable increase in tone such that passive movement is difficult, and 4 for rigidity in flexion and extension.

ASIEP *See* Autism Screening Instrument for Educational Planning.

ASL *See* American Sign Language.

ASP disorder *See* antisocial personality disorder.

Asperger syndrome A behavioral syndrome with eccentric and obsessive interests, impaired social interactions, average to above-average intelligence, gross-motor clumsiness, and communicative deviance. Children with Asperger syndrome occupy the mild end of the autistic spectrum, with the major differential points being the absence of early language delay, the absence of mental retardation, and the presence of motor clumsiness. Incidence is estimated at 2 per 1,000 with a 7 to 1 male predominance.

asphyxia Suffocation; lack of oxygenation. When asphyxia is mentioned as a possible cause of developmental disability, it must be of sufficient duration and severity to produce the death of nerve cells. For perinatal asphyxia to be seriously considered as a cause of brain damage, the Apgar score should be 0–3 at 10 minutes, and there should also be severe hypotonia (decreased muscle tone) and seizures.

aspiration Literally, breathing or inhalation. The medical procedure of aspiration is the removal of a substance from the body by suction. Aspiration pneumonia is a lung infection caused by breathing (aspirating) an irritating substance into the lungs. Aspiration pneumonias are common with tracheoesophageal fistulas and neuromotor disorders with an oromotor or swallowing problem. Meconium aspiration is common with fetal stress and postmature deliveries. Foreign body (e.g., a peanut) aspiration can produce severe lung disease.

aspirin sensitivity Allergic asthma, nasal polyps, and severe intolerance to aspirin is a widely recognized syndrome in adults. The widespread presence of salicylate (the active ingredient in aspirin, ASA) in foods has contributed to salicylates being included on the list of substances to be avoided in almost all of the dietary regimens claiming to treat disorders of attention and learning. Evidence supporting this latter association remains anecdotal.

Assessing Prelinguistic and Early Linguistic Behaviors in Developmentally Young Children A set of five early language skills that assesses cognitive antecedents to word meaning, play, communication intention, language comprehension, and language production.

Assessing Semantic Skills through Everyday Themes (ASSET) A test of receptive and expressive vocabulary for 3- to 9-year-old children in 10 areas: understanding labels, identifying categories, identifying attributes, identifying functions, understanding definitions, expressing labels, expressing categories, expressing attributes, expressing functions, and expressing definitions.

assessment Information gathering aimed at 1) evaluating previous performance, 2) describing current behavior, and 3) predicting future behaviors. A comprehensive assessment synthesizes past records, evaluations, interviews with significant people, observations of current behavior, results of standardized tests, and other special procedures. Assessment differs from testing in that testing reflects performance at a particular time, whereas assessment requires clinical judgment to give meaning to the overall pattern and interrelationships among the various results.

Assessment of Children's Language Comprehension (ACLC) A test that uses a picture-pointing task to relate single-word vocabulary to the comprehension of two-, three-, and four-word phrases.

Assessment of Phonological Processes–– Revised (APP–R) A 20-minute assessment of phonological processes that can be used for intervention planning.

Assessment of Preterm Infant Behavior (APIB) An adaptation of the Brazelton Neonatal Behavioral Assessment Scale for use with newborns under 37 weeks' gestational age. The APIB rates behaviors in visual, auditory, tactile, organization, and reflex categories. It is used with medically stable premature infants until they react to the environment in a manner similar to full-term infants.

ASSET *See* Assessing Semantic Skills through Everyday Themes.

assimilation A learning process that applies a general cognitive structure to particular environmental data and modifies the data to suit that internal cognitive structure.

assistive technology device An item, piece of (re)habilitation equipment, or product system used to increase, maintain, or improve the functional capabilities of individuals with disabilities. Examples of such devices are orthotics, wheelchairs, and adaptive seating. PL 103-218, the Technology-Related Assistance for Individuals with Disabilities Amendments of 1994, encourages and assists states in developing programs of technology-related assistance and extending the availability of assistive technology to individuals with disabilities and their families.

associated deficits Neurobehavioral findings that do not derive directly from the primary developmental diagnosis but, rather, indicate more diffuse brain involvement and suggest the possibility of other developmental diagnoses. Associated deficits may be more disabling than the primary diagnosis, their impact on functioning is more than additive, and they reflect the underlying continuum of developmental disabilities.

associated movements Overflow movements; extraneous or adventitious movements that occur in the performance of a motor act, such as tongue protrusion when writing. Mirror movements are contralateral (opposite) associated movements; synkinesis refers to ipsilateral (on the same side) associated movements. Associated movements decrease with age and increase with many developmental disabilities; they are inversely correlated with intelligence level. Associated movements are included with soft neurological signs or signs of minor neurological dysfunction.

associated reactions Movements seen on the affected side of a hemiplegia (paralysis of half the body) or hemisyndrome in response to voluntary forceful movements in other parts of the body.

association Also known as *syntropy,* a nonrandom occurrence of multiple anomalies (malformation, deformation, disruption, or dysplasia) in more than two individuals. There is a purely statistical relationship between the anomalies. Examples include VATERS, MURCS, and CHARGE, all acronyms denoting typical associations. Understanding of the relationship between anomalies in an association is weaker than in a syndrome, although an association such as VATERS may occur as part of a syndrome, such as trisomy 18.

association area The primary visual, auditory, sensory, and motor areas of the cerebral cortex (Brodmann areas 1, 2, 3, 4, 17, and 41) are bounded by association areas (e.g., 5, 6, 7, 18, and 42) in which the incoming sensations and outgoing motor actions are interpreted or initiated by the subject. Problems with higher-order thinking (such as occur with learning disabilities) are often localized to the association areas.

Association for Children and Adults with Learning Disabilities (ACLD) *See* Learning Disabilities Association of America.

Association for the Gifted One of 13 divisions of the Council for Exceptional Children (TAG—The Association for the Gifted). Founded in 1958, the division strives to promote an understanding of gifted and talented students and their educational needs, to disseminate current knowledge of the gifted, to expand existing knowledge, and to advocate for policies and legislation on all levels that address the needs of the gifted. The association publishes the *Journal for the Education of the Gifted* and the *TAG-UP-DATE,* the association's newsletter.

associationism A theory of learning suggesting that once two stimuli are presented together, one of them will remind the learner of the other. Basic principles of associationism are 1) contiguous stimuli (occurring close together) are more likely to be associated than those occurring far apart; and 2) the more frequently the paired stimuli are repeated, the more strongly they will be associated.

assortative mating The tendency of individuals with cognitive and emotional disorders to form relationships with each other. Although the majority of pairing occurs between like types—for example, between people with schizophrenic disorders—there are also documented pairings of people with complementary or nonrelated disorders. For example, people with sociopathic tendencies and those described as hysteric often couple. Such mating thus increases the genetic probability that their offspring will be similarly affected. Although not documented within the population with learning disabilities, it is reasonable to assume that a similar process occurs and increases the likelihood or genetic risk of the offspring having learning or other developmental disabilities. Whereas this phenomenon applies to some extent to people with mental retardation, there is usually a cognitive level difference (one member of the couple being more functional than the other) that allows for their adaptive existence as a couple and as a family. In some cases assortative mating is enhanced by prolonged association with a particular social reference group (e.g., mental health facility, group therapy, sheltered workshop). However, research also indicates the existence of this phenomenon independent of prolonged affiliation.

astasia An inability to stand due to motor incoordination; this neurological finding can manifest itself in episodes of sudden collapse, with loss of support of the weight of the body. Astasia can be observed in typically developing infants at 4–5 months of age; physiologically it precedes abasia.

astatic seizure *See* akinetic seizure and atonic seizure.

astereognosis Congenital or acquired difficulty with stereognosis (solid form recognition by touch).

asthenic body type A long, slender habitus (appearance).

asthma A disorder with recurrent episodes of wheezing and shortness of breath (dyspnea) precipitated by allergy, infection, and physical or emotional stress. The incidence is 2%–5% with a prevalence of 2%; there is a male predominance. As a chronic disease in childhood, asthma accounts for a significant percentage of school absence; however, students with asthma tend to be academic overachievers. When associated with allergies, atopic asthma represents one of the more severe allergic disorders of childhood; yet the incidence of learning and behavior disorders in this condition does not appear to be elevated over that of the general population. This gives rise to serious doubt that allergy plays any significant role in the etiology of neurobehavioral syndromes.

asymmetrical tonic neck reflex (ATNR) A primitive reflex in which turning the baby's head to one side causes the arm and leg on that side to extend while the opposite arm and leg tend to flex, producing a "fencing posture." This is a physiological (normal) response in newborn babies that gradually disappears during the first 6 months of life. However, even late in the first year when the reflex is no longer visible, it can significantly influence tone and other reflex responses, facilitating extension on the face side and flexion on the occiput side. Any examination of the neuromotor system in infancy should therefore be performed with the baby's head in midline. With an obligatory response, the child would be unable to break out of the ATNR pattern so long as the head remained turned to the side; such a response should be considered pathological.

ATNR

asymptomatic Without symptoms. Appearing healthy and without disabilities when in reality there is a disease condition present. Some carriers of infectious diseases remain asymptomatic while spreading the disease; others become symptomatic. Genetic carriers of autosomal recessive conditions may have no symptoms or only mild symptoms compared to homozygotes. Many diseases of various etiologies have quiet phases or asymptomatic stages. Screening tests often attempt to diagnose asymptomatic disorders. An asymptomatic impairment should not produce disability, but if identified, might engender a disability (*see* prodrome). Many definitions of health equate health with being asymptomatic. Such a definition is controversial, in that it ignores those conditions just mentioned.

ataxia Literally, "lack of order"; in developmental disabilities, absence or loss of muscular coordination leading to clumsy and uncertain standing, walking, and reaching. An ataxic (unsteady) gait is wide-based, staggering, almost drunken; the difficulty is exaggerated when walking with the eyes closed. Significant ataxia is usually associated with disorders of the cerebellum.

ataxia telangiectasia Louis-Bar syndrome; a progressive, ultimately fatal genetic disorder with marked coordination problems (ataxia); dilation of the small vessels (telangiectasia) of the eyes, nose, and ears; frequent infections (secondary to an immune system limitation); and, in approximately half of the cases, mental deficiency in the later stages of the disease. Incidence is rare, with inheritance following an autosomal recessive pattern.

ataxic cerebral palsy One of the physiological subtypes of cerebral palsy in which the prominent motor signs are early hypotonia (decreased muscle tone) and later ataxia (unsteady gait). When ataxia is the prevailing motor symptom and it exhibits constant improvement with age, congenital cerebellar involvement is typical, with some degree of cerebellar hypoplasia or agenesis (absence of formation) usually being demonstrable on neuroradiological investigation. The most frequent associated deficit with cerebellar cerebral palsy is mild cognitive limitation; tremor and articulation disorders are not uncommon. This is one of the rarer subtypes of extrapyramidal cerebral palsy.

atelectasis A collapse of a segment of the lung; its presence is usually associated with preexisting or underlying lung disease, and its occurrence is usually marked by increased respiratory distress.

athetoid posturing An abnormal movement pattern of the hand and fingers (and sometimes of the foot and toes) involving splaying of the digits, spooning, and an "almost withdrawal" or "avoidance" posture when attempting to grasp an object (and sometimes spontaneously). Athetoid posturing of the feet contributes to the "spontaneous Babinski" of extrapyramidal cerebral palsy.

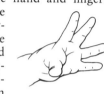
athetoid posturing

athetosis Literally, "without position"; in motor disabilities, a pattern of movement disorder characterized by involuntary, slow, writhing, and undulating movements of flexion, extension, pronation, and supination—more peripheral than central, sometimes called vermicular or wormlike. When the associated motor delay is serious, the type of extrapyramidal cerebral palsy present is usually described as choreoathetoid. More purely athetoid movements are slower and more sustained than choreiform (involuntary twitching) movements. *See also* choreoathetosis.

Ativan *See* lorazepam.

atlantoaxial instability An enlargement of the distance between the first two cervical (neck) vertebrae that leaves the individual susceptible to spinal cord compression, neurological involvement (transient or permanent weakness or paralysis), and death. Children with Down syndrome are at increased risk for atlantoaxial instability. Periodic radiologic screening (cervical spine X rays), close neurological monitoring, and caution with regard to contact sports and other activities that might precipitate cord compression are indicated.

ATNR *See* asymmetrical tonic neck reflex.

atonic cerebral palsy *See* hypotonic cerebral palsy.

atonic seizure Akinetic or astatic seizures; seizures characterized by sudden loss of posture and tone. In infants who do not stand independently, these seizures are manifested in the "salaam seizures" during which the infant suddenly drops his or her head and neck forward. In older children, the loss of postural tone results in a sudden drop to the ground ("drop attack"). Although there is only a brief loss of consciousness, head injuries commonly occur after such events. Atonic spells are most common in the morning shortly after waking, but can occur frequently during the day. Atonic seizures are part of Lennox-Gastaut syndrome, which has a poor prognosis for seizure control and cognitive development. *See also* Lennox-Gastaut syndrome.

atopy Literally, "strangeness." A group of allergic diseases with common features. Atopic diseases include hay fever, allergic asthma, certain cases of eczema, and some cases of urticaria (hives). These have a definite familial or genetic tendency, but not to specific diseases or allergens.

atresia The congenital absence of or failure to develop a normally present body cavity or canal.

atrophy Shrinkage; wasting away. A decrease in size of an anatomical structure (body part or organ).

attention Selective, goal-directed perception. Neuropsychological theories and (neuro)physiological correlates of arousal and attention remain confusing and disappointing. Whatever the operational definition of *attention*, the length of time a child can attend to a stimulus (attention span) increases with age, interest, and intelligence level.

attention-deficit/hyperactivity disorder (ADHD) Formerly, attention deficit disorder (ADD) with or without hyperactivity (H). This disorder is a neurobehavioral syndrome characterized by short attention span, distractibility, impulsivity, and hyperactivity. Frequently this disorder (either ADHD or ADD) overlaps with learning disabilities. Diagnosis is by interview, observation, and behavioral questionnaires. The child or adult should, over a prolonged period of time, demonstrate a behavioral pattern that includes the following: fidgeting, difficulty remaining seated, distractibility, difficulty waiting turns, blurting out answers, failure to complete assignments, poorly sustained attention, excessive shifting, noisiness, excessive talking ("motor mouth"), intrusiveness, failure to listen, frequently losing things, and physically dangerous behavior. There is some overlap with oppositional defiant disorder. Motor clumsiness and visual perceptual motor disorders are also common in this condition. Current prevalence estimates suggest that 5%–10% of all children exhibit some form of ADHD, with 20% of these exhibiting a severe form. Although familial in occurrence, transmission patterns are not yet fully delineated.

attribution retraining Experimental programs based on attribution theory are designed to teach children how to change their performances by changing their perception of the cause of success or failure from an uncontrollable factor, such as ability, to a controllable factor, such as effort. Students are given feedback regarding their effort on tasks, such as "You were trying hard" or "We usually fail because we don't try hard enough." It is important that the tasks undertaken be consistent with the students' abilities.

attribution theory A social psychology theory that explores the cognitive rules typically used by individuals to explain observed social behavior. People develop a repertoire of causal schemata, defined as a general conception of how certain kinds of causes interact. A major division separates those who blame themselves (internal causation) from those who blame others or their environment (external causation). A person's explanations for feelings, successes, failures, or other outcomes may be enhanced or inhibited by his or her position on the internal versus external causal axis.

audile   Describes a person who learns best by listening (e.g., rather than by looking).

audiogram   A record showing hearing level by sound frequency. A clinical audiogram should show hearing thresholds measured by both air conduction and bone conduction. Better hearing by bone conduction than air conduction indicates an air–bone gap, a sign of conductive hearing loss.

audiologist   An individual who holds a degree and/or a certification in audiology and who is concerned with the identification, assessment, and rehabilitation of hearing impairments.

audiology   The study of hearing and hearing disorders; specifically, the assessment of the nature and degree of hearing loss, hearing conservation, and the rehabilitation of individuals with hearing impairments. Clinical audiology considers hearing to be the foundation of learning and utilization of language skills; thus, emphasis is placed on understanding the social uses of hearing and on maximizing the ability of individuals with hearing impairments to cope with the demands of communication.

auditory   Relating to hearing or audition.

auditory brain-stem response (ABR)   *See* brain-stem auditory-evoked response.

auditory discrimination   The (brain's) ability to tell the difference between very similar sounds. People with problems in auditory discrimination have difficulty distinguishing between words that sound alike or differ in a single phoneme. Such words as "tow" and "toll," and "whim" and "win," may sound identical to them. An impairment in auditory discrimination can interfere with verbal comprehension and the development of functional read-

ing skills. In addition, a serious weakness in auditory discrimination in the classroom setting can be confused with inattention, as the child appears not to have listened closely. *See also* Wepman Auditory Discrimination Test.

auditory memory   The ability to store and retrieve information presented verbally as sounds or in the form of sound symbols, which may involve auditory sequential memory (remembering details in a particular order). Auditory memory relates to the acquisition and use of both expressive and receptive language vocabulary. Expressive vocabulary may partially depend on an ability to recall and retrieve particular words at the appropriate time, whereas receptive vocabulary may constitute a form of auditory recognition, retention, and association. *See also* auditory sequential memory.

auditory motor   *See* perceptual-motor.

auditory nerve   Also known as the acoustic nerve; the eighth cranial nerve. Cranial nerve VIII has two major branches: the cochlear nerve for hearing and the vestibular nerve for balance.

auditory perception   The ability of the brain to interpret information that enters the body through the ears. Auditory perception is not directly related to auditory acuity or sharpness but to the process by which the brain discriminates sounds from each other and identifies meaningful units of sound.

Auditory Projective Test   *See* Braverman–Chevigny Auditory Projective Test.

auditory sequential memory   The ability to retain verbally presented information in a particular order. Auditory sequential memory is measured by tests such as digit span and memory for sentences and nonsense syllables. People with auditory sequential memory problems may also have difficulty following a series of instructions. However, such a difficulty may be confused with or may coexist with attentional limitations, which may also be manifested by an inability to respond correctly to an ordered series of verbal directions.

auditory training The process of teaching a person with a hearing impairment how to make the best use of residual acoustic cues (i.e., how to listen, localize, and discriminate). Auditory training is not to be confused with auditory process training, a method of ameliorating learning disabilities prevalent in the 1960s.

augmentative communication Any procedure or device that facilitates speech or spoken language.

augmentative and alternative communication (AAC) Temporary or permanent compensation techniques of individuals with severe expressive communication disorders. AAC interventions should utilize an integrated group of components, including the symbols, aids, strategies, and techniques used by individuals to enhance communication. In this definition, "symbols" refer to the methods used to facilitate communication by representing conventional concepts (e.g., gestures, photographs, manual sign systems, printed words, spoken words). The term "aids" refers to a physical object or device to assist with the communication process (e.g., board, chart, device, computer). "Strategies" are the specific ways AAC aids and techniques are used to enhance communication (e.g., role playing, classroom learning), and "techniques" refer to the way in which the messages are transmitted (e.g., scanning, encoding, signing, natural gestures). All these interventions come from both augmentative and alternative communication approaches.

augmentative communication system Aggregate communication process for an individual with verbal communication difficulty.

aura A sensation that may precede a seizure or migraine headache. This may be caused by vasodilation (increase in diameter) of the blood vessels of the brain in migraines. The auras present in migraine headaches include vomiting; visual disturbance; tingling; or transient hemi-

plegia (paralysis of half the body), aphasia (loss of language skills), or ataxia (unsteady gait). Auras preceding seizures—generally complex partial seizures—are often olfactory (smell), a gastric "rising" sensation, fear, visual hallucinations, or, rarely, rage reactions. The frequency of auras appears to increase with age; however, this may reflect the ability of a child to describe the phenomenon.

aural rehabilitation Educational procedures used with individuals with hearing impairments to improve their overall ability to communicate. Rehabilitation includes developing, utilizing, and integrating existing receptive and expressive modalities such as utilizing auditory, tactile, visual, and kinesthetic channels. All the techniques are based on two methodologies: 1) the analytic method, which is a sequential approach that stresses mastery of the parts of the technique for assimilating information into a comprehensive picture; and 2) the synthetic method, which promotes the use of language in spontaneous, simultaneous situations through speech, reading, and writing before the language is presented formally.

auricle The external ear, or pinna. The term is also an old synonym, little used, for the heart chamber now called the atrium.

auscultation Listening; a diagnostic procedure to listen to the body's internal sounds; examples include the use of a stethoscope to auscultate heart sounds and breath sounds or a fetoscope to auscultate the unborn baby's heart rate.

autism Kanner syndrome, autistic disorder, early infantile autism. A neurobiological syndrome characterized by extremely deviant behavior including failure to develop social relationships, language delay and deviance, hyperactivity, tactile defensiveness, stereotypies, insistence on the preservation of sameness, and, in approximately 85% of cases, mental retardation. This rare developmental disorder was first described by Leo Kanner (1894–1981) in 1943 and was, for many years, thought to reflect maternal ambivalence toward the child. It is now generally recognized to be a severe organic brain disorder with many different etiologies (causes) such as rubella, neurofibromatosis, and fragile X syndrome. Incidence is estimated at 0.02%. Treatment is generally through the educational system using highly structured, nonstimulating environments, behavior management techniques, and a language-based curriculum. Prognosis for adult functional outcome is related to IQ and the degree of language impairment. Autism has been diagnostically categorized as a pervasive developmental disorder.

Autism Screening Instrument for Educational Planning (ASIEP) A classroom assessment and educational planning system for persons with autism, severe disabilities, and developmental disabilities who are between 18 months of age and adulthood and who have low language abilities. The ASIEP includes five components: autism behavior checklist (ABC); sample of vocal behavior; interaction assessment (including self-stimulation, crying, laughing, gesturing, manipulation of toys, conversation, and tantrums); educational assessment; and prognosis of learning rate.

autistic features Behavioral deviance frequently seen in children with autism, deafness, or other developmental disorders with somewhat atypical presentations. These features can include language delay, noncommunicative language, reference to self in third person, pronominal reversal, neologisms (introduction of new words or new senses of words), echolalia (repetition of what is heard), poor eye contact, lack of cuddliness as a baby, not responding to auditory input, good rote memory, acting as though off in own world, treating people like furniture, laughing for no reason, odd play, no peer interactions, water play, toe walking (an equinus [an involuntary foot extension] gait), rocking, twirling, spinning, perseveration (unable to move to another thought or idea), hyperactivity, unusual object attachment, hand regard, hand flapping, stereotypies, and preservation of sameness.

autognosis Diagnosis through the awareness of the feelings that the individual en-

genders in the examiner. For example, an interview with a depressed person may leave the physician feeling depressed.

automatic processing Behavioral sequences that, after prolonged practice, no longer require attention. Some processes are susceptible to this type of learning, whereas others may be intrinsically incapable of automatization. Although automatic processes are rapid and efficient, once learned they are inflexible and difficult to change. In a learning situation, automatization failure and deficiency refer to the fact that a person must still devote conscious attention to learning tasks that have become automatic for others. For example, having to consciously decode words hinders comprehension, and having to consciously compute math facts decreases the attention available for processing new concepts. In everyday life, whereas the process of learning to drive requires conscious attention, once the process becomes automatic, little thought is given to the specific actions necessary.

automatisms Semipurposeful movements or activities that occur frequently with complex partial seizures. These are generally stereotypic movements that may be related to the activity in progress before the onset of the seizure or may begin after the onset. Automatisms can be described in five groups based on the characteristics of the activity. These groups include gestural motions (picking at clothing), alimentary motions (chewing or lip smacking), mimicking (facial grimaces), verbal occurrences (yelling, laughing, or repetitive speech), and ambulatory movements (walking or running). In general, automatisms occur after consciousness has been lost and children do not remember them.

automatization The point at which information processing becomes effortless and more efficient due to practice or increased expertise.

autonomic nervous system The involuntary nervous system; that division of the nervous system that controls the unconscious functioning of the cardiovascular, respiratory, digestive, and reproductive systems; sometimes referred to as brainstem, vegetative, or life-sustaining functions. There are two major subdivisions to the autonomic nervous system: 1) the sympathetic (adrenergic), and 2) the parasympathetic (cholinergic) nervous systems.

autosomal dominant Describes the inheritance pattern for a trait that appears in every generation, is transmitted by an affected person (one parent), but never by an unaffected person. Transmission and occurrence are not affected by sex. Neurofibromatosis is an example of an autosomal dominant trait.

autosomal recessive Describes the inheritance pattern for a trait that is inherited when a child receives two genes for the trait, one from each parent, both of whom must carry the gene for that trait although they are not necessarily affected by it. Every human probably carries several harmful recessive genes, but these genes are usually present in the general population at a relatively low prevalence. A specific harmful gene may be present in a particular population at a higher rate than that of the general population. For example, although Tay-Sachs disease is present in all populations, it occurs at a greater rate in the Ashkenazic Jewish population. Inbreeding among ethnically, religiously, or geographically isolated populations results in an increase in the number of individuals with rare recessive disorders. *See* consanguinity.

autosome Any chromosome other than a sex chromosome. Humans have 22 pairs of autosomal chromosomes and one pair of sex chromosomes.

auxology The study or science of (human) growth. The term was introduced by Paul Godin (1860–1935) in 1919 and was popularized by J.M. Tanner in the 1970s to refer to the whole subject of physical and physiological growth and development.

aversive stimulus A stimulus that, applied to a response, decreases the tendency of that response to recur; a noxious stimulus.

axial Central in the body; along the axis of the head and trunk; axial tone (especially hypotonia [decreased muscle tone]) is often distinguished from appendicular tone.

axilla The armpit.

B

babbling The second stage of infant vocalization following cooing and preceding first words. Consonant and vowel combinations are used repetitively to produce such sequences as "gagaga" and "dadadada." Babbling is a maturational phenomenon that occurs over time (6–7 months) even in children who are deaf but is delayed in children with developmental disabilities such as mental retardation and language disorders. Absent or delayed babbling is part of the syndrome of the quiet baby.

Babinski sign A plantar (foot) reflex in which the toes flex (turn down) when the lateral (outside) of the sole is stimulated. An abnormal (termed *positive*) Babinski sign is an upgoing (extension) movement of the toes (dorsiflexion). A positive response is not uncommon in the first year of life. A normal (termed *negative*) Babinski reflex is described as flexion (downgoing) and plantar flexion. The first movement of the hallux (big toe) and the presence of flaring of the toes are important points in equivocal or uncertain Babinski responses. Positive Babinski responses are signs of pyramidal tract involvement in spastic cerebral palsy, and spontaneous (unstimulated) upgoing Babinskis can be observed in extrapyramidal cerebral palsy. Joseph François Felix Babinski (1857–1932) first described this reflex.

Babinski sign

Babkin reflex A newborn reflex pattern in which squeezing the infant's palms produces mouth opening, eye closing, and turning and flexing of the head. This palmomandibular sign weakens in the first month and is absent after 4 months of age.

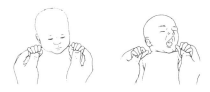

Babkin reflex

back pain In adults, back pain is a frequent complaint and is often related to physical exertion or psychosomatic stress. In children, back pain is almost always associated with significant organic pathology. Rarely does it accompany the psychosomatic triad of headache, abdominal pain, and leg pains often found together in children.

backward An antiquated and inexact term used to describe mild mental retardation, borderline intelligence, or academic underachievement.

backward reader An outdated term broadly used to refer to anyone with a significant reading problem. The term was derived from the normal tendency of young children, and the residual tendency of older children with reading difficulties, to reverse letters and words when learning to read. The term was used with great regularity in school psychology as late as 1970 and reportedly still appears infrequently in the literature. If encountered in contemporary special education settings, the user must be asked to define its context. Like its modern counterpart, *dyslexia*, the term *backward reader* can easily be misinterpreted.

baclofen A centrally acting muscle-relaxant drug that is sometimes used in severe cases of cerebral palsy; indications and efficacy remain unclear. One proposed method of improving the efficacy of baclofen is by continuous intrathecal baclofen infusion (CIBI). Baclofen also has been used to treat self-injurious behavior.

BAER *See* brain-stem auditory-evoked response.

Baller-Gerold syndrome A rare genetic syndrome with craniosynostosis (premature fusion of skull sutures), growth deficiency, abnormalities of the forearm and anus, and, in approximately half the cases, mental retardation. Inheritance follows an autosomal recessive pattern.

ballismus Rotary flailing; irregular, violent, flinging, hurling, large rapid movements at the shoulder or hip. The condition is typically unilateral (hemiballismus) and represents a rare variant of choreiform (involuntary twitching) extrapyramidal cerebral palsy.

Balthazar Scales of Adaptive Behavior (BSAB) A rating scale for adaptive behavior in institutionalized children and adults with mental retardation.

banding A technique of staining chromosomes that produces characteristic but different patterns of cross-bands. G-banding uses Giemsa staining; Q-banding uses quinacrine fluorescence.

Bankson-Bernthal Test of Phonology (BBTOP) An assessment of articulation and phonological processes among children 3–9 years of age.

Bankson Language Test–Second Edition (BLT–2) A test of language for children from 3 to 7 years of age with results organized into three general categories: semantic (meaning systems) knowledge, morphological/syntactic (language structure) rules, and pragmatics.

Bannatyne classification A heuristic recategorization of Wechsler subtests in an attempt to assist in the evaluation of children believed to have learning disabilities. The spatial category (picture completion, block design, and object assembly) taps the ability to manipulate objects in space. The conceptual category (comprehension, similarities, and vocabulary) addresses abilities involved in language development. The sequential category (arithmetic, digit span, coding) is the same as the Wechsler freedom from distractibility factor; it measures the ability to remember and utilize auditory and memory stimuli sequences in short-term memory storage. The acquired knowledge category (information, arithmetic, vocabulary) evaluates abilities usually learned at home and school. Bannatyne's categorization is based on examination of the subtest, rather than factor-analytic studies. Designed to aid in test interpretation, the pattern proposed as generally typical of learning disability is spatial-conceptual-sequential. However, no single, unique Wechsler profile for children with learning disabilities has been demonstrated. This is not surprising, because children with learning disabilities are a heterogeneous group. Bannatyne's classifications have not succeeded at either differentiating children with visual-perceptual limitations from those with auditory-perceptual limitations or discriminating children with learning disabilities from groups of children with other disabilities.

barbiturate A group of addictive drugs that act as central nervous system depressants; they can be used for sedation and seizure control.

Bardet-Biedl syndrome A genetic syndrome with polydactyly (extra fingers or toes), syndactyly (webbing of the fingers or toes), obesity, retinitis pigmentosa (with night blindness in childhood progressing to complete blindness by age 20 in three fourths of cases), and mild to moderate mental retardation in 85% of cases. Cardiac, renal, and ophthalmological follow-up is indicated. Inheritance follows an autosomal recessive pattern. Recurrence risk is 25%.

Barlow maneuver A test of hip stability used to screen for congenital hip dislocation in infants; medial to lateral (outside) pressure is applied to the proximal femur (thigh bone). Testing for hip dislocation is a routine component of the pediatric examination in early infancy.

barrier-free Describing a building, facility, or area that is accessible to people with impaired mobility. Barrier-free access provides ramps or elevators to supplement steps or stairs. Doorways are wide enough to accommodate wheelchairs, and bathrooms are equipped to accommodate people with impaired mobility. The term is also used to refer to removing barriers that limit access of people with other disabilities by, for example, printing all signs in braille for people with visual impairment.

basal The point below which test items are assumed to be correct. To shorten test administration time, particularly when the test covers a wide age range, administration procedures often indicate an item to begin with, based on age or grade. Basals are described specifically for each test and are often a set number of consecutive items answered correctly. If, for example, the basal is four consecutive correct answers and the subject misses one of the first four items administered, easier items are administered until the criteria are met. In scoring, items below the basal, regardless of whether they are correct, are scored as correct. A variation of this rule is sometimes referred to as a "double basal," in which two basals are obtained with errors between them. The Peabody Picture Vocabulary Test— Revised requires that the higher basal be used; other tests may not address this phenomenon. Because scoring procedures differ by tests, instruction manuals should be consulted.

basal ganglia A group of nuclei (control centers) in the brain whose major function is to regulate voluntary motor activity through the extrapyramidal motor system. These nuclei include the striatum (caudate nucleus and putamen), globus pallidus, and substantia nigra. They are very susceptible to damage by hyperbilirubinemia (high levels of bilirubin in the blood), which can occur in neonatal jaundice (yellowing of the skin) (e.g., in Rh incompatibility [erythroblastosis fetalis]). Immediate pathological effects might include opisthotonos (an arching of the back) with kernicterus; long-term effects are reflected in choreoathetoid cerebral palsy.

Basal readers series A series of books containing a collection of stories in which vocabulary is controlled. The books are typically used with groups of children and represent different reading levels. The series also includes teachers' manuals, workbooks, placement and achievement tests, and various audiovisual and duplicating materials.

base pair *See* deoxyribonucleic acid (DNA).

baseline A record of the frequency, duration, or intensity with which a behavior occurs over a period of time before an attempt to change the behavior is initiated. For example, the number of times a student talks out in class is recorded over a period of 3 days. This represents baseline data. Continuing to monitor the behavior while a specific method of behavior management is in place or charting it again over a 3-day period at a later date and comparing it to the baseline data will indicate the effectiveness of the intervention. This method may also be used to assess the effectiveness of an academic intervention. For example, the number of words read correctly per minute may be charted. Baseline behaviors can include physiological measures such as heart rate.

baseline exaggeration A phenomenon in which acute psychiatric symptoms are an exaggeration of preexisting behavior problems in people with mental retardation.

Basic Achievement Skills Individual Screener (BASIS) An individually administered test designed to assess students' basic skills in mathematics, reading, spelling, and writing. The skills are assessed from first- through eighth-grade levels. Administration time is approximately 1 hour. Both norm-referenced (standard scores, percentile ranks, stanines, grade equivalents, age equivalents, and normal curve equivalents) and criterion-referenced (Grade Referenced Placement Score) scores are provided for mathematics, reading, and spelling. Writing samples are scored holistically and are rated as average, below average, or above average. People with disabilities were included in the standardization sample, although several modifications are recommended with these populations.

Basic School Skills Inventory–Diagnostic (BSSI–D) Both a norm- and criterion-referenced test for children ages 4-0 to 7-5. The BSSI–D uses 110 items to measure the following six areas of school performance: 1) daily living skills, 2) spoken language, 3) reading readiness, 4) writing readiness, 5) math readiness, and 6) classroom behavior.

basic skill A fundamental ability. The mastery of basic skills is necessary to progress to higher levels of achievement. Basic skills are considered to be the activities necessary for functioning on a daily basis. Academically, basic skills include speaking, spelling, reading, writing, and arithmetic. The basic skills of individuals with learning disabilities are often not uniformly developed or are attained through one predominant processing style or channel, making the achievement of more-advanced academic abilities, such as integration of information or problem solving, even more difficult to achieve. In addition, for children with learning and other developmental disabilities, basic skills training may also emphasize social skills, study habits, attention training, and other specific tasks that assist in the development of independence and self-esteem.

basic trust In Eric Erikson's version of psychoanalysis, the major achievement of the first year of life; repeated interactions with a caregiver (typically the mother) teach the infant a positive orientation toward the world. The major importance of this theoretical construct lies in the long-term impact of a failure in its development: children who are severely neglected in infancy remain at risk in later life of exhibiting significant sociopathy. Extrapolation of this association to the milder end of the spectrum of parenting disorders is less well documented.

basilect Dialect that varies considerably from standard English; common in cultural groups that are not frequently exposed or readily inclined to adopt standard English (e.g., English spoken in ethnic communities).

BASIS *See* Basic Achievement Skills Individual Screener.

Bassen-Kornzweig disease *See* abetalipoproteinemia.

Battelle Developmental Inventory (BDI) A comprehensive, standardized, 341-item assessment for children from birth to 8 years of age in the domains of personal-social, adaptability, motor, communication, and cognition. Administration time is 1–2 hours. A Spanish version is available.

Battelle Developmental Inventory Screening Test (BDIST) A 96-item developmental screening test for children from birth to 8 years of age that yields a total test score and seven subtest scores in the following domains: personal-social, adaptive, gross motor, fine motor, receptive language, expressive language, and cognitive. Derived from the BDI (Battelle Developmental Inventory), the test allows the use of alternative screening cutoffs. Administration time is approximately a half hour.

battered child syndrome Also known as Caffey syndrome, Caffey-Kempe syndrome; refers to a specific pattern of lesions to the bones found on X-ray examination that indicates a child is being criminally beaten by his or her caregivers. These radiographic findings may be accompanied by bruises, burns, black eyes, cuts, and abrasions leading to suspicion of the etiology (cause).

battery Specific groups of diagnostic tests used in evaluating an individual for a variety of conditions and in a number of situations. Psychological, educational, neurological, and developmental evaluations include test batteries. Individual tests in a battery focus on different but related skills or on particular aspects of a given skill, providing the examiner with a significant amount of data. Those data, in combination with history information, behavioral observation, and clinical judgment, are used to formulate a diagnosis and, subsequently, to suggest directions for intervention.

Bayes theorem/Bayesian analysis　A probabilistic approach to assessing the effectiveness of a screening test or diagnostic procedure; the approach attempts to allow for the prevalence of the condition being tested for in the population. If the joint probability is prevalence multiplied by sensitivity, then the final, or posterior, probability is the joint probability divided by the sum of the joint probability and the product of the false positive rate multiplied by [1 minus the prevalence rate] or

$$\text{probability} = \frac{\text{joint probability}}{\text{joint probability} + (\text{false positive rate} \times [1 - \text{prevalence rate}])}$$

For example, if a disorder has a 3% prevalence rate and a screening test has a sensitivity (true positive rate) of 95% and a false negative (underreferral rate) of 10%, then the posterior probability that the disorder is present when the screening test is positive is only 37%.

Bayley Scales of Infant Development–Second Edition (BSID–II)　A measure of cognitive and motor development for children from 1 to 42 months of age. Originally developed by Nancy Bayley, the following two standard scores are obtained: 1) a mental development index from the mental scale, and 2) a psychomotor developmental index from the motor scale. The mental scale assesses shape discrimination, sustained attention, imitation, comprehension, problem solving, memory, vocalization, and naming objects. The motor scale assesses fine- and gross-motor abilities, including grasping, sitting, and walking. There is also a Behavior Rating Scale, which systematically rates 11 areas of social and affective behavior. Behaviors related to cognitive tasks (i.e., attention span, reactivity, and goal directedness) have been found to relate to mental scores, whereas social extraversion behaviors (i.e., cooperativeness, emotional tone, and social orientation to the examiner) have been found to

have little predictive validity. Standard scores on the Bayley have a mean of 100 and a standard deviation of 16. The average length of testing is 45 minutes. Proper administration of the scales requires considerable practice and experience. As of 1996, the scale was regarded as the best available measure of infant development, owing to its psychometric properties.

Bayley II　*See* Bayley Scales of Infant Development–Second Edition.

BBCS　*See* Bracken Basic Concept Scale.

BBTOP　*See* Bankson-Bernthal Test of Phonology.

BDI　*See* Battelle Developmental Inventory; *see also* Beck Depression Inventory.

BDIST　*See* Battelle Developmental Inventory Screening Test.

BE　Below elbow.

BEAM　*See* brain electrical activity mapping.

Beck Depression Inventory (BDI)　A self-administered questionnaire with 21 items rated on a four-point scale to screen for and assess the intensity of depression in persons 17–80 years of age. A version for children is also available.

Becker muscular dystrophy　*See* muscular dystrophy.

Beckwith-Wiedemann syndrome (Beckwith syndrome)　A dysmorphic syndrome of unknown etiology (cause) characterized by exomphalos (umbilical abnormality), macroglossia (large tongue), and gigantism (macosomia [large body size] often present from birth). Mental retardation is an occasional finding. There is a characteristic facies with a birthmark on the forehead and a linear groove in the lobule of the ear. Hypoglycemia (low blood sugar level) and Wilms' tumor (a malignancy of the kidney) are among the potential complications; thus, regular medical follow-up for these conditions is warranted. Inheritance pattern is unclear.

bed-wetting *See* enuresis.

Beery and Buktenica Developmental Test of Visual-Motor Integration A visual perceptual motor test for children 2–16 years of age.

Beery Developmental Test of Visual-Motor Integration (DTVMI) *See* Developmental Test of Visual-Motor Integration.

BEH *See* Bureau of Education for the Handicapped.

behavior disorder A practical term referring to observable behavior that deviates from the norm. In special education, the term is often used synonymously with the terms *emotionally disturbed* and *emotionally handicapped*. PL 94-142, the Education for All Handicapped Children Act of 1975, uses the term "seriously emotionally disturbed" when providing criteria for eligibility for services. (PL 94-142 was reauthorized in 1990 as PL 101-476, the Individuals with Disabilities Education Act [IDEA]). This latter term does not include children with social maladjustments unless it is determined that they also have serious emotional disturbances. States, however, use a variety of terms, including *behaviorally disordered*, in their legal language when defining criteria for services. The interchangeable use of these terms is confusing, if not contradictory. A serious emotional disturbance encompasses a range of childhood psychopathology, including schizophrenia, whereas a behavior disorder implies behavior that is unacceptable to an environmental norm. The vagueness of *behavior disorder* as a categorical descriptor makes it difficult to define appropriate intervention strategies. In addition, describing and attempting to modify specific behaviors without questioning etiology (cause) may overlook learning or language disorders as causative factors. *Behavior disorder* connotes a diagnosis that is based on the presence of one or more deviant or problem behaviors.

Behavior Evaluation Scale (BES) A checklist of six developmental areas and one problem area to help plan educational interventions for children with autism.

Behavior Evaluation Scale–2 (BES–2) A behavior assessment for children in grades kindergarten through 12. The BES–2 measures five dimensions corresponding to the five characteristics of behavior disorders/emotional disturbance in PL 94-142, the Education for All Handicapped Children Act of 1975 (since reauthorized as PL 101-476, the Individuals with Disabilities Education Act [IDEA] of 1990): learning problems, interpersonal difficulties, inappropriate behavior, unhappiness/depression, and physical symptoms/fears. Examiner qualifications are minimal. A seven-point scale is used to rate 76 items according to the frequency with which indicated behaviors are observed. Standard scores with a mean of 10 and a standard deviation of 3 are derived for each subscale, and a behavior quotient with a mean of 100 and a standard deviation of 15 is derived from the sum of the subscale standard scores. Percentiles may be obtained for each of the five subscales and the total scale. The BES–2 is not to be confused with Kozloff's Behavior Evaluation Scale, which is an entirely different instrument.

behavior management An approach to child rearing/parent training that moves the focus of behavior intervention from a reactive stimulus–response approach to a proactive preventive management approach. Such an approach eliminates environmental support for inappropriate or negative behaviors and provides environmental support for positive behaviors. For children with neurological problems, ordinary parenting techniques that communicate a "Don't do that again" message in response to an inappropriate behavior are usually ineffective. In a structured behavior management approach, misbehaviors are anticipated, and preventive measures are instituted. Thus, children who are neurologically driven (i.e., children with attention-deficit/hyperactivity disorder [ADHD]) can avoid the experience of constant reprimands while enjoying positive reinforcement for good behaviors.

behavior modeling A training intervention popularized by social learning theory.

A practitioner demonstrates (models) the appropriate behavior or uses a visual representation. Behavior modeling is a useful instructional procedure that requires its users to follow specific, but not difficult, procedures to produce maximum results.

behavior modification A set of techniques based on the systematic application of learning theory. Common to all models of learning theory is the notion that positive reinforcement will increase a behavior and that negative reinforcement or punishment will decrease a behavior. From these fundamental tenets, a number of psychotherapeutic techniques and parent-training models have been developed to help parents handle the tasks of child rearing more systematically. Although these tools are useful for parents of neurologically normal children, they often fail to modify the organically driven behavior of a child with neurological problems (e.g., a child with attention-deficit/hyperactivity disorder [ADHD] or Prader-Willi syndrome). These children may cognitively associate a behavior with an expected consequence, but the neurological substrate of their behavior remains unmanaged. An injudicious application of these techniques and their subsequent failure can lead to secondary emotional and family problems.

Behavior Observation Scale for Autism (BOS) A 67-item direct observation scale used to diagnose autism.

Behavior Rating Instrument for Autistic and Atypical Children (BRIAAC) A behavior rating scale that generates the following eight subscales: relationship to an adult, communication, drive for mastery, vocalization and expressive speech, sound and speech reception, social responsiveness, body movement, and psychobiological development. The resulting profile is used for diagnosis, prognosis, and programming.

Behavior Rating Profile (BRP) A 124-item questionnaire that includes student rating scales, teacher rating scales, parent rating scales, and a sociogram. The instrument attempts to assess children's behavior in a variety of settings and from different points of view.

behavioral genetics A field of study concerned with the effects of genes on the expression of behavior. Although nature versus nurture issues continue to be a central controversy in the study of human behavior, recently a convergence of factors has permitted a quantitative measurement of the genetic aspects of the nature versus nurture interdependence in producing states of behavioral health or unhealth. These factors include the following: 1) an availability of adequate family pedigrees in countries that have standardized national health records, 2) standardized diagnostic criteria, 3) molecular genetic technology, and 4) computer modeling. The prototype for such studies is the research on the genetic determinants of alcoholism. Behavioral geneticists have focused on developmental difficulties such as Tourette syndrome, attention-deficit/hyperactivity disorder [ADHD], language deviance, and dyslexia and have described a number of chromosomal and environmental interactions.

behavioral observation audiometry A hearing assessment procedure used primarily with infants and young children. The child is behaviorally conditioned to perform a certain task in response to sound in order to obtain hearing thresholds. In testing infants, reflex responses are elicited and utilized; the following three types are typically employed: 1) the hear-turn technique, 2) the high-amplitude sucking technique, and 3) the starter technique. The infant's response is used to determine speech–sound discrimination. Play conditioning for 3- to 4-year-olds pairs a fun activity (e.g., building pegboard figures, dropping coins in a bank) with preservation of sound produced by a pure tone audiometer.

behaviorism Within the discipline of psychology, a theory of behavior that views learning as the central focus of human psychology. Learning is defined as the acquisition of specific responses (R) to specific stimuli (S). This theoretical formulation traditionally viewed any discussion of brain mediation of the *S–R* chain through cognition, consciousness, or instinct as irrelevant and unscientific, because it was unobservable and therefore nonobjectifiable. Recent theoretical reformulations, however, have readmitted the role of the brain's mediation, using the person him- or herself as a scientific observer. Within the same fundamental framework, the concepts of cognitive behaviorism have developed. These concepts and the resulting methods of therapeutic intervention have now begun to interact with other language and cognitive processing theories, such as information, hemispheric lateralization, and neurolinguistic theories. Although no single theoretical framework has emerged, the interactions are providing a base for developing interventions for children with mental retardation, language impairments, and developmental disabilities.

Behr disease An inherited spastic paraplegia with optic atrophy (wasting); a rare hereditary degenerative disease characterized by ataxia (unsteady gait), mental retardation, optic atrophy, nystagmus (involuntary eye movements), and peripheral neuropathy that begins in infancy. Inheritance follows an autosomal recessive pattern.

Bell palsy Paralysis (usually temporary) of the facial (seventh cranial) nerve leading to sagging of the face on the involved side with an ironing out of the usual facial lines.

Benadryl *See* diphenhydramine.

Bender Face Hand Test An examination procedure to test for extinction (failure to perceive). *Stimulus:* The individual is lightly touched on one or both cheeks and/or hands and on the ipsilateral (on the same side)/contralateral (opposite) cheek and/or hand. *Response:* With eyes closed, the individual is asked to identify the body parts touched. The most common failure involves the extinction of the distal stimulus (hand) when the ipsilateral hand and cheek are touched.

Bender Visual Motor Gestalt Test (Bender Gestalt) A measure of visual-motor ability adapted in 1938 by Lauretta Bender from drawings used by Max Wertheimer in his studies of the gestalt concepts involved in visual perception. The Bender Gestalt is a nonverbal test with a range of applications to all age groups and to populations with diverse cultural and experiential backgrounds. The subject is asked to copy on a blank piece of paper nine figures of varying complexity that are presented one at a time. The subject is subsequently asked to reproduce the figures from memory, adding a visual retention component to the test. A significant relationship exists between intelligence and the accuracy of Bender-Gestalt reproductions. The child supplies clues to his or her learning approach, to the ease with which psychomotor skills are acquired, and to how well he or she organizes written work on a page. The Bender-Gestalt drawings help to provide important information about developmental lags, neurological impairment, mental retardation, and emotional disorders. The test takes approximately 5 minutes to administer. The Koppitz Developmental Bender Scoring System is typically used to evaluate the test. The following four categories identify errors on the developmental scoring scale: 1) distortion of shape, 2) rotation, 3) integration difficulties, and 4) perseveration. Percentile norms are available for children ages 5-0 through 11-11. There is also a score based upon 12 emotional indicators, but little is known about their validity.

benign childhood epilepsy *See* benign rolandic epilepsy.

benign rolandic epilepsy Also called midtemporal epilepsy, sylvian epilepsy, and benign childhood epilepsy with centrotemporal spikes (sharp, pointed deviations). A seizure disorder with infrequent seizures beginning between ages 5 and 10 years. Typically, the seizure is preceded by a sensory aura in the mouth (tongue, cheek, or gums), followed by salivation, speech arrest, and tonic (increased muscle tone) or tonic-clonic (relaxation of muscle tone) movements of the face. Consciousness is preserved in more than half the cases. Seizures occur frequently during sleep. The electroencephalogram (EEG) shows mid-temporal spikes. Prognosis for this type of seizure disorder is excellent, as most children respond to anticonvulsants and are generally seizure-free after middle childhood by the onset of puberty.

Benton Right-Left Discrimination Test   A 20-item test in which children who are 6 years of age are expected to identify the right and left sides of their bodies, children who are 7 years old are expected to touch right-sided or left-sided body parts with the ipsilateral (on the same side) hand, and children who are 9 years of age perform the same motion with the contralateral (opposite) hand. Eleven-year-old children are expected to identify the examiner's right and left, and children who are 12 years of age are expected to identify the examiner's right and left with the children's right or left hands.

Benton Visual Retention Test–Fifth Edition   A test of visual-motor coordination and visual memory with direct copying and delayed memory administrations. The number of correct reproductions and the error score can be compared to age norms for children as young as 6 years, with expected scores being given for different IQ levels. The results obtained with this instrument do not discriminate among the impact of visual attention, visual memory, and visual-perceptual motor skill areas.

benzodiazepine   A class of antianxiety drugs including diazepam, lorazepam, clonazepam, clorazepate, nitrazepam, and acetazolamide. Diazepam and lorazepam are also used in the treatment of status epilepticus. Clonazepam is useful in minor motor seizures, mixed seizure disorders (e.g., Lennox-Gastaut, infantile spasms), and atypical absence seizures. Clorazepate is used as an adjunct to other anticonvulsants in the treatment of refractory partial and generalized seizures. Nitrazepam is effective in minor motor seizures and infantile spasms, but is not used in the United States because of its liver toxicity. Acetazolamide has clinical use in many kinds of seizures including absence, menstruation-related generalized, and complex partial seizures. It is especially useful in refractory seizures. In general, side effects of the benzodiazepines include sedation, ataxia (unsteady gait), and respiratory depression. They must be administered 2–4 times a day and can lose their antianxiety effectiveness over time.

BES   *See* Behavior Evaluation Scale.

BES–2   *See* Behavior Evaluation Scale–2.

bethanechol   A cholinergic agonist that stimulates the parasympathetic nervous system (trade name, Urecholine). It is used in the treatment of gastroesophageal reflux.

bezoar   A stomach mass that is composed of ingested nonfood items and that may cause symptoms of gastrointestinal obstruction and, rarely, perforation. (A *trichobezoar* is a hair ball.)

BIDS syndrome   IBIDS syndrome without ichthyosis (very dry skin).

bilateral   Pertaining to both sides of the body.

bilateral integration dysfunction   *See* vestibular-bilateral disorder.

bilingual   Fluency of verbal communication processes in two or more languages. A key issue in education concerns the impact of bilinguality on the educational process. The younger the person, the easier it appears to be to learn multiple languages; however, it has been suggested that the educational process in other content areas becomes confused when more than one language has been acquired.

Bilingual Syntax Measure I and II (BSM)   A criterion-referenced measure of oral syntactic (language) structures. Available in both English and Spanish versions.

Binder syndrome   *See* maxillonasal dysplasia.

binocularity   The use of both eyes to focus on an object and allow the brain to form a clear three-dimensional picture of the object.

biofeedback A term used to denote both the process and the outcome of the application of operant conditioning methods, such that a person acquires the ability to shift autonomic nervous system–based physiological functions (both visceral and central) to the control of higher cortical processes. For example, the autonomic vasoconstriction (narrowing of blood vessels) substrate of migraine headache processes is brought into conscious volitional control so that when vasoconstriction begins, the affected person begins the biofeedback processes to redilate the vessels. These training processes include bringing these autonomic questions into awareness by electronic monitors that "feed back" to the subject information on such body processes as skin temperature, heart rate, and skin sweat response. The person learns to change the rate or degree of these body processes as reflected in the electronic indicators by conscious monitoring and body feedback. Biofeedback has been used in people with developmental disabilities in such areas as facilitating continence in the presence of spinal cord lesions such as those that occur in myelomeningocele (protuberance of both the spinal cord and its lining).

biosocial Pertaining to both biological and social phenomena, especially the interrelationship between the two and usually with an emphasis on the social.

biotinidase deficiency Also known as multiple carboxylase deficiency. A hereditary metabolic condition in which the clinical signs and symptoms are extremely variable but can include myoclonic seizures, developmental delay, ataxia (unsteady gait), sensorineural hearing loss, hypotonia (decreased muscle tone), dermatitis, alopecia (hair loss), and optic atrophy (wasting). The incidence of this syndrome is approximately 1 in 75,000. Inheritance follows an autosomal recessive pattern.

biparietal diameter A measurement of the width of the fetal skull made by ultrasound; this length is used to estimate gestational age.

bipolar illness A psychiatric disorder characterized by extremes of happiness and sadness of mood and excessive behaviors that reflect the mood. Previously termed *manic-depressive disorder*, the name change to *bipolar illness* more accurately reflects the extremes of mood and behavior experienced by those with the disease. In the depressive phase, the affected person may reach a complete vegetative depression and see life as a black hole from which there is no escape and for which there is no hope. While in this "pole" of the disorder, the person may stop eating, stay in bed, and may attempt suicide. As the depression remits, the person often swings to the alternate "pole" where happiness and enthusiasm give way to unrealistic euphoria, untempered enthusiasm and optimism, and behavioral excesses. Thus, in this polar end of the illness, the affected person may not sleep for days or weeks, may talk for hours (or days) on end, may go on spending sprees of hundreds of thousands of dollars, and may engage in excesses of sexual appetite (both in quantity and number of partners). Persons with bipolar illness have a failure of the emotional modulating system combined with both thought processes and behavior components that reflect the unrealistic polar extremes of the disorder. Thought to be genetic in origin, the disease exhibits familial expression. Furthermore, many developmental and learning disorders, such as autism and reading problems, appear in excess in families with bipolar illness.

bird-headed dwarfism *See* Seckel syndrome.

birth defect A congenital disability. The use of the term *birth defect* is now discouraged because it implies that the person is damaged and may have contributed to the condition by the process of being born.

Birth to Three Developmental Scales A developmental profile for children from birth to 3 years of age that uses observation, direction following, motor and verbal imitation, object and picture naming, and pointing.

bite reflex An oral reflex in which tactile (touch) stimulation in the oral area (gums, teeth, or tongue) produces a rhythmic opening and closing of the mouth; a primitive reflex apparent between birth and 6 months of age, after which it is replaced by rotary chewing.

bivalve cast A cast in two pieces connected at their margins like a bivalve or clam shell; such a cast allows ready access to the casted body part.

BK Below knee.

BLAT *See* Blind Learning Aptitude Test.

blended family A nuclear family formed by the joining of two previously unrelated families. For example, a woman and her two biological children may join (usually by marriage) with a man and his two biological children to form a blended family with four children. Blending requires not only the working out of the adults' relationship, both as intimate partners and as parents, but also the working out of relationships between previously unrelated children to each other and to previously unrelated adults who are now, de facto, authority figures. Often this process is further complicated when one or more of the children maintains a principal residence with the other parent and is part of the blended family on an irregular basis.

blepharophimosis, camptodactyly, short stature, mental retardation, and inner hearing impairment syndrome A dysmorphic syndrome with peculiar facies including short palpebral fissures (eye slits), camptodactyly (permanent flexion of the fingers or toes), short stature, severe mental retardation, and hearing loss.

Blind Learning Aptitude Test (BLAT) A 61-item verbal-touch test of tactile (touch) discrimination for children who are blind and ages 6–16 years. The examiner guides the child's hands over pages of patterned dots and lines and the child is asked to describe what is felt. Learning aptitude is assessed through recognition of differences and similarities, identification of progressions and missing elements, and the ability to complete a figure. Administration time is approximately 45 minutes. The

BLAT appears to be most useful for children between the ages of 6 and 12. Standard scores are provided (with a mean of 100 and a standard deviation of 15). In conjunction with the use of verbal measures, the BLAT is a supplementary test for evaluating the nonverbal cognitive abilities of children who are blind.

blindism A self-stimulatory behavior typically exhibited in people who are blind, such as eye gouging or eye rubbing noted in preschool children who are blind (*see* digito-ocular sign of Franceschetti). Other such socially inappropriate behaviors include rocking, hand movements, smelling, and autistic stereotypies (constantly repeated meaningless gestures or movements).

blindness A person is termed blind when there is corrected visual acuity worse than 20/200 in the better eye. It has been recommended that the definition of the term *blind* be restricted to the absence of light perception and that "visual impairment" and "low vision" be extended to describe persons with vision worse than 20/200 but who retain light perception.

Blissymbolics A graphic symbol system created by Charles Bliss in 1942. In this system, symbols are combined in a logical manner to depict aspects of human experience. Blissymbolics use photographs (symbols that look like what they represent), ideographs (symbols representing ideas), and symbols depicting characteristics of the word (i.e., plural or action) to construct compound symbols, providing for a large vocabulary. Blissymbolics are particularly useful to those who are unable to use traditional written language but who can learn and employ a large vocabulary. The system is an aided augmentative communication approach for nonvocal individuals with physical disabilities; it has also been used successfully with individuals with mental retardation or hearing impairments and adults with aphasia (loss of language skills).

Blitz-Nick-Salaamkrampfe syndrome *See* West syndrome.

Bloch-Sulzberger syndrome *See* incontinentia pigmenti syndrome.

blood–brain barrier The relative impermeability of the adult brain to certain metabolites and especially to sudden fluctuations in the levels of these metabolites that occur in the bloodstream; the brains of premature and very young infants are more susceptible to such changes.

Bloom syndrome A genetic syndrome with a short stature, facial erythema (inflammation) with a butterfly distribution (exaggerated by sunlight), midface hypoplasia (flattening), and occasionally mild mental retardation. There is a high incidence of immune defects and of cancer. Inheritance follows an autosomal recessive pattern. Risks for this disorder are increased among Ashkenazic Jewish populations, of whom 1 in 100 is thought to be a carrier of the gene for Bloom syndrome.

Blount disease Genu varum (bow legs), from an abnormality of the tibia (calf bone).

BLT–2 *See* Bankson Language Test–Second Edition.

blue sclera A bluish tinge to the whites of the eyes that occurs in premature infants and persons with glaucoma (increased pressure in the eye, often hereditary); it is also noted in the following systemic disorders: osteogenesis imperfecta (fragile bone disease), Marfan syndrome, Hallermann-Streiff syndrome, Crouzon syndrome, Turner syndrome, and a syndrome of hyperextensibility of the joints with hearing impairment.

Brazelton NBAS *See* Brazelton Neonatal Behavioral Assessment Scale.

BNT *See* Boston Naming Test.

Bobath *See* neurodevelopmental therapy.

bobble-head doll syndrome A peculiar head-bobbing behavior (2–4 times/second) associated with a third ventricle cyst (hydrocephalus [excess fluid in the brain]); it may be the presenting sign for this latter condition. To be distinguished from spasmus nutans.

Boder Test of Reading-Spelling Patterns A criterion-referenced diagnostic test to identify the following three subtypes of reading disability originally described by Elena Boder: 1) a dysphonetic pattern (inability to sound out and blend component letters and syllables of a word), 2) a dyseidetic pattern (limitations in visual memory and visual discrimination), and 3) a mixed pattern (incorporating both types of errors). Results are reported in terms of reading level, reading age, mental age, and reading quotient (based on sight-word vocabulary), spelling test score, and reading-spelling pattern (normal, nonspecific reading disability, dysphonetic, dyseidetic, mixed dysphonetic/dyseidetic, and undetermined). The Boder was designed for screening and clinical use and is not standardized.

Boehm Test of Basic Concepts–Revised (Boehm–R)(BTBC–R) A group test for children in kindergarten through grade two to assess conceptual mastery for early school success and pinpoint areas in need of remediation. There is also an individually administered preschool version for children 3–5 years of age.

bolus A globular mass; it can refer to food ready to be swallowed or drugs to be injected intravenously in a single dose or administered over a short time period.

bone age Also known as anatomical age. Skeletal growth age as determined by the X-ray appearance of the bones compared with standards for different ages; the most commonly used standards are those of Greulich and Pyle for the hand. In children with short stature, chronological age, bone age, height age, and midparental height can be used to predict final adult height.

BOR syndrome *See* Melnick-Fraser syndrome.

borderline intellectual functioning The presence of an IQ between 70 and 85 in the absence of functional or adaptive impairment. Sometimes equated with the slow learner educational category. Earlier classifications referred to this IQ range as borderline mental retardation; there is no association of either with borderline personality disorder.

Börjeson-Forssman-Lehmann syndrome An X-linked genetic syndrome characterized by severe to profound mental retardation, hypotonia (decreased muscle tone), hypogonadism (small testicles), and microcephaly (abnormally small head) with a coarse facies and large ears. Inheritance follows a recessive pattern.

BOS *See* Behavior Observation Scale for Autism.

Boston Naming Test (BNT) An aphasia test with 60 stimulus picture cards for use with subjects above 5 years of age.

BOTMP *See* Bruininks-Oseretsky Test of Motor Proficiency.

Botox *See* botulinus A toxin.

bottom shuffling *See* scooting.

bottom-up processing (stimulus-driven) A term found in cognitive psychological theory referring to processing directly affected by stimulus input. In bottom-up processing, perception is based on a detailed analysis of stimulus information. Perception is largely bottom-up when viewing (or listening) conditions are clear, but may increasingly involve top-down processing as conditions deteriorate. For example, a word that is clearly written (and recognized by the reader) can be processed on its own merits (bottom-up). However, if it is not clear to the reader, context clues and expectations based upon previous experience must be utilized (*see* top-down processing). In most circumstances, perception involves the interaction of bottom-up and top-down processing.

botulinus A toxin (Botox) The neurotoxin that produces botulism (food poisoning). This neurotoxin can be used in the treatment of neuromuscular disorders such as rigidity and spasticity.

boundaries Emotional and interactional barriers that protect and enhance the integrity of individuals, relationships, and families. Boundaries are unwritten rules that function as invisible lines defining both closeness and distance in a relationship, authority structures in the family, and the relationship of the family to the outside world. Boundaries can be too rigid to allow growth, they can be appropriately clear and flexible, or they can be too loose to protect the family. When too rigid or too loose, family therapy may be necessary to redefine, loosen, or strengthen boundaries.

Bourneville-Pringle syndrome *See* tuberous sclerosis syndrome.

bow legs Genu varum; mild bowing of the legs is physiological (normal) in late infancy. In this mild form, gross motor development is not affected; hence, significant motor delay should prompt a search for other causal factors. *See* genu varum.

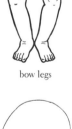

bow legs

bowing reflex *See* Gamper reflex.

BPD *See* bronchopulmonary dysplasia.

brachial Relating to the arm.

brachycephaly A disproportionately short head (high cephalic index).

brachycephaly

brachydactyly Short fingers; can be an autosomal dominant trait with or without other developmental or syndromic associations. Short fifth fingers that do not reach the distal interphalangeal crease of the fourth finger are a minor dysmorphic feature that may reflect the presence of a neurodevelopmental disorder.

Bracken Basic Concept Scale (BBCS) An educational diagnostic instrument that measures 258 basic concepts in 11 subtest categories for children 2–6-8 years of age in order to assess school readiness as reflected in receptive language. Administration is individual or group. Responses may be verbal (stating the number that corresponds to the answer) or nonverbal (pointing to the correct option). Standard scores (mean of 100, standard deviation of 15) by age, percentile bands, normal curve equivalents, stanine scores (a scoring system with scores expressed as whole numbers from 1 to 9 with a mean of 5 and a standard deviation of 2), and mental age scores are provided. Two short screening tests are used to identify children who would benefit from the full scale.

brain The part of the central nervous system contained in the skull or cranium. It performs a multitude of tasks, from control of basic functions (e.g., breathing) to higher cortical functions (e.g., intellect and learning). The brain is divided into

brain

the following four major parts: 1) brain stem, 2) diencephalon, 3) cerebrum, and 4) cerebellum. The brain is also divided into halves, called hemispheres, that are connected by the corpus callosum. For protection, the brain is surrounded by a layer of tissue called the meninges, and is further protected by a fluid, the cerebral spinal fluid (CSF), that flows through the brain in a system of conduits called ventricles. Blockage of these ventricles can cause hydrocephalus (excess fluid in the brain).

brain electrical activity mapping (BEAM) A complex computer technology that uses electroencephalographic (EEG) readings to map the electrical activity of the brain. BEAM is a potentially useful research tool in the evaluation of children with learning disabilities.

brain-stem auditory-evoked potentials (BAEP, BAER, ABR) A test using auditory stimuli (sound) to measure the passage of the message along the auditory nerve (cranial nerve VIII) to the brain stem and associated areas of the brain. This gives information about the intactness of the system but not about the perception of the sound. Damage to hearing resulting in an abnormal BAEP can be caused by meningitis (inflammation of the spinal cord and brain membranes), hyperbilirubinemia (high levels of bilirubin in the blood), perinatal asphyxia (lack of oxygen), or central nervous system disorders like leukodystrophy. It can be used to assess hearing in children who are too young to cooperate for a behavioral hearing test.

brain-stem auditory-evoked response (BAER) Also known as ABR (auditory brain-stem response) or BSER (brain-stem evoked response). A test of the intactness of the auditory nerve (cranial nerve VIII) and its tract in the brain stem. The test gives information only about brain-stem structures and therefore reveals nothing about cortical defects in auditory perception. It is performed by introducing a set of clicks to one ear and tracing the resulting electrical activity from the eighth cranial nerve sequentially to the following structures in the brain stem: cochlear nucleus, superior olivary nucleus, the nucleus of the lateral lemniscus, and the inferior colliculus. Abnormal BAERs are found with brain-stem damage resulting from meningitis (inflammation of the spinal cord and brain membranes) or encephalitis (brain inflammation), neonatal jaundice (yellowing of the skin), or perinatal asphyxia (lack of oxygen). Hereditary degenerative diseases like Friedreich ataxia can show subclinical abnormalities of the eighth nerve. Abnormal BAERs can also be the result of middle-ear disease that impedes the activation of the eighth cranial nerve.

branchial arch An anatomical anlage (predisposition) that evolved from gills in fish into structures of the ear and neck in humans. Abnormalities in fetal branchial arch development give rise to branchial cysts deep within the neck and to conditions such as the Treacher Collins and Goldenhar syndromes.

branchio-oto-renal syndrome *See* Melnick-Fraser syndrome.

Braverman-Chevigny Auditory Projective Test An adaptation of the Thematic Apperception Test (TAT) for persons with visual impairments; the stimulus is a conversation with garbled language.

Brazelton Neonatal Behavioral Assessment Scale (NBAS) A tool for the behavioral assessment of newborn infants. The 37 items include a careful description of state, visual and auditory alertness and orientation, tone and posture, cuddliness and consolability, as well as startle and self-quieting. Elicited responses (primitive reflexes) are scored separately.

breathholding spell A paroxysmal behavior observed in preschool children after severe crying following an identifiable emotional upset; it may end in unconsciousness with a brief clonic (rhythmic contraction and relaxation) asphyxic seizure. Breathholding spells should be treated behaviorally rather than with anticonvulsant medication.

breech The delivery of a baby feet first rather than head first. In a frank breech presentation, the baby's pelvis comes out first with the legs flexed (turned down) on the body; in footling breech, the feet themselves come out first. The neonatal mortality rate, incidence of prematurity, specific genetic syndromes, major organ malformations, and the later presence of neurological abnormalities are significantly higher in children born by breech presentation. Breech presentation accounts for approximately 3% of all deliveries. The major obstetrical risk in a breech delivery is that the umbilical cord may be compressed during the relatively prolonged delivery of the largest part of the baby, the head.

BRIAAC *See* Behavior Rating Instrument for Autistic and Atypical Children.

bridge A three-block construction that can be imitated by a child at 3 years of age; a fine-motor milestone.

bridge

Brill Educational Achievement Test for Secondary Age Deaf Students An academic screening test for adolescents who are deaf and 13–20 years of age.

Broca's aphasia Expressive aphasia; motor aphasia; the loss of the ability to speak secondary to damage to a specific area of the left frontal lobe (Brodmann area 44, Broca's area, inferior frontal gyrus, anterior speech cortex). Residual speech is characterized by agrammatism.

Broderick decision *Halderman v. Pennhurst State School and Hospital, et al.; A* 1978 court decision rendered by U.S. District Court Judge Raymond Broderick stipulating that keeping individuals with mental retardation in institutions isolated from the rest of society violated their constitutional rights. This ruling was the result of a class-action suit filed in May 1974 by parents of clients at the Pennhurst School for the Mentally Retarded in Pennsylvania. Judge Broderick argued that institutionalization violated these individuals' rights under the Fourteenth Amendment to the U.S. Constitution.

Brodmann areas A system to numerically map the functional areas of the human cortex: sensory reception—1, 2, 3; primary motor—4; sensory association—5, 6, 7; visual reception—17; visual association—18; speech reception (Wernicke)—39; auditory reception—41; auditory association—42; speech motor (Broca)—44.

Brodmann areas

bronchopulmonary dysplasia (BPD) Severe chronic lung disease secondary to respiratory distress syndrome and the toxic effects of prolonged high oxygen on the immature lung. Developmental problems associated with BPD are twofold: 1) cardiopulmonary insufficiency has a direct, slowing effect on motor development and 2) most infants who develop BPD have survived neonatal courses replete with other events potentially traumatic to the central nervous system. Some infants with BPD develop a movement disorder characterized by chorea and oral motor problems.

BRP *See* Behavior Rating Profile.

Bruininks-Oseretsky Test of Motor Proficiency (BOTMP) An instrument to differentially assess fine- and gross-motor skills in children 4½–14½ years of age; the eight subtests take less than 1 hour to administer. The test represents a major standardized tool to evaluate motor skills in the areas of running speed and agility, balance, bilateral coordination, strength, upper-limb coordination, response speed, visual-motor control, and upper-limb speed and dexterity. It is an adaptation of the earlier Lincoln-Oseretsky Tests of Motor Proficiency.

bruit Noise; an abnormal sound heard on auscultation (listening with a stethoscope); a cranial bruit may be heard in the presence of an intracranial vascular (blood vessel) malformation or tumor, hyperthyroidism, heart disease, or fever. Pathological bruits have the quality of "footsteps in an empty church."

Brunnstrom A system of physical therapy for the treatment of cerebral palsy. Developed by Signe Brunnstrom to treat hemiplegia (paralysis of half the body), this approach induces primitive (fetal) synergistic movement patterns to help teach purposeful movements.

bruxism Teeth grinding; can reflect a sleep disorder or nervous habit in children. In children with more severe developmental disabilities, this self-stimulatory behavior can lead to severe dental impairment, with teeth being ground flat. Teeth grinding when awake is often associated with mental retardation.

BSER Brain-stem evoked response. *See* brain-stem auditory-evoked response.

BSID–II *See* Bayley Scales of Infant Development–Second Edition.

BSM *See* Bilingual Syntax Measure I and II.

BSSI–D *See* Basic School Skills Inventory Diagnostic.

BTBC–R *See* Boehm Test of Basic Concepts–Revised.

bulbar syndrome *See* pseudobulbar palsy.

burden A term used in clinical genetics to describe the total impact of a disorder on an individual, his or her family, and society. In genetic counseling, the impact of the burden of a child with disabilities generally outweighs the probability of recurrence in determining whether to have additional children.

Bureau of Education for the Handicapped (BEH) Former name for the U.S. Department of Education's Office of Special Education and Rehabilitative Services.

Burks Behavior Rating Scale A 110-item written inventory used to identify patterns of behavior problems in children grades one through nine. A parent or teacher rates descriptive statements regarding the child's observed behavior. Subscales measure a broad spectrum of behavioral tendencies: 1) anxiety, 2) withdrawal, 3) sense of persecution, 4) aggressiveness, 5) attention, 6) impulse control, 7) anger control, 8) reality contact, and 9) social conformity. The rating scale can be completed in 15–20 minutes. Guides for parents and teachers define each subscale, suggest possible causes for problem behavior, and offer suggestions for addressing undesirable behaviors from both perspectives. The manual provides instructions for use with particular groups including persons with mild mental retardation, learning disabilities, speech and hearing impairments, and physical disabilities.

Burks Behavior Rating Scales, Preschool and Kindergarten Edition A downward extension of the Burks Behavior Rating Scale for use with children ages 3–6 years. The Preschool and Kindergarten Edition consists of 105 descriptive statements for a parent or teacher to rate. This scale includes all of the subscales of the Burks Behavior Rating Scale, with the exception of academics.

butyrophenone A group of major tranquilizers such as haloperidol (Haldol). These drugs are used to treat psychosis.

C

CA *See* chronological age.

cachexia Wasting, weakness, or emaciation. In children with unusually severe failure to thrive (poor growth), cachexia suggests the likelihood of an underlying physical disease.

cadence The number of steps per minute; one of the measures taken in a gait analysis.

CADeT *See* Communication Abilities Diagnostic Test.

CADL *See* Communicative Activities of Daily Living.

caffeine A central nervous system stimulant found in coffee, chocolate, and tea; its usage is of minimal to no therapeutic value in the treatment of attention-deficit/hyperactivity disorder (ADHD).

Caffey-Kempe syndrome *See* shaken baby syndrome.

CAI *See* computer-assisted instruction.

Cain-Levine Social Competency Scale A social adaptive scale for school-age children with moderate mental retardation.

calcaneus Heel bone.

calcaneus deformity An orthopedic abnormality in which the forefoot is pulled upward and the heel downward; the resulting appearance resembles a heel-walking stance.

calendar age *See* chronological age.

calcaneus
deformity

Callier-Azusa Scale An adaptive checklist for use with children who are deaf and blind up to a developmental age of 7 years. The five subscales (motor, daily living, language, perceptual, and socialization) involve the observation of spontaneous behavior in structured and unstructured situations over a period of 2 weeks.

calvaria The roof of the skull, or the cranial vault.

camptodactyly Fixed flexion contracture of a finger; a physical feature found in a number of syndromes.

Camurati-Englemann syndrome A rare genetic syndrome with a progressive bone disorder leading to leg pain, weakness, a waddling gait, an asthenic (slender or slight) malnourished habitus (appearance), and, occasionally, compromise of optic and auditory nerve functions. Inheritance follows an autosomal dominant pattern.

cancellation of rapidly recurring target figures A test to differentiate dyslexia from other learning disabilities and to detect poor concentration. A diamond and the number 592 must be identified in an array of 140 figures and numbers. Visual discrimination problems may also affect the scores on this test.

cancellation test A timed test requiring the subject to eliminate a certain letter, number, or shape whenever it appears scattered at random among an array of similar symbols.

Candida albicans A common yeast or fungus that typically resides on human skin and mucous membranes but that may give rise to thrush (a mouth infection in young babies), candidiasis (a diaper rash), and vaginal yeast infections. Subclinical yeast infections have been alleged to play a role in migraine, depression, fatigue, irritability, attention deficits, hyperactivity, autism, and other neurobehavioral syndromes. A yeast toxin is hypothesized to produce these symptoms; the treatment for this "yeast connection" includes a diet low in sugar and refined carbohydrates, and the antifungal drug nystatin. Support for this approach remains anecdotal; the treatment is unproven and controversial.

candle-drippings   A term describing the shape of nodules protruding into the ventricles (fluid-containing spaces) of the brain in tuberous sclerosis.

candling   *See* transillumination.

canities   Graying of scalp hair and beard hair.

Cantelli sign   *See* doll eyes maneuver.

canthus   The corner of the palpebral fissure (eye slit). Each eye has an inner (nasal or epicanthus) and an outer (lateral or telecanthus) canthus. The inner canthal distance is a measurement used to assess the presence of a minor dysmorphic feature—increased inner canthal distance.

cao gio   *See* coining.

caput succedaneum   Soft-tissue swelling of the scalp when a baby is born in the vertex presentation (head first); the margins of swelling are not limited by suture lines; sometimes referred to just as caput.

Capute Aptitude Test (CAT)   A measure of problem-solving skills in children birth to 2 years of age. The CAT is not intended for use by itself, but, rather, as part of a more comprehensive pediatric neurodevelopmental assessment that includes CLAMS (Clinical Linguistic and Auditory Milestone Scale), a motor evaluation, and a detailed examination for minor dysmorphic features.

carbamazepine (CBZ)   Trade name Tegretol. An anticonvulsant also effective in treating movement disorders and some psychiatric conditions in people with severe developmental disorders. The chemical structure is similar to the tricyclic antidepressants. Carbamazepine is used to treat partial and generalized tonic-clonic seizures; it is not effective in absence seizures. Estimates of complete seizure control using carbamazepine only are 80%. In practice, the beginning dose of carbamazepine is 10 milligrams per kilogram of body weight per day and is gradually increased by increments of 5 milligrams per kilogram of body weight per day to a maintenance dosage of 40 milligrams per kilogram of body weight per day, generally yielding a therapeutic blood level of 4–12 micrograms per milliliter. Children must take the medication three or four times a day, whereas adolescents and adults may only require twice daily dosages. Carbamazepine has not been reported to produce the deleterious effects on cognition and behavior noted in older anticonvulsants such as phenobarbital. Rather, improvements in memory, mood, perceptual and motor speed, and decision making have been described. Side effects include drowsiness and rashes. Blood problems, such as aplastic anemia or leukopenia (i.e., certain types of blood cells are not formed, producing low blood counts), have been described, as has liver damage with jaundice (yellowing of the skin). The use of carbamazepine has increased in light of its successful treatment of seizures and its positive effects on cognition.

cardiac   Relating to the heart.

cardinal points reflex   *See* rooting reflex.

cardiomegaly   Enlarged heart.

cardiopulmonary   Pertaining to the heart and lungs.

cardiorespiratory   Pertaining to the heart and lungs.

cardiovascular   Relating to the heart, blood vessels, or circulatory system.

caries   Tooth decay and death of bone from bacterial action; dental caries are decayed and rotting teeth secondary to poor oral hygiene.

Carl D. Perkins Vocational and Applied Technology Education Act of 1990 (PL 101-392) This law amended and renamed the Carl D. Perkins Vocational Educational Act of 1984 (PL 98-524). The purpose of PL 101-392 was to make the United States more productive and competitive in the world economy by more fully developing the educational and vocational skills of all segments of the population. The definition of "special populations" has been expanded to include individuals with disabilities, those who are economically and educationally disadvantaged (including migrant and foster children), individuals with limited English proficiency, those who are in jeopardy of experiencing sex bias, and those in correctional institutions. This law requires that individuals with disabilities, like their counterparts without disabilities, be provided vocational education in the least restrictive environment, and that they be granted equal access to all aspects of vocational programs and placement activities. PL 101-392 is closely aligned and interwoven with PL 101-476, the Individuals with Disabilities Education Act (IDEA) of 1990 to guarantee full vocational education opportunities for youth with disabilities.

carnitine A chemical found in food and produced in the liver and other tissues that helps in the breakdown of long-chain fatty acids. Carnitine also acts to protect the cell against certain normal breakdown products (Acyl-CoA derivatives) that can be toxic to the cell. Carnitine is used in some metabolic disorders (generally, enzyme deficiencies) such as carnitine palmityl transferase deficiency, organic acidopathies, disorders of fatty acid breakdown, acute exacerbations of some amino acidopathies, and sometimes in acute and chronic valproic acid toxicity. Other postulated uses include nutritional supplementation in chronic renal (kidney) disease or premature babies or in some cases of idiopathic cardiomyopathy (enlarged heart). The function and clinical use of carnitine are under continuing investigation.

carnitine deficiency 1. Systemic carnitine deficiency is characterized by muscle weakness of varying severity and a pro-
gressive age of presentation. There is an increase in number and size of mitochondria, and the mitochondria have abnormal morphology (structure and form) and increased inclusions. Although carnitine levels are low in blood, liver, and muscle, carnitine supplementation has resulted in improvement in only one third of people. 2. Muscle carnitine deficiency is an autosomal recessive disorder that presents in childhood with progressive weakness. Blood carnitine levels are normal, but muscle levels are low. Carnitine supplementation improves the weakness in about two thirds of cases without increasing muscle carnitine levels.

Carolina Curriculum for Infants and Toddlers with Special Needs (CCITSN) An approach to providing appropriate intervention strategies for children with developmental delays functioning in the birth to 24-month developmental range; 24 areas are assessed by observation or parent reporting, and the results are used to generate specific teaching interventions.

Carolina Curriculum for Preschoolers with Special Needs (CCPSN) An upward extension of the Carolina Curriculum for Infants and Toddlers with Special Needs, with a greater emphasis on intervention activities in group settings.

Carolina Picture Vocabulary Test (CPVT) A norm-referenced test of receptive sign vocabulary for children between 4 and 11-6 years of age who are deaf or have hearing impairments.

carotenemia A yellow tinge to the skin resulting from an excess of carotene in the blood. This is secondary to a diet high in yellow/orange (vitamin-A–containing) foods. This yellow coloring may be distinguished from jaundice (a yellowing of the skin) clinically, in that it does not involve the whites of the eyes (i.e., pseudojaundice).

carp mouth The combination of downturned corners of the mouth (relative overgrowth of the upper lip), a thick lower lip, and a short philtrum (indentation in upper lip below nose); carp mouth can be found in a number of syndromes.

Carpenter syndrome Acrocephalopoly-syndactyly. A genetic syndrome with a "tower-shaped" skull from craniosynostosis (premature fusion of skull sutures), polydactyly (extra fingers or toes), syndactyly (webbing of the fingers or toes), and lateral displacement of the inner canthi (i.e., dystopia canthorum) contributing to a "downthrust" gaze appearance and mild obesity. Occasionally, there is mild mental retardation. Surgical correction of the craniofacial malformation is indicated, along with audiological monitoring and speech-language therapy. Inheritance is thought to follow an autosomal recessive pattern.

carpus Wrist. The wrist is composed of eight small carpal bones arranged in two rows.

carrier An individual who is heterozygous for a trait. In reference to a disease or genetic syndrome, an individual who is heterozygous has on his or her chromosome pair one normal gene and one abnormal gene that carries the gene for that trait. Although carriers appear normal, the presence of abnormal genes can sometimes be detected by laboratory methods. Disorders transmitted by way of carriers are usually recessive and thus require the mating of two carriers to produce a disease state (i.e., two abnormal genes must be present). Every individual is probably a carrier for a few rare, recessive disorders. Certain population groups have many carriers of particular disease genes, such as Tay-Sachs in Ashkenazic Jewish people or sickle cell trait in African American people or Caucasian people of Mediterranean descent. The carrier state may produce some protection from disease. For instance, carriers of sickle cell trait are protected from malaria.

Carrow Auditory-Visual Abilities Test (CAVAT) A norm-referenced test wih 14 subtests to measure auditory and visual-perceptual, motor, and memory skills for chldren ages 4–10 years. Test administration time is 1½ hours.

Carrow Elicited Language Inventory (CELI) A norm-referenced measure of productive use of grammar for children ages 3 through 7-11 with 52 items ranging from 2-word phrases to 10-word sentences. Children are asked to repeat the items, and their responses are scored and analyzed in terms of grammar, structure, error type, and production of verb forms. The inventory is used to diagnose expressive language delays and grammatical disorders.

carrying angle The angle of the forearm on the upper arm; the angle at the elbow. Absent sex chromosomes increase the carrying angle; extra sex chromosomes decrease the carrying angle.

CARS *See* Childhood Autism Rating Scale.

case definition Clinical diagnostic criteria that serve as a template against which to match the presenting signs and symptoms of an individual in determining the nature of his or her illness and the appropriate treatment. In contrast to clinical practice, where a working diagnosis may be sufficient for initiating clinical management procedures, case definition must more clearly delineate operating diagnostic criteria. For epidemiological purposes, the following questions must be answered: When in the prodromal phase does the person actually become a "case"? When in the clinical course is a "case" cured and therefore no longer a "case"? and "Is a subclinical or atypical manifestation of a disease also a "case"? The answers to these questions for any given disease determine who is counted in epidemiological measures of incidence and prevalence.

case history The cumulative medical, psychological, educational, familial, and social record of an individual.

case identification Assignment of a diagnosis to a set of signs and symptoms. Epidemiologists study the occurrence and determinants of diseases in groups of people. Thus, they must count the number of identified cases in any investigation of who, where, when, and how people contract specific diseases. Accurate reporting is also essential in plotting disease patterns. Although accurate case identification is contingent on good case definition, other variables in case identification may impede accurate counting of a disease in a population. These include the following: 1) the extent to which people in a community use the medical establishment, 2) the extent to which physicians correctly diagnose their patients, and 3) the extent to which accurately diagnosed cases can be ascertained on a community-wide scale.

case management A procedure for coordinating multiple service activities to a client or client system. Case management is most effective for clients who need multiple services, long-term service, or both. The case manager coordinates the activities of multiple service providers who are simultaneously serving the needs of one client, thereby helping to eliminate duplication and fragmentation of service. In addition, case management can alleviate the difficulties associated with staff turnover. Case management can occur within a single agency or at the community level, where services are coordinated among agencies.

cast A molded casing composed of plaster of paris, fiberglass, or plastic, used to immobilize a body part.

CAT *See* Capute Aptitude Test. *See also* Children's Apperception Test.

cat-cry syndrome *See* cri-du-chat syndrome.

cat posture *See* symmetric tonic neck reflex.

CAT scan Also called CT scan. *See* computed tomography.

Catapres Trade name for clonidine.

cataract An opacity of the lens of the eye that blocks normal vision. Cataracts can be congenital or acquired and can be associated with congenital infections, such as congenital rubella syndrome, or metabolic disorders such as galactosemia. Cataracts may also be inherited and are part of many genetic syndromes. The de-crease in vision in the eye with a large cataract may produce amblyopia (poorer vision in one eye) and strabismus (squint). Small cataracts may not significantly impair vision. Early diagnosis is critical; in infants, surgery, laser therapy, or other methods of removing the cataract should be performed in the first months of life.

CATCH An acronym for the syndromic association of congenital heart disease (conotruncal defect), atypical facies, thymic hypoplasia (atypical tissue development), cleft lip/palate, and hypocalcemia (low blood calcium) that can occur with chromosome 22 q11 deletions.

catecholamines A group of chemicals that influences the activity of the nervous system; these chemicals include epinephrine, norepinephrine, and dopamine.

Cattell Developmental and Intelligence Scale A modification of the Gesell schedules for children 3 months to 30 months of age; it yields a ratio IQ.

caudal regression syndrome A congenital malformation syndrome that involves varying degrees of agenesis (absence of formation) of the lower extremities, pelvis, sacrum, and spinal cord. Gait disorders, incontinence, imperforate (not open) anus, renal (kidney) agenesis, and abnormalities of the external genitalia are also manifestations of this syndrome, which most commonly occurs in infants of mothers with diabetes. In infants who survive, long-term orthopedic, urological, and neurological management is necessary.

CAVAT *See* Carrow Auditory-Visual Abilities Test.

cavus foot A foot with an extremely high arch (the opposite of flat foot); this painful foot deformity may be part of a syndrome, such as Friedreich ataxia, or an early sign of a spinal cord tumor.

CBC *See* complete blood count.

CBP *See* Child Behavior Profile.

CBT Cognitive behavior therapy; *see* cognitive therapy.

CBZ *See* carbamazepine.

CC *See* chief complaint.

CCC *See* Certificate of Clinical Competence.

CCITSN *See* Carolina Curriculum for Infants and Toddlers with Special Needs.

CCPSN *See* Carolina Curriculum for Preschoolers with Special Needs.

CCS *See* Crippled Children's Services.

CCSPEA *See* Classroom Communication Screening Procedure for Early Adolescents.

CDH *See* congenital dislocation of the hip; *see also* developmental dysplasia of the hip.

CEC *See* Council for Exceptional Children.

ceiling The point above which test items are assumed to be incorrect. Testing procedures often include a starting point based on age or grade, a basal, and a ceiling. Ceilings are described specifically for each test and are often a set number of consecutive items answered incorrectly; testing is stopped when that criterion is met. In scoring, items above the ceiling, regardless of whether they have been administered or whether they are correct, are scored as incorrect.

CELF–R *See* Clinical Evaluation of Language Fundamentals–Revised.

CELI *See* Carrow Elicited Language Inventory.

cell migration A step in the sequence of embryogenesis in which cells move from their original area to their final anatomical location. This process is complex and subject to damage by teratogens (toxic agents), as occurs in myelomeningocele (protuberance of both the spinal cord and its lining).

cell therapy Sicca cell therapy.

center-based program Intervention that focuses on exposing children to an educationally stimulating environment outside the home with the aim of facilitating the development of intellectual and social competence. For young children with special needs, there is often a home-based component to the center-based program. Although *center-based program* most often refers to early childhood special education (ECSE) programs, the term can also apply to services offered at a centralized location for other populations.

central axis Midline of the body.

central blindness Blindness caused by damage to the visual cortex in the occipital lobe. Often visual perception is more affected than actual vision. People with central blindness are not blind in the sense that they have no vision but have visual impairments because their perception of light images is inaccurate and inconsistent. This phenomenon is also known as cortical blindness.

central deafness A hearing loss resulting from damage to the auditory nerve pathways in the brain stem or cerebral cortex, resulting in the ability to hear pure tones but not necessarily to understand sounds or speech. An example is Wernicke aphasia (a receptive aphasia with impaired auditory comprehension resulting from damage to Wernicke's area—the posterior first temporal gyrus of the dominant cerebral hemisphere, generally the left). People with this problem often have word-finding problems and paraphasia (transposition or substitution of sounds, morphemes, or words). Central deafness is also known as cortical deafness.

central nervous system (CNS) The composite system formed by the brain and spinal cord, as contrasted with the peripheral nervous system (the system of nerves running throughout the body). The CNS is the center of control for the entire nervous system and has the additional function of controlling voluntary movement and thought. Developmental disorders reflect chronic impairment to the brain and not to the spinal cord or peripheral nervous system, although impairment of the latter may also be involved, as in myelomeningocele (protuberance of both the spinal cord and its lining). The CNS receives sensory information from the body and sends out nerve impulses that respond to the input by stimulating muscle contractions. For example, when a teacher asks a student to draw a circle, the sensory input is the verbal instruction that is detected through the eighth, or auditory, cranial nerve. This information goes to the auditory association area where the stimulus is interpreted. A sequence of signals is then sent to the appropriate motor area, from which an impulse is sent to the student's hand. The hand and arm muscles contract to draw a circle. *See also* cortex.

centration   Focusing on one aspect of a problem when more than one are important.

cephalic index   The ratio of the maximal breadth to the maximal length of the skull; a decreasing value suggests scaphocephaly (projected head), whereas an increasing value indicates brachycephaly (irregular, flat head shape). When not associated with craniosynostosis (premature fusion of skull sutures) or microcephaly (abnormally small head), many varieties of skull shape are racial or normal variants.

cephalocaudal   Literally, "head to tail." In describing the human body, cephalocaudal means going in a head to tail direction. The emergence of voluntary motor control follows a law of cephalocaudal progression, with head control being achieved in the first months of life and independent ambulation occurring late in the first or early in the second year of life.

cephalohematoma   Subperiosteal hemorrhage (bleeding) of the skull often associated with a hairline fracture incurred during delivery. So much blood may be lost into the swelling that a blood transfusion may be required. Unlike caput succedaneum, the swelling is limited by the suture lines of the skull. Calcification of this tumor can take months to resolve; the hard edge with a soft center may give the mis-

leading impression of a depressed skull fracture.

cephalopelvic disproportion (CPD)   A head–pelvis disproportion; a fetal head that is too large relative to the maternal pelvis to safely allow vaginal delivery; prolonged labor is one major sign of CPD.

cerea flexibilitas   "Waxy flexibility" sometimes seen in young children with severe environmental deprivation; an arm or leg passively placed in a given position remains there for a long time. This bizarre behavior is often seen in adults with catatonic schizophrenia.

cerebellar cerebral palsy   *See* ataxic cerebral palsy.

cerebellar function   The coordination and smoothing out of movements by the most posterior part of the brain. Dysfunction is characterized by dysdiadochokinesia (inability to perform rapidly alternating movements), titubation (staggering gait), intention tremor (trembling that accompanies voluntary movement), and ataxia (unsteady gait).

cerebellar stimulation   A controversial neurosurgical method of treating severe movement disorders (e.g., cerebral palsy) by implanting electrodes in the cerebellum and subjecting that part of the brain to continuous patterned electrical currents. As with other controversial therapies, claims for the success of this method have been extended to include the treatment of seizures, mental retardation, and other developmental disorders.

cerebral gigantism   *See* Sotos syndrome.

cerebral palsy   A family of syndromes with disordered movement and posture, delayed motor development, and atypical motoric findings on neurological examination. The etiology (cause) of the motor problem is located in the brain, rather than in the spinal cord or peripheral nervous system (the system of nerves running throughout the body). Although the brain injury is usually prenatal and rarely postnatal, cerebral palsy is rarely diagnosed in the first year of life. The full clinical picture only becomes clear in the second year of life. These disorders are all chronic but nonprogressive; with the exception of orthopedic complications, most children with cerebral palsy do not deteriorate functionally as they get older. The incidence of associated deficits in cerebral palsy is quite high: Mental retardation (50%–70%), seizures, and visual and auditory impairments are common. Dysarthria (difficulty pronouncing words), strabismus (crossed eyes or squint), feeding disorders, poor physical growth, asymmetrical growth, and asymmetrical neurological findings are not uncommon. The overall incidence of cerebral palsy is just under 0.5%. As stated, few cases are postnatal in onset, and most cases that were previously thought to be perinatal are now considered to be prenatal in etiology. The types of cerebral palsy are grouped under the following two major headings: 1) the physiological (or neuroanatomical, as defined by the tone and movement pattern); and 2) the topographical (as defined by which parts of the body are more involved). These may be outlined as in the table below.

Types of cerebral palsy

Physiological	Topographical
Spastic	Monoplegia
	Hemiplegia
	Diplegia
	Triplegia
	Quadriplegia
	Paraplegia
Extrapyramidal movement	(Choreo)athetoid
	Ataxic/cerebellar
	Tremor
tone	Rigid
	Hypotonic/atonic

cerebrohepatorenal syndrome Zellweger syndrome; a very rare genetic syndrome causing a peroxisomal enzyme deficiency leading to hypotonia (decreased muscle tone), high forehead, flat facies, brain abnormalities, hepatomegaly (liver enlarge-

ment), and kidney cysts. Breech presentation, intrauterine and postnatal failure to thrive (poor growth), and death within the first 6 months of life are characteristic. Inheritance is thought to follow an autosomal recessive pattern.

cerebrospinal fluid (CSF) The fluid that fills the ventricles of the brain and the space around the spinal cord. It can be removed from the body for diagnostic testing by a procedure called a lumbar puncture (LP). CSF may contain white blood cells indicating infection (e.g., meningitis [inflammation of the spinal cord and brain membranes]), red blood cells indicating a hemorrhage (bleeding), or too much protein, as in neurodegenerative diseases or tumor cells (e.g., leukemia, medulloblastoma). CSF examination is often helpful in making diagnoses of central nervous system diseases.

cerebrovascular accident (CVA) *See* stroke.

Certificate of Clinical Competence (CCC) A post-master's certification in audiology (CCC-A) or speech-language pathology (CCC-SP).

certificate of high school equivalency A formal document certifying that an individual has met the state requirements for high school graduation by attaining satisfactory scores on the tests of the general equivalency diploma (GED) or other state-specified examinations. These certificates are often accepted in the same manner as high school diplomas.

certification A recognition of qualification to perform certain professional tasks and duties. Certification is less stringent than licensing and requires only the attainment of specified education or experience standards with no accompanying assessment or monitoring of competence. Certification through a professional organization implies just the opposite: attainment of a level of competence.

ceruminosis Impacted cerumen (ear wax). Ceruminosis can contribute to hearing impairment; it is especially common in people with a narrow external ear canal, which occurs in Down syndrome. Drugs are used to liquefy the wax.

cervical Relating to any necklike structure, as in cervical vertebrae, which support the head upon the body, or cervical cancer, which is located in the neck (cervix) of the uterus.

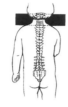

cervical spine

cervical auscultation A clinical technique that uses a stethoscope to listen to the sounds of swallowing. Aspiration is thought to be associated with sounds that are less sharp or that have a bubbling quality. The technique is of limited application.

cesarean section The delivery of a fetus by an incision through the abdominal wall into the uterus; it is usually performed because of specific indications such as fetal distress, breech presentation, bleeding, cephalopelvic disproportion, or "repeat C-section." (This last indication is no longer considered obligatory). In general, a history of cesarean section does not affect a baby's risk for later developmental disability; more important to consider are the reasons for performing the section and the baby's postnatal course.

C4b protein A plasma protein that is low in the presence of autoimmune diseases. This protein may also be low in people with autism, suggesting a possible autoimmune mechanism in the etiology of autism.

Chaddock sign Stimulating the skin in the region of the external (lateral) malleolus causes the big toe to extend; it may be considered a sign of pyramidal tract involvement and a variation of the Babinski sign.

chaining The linking together of two or more responses into a single complex behavioral sequence by a training program that twins each successive response into the stimulus for the next response in the sequence.

chalasia A transient, benign form of gastroesophageal reflux; postprandial regurgitation (spitting up after meals) in early infancy, usually successfully treated by upright positioning, thickened feedings, and smaller feedings.

CHAMPUS *See* Civilian Health and Medical Program of the Uniformed Services.

Chandler Movement Assessment of Infancy–Screening Test (CMAI–ST) A 10-minute screening version of the Movement Assessment of Infants (MAI).

channeling Continued growth of an infant along any given percentile of the growth curves for length, weight, and head circumference. A failure of channeling involves switching or crossing growth curves to a lower percentile.

chaotic family A family characterized by chronic and severe lack of structure and organization. Individuals in such a family function autonomously with little commitment to or support from the family unit. A child with developmental disabilities in this type of family often experiences understimulation and isolation, owing to inability of the family to work together to meet the child's constant and special needs.

Chapter 1 of the Education Consolidation and Improvement Act of 1981 (PL 98-211) A mandated program of compensatory education for children with educational disadvantages in schools with concentrations of children from low-income families; formerly known as Title 1 of the Elementary and Secondary Education Act. Federal grants are made through state education departments to local school districts based on the number of children from families in poverty. Services are then provided based on the extent of the student's educational deprivation. The law allows for a range of services, including instructional services, purchase of materials and equipment, teacher training, construction, and social and health services.

Charcot-Marie-Tooth syndrome Peroneal muscular atrophy (wasting), HMSN I (hereditary motor and sensory neuropathy). A genetic syndrome of progressive distal muscle atrophy and progressive sensorineural hearing loss. Prevalence rates are estimated at 4 per 100,000. Inheritance follows an autosomal dominant pattern with high penetrance expression. Lemieux-Neemeh syndrome is Charcot-Marie-Tooth syndrome with the addition of chronic nephritis (kidney disease). Jean M. Charcot (1825–1893) and Pierre Marie (1853–1940) were French neurologists; Howard M. Tooth (1856–1925) was an English neurologist.

CHARGE association Acronym representing the congenital malformations of coloboma (absence of part of the eye or retina), heart disease, choanal atresia (nasal blockage), retarded growth and development with mild to profound mental retardation, genital anomalies, and ear anomalies and deafness. Mental retardation, and visual and auditory problems frequently impair cognitive functioning.

Chédiak-Higashi syndrome Chédiak-Steinbrinck-Higashi syndrome. A rare genetic syndrome with partial albinism leading to reduced visual acuity; immune defects in the white blood cells then contribute to recurrent infections, progressive cranial and peripheral neuropathy, and occasional mental retardation. Therapy includes diligent and aggressive treatment of the recurrent infections; nonetheless, most affected persons do not survive childhood. Inheritance is autosomal recessive with a high frequency of consanguinity noted in the families of affected individuals.

chelion Corner of the mouth.

chemotherapy Treatment with chemicals or drugs; usually refers to highly toxic substances used to treat cancer.

cherry red spot A red patch seen on the retina in children with various neuronal storage diseases, such as Tay-Sachs disease. The lipid compounds that cannot be broken down or excreted are found in the neuron, giving it a grayish color. The red spot is an area that does not contain any nerve cells and therefore is red (the normal color), not gray.

cherubism A genetic disorder that causes swelling of the mandible (jaw) along with a "heavenward" glance to produce a cherubic or angelic appearance. Articulation disorders may result from oral structural problems. Inheritance follows an autosomal dominant pattern with variable expression and incomplete penetrance in females; thus, males with the syndrome are more affected than females with the syndrome.

chi square A frequently used statistic that is employed in the following two ways: 1) to test whether observed results are of such dimensions that they could not have occurred by chance alone, and 2) to test the possibility of a relationship (termed *association*) between two variables. The chi square is an easy-to-use and powerful statistical tool when appropriately applied.

chickenpox *See* varicella.

chief complaint (CC) The principal symptom or subjective concern leading to a self-referral for diagnostic assessment and treatment. Often the final diagnosis is one commonly associated with the chief complaint, but sometimes this diagnosis is one rarely associated with this symptom. A caveat of diagnosis is that "uncommon presentations of common disorders are more common than common presentations of uncommon disorders."

chignon An artificial caput succedaneum or subcutaneous edema (swelling) of the scalp often secondary to vacuum extraction of a newborn.

Child Behavior Profile (CBP) A group of standardized and normed questionnaires that includes the Child Behavior Checklist (CBCL), the Teacher Report Form (TRF), the Direct Observation Form (DOF), and the Youth Self-Report Form (YSRF). The CBCL can help in the diagnosis of attention disorders, depression, and other childhood behavior problems and psychopathology.

Child Find Organized efforts to locate children with developmental disabilities or children who are at risk for developmental disabilities. Two federal enactments have given such efforts increased importance: 1) PL 93-380, the Education of the Handicapped Act Amendments of 1974, requires states to develop and implement systematic procedures for locating all individuals with disabilities from birth to age 21. The mandate particularly focuses on children not enrolled in school programs in order to facilitate an accurate child count for planning intervention programs and to document the need for additional early intervention programs. 2) PL 94-142, the Education for All Handicapped Children Act of 1975, and its amendments, list specific features of a free and appropriate public education (FAPE) in the least restrictive environment (LRE), the provision of services to all children with disabilities from birth, and the locating of unserved children.

child life specialist A professional who interacts with hospitalized children with a major focus on providing materials, guidance, and an appropriate environment for play activities; there is an additional emphasis on meeting the child's emotional needs and on psychiatric adjustment to hospitalization.

Childhood Autism Rating Scale (CARS) A 15-factor diagnostic instrument for autism that rates children's behavior in the presence of an adult and during independent play.

Children with Special Health Care Needs (CSHCN) Category includes children eligible for Supplemental Security Income (SSI) benefits, for services under Part H of IDEA, foster children, and children previously covered under CCS (Crippled Children's Services) because of developmental disabilities and chronic illness.

Children's Apperception Test (CAT) Three oral response projective tests measuring the traits, attitudes, and psychodynamics involved in the personality development of children. The measures are used to assess personality in children ages 3–10 years for clinical and diagnostic purposes. The CAT–A consists of 10 pictures of animals in a human social context; the child is asked to tell a story about the pictures. The CAT–H is composed of 10 pictures of human figures in situations of concern to children. The CAT–S is a supplemental form presenting 10 animal figures in family situations that are common but not as universal as those depicted in the two other forms. The picture plates resemble pieces of a jigsaw puzzle, so that children who do not relate stories can manipulate the test items in play techniques. Administration for each form of the test takes approximately 30 minutes.

Children's Version of the Family Environment Scale (CVFES) A downward extension of the Moos Family Environment Scale to elementary school-age children; subjects respond to 30 questions by selecting one of three pictures that best represents their family; scores are generated for cohesion, expressiveness, conflict, independence, achievement orientation, intellectual-cultural orientation, active-recreation orientation, moral-religious emphasis, organization, and control. Caution should be used in interpreting these results in children with attention and learning problems.

chloral hydrate A nonbarbiturate, nonbenzodiazepine sedative-hypnotic; a relatively safe sleep-inducing drug often used to prepare children for surgery or other procedures such as an electroencephalogram (EEG).

chloride-deficient formula In 1978 and 1979 two soy-based infant formulas (Neomullsoy and CHO-free) lacked adequate dietary chloride and produced serious illness (i.e., metabolic alkalosis) in a small number of children. It has been hypothesized that subclinical metabolic abnormalities due to these formulas may be associated with later neurodevelopmental disability for infants who had used these formulas in 1978 and 1979. Research data do not support more than a very mild impact on learning.

chlorpromazine   Trade name Thorazine. A phenothiazine drug used to treat severe behavior disorders in children. Side effects include tardive dyskinesia (slow, rhythmic automatic movements), photosensitivity, and blood and liver chemistry problems.

chondrodysplasia   punctata   Conradi-Hunermann syndrome; a genetic syndrome with asymmetric shortening of limbs, scoliosis (spinal curvature), and a characteristic facies with saddle-nose deformity and malar hypoplasia (undergrowth of the midface with cheekbones flat or depressed). Growth problems such as failure to thrive (poor growth) and short stature are common. Mild to moderate mental retardation and cataracts can occur. Incidence is estimated at 2.5 per million. Inheritance follows both autosomal dominant and autosomal recessive patterns. The autosomal recessive form is more severe and usually results in death before 1 year of age; autosomal dominant forms have a milder course. There is also an X-linked form lethal in males.

chondroectodermal dysplasia   Ellis-van Creveld syndrome; a genetic syndrome with short arms and legs leading to short stature, polydactyly (extra fingers or toes), and nail hypoplasia (atypical tissue development). Mental retardation is occasional. Congenital heart disease and abnormalities of the teeth and mouth are frequent. Many affected individuals die in early infancy from cardiorespiratory problems. Inheritance follows an autosomal recessive pattern with a consanguinity rate of 30%.

chorda tympani section   A surgical procedure that disrupts parasympathetic innervation to sublingual and submandibular glands as a treatment for drooling; it is usually performed bilaterally (both sides of the mouth) and combined with a tympanic neurectomy.

chorea   Literally, "dance." In the field of neurological dysfunction, chorea refers to a pattern of movement disorder characterized by spasmodic, irregular, unpredictable, involuntary, and purposeless movements also including large central twitches or jerking movements. Mild isolated chorea may be seen in the choreiform (involuntary twitching) syndrome; with more severe motor delay and chorea, the resulting type of extrapyramidal cerebral palsy is usually described as choreoathetoid. Choreiform movements are quicker and less fluid than athetoid movements.

chorea minor   Sydenham chorea (chorea major refers to chorea of a hysterical nature). A transient chorea that follows rheumatic fever.

choreic hand   When the arms are extended horizontally, the wrists flex and the wrist and finger joints are overextended; exaggerated spooning.

choreic hand

choreiform syndrome   The presence of mild choreiform (involuntary twitching) movements in the outstretched arms of boys standing at attention with their eyes closed. In late school-age and early adolescent boys, this was originally thought to be a marker for future (or present) juvenile delinquency and thus was named a "syndrome." This association has not held up well, and the neuromotor finding is considered a nonspecific sign of minor motor dysfunction.

choreoathetosis   One of the physiological subtypes of extrapyramidal cerebral palsy in which involvement of the basal ganglia produces a movement disorder with features of both chorea and athetosis (involuntary twisting of the upper extremities). Prior to the era of exchange transfusion for Rh incompatibility, basal ganglia involvement was most commonly seen following bilirubin encephalopathy (brain damage due to lack of oxygen) or kernicterus. Many of these children had a relatively pure motor disability with few associated deficits. Most cases of basal ganglia involvement are subsumed under more diffuse asphyxic brain damage, so that these children have associated deficits of increased severity. A choreathetoid cerebral palsy with prominent superimposed rigidity is sometimes referred to as a tension athetosis.

chorioretinitis An inflammation of the back of the eye or retina characterized by pigmentary changes and scarring in the retina. Chorioretinitis is common in some intrauterine infections such as toxoplasmosis, cytomegalovirus (CMV), and congenital rubella. These congenital infections can be associated with mental retardation, impairments of vision and hearing, and failure to thrive (poor growth).

Chotzen syndrome *See* Saethre-Chotzen syndrome.

chromosomal aberration An abnormal number or structure of chromosomes that may produce an abnormal phenotype. A trisomy such as Down syndrome is an example of an abnormal number of chromosomes (47), usually producing mental retardation as well as other physical defects. An example of a chromosomal abnormality that has no physical manifestations is a balanced translocation where two chromosomes of different numbers exchange pieces but no genes are lost.

chromosomal abnormality *See* chromosomal aberration.

chronic sorrow Chronic grief; parental response to a child's chronic disability or illness. This grief can be quite variable and can progress through stages of helplessness, hopelessness, and dependency. This sorrow or grief tends to be acutely reactivated with each new developmental stage that the child would normally experience were it not for the disability or illness (e.g., entering school, adolescence, leaving home).

chronic subdural hematoma A collection of bloody fluid under the dura (outer layer of the brain) produced by trauma to the head. Chronic subdural hematomas are most common in adolescents, and there is not generally a history of head trauma. Clinical presentation includes headaches and changes in personality and alertness. This can progress rapidly to loss of consciousness and seizures. Diagnosis is by magnetic resonance imaging (MRI) or computed tomography (CT) scan. Treatment involves removing the

fluid to relieve the pressure on the brain. Subdural effusions (fluid under one of the meningeal layers) in infants can be acute or chronic and are commonly associated with nonaccidental trauma (abuse). Clinical symptoms in infants are less specific and include failure to gain weight, irritability, lethargy, and vomiting. CT scans often reveal not only a subdural hematoma but also an associated skull fracture. In infants, repeated removal of the fluid with a needle can sometimes eliminate the need for surgery. Prognosis in subdural hematoma is correlated with the amount of underlying brain damage. The prognosis tends to be worse in children who have been abused. Residual neurological signs are related to the area of the brain that has been damaged.

chronological age (CA) The actual age of an individual derived from his or her date of birth. Chronological age is expressed in years, months, and days. It is used in psychometrics as a comparison standard for various measures of performance and is the denominator in the equation for determining an intelligence quotient by the ratio method: mental age (MA)/CA $\times$ 100 = IQ.

Chun Gun A sophisticated, high-intensity light source; the instrument is used in the transillumination of an infant's head to detect structural brain abnormalities.

CIBI Continuous intrathecal baclofen infusion. *See* baclofen.

cicatrix A scar.

ciliary reflex Eyelash reflex; an infant reflex in which touching an eyelash (stimulus) produces bilateral blinking (response).

cimetidine Trade name Tagamet; an H_2-receptor antagonist that suppresses gastric acid production. It is often used in the treatment of gastroesophageal reflux.

CIP *See* Comprehensive Identification Process.

circumduction A circular movement; in a hemiplegic gait, the involved leg, instead of being flexed directly forward, is extended, abducted, and dragged ahead through an outward semicircle with increasing flexion and adduction.

Civilian Health and Medical Program of the Uniformed Services (CHAMPUS) A federally funded health insurance for the dependents of active and retired military personnel. Health care services are purchased by CHAMPUS from private non-military providers when such services are not available or not accessible through the military system.

CLAMS *See* Clinical Linguistic and Auditory Milestone Scale.

Clancy Scale A 54-item questionnaire to identify autism in children. The items are grouped into 14 categories that reflect an expansion and refinement of the nine diagnostic points checklist. The 14 descriptors include difficulty with peer relationships, acting as if deaf, resistance to learning, lack of realistic fear, resistance to change in routine, preferring to communicate with gestures, inappropriate laughter, lack of cuddliness as a baby, hyperactivity, poor eye contact, unusual object attachment, spinning of objects, repetitive and sustained odd play, and standoffish manner.

class within a class (CWC) A service delivery model in which students with mild disabilities are educated in the general classroom using a collaborative educational program provided by general and special education teachers. Programs include 1) collaborative curriculum development in which teachers of students with learning disabilities and general education teachers write curricula and plan teaching strategies, 2) a service delivery model that places teachers of students with learning disabilities in the general classroom to promote collaboration between general and special educators, and 3) development of a curriculum to provide students with learning disabilities instruction in learning strategies and study skills.

classification The process of grouping and defining the criteria for group inclusion or exclusion.

Classroom Communication Screening Procedure for Early Adolescents (CCSPEA) A language screening instrument for underachieving upper elementary students prior to entering junior high school. CCSPEA assesses the ability to scan an assignment for answers, follow oral and multipart written directions, use metalinguistic and metacognitive skills, and match vocabulary items with definitions/synonyms.

clavicle Collar bone.

claw grasp Three- or four-finger grasp or jaw chuck; an advance in the radial (thumb and forefinger) rake that is not yet a pincer (two-finger) grasp.

CLD *See* Council for Learning Disabilities.

cleft lip An embryonic defect that presents in the newborn with varying degrees of failure of the upper lip to fuse appropriately. It can be associated with cleft palate, hypertelorism (widely spaced eyes), speech disorders, recurrent otitis media (middle-ear infection), and conductive (involving the middle and outer ear) hearing loss. Etiology (cause) is genetic with a polygenic pattern and varying recurrence risks; about one third of cases of cleft lip are part of another syndrome that may have other associated features and a more definable recurrence rate.

cleft lip

cleft palate A congenital defect in which the palate (bony roof of the mouth) has not closed or fused in the midline during fetal development. Cleft palate is associated with feeding and swallowing problems, failure to thrive (poor growth), aspiration, recurrent ear infections, and hypernasal dysarticulate speech. Cleft palate has multifactorial inheritance; cleft palate with cleft lip also has multifactorial inheritance, but is pathophysiologically distinct from isolated cleft palate. Clefting can occur as an isolated oral cavity malformation or as part of many genetic and teratogenic (causing malformation) syndromes.

cleidocranial dysostosis Scheuthauer-Marie syndrome; a genetic syndrome with variable expression of bone defects (i.e., dysostosis) affecting the clavicle (cleido), delayed eruption of teeth, and late ossification of the skull (cranial) sutures. Because of incomplete clavicles, people can often approximate their shoulders in front of their chest. One of the earliest signs noted may be late closure of a large anterior (front) fontanel (soft spot). Cognition is normal; audiological and dental monitoring is indicated. Inheritance follows an autosomal dominant pattern; however, one third of the cases represent fresh mutations.

client A social-work term denoting an individual, family, group, or community receiving services. In contrast to the medical term *patient*, the term *client* highlights the elements of mutuality, self-determination, and the aspect of being an informed consumer of the helping process.

Client Assistance Program The state agency responsible for providing legal, administrative, and other assistance to individuals seeking and receiving vocational rehabilitation services.

Clinical Evaluation of Language Fundamentals—Revised (CELF–R) A revised and restandardized (1987) version of the CELF that is designed to identify children ages 5–16 years who lack basic language skills. The CELF–R consists of 11 subtests for ages 5-7 and 8-16 that provide receptive, expressive, and total language scores. Five supplementary subtests are available for additional diagnostic information. Norms include standard scores by age for subtests as well as composite scores, percentile ranks (by age) for subtests, and composite scores and age-equivalent scores for total language scores. A screening version is also available.

Clinical Linguistic and Auditory Milestone Scale (CLAMS) A test of early language development (birth to 2 years of age) that uses a parent or caregiver interview and yields an expressive language quotient (ELQ) and a receptive language quotient (RLO). Although normative data have been published to allow use of the CLAMS as a screening test, the instrument is intended for use in a more comprehensive diagnostic approach (CAT-CLAMS).

clinical psychology A branch of the study of human behavior concerned with testing, diagnosing, researching, and treating mental disorders and interpersonal problems.

clinician A professional who is directly involved with the examination, diagnosis, and treatment of patients or clients.

clinodactyly Lateral or medial turning of a finger; a physical feature found in a number of syndromes; clinodactyly (inturning) of the fifth finger is a common nonspecific minor dysmorphic (atypical) feature.

clock-training Pseudo toilet training where the caregiver, rather than the child, is trained. The child is placed on the toilet/potty at regular intervals to catch bowel movements. This reflects more a caregiving refinement than an early stage of genuine bowel regulation. Children do not need long periods of repetitious exposure to the potty to accustom them to its use. When successful, clock-training decreases the expense for diapers and the caregiver's need to clean the child.

clonazepam Trade name Klonopin; an anticonvulsant medication; also used to treat hypomanic states, self-injurious behavior, and severe maladaptive behavior in persons with severe mental retardation. Clonazepam is dosed three to four times a day and has good seizure control; seizures decrease over the first month of treatment in 30%–50% of persons treated for the disorder. Side effects include sedation, ataxia (unsteady gait), dysarthria (difficulty pronouncing words), emotional irritability, and weight gain. Clonazepam is useful in treatment of Lennox-Gastaut syndrome, but its efficacy in infantile spasms is debated.

clonidine Trade name Catapres; an antihypertensive drug (used to treat high blood pressure) that is also used to treat Gilles de la Tourette syndrome and as an adjunct for attention-deficit/hyperactivity disorder (ADHD). Clonidine can be given in delayed release transdermal (absorbed through the skin) dosage form. The main side effect is tiredness.

clonus Rapidly alternating muscle contraction and relaxation, leading to repetitive flexion and extension.

closure A law of gestalt perceptual psychology asserting that mental processes tend to produce completeness and symmetry; for example, a circle that is missing a few degrees of its circumference is perceived as a circle rather than an arc.

cloudy cornea Haziness of the normally translucent cornea of the eye. Cloudy cornea is a sign that can occur in congenital syphilis, mucopolysaccharidosis, and mucolipidosis.

cloverleaf skull syndrome Also known as kleeblattshädel syndrome; a syndrome of premature synostosis (closure) of the cranial sutures producing upward and lateral outpouchings of the skull in a three-leaf clover outline; hydrocephalus (excess fluid in the brain), developmental delay, and early death are associated features.

cloze technique A procedure for teaching and assessing reading comprehension based on the construct of perception and closure as defined in gestalt psychology. In general, using this technique, in a reading selection of 250 words, every 10th lexical word would be deleted and the reader would be asked to fill it in. This requires various reading skills, including context clues, knowledge of linguistic patterns, and general reading comprehension.

clubbing A convex curvature of the nail and top of the digit found in chronic disease, especially pulmonary disease.

clubbing

clubfoot *See* talipes equinovarus.

clumsy child syndrome An age-inappropriate difficulty in performing skilled motor movements. This may include both fine- and gross-motor movements. Mild motor delay may be an early sign of later clumsy child syndrome. Developmental apraxia (inability to perform purposeful movements) may be synonymous with clumsy child syndrome, but the latter usually refers more specifically to problems with fine-motor skills. In school-age children, developmental disorders of written language or dysgraphia (impaired writing) represent prominent symptoms. Clumsy child syndrome is sometimes referred to as minimal cerebral palsy.

cluttering Speech that is so excited and rapid that words run together with syllables omitted; the fast rate and irregular clustering of phrases lead to difficulties with intelligibility. Cluttering can occur in isolation or be associated with disorders in articulation, language, learning, and attention.

CMAI–ST *See* Chandler Movement Assessment of Infancy–Screening Test.

CMMS *See* Columbia Mental Maturity Scale.

CMV Cytomegalovirus. *See* fetal cytomegalovirus syndrome.

CNS *See* central nervous system.

coarse facies A facial appearance characterized by swelling of the lips, thickening of the subcutaneous (inner) tissue, and broadening of the nose; this can develop as a side effect of chronic phenytoin (Dilantin) treatment.

coarse facies

Cobb angle A measure of the degree of curvature in scoliosis (spinal curvature), using horizontal lines to vertebral bodies as drawn on X rays. Angles of 20–40 degrees suggest mild scoliosis; angles of 40–60 degrees suggest moderate scoliosis; and angles of greater than 60 degrees suggest severe scoliosis.

cocaine baby *See* infant of drug-addicted mother; infant of substance-abusing mother.

cochlear implant An electronic device that is placed in the skull and that, in combination with a hearing aid worn on the body, enhances the detection of sound by a person who cannot use conventional hearing aids. Im-

cochlear implant

plantation of the device is the easiest part of using a cochlear implant. Thereafter, intense work is required to learn speech detection. In the ideal situation, the cochlear implant allows detection of speech by a person who might only have been able to read lips. As technology improves, the addition of more channels to the implant will also improve the quality of speech detection.

Cockayne syndrome A genetic degenerative syndrome with cachectic (starvation) dwarfism, premature senility, retinal degeneration, sensorineural hearing loss, mental retardation, and skin photosensitivity. The lack of subcutaneous (inner) fat contributes to a wizened, sunken-eyed appearance. The life span is considerably shortened for affected individuals. Inheritance follows an autosomal recessive pattern.

cocontraction Simultaneous contraction of all the muscles around a joint (agonists and antagonists) to produce stability.

Coffin-Lowry syndrome A genetic syndrome with severe mental retardation, coarse peculiar facies (bulbous nose, antimongoloid slant, pouting lower lip), tapering fingers, and short stature. Inheritance points toward an X-linked semidominant pattern with many sporadic cases.

Coffin-Siris syndrome Fifth digit syndrome; a syndrome characterized by hypoplastic (short to absent) fifth-digit nails, microcephaly (abnormally small head) with coarse facies but very full lips, intrauterine and postnatal growth defi-

ciency, mental retardation, and hirsutism (excessive hair growth) combined with sparse scalp hair growth. Inheritance appears to be autosomal recessive; however, confirming evidence is still scanty.

cognate A blood relative through the mother's side of the family.

cognitive behavior therapy (CBT) *See* cognitive therapy.

cognitive style 1. The preferred method for approaching a learning or problem-solving situation. Cognitive style is often described in terms of modality, such as visual, auditory, or kinesthetic, referring to the preferred method of acquiring information. 2. The preferred method of information processing (i.e., whether the individual prefers information presented in a part-to-whole, linear fashion or, conversely, in a whole-to-part, simultaneous fashion). Current theories and descriptions of cognitive style are drawn from earlier work in perception and decision-making styles such as field dependence–independence, leveling-sharpening, and repression–sensitization. Most individuals, although indicating a preference, can use a variety of styles. Cognitive style in an individual with a disability, however, is often a reflection of an innate neurological profile. In this case, the choice is not based on the most efficient method for the situation, but on the limited options available to the learner. Learning style theories expand the cognitive style concept to include environmental variables.

cognitive therapy Also termed *cognitive behavior therapy* (CBT); a psychological treatment based on a cognitive model of emotional functioning. In contrast to drive-based and conflict-motivated models of emotional functioning, cognitive models assert that emotions and behaviors are mediated by specific cognitions in response to an event. Emotional disorders, such as depression, are seen as the outcome of learned, habitual, dysfunctional thinking processes and patterns that have become so automatic in their mediational function that they are no longer in conscious awareness. The automatic filtering of events through the learned, habitual, yet dysfunctional, thinking processes leads to a distorted interpretation of the event and thus a distorted emotional response. In the case of depression, these distortions are negatively loaded and lead to a negative emotional response. Cognitive therapies aim to expose both the content and process of dysfunctional thinking and, once exposed, to remove or replace them with more functional processes leading to less-distorted and less-toxic emotional outcomes.

Cohen syndrome A genetic syndrome with a peculiar facies (e.g., open mouth, short philtrum [indentation in upper lip below nose], prominent incisors, micrognathia [small jaw]), mental retardation, hypotonia (decreased muscle tone), short stature, obesity of mid-childhood onset, and long slender fingers and toes. Inheritance follows an autosomal recessive pattern.

coining Cao gio; an Asian folk medicine practice of rubbing the involved area of the body with a coin. This dermabrasion technique can produce welts and superficial bruises that may be misinterpreted as signs of child abuse.

colic Also known as evening colic, 3 months' colic. A condition of unknown etiology (cause) occurring in infants in the first 3 months of life during which time they exhibit restlessness, crying, and apparent pain at a regular part of the day (usually every evening). Colic may be ameliorated with drugs, but the condition spontaneously resolves as the babies begin their fourth month; it has no long-term or developmental implications. However, in a colicky, irritable infant who cries and refuses to be comforted at all hours of the day after the first 3 months of life, brain damage may be suspected, especially if the infant cry is shrill and high pitched.

collateral A small side branch.

Collier sign Supranuclear lid retraction, "posterior fossa (furrowed) stare"; may

contribute to a hyperalert appearance and suggests a midbrain lesion (as in the diencephalic syndrome).

coloboma A cleft, slit, gap, or fissure in any eye structure. Refractive errors and retinal detachments are potential complications of certain types of coloboma. Iris colobomas are readily visible to inspection; retinal colobomas require ophthalmological examination to be detected. Colobomas are often part of a larger genetic or malformation syndrome. Iris colobomas suggest the need for chromosome analysis.

colon The large intestine; the part of the digestive tract that connects the small intestine to the rectum. The colon is mainly responsible for the absorption of water from fecal material.

color blindness A sex-linked inability to discriminate colors (either red-green or all colors), occurring in 8% of boys and 0.5% of girls. The presence of color blindness does not relate to the occurrence of learning disabilities. *See also* Ishihara test.

colostomy A surgical operation and its result in which the large intestine is brought through the abdominal wall to empty into an appliance that has a plastic bag; the procedure is used to treat cancer, obstruction, and incontinence related to rectal dysfunction that may be secondary to spinal cord damage or dysfunction.

Columbia Mental Maturity Scale (CMMS) A multiple-choice test measuring global intelligence and requiring no verbal and little motor response, for use in nonverbal children or in children with physical disabilities who are between 3-6 and 10 years of age. A card of symbols is presented to the child, who must identify which of the pictures is different, according to color, shape, use, or symbol. Administration time is less than 20 minutes. The results generate an IQ with a mean of 100 and a standard deviation of 16. Because minimal motor response is required, the test helps in assessing children with severe physical impairments.

columella nasi The lower margin of the nasal septum. A short columella contributes to an apparent flat nose in a number of syndromes.

coma A state of decreased consciousness, with unresponsiveness even to painful stimuli.

common sense The ability to demonstrate knowledge of information thought to be widely understood. Generally, common sense is a compilation of cultural traditions or folk knowledge constituting a body of shared and relatively standardized interpretations of a variety of phenomena—from natural occurrences to social behavior—and containing solutions to everyday problems. As opposed to "book knowledge" or "school smarts," common sense is pragmatic and relies heavily on problem-solving skills applied to "real life." Occasionally, parents and teachers are baffled at a child's solid common sense but simultaneous failure in the classroom. Many people with learning disabilities and attention disorders appear to lack common sense. Knowing to "come in out of the rain" and to "look before one leaps" are the type of "givens" common sense is assumed to make obvious to everyone.

Communication Abilities Diagnostic Test (CADeT) An informal norm-referenced test of language development for children ages 3–9 years that uses stories, board games, and conversational context to assess syntax (grammar), semantics (the meaning of words), and pragmatic language.

Communication and Symbolic Behavior Scales (CSBS) A norm-referenced assessment of language for children whose functional communication ages are 9 months to 2 years. A caregiver questionnaire, direct sampling of verbal and nonverbal communicative behaviors, and observation of relatively unstructured play activities generate 16 communication scales and 4 symbolic behavior scales.

communication board An apparatus on which letters, numbers, and commonly used words are represented to assist individuals for whom oral expression is difficult or impossible. There are several types of boards, including 1) a direct-selection board, with a one-to-one correspondence between what the sender wants to express and the elements the board provides; 2) an encoding board, requiring the acquisition of input techniques before the device can be used; and 3) a scanning board on which message elements are presented, with matching components indicated by a prearranged signal (i.e., arm, hand, or eye movement), thus requiring a minimum amount of physical control by the user.

Letters		A	B
		C	D
E	F	G	H
I	J	K	L
M	N	O	P
Q	R	S	T
U	V	W	X
Y	Z		

communication board

communication disorder A problem with hearing, language, and/or speech, including articulation, voice, and fluency.

Communicative Activities of Daily Living (CADL) A test of the knowledge and use of functional language in daily life activities. Originally developed for use with people with aphasia (loss of language skills), this instrument has subsequently been normed for use for people with mental retardation. Simulated life activities, such as label reading, transportation, ability to tell time, and understanding of common signs, are assessed to determine the functional language and adaptive skills needs of the person with mental retardation.

communicology Speech-language pathology.

compensation An adjustment or series of adjustments to counteract or mitigate the effect of some anomaly (malformation, deformation, disruption, or dysplasia), impairment, or disability. Both the difficulty and the adjustment can be neural, motoric, psychological, physical, or social in nature, and may not be readily apparent. Seeking achievement in other areas, working harder than others, or implementing bypass strategies to circumvent weaknesses are examples of compensatory techniques. Because developmental disabilities are permanent and can vary in expression over the life span, compensatory techniques are necessary to facilitate daily function and may vary in response to changing needs. The more that is known about the individual's difficulty, the easier it may be to identify strengths and devise compensatory techniques.

compensation A theory of recovery from brain damage that suggests that the functions of a damaged circuit may be assumed by other circuits and pathways, as opposed to true recovery of the original damaged circuits.

compensatory methodology Accomplishing instructional objectives by circumventing weaknesses and utilizing strengths of the student. Commonly used in reference to educating students with disabilities, such as those who are deaf, blind, or have learning disabilities.

complete blood count (CBC) A battery of tests of the blood, including hemoglobin (oxygen-carrying red blood cells), hematocrit (the volume of packed red cells), red and white blood counts, red cell indices, and a differential white blood cell count (percentages of different white blood cells).

completion test A test that requires the subject to fill in blank spaces of test items such as incomplete sentences.

complex partial seizure A type of partial seizure that includes altered consciousness and often automatisms (robotic behaviors, such as running, fumbling with objects or clothing, or lip smacking). A complex partial seizure is often preceded by a simple partial seizure. Recognition of this fact helps to diagnose the seizure type, warns the person that he or she is about to have a seizure that alters consciousness, and may help to localize the brain focus of the seizure. Frequently, seizures with automatisms begin in the temporal lobe. Complex partial status epilepticus is rare; complex partial seizures can generalize to tonic-clonic seizures. Complex partial seizures are

treated with carbamazepine (Tegretol), phenobarbital, valproic acid (Valproate), phenytoin (Dilantin), primidone (Mysoline), or mephobarbital (Mebaral).

Comprehensive Identification Process (CIP) A screening test for children from 2½ to 5½ years of age who are not participating in an organized preschool program. Motor, cognitive, and speech-language areas are assessed. Administration time is approximately 1 hour for relatively skilled personnel; 30% of children are subsequently referred for further testing.

Comprehensive Test of Visual Functioning (CTVF) An assessment device for visual function in children ages 8 to 16-0 that includes subtests on visual acuity, visual processing/figure–ground, visual tracking, reading word analysis, visual/ letter integration, visual/writing integration, nonverbal visual closure, nonverbal visual reasoning/memory, spatial orientation/memory/motor, spatial orientation/motor, visual design/motor, and visual design/memory/motor.

computed tomography (CT) Computed axial tomography (CAT) scan; a radiological technique in which rays are passed through the brain (or other body part) to produce a picture that shows the body part in cross section. Serial sections that look at different areas of the brain are possible. Head CT scans are used to delineate location of brain damage secondary to tumor, stroke, congenital malformations, or infection. A CT scan can be completed in 30 minutes. It does, however, require stillness; thus, many younger children must be sedated.

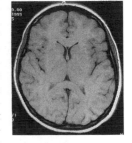

computed tomography scan

computer-assisted instruction (CAI) The use of computer programs to teach people with and without developmental disabilities.

conative Volitional, as opposed to cognitive.

concave A hollowed-out, or depressed, surface; often used in descriptions of corrective lenses and spinal curvatures.

concentric power The ability to resist force as the muscle is shortened.

concept A regularity in events or objects designated by some label. For example, the concept of *chair* includes easy chairs, desk chairs, straight-backed chairs, and so forth. The concept of *chair* is itself part of a concept called *furniture*. Concepts may be described as nonverbal or verbal. Nonverbal concepts are groups of ideas that go together and are easier to picture than to describe. For example, to understand fractions, it might be easier to picture a pizza being divided than to explain it in words. Verbal concepts refer to associated ideas that are readily described through language (e.g., *friendship*). Concrete concepts refer to objects that can be seen or felt, such as the concept of *dog*. Abstract concepts refer to ideas, rather than objects. For example, *democracy, evaporation*, and *creativity* are examples of abstract concepts. Students with learning disabilities can have difficulty understanding concepts if they are presented by a method not suited to their cognitive strengths. For example, students with language impairments are helped by a visual representation of a concept; abstract concepts are often stumbling blocks for such students.

concordant A term used in twin studies meaning that both twins have a certain trait.

concrete operations Piagetian stage in cognitive development in which induction (logical thinking) emerges but is limited to what is immediately perceived. This approach remains prominent from 6 to 12 years of age.

concretism A style of thinking and behavior in which an individual views each situation as new and unique, with a failure or inability to see fundamental similarities and relationships between situations that others recognize as similar or analogous. In concretism, general knowledge, problem-solving strategies, and comparable components are neither generalized nor assimilated into a cognitive structure to be assessed at a later date. Concretism is characteristic of some individuals with mental retardation.

concussion Transient neuronal dysfunction that immediately follows head trauma with or without retrograde (before the injury) amnesia (impaired memory); it is less severe than contusion. Associated symptoms may include drowsiness, vomiting, seizures, and other neurological findings.

conditioned dysphagia A learned difficulty with food acceptance and feeding that results from an aversion to swallowing.

conditioned reflex A learned response to a neutral stimulus; the linking of a neutral stimulus to a stimulus that elicits an unconditioned reflex response.

conduct disorder A persistent behavior pattern of violating others' rights and ignoring age-appropriate social standards. Specific behaviors include lying, theft, arson, running away from home, aggression, truancy, burglary, cruelty to animals, and fighting. This disorder is distinguished from oppositional defiant disorder by the increased severity of the behaviors and their occurrence independent of an event occasioning opposition. Attention-deficit/hyperactivity disorder (ADHD) is frequently associated with or misdiagnosed as conduct disorder. There is a marked male predominance in incidence.

conductive deafness Hearing loss because of an inability to transmit sound from the air to the tympanic membrane (ear drum) in order to activate the auditory nerve (cranial nerve VIII). This is generally the result of a problem with the outer or middle ear; the inner ear is usually normal. Causative factors range from congenital malformations of the outer ear to fluid in the middle ear because of an ear infection. Some causes of conductive losses can be treated and cured.

conductive education A school of physical therapy for cerebral palsy; *see also* Peto.

co-negativity Specificity.

confabulation Fabrication; differs from lying in that the subject believes what is being said; observed in adults with organic brain syndromes and in children with attention disorders.

confidence interval *See* error of measurement.

confidentiality A legal and ethical professional practice principle whereby such professionals may not disclose or discuss information regarding a client or patient; including the diagnostic and treatment services rendered, without the express written consent of the client or patient. This restriction includes the identity of the client or patient, records, opinions, or behaviors. Violation of this principle is considered malpractice. Confidentiality, however, may be set aside when there is danger of suicide, homicide, or child abuse (i.e., when there is a clear and present danger of harm to self or others).

confusion reflex *See* flexor withdrawal reflex.

congenital Present at birth; either genetic or acquired in utero due to teratogens (toxic agents) or mechanical factors.

congenital cytomegalic inclusion disease *See* fetal cytomegalovirus (CMV) syndrome.

congenital dislocation of the hip (CDH) *See* developmental dysplasia of the hip.

congenital rubella *See* fetal rubella syndrome.

congenital vertical talus Rocker-bottom foot; a rigid flat foot that has a high association with other congenital anomalies and genetic syndromes, CNS disorders (especially myelodysplasia), congenital hip dislocation, and arthrogryposis (fixation of the joints).

Conners Rating Scales A group of normed questionnaires to assess hyperactivity and inattention. The Conners Parent Rating Scale (CPRS) and the Conners Teachers Rating Scale (CTRS) are used for children 6–14 years of age; the shorter Conners Parent Rating Scale–Revised (CPRS–R) and Conners Teachers Rating Scale–Revised (CTRS–R) are used for children 3–17 years of age. These instruments are used both for diagnostic purposes and to monitor the response to stimulant drug therapy for hyperactivity.

Conradi-Hunermann syndrome *See* chondrodysplasia punctata.

consanguinity Having a common ancestor; a blood relationship. Rare recessive disorders are more likely to occur from a consanguineous relationship, since the two people involved tend to carry similar genes. Throughout history, laws have prohibited consanguineous marriages because of the knowledge that these marriages produced a greater number of children with mental retardation and deformities.

consensual light reflex The contraction of a shaded pupil (protected from the light) when the other pupil is stimulated by light.

consequent stimulus event (CSE) The effect produced in the environment by an operant behavior. The CSE always follows the operant and serves to strengthen, weaken, or maintain the behavior.

consensual light reflex

CSEs that strengthen operant behaviors are called reinforcers and may be positive or negative. Positive CSEs strengthen the operant by immediately following it with a reward. Negative CSEs strengthen an operant by immediately following it with the removal, or avoidance, of something a person does not like. During the initial stages of learning, it is important that the CSE follow the operant immediately. A delay may prevent the association of the CSE with the operant, and the CSE may then not have any effect on the operant. A CSE that weakens a behavior is called a punisher or aversive stimulus event (ASE). Negative reinforcement and punishment are often confused but are quite different. Punishment serves to weaken undesirable behavior by presenting an ASE after the behavior occurs; negative reinforcement serves to strengthen desirable behavior by removing an ASE after the desirable behavior occurs. Reinforcers and punishers may be primary (unlearned or unconditioned) such as food or physical pain, or secondary (learned or conditioned). Secondary reinforcers or punishers usually require pairing with a primary or an established reinforcer or punisher to become effective. For example, a frown becomes effective through an initial pairing with a "time-out."

conservator A court-appointed person who maintains responsibility for and power over the financial affairs of another individual who has been legally judged incapacitated. In terms of finances, a person may need a conservator only when he or she has a physical impairment and thus is unable to negotiate financial matters easily or in a timely manner. A person who is mentally incapacitated (by illness, accident, or mental retardation), however, may have a conservator for financial matters and a guardian to oversee other areas of life decision making.

consolability An infant's capacity to quiet following a period of crying. The degree of intervention necessary to help the infant to quiet may reflect the ability to regulate state changes.

contagion The spread of disease from one individual to another.

contagious Relating to the spread of a disease from one individual to another. Different infectious diseases have greater or lesser degrees of contagiousness; some spread rapidly, whereas others can only be spread by prolonged intimate contact. Developmental disabilities are not contagious.

contextual clues A word attack skill using the relationship of words to their uses in phrases, sentences, and paragraphs to help decode unknown words. Closure activities (filling in missing words) are often used both to teach and to test the use of contextual clues. For example: "The _____ man shouted and stomped his foot" (from Woodcock-Johnson Psycho-Educational Battery–Revised).

contiguous gene syndrome The presence of multiple anomalies due to deletions of gene(s) next to each other on the same chromosome. For example, WAGR syndrome, an acronym for the combination of conditions including Wilms' tumor (a malignancy of the kidney), aniridia (absent irises), genitourinary abnormalities, and mental retardation, is caused by a deletion of chromosome 11p. This deletion is in a similar location as the deletion in Beckwith-Weidemann syndrome, which also includes Wilms' tumor and genitourinary abnormalities.

contingency A term from behaviorist learning theory that refers to the conditions in which a consequent stimulus event (CSE) occurs. The contingency is what the child must do before the CSE is presented. For example, a teacher might want a student to write the three times table (the operant behavior) with 100% accuracy in order to receive 15 minutes of free time. The contingency would be writing the three times table with 100% accuracy.

contingency contracting A specific type of behavior modification program. A teacher makes a contract with a student, who agrees to perform a specific behavior, such as finishing an assignment, in return for an agreed-upon reward.

continuous performance test (CPT) A research technology to quantitate attention span, concentration, and impulsivity by having the subject identify a specific letter sequence in a rapidly changing stream of randomized letters; error score and reaction time are electronically calculated.

continuous positive airway pressure (CPAP) A type of assisted ventilation used in newborns with respiratory distress.

continuum of developmental disabilities
An approach to the major categories of developmental disabilities that focuses on their similarities (as opposed to the spectrum that emphasizes their differences). In many cases of a given developmental diagnostic category, associated findings suggest one or more other developmental diagnoses. Thus, children whose primary diagnosis is mental retardation often exhibit some motor findings common to children with cerebral palsy; children with cerebral palsy often have varying degrees of mental retardation; and children with severe learning disabilities have a variety of motor and cognitive abnormalities.

continuum of reproductive casualty The entire range of fetal and maternal disorders associated with pregnancy, labor, and delivery; in 1956 Benjamin Pasamanick described this continuum as a risk factor in later developmental disabilities.

contracture A permanent muscular or other soft-tissue contraction (fixed increased resistance to passive stretch) due to tonic spasm or shortening. Contracture at a joint prevents movement through the full range of motion. Contractures arise earlier in spastic cerebral palsy and later in extrapyramidal cerebral palsy. Contractures may be prevented by physical therapy, positioning, and bracing; they may be treated by serial casting and surgery. Congenital contractures occur in arthrogryposis (fixation of the joints).

contraindication Prohibition; a reason not to do something; any symptom or special circumstance that renders a treatment or surgical procedure inadvisable. Contraindications may be relative or absolute. For example, surgery may be delayed until the individual is in an optimal nutritional state; elective procedures in infants are usually not carried out until the baby weighs 10 pounds. In the area of developmental disabilities, tics and Gilles de la Tourette syndrome represent relative contraindications to the use of methylphenidate for attention-deficit/hyperactivity disorder (ADHD).

contralateral On the opposite side of the body. Because motor nerve fibers from the brain cross the midline, the right brain controls motor movements on the left side of the body; similarly, the left brain controls motor movements on the contralateral, or right side, of the body.

contralateral

contrecoup injury An injury that occurs when the force of a blow to one side of the body causes damage to the other side of the body; this is especially common in head injuries because the brain is constrained within the skull.

contusion A head injury (more severe than a concussion) that results in bleeding into the brain. Associated symptoms may include loss of consciousness, vomiting, skull fracture, seizures, papilledema (edema and inflammation of the optic nerve), and neurological residua.

conversation board *See* communication board.

convex Rounded, bulging outward; often used in the description of corrective lenses and spinal curvatures.

convulsion A violent involuntary muscular contraction that can be due to a neurological seizure disorder. Recurrent seizures define epilepsy.

cooing The first stage of infant vocalization consisting of vowel sounds. It may be present near birth in the form of short, squealing sounds, and should be easily noticed by 3 months of age. By 6 months of age, cooing evolves into fairly musical play with complex vowel patterns. The absence or significant delay of this vocalization pattern, as seen in the quiet baby, should be considered an early marker for developmental disorders, especially mental retardation or language disorders. Since cooing is preprogrammed, it is not dependent on external auditory stimuli and will occur on time in children deaf from birth.

Cooperative Preschool Inventory–Revised A brief screening test for school readiness in children of 3–6 years of age, with an administration time of 15 minutes. The instrument has been used principally to measure the effects of early intervention programs in low socioeconomic populations.

Coopersmith Self-Esteem Inventory (CSEI) A measure of an individual's feelings and attitudes about him- or herself. There are two forms of the measure: Form A comprises five subscales with 58 items that address general self, social self, peers, home-parents, school-academic, and a lie scale. Form B is briefer and is not divided into subscales. Norms are provided for children ages 9–15 and for young adults.

co-positivity Sensitivity.

coprolalia The obsessive and compulsive use of obscene words; this symptom occurs late in the course of Gilles de la Tourette syndrome. Related findings in Tourette syndrome include copropraxia (obscene gestures) and coprographia (obscene drawings and writings).

corectopia A pupil that is not centered in the iris.

cornea The transparent, clear anterior (front) covering of the eye.

corneal light reflex test *See* Hirschberg test.

Cornelia de Lange syndrome Brachmann-de Lange or de Lange syndrome; typus degenerativus amstelodamensis. A syndrome of mental retardation, hirsutism (excessive hair growth), microcephaly (abnormally small head), very short stature of prenatal onset with micromelia (small extremities), thin downturning and long upper lip, and a small nose with anteverted nares (nostrils). The hirsutism is especially prominent with the bushy eyebrows that tend to be confluent across the midline (synophrys). The degree of mental retardation tends to be severe, with marked speech and language problems and occasional hearing impairments and autistic features. Recurrence risk is negli-gible, but rare cases of autosomal dominant inheritance have been reported. Duplication of part of the long arm of chromosome 3 can produce a phenotype similar to de Lange syndrome. Named after the Dutch pediatrician Cornelia de Lange (1871–1950).

coronal plane An anatomical plane that divides the body into an anterior (front) and posterior (back) half.

corporal punishment A form of punishment in which physical pain or discomfort is administered. Although it is not uncommon for schools and school systems in the United States to condone and administer corporal punishment, little is known about its effectiveness due to the lack of research in this area. Research has, however, indicated negative side effects related to corporal punishment. The use of punishment has been demonstrated to produce strong emotional side effects in children, sometimes resulting in behavior more deviant or disruptive than the original. Instances of aggressive behavior directed toward the punisher, innocent bystanders, and inanimate objects have been demonstrated after corporal punishment was applied. Any behavior that provides escape from the punishment (e.g., lying, hiding, cheating) is negatively reinforced, and may become part of a child's repertoire. Corporal punishment also provides a model of aggressive behavior that is imitated by young children. The adult administering the punishment may be teaching the student that it is acceptable to hurt others if you are an adult or if you do not get caught. Some consider corporal punishment justified only when the individual's behavior is potentially more damaging to him or her than the punishment (e.g., a young child who is about to touch a hot stove, or self-injurious behavior of some youth with severe disabilities).

corpus callosum The portion of the brain that connects the two hemispheres. Agenesis (absence of formation) of this connection or surgical severing to control seizures often affects the ability to exchange information between the hemispheres. People with such "split brains" tend to give different responses to a stimulus depending on which side of the body receives the stimulus. For example, if an object is presented to the left side of the brain, then the response is a verbal calling of the object name. On presentation to the right side, the individual reports seeing nothing, but is able to select that object from other objects. Congenital absence of the corpus callosum can be associated with other abnormalities of the central nervous system and cognition.

cortex   Gray matter; the outermost, half-inch-thick layer of the cerebrum, or largest and topmost division of the brain; this surface is marked by numerous gyri (hills) and sulci (valleys and ridges). Localization of specific functional areas on the cortex can be by Brodmann numbers, von Economo lettering, or neuroanatomical nomenclature. Some of the major areas are noted in the table below.

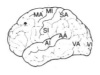
cortex: von Economo lettering

cortical blindness   Also known as central blindness. Visual impairment secondary to damage to the occipital cortex in the presence of an intact visual system including an eyeball, lens, retina, and optic nerve pathway. Cortical blindness following head trauma may be transient.

cortical deafness   *See* central deafness.

cortical thumb   Fisting with the thumb flexed inside the clenched palm. This is often re-

cortical thumb

garded as a sign of abnormal hypertonicity (increased muscle tone); however, cortical thumbing can be normal in the first 3 months of life, during which time fisting is itself normal. A frequently used synonym is cerebral thumb.

cost contingency (response cost)   A form of punishment in which the student loses something of value he or she has previously earned or is normally given. For example, detention is the loss of free time as a result of undesirable behavior. This form of behavior modification has been more successful with children who have attention deficit/hyperactivity disorder (ADHD) and do not respond to other forms of behavior management in the same way as other children. Children with ADHD often focus on the reinforcer rather than the task being reinforced. For cost contingency to be effective, the loss must be immediate and related to a specific behavior. For example, the child might lose 1 of 10 tokens with the explanation, "You were looking out the window." Care must be taken that this be perceived by the child as a way of helping him or her control attention and not as a punitive action.

costa   Rib.

Cotrel Dubousset procedure   A modification of the Harrington rod for the orthopedic surgery treatment of scoliosis (spinal curvature).

Council for Exceptional Children (CEC)   Founded in 1922, CEC is the world's largest professional organization concerned with exceptional (exceptional in any respect, as in children who have learning disabilities, physical impair-

Heteromodal bifrontal associative areas

MI	motor, idiotypic cortex	Idiotypic—primary sensory and motor area
SI	sensory, idiotypic cortex	Idiotypic—primary sensory and motor area
AI	auditory, idiotypic cortex	Idiotypic—primary sensory and motor area
VI	visual, idiotypic cortex	Idiotypic—primary sensory and motor area
MA	motor, associative area	Homotypical isocortex—modal specific unimodal associative area
SA	sensory, associative area	Homotypical isocortex—modal specific unimodal associative area
AA	auditory, associative area	Homotypical isocortex—modal specific unimodal associative area
VA	visual, associative area	Homotypical isocortex—modal specific unimodal associative area

ments, or special gifts). The organization is divided into special interest groups including divisions on physical disabilities, behavior disorders, mental retardation, communication disorders, learning disabilities, visual impairments, talented and gifted, early childhood education, special education administration, career development, technology and media, and educational diagnostic services. The CEC sponsors national and state conventions and issues two periodicals: *Exceptional Children* and *Teaching Exceptional Children*.

Council for Learning Disabilities (CLD) Originally formed in 1968 as the Division for Children with Learning Disabilities, within the Council for Exceptional Children (CEC). With the realization in the early 1980s that adults also have learning disabilities, the name was changed to its present form, and the CLD also became a separate and independent organization, rather than a division of CEC. The official journal of the CLD is the *Learning Disability Quarterly*.

cover/uncover test A screening test for strabismus (squint); the patient fixates (stares at) a light or other interesting toy or object, and each eye is alternately covered and uncovered; the deviation (inward or outward) of either eye under any of the test conditions yields information useful to the diagnosis of strabismus; this technique can be used in infants as well as adults. This test is also known as the crossed patch test.

cowlick An accessory hair whorl producing an unusual upward sweep of hair. An example of a minor dysmorphic (atypical appearance) feature.

coxa The hip.

Coxsackie virus A group of ribonucleic acid (RNA) viruses associated with a range of disorders, including colds, aseptic meningitis (inflammation of the spinal cord and brain membranes), and cardiac disease.

CPAP *See* continuous positive airway pressure.

CPD *See* cephalopelvic disproportion.

CPK *See* creatine phosphokinase.

CPT *See* continuous performance test.

CPVT *See* Carolina Picture Vocabulary Test.

crack A street term for an inexpensive form of freebase cocaine; *see also* infant of substance abusing mother.

cracked-pot sound *See* Macewen sign.

Craig Lipreading Inventory A measure of single phonemes and more complete language pattern discernment. The test has been broadly used to assess the lipreading performance of people with deafness. The inventory may be presented by an examiner or a filmed version with soundtrack can be used, permitting the use of the test for lipreaders alone or for people who have residual hearing. Because many factors, including hearing loss, educational experience, and mental age, contribute to lipreading competency, tests of this skill are best used to compare groups, rather than to attain established norms.

cranial nerve Any of the set of 12 pairs of nerves that exit from the base of the skull. The nerves are numbered with Roman numerals in addition to their names, as indicated in the table on page 75.

craniectomy Excision of a portion of the skull. In the presence of craniosynostosis (premature fusion of skull sutures), the reopening of sutures by a morcellation procedure (bit-by-bit removal of a linear strip of bone, and treating the edges so they do not grow together again) is more for cosmetics (*see* Crouzon syndrome).

craniofacial dysostosis *See* Crouzon syndrome.

craniosynostosis Also termed craniostosis. Premature closure (fusion or ossification) of the skull sutures, thus slowing or stopping the growth of the skull and presumably inhibiting further brain growth and contributing to the evolution of developmental disabilities. Continued brain

Cranial nerves

Cranial nerve	Function	Dysfunction
I Olfactory	Sense of smell	Loss may indicate a tumor or Kallmann syndrome
II Optic	Vision	Blindness
III Oculomotor	Helps move eye and eyelid	Strabismus, ptosis
IV Trochlear	Helps move eye	Strabismus
V Trigeminal	Sensation from lower eyelid to maxilla (upper mouth); chewing	Loss of sensation, dysarthria
VI Abducent	Helps move eye outward	Strabismus
VII Facial	Gustatory sense; facial movements	Facial palsy, loss of taste
VIII Vestibulocochlear	Hearing and balance	Deafness, vertigo (dizzy)
IX Glossopharyngeal	Swallowing	Dysphonia
X Vagus	Nerve to larynx and gut	Dysphonia
XI Accessory	Swallowing	Dysarthria
XII Hypoglossal	Tongue movements	Dysarthria

growth is the major inhibitor of suture closure, so that most occurrences of craniosynostosis reflect primary arrest of brain development. In the absence of signs of increased intracranial pressure, surgical intervention (i.e., craniectomy) to allow the skull to continue to grow is rarely helpful other than cosmetically (*see also* Crouzon syndrome). When only selected sutures, as opposed to all sutures, prematurely fuse, total intracranial volume is most likely to be within the normal range.

crawling Locomotion in quadriped; regional variations in usage do not clearly distinguish crawling from creeping. Delayed crawling (past the age of walking), so that the child walks before crawling, has little significance as an isolated finding.

crawling

creatine phosphokinase (CPK) An enzyme; an elevated CPK level may indicate muscular dystrophy.

Credé maneuver A technique for manually expressing urine from the bladder of paralyzed individuals.

credibility The degree to which information provided is trustworthy and believable. This is an especially important consideration when evaluating a child for some types of developmental disabilities, since diagnosis is partially based on developmental history as given by parents and other significant caregivers. Individuals are characterized as good or bad historians based upon the quality and consistency of the information they are able to provide.

creeping Locomotion in prone; regional variations in usage do not clearly distinguish creeping from crawling.

cretinism *See* hypothyroidism, congenital.

crib-o-gram An instrument used to assess hearing in premature and newborn infants by recording movement in response to loud sound stimuli. The instrument has high false-positive and high false-negative rates and only detects profound bilateral hearing loss.

cri-du-chat syndrome 5p-syndrome, cat-cry syndrome; a genetic syndrome with poor growth and a mewing catlike cry in infancy, microcephaly (abnormally small head), a rounded, moon facies with hypertelorism (widely spaced eyes), epicanthal folds, and downward slanting of the palpebral fissures (eye slits). The level of mental retardation is severe to profound. Most cases represent spontaneous partial deletions of the short arm of chromosome

5, but 10%–15% are secondary to a parental balanced translocation with an increased recurrence risk. Incidence is estimated at 1 per 20,000.

Crippled Children's Services (CCS) Federally subsidized state programs for the diagnosis and treatment of children with developmental disabilities, especially those with physical disabilities and other medical complications. In some states, this program has been renamed Children with Special Health Care Needs (CSHCN). *See also* Children with Special Health Care Needs.

crisis A debilitating mental or emotional state elicited in response to an event perceived to be so threatening that the usual coping skills are insufficient and ineffective. A crisis can often be the decisive turning point or culmination of a series of events when it forces a response to a situation that cannot persist indefinitely because of its stressful nature. Thus, the possibility of seeking assistance and initiating therapy is enhanced. For example, the birth of a baby with a disability is a major family crisis. Feelings of guilt, blame, anger, and resentment are typical, as well as concern regarding the child's health. In some cases, when the disability or defect is readily apparent, there is tremendous disappointment at not having pregnancy result in a "normal" child. Parents are often isolated from outsiders and each other while they face a frightening and exhausting period. Education, support, and understanding for the family can help to alleviate the impact of the crisis and allow the family to determine a level at which they will be able to function.

criterion A predetermined level of performance to be achieved; a targeted standard.

critical period A time period early in the life of an organism when learning essential to normal adult functioning must occur. There is an implication of irreversibility; if this temporal gate is missed due to environmental deprivation or deviance, the organism will never be able to later achieve that learning. This concept is derived from ethology (the study of animal

behavior) and probably does not have a human equivalent. Sensitive periods and plasticity probably better characterize human development. Biologically, there are critical periods in brain development, but these are mostly prenatal.

cross-categorical The grouping together of students with disabilities without reference to a particular label or category of exceptionality. Rather than considering each category of special education as distinct, common characteristics are emphasized and student instruction is viewed from this perspective. Since categories of disabilities are not mutually exclusive and children with varying conditions are not always easily differentiated from each other, placement in a common class is advocated by some educators as a viable and practical alternative. Furthermore, assessment and treatment procedures for various categories often overlap, illustrating considerable commonality among some categories. Other educators are opposed to such grouping and advocate separate placement for students with different disabilities. These educators are concerned that individual needs will be overlooked, and they view diversity as an impediment to instruction.

crossed extension A primitive reflex in which a noxious stimulus applied to one foot produces a flexion/extension re-

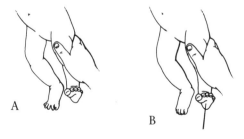

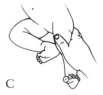

crossed extension

sponse in the other foot. Absence or asymmetry of the response is abnormal and indicates damage to the motor system of the side that does not respond.

crossed extension pattern The simultaneous forward movement of one arm and the contralateral (opposite) leg in creeping, crawling, and walking.

crossed patch test *See* cover/uncover test.

croup An acute viral respiratory syndrome characterized by a croaky, honking cough; the differential diagnosis includes epiglottitis (inflammation of the epiglottis), laryngotracheobronchitis (inflammation of the wind pipe), and spasmodic laryngitis, with the first of these representing a life-threatening medical emergency. The asphyxia (lack of oxygen) sometimes occurring with epiglottitis can produce brain damage or death.

Crouzon syndrome Craniofacial dysostosis. A genetic syndrome with premature craniosynostosis (fusion of skull sutures) leading to brachycephaly (irregular, flat head shape), mid-face hypoplasia (atypical tissue development), and shallow orbits with exophthalmos or proptosis (a pop-eyed look). The nose is parrot beaked with a relative prognathism (a prominent jaw). The head and face in Crouzon syndrome resemble their appearance in Apert syndrome, but Apert syndrome has a 100% occurrence of neurocognitive problems, whereas in Crouzon syndrome, such problems are absent unless increased intracranial pressure is left untreated. One third to half of all cases have a conductive (involving the middle and outer ear) hearing loss. Inheritance follows an autosomal dominant pattern, with, however, extremely variable expression; about one quarter of cases represent spontaneous mutations. Recurrence risk is either zero or 50%.

crown-rump length The distance from the top of the head to the bottom of the buttocks; one of the standard measures of fetal size.

cry A prelinguistic vocalization pattern that can be reflex (e.g., birth cry), communicative (e.g., pain, anger, exercise, hunger, fatigue, fretfulness), or pathological (e.g., colic). Tears do not usually accompany crying until 6 weeks of age. Prolonged primitive crying may reflect underlying brain damage or mental retardation, and certain cry patterns can point toward specific diagnoses: a shrill, high-pitched cry suggests cerebral irritability (e.g., encephalitis [brain inflammation], meningitis [inflammation of the spinal cord and brain membranes], hydrocephalus [excess fluid in the brain]), a mewing cat cry suggests cri-du-chat syndrome (this cry disappears in older children), a bleating lamb cry suggests Cornelia de Lange syndrome, and a hoarse cry is noted in hypothyroidism. Sound spectrographic analysis has confirmed the specificity of these cry patterns.

cryptophthalmus Hidden eye. The absence of a palpebral fissure (eye slits), and, by extension, the absence of eyelashes and eyebrows. Cryptophthalmus can be associated with mental retardation, genital anomaly, and ear and kidney defects (Fraser syndrome).

cryptorchidism Undescended testes; may be unilateral or bilateral. This can be an isolated finding or a component of an identifiable genetic syndrome. Treatment can be medical (with hormones) or surgical (orchiopexy).

crystallized ability A term from the Horn-Cattell theory of intellectual processing. Crystallized ability refers to intellectual functioning or tasks utilizing previous training, education, and acculturation. A measure of crystallized ability may represent individual differences in knowledge, including verbal abilities; in the information on which judgment, sophistication, and wisdom are based; and in the types of reasoning based on previously learned procedures. The Woodcock-Johnson Psycho-Educational Battery–Revised (WJ–R) Test of Cognitive Ability is based upon the Horn-Cattell theory. The Kaufman Assessment Battery for Children (K-ABC) also provides, to some extent, a framework for assessing crystallized and fluid abilities. *See also* fluid intelligence.

CSBS *See* Communication and Symbolic Behavior Scales.

CSE *See* consequent stimulus event.

CSEI *See* Coopersmith Self-Esteem Inventory.

CSF *See* cerebrospinal fluid.

CSHCN *See* Children with Special Health Care Needs.

ctenoid A specific electroencephalographic (EEG) finding with 14- and 6-persecond positive spikes (sharp pointed deviations); ctenoids are not pathognomonic (indicative) but are slightly more frequent in people with learning, behavior, and attention disorders.

CTLSHO Cervical-thoraco-lumbar-spinal and hip orthosis, or in-chair orthosis for scoliosis (spinal curvature).

CTLSO Cervical-thoraco-lumbar-spinal orthosis; *see also* Milwaukee brace.

CTVF *See* Comprehensive Test of Visual Functioning.

cubitus valgus Increased carrying angle, as seen in Turner syndrome.

cued speech A system of manual cues used in conjunction with speech reading. The system was developed in 1967 at Gallaudet College in Washington, D.C. Cued speech was designed to lessen ambiguity experienced by individuals with severe and profound hearing impairments using speech reading to understand spoken language. Since many sounds appear visually similar, cued speech attempts to avoid phoneme confusion by providing a visual element to speech reading. Twelve hand signals or cues comprise the system: four cues are hand positions that differentiate between groups of vowel sounds; eight cues, based on Arkan Sign Language hand shapes, are used to visually discriminate between groups of consonants.

cultural bias The use of material that is familiar to one social or economic group but remote from the experiences of an-

other group. For example, there is evidence to suggest that items on most intelligence tests are more familiar to Caucasian, middle-class children than to their lower-class and/or ethnically different peers, resulting in measurably higher performance by the Caucasian middle-class children.

cultural sensitivity Knowledge of cultural differences and the corresponding usage of verbal and nonverbal behavior that optimizes interactions with people from a different cultural background.

custodial care Institutional placement with no therapeutic service components as part of the care.

cutaneous Relating to the skin.

cutaneous facilitation Skin stimulation as a component of neuromuscular therapy; such stimuli include light-moving touch, fast brushing, and applying ice to skin.

CVA Cerebrovascular accident. *See* stroke.

CVFES *See* Children's Version of the Family Environment Scale.

CWC *See* class within a class.

cyanosis A blue tinge or color to the skin, especially noted peripherally in the lips and fingernails; it can occur with cold, shock, disease of the heart or lungs, and seizures. The blueness derives from decreased oxygen leading to an increase of reduced hemoglobin (oxygen-carrying red blood cells).

cybernetics The study of regulating mechanisms in closed systems, particularly the flow of information and feedback loops in those systems.

Cylert Trade name for pemoline.

cynotrichous Straight, curly, or wavy hair as found in Caucasian races.

cystic encephalomalacia A brain condition characterized by the formation of cystic cavities (holes) in the white matter of the brain. Generally a result of severe asphyxia (lack of oxygen), cystic encephalomalacia can be found after viral encephalitis (brain inflammation). The brain-stem nuclei and the thalamus tend to be affected initially, with further damage extending to the basal ganglia and the cerebral cortex. The brain damage can be seen on ultrasound and on computed tomography (CT) and magnetic resonance imaging (MRI) scans. The outcome of this type of insult is usually cerebral palsy with mental retardation. Spastic quadriplegia is the most common type of cerebral palsy associated with cystic encephalomalacia.

cytomegalovirus (CMV)   *See* fetal cytomegalovirus syndrome.

D

DA *See* dextroamphetamine.

DAB–2 *See* Daberon–2 Screening for School Readiness; *see also* Diagnostic Achievement Battery–2.

Daberon–2 Screening for School Readiness (DAB–2) A standardized measure of school readiness for children 4–6 years of age or children with learning or behavior problems who are functioning at the early elementary school level. The test samples knowledge of body parts, color and number concepts, gross-motor development, categorization, and other developmental abilities. It is individually administered in 20–40 minutes.

dacryostenosis *See* lacrimal duct stenosis.

dactylology Fingerspelling for the purpose of talking; American one-hand manual alphabet with a configuration for each of the 26 letters.

Dallas Preschool Screening Test (DPST) A brief screening test of "primary" learning areas, including speech-language, problem solving, and motor skills. Administration time is 15 minutes.

Dandy-Walker syndrome A brain malformation resulting in an enlargement of the fourth ventricle that pushes into the cerebellum and prevents the normal formation of the central portion of the cerebellum. This is often associated with hydrocephalus (excess fluid in the brain), as well as other brain and systemic (body) malformations, such as cleft palate, enlarged kidneys with cysts, agenesis (absence of formation) of the corpus callosum (a part of the brain), or an occipital encephalocele (protrusion of the brain out the back of the skull).

dantrolene sodium Trade name Dantrium; a drug whose peripheral (noncentral) action reduces spasticity in cerebral palsy.

DAS *See* Differential Ability Scales.

DASE *See* Denver Articulation Screening Exam.

DASG *See* Developmental Assessment of Spanish Grammar.

DASI *See* Developmental Activities Screening Inventory.

day care Facilities and programs providing care, stimulation, and socialization to children, older adults, people with developmental disabilities, and other dependents on a nonresidential basis. Care is provided during the day, and the clients return to their homes each evening. Long used with children, the concept was extended to other populations in the 1980s.

day hospital Facilities and programs for people with mental illness and older adults; these programs provide health, mental health, and social services during the day, but allow individuals to return to their homes at night, thus averting institutionalization.

daydream A fantasy occurring in a wakeful state, independent of external stimulus, that can serve to gratify wishes not satisfied in real life. Although often dismissed as a waste of time or as escapism, daydreaming is not inherently pathological. In fact, it is frequently associated with creativity, visual production, and problem solving. Daydreaming is common among young people, and is noted particularly when it occurs in school. Daydreaming is antithetical to concentration and performing mental operations, including information integration and calculations. Such activities are routinely encountered in school, making children with attention deficits and other learning difficulties, who often tend to daydream, subject to questions concerning their desire to learn and their level of cooperation and motivation for school. In addition to contributing to school problems, daydreaming may occur as a result of previously experienced school and social failure, since it can be considered an adaptive way of coping with frustration and boredom. Typically associated with children who have attention-deficit/hyperactivity disorder (ADHD), daydreaming is also commonly reported among the gifted (those who have superior general intellectual ability).

dB *See* decibel.

DCB *See* Devereux Child Behavior Rating Scale.

DCC *See* Developmental Communication Curriculum.

DDH Developmental dysplasia of the hip; *see* congenital dislocation of the hip (CDH).

DDST *See* Denver Developmental Screening Test.

deaf Having nonfunctional hearing, with or without amplification, for the ordinary purposes of daily living. Deafness is characterized by a pure tone loss greater than 90 decibels—over the speech-range frequency of 500, 1,000, and 2,000 hertz. Hearing loss is expressed in a spectrum of degrees ranging from mild to profound. An individual formerly referred to as being deaf is now classified as having a profound hearing loss. *Profound hearing loss* is preferred because *deaf* (as well as *dumb* and *deaf mute*) implies that mental incapacitation occurs with hearing loss and speech impairment, thus suggesting a disability extending beyond absence of functional hearing.

deaf mute (deaf and dumb) Antiquated term for an individual who can neither hear nor speak, usually one born with (i.e., congenital) severe to profound hearing loss. The term is objectionable because it implies that mental incapacitation accompanies the inability to hear or speak.

deafism A self-stimulating behavior in a person with a hearing impairment; such behaviors as poking at one's ear may produce auditory feedback.

deafness Profound degree of hearing loss that prevents understanding of speech through the ear. Deafness is the inability to hear, without reference to the etiology (cause) of the loss. Hearing impairment is the preferred generic term to indicate any degree of hearing loss.

Deaver A system of physical therapy developed by the physiatrist George D. Deaver for the treatment of cerebral palsy. This approach utilizes extensive bracing and focuses on the achievement of functional activities of daily living (ADL). The Deaver system also places a high value on achieving a typical appearance (e.g., by working to control grimacing).

deceleration Decrease in fetal heart rate, relative to uterine contractions during delivery. There are three types: early (type I dip), late (type II dip), and variable (type III dip). The duration of the contractions and the degree to which fetal heart rate decreases help the obstetrician to assess fetal hypoxia (oxygen deficiency).

decerebrate posture The posture assumed when the cortex and cerebrum of the brain are removed or extremely damaged; decerebrate posture is similar to the decorticate posture, except that the upper extremities are extended instead of flexed.

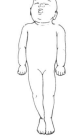

decerebrate posture

decibel (dB) A quantitative measure of sound intensity or loudness. In audiology, sound intensity is a ratio of the sound being measured to a standard reference sound level. The relative intensity of sounds is expressed on a decibel (dB) scale. Whispering measures about 30 dB, normal conversation is gauged between 50 and 65 dB, and a hairdryer registers 70 dB.

declarative knowledge A hypothetical construct of the way in which certain information is represented in memory. Within this model, knowledge is 1) represented by declarative propositions, which are the basic units of information, each corresponding roughly to one idea; and 2) knowing that something is the case. The organization of declarative knowledge is similar to the semantic (meaning systems) memory network in which all ideas are ultimately associated with all other ideas. Propositions have varying levels of activity, most being inactive at any specific time and representing a long-term memory store. The few propositions that are active at any one time are old knowledge that is in conscious awareness. This small part of the propositional network comprises one part of working memory. *See* memory, procedural knowledge.

decoding Word calling; the ability to pronounce written letters and words. Decoding is distinguished from comprehension, which implies an understanding of the material read.

decorticate posture The posture assumed when the cortex of the brain is removed or extensively damaged; it is similar to the tonic labyrinthine supine posture (extension of all four extremities) and includes flexion of the upper extremities, shoulder adduction/retraction, and extension of the lower extremities.

decorticate posture

decubiti Bedsores secondary to pressure and decreased mobility; decubitus ulcers, or pressure sores, can be prevented by proper hygiene and by relieving pressure on bony prominences by frequent repositioning of the individual with limited mobility; specialized beds, mattresses, pads, and cushions can also be used.

deductive reasoning To draw a specific conclusion from a general rule or to apply a general rule to a specific situation. *See* top-down processing (conceptually driven).

deep-tendon reflex (DTR) When a tendon is tapped with a reflex hammer, a sudden stretch is applied to the attached muscle; this stimulus produces a reflex contraction that can be observed or felt. A number of different DTRs are routinely elicited on neurological examination: the biceps, triceps, and ankle and knee jerks (the last is sometimes referred to as the *patellar reflex*). The response is graded on a 5-point scale from 0 (pathologically absent) through 2+ (physiological/normal response) to 4+ (pathologically brisk/exaggerated). Asymmetries should be noted.

defect theory *See* difference approach.

defectology A Russian term for the scientific study of mental retardation.

defense mechanism A psychoanalytic term for various psychic operations used by the ego to avoid awareness of unpleasant and anxiety-provoking stimuli. The ego selectively uses defense mechanisms to ward off conflict originating in the id, the superego, or dangers in external reality. Common defense mechanisms include denial, rationalization, repression, and projection. Defense mechanisms can represent quite healthy responses to stress.

deformation Abnormal form, shape, or position of a part of the body caused by mechanical forces; prenatal deformations include abnormal foot positions related to oligohydramnios (too little amniotic fluid) or fetal central nervous system defects; plagiocephaly is a postnatal skull (cranial) deformation.

degenerative disorders *See* heredodegenerative diseases.

deglutition Swallowing.

dehiscence The splitting apart or opening of a closed (surgical) wound.

deinstitutionalization The relocation of persons with developmental disabilities and psychiatric problems from institutional settings to community placements; one component of normalization. The movement toward deinstitutionalization and normalization of people with mental retardation or developmental disabilities occurred during much of the late 1970s and early 1980s.

de Lange syndrome *See* Cornelia de Lange syndrome.

deletion The absence of a single base pair or a small part of a segment of base pairs along a chromosome. The deletion interferes with the proper coding of an enzyme or protein and causes the product to be inactive. Many genetic disorders that previously had no identifiable chromosomal abnormalities are caused by deletions. For example, Prader-Willi syndrome is associated with a deletion on chromosome 15. The deletion is part of the structure of the chromosome and, therefore, is passed on with the chromosome. The presence or absence of the disorder is dependent on whether the trait is recessive or dominant and, sometimes, from which parent it originates. A deletion on chromosome 15 that is inherited from the father will produce Prader-Willi syndrome. That same deletion inherited from the mother produces Angelman syndrome.

dementia A marked deterioration of mental processes that is organic in origin. Dementia is characterized by faulty judgment, impaired memory content and processes, concreteness and rigidity of thinking, and, ultimately, personality changes. Although some dementias are treatable, such as those due to malnutrition or adverse drug reactions, most indicate an underlying degenerative process that is irremediable. These processes typically occur in adults. When such processes are noted in children, they are usually referred to as degenerative processes or developmental regressions.

de Morsier syndrome *See* septo-optic dysplasia.

denial A defense mechanism that allows for rejection of elements of reality that would be intolerable if allowed to remain in the conscious realm. Denial is also the negation of experiences of reality through refusal to accept them. Denial can serve a positive function in families with children who have disabilities. As an initial response, denial provides an opportunity for family life to proceed as usual. At the time of diagnosis, a degree of denial (particularly if the disability is severe) allows parents to maintain a positive view of their child. Denial is often a response to misinformation or a lack of information regarding what a disability is or what may be realistically expected from the child. Providing information, support, and guidance often helps a family to acknowledge and adjust to their child's disability. The energy spent denying a problem can then be used to advocate for the child and to experience the other feelings that accompany living with a child with a disability. In extreme cases, denial is the family's consistent and unwavering response to the diagnosis; despite information and assistance, they contend that there is "nothing wrong" with their child and may engage in doctor shopping. The latter often leads to multiple contacts with different professionals and seriously hampers the development of the child's and the family's functioning.

Dennyson-Fulford procedure An orthopedic surgery operation that is a modification of the Grice subtalar arthrodesis (surgical immobilization below the ankle) used to treat valgus deformity of the foot.

Denver Articulation Screening Exam (DASE) A brief screening test to assess speech (pronunciation) in children 2½–6 years of age by the production of 30 sounds contained in 22 separate words that the child is asked to repeat. The number of correctly produced sounds is charted on an age graph on the reverse side of the test form, and scores below the 15th percentile for age are referred for more detailed evaluation by a speech-language pathologist.

Denver Developmental Screening Test (DDST) A screening test for developmental delay in children from birth to 6 years of age that divides test items into the Gesell streams of development (i.e., gross-motor, fine-motor, language, and personal social skills) and classifies children's performances as "normal," "questionable," or "abnormal." The test depends heavily on the caregiver's report. A recent revision (Denver II, 1990) is attempting to improve the test's validity in children from birth to 3 years of age. The DDST remains the most widely used developmental screening test for preschool children; much of the criticism directed at it reflects limitations in the screening endeavor. The Denver Developmental Screening Test–Revised (DDST–R) differs from the original (itself a revision) only in format and minor details of scoring. Some clinics use the Revised Prescreening Developmental Questionnaire (R–PDQ) as a first-stage screening and the DDST as a second-stage screening.

Denver Eye Screening Test (DEST)   A protocol for the assessment of eye functioning in children birth to 6 years of age. It includes a vision test (three types for different age groups: fixation test, picture card test, and *E* test) and three tests for nonstraight eyes (parent questionnaire, cover test, and pupillary light reflex test).

DENVER II   The 1990 revision of the Denver Developmental Screening Test (DDST) with 125 items; the increase in items (from 105) was mainly in the area of language.

deoxyribonucleic acid (DNA)   The basic biochemical unit of genes; the chemical system of nucleotide base pairs connected by sugar-phosphate moieties (parts of divisible items) present in a double helix form in the genes; DNA codes all the proteins and enzymes found in the body. Some inherited disorders (e.g., sickle cell anemia) result from the substitution of one different base pair for the correct one; other disorders are caused by a deletion or addition of one or more base pairs.

DNA

Depakene   *See* valproic acid.

Department of Health and Human Services (DHHS)   The federal agency that houses the Social Security Administration, the Office of Human Development, the Health Care Financing Administration, the Family Services Administration, the Developmental Disabilities Administration, and the Public Health Service. The Department of Health and Human Services was formed in 1979 when the Department of Education was separated from the Department of Health, Education & Welfare (HEW) to become an independent agency.

departmentalization   The teaching of different subjects by different specialized teachers; this may be in the same classroom (teachers rotate, pupils remain) or different classrooms (teachers remain, pupils rotate). The onset of departmentalization frequently exacerbates the difficulties experienced by children with learning disabilities, as well as by those with attention-deficit/hyperactivity disorder (ADHD), who have poor organizational skills.

dependency   Behavior characterized by an overreliance (warranted or unwarranted) on another person or system. The reliance can be emotional, physical, or financial. The dependent person fails to utilize his or her own skills and abilities, passively leaning on another person or system to care for his or her needs. The threat of removal or of withdrawal of support is experienced as a psychological threat of loss to the dependent person, who views him- or herself as personally incapable of meeting these needs.

Depo-Provera   *See* progestin.

depression   Mood of sadness, despair, and discouragement. Overt manifestations are highly variable and can be culturally specific. Depression may be a symptom of a number of mental and physical disorders, a syndrome of associated symptoms secondary to an underlying disorder, or a specific psychiatric disorder. Slowed thinking, a decrease in pleasure, feelings of guilt and hopelessness, decreased physical activity, and disruption of eating and sleeping are common disruptive characteristics. Depression is classified by severity, recurrence, and association with mania. In children, depression may be demonstrated through refusal to go to school, antisocial behavior, excessive reaction to separation from parental figures, anxiety, and somatic complaints. Children are more difficult to diagnose with depression, because symptoms are more variable, diagnostic criteria are not universally agreed upon, and comorbidity with more apparent or overt difficulties (attention-deficit/hyperactivity disorder [ADHD], conduct disorder) may mask the presence of depression.

deprivation A state of chronic unmet or incompletely met physical, social, or emotional needs. *See* maternal deprivation.

depth perception The ability of the visual system to interpret shape and position of a three-dimensional world while only being provided with two-dimensional sensory input. The use of shadow, size, interference patterns, and other learned visual cues allows the presence of depth perception even in the absence of binocular (two eyes) stereoscopic vision.

derived score Any score obtained by a statistical treatment or other manipulation of raw score or raw data.

dermal sinus A midline skin pit along the spine, which may connect with an underlying sinus and represent a risk for infection. A dermal sinus may reflect an underlying spinal abnormality.

dermatitis Rash.

dermatoglyphics Fingerprints and palm prints; surface skin marking patterns on the fingers and toes, palms and soles that allow unique identification of each individual; dermatoglyphic anomalies (malformations, deformations, disruptions, or

loop   arch   whorl
finger dermatoglyphics

dysplasias) can be components of specific syndromes.

dermatome The area of the skin enervated (supplied) by a single dorsal nerve root for sensation and motor response.

derotative righting A postural response in which 1) voluntary or passive turning of the head is followed by a segmental or corkscrew (un)rolling of the rest of the body; or 2) voluntary or passive rotation of the pelvis segmentally rolls the trunk, shoulders, neck, and head. This movement pattern is a prerequisite to voluntary rolling over.

de Sanctis-Cacchione syndrome A genetic syndrome with xeroderma pigmentosa (extreme sensitivity of the skin to light), mental retardation, gonadal hypoplasia (defective reproductive tissue development), microcephaly (abnormally small head), and neurological complications. Inheritance is autosomal recessive.

desensitization A treatment technique employed to help clients overcome inordinate and disabling learned fears, such as fear of flying and fear of heights, or exaggerated physiological responses such as a hypersensitive gag reflex. A series of successive and closer approximations to the triggering stimulus is paired with relaxation techniques and biofeedback, thus allowing the client to effectively manage or completely eliminate the fear. Desensitization procedures are also used to decrease exaggerated physiological responses that interfere with appropriate functioning (e.g., oral motor desensitization).

desipramine A tricyclic antidepressant; one of the drugs used to treat attention-deficit/hyperactivity disorder (ADHD).

DEST *See* Denver Eye Screening Test.

Detroit Tests of Learning Aptitude–Revised (DTLA–3) A criterion-referenced test of specific mental abilities, composed of 11 subtests: word opposites, sentence imitation, oral directions, word sequences, story construction, design reproduction, object sequences, symbolic relations, conceptual matching, word fragments, and letter sequences. The subtests are grouped into four domains: linguistic, including verbal and nonverbal composites; cognitive, including structural and conceptual composites; attentional, including attention-enhanced and attention-reduced composites; and motoric, including motor-enhanced and motor-reduced composites. A general intelligence quotient (GIQ) is derived from the standard scores of all the subtests. The DTLA-3 is designed for children 6–17 years of age and takes 50 minutes to 2 hours to administer. It is used to diagnose learning disabilities and mental retardation. There is a 100-item (six-subtest) Detroit Tests of Learning Aptitude–Primary 2 (DTLA–P2) for children 3–9 years of age, as well as a Detroit Tests of Learning Aptitude–Adult (DTLA–A) for people 16–79 years of age.

Developmental Activities Screening Inventory (DASI) A cognitive screening measure for children 6 months to 5 years of age; it can be adapted for use with preschool children who have visual impairments, hearing impairments, and multiple disabilities.

developmental approach The theory that persons with mild mental retardation (cultural-familial retardation, retardation due to psychosocial disadvantage) without evidence of organic brain damage behave and learn exactly in the same manner as mental-age–matched controls without mental retardation, except for the impact of personality variables, such as wariness and outerdirectedness. The developmental approach has been referred to as a motivational or social learning theory of mental retardation.

Developmental Assessment of Spanish Grammar (DASG) An adaptation of a developmental sentence-scoring technique for Spanish-speaking children.

Developmental Communication Curriculum (DCC) A language curriculum for children who are developmental ages birth–5 years. The DCC includes the Developmental Communication Inventory

(DCI) to assess prelinguistic, symbolic, symbolic relationships, and complex symbolic relationships in play contexts.

developmental coordination disorder *See* dyspraxia.

developmental-difference controversy *See* developmental approach, difference approach, two group approach.

Developmental Disabilities and Bill of Rights Act Amendments of 1987 (PL 100-146) Legislation that amended PL 88-164, the Mental Retardation Facilities and Community Mental Health Centers Construction Act of 1963, and contained a Bill of Rights section for people with developmental disabilities. PL 100-146 expanded the definition of *developmental disabilities* to include individuals with mental retardation, autism, cerebral palsy, and seizure disorders. It also authorized funding for a wide variety of programs and services affecting individuals with developmental disabilities, to enable them to "achieve their maximum potential through increased independence, productivity, and integration into the community."

Developmental Disabilities Assistance and Bill of Rights Act of 1975 (PL 94-103) A federal law that extended the definition of *developmental disabilities* to include autism and selected types of dyslexia; it also set up a task force on the definition of *developmental disabilities* that, in 1977, further broadened the definition by using a generic or functional approach that cut across specific categories or diagnoses. This act also mandated each state and territory to establish a protection and advocacy (P&A) system as a condition of receiving federal funding under this law. Advocacy agencies are authorized to pursue legal, administrative, and other remedies to protect the rights of individuals with developmental disabilities. Each state's governor designates a program to serve as the P&A system and must ensure that it is independent of any service provider. The Administration on Developmental Disabilities, within the Department of Health and Human Services, is responsible for administering a P&A program for people with developmental disabilities at the federal level.

Developmental Disabilities Assistance and Bill of Rights Act of 1990 (PL 101-496) Legislation that amended PL 88-164 and PL 100-146 to add the goals of interdependence, community acceptance, and inclusion for all people with developmental disabilities. It also authorized grants to support the planning, coordination, and delivery of increasingly specialized services to all people with developmental disabilities, and expanded several existing programs, including the protection and advocacy (P&A) system and university affiliated programs (UAPs).

Developmental Disabilities Services and Facilities Construction Act of 1970 (PL 91-517) A federal law that expanded PL 88-164, the Mental Retardation Facilities and Community Mental Health Centers Construction Act of 1961, to include services for people with cerebral palsy and seizure disorders. This law introduced the concept of "developmental disability" and replaced "clinical training" with "interdisciplinary training." PL 91-517 also created a program of state formula grants to establish councils to plan government activities related to service delivery.

developmental disability A condition in which a static encephalopathy (brain damage due to lack of oxygen) or brain injury leads to a serious impairment or limitation of one or more functions controlled by the brain. The "injury" may be structurally programmed into the developing brain. All developmental disabilities bear a "family resemblance" because of their common grounding in brain pathology (origin). The onset of a developmental disability must be during the developmental period—variously defined as birth to 12 or birth to 22 years of age. Federal legislation defines developmental disability as "a severe, chronic disability of a person 5 years of age or older, which is attributable to a mental or physical impairment or combination of mental and physical impairments; is manifested before the person attains age 22; is likely to continue indefinitely; results in substan-

tial functional limitations in three or more areas of major life activity: 1) self-care, 2) receptive and expressive language, 3) learning, 4) mobility, 5) self-direction, 6) capacity for independent living, and 7) economic self-sufficiency; and reflects the person's need for a combination and sequence of special, interdisciplinary, or generic care, treatment, or other services that are of lifelong or extended duration and are individually planned and coordinated." The federal definition also states that developmental disability can also be applied to infants and young children from birth to age 5, "who have substantial developmental delay or specific congenital or acquired conditions with a high probability of resulting in developmental disabilities if services are not provided." Individual states may expand and modify the definition to more fully meet the needs of their citizens.

developmental dysplasia of the hip (DDH) Luxatio coxae congenita; previously referred to as congenital dislocation of the hip. A congenital abnormality of the hip that renders it unstable with regard to keeping the femur (thigh bone) in the joint. Present at birth, the defect leads to limitation of hip abduction, asymmetry of thigh folds, leg shortening, and persistent adduction of the involved side. It is more common in females and after breech delivery. The Ortolani and Barlow tests are used to routinely screen for DDH; later, it will show up as a limp and a positive Trendelenburg sign. CDH is often an isolated anomaly (malformation, deformation, disruption, or dysplasia), but it may occur as part of a more generalized syndrome.

developmental hesitation Benign and typical stumblings, repetitions, and prolongations in the speech of a child learning to talk.

Developmental Indicators for Assessment of Learning–Revised (DIAL–R) A preschool and prekindergarten developmental screening test for children 2–6 years of age. Its three subtests measure gross- and fine-motor skills, expressive and receptive language, and cognitive-academic skills. Administration time is approximately 30 minutes. The acronym DIAL–R also refers to the rotating discs with which visual stimuli for certain test item groups are presented.

developmental output failure A group of learning disabilities in which the specific nature of the problem does not cause school failure or underachievement until the demand for specific outputs increases, especially the marked increase in written work in fourth grade.

Developmental Profile II A 186-item questionnaire that yields developmental ages in five areas (physical, self-help, social, academic, and communication), as well as an IQ equivalence score for children from birth to 9½ years.

Developmental Screening Inventory (DSI) A screening test for developmental disabilities in children 1–18 months of age. The test is a clinical selection of items from the Gesell Developmental Schedules, for use by relatively sophisticated examiners; it is more a clinical procedure than a standardized test. The revised form (the RDSI) has been extended to an age range of 36 months and has a first-stage prescreening questionnaire, the Revised Parent Developmental Questionnaire (RPDQ) (not to be confused with the Revised Prescreening Developmental Questionnaire, R–PDQ).

Developmental Test of Visual-Motor Integration (DTVMI) Beery. A measure used to assess perceptual-motor ability in children 4–13 years of age. The child is asked to copy up to 24 geometric figures selected from other developmental tests including the Bender-Gestalt, Cattell, Gesell, and Stanford-Binet. The figures are arranged in order of increasing difficulty, beginning with a simple figure like a circle or square and becoming progressively more complex. Each design is scored on a pass/fail basis, and testing may be discontinued after three consecutive failures. A large number of scoring judgments are subjective, leading to substantial disagreement regarding scoring. The DTVMI was originally normed in

1974 and was renormed by Buktenika in 1981. Raw scores are converted into standard scores with a mean of 10 and a standard deviation of 3. Many of the interpretive rationales described for the Bender-Gestalt are also applicable to the DTVMI. Administration time is 15 minutes.

Developmental Test of Visual Perception (DTVP) Frostig. A battery of five visual-perceptual-motor subtests used to identify the underlying disorder in learning disabilities and to formulate a specific visual-perceptual-motor training program to remediate learning disabilities in children 3–8 years of age. Its component subtests include measures of visual-motor coordination (drawing a straight line between successively closer parallel lines), figure–ground discrimination (differentiation between foreground and background), form constancy, spatial relationships, and position in space. The associated therapy (Frostig Program) improves performance on the test battery, but this has not been shown to spill over into the area of learning.

Devereux Child Behavior Rating Scale (DCB) A checklist of about 100 behaviors that yields a number of interpretable factors. The behaviors are scored on a 5-point Likert-type scale. The DCB is meant to be used by caregivers in institutional settings to refine descriptions of symptom behaviors in children 8–12 years of age. Administration time is 15 minutes. The instrument has good reliability but only face validity.

deviation IQ Normalized standard score with a mean of 100 and a standard deviation of 15 or 16, depending on the measure employed. The deviation IQ expresses the deviation of the ratio IQ from the mean ratio IQ at each age level. It is not an absolute measure of performance, but, rather, the relative position of a particular measure of intelligence on a normal, or gaussian, curve. Each individual IQ score is given meaning by relating it to the distribution of all relevant IQs and to where in that distribution the given IQ is located. The deviation IQ has replaced the ratio IQ because it controls for the variability of IQ distribution across the age range.

dexamethasone suppression test (DST) The administration of the steroid dexamethasone typically suppresses plasma cortisol levels; many people with major depression do not respond to dexamethasone, but continue to produce excess cortisol. This test can be helpful in diagnosing depression in people with mental retardation and atypical presentations of depression.

Dexedrine Trade name for dextroamphetamine sulfate.

dextroamphetamine (DA) Trade name Dexedrine; a short-acting stimulant medication that is occasionally still used in the treatment of attention deficit disorders and hyperactivity in children and adults. It is manufactured in multiples of 5 milligrams (5, 10, and 15) and is available in a sustained-action formula. Because of its addictive potential, dextroamphetamine is treated as a controlled substance; however, addiction is not a problem in subjects with attention problems. Side effects include stomachache, headache, anorexia (loss of appetite), poor growth, and sleep problems. Side effects can usually be managed by titrating the dosage.

DHHS *See* Department of Health and Human Services.

diadochokinesis Rapid alternating movements (RAM); the normal power of alternately bringing a limb into alternate positions, as of flexion and extension or of pronation and supination. This facet of motor coordination can be tested in individuals by requesting that they pat their knees with the rapidly alternating palmar and dorsal surfaces of their hands. Performance of the dominant hand is usually slightly superior to that of the nondominant hand. Difficulty in performing this test is referred to as dysdiadochokinesis.

diagnosis Diagnosis is both a process and an outcome. It is the process of compiling and categorizing signs and symptoms (medical, emotional, or social) exhibited by an individual and formulating a solution based on that compilation. Diagnosis also involves eliminating other possible categorizations and causes in order to identify a specific pathological condition. The term *diagnosis* has tended to be restricted to the process engaged in by medical doctors. Social workers, psychologists, nurses, and educators more frequently use the term *assessment*.

Diagnostic Achievement Battery–2 (DAB–2) An individually administered academic achievement test that provides a profile of abilities in listening, speaking, reading, writing, and mathematics. Subtests include story comprehension, characteristics, synonyms, grammatic completion, alphabet/word knowledge, reading comprehension, capitalization, punctuation, spelling, writing composition, and mathematical reasoning and calculations. Writing composition, spelling, capitalization, punctuation, and math calculation subtests may be given to small groups. Subtest scores convert to standard scores (with a mean of 10 and a standard deviation of 3) and percentile ranks. Composite scores (with a mean of 100 and a standard deviation of 15) in listening, speaking, reading, writing, mathematics, spoken language, written language, and total achievement are generated by combining subtests.

***Diagnostic and Statistical Manual of Mental Disorders* (DSM)** The most commonly used classification system for abnormal behaviors and mental disorders. Published by the American Psychiatric Association, the DSM is the system generally used in the United States for official diagnostic and record-keeping purposes. The first version of the DSM was published in 1952 and reflected a psychobiological perspective that viewed mental disorders as the reaction of the person to psychological, social, and biological factors. Subsequent editions have classifications compatible with the International Classification of Diseases (ICD) and do not specifically imply any particular theoretical framework for understanding nonorganic mental disorders. DSM-IV (1994) contains specific diagnostic criteria, a multiaxial classification system, and an increased emphasis on descriptive determinants of mental and physical disorders. Even though DSM-IV categories are more behaviorally explicit than prior editions, clinical judgment is still required. For example, some of the diagnostic criteria require that a child's symptoms be inappropriate for age. Since the DSM-IV does not provide age norms, base rate, or treatment recommendations for any of its diagnostic conditions, judgment must be used to decide whether a child's behavior is in fact deviant. Inclusion of specific developmental disorders is considered controversial by some because many children with these disorders have no other form of mental disorder. DSM-IV does require that standardized, individually administered educational achievement and intelligence tests be used to diagnose such developmental disorders.

Diagnostic Checklist for Behavior-Disturbed Children (Form E-2) The earliest objective behavior checklist used in the diagnosis of autism; it was first used to document a decrease in autistic symptomatology after 5 years of age.

Diagnostic Interview Schedule (DIS) A structured, standardized interview designed to elicit the information required to make certain DSM diagnoses. Versions of the DIS have been periodically created and contain procedures and probes for use in identifying specific clusters of symptoms not previously included in the schedule. The DIS can be administered by both professional and lay interviewers.

Diagnostic Reading Scales (revised edition) An integrated series of tests designed to provide a standardized evaluation of a student's silent and oral reading levels (from elementary level for poor readers through high school for normal-ability readers) and auditory comprehension. The battery measures the nature and extent of word skills and provides an estimate of the student's instructional level.

diagnostic teaching An informal method of assessing learning abilities when formal diagnostic methods are ineffective or incomplete. It involves observation and instruction to determine if the student possesses and can utilize the skills being assessed or if remediation and development of compensatory techniques are necessary. "Trial lessons," or "teaching probes," are used to simultaneously test and teach by recording and interpreting the student's reaction to and progress with the material. Diagnostic teaching can be employed by many disciplines involved with persons with developmental disabilities.

DIAL–R *See* Developmental Indicators for Assessment of Learning–Revised.

dialect A distinct form of a language spoken in a specific geographical area, varying uniquely from the official standard of the larger surrounding community in, for example, pronunciation, word usage, and grammar. The dialect is different enough to be regarded as a unique entity, but not sufficiently different to be considered a separate language.

diaschisis theory The theory that the return of function following brain damage occurs as the nervous system recovers from a period of shock, since the shock had widespread effects on areas of the brain not directly damaged. In this theory a significant amount of brain damage symptomatology is attributed to nonspecific shock as opposed to specific brain lesions.

diastema A split; a wide space between the upper central incisors ("two front teeth"); associated in folklore with marrying wealth.

diastematomyelia A developmental malformation in the spinal cord often found with myelomeningocele (protuberance of both the spinal cord and its lining). It consists of a splitting of the spinal cord without duplication. A bony spur is often found between the split pieces of cord.

diathesis An inherited predisposition or tendency to develop certain diseases or disorders. For example, the members of a certain family may be more likely to become alcoholics. In other families, there may be a predisposition to the development of otosclerosis (chronic progressive deafness) and progressive hearing loss.

diazepam   Trade name Valium; a benzodiazepine that is used as an antianxiety drug, a muscle relaxant (for spasticity), and an anticonvulsant. It can also be administered intravenously to stop prolonged, uncontrollable seizures (status epilepticus).

dichotic listening   A test of speech lateralization in children in which different stimuli are stereophonically presented to both ears (dichotic); the stimulus that is correctly discriminated indicates the relative efficiency of the processing auditory input of the right versus the left cerebral hemispheres, so that a right-ear advantage is consistent with left hemisphere language localization.

diencephalic syndrome   Progressive emaciation in a euphoric, hyperactive, hyperalert infant with a brain tumor (usually astrocytoma in type) of the hypothalamus or third ventricle. It presents as a disorder of growth, with neurological and neurodevelopmental findings occurring later.

difference approach   Defect theory; the theory that people with moderate to profound mental retardation as well as those with mental retardation with independent evidence of organic brain damage may not behave and learn in the same way as mental-age–matched controls without mental retardation. There are qualitative as well as quantitative (mental age, IQ) differences between people with and without mental disabilities. *See also* developmental approach, two group approach.

Differential Ability Scales (DAS)   A cognitive abilities battery for children and adolescents 2-6 to 17-11 years of age. It is composed of 17 cognitive subtests in verbal and nonverbal areas, as well as diagnostic subtests (basic number skills, spelling, and word reading). Administration time is 1–1½ hours.

Digit Span   A supplementary verbal subtest of the Wechsler Intelligence Scale for Children–III, in which the child listens to a series of numbers and then repeats them. The subtest, in two parts, assesses sequential memory, short-term memory, and attention. The first part of the subtest, called *digits forward*, contains a series of items varying in length from 3 to 9 numbers. The second part, called *digits backward*, contains a series of items ranging in length from 2 to 8 numbers. There are two series of numbers for each sequence length; digits forward is administered first, followed by digits backward. Digits forward predominantly involves rote learning, memory, and sequential processing, whereas digits backward requires sequential processing, planning ability, and an ability to retain and manipulate the mental image of the object for a longer time period. Difficulty with digit span may suggest or relate to anxiety, attention deficits, memory, and auditory processing problems. The pattern of errors (omissions, reversals) can provide some clue as to what type of processing problems the child may have.

digit span test   A test in which the subject is required to repeat a series of random numbers immediately after a single presentation; also known as *digits forward*. The number of digits a child can repeat increases with age, intelligence level, and rote sequential memory skills. Compared to digits backward (*see* Digit Span), digits forward appears to be a more left-brain function.

digito-ocular sign of Franceschetti   Poking at the eyes; "eye boring" or pressing the fists, knuckles, or fingers into the orbits of the eyes. This behavior is an example of a "blindism," an activity common in preschool-age children who are blind; it can also occur in children with mental retardation who have no eye pathology, and can accompany other self-stimulatory behaviors in institutionalized persons. It is probably only mildly specific for visual impairment (as with ear boxing for hearing impairment), and occupies a position on the nonspecific spectrum of self-stimulatory–self-injurious behaviors.

diglossia A bifid or forked tongue; a congenital anomaly (malformation, deformation, disruption, or dysplasia) of the tongue.

diglossia Occurs when a young child can recognize that two varieties of a language are each to be used in different social settings.

DIP joint See distal interphalangeal joint.

diphenhydramine Trade name Benadryl; an antihistamine that can be used to treat allergic symptoms. Because of the side effect of drowsiness, it can also be used to treat mild sleep disorders.

diphenylmethanes A group of minor tranquilizers that includes hydroxyzine hydrochloride (Atarax) and hydroxyzine pamoate (Vistaril), used in the treatment of anxiety.

diplegia Little disease; literally, "two palsy." A topographical subtype of spastic cerebral palsy in which all four extremities (arms and legs) are involved, but the upper extremities are less involved than the lower extremities. Therefore, sitting is not as delayed as walking. It is a common sequela to prematurity and can exhibit a fairly benign course. Toe walking, scissoring, strabismus (squint), and normal intelligence are common associated findings. Probably the most common single subtype of cerebral palsy.

diplomyelia A developmental malformation of the spinal cord often found with myelomeningocele (protuberance of both the spinal cord and its lining). It is a complete duplication of the cord over several segments.

diplopia Double vision; a neuro-ophthalmological finding.

Direct Instruction Systems for Teaching Arithmetic and Reading (DISTAR) A reading method that was developed as an outgrowth of a program established primarily as a compensatory effort to prepare disadvantaged Black children for entrance into traditional middle-class, White-oriented school programs. It is highly structured, fast-paced, and directive. The beginning level starts with sound identification, left-to-right sequencing, and oral sound blending. Children learn to read by sounding out words, then by reading groups of words as complete thoughts. The second level expands the beginning level. Reading III, the third level, is described as a basal reader program for third grade or for a remedial reading program. The first and second levels are designed for use in small groups, but much of level III is designed for use with 30 children at a time. A detailed teachers guide is provided.

directionality Internal awareness of the right and left sides of the body and the ability to apply this realization to external objects. Individuals with directionality problems frequently reverse letters or numbers (*b* for *d* and vice versa) because they cannot consistently perceive or determine that the particular symbol is pointed in a particular direction (*b* to the right and *d* to the left). Difficulty with directionality is sometimes referred to as *right/left confusion.*

DIS See Diagnostic Interview Schedule.

disability Any restriction or lack of ability (resulting from an impairment) to perform an activity in the manner or within the range considered usual for a human being. Disability may be temporary or permanent, reversible or irreversible, and progressive or regressive. Disability may arise as a direct consequence of impairment or as a response by the individual, particularly psychologically, to a physical, sensory, or other impairment. Disability represents the objectification of an impairment and, as such, reflects disturbances at the level of the person. The World Health Organization defines disability as the second level of a continuum: impairment, disability, and handicap based on health experience. Thus, its definition is, "In the context of health experience, a disability is any restriction or lack (resulting from an impairment) of ability to perform an activity in the manner or within the range considered normal for a human being."

disability etiquette Preferred word usage and behavior when writing about, meeting, socializing with, or assisting people with disabilities. Although some specific terminology is still debated among groups of people with disabilities and their advocates, agreement has been reached regarding some general rules. These include emphasizing abilities, not limitations; avoiding words with negative or judgmental connotations; demonstrating patience; and asking if assistance is needed before giving it. The goal of enlightened language usage and treatment is to more fully integrate people with disabilities into society and to lessen misunderstanding and ignorance among the population without disabilities.

disability, secondary A disability or adverse circumstance that does not necessarily follow as a direct consequence of a primary disability but for which the primary condition is a risk factor.

discharge planning An interdisciplinary process for facilitating reintegration into the community after a major illness (accidental, physical, or mental). A discharge plan may include environmental modification (e.g., ramps), adaptive equipment (e.g., a walker), psychological counseling to facilitate adjustment, vocational rehabilitation for work adaptations, visiting nurses for ongoing care, and special transportation arrangements. A discharge plan should be safe and realistic, and should allow the person to resume as normal a life as possible.

discipline An area of training and practice. Training, certification, and licensure vary greatly among disciplines, and the degree of autonomous independent practice allowed differs among states and clinical settings. For example, medicine is sometimes considered a single discipline; at other times the various medical and surgical specialties and subspecialties are considered separate disciplines.

discipline From the Latin "disciplino," meaning teaching and learning. In a broader sense, disciplining of children is the inculcation of the mores of a culture by families first and continuing through various educational settings. However, common usage of the word connotes limit setting, with rewards for compliance and punishment for transgressions. Whereas discipline may include many methods for reaching the goal of self-control, punishment may actually be detrimental in its long-term effects.

DISCO *See* Dyskinesia Identification System–Coldwater.

discordant A term used in studies of twins where one twin has the trait being investigated and the other does not. *See also* concordant.

disease Literally, "without ease," "uncomfortable"; a failure of an organism to adequately adapt to stress, resulting in a disturbance in structure or function. A disease is a definite entity with a single cause (even if unknown) and recognizable signs and symptoms from which it can be diagnosed.

disengagement A pattern of family relations characterized by extreme emotional distance and detachment, rigid boundaries, and strong individual autonomy rather than family closeness. Although not necessarily pathological if all members are comfortable with such a style of relating, the pattern can indicate a number of relationship difficulties, including little interaction or exchange of feeling, and lack of a sense of belonging. Families with children who have developmental disabilities often develop a style of relating in which one parent (usually the mother) becomes overly close and involved with the affected child to the exclusion of other family members, who then drift into a pattern of disengagement.

disfluency *See* dysfluency.

dislocation Luxatio; complete and persistent displacement of a bone from its joint; dislocation is accompanied by pain, shortening, and loss of function.

displaced speech Talking that refers to past or future events and not to the immediate present. In the development of children's language, references to the present represent the earliest stage, followed by references to the past, and finally reference to the future.

distal   Farthest from the center.

distal interphalangeal joint (DIP joint) The joint nearest the tip of the finger or toes.

distal transverse palmar crease   A flexion crease on the palm of the hand; the "heart line" of palmistry. Variations in this crease pattern occur in genetic syndromes and nonspecifically in developmental disabilities.

distal transverse palmar crease

DISTAR   *See* Direct Instruction Systems for Teaching Arithmetic and Reading.

Ditropan   *See* oxybutynin.

dizygotic twins   Fraternal twins; two individuals born at the same time to the same mother, but having different genetic makeups. Dizygotic twins occur when two ova are fertilized at the same time. Such twins are no closer to each other genetically than two siblings born from different pregnancies.

DMD   Duchenne muscular dystrophy; *see* muscular dystrophy.

DNA   *See* deoxyribonucleic acid.

Dolch Word List   A list, developed by Edward W. Dolch, of 220 words that constitute more than 65% of all words found in elementary reading materials and 50% of the words found in all reading materials. It includes prepositions, conjunctions, pronouns, adjectives, adverbs, and the most common verbs, but no nouns. Thus, the list comprises structure words that hold language together, rather than content words; it is often taught as a sight word vocabulary. Many of the words have irregular spellings and cannot be learned by picture clues.

dolichocephaly   A disproportionately long head; a low cephalic (head) index secondary to premature closure of sagittal (median) sutures, producing craniosynostosis (premature fusion of skull sutures) and linked with scaphocephaly (projected head). A common skull shape in premature infants.

dolichocephaly

doll eyes maneuver   Cantelli sign; eye movements normally follow head movements; when the head is rotated and the eyes do not follow or actually go in the opposite direction, then the "doll eyes" phenomenon is present. This indicates the absence of the eye righting reflex, with probable brain-stem injury.

Doman-Delacato approach   *See* patterning.

Doman-Delacato Developmental Profile An instrument used to measure improvement during patterning therapy.

dominance   A tendency to preferentially use one side of the body, usually reflecting a preferred development of one side of the brain for particular functions. Hand dominance is typically established and clearly evident by 2 years of age. Strong hand dominance before 18 months of age is usually suggestive of a motor impairment of the nondominant side. Neuromaturational delay in expression of dominance can occur with children who have learning disabilities or mental retardation.

Donohoe syndrome   *See* leprechaunism.

dorsum   The back; the posterior or superior surface. Dorsal is the opposite of ventral.

double blind   A method of studying treatment efficacy in which neither the person administering and evaluating the treatment nor the person receiving the treatment is aware of whether an active or inactive treatment (placebo) is being administered.

double hemiplegia   A type of spastic cerebral palsy in which both arms appear to be more severely involved than both legs. Because the functional and practical implications of this do not significantly differ from quadriplegia (paralysis of all four extremities), the condition is probably just as well described as an asymmetrical quadriplegia.

"downers" A slang term for drugs (legal or illegal) that depress the central nervous system. Such drugs include tranquilizers, alcohol, and sleep medications.

Down syndrome (DS) Trisomy 21, trisomy G. A chromosomal disorder with hypotonia (decreased muscle tone), short stature, flat facial profile, epicanthal folds, upslanting palpebral fissures (eye slits), small ears, speckling (Brushfield spots) of the iris (the colored part of the eye that surrounds the pupil), short fingers, single transverse palmar crease (simian crease), cardiac defects, duodenal atresia, atlantoaxial instability, thyroid disorders, conductive hearing loss, and mental retardation. Because people with Down syndrome have an extra chromosome 21, they have a total chromosome count of 47 instead of the usual 46. The multisystem involvement in this disorder requires ongoing follow-up in a multidisciplinary specialty (DS) clinic setting. Incidence is 1 in 660 (1 in 1,500 for mothers under 30 years of age to 1 in 25 for mothers over 45 years of age). The recurrence risk of DS is 1%, although it may be higher in the presence of a parental translocation carrier. Originally described by John Langdon Down (1828–1896) in 1866, Down syndrome was not clearly differentiated from cretinism (hypothyroidism) and other dysmorphology (atypical features) syndromes until 1959, when Jerome Lejeune demonstrated the atypical chromosome count.

DPST *See* Dallas Preschool Screening Test.

DPT Combined diphtheria, pertussis (whooping cough), and tetanus immunizations; diphtheria and tetanus toxoids with pertussis vaccine. The existence of developmental disabilities should not be a contraindication to the routine administration of DPT; adverse events following

a first dose and a progressively deteriorating neurological status are the only recognized contraindications.

Draw-a-Man Test *See* Goodenough-Harris Drawing Test.

drug Any nonfood substance that affects living tissue.

drug-free period *See* drug holiday.

drug holiday Discontinuing a drug in order to reevaluate baseline (before intervention) behavior and drug/dose responsiveness. The use of the term *holiday* unfortunately connotes that the drug was bad or unnecessary in the first place. A drug holiday is an important tool in the management of psychotropic medication.

DS *See* Down syndrome.

DSI *See* Developmental Screening Inventory.

DSM *See Diagnostic and Statistical Manual of Mental Disorders.*

DST *See* dexamethasone suppression test.

DTLA–3 *See* Detroit Test of Learning Aptitude–Revised.

DTP *See* DPT.

DTR *See* deep-tendon reflex.

DTVMI *See* Developmental Test of Visual-Motor Integration.

DTVP *See* Developmental Test of Visual Perception.

Dubowitz Neurological Assessment A brief (10-minute) neurological screening of infants that can be used to monitor the progress of central nervous system insults in infants at high risk.

Dubowitz Scale Dubowitz score; an instrument to determine gestational age by examining 11 physical characteristics and 10 neurological findings.

Dubowitz syndrome A genetic syndrome with eczema (skin rash), short stature, a peculiar facies (somewhat similar to that seen in persons with fetal alcohol syndrome), and a range of cognitive functioning from average intelligence to severe mental retardation. Inheritance is autosomal recessive.

Duchenne muscular dystrophy (DMD) *See* muscular dystrophy.

due process *See* impartial due process hearing.

duodenal atresia A congenital malformation of the first portion of the small intestine with complete blockage; unless surgically corrected, duodenal atresia leads to death from aspiration—if the baby is fed—or from starvation if the baby is not fed. Duodenal atresia is more common among infants with Down syndrome than among other infants.

duodenum The first part of the small intestine, connecting the pylorus (lower end of the stomach) to the jejunum (middle of the small intestine); it is a major site for digestion and ulcerations.

dwarfism Outdated term, with a pejorative connotation, referring to extremely short stature on the basis of endocrinological (hormonal) or genetic etiology (cause). In general, although poor growth is frequently associated with severe developmental disorders, most individuals with syndromes typically referred to under the rubric of *dwarfism* exhibit normal intelligence and no associated developmental disabilities.

Dwyer instrumentation An anterior (front) cable orthopedic surgery procedure for treatment of scoliosis (spinal curvature).

Dycem A nonslip material used to cover handles and trays.

Dyggve-Melchior-Clausen syndrome A genetic syndrome with disproportionately short trunk, dwarfism, microcephaly (abnormally small head), mental retardation, and a variety of bone and joint abnormalities including atlantoaxial instability. Inheritance is autosomal recessive.

Dyke-Davidhoff-Masson syndrome A nongenetic syndrome including facial asymmetry (with X-ray confirmation of underlying asymmetrical skull [cranial] abnormalities), contralateral hemiplegia (paralysis of one half of the body), mixed seizure disorder, and varying degrees of mental retardation.

dynamic Describes an orthopedic deformity, with abnormal positioning of extremities (arms or legs), that can be passively corrected; characterizes a flexible or nonfixed deformity.

dysarthria Generic name for a collection of motor speech problems caused by various impairments of the central or peripheral nervous systems. Faulty speech production, characterized by imprecise consonants and irregular articulation, is typical of the disorder. Respiration, voice, fluency, and prosody (melody of speech) are usually hindered as well. Both volitional and automatic actions, including chewing, swallowing, and other oral-motor movements, may also be deviant. Children with cerebral palsy can show marked delays in achieving articulation comparable to that of their age peers. Most adults acquire dysarthria as the result of cerebral vascular accidents (strokes) or degenerative disease after a lifetime of normal speech. Anarthria, or the inability to articulate at all, is the result of severe neuromuscular involvement.

dysautonomia *See* Riley-Day syndrome.

dyscalculia Mathematics disability; a learning disability in which mathematics is the only or the most severely involved subject area. A mathematics disability that begins in the fourth grade may be secondary to a reading disability. Mathematics errors, such as misreading operational signs (addition for subtraction) or reversing numerical order, may reflect either a mathematics or a reading problem. Difficulty with mathematics often reflects right-brain impairment.

dysdiadochokinesis A neurological finding in which the individual has difficulty with rapidly alternating pronation and supination of the arms.

dyseidetic One of the three dyslexic subtypes—the other two being dysphonetic and mixed—identified by Elena Boder. These subtypes are based on specific reading-spelling error patterns. Dyseidetic readers show strength in the auditory analytic function and weakness in the visual gestalt function. They have poor memory for visual configurations of letters and words and read laboriously, sounding out familiar as well as unfamiliar words. Typical misspellings are phonetically accurate. They also write good phonetic (representing sounds) equivalents of words that they could not read. For example, "talk" might be read as "talc" and spelled as "tok." The mixed group exhibits weaknesses in both the visual gestalt and the auditory analytical functions, with resulting disability in developing both sight vocabulary and phonic skills. The Boder Test of Reading-Spelling Patterns is based on these error patterns. *See also* dysphonetic.

dysfluency Any type of speech characterized by an interruption in the flow of sounds. Such speech is marked with prolongations, hesitations, repetitions, and other rhythmic disturbances. Dysfluency can refer to the developmental hesitation of a child or the dysprosody (loss of melody of speech) of an individual who stutters.

dysfunction Abnormality or malfunctioning of a system.

dysfunctional family A family unable to effectively carry out its tasks or emotional functions. Such families tend to respond to stress situations with rigid, unyielding, patterned behavior, rather than effectively accommodating themselves to the demands of the situation. Frequently, boundaries between individual members are either too loose, too rigid, or too distant for cooperation and support to occur. When stress levels reach unmanageable proportions, frequently one member develops symptomatology that forces the family to initiate treatment.

dysgraphia Poor pencil and paper (handwriting and drawing) skills for age; the condition is usually congenital in children and may be part of a learning disability syndrome. Dysmorphisms can be an isolated problem reflecting poor motor planning or execution, or a component of a developmental disorder of written language.

dyskinesia Any impairment of voluntary movement.

Dyskinesia Identification System–Coldwater (DISCO) A 34-item movement rating scale used in the diagnosis of dyskinesia.

dyslexia Reading disability; a term loosely employed to describe any learning disability in which reading, writing, and spelling are more severely involved than other subject areas. In the strict sense, dyslexia refers to a pure reading disorder with no other subjects involved, and no attentional or other neurological problems. Such pure dyslexia is rare, often familial, and predominantly male. There are no diagnostic markers, such as letter reversals, specific to dyslexia.

dysmaturity The impact of placental insufficiency on a term or preterm infant includes generalized growth retardation; dry, peeling, cracked skin; meconium staining; and a wide-awake, hyperalert expression. Dysmaturity is sometimes used more generally to refer to any situation in which birth weight is low for gestational age secondary to placental insufficiency; it would then include postmaturity but not all cases of prematurity.

dysmorphology The science or study (*logy*) of abnormalities (*dys*) of shape, form, or structure (*morpho*); in human beings most disorders of morphogenesis (the development of form and structure) are congenital—either genetic or the result of other prenatal influences. The visual recognition of dysmorphic features is an important component in the identification of genetic and other syndromes (syndromology), sequences, and associations. A cumulative number of mild superficial malformations (minor dysmorphic features) may be of developmental significance even in the absence of an identifiable syndrome.

dysnomia A weakness or inability to name objects (word finding), not as severe as anomia; a frequent component of a language or learning disability.

dysphagia Difficulty swallowing; one of the signs of oromotor dysfunction that is common in cerebral palsy and can contribute to feeding disorders and poor growth.

dysphonetic One of three dyslexic subtypes identified by Elena Boder. These subtypes are based on specific reading-spelling error patterns. Dysphonetic readers show strength in the visual gestalt function and weakness in the auditory analytical function. They typically have a functional, although relatively limited, sight word vocabulary but lack phonic word analysis skills. Their most striking error is semantic substitution (i.e., substituting a word similar in meaning to the original word but unlike it phonetically, such as "sweater" for "jacket"). Their misspellings are phonetically inaccurate and include such errors as extraneous letters, omitted syllables, auditory discrimination errors, syllable reversals, letter-order errors, and other auditory sequencing errors. The other dyslexic patterns are dyseidetic and mixed. The mixed group has weaknesses in both the visual gestalt and auditory analytical functions, with resulting disability in developing both sight vocabulary and phonic skills. The Boder Test of Reading-Spelling Patterns is based on these error patterns.

dysphonia Disorder of voice quality that includes hoarseness due to chronic laryngitis and, rarely, to papillomata (tumors on the larynx [windpipe]).

dysplasia Abnormal development in shape and size, especially at the cellular level.

dyspraxia Partial loss of or failure to develop the ability to perform coordinated movements, not explainable by mental retardation; also known as developmental coordination disorder.

dysraphism An abnormality of the axial skeleton including the skull (cranial) and spinal column. Dysraphic states include anencephaly (no brain or absent top of skull), myelomeningocele (protuberance of both the spinal cord and its lining), and duplications or split spinal cords (diastematomyelia or diplomyelia). These disorders generally involve neurological dysfunction as well as skeletal abnormalities. The abnormal formations occur early in fetal life and have a genetic component.

dysrhythmia Stammering due to an incoordination between breathing and speech.

dyssemia A disorder of socialization characterized by problems with respecting boundaries, interpreting gestural language (including facial expressions), vocal loudness, rhythm, and dress.

dysthymic disorder A specific depressive disorder characterized by a constant and chronic disturbance of mood involving either depressed or irritable mood (particularly in children and adolescents) for at least a year (2 years for adults). Although there may be brief periods of relief, dysthymic depression is present for most of the day more days than not. In addition, there may be other associated symptoms, including appetite disturbances, sleep disturbances, chronic fatigue, concentration and problem-solving difficulties, low self-esteem, and feelings of helplessness and hopelessness. Young people with developmental disabilities are especially vulnerable to this disorder. Often these youth are subject to constant demands that exceed their capabilities, leading to a constant sense of failure and, ultimately, chronic depression or dysthymia. Too often, this treatable disorder gets reinforced when it is seen by teachers, parents, and others as "lack of motivation."

dystocia Abnormal labor; usually refers to maternal dystocia or structural abnormalities of the uterus giving rise to premature or prolonged labor.

dystonia Abnormality of muscle tone often leading to unusual posturing (dystonic movements). A number of transient dystonia syndromes have been described in premature infants, and dystonia is one of the motor complications of antipsychotic drugs frequently used to treat severe maladaptive behaviors in people with developmental disabilities.

dystonia musculorum deformans A disorder—frequently genetic—of movement and posture characterized by progressive, intermittent, or continuous muscle spasms including torticollis (stiff neck).

dystonic attack Opisthotonic attack; an intermittent, exaggerated, involuntary total body extension pattern with the head thrown backward in an arching posture. These episodes occur in children with severe motor abnormalities (e.g., cerebral palsy), almost always when the child is supine or the head has been extended, so that the episodes can be mistaken for seizures. Modifications in handling usually decrease the incidence of such pseudoseizures.

E

EAP   *See* employee assistance program.

EAR   *See* early automated responses.

Early and Periodic Screening, Diagnosis, and Treatment (EPSDT)   A federal program to fund routine medical and developmental services for Medicaid-eligible persons under 21 years of age.

early automated responses (EAR)   A grouping of infantile reflex patterns that includes EAR–I (primitive reflexes) and EAR–II (postural responses).

Early Childhood Special Education Act of 1986   *See* Education of the Handicapped Act Amendments of 1986 (PL 99-457).

Early Detection Inventory (EDI)   A screening test for children between 3½ and 7½ years of age in the areas of motor, social, behavioral, and academic skills.

Early Intervention Amendments to PL 94-142   *See* Education of the Handicapped Act Amendments of 1986 (PL 99-457).

Early Intervention Development Profile (EIDP)   A criterion-referenced assessment scale for infants from birth to 30 months; its six scales tap perceptual and fine-motor, cognitive, language, social and emotional, adaptive, and gross-motor skills. The cognitive scale in this battery is based on Piagetian theory.

Early Language Milestones Scale–Second Edition (ELM Scale–2)   A language screening test for children from birth to 3 years of age, as well as older children with developmental delays whose functional level is within this range; it uses a Denver Developmental Screening Test format and divides language into three streams: auditory expressive, auditory receptive, and visual. Administration time is less than 10 minutes.

Early Screening Inventory (ESI)   A developmental screening test to identify children 4–6 years of age who will need special education intervention. Items are derived from the Stanford-Binet Intelligence Scale, Denver Developmental Screening Test, Illinois Test of Psycholinguistic Abilities, and the Purdue Perceptual Motor Survey. The instrument also includes a parent questionnaire.

Early Screening Profiles (ESP)   A comprehensive screening instrument for children ages 2-0 to 6-11 years. The ESP yields screening indexes or standard scores in cognitive/language, motor, or self-help/social areas to identify children at risk or gifted children (those who have superior general intellectual ability).

EASIC   *See* Evaluating Acquired Skills in Communication.

Easter Seal Society   A private fundraising and service organization for children and adults with disabilities. Founded in 1919, this national organization's mission is to help people with disabilities achieve independence. The society strives to do so through the provision of rehabilitative services, technical assistance, disability prevention, advocacy, and public education. The National Easter Seal Society publishes a quarterly newsletter, the *Communicator*; other publications and informational materials are available upon request.

eccentric power   The ability to resist force as a muscle is lengthened.

ecchymosis   Bruise or contusion. The skin discoloration (red, blue, brown, yellow) in stages of healing that suggest the age of the injury. Ecchymosis can be due to accidents, (child) abuse, bleeding disorders, and other disease processes that cause blood to escape from vessels into surrounding tissue.

echolalia Parroting; repeating words, phrases, and sentences. Echolalia can be immediate or delayed, with the latter being more pathological. In children without disabilities, this imitative phase is transitory between the ages of 18 and 24 months. In children with mental retardation, language disorders, and autism, the echolalic phase is more prominent, prolonged, and correlated with a mental age closer to 30 months. Echolalia spontaneously observed in clinical situations should give rise to a more detailed assessment of language function. Echolalia after the appropriate developmental stage is a sign of language deviance.

echopraxia The tendency to mimic the actions of others; a subtype of echolalia noted in Gilles de la Tourette syndrome.

eclampsia The convulsive stage of toxemia of pregnancy. Eclampsia/toxemia can affect the oxygen delivered to the brain of the baby and contribute to later developmental disorders.

ECMO therapy *See* extracorporeal membrane oxygenation therapy.

ECO Scales Five separate scales used to assess social play, turn taking, preverbal communication, language, and conversation. Administration time is 10–30 minutes, with the results used to address developmental goals and adult–child interaction patterns.

ecogenetic disorder A disease caused by the interaction of a genetic predisposition with an environmental factor; for example, emphysema in alpha-1-antitrypsin (a specific enzyme inhibitor) deficiency and smoking.

ectodermal Refers to parts of the body derived from the outermost layer (ectoderm) of embryonic cells. Human ectodermal derivatives include skin, hair, and

nervous system. Their common embryonic origin suggests a rationale for the nonspecific association between minor dysmorphic (atypical) features and mild learning, attention, and behavior disorders, as well as more severe developmental problems.

ectodermal dysplasia A group of genetic syndromes with involvement of ectodermal derivatives—hair, teeth, and nails. Despite dysmorphic (atypical) facies, neurodevelopmental problems—other than an occasional hearing impairment—are unlikely with the exception of xeroderma pigmentosa (extreme sensitivity of the skin to light).

ectomorph A thin, asthenic (slender or slight) body type or build; leptosome.

ectopia lentis Dislocation of the lens of the eye, which can be inherited in isolation or as part of several syndromes, such as Marfan syndrome or homocystinuria.

ectropion Eversion (turning out) of the eyelid; congenital ectropion is seen in one third of the cases of Down syndrome.

eczema A skin disorder characterized by erythema (redness), vesiculation (blisters), and flaking or scaling; it sometimes becomes exudative (weeping). Often a sign of atopy (allergy), it is also a component of many syndromes and systemic disorders.

edema Fluid accumulation with swelling. Common causes of edema include injury and cardiac and renal disorders.

EDI *See* Early Detection Inventory.

EDPA *See* Erhardt Developmental Prehension Assessment.

EDTA *See* ethylenediaminetetraacetic acid.

educable mentally handicapped (EMH) *See* mild mental retardation.

educable mentally retarded (EMR) *See* mild mental retardation. Although *people with mild mental retardation* is the preferred terminology, the terms *educable* *mentally retarded* and *educable mentally handicapped (EMH)* are still in use, particularly in special education settings with regard to the level of learning support indicated.

Education Amendments of 1974 (PL 93-380) Amendments to the Elementary and Secondary Education Act (ESEA), which included a variety of changes to existing federal education programs and contained two important laws. One of the amendments renamed Title VI of the ESEA to the Education of the Handicapped Act Amendments of 1974. This law required states to establish a timetable for achieving full educational opportunity for all children with disabilities. The act included procedural safeguards to be used in identifying, evaluating, and placing children with disabilities. It mandated that children be integrated into general classes when feasible, and required that testing and evaluation materials be chosen and used on a nondiscriminatory basis. The second major law, the Family Education Rights and Privacy Act (FERPA), also called the Buckley Amendment, gave parents of students under the age of 18, and students 18 years of age and over, the right to examine and comment on the records contained in a student's personal file. FERPA applied to all students, including those in postsecondary education. When a file contains material the parent or eligible student views as inaccurate, misleading, or in violation of his or her rights, provisions are made to challenge and remove the information in question. If school staff and parents disagree about the accuracy or relevance of material, mechanisms for a hearing are stipulated. PL 93-380 began to focus upon and stress the need to fully educate all children with disabilities and to ensure their active participation in this process.

Education for All Handicapped Children Act of 1975 (PL 94-142) A federal law that grew out of and strengthened previous acts including the Education of the Handicapped Act of 1970 (PL 91-230), Title VI of the Education Amendments of 1974 (PL 93-380), and other legislation

of similar names. PL 94-142 became fully effective in September of 1978 and was designed to ensure that all children with disabilities have available to them a free, appropriate public education (FAPE); the law provided for impartial and objective decision making, appropriate educational funding, individualized education programming, accountability at all levels of government, and federal financial assistance to state and local school districts. Major provisions of the law included 1) the process for determining that a child has a disability and is in need of special education and related services; 2) developing an individualized education program (IEP) to meet the unique needs of the child with a disability, including provision of "related services" that may be necessary to assist a child in benefiting from special education services; 3) a requirement that students be placed to the maximum extent possible in the least restrictive environment (LRE) that addresses their needs; and 4) creation of safeguards to be used by parents or guardians of children with disabilities. These safeguards allow parents or guardians to examine relevant records on the identification, evaluation, and educational placement of their child; and require that parents or guardians be given prior written notice when an educational agency changes or refuses to change the identification, evaluation, or educational placement of their child. PL 94-142 is the core of federal funding for special education.

In 1990, PL 94-142 was reauthorized and expanded under PL 101-476, the Education of the Handicapped Act Amendments of 1990, and was renamed the Individuals with Disabilities Education Act (IDEA). The law's name reflects a change in terminology; PL 101-476 employs "people-first" language, replacing "handicapped children" with "individuals with disabilities."

Education of the Handicapped Act of 1970 (PL 91-230) A federal law that consolidated previous legislation and established a new Title VI to replace the one enacted in PL 89-750, the Elementary and Secondary Education Amendments of 1966.

This new authorization of Title VI, which became known as Part B, established a core grant program for educational agencies at the local level. Part B was the precursor to the Education for All Handicapped Children Act of 1975 (PL 94-142), which significantly expanded the educational rights and opportunities for children and youth with disabilities.

Education of the Handicapped Act Amendments of 1974 *See* Education Amendments of 1974 (PL 93-380).

Education of the Handicapped Act Amendments of 1983 (PL 98-199) Federal legislation that arranged and reauthorized discretionary programs for individuals with disabilities by expanding the means for providing transition services from school to work for students with disabilities; establishing and funding parent training and information centers to help parents guarantee their children's rights under PL 94-142; and providing financial incentives for increasing research and implementation of preschool education and early intervention programs. All of these programs fell under the auspices of the Office of Special Education Programs (OSEP), which had replaced the Bureau of Education for the Handicapped (BEH).

Education of the Handicapped Act Amendments of 1986 (PL 99-457) Federal legislation that lowered the age of eligibility for special education and related services for all children with disabilities to 3 years of age. This initiative was known as Section 619 in Part B, and mandated that, in order to receive federal funding, states had to begin providing services to preschool children by October 1991. All states have since complied. This act also included a Part H, which created a comprehensive early intervention program for infants, toddlers, and their families. This program is directed to the needs of children from birth to 3 years of age who are identified as needing early intervention services and requires the development and implementation of an individualized family service plan (IFSP) for each participating child and his or her family. State definitions of eligibility under this pro-

gram may vary, but to receive federal funding a state must have an acceptable service delivery system in place by its fifth year of participation in the program.

PL 99-457 reiterated the requirements and stipulations found in the Education of the Handicapped Act of 1970 (PL 91-230), its amendments, and the Education for All Handicapped Children Act of 1975 (PL 94-142), including the rights of children and youth with disabilities—regardless of severity—to a free, appropriate public education and to an individualized education program (IEP) or IFSP developed and implemented to enumerate the special education, early intervention, and related services a child, youth, and/or family is to receive. Parents' rights were also delineated, including the rights to participate in all aspects of the identification, evaluation, and placement processes; to give consent for initial evaluation and placement; and to dispute any aspect of the process with specified due process procedures. This law also reauthorized discretionary programming and expanded school-to-work transition programs.

In 1991, the act was reauthorized as PL 102-119, the Individuals with Disabilities Education Act Amendments.

Education of the Handicapped Act Amendments of 1990 (PL 101-476) Also called the Individuals with Disabilities Education Act (IDEA) of 1990. A federal law that amended and expanded PL 94-142, the Education for All Handicapped Children Act of 1975. The law renamed and combined the original act and its amendments. The term "handicapped children" was replaced by "individuals with disabilities," and the general definition of those with disabilities was expanded to include people with autism and traumatic brain injury (TBI) as separate categories. Other major changes included the addition of programs to promote research and the use of technology; transition programs beginning after high school; a program to serve children with emotional disorders; greater emphasis on addressing the needs of culturally and ethnically diverse children with disabilities; and waiving a state's traditional immunity from private litigation.

educational sign systems Manual equivalents of spoken English. Seeing Essential English (SEE₁) and Signing Exact English (SEE₂) are two pedagogical sign systems frequently used with populations of nonvocal people with disabilities. Unlike American Sign Language, which deviates from oral language, educational sign systems consist of manual translations of spoken English, maintaining its syntax (grammar), structure, and morphology (word structure). These systems can also be part of a total communication system.

Edwards syndrome *See* trisomy 18 syndrome.

EEC syndrome A genetic syndrome standing for ectrodactyly (cleft hands and/or feet), ectodermal dysplasia (a skin disorder), and clefting (cleft lip/cleft palate); it is frequently accompanied by urinary tract abnormalities and conductive (involving the middle and outer ear) hearing loss. Inheritance is probably autosomal dominant with variable expressivity.

EEG *See* electroencephalogram.

EFA *See* Epilepsy Foundation of America.

EFT *See* Embedded Figures Test.

Eggers procedure An orthopedic surgery operation for knee flexion deformity in cerebral palsy; used only in modified fashion.

egocentrism A young child's inability to understand another's point of view. In Piaget's theory of early development, this describes a cognitive limitation without the pejorative connotation the same behavior would imply in an adult.

EIDP *See* Early Intervention Development Profile.

18p− Deletion of the short arm of chromosome 18; a chromosomal disorder with mental retardation (with language abilities being relatively more severely im-

paired), growth deficiency, and a peculiar facies (including jug-handle ears).

18q− Deletion of the long arm of chromosome 18; a chromosomal disorder with mental retardation, hearing impairment, growth deficiency, mid-facial hypoplasia (underdevelopment), a prominent antihelix (part of the external ear), occasional behavioral abnormalities, and eye defects.

eikonometer *See* aniseikonia.

ELBW Acronym for infants of extremely low birth weight (i.e., below 1,000 grams).

elective Optional, nonemergency. Most cosmetic surgery is elective. Most elective surgery in children is scheduled so that they miss the least amount of school as possible.

electric hair Uncombable or fly-away hair, a minor dysmorphic (atypical) feature; multiple cowlicks can give the same appearance.

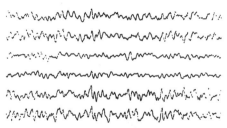

electric hair

electroencephalogram (EEG) A brainwave test. A clinical tool used to measure brain electrical activity between different areas of the scalp and a reference point. An EEG should include measurements made in drowsy, sleep, and awake states, and, if possible, with hyperventilation (rapid breathing) and photic (light) stimulation. Combined with the clinical history, an EEG can support the diagnosis of a seizure disorder, help classify the focus (location) and type of seizure disorder, and contribute to the selection of appropriate anticonvulsive therapy. In some instances an EEG can clarify prognosis.

electroencephalogram (EEG)

electrolyte A chemical in the blood that can conduct an electric current. Serum electrolytes refers to a battery of tests to determine the levels of these chemicals in the blood. The resulting patterns provide much information on the individual's status and the body's acute and chronic response to a variety of disease states. The most important electrolytes are sodium (Na), potassium (K), calcium (Ca), magnesium (Mg), chloride (Cl), bicarbonate (HCO_3), and phosphate (PO_4).

electromyography (EMG) A study recording the electrical activity in a muscle. It is used to identify and help classify the type of myopathy (disorder of voluntary muscle), neuromuscular disease, or lower motor neuron (nerve from spinal cord to muscle) present. The pattern of muscle response to the electrical stimulation varies with condition(s).

electroretinography (ERG) A measure of retinal (eye) function documented by changes in electrical potentials when light hits the eye. The pattern of sequence of electrical changes and the amplitude of response can be used to diagnose eye diseases that may cause blindness, such as retinal detachment, which occurs in some premature babies with retinopathy of prematurity (ROP).

Elementary and Secondary Education Act (ESEA) of 1965 (PL 89-10) A federal law designed to strengthen and improve educational quality and opportunity for the nation's elementary and secondary students, particularly for economically underprivileged children. This act paved the way for direct federal support for the education of children with disabilities and was the statutory basis upon which early legislation addressing special education was drafted.

Elementary and Secondary Education Act Amendments of 1965 (PL 89-313) Federal legislation that authorized the first federal grant program specifically targeted for children and youth with disabilities. Grants were awarded to state agencies to educate students with disabilities in state-supported or state-operated schools and facilities.

Elementary and Secondary Education Act Amendments of 1966 (PL 89-750) This law amended Title VI of PL 89-10 by authorizing the first federal grant program for the education of children with disabilities at the local school level, rather than providing assistance solely to state-operated programs. PL 89-750 established the Bureau of Education for the Handicapped (BEH) (now known as the Office of Special Education Programs [OSEP]) to implement, monitor, and evaluate federally funded special education programs. The law also created the National Advisory Council, now called the Council on Disability.

Elementary and Secondary Education Act Amendments of 1968 (PL 90-247) The final piece of federal legislation in the 1960s to address special education. This law established a set of what became known as "discretionary" programs designed to supplement existing special education services. Among supportive services were funding for regional resource centers, services for children with sensory impairments, special education research, and the groundwork for continuing education and informational resources.

Elementary and Secondary Education Act Amendments of 1978 (PL 95-561) Part A of Title IX of this federal law is known as the Gifted and Talented Children's Act. The statute and its regulations defined *gifted and talented children* and described the special education services to which they were entitled by virtue of their demonstrated or potential abilities in the arenas of academic, creative, leadership, or visual and performing arts achievement.

elephant man disease *See* neurofibromatosis. Neurofibromatosis was formerly and derogatorily referred to as elephant man disease because of the famous case of Joseph Merrick (1862–1890), whose deformity led him to a circus career where he was billed as "The Elephant Man." His condition was described by Sir Frederick Treves (1853–1923) in 1885.

Merrick was later made the subject of an award-winning play and movie, which reinforced the often striking discrepancy between severe physical deformity and intelligence.

elfin facies   A facial appearance associated with a number of syndromes, such as leprechaunism and Williams syndrome.

ELIP   *See* Environmental Language Intervention Program.

Ellis-Van Creveld syndrome   *See* chondroectodermal dysplasia.

ELM Scale–2   *See* Early Language Milestones Scale–Second Edition.

emaciation   Lean muscle mass wasting and fat depletion, with starvation.

Embedded Figures Test (EFT)   A measure of cognitive style that requires the subject to find simple geometric figures in complex, colored designs. Several versions of the EFT exist, including preschool (PEFT), children's (CEFT), and group (GEFT) tests. Field dependence and disembedding have been related to problem-solving style and a number of other variables.

embryo   The product of conception from fertilization to birth; in the later stages of development the embryo is referred to as a fetus. Sometimes the term *embryo* is restricted to development prior to the fetal stage, rather than to the entire period of gestation. The major organ systems are formed during this early stage; disturbances in the developmental process at this time contribute to fetal wastage (spontaneous miscarriage) or major organ system malformations.

embryogenesis   The process in a fetus where cells multiply and specialize to form a particular organ or organ system, such as the brain and central nervous system (CNS). This process is a complex progression from induction (where cells divide) to migration and organization into specialized layers. The critical period of fetal (before birth) development is during embryogenesis, when the cells are particularly vulnerable to damage by a`te-

ratogen (toxic agent), thus disrupting the normal pattern of events. This leads to CNS malformations that cause a large number of fetal, neonatal, and infant deaths. It is estimated that 3% of neonates have a significant CNS or other systemic malformation. Genetic abnormalities, maternal infection, drugs, and illness account for 40% of malformations. However, the cause in the remaining 60% is unknown.

EMG   *See* electromyography.

EMH   Educable mentally handicapped; *see* mild mental retardation.

emotion   A set of subjective feelings often accompanied by physiological changes that can impel one toward action. Examples of emotions include fear, love, surprise, and hate. *See also* affect.

empathy   Insightful awareness. The objective or intellectual recognition of the nature and significance of another's emotions and behaviors or of their experience of a specific situation. Empathy allows a helping professional to view events from a client's or patient's perspective. Empathy differs from sympathy, which stems from having a similar personal, cognitive, or affective experience (i.e., "I know how you feel").

employee assistance program (EAP)   Employer-based services to employees to help with life stresses and problems that negatively affect job performance through such things as accidents, absenteeism, attitude difficulties, emotional problems, or substance abuse. Employee assistance services may include drug treatment, family services (e.g., helping with nursing home or group home placement), and marital or family therapy. The philosophy is one of treatment to enhance job performance rather than punishment for poor performance.

EMR   Educable mentally retarded; *see* mild mental retardation.

enanthem   A rash on the mucous membrane (e.g., inside the mouth), usually associated with an exanthem (a skin rash) in the presence of systemic (body) disease. The Koplik spots of measles are an example.

encephalofacial angiomatosis *See* Sturge-Weber syndrome.

encephalopathy Brain abnormality; typically subdivided into static and progressive. The effects of static encephalopathies include the entire spectrum and continuum of developmental disabilities.

encopresis Fecal soiling, fecal incontinence. Lack of or incomplete bowel control can be primary, when the child has never achieved such control, or secondary, when the child previously achieved bowel control but then later lost it. Age-appropriate lack of bowel control should not be referred to as encopresis. Even in older children, if the absence of toilet training is developmentally appropriate, the term *encopresis* should be avoided because it connotes severe emotional pathology (origin). Secondary encopresis in otherwise normal children is often "overflow diarrhea," leakage around fecal impaction associated with prolonged constipation. Secondary encopresis that is more than occasional or transiently associated with emotional stress should be considered a major psychiatric symptom and potentially reflective of severe psychopathology.

endemic A disease or disorder that is peculiar to, or occurs at high rates in, a given population or geographic area (e.g., lead poisoning in inner-city children, histoplasmosis infection in the Mississippi Valley, myelomeningocele [protuberance of both the spinal cord and its lining] in the Irish).

endogenous Disease or illness that comes from within rather than being caused by external sources (e.g., depression resulting from unresolved emotional conflict rather than in response to a specific sad experience).

endomorph A body type tending to be short, stocky, rounded, well padded; pyknic.

endorphin An opiate that occurs naturally in the body and is involved in the perception of pleasure and pain; the ability of certain drugs to affect endorphin levels is being explored in the etiology and treatment of self-injurious behavior.

engram Memory trace; a hypothetical physical modification of the brain that accounts for memory retention. This is a research, rather than a clinical, term.

enmeshment A term describing a pattern of family relating characterized by strong allegiance and closeness, few or extremely permeable hierarchies and boundaries, and little individual autonomy. Often such a pattern of relating has strong ethnic and cultural origins. When culturally determined, this pattern is less often pathological. When a family is enmeshed to protect itself from psychological pain, that family can become extremely toxic and pathological. Often a family member must become symptomatic in order to prompt the family to secure help and enable the opportunity to grow. Families who have children with developmental disabilities often develop enmeshed patterns as a way of protecting the child and themselves from hurt. This protection can become a stranglehold, with neither the child nor the family able to mature.

enrichment Providing children with extra social, emotional, and cognitive stimulation, as well as improved nutrition, sanitary conditions, and regular and preventive medical and dental care. Enrichment is often used generically to refer to any supplementary activity, intervention, or opportunity added to a child's daily life experiences. Enrichment activities are routinely part of early childhood special education, including home-based programs, which encourage parental involvement and teach parents ways to enhance their child's development. Enrichment is also used to refer to supplementary educational experiences and programming for gifted children (those who have superior general intellectual ability).

ENT Ears, nose, and throat; *see* otolaryngology.

enteral feeding Tube feeding; examples include nasogastric and gastrostomy tube feedings.

entropion Inversion (turning in) of the eyelid; it can be associated with mental retardation and a variety of congenital defects.

enuresis Urinary incontinence after 5 years of age. Nocturnal enuresis is nighttime bed-wetting; diurnal enuresis is urinary incontinence when awake during the day. Primary enuresis is defined as uninterrupted lack of bladder control for at least 1 year; secondary enuresis is defined as being preceded by at least 1 year of dryness. Most primary nocturnal enuresis is familial, which can be confirmed by a detailed family history. Regressive secondary enuresis may indicate urinary tract infection or severe emotional stress; it may be a presenting sign of child sexual abuse. Daytime bladder control can be influenced by mental age and the presence of inattentive, impulsive behavior. Primary enuresis is associated with a small bladder and/or a sleep disorder (e.g., a deep sleeper). Primary enuresis is more likely to be a neurodevelopmental phenomenon, whereas secondary enuresis often reflects intrapsychic stress.

Environmental Language Intervention Program (ELIP) An assessment/diagnostic remediation program for prelanguage and early language skills. The Environmental Prelanguage Battery (EPB) assesses readiness behaviors such as play in children who have no oral language skills. The Environmental Language Inventory (ELI) assesses language development (two or more word phrases) in conversation, imitation, and free play.

eosinophilia An excessively high number of a specific type of eosin (red) staining white blood cells; of the variety of conditions associated with eosinophilia, the most common in children are allergy, parasites (worms), and cancer.

EOWPVT Expressive One-Word Picture Vocabulary Test; *see* One-Word Picture Vocabulary Tests.

EPEC *See* Evaluation and Prescription for Exceptional Children.

ephedrine An adrenergic drug that increases bladder muscle tone and can be used in the treatment of neurogenic bladder.

epicanthus/epicanthal fold A semilunar (crescent-shaped) fold of skin extending downward from the side of the nose (upper) to the lower lid and partially covering the inner canthus. An epicanthal fold is most commonly an isolated autosomal dominant feature; it is also associated with Down syndrome and many other genetic syndromes. It is present in the normal fetus from the third to the sixth month, so its postnatal presence may be considered a sign of developmental immaturity. Up to one third of normal infants under 1 year of age exhibit persistent epicanthus. It is one of a number of minor dysmorphic (mildly atypical) features that, in combination, may have developmental significance. It does not affect vision but its presence may produce the mistaken impression of strabismus (squint) by concealing the medial sclerae (pseudostrabismus).

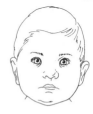

epicanthus

epicritic Pertaining to the mild sensation of pressure, touch, and temperature.

epidemic A disease or disorder with an occurrence rate that massively exceeds normal rates either in the numbers affected or in the rapidity of occurrence. Current examples include acquired immunodeficiency syndrome (AIDS) and lead intoxication in children.

epidemiology The study of the distribution, determinants, and deterrents of disease. Epidemiologists study disease at the macro perspective (in large groups of people), whereas clinical medicine pathologists study disease at the micro level (in single individuals). Epidemiologists study groups with a disease and groups without the disease in order to determine the difference between those affected and those spared. For example, to gauge distribution, epidemiologists might study whether the disease is more prevalent in men or women, northerners or southerners. To isolate its determinants, they might try to find out whether it is genetically transmitted or the result of behavioral habits. To identify deterrents, they might ask whether some diets prevent the disease more than others. Many people with developmental disabilities have been epidemiologically investigated.

epigenetic Relating to the appearance of new genetic phenomena not present at previous stages of development.

epigenetic sequence The biological and psychological development of the individual in an ordered and sequential series of stages.

Epilepsy Foundation of America (EFA) A nonprofit, voluntary organization dedicated to epilepsy treatment, research, and education. The national foundation and its local chapters provide information regarding epilepsy, its treatment, and related issues including employment, advocacy, and educational programming.

epileptic Relating to a seizure or seizure disorder.

epileptic syndrome A seizure disorder characterized by a pattern of findings that occurs together. These can include age of onset, etiology (cause), types of seizures, electroencephalography (EEG) findings, precipitating factors, family history, evaluation, and prognosis. For example, West syndrome consists of infantile spasms (onset and seizure type), hypsarrhythmia (a continuous disorganized pattern of high-voltage slow waves [sharp pointed deviations]), and developmental delay.

epiloia *See* tuberous sclerosis syndrome.

episodic memory A component of memory hypothesized by memory theorists to consist of an experiential record of events and occurrences. Episodic memory has an autobiographical flavor and usually contains spatial-temporal information, such as memory for specific episodes (e.g., what one had for dinner the previous night). Repeated exposure to certain kinds of information seems to produce a shift from episodic to semantic (meaning systems) memory. Being told there is a snake called a rattlesnake would presumably be stored initially in episodic memory (e.g., "Uncle Bob told me about a rattlesnake when we were sitting on the porch last night"). Eventually, the idea of rattlesnake would become a part of semantic memory as a type of reptile.

eponym The naming of a syndrome (or sign or symptom) after the person who first defined, described, or popularized its importance. Use of the possessive to title the syndrome is obsolete (i.e., Down syndrome, not Down's syndrome). The more neutral historical term is the preferred usage before the true etiology (cause) is known. Once, however, the underlying scientific basis is discovered, nomenclature should reflect that knowledge. Thus, Down syndrome would become trisomy 21.

EPSDT *See* Early and Periodic Screening, Diagnosis, and Treatment.

equilibration The tendency of biological organization and mental development to progress toward more complex and more stable levels through a balanced interaction between assimilation and accommodation.

equilibrium The process of maintaining an upright posture. Equilibrium reactions are a subgroup of postural reactions facilitating the development of voluntary movement late in the first year of life, enabling the infant to compensate for changes in the body's center of gravity and thus achieve successful head control, sitting, and standing.

equinovalgus Rocker-bottom foot deformity.

equinovarus *See* clubfoot.

equinus The foot position in toe-walking, resembling the posture naturally assumed by a horse's hoof; plantar flexion.

equinus deformity An orthopedic abnormality in which the heel of the foot is pulled upward and the forefoot downward.

equipotentiality A hypothetical mechanism of recovery after brain damage that involves the assumption of control by undamaged parts of the same neural system.

Erb palsy Paralysis of the upper arm due to injury to the upper brachial plexus (nerves to the arm), usually sustained by an infant during childbirth. The arm lies limp at the infant's side with the hand pronated in the "policeman's tip" position. This peripheral nervous system injury (nerves running  throughout the body) should not be confused with a central monoplegia; named after Wilhelm Heinrich Erb (1840–1921).

Erb palsy

ERG *See* electroretinography.

Erhardt Developmental Prehension Assessment (EDPA) A criterion-referenced assessment for hand function development for children from birth to 6 years of age that yields age levels for three areas: involuntary hand-arm movements, voluntary movements, and prewriting skills. Administration time is up to 1 hour.

ERP *See* event-related potential.

error of measurement The standard deviation of the difference between the obtained score and the true score. Such a difference is attributed to the unreliability/variability in the test instrument or the examiner. The error of measurement is often expressed in the form of confidence bands. For example, if the mean score on a test is 100, the standard deviation 15, and the standard error of measurement 3, then the confidence interval at the 68 percent level for a test score of 100 is 100 ± 3, or 97 to 103. (There is a 68% chance that the subject's true score lies in the range of scores from 97 to 103.) For the 95% level, the range will be defined as the mean ± 1.96 (standard error), or 100 ± 6. (The chances are 95 out of 100 that the subject's true score falls in the range 94 to 106.)

erythema Redness of the skin; one of the cardinal signs of inflammation; a component of many skin diseases.

erythema infectiosum Fifth disease (socalled relative to an older system of numbering common exanthems [skin rashes] in children); a viral exanthem in which an otherwise well child has red flushed cheeks. This "slapped cheeks" appearance should not be interpreted as a sign of child abuse.

erythroblastosis fetalis Hemolytic disease of the newborn; a blood group incompatibility (usually Rh) between mother and baby causes an anemia in the baby; erythroblasts (blood cells that produce red blood cells) then increase in the circulation where they are normally rare; the increased breakdown of red blood cells contributes to jaundice (yellowing of the skin), liver enlargement, and generalized edema (fluid-filled swelling) (hydrops fetalis). With immunological treatment of Rh negative mothers, this condition is usually preventable.

erythrocyte sedimentation rate (ESR) A blood test that nonspecifically indicates inflammation or disease.

Escalante syndrome *See* fragile X syndrome.

ESI *See* Early Screening Inventory.

esophageal atresia A congenital malformation in which the gullet ends in a blind pouch and does not communicate with the stomach; part of the VATER association and other malformation syndromes.

esophagus Throat, gullet; the part of the gastrointestinal tract that connects the pharynx (back of the throat) with the stomach.

esophoria An inturning of one eye after its vision has been covered and uncovered. This is demonstrable by using the crossed-patch test, which alternately covers and uncovers each eye while looking for deviation in the covered eye.

esotropia Cross-eye; internal or convergent strabismus or squint. The sixth cranial nerve supplies the lateral rectus muscle of the eye; if this is damaged, the unopposed medial rectus muscle pulls the eye inward. Increased intracranial pressure such as occurs in hydrocephalus (excess fluid in the brain) frequently affects this sixth nerve function.

ESP See Early Screening Profiles.

ESR See erythrocyte sedimentation rate.

ethnicity Shared origins, characteristics, values, customs, and traditions. An ethnic group is a distinct group of people who share a common race, language, customs, and other traditions.

ethosuximide Trade name Zarontin; an anticonvulsant used to treat absence seizures; it is not effective against other kinds of seizures. Ethosuximide is generally given twice a day. Minor side effects include stomachache, rash, headache, and a reversible blood problem. Unusual side effects at high dosages include hiccups or neurotoxicity with lethargy or hallucinations. Therapeutic blood levels are used to monitor treatment.

ethylenediaminetetraacetic acid (EDTA) A drug with salts that is injected intramuscularly to treat lead poisoning.

etiology Cause; medically, this refers to the underlying pathology. Traditional medical etiologies are characterized as belonging to one of the following groups: genetic, infection, trauma, tumor, and toxin (poison).

eugenics A social engineering philosophy with scientific pretensions to improve racial hereditary characteristics. Negative eugenics is concerned with the sterilization of "carriers" of "undesirable" genetic traits; positive eugenics promotes matings between carriers of "desirable" genetic traits. The "eugenics scare" of the early 20th century gave rise to the compulsory sterilization of people with mental retardation in the United States, and contributed to the racial theories and holocaust atrocities of the National Socialist Party in Nazi Germany. Any discussion of eugenics must carefully distinguish its narrow scientific base from its broader unproven pseudoscientific assumptions.

euthanasia Permitting or facilitating dying, usually in a person with a terminal illness or in a persistently vegetative state.

Evaluating Acquired Skills in Communication (EASIC) A criterion-referenced assessment for children with severe impairments who are 3 months to 8 years of age. The EASIC rates the following behaviors: prelanguage, receptive I (noun labels, action verbs, and basic concepts), expressive I (emerging modes of communication), receptive II (more complex language forms), and expressive II (using more complex communication).

Evaluation and Prescription for Exceptional Children (EPEC) An educational planning assessment for preschool children.

evaluation, educational A diagnostic procedure by which students are assessed with regard to their eligibility and specific needs for special education services. Federal law requires parents' consent for any initial preplacement evaluation. Under federal law (most recently, the Individuals with Disabilities Education Act [IDEA]), all tests and other evaluation materials must be administered in a child's native language, validated for the specific purpose for which they are used, and administered by trained personnel in accordance with proper instructions. No single test shall be used as the sole basis for determining appropriate educational placement. The evaluation is to be made by a multidisciplinary team and is to include areas appropriate to the individual student. Reevaluation is required at least every 3 years and may be done more often, but not more than once per calendar year.

event-related potential (ERP) A wave generated on electrophysiological monitoring of brain response to a specific stimulus. ERPs have been used in research on the efficacy of stimulant medication in the treatment of attention disorders.

eversion Turning the sole of the foot outward from the mid-line of the body; the foot posture utilized in the indirect Fog test (a gait test that involves walking on the insoles of the feet).

exanthem A skin eruption that is a symptom of a more general disease such as roseola (measles) or scarlet fever. Viral exanthems before the age of 3 years (especially around 2 years of age in boys) have been correlated with specific learning disabilities.

exanthema subitum *See* roseola.

exceptional child Term used equally to describe a child who is gifted (with superior general intellectual ability) or a child who has a disability.

exclusionary discipline The practice of removing a student from the routine school environment for a specified period of time; it includes both supervision and expulsion. When children with disabilities achieve a predefined cumulative total time of exclusion, an individualized education program (IEP) review is mandated.

exophoria A latent outward turning of one eye after its vision has been blocked. This is provoked by the cover–uncover test.

exophthalmos Pop eyes; abnormal protrusion of the eyeballs; bilateral (both eyes) exophthalmos is usually a sign of hyperthyroidism, whereas unilateral (one eye) exophthalmos often reflects localized orbital or neurological disease (e.g., a tumor).

exotropia Walleyedness; external or divergent strabismus or squint. The third cranial nerve controls the medial rectus muscle of the eye; impairment of that nerve often produces some degree of strabismus sometimes accompanied by ptosis, or drooping, of the eyelid.

exotropia

expectant An approach to diagnosis and therapy that does not involve any test or intervention other than waiting and watching; there is an implication that such waiting is "hopeful." In young infants, the diagnosis of developmental disabilities may sometimes be partially expectant.

expectorant A cough medicine that promotes the expulsion of bronchial (chest) secretions.

Expressive One-Word Picture Vocabulary Test (EOWPVT) *See* One-Word Picture Vocabulary Tests.

expressivity The extent to which a gene manifests its effects. Variable expressivity means that some individuals may show only mild manifestations of the gene, whereas others show severe ones. When discussing the expressivity of a genotype, there are no individuals that do not express some characteristic of the trait. *See also* penetrance.

extended family A family unit including parents, children, and other relatives, perhaps representing several generations. In some cultures, close or long-term family friends are part of the extended family. A natural support system, extended family members often share the caregiving responsibilities of a child with disabilities, and, depending on the extent of their involvement, should be included in varying degrees in the child's intervention plan.

extension Straightening of a joint.

extensor thrust Sudden extension of the neck, back, hips, and knees so that the body is arched back like a bow; tonic spasm.

external motivation Engaging in a task in order to meet a goal separate from both the task itself and the feeling of accomplishment engendered by successful completion. Completing a task to please others, to get a good grade, or to receive a reward are examples of external motivation goals. Rewards for learning should be used judiciously because, in some instances, they decrease interest in a task. Once the reward is perceived as the reason for engaging in an activity, an individual may engage in that activity only when the reward is available. Moreover, rewards that are theoretically but not actually available give negative reinforcement and undermine intrinsic motivation (e.g., the *A* grades that some children can never achieve). Extrinsic rewards are appropriate and effective for tasks that have limited intrinsic appeal; many rote tasks fall into this category. Rewards that are contingent on a specific level of performance, and that provide information regarding level of mastery, are less likely to undermine interest. In a classroom setting, rewards are often necessary as incentives to prod students into engaging in tasks in which they have little initial interest. Once begun, an attempt should be made to shift attention to intrinsic rewards by making the task interesting and challenging but achievable, with the value of the skill being made apparent.

external rotation Turning a limb away from the mid-line of the body.

externalization Attributing cause for feelings or behaviors to external sources.

extinction The process of discontinuing reinforcement to reduce a conditional response to its preconditional level. For example, Penelope cries until her parents bring her an after-bedtime drink of water. Her parents stop bringing her the water and ignore her crying. The crying behavior eventually stops or is extinguished because it is no longer reinforced.

extracorporeal membrane oxygenation therapy (ECMO) A method of delivering oxygen to infants with respiratory compromise that uses a heart-lung bypass system and allows the lungs to rest and heal without the negative pulmonary effects of high oxygen levels and the complications of ventilator therapy.

extrapyramidal cerebral palsy Any of the clinical physiological subtypes of cerebral palsy that do not reflect predominantly pyramidal tract involvement (spastic cerebral palsy). Ataxic/cerebellar, choreoathetoid, hypotonic or atonic (decreased or no muscle tone), rigid, and tremor are the principal members of this group. In general, for similar degrees of motor involvement, the degree of the motor delay is more severe for extrapyramidal than for spastic cerebral palsy. This appears to be due to the more frequent impairment of equilibrium and balance reactions as well as the more variable tone in extrapyramidal cerebral palsy; extreme variations in tone in this type of palsy also contribute to the decreased incidence and later onset of contractures. Facial grimacing is more common in extrapyramidal cerebral palsy than in spastic cerebral palsy.

extrapyramidal system Voluntary muscle reactions are a result of cooperation between the cortically controlled pyramidal system and three nonpyramidal systems: the vestibular system, the cerebellar system, and the striatal system. This last system, often referred to as the extrapyramidal system, includes such structures as the caudate nucleus, putamen, globus pallidus, and substantia nigra. Damage to these extrapyramidal centers (basal ganglia) produce movement disorders such as Parkinson disease, Huntington chorea, and choreoathetoid cerebral palsy.

eye color An inherited characteristic that has been suggested as a biological marker for learning style, with light- (blue) eyed persons being more self-paced and dark- (brown) eyed persons being more socially reactive. Dark-eyed children are thought to exhibit better perceptual motor speed and accuracy and have a lower prevalence of learning disabilities than light-eyed children. Light-eyed children in turn may have a higher incidence of autism and do better on learning skills that involve language, numbers, and pencil and paper tasks.

eye exercises *See* optometric training.

eye–hand coordination Refers to the direction of fine-motor activities of the hand in interaction with the visual system. Activities requiring eye–hand coordination include tracing, drawing, writing, lacing, and use of scissors. Direct training of eye–hand coordination has been attempted to remediate academic failure. Research has not proven this approach to be effective.

F

Fabry disease A genetic syndrome characterized by attacks of burning pain in the hands and feet, dark nodular skin lesions, and progressive renal insufficiency. Symptoms are secondary to an enzyme deficiency and can include cerebrovascular (stroke) findings such as seizures, hemiplegia (paralysis of half the body), and mental retardation.

face validity A test is said to have face validity if a reading of the items appears to reflect the areas that the test purports to measure. Face validity alone is insufficient to judge the value of the test. It is but one aspect of content validity, which can be evaluated by a panel of experts.

FACES *See* Family Adaptability and Cohesion Evaluation Scales.

facial index Ratio of facial height to facial width. A measurement sometimes used in syndrome descriptions.

facial nerve The seventh cranial nerve; cranial nerve VII is responsible for facial movement and expression and taste at the front of the tongue.

facies Face, countenance, expression. A facial expression suggestive, diagnostic, or pathognomonic (indicative) of a specific diagnosis or condition. For example, the hippocratic facies with a pinched expression, sunken eyes, hollow cheeks, and a leaden complexion is seen in people about to die. Numerous genetic syndromes have characteristic facies, and many children with minor dysmorphic (atypical) features have a peculiar, if nondiagnostic, facies. A leonine facies characterizes craniometaphysial dysplasia; a pugilistic facies characterizes the otopalatodigital syndrome; a triangular facies characterizes the multiple lentigines syndrome; and a myopathic facies is a relaxed, droopy appearance seen in myasthenia gravis.

facilitated communication Attempts by a person with a disability to convey thoughts and feelings through means other than spoken language, often assisted by another person who interprets signs or symbols, or through some sort of assistive technology or device. The term *facilitated communication* is most often used today in reference to people with autism and is considered a controversial system.

facilitator A person (e.g., social worker, psychologist, counselor) who enables change by assisting with communication, linking or strengthening existing systems, initiating new systems, channeling or developing resources, and acting as or arranging for an expert consultant. Among other activities, facilitators convene linkage meetings, encourage expression of feelings and opinions, gather and disseminate information, brainstorm, provide support, and advocate and lobby.

factitious disorder The reporting of or presence of symptoms of an actual mental or physical disorder that, on investigation, are found to be purposely created by the patient. *See also* Münchausen syndrome by proxy and malingering.

factor analysis A mathematical procedure for analyzing the intercorrelations of a group of variables that have been administered to a large number of individuals. The procedure is based on the assumption that intercorrelation can be accounted for by some underlying set of unobservable facts that are fewer in number than the variables themselves. The output of factor analysis is a factor matrix indicating the extent to which each test is correlated with, or "loads on," one or more factors. Factor loadings are correlations between factors and tests. Loadings indicate the weight of each factor in determining performance on each test. The naming of the factor depends upon the content of the tests that have loaded on the factor. For example, a factor analysis of the standardization group of the Wechsler Intelligence Scale for Children–Revised (WISC–R) resulted in the factors labeled verbal comprehension, perceptual organization, and freedom from distractibility, often referred to as the Kaufman factors.

faculty psychology A discredited doctrine that the mind is composed of various powers (faculties) that produce mental activities such that the intellect knows, the will desires, and so forth. Such a verbal approach may, however, be rooted in language—in how mental activities are discussed—and is therefore to a certain degree inescapable, accounting for the continual reappearance of faculty psychology in a variety of guises. Sometimes referred to as a modern equivalent of phrenology—the pseudoscience that claimed to interpret personality traits by palpating bumps on the surface of the head.

fading The process of slowly removing prompts until the desired response can be completed without any prompts. For example, in preparing a child to move from a structured to a less-structured classroom setting, the structure (study carrel, behavior charts, tokens) is gradually removed so that the old setting becomes more like the new one.

Fagan Test of Infant Intelligence (FTII) A screening device used to evaluate cognitive function in 6- to 12-month-old infants. Computerized technology is used to measure visual attention to novel stimuli. This nonmotor test would appear to be especially useful in assessing intelligence in infants with severe motor impairments.

failure to thrive (FTT) A presenting symptom (not a diagnosis) in which a child under 2 years of age (and usually under 1 year of age) exhibits some degree of growth failure in the absence of an obvious cause. The degree of growth failure necessary to raise concern of an underlying illness has never been clearly defined. In the past it was common to distinguish organic FTT (in which a physical disease was causing the growth failure) from nonorganic FTT (in which the poor growth was a result of a feeding problem or disorder of parenting). It is now recognized that many cases of FTT are not subject to this dichotomy.

fall away A test for tone in which an infant is suspended upside down and alternately each leg is released. The speed of fall of each lower extremity is compared; the leg that falls faster is considered to have relatively decreased tone.

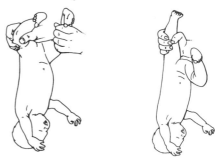

fall away

family A group of individuals related by blood, adoption, or marriage; in systems theory, a special group of individuals related to each other through reciprocal affections and loyalties. Admission to a family occurs through birth, marriage, or adoption, and members exit only by death. A family differs from other social groups in three important ways. A family has 1) a shared and relatively predictable cycle of life experiences, 2) permanency of membership, and 3) the paramount importance of the affectional ties of attachment, loyalty, and positive regard. Thus, even in the absence of biological or legal ties, people may consider themselves and be considered a family based on their mutual support, involvement, and affection for each other.

Family Adaptability and Cohesion Evaluation Scales (FACES) A 40-item self-report questionnaire used to indicate a family member's perception of his or her family's cohesion and adaptability. Each family member completes the instrument twice, once indicating current perceptions of the family (real) and once indicating how he or she would like the family to be (ideal). To the extent that the real and ideal differ, satisfaction can be estimated. The instrument has a sound theoretical base and has been well normed across diverse populations. FACES III is a shortened 20-item screening revision that limits the amount of information gathered, and thus the instrument's validity, but is quicker to administer. It is a screening tool for clinical settings.

Family Educational Rights and Privacy Act of 1974 *See* Education Amendments of 1974 (PL 93-380). This law incorporated student school records within the right to privacy.

Family Inventory of Life Events (FILE) A 71-item self-report instrument designed to assess both normative and nonnormative life situations and changes experienced by a family within the preceding year, as well as certain family experiences prior to the past year. The inventory is concerned with the number and duration of stressful events that tax a family's resources and that may be sources of dysfunction or distress. Such information is helpful in determining a family's coping abilities and in recognizing the life events that may hamper or facilitate the family's capacity to care for a child with developmental disabilities.

family life cycle The sequence of developmental and transitional changes in family structure and relationships from the time families are joined through the marriage of young adults until the death of the marital partners, when the process continues with their children. Families of children with mental retardation or other severe disabilities experience a series of crises as the child reaches various developmental stages. Many surveyed parents describe life with a child with mental retardation as a series of ups and progressively greater downs. The unmet needs of

parents and the degree of family stress seem to form a U-shaped curve. Demands and stresses are high among parents of preschoolers. These stresses drop off when children enter school programs, and they rise again beyond their original levels when the children become older; entry into both adolescence and young adulthood appears to be particularly stressful. It is important to realize that parents never fully resolve the complexity of feelings about their child's mental retardation or other form of developmental disability. The entire family and its subsequent life events and experiences are tempered by the presence of a child with a disability.

family of origin A family or kinship group related by blood or genetic ties.

family planning Voluntary and deliberate decisions regarding reproduction prior to conception. The number of children, the timing of children's births, the origin of children (biological or adoptive), and any methods of preconception birth control are dimensions of family planning. Although usually discussed within the context of a couple, many single adults are opting for families independent of their plans for coupling. Thus, technological reproductive methods may also become part of such adults' family planning strategies.

family therapist A therapist who works with the whole family as the unit of treatment or intervention.

family therapy Therapy in which the family is the unit of treatment or intervention. During the course of therapy, many or all members may be seen. Sessions may involve one or two members or the whole family. Sessions may focus on individual members or relationship pairs within the family; however, the focus is a change in interaction patterns at the family level.

Fanconi pancytopenia syndrome A genetic disorder with growth deficiency, a peculiar facies, microcephaly (abnormally small head), mild mental retardation (in one fourth of cases), thumb/radial hypoplasia (atypical tissue development), hyperpigmentation, and a diffuse blood disorder. Inheritance is autosomal recessive.

FAS *See* fetal alcohol syndrome.

fasciculation Visible involuntary twitching of muscles. When accompanied by muscle wasting, it may indicate a spinal cord or neuromuscular disorder.

Fay, Temple *See* patterning.

febrile seizure A seizure occurring simultaneously with a fever in the absence of other central nervous system disease. In most children, the seizure is precipitated by the presence of a high fever. In children with febrile seizures, 96.9% do not have other kinds of seizures or cognitive impairments. Acute treatment includes lowering the fever and treating its cause. Chronic treatment with anticonvulsants is only considered in children with complicated febrile seizures, since the medication does not lessen the chance of recurrence, and side effects related to behavior and intelligence are common.

feeble-minded Obsolete and unacceptable term describing individuals with mental retardation and an IQ between 50 and 70; sometimes generically used for all IQs below 70. The term *absolute feeble-mindedness* has been used to refer to mental retardation with an organic basis; *relative feeble-mindedness* has been used to refer to mental retardation due to environmental or unknown causes.

Feingold diet/hypothesis The unproven claim that trace amounts of salicylates, preservatives, and food dyes and coloring can produce behavioral symptoms, attention deficits, hyperactivity, and learning disabilities in children, and that many such neurobehavioral problems can be treated or prevented by a diet that strictly avoids the offending small-molecule additives. Although Benjamin Feingold (1900–1982), who developed this dietary theory, was an allergist, he did not hypothesize an allergic mechanism. The Feingold Association promotes this dietary approach.

femoral anteversion An orthopedic deformity in which the thighbones turn inward so that the knees and feet both turn in; common in spastic cerebral palsy.

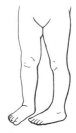

femur Thighbone.

FEP *See* free erythrocyte protoporphyrin.

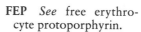

femoral anteversion

feral child A child allegedly raised by animals, such as a wolf-child. There are no documented cases of such an occurrence. Unproven legends and anecdotes about such children have acquired mythical status in modern thinking, but should not be adduced as evidence in any discussion of the impact of early nurturance or deprivation on later development.

Fernald Word Learning Technique (VAKT) A multisensory approach to reading that incorporates visual, auditory, kinesthetic, and tactile (VAKT) components. Words selected by the student are written by the instructor in cursive writing. The child says the word while tracing it with his or her finger in contact with the paper until the child can write the word without looking at the model. When the child has internalized that he or she can write and recognize words, the child is encouraged to write a story. The story is typed immediately, and the child reads it in typed form while it is fresh in his or her mind. Once the story is complete and a new word has been used in a meaningful way, the word is filed alphabetically in the child's word list. After a period of time, tracing is done mentally, and file words are typed. After the child is able to learn the typed version of new words, the reading approach becomes similar to others. The Fernald procedure also calls for "positive reconditioning" for children who have experienced school failure. Positive reconditioning specifically avoids 1) calling attention to emotionally loaded situations (reminding the child of the supposed importance of academic success), 2) using methods that previous experience suggests are likely to be ineffective, 3) permitting conditions that may cause embarrassment, and 4) directing attention to what the child cannot do. Grace Maxwell Fernald (1879–1950) was the psychologist who pioneered this approach.

fertility rate The number of live births in a given population during a specific time period. Fertility rates are one indicator of the health status of a given population.

fetal alcohol syndrome (FAS) Smith syndrome; a syndrome resulting from the teratogenic (causing malformations in the developing fetus) effects of maternal alcohol ingestion. Findings include prenatal onset of growth deficiency with microcephaly (abnormally small head) and short stature, cognitive impairments, and a characteristic facies with short palpebral fissures (eye slits) and a smooth philtrum (indentation in upper lip below nose). When present, mental retardation tends to be mild, but the entire spectrum of cognitive and neurobehavioral disabilities is represented by the frequent occurrence of attention-deficit/hyperactivity disorder (ADHD), articulation problems (related to mid-face hypoplasia [flattening] and cleft lip and palate deformities), language disorders, and specific learning disabilities. Cardiac and skeletal abnormalities are common. Incidence figures suggest that 1 in 300 babies show some effect (fetal alcohol effect, FAE) of maternal ingestion of alcohol, and more than 1 in 1,000 babies exhibit the full-blown syndrome. Greater than 10% of mild mental retardation may be secondary to ethanol toxicity to early neuronal migration and nerve cell development, making alcohol the most common severe teratogen (toxic agent) to which the fetus is exposed. The severity of the dysmorphic (atypical) features tends to correlate with the severity of the cognitive dysfunction.

fetal antiepileptic drug syndrome A constellation of congenital abnormalities associated with maternal use of an antiepileptic (anticonvulsant) drug, such as phenytoin, during pregnancy. *See*, for example, fetal Dilantin (phenytoin) syndrome.

fetal cytomegalovirus (CMV) syndrome Congenital cytomegalic inclusion disease; a syndrome of growth retardation, mental retardation, microcephaly (abnormally small head), brain (periventricular) calcifications (less than 10% of cases), hearing loss (50% of cases) and chorioretinitis (inflammation of the choroid and the retina [light-sensitive inner back wall]) that can follow on maternal (and fetal) infection by this herpes group virus. "Blueberry muffin spots" may be noted secondary to a blood disorder. Congenital CMV infection is common, but most cases are asymptomatic. Postnatal CMV infection may be involved in progressive sensorineural (involving the inner ear or the auditory nerve) hearing loss. The interpretation of serologic (serum) and culture tests is not conclusive.

fetal Dilantin (phenytoin) syndrome Fetal hydantoin effect; a pattern of fetal malformation caused by maternal use of Dilantin (an antiseizure medication) during the first trimester of pregnancy. This pattern includes poor growth, mild cognitive impairments, unusual facies, and digit and nail hypoplasia (failure of fingers and nails to develop completely). The facial features include hypertelorism (widely spaced eyes); a broad, flat nasal bridge; short nose; bow-shaped lip; and often a cleft lip and palate. Eye problems including coloboma (absence of part of the eye or retina [light-sensitive inner back wall]), strabismus (squint), ptosis (drooping), or slanting of the eyes may be seen. The digits (fingers and toes) are often small at the tip with small nails. Approximately 10% of exposed fetuses exhibit the syndrome, and one third demonstrate isolated effects. Fetal susceptibility to hydantoin exposure appears to be genetic. Clefting and congenital heart disease are increased in children of mothers with epilepsy independent of anticonvulsant exposure. Although only hydantoins (Dilantin) have been studied, there is some concern that combinations of hydantoins and barbiturates increase the risk to the fetus of developing this syndrome.

fetal face syndrome Robinow-Silverman syndrome; a syndrome with short forearms, hemivertebrae (absence of half of vertebrae), hypoplastic (with atypical tissue development) genitalia, and a facies that resembles that of an 8-week-old fetus. Intelligence is usually normal, but language disorders have been noted.

fetal hydantoin effect *See* fetal Dilantin (phenytoin) syndrome.

fetal phenytoin syndrome *See* fetal Dilantin syndrome.

fetal rubella syndrome Congenital rubella; Gregg syndrome; rubella embryopathy. A syndrome of deafness, cataracts, and cardiac and central nervous system abnormalities. German measles (rubella) transmitted from the mother to the fetus in the first or second trimester of pregnancy produces these abnormalities in the baby; maternal vaccination with attenuated (diluted) rubella represents primary prevention. Gamma globulin can be administered as secondary prevention when a nonimmune pregnant woman is exposed. Mental retardation occurs in about one third of patients; learning disabilities, language disorders, autism, impulsivity, and behavior disorders are also common. The last major rubella epidemic in the United States was in 1964–1965.

fetal Tridione syndrome *See* fetal trimethadione syndrome.

fetal trimethadione syndrome Fetal Tridione syndrome; a pattern of malformations described in children of mothers who used trimethadione (Tridione), an anticonvulsant medication used to treat absence seizures that do not respond to other agents. The syndrome includes growth failure, mental retardation, abnormal facial features, heart disease, and abnormal genitalia. The facial features consist of brachycephaly (irregular, flat head shape), small mid-face, upturned nose, Λ-shaped eyebrows, and a prominent forehead. Eyes may show strabismus (squint) or ptosis (drooping), and the external ear is generally malformed. The heart disease is tetralogy of Fallot and the genitalia are ambiguous (girls have a large clitoris or boys have a small penis with an abnormally placed urethral opening). The frequency of severity of defects associated with the use of this drug during pregnancy is significant.

fetal wastage A maternal history of losing previous pregnancies; the cause for high fetal wastage (such as genetic risk or congenital malformations) tends to persist and may be taken as a risk factor for a pregnancy that goes to term.

fetoscope *See* auscultation.

fetus The product of conception (embryo) from the eighth week of gestation to the moment of birth.

Feuerstein, Reuven An Israeli psychologist who developed the theory of cognitive modifiability. Factors influencing Feuerstein's views include his early experiences in a concentration camp, studying under Jean Piaget and Andre Rey at the University of Geneva, and working with Youth Aliyah, an agency responsible for the integration of Jewish children from many cultures into a technologically advanced society. Feuerstein views intelligence as not being static but changeable, and has formulated specific "mediated learning experiences" that are reportedly successful in teaching slow-learning adolescents to perform substantially higher, level cognitive tasks. He has created an assessment instrument known as the Learning Potential Assessment Device (LPAD), as well as a teaching method called Instrumental Enrichment (IE). The theory of cognitive modifiability is controversial with regard to the degree in which genetic mental retardation can be altered.

fever A body temperature above 98.6°F (37°C). Fever is not an illness or a diagnosis, but a sign. For diseases of similar severity, children tend to run relatively higher fevers than do adults. High fever in susceptible young children may precipitate febrile convulsions. Some of the highest fevers in childhood are associated with roseola (measles), otitis media (middle-ear infections), and urinary tract infections.

fever of unknown origin (FUO) Prolonged episode of fever without a readily apparent explanation. In infants and young children, this symptom often leads to a sepsis (infection) workup.

FFD *See* freedom from distractibility.

FG syndrome A genetic syndrome with mental retardation, hypotonia (decreased muscle tone), seizures, hyperactivity, outgoing personality, short stature, peculiar facies with prominent forehead, and imperforate (not open) anus. Inheritance is X-linked recessive.

fibula Calf bone; the smaller of the two leg bones.

field theory The application of gestalt psychology to the study of mental retardation.

fifth disease Erythema infectiosum.

figure–ground discrimination Recognition of the difference between foreground and background in the context of any given set of visual or auditory stimuli. Individuals with visual figure–ground discrimination may confuse printed words with the paper upon which they are printed, or may give undue significance to ancillary sections of the page rather than attending to the most prominent shape or figure. Those with auditory figure–ground problems have difficulty discerning the teacher's voice from other noises in the classroom. Figure–ground limitations refer to difficulty distinguishing a particular sight or sound from a larger group of shapes or sounds that constitute the background.

FILE *See* Family Inventory of Life Events.

fine-finger movements A test of fine-motor integration in which the thumb is repetitively tapped against the index finger or is successively tapped against each of the other four fingers in series. The task can be administered as a timed test of motor coordination, or the results can be interpreted as signs of minor neurological dysfunction according to the degree of clumsiness and the presence of spillover to the opposite side (mirror movements). Asymmetrical performance may be a significant indicator of asymmetrical central nervous system dysfunction.

fine-motor skills Activities that require the coordination of the small muscles of the body, especially those of the hand. Eye–hand coordination in infancy; problem solving with toys and puzzles in early childhood; and graphomotor/drawing and dressing skills in middle childhood are used to assess fine-motor skills.

finger-to-nose test The tip of the forefinger (index finger or pointer) is rapidly moved from the tip of the nose to either the examiner's fingertip or to an extended reach position. Dyssynergia (incoordination) or terminal tremor are often interpreted as indicating cerebellar disease; however, they may also occur with dysfunction of the cerebral cortex. Asymmetric performance should be noted.

fingerspelling Dactylology, dactyl speech. A form of unaided augmentative communication with finger movements that uses the conventional language system and its vocabulary, spelling, and grammar; the American Manual Alphabet is a fingerspelling system. Fingerspelling is generally used as an adjunct to sign language, where signs represent words or word parts, not letters. Fingerspelling allows for the rendering of proper names, specialized terms for which no signs exist, and slang.

first-arch syndrome Any of a large group of syndromes that involve derivatives of the first brachial arch (an embryologic structure); these include Treacher-Collins syndrome, mandibulofacial dyostosis, Pierre Robin syndrome, cleft lip and palate, and deafness associated with ear deformities.

first-degree relative Parent, child, sibling; an individual who has half of his or her genes in common with the index case (also includes identical twins with all genes in common).

first-order change In general-systems theories and family therapy based on these system theories, first-order change is behavior change with no real systemwide change. First-order change is viewed as superficial by many theorists; however, it is often a necessary precursor to more fundamental system change (termed second-order change).

Fisher-Logemann Test of Articulation Competence   A test of pronunciation that includes picture and sentence tasks for examining all English phonemes according to syllabic function in preschoolers to adult.

fisting   Hand position with fingers flexed in a clenched palm. This is the normal posture for the first 3 months of life, after which the hand begins to be open or unfisted most of the time. Persistence of fisting past this time is often a sign of hypertonicity (increased muscle tone) or spasticity.

fisting

fit   *See* seizure.

5p–   *See* cri-du-chat syndrome.

fixed   Describes an orthopedic deformity (or abnormal positioning of extremities) that cannot be passively corrected.

flaccid   Floppy, hypotonic (decreased) muscle tone due to neuromuscular dysfunction.

"flaky"   Informal, nonspecific term describing a mild to moderate state of psychological disorganization that may be demonstrated through trouble organizing thoughts, remembering plans, formulating intentions, and carrying out everyday affairs. The term is often used to refer to individuals who probably have undiagnosed learning and attention disabilities or to characterize an aspect of task performance (e.g., "flaky" sentence structure or word association). With respect to developmental assessment, "flaky" is a partial clinical impression or initial indicator that becomes refined, quantified, and objectively defined by standardized tests and neurodevelopmental examination.

flat affect   Lack of expressed emotion or a fixed emotional state with no range of variability or emotion. Thus, a person appears to have no reaction to obvious humor, or to hearing good news or bad news. Flat affect should be investigated, since it may be symptomatic of depression. Children with learning disabilities who are developing secondary emotional disorders often present with a flat affect.

Flesch index   An index of the reading difficulty of a passage; it is calculated from empirically derived regression formulas that use counts of words per sentence, syllables per 100 words, and frequency of personal words to generate reading ease and human interest scores and to calculate grade levels.

flexion   Bending of a joint.

flexor   Any muscle that bends a joint. Flexor tone refers to the degree to which the predominant muscle tone produces a flexor habitus (appearance).

flexor withdrawal reflex   A procedure to induce active foot dorsiflexion (upgoing movement of the toes); in a sitting position, the patient is asked to flex the hip (lift the thigh) against resistance; a positive response is automatic dorsiflexion of the foot at the ankle.

flight of ideas   A continuous change of subject and thought content with little apparent connection among the topics and little external stimulation for the change. This may be one manifestation of attention-deficit/hyperactivity disorder (ADHD).

FLK   *See* funny-looking kid.

floppy infant   Hypotonia (decreased muscle tone) with motor delay in the first 1–2 years of life. This may be an early presentation for a variety of cognitive or neuromotor disorders. Rarely, the floppy infant is diagnosed as having a congenital myopathy (disorder of voluntary muscle) or neuromuscular disorder via nerve conduction studies and electromyography. More commonly, hypotonia evolves into

floppy infant

spastic cerebral palsy by late in the first year of life or extrapyramidal cerebral palsy by late in the second year of life. In the absence of any of these outcomes, the floppy infant most commonly has benign cerebral hypotonia, a motor condition that will be outgrown. The more severe and prolonged the hypotonia, the greater the likelihood of more-pervasive cognitive and motor dysfunction. *See also* Prader-Willi syndrome.

flora   Vegetation; can refer to bacteria normally residing on or in the body.

fluency disorder   Any condition resulting in an interruption in the flow of oral language; this includes, but is not restricted to, stuttering and cluttering.

fluid intelligence   A term for the Horn-Cattell theory of intellectual processing. Fluid intelligence is the ability to infer relationships and correlations; it is best measured by novel tests, particularly when adaptation and flexibility are involved. Tasks intended to measure fluid intelligence should not depend on previously acquired knowledge or earlier-learned problem-solving procedures; rather, they should require the discovery of the essential correlations of a task for the first time and the drawing of inferences that could not have been worked out previously. The Woodcock-Johnson Psycho-Educational Battery– Revised (WJ–R) Tests of Cognitive Ability are based upon the Horn-Cattell theory. The Kaufman Assessment Battery for Children (K–ABC) also provides, to some extent, a framework for assessing crystallized and fluid abilities.

fluoxetine   Trade name Prozac; an antidepressant drug.

FO   *See* foot orthoses.

folic acid   A B-complex vitamin implicated in neural tube defects; when a pregnant woman has a low folic acid level, the fetus may be more inclined to develop spina bifida (open neural tube defects).

fontanel   A "soft-spot" on a baby's head; there are two palpable fontaneles at birth

fontanel

(anterior [front] and posterior [back]), but usually only the anterior one is followed clinically. Each fontanel represents a membranous interval at the angles of the cranial bones in the infant. The anterior fontanel closes between 8 and 15 months of life; the posterior one by 4 months. Premature closure of the fontanel may result from craniosynostosis (premature fusion of skull sutures); this should be of special concern when associated with decreasing head growth or microcephaly (abnormally small head). An enlarging anterior fontanel may reflect hydrocephalus (excess fluid in the brain) or vitamin-A toxicity, especially with an enlarging head circumference. A persistent anterior fontanel may occur in a variety of genetic, metabolic, and bone disorders. In young infants, the anterior fontanel may pulsate with the heartbeat; dramatic visual pulsations may be seen in increased intracranial pressure and a variety of heart conditions.

foot orthoses (FO)   Orthopedic corrections including arch supports, shoe inserts, and corrective or orthopedic shoes.

foot-switch system   A component of gait analysis that allows recording of the foot-to-floor contact patterns for each leg.

Forestown boot   A foot orthosis to treat equinus (involuntary foot extension).

formal operations   The final Piagetian stage of cognitive development characterized by achievement of formal logic (induction and deduction) and abstract reasoning; it usually emerges at adolescence (12–15 years of age). People with mental retardation do not reach the formal stage of operations.

Formal Reading Inventory (FRI)   A method for assessing silent reading comprehension and oral reading miscues for individuals ages 6-6 to 17-11. The inventory includes four forms. Each form has 13 developmentally sequenced passages with five literal, inferential, critical, and affective multiple-choice questions following each story. Silent reading quotients (with a mean of 100 and a standard deviation of 15) and percentiles are provided for all four forms. However, the manual suggests that forms A and C be read silently and that forms B and D be read orally (forms C and D providing a posttest). Quotients are not provided for orally read passages. Oral reading miscues may be noted and characterized as: 1) meaning similarity—the ability to use comprehension strategies; 2) function similarity—the ability to use appropriate grammar forms; 3) graphic/phonemic similarity—the ability to use word-attack strategies; 4) multiple sources—the category used when a miscue fits several of the miscue types; and 5) self-correction—the ability to recognize errors and provide an accurate response without help.

formboard A flat board of various dimensions with a number of (usually different) geometric shapes cut out and matching shapes (usually slightly thicker than the board) that can be inserted in the board. Formboards were invented by Edouard Seguin (1812–1880) as a visual-perceptual motor training device, and later were incorporated into many intelligence tests for preschool children.

forme fruste An incomplete or abortive form or manifestation of a condition or disease.

4p– syndrome Deletion of all or part of the short arm of chromosome 4 syndrome; a chromosomal disorder with profound mental retardation, seizures, growth deficiency, and a peculiar facies.

fragile X syndrome Martin-Bell syndrome, Marker X syndrome, Escalante syndrome. A genetic syndrome with the familial occurrence of moderate mental retardation, predominantly in males, who also demonstrate a long narrow face with thick features, prognathism (a prominent jaw), blue eyes, and, early in life, macro-

fragile X syndrome

somia (large body size), and later in life, macro-orchidism (large testicles). This is an X-linked disorder with a fragile site (FMR—1 gene) on the long arm of the X chromosome (Xq 27). The 30% of female carriers who are affected appear to be more mildly involved, with shyness, anxiety, and panic attacks. The syndrome accounts for approximately 5% of mental retardation in males, but has also been reported with learning disabilities, autism, speech and language disorders, and mathematics and motor disabilities. A carrier female has a 38% risk of producing a son with mental retardation and a 16% chance of producing a daughter with mental retardation.

frame An orthopedic device for a bed; the frame is either on or around the bed or is itself a specialized bed. The frame allows extrinsic support (such as a pulley system) for positioning.

Franceschetti-Klein syndrome *See* Treacher Collins syndrome.

Fraser syndrome *See* cryptophthalmus.

free association A term originally applied to a therapeutic technique most often used by psychoanalytically oriented psychotherapists in which the client is instructed to say whatever thought, feeling, or image comes to mind. Free association has become a component of many psychological and educational tests.

free erythrocyte protoporphyrin (FEP) A component of hemoglobin; when its level is high, lead poisoning or iron deficiency can be suspected. The FEP level is not sufficiently sensitive to be used any longer, given the current lowered limits for lead exposure of the Centers for Disease Control (CDC).

free-floating anxiety Pervasive and ever-present tensions and insecurities unrelated to specific events, situations, or threats.

freedom from distractibility (FFD) The Wechsler Intelligence Scale for Children (WISC) Kaufman factor score that attempts to measure the ability to concentrate and to remain attentive. The factor score is obtained by totaling the scaled scores of the arithmetic, digit span, and coding subtests. A high FFD score suggests good short-term memory, the ability to maintain attention, good encoding ability, and the capacity to self-monitor. A low FFD score suggests distractibility, poor rehearsal strategies, anxiety, and difficulty with encoding and shifting mental processes when manipulating symbolic material. The FFD score can be difficult to interpret, and it may not capture all of the skills and complex processes that contribute to attention.

Freeman-Sheldon syndrome *See* whistling face syndrome.

frenulum linguae The lingual frenulum; a fold of tissue from the floor of the mouth to the mid-line of the undersurface of the tongue. A short lingual frenulum is described as tongue-tie, which can affect the elevation of the tongue tip to the palate for production of specific sounds (generally *L, T, D*), but is rarely clinically significant.

frequency Measurement of the pitch of a sound. The number of complete cycles a sound wave makes over a period of time, expressed in hertz (Hz). Human beings with average hearing can detect frequencies from approximately 20 to 20,000 Hz.

FRI *See* Formal Reading Inventory.

Friedreich ataxia A heredodegenerative disorder characterized by ataxia (unsteady gait), nystagmus (involuntary eye movements), kyphoscoliosis, and pes cavus (a foot deformity). Degeneration occurs in the axons of the nerve cells of the spinal cord long tracts, and occasionally in other parts of the nervous system (cerebellum, brain stem, and vestibular [balance] and auditory systems). Progressive ataxia involves the legs more than the arms. Speech can be affected because of a dyscoordination between breathing and phonating (sound production). Lateral nystagmus (a jerky movement of the eyes) is present, as is optic atrophy. Visual-

evoked potentials (VEPs) are abnormal in two thirds of patients, but electroretinograms are normal. Weakness and wasting of the distal muscles are common, as are abnormal sensations such as paresthesias (numbness, tingling, or heightened sensitivity). Intelligence is preserved. Heart problems and diabetes are common. Life expectancy is to the 40s or 50s; individuals with advanced cases are often confined to bed with swallowing difficulties. Inheritance is autosomal recessive.

frog posture Refers to posture of a pithed, or debrained, frog. A posture that indicates extreme hypotonia (decreased muscle tone) or floppiness:

frog posture

an infant lies flat with arms in a surrender posture, legs flexed, feet everted, and hips abducted (turned outward). Bilateral hip abduction deformity is the "frog leg" posture.

frontal lobe The anterior portion of the brain just behind the forehead; the area of the cerebrum in front of the central sulcus (fissure of Rolando, one of the major indentations on the brain). It comprises much of the front part on the brain. Loss

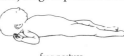
frontal cortex

of the frontal lobes can result in passivity and loss of motivation. The posterior (back) part of the frontal lobe contains the motor cortex, which is involved in voluntary movement.

frontal lobe syndrome A behavioral profile that follows severe, diffuse bilateral damage to the frontal lobe and includes disturbances in voluntary action, speech initiation, and sustained interest or affect; apathico-akinetico-abulic syndrome.

frontometaphysial dysplasia A genetic syndrome with prominent supraorbital (just above the eye or brow) ridges, joint limitations, and bone abnormalities; progressive hearing loss, and occasional mental retardation. Inheritance is X-linked.

frontonasal dysplasia Median cleft face syndrome.

frustration A feeling of discomfort, disappointment, or insecurity aroused by a blocking of gratification or by the existence of unresolved problems. Children and adults with developmental disabilities often experience frustration in academic, vocational, and social situations, because they are frequently unable to meet the expectations of themselves or others. Frustration can be exacerbated by an inability to express the feeling as such, by exposure to consistently unrealistic or inappropriate expectations, and by a misunderstanding of the nature or extent of the individual's disability. If frustration is unchecked indefinitely, it may evolve into learned helplessness (a belief that external stresses are beyond the individual's ability to cope with all stress, including that which is controllable). Emotional and behavior problems secondary to the disability and associated frustration may develop as well. Several theories contend that frustration arouses, and may result in, aggression.

FTII *See* Fagan Test of Infant Intelligence.

FTT *See* failure to thrive.

functional Having an emotional or psychiatric cause.

Functional Independence Measure for Children (WeeFIM) A measure of the severity of disability in children and adults with developmental levels between 6 months and 7 years; performance on each of 18 items in six domains (self-care, sphincter control, mobility, locomotion, communication, and serial cognition) is assigned to one of seven levels on an ordinal scale, with scores ranging from complete independence (level seven) to complete dependence on a helping person (level one).

functional skills training Direct training in the skills and competencies necessary for everyday living. These skills may include the use of adaptive equipment, counting change, reading single words, balancing a checkbook, and completing a job application.

fundus The bottom or base of an organ; the part of a hollow organ that is farthest from its opening.

funny-looking kid (FLK) Antiquated medical colloquialism for a child with sufficient minor (or major) dysmorphic (atypical) features to support the need for genetic evaluation and the possible presence of an identifiable syndrome. "Funny" does not infer that the patient is to be laughed at, but, rather, that the presence of the malformations make the examiner feel "funny"—uncomfortable and uncertain for overlooking, or failing to diagnose, a rare syndrome or variant. Such children are now more accurately characterized as dysmorphic.

FUO *See* fever of unknown origin.

G

gag reflex A tactile (touch) stimulus to the posterior (back) tongue or pharynx (throat) that produces the response of tongue protrusion, head and jaw protrusion, and pharyngeal contractions; the reflex is present by 6½ months of gestation, is strong at birth, is hyperactive in neurologically impaired children, and is hypoactive with ataxia (unsteady gait). The persistence of this reflex is a component of the neurological examination of cranial nerves IX and X.

gait Walk; pattern of walking; test of walking. An ataxic, or cerebellar, gait is staggering and drunken; in a hemiplegic gait, the affected foot is circumducted (swung forward in a half-circle); an equinus gait is toe walking. Gait tests include walking, running, skipping, hopping (on one foot), heel walking, toe walking, tandem (heel to toe) walking, and Fog tests. Disturbances in gait can reflect major motor system involvement (e.g., cerebral palsy), or milder motor system involvement, such as clumsy child syndrome.

gait analysis A quantitative description of gait (walk) as performed in a gait analysis laboratory that uses an optical, or visual, recording system and an electric system comprising a floor plate (floor pressure sensor) and a variety of electromyogram (EMG) components; the large amount of data generated is analyzed by specially designed computer programs.

gait cycle The interval between foot contacts of the same leg while walking; the gait cycle is divided into swing and stance phases. One complete gait cycle covers one stride length (two steps).

GAL *See* guardian ad litem.

galactosemia Hereditary galactose intolerance. An autosomal recessive inborn error of metabolism characterized by hepatomegaly (liver enlargement), splenomegaly (large spleen), and failure to thrive. Infants are normal at birth but soon develop vomiting and lethargy. Some have prolonged prevalence in the neonatal period. Untreated, these children develop cataracts in addition to poor physical growth and mental retardation. One type of galactosemia is not diagnosed until 2–3 years of age with the presentation of mental retardation and IQ scores typically ranging from 50 to 70. Etiology involves a defect in the activity of the enzyme galactose-1-phosphate uridyl transferase. Diagnosis is suspected with an increased amount of reducing substances and galactose in the urine and is confirmed by measuring the enzyme's activity level in red blood cells. Many states include galactosemia in routine newborn screening. Treatment requires dietary manipulation to avoid galactose. In general, the earlier treatment is initiated, the better the cognitive outcome. However, electroencephalogram (EEG) abnormalities and visual-perceptual limitations have been identified in at least half of children treated from birth.

Galant reflex A primitive reflex observed in infants, elicited by holding the baby in prone (front) suspension and stroking the back paravertebrally (to one side of the spine) from top to bottom. The response to this stimulus is an arching or incurving of the trunk toward the stimulated side. An asymmetrical or extremely strong Galant reflex is thought to increase the risk for hip dislocation in children with cerebral palsy. It is named after the researcher S. Galant who au-

Galant reflex

thored the most extensive early description of the reflex.

Galeazzi sign One knee lower than the other when the child is supine on a flat surface and the knees are flexed to 90 degrees; this sign occurs with hip dislocation.

Gallaudet University The only liberal arts college for people with hearing impairment in the world. Founded as a department of the Columbia Institute for the Deaf in 1864 by Amos Kendall (1789–1869) and Edward Miner Gallaudet (1837–1917), the college was established through federal legislation signed by Abraham Lincoln. In 1894, the department became Gallaudet College, named in honor of Edward Gallaudet's father, Thomas Hopkins Gallaudet, who had established the first school for the deaf in the United States. Located in Washington, D.C., Gallaudet University has a distinguished record of success and has produced many leaders in the education of people with hearing impairment in the United States.

galvanic skin response (GSR) The measured resistance to the passage of a weak electric current; an electrophysiological variable used in the research quantification of responsiveness to different stimuli.

Gamper reflex Bowing reflex; the infant is placed in a supine (back) position and the thighs are extended at the hips, causing the baby to come to a sitting "bow" position. This reflex is rare in premature infants, but common in babies with anencephaly (no brain or absent top of skull).

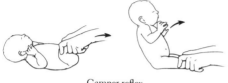

Gamper reflex

gangliosidoses A group of hereditary disorders characterized by progressive storage of gangliosides (chemicals) in the gray matter of the brain. The buildup of the product occurs because of an enzyme that is present only in an inactive form. At least 10 of these disorders have been described, and they present clinically with intellectual deterioration that may be associated with an enlarged liver. Motor findings include dystonia (impaired muscle tone), hypotonia (decreased muscle tone), ataxia (unsteady gait), or myoclonus (muscle twitching). Seizures and optic atrophy (wasting) are frequent. A common physical finding is a cherry red spot in the back of the eye. The rapidity of deterioration and presence of motor and visual problems are specific to the type of enzyme deficiency. Gangliosidoses include Tay-Sachs disease, Niemann-Pick disease, and types of amaurotic (loss of vision unrelated to an eye condition) idiocy, lipofuscinoses, lipidoses, and Gaucher disease. Inheritance is generally autosomal recessive.

Gardner Social Maturity Scale (GSMS) A brief, 15-minute estimate of how a child compares socially with chronological age peers 3–13 years old.

gastrocnemius Calf muscle.

gastroesophageal reflux (GER) The regurgitation of stomach contents back into the esophagus (throat). This can be an occasional typical variant of little significance, or it can be a chronically recurring problem that contributes to aspiration and failure to thrive (poor growth). GER may be associated with significant neurological impairment or a genetic syndrome, and may require surgical correction (a Nissen fundoplication).

gastrostomy A surgical operation that creates an artificial opening into the stomach, usually for the insertion of a feeding tube.

gate A test item that assesses nonverbal problem-solving ability; it involves the imitation of a five-block construction. Fine-motor problems limit the interpretation of this item as a measure of intelligence. It can usually be achieved by children 4 years of age.

gate

gate control A theory of pain that postulates that neural mechanisms in the spinal cord act like a gate to modulate the flow of nerve impulses from the peripheral (noncentral) fibers to the brain. Such gate mechanisms are influenced by descending nerve impulses that refer to past experience, so that the same degree of pain stimulus may be interpreted quite differently.

Gaucher disease A progressive condition in which cerebrosides are stored in the reticuloendothelial system (bone marrow, spleen, etc.) and sometimes in the nervous system. There are three clinical types: chronic, infantile, and juvenile. Chronic Gaucher disease is slowly progressive with organ involvement (liver and spleen), but no neurological involvement occurring until late in life. Infantile Gaucher disease has marked central nervous system involvement and a rapidly progressive downhill course leading to early death. The clinical features of juvenile Gaucher disease are splenomegaly (large spleen), anemia, and neurological involvement (with ataxia [unsteady gait], intellectual deterioration, myoclonic seizures, and spasticity) presenting in the first decade of life. The enzyme acid phosphatase is elevated in the blood. Diagnosis is made by identifying Gaucher cells in bone marrow tissue. Attempts at treatment for the chronic form have included enzyme replacement therapy (Alglucerase/Ceredase) and bone marrow transplant. Inheritance is autosomal recessive, with a recurrence risk of 25%. Two thirds of people with chronic Gaucher disease are of Ashkenazic Jewish ancestry. Named for the French dermatologist Phillipe C.E. Gaucher (1854–1918).

gavage Feeding by a tube inserted into the stomach; the tube may be a nasogastric, orogastric, or gastrostomy tube. When for a variety of reasons (usually related to the presence of neurological impairment that affects the individual's ability to swallow) tube feeding is used, the orogastric and nasogastric tubes usually represent short-term approaches and the gastrostomy tube a long-term approach.

GBS infection *See* group B streptococcal infection.

GED *See* Tests of General Educational Development.

gelastic seizure An unusual seizure type with paroxysmal laughter and transient loss of consciousness.

gene A unit of heredity located on a specific chromosome site (locus) and comprising the cell's DNA (deoxyribonucleic acid).

generalization The ability to apply a rule to cases or situations other than those in which it has been learned. This process does not always occur automatically in students with disabilities. For example, a student may learn to raise his or her hand consistently in a resource room, but will not do so in a general classroom. Generalization is more likely to occur if it is a component of the training process itself.

generalized seizure Grand mal seizure; tonic-clonic seizure; a seizure with electrical changes in both sides of the brain (both hemispheres). Generalized seizures are characterized by loss of consciousness with tonic (increased muscle tone) and then clonic (rhythmic contraction and relaxation) movements. Seizure types in this category include absence, tonic, clonic, tonic-clonic, atonic, and myoclonic. The duration can range from a few seconds to half an hour or more. A postictal period of disorientation and poor coordination is common. Generalized seizures can be the primary seizure or may follow a partial seizure. In the latter case, an aura, or warning, may precede the seizure. Generalized tonic-clonic, or major motor, seizures can occur with fever (febrile seizure), prior to menstrual periods, with infections such as meningitis (inflammation of the spinal cord and brain membranes), or with certain drugs. Diagnosis is by electroencephalogram (EEG) with clinical correlation, and treatment includes use of appropriate anticonvulsants.

generic The name of a chemical structure (e.g., drug) not protected by patent; the official name, or the nonproprietary name. Thus, a generic drug name is the chemical name, whereas the brand name is the proprietary name.

genetic The etiology (cause) of a disorder determined to be in the structure of an individual's genes, which exhibit extra, missing, or rearranged DNA (deoxyribonucleic acid). Genetics is that branch of medicine concerned with the heredity of disease conditions, the prediction of recurrence risks, and the counseling of families about such risks.

genetic counseling A process to help individuals and families understand the ramifications associated with the present occurrence of a genetic disorder in the family and the risk of recurrence of the disorder. More specifically, genetic counseling involves an attempt by one or more trained people to help at-risk or affected individuals and families to 1) comprehend the medical facts including the diagnosis of a disorder, its probable course, and the available management; 2) appreciate the way heredity contributes to the disorder and the risk of recurrence in specific relatives; 3) understand the options for dealing with the risk of recurrence; 4) choose the course of action that seems appropriate in view of the family's risk and goals, and act in accordance with that decision; and 5) make the best possible adjustment to the disorder in an affected family member and/or to the risk of recurrence of that disorder. Genetic counselors must meet both educational and competency criteria as determined by passing an examination. In 1992, the new American Board of Genetic Counselors became an independent body after separating from the American Board of Medical Genetics medical subspecialty board.

genetic screening Testing in a particular population to identify individuals at high risk for carrying or having a specific disorder. For example, testing for carriers of Tay-Sachs among the Ashkenazic Jewish population targets a particular subgroup, whereas the blood test for phenylketonuria (PKU) is used in the general population. Other genetic screening tests include chromosome mapping for single gene disorders such as cystic fibrosis or Duchenne muscular dystrophy.

genogram A diagram delineating family composition and stucture for three or more generations. It is used in family systems theory to indicate the types of relationships among individuals as well as genetic diseases and behavioral habits such as alcoholism. Biological, legal, and functional family members and the nature of their relationships are graphically depicted together with pertinent dates, issues, and information in a one-page format. Once structure is mapped, probing for disorders in each of these family members can be helpful in determining familiarity and possible genetic inheritance patterns of a particular disorder. The genogram can serve to summarize large amounts of dynamic and factual information concerning biological and psychological risks, illness and dysfunction, as well as to indicate areas of strength and resources. (*See* example on p. 131).

genomic imprinting *See* imprinting, genomic.

genotype The genes that are present on an individual's chromosomes, the expression of which produces the phenotype (appearance). A carrier genotype for an autosomal recessive disorder would have one disease gene and one normal gene. The expression of that, the phenotype, is usually a typical individual.

genu Knee.

genu recurvatum Back-knee; the ability of the knee to bend backward. Secondary to general joint laxity, this may be a component of a more generalized genetic disorder.

genu valgum Knock-knee; the distance between the knees is decreased whereas that between the ankles is increased. Many children have knock-knees

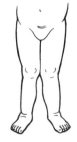

genu valgum

Genogram Key

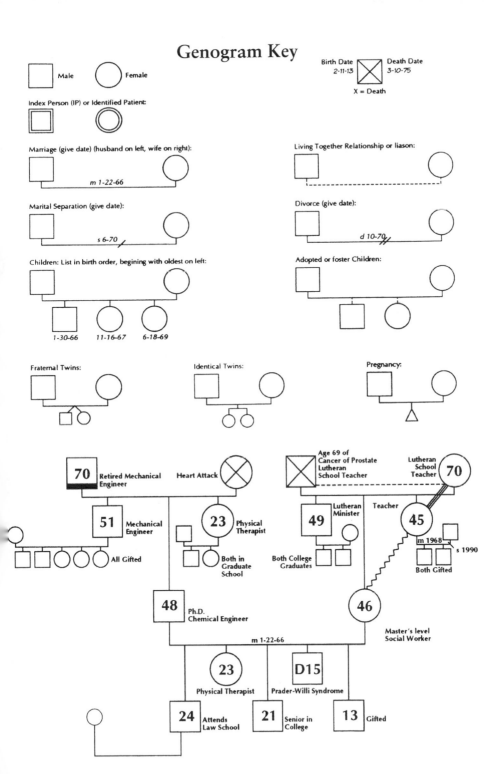

Male □   **Female** ○

Birth Date 2-11-13   ⊠   Death Date 3-10-75
X = Death

Index Person (IP) or Identified Patient:

Marriage (give date) (husband on left, wife on right):
m 1-22-66

Living Together Relationship or liason:

Marital Separation (give date):
s 6-70

Divorce (give date):
d 10-70

Children: List in birth order, begining with oldest on left:
1-30-66   11-16-67   6-18-69

Adopted or foster Children:

Fraternal Twins:

Identical Twins:

Pregnancy:

---

70 Retired Mechanical Engineer   Heart Attack ⊗   Age 69 of Cancer of Prostate Lutheran School Teacher ⊠   Lutheran School Teacher 70

51 Mechanical Engineer   23 Physical Therapist   49 Lutheran Minister   Teacher   45

All Gifted   Both in Graduate School   Both College Graduates   m 1968   s 1990   Both Gifted

48 Ph.D. Chemical Engineer   46

Master's level Social Worker

m 1-22-66

23 Physical Therapist   D15 Prader-Willi Syndrome

24 Attends Law School   21 Senior in College   13 Gifted

when they start school; this corrects spontaneously by 9 years of age.

genu varum Bow legs; the distance between the knees is increased. Children are usually bowlegged when they first walk; knock-knee develops late in the preschool period.

geographic tongue Varying areas of smoothness and roughness on the tongue's surface, giving the impression of a map with contours suggesting land–sea boundaries. Although geographic tongue does occur as a minor dysmorphic (atypical) feature, it is most often a typical variant. Within a fairly short time period, the map's appearance can alter strikingly.

GER *See* gastroesophageal reflux.

German measles *See* rubella.

Gerstmann syndrome A neurological syndrome resulting from damage to the dominant parietal lobe and leading to the following signs: finger agnosia (inability to name the finger touched with eyes closed), dysgraphia (impaired writing), dyscalculia (impaired mathematics), and right–left and other spatial disorientation. The same constellation occurring in children without obvious brain injury is referred to as developmental Gerstmann syndrome; it accounts for a very small percentage of learning disability patterns in children.

Gesell, Arnold Lucius (1880–1961) A pediatrician and psychologist whose careful observational studies of infant and child development provided the basis for the maturational theory of development. Gesell originated the description of infant milestones along four major streams, and his infant testing procedures provided the basis for almost all later infant tests. *See also* maturational theory of development; infant milestones.

Gesell Developmental Schedules A standardized procedure to assess development in the areas of motor (gross and fine), adaptive (problem solving), language (ex-

pressive and receptive), and personal-social (self-help) functioning for children 4 weeks to 6 years of age. The independent assessment of these four areas allows the interpretation of dissociation between streams as well as global delay. Almost all existing infant (screening and diagnostic) tests have been adapted from the Gesell schedules.

gestalt A typical perceptual experience in which the whole is understood as something more than the sum of the parts. Furthermore, this gestalt may be perceived before the parts comprising it. Gestalt psychology formulated several laws of perceptual organization: first, the law of proximity, whereby visual elements tend to be grouped together if they are close to each other; second, the law of similarity, whereby elements will be grouped perceptually if they are similar to each other; third, the law of good continuation, whereby elements requiring the fewest changes, or interruptions—in straight or smooth, curving lines, or contours—will be grouped together; fourth, the law of closure, whereby missing parts of a figure are filled in to complete the figure; and fifth, the law of Pragnanz, whereby psychological organization will always be as "good" as prevailing conditions allow, where "good" describes a figure that is highly predictable from the parts that can be seen. When figures become complex or when labeling of incomplete visual or auditory stimuli is required, a similar configuration may be interpreted differently by different individuals based on past experience. The concept of closure is utilized by the Gestalt Closure subtest of the Kaufmann Assessment Battery for Children (K–ABC) and the Incomplete Words and Visual Closure subtests of the Woodcock-Johnson Psycho-Educational Battery–Revised (WJ–R). In each of these tests, the experiential factor is taken into consideration by allowing credit for diverse answers. In education, the term *gestalt* may be used to describe recognition of a word as a whole without analyzing it phonetically. Gestalt may also refer to grasping an overall concept without understanding the details relating to that concept. This pattern is frequently seen in children with learning disabilities who have sequential processing limitations.

gestalt

gestation Pregnancy; in humans the 40-week period (plus or minus 2 weeks) from conception to birth. A gestation period shorter than 38 weeks indicates prematurity, whereas one longer than 42 weeks indicates postmaturity.

gesture Movement of any part of the body to emphasize or express an idea, emotion, or function. The term does not include formalized symbolic methods of communication, such as fingerspelling, American Sign Language (ASL), or other forms of unaided augmentative communication. Gestures are an informal method of communication; their meanings are often concrete and facilitate learning, comprehension, and retention. Natural gestures can frequently be used and understood with minimal training. Gestures and facial expressions typically require less motor control than formal sign language systems. Though relatively easy to learn and use, information communicated solely through gestures is typically limited and constrained. Most often, gestures and facial expressions supplement other augmentative communication systems or are employed as a temporary method of communication. Amer-Ind is a comprehensive gestural system based on American Indian hand talk used for fundamental intertribal communication.

g factor Index of general mental ability or intelligence that largely represents the reasoning and abstracting aspects of mental ability, as opposed to lesser aspects of mental ability. Tests with high g loadings require complex mental effort, such as comprehension and hypothesis-testing tasks; tests with low g loadings require less-complex abilities and involve recall, recognition, and dexterity. There is general agreement that several distinct aspects of mental ability are correlated with each other, and that the correlation among the distinct factors represents a large general factor. However, this does not necessarily suggest that g is an actual entity. Thus, the disagreement regarding factor theories of intelligence now centers on which factor(s) is (are) most important—the multiple specific factors or the underlying general factor g.

G-FTA *See* Goldman-Fristoe Test of Articulation.

GFW *See* Goldman-Fristoe-Woodcock Test of Auditory Discrimination.

GFW–Battery *See* Goldman-Fristoe-Woodcock Auditory Skills Test Battery.

gibbus Extreme kyphosis (curvature of the spine); humpback.

Giemsa banding A staining technique that produces characteristic light and dark bands that are unique for each chromosome pair.

gifted Refers to superior ability and/or functioning in at least one specific area. PL 97-35, the Educational Consolidation and Improvement Act of 1938, defined the gifted as "children who give evidence of high performance capabilities in areas such as intellectual, creative, artistic, leadership capacity, or specific academic fields, and who require services or activities not normally provided by the school in order to fully develop such capabilities." Elsewhere, the concept of giftedness has been variously defined. Some definitions separate gifted children (those who have superior general intellectual ability) from talented (those who show signs of special aptitude or ability in a specific area of the arts, sciences, or business). Some conceptualizations also include high levels of task commitment, creativity, and a self-concept that recognizes and accepts special talents. Gifted learners occur in nearly every population of students with disabilities. One recently recognized group is gifted students with learning disabilities. Individuals in this specific group often go unrecognized or are mislabeled as "unmotivated." In addition to identification, programming for these students is challenging.

Gifted and Talented Children's Act of 1978
See Elementary and Secondary Education
Act Amendments of 1978 (PL 95-561).

Gilles de la Tourette syndrome A condition that starts in middle childhood with multifocal tics (usually facial) that progress to vocal tics, coughing and throat clearing, animal noises, echolalia (repetition of what is heard), and coprolalia (unprovoked obscene language). Attention-deficit/hyperactivity disorder (ADHD), learning disorders, sleep disturbances, and obsessive-compulsive traits such as self-mutilation are reported. Although a specific neurotransmitter abnormality has not been identified, the often dramatic eradication of symptoms by the drug haloperidol supports an organic disorder. The syndrome's relationship to the full spectrum of developmental disabilities remains unclear. About one third of cases are familial, with an autosomal dominant mode of inheritance. Named after the French neurologist Gilles de la Tourette (1855–1904).

Gillingham approach/reading method *See* Orton-Gillingham reading method.

Gillingham-Stillman reading method *See* Orton-Gillingham reading method.

gingival fibromatosis-hypertrichosis syndrome A genetic syndrome with generalized hypertrichosis (excessive amount of dark hair, including eyebrows and eyelashes), and gingival hyperplasia (overgrowth of gums). Inheritance is usually autosomal dominant; seizure disorders and mental retardation are more common in the sporadic (probably autosomal recessive) cases.

gingival hyperplasia Overgrowth of the gums; the two most common causes of gingival hyperplasia are acute leukemia and chronic Dilantin (diphenylhydantoin) drug treatment for seizure disorders.

glabellar tap A finger tap on the junction between the nose and the forehead (glabella) causes eyelid blinking. A nonspecific sign of neurological integrity in a newborn.

Glasgow Coma Scale A standardized quantitative scale to rate the ability of the person with neurological impairment to open eyes (*E*, scored 1–4), talk (*V*, scored 1–5), and move (*M*, scored 1–6); the total score is used to predict mortality and morbidity following a head injury. Low scores (below 8) indicate coma; high scores (above 8) rule out coma.

glass frustration An item on infant tests; a toy in which the child shows interest is placed behind a pane of clear glass, and the child's ability to obtain the toy by reaching around the glass is assessed. Success usually occurs at 13 months of age.

glaucoma A disorder of the eye in which increased pressure within the eye produces pain and varying degrees of loss of vision if left untreated.

glenohumeral joint Shoulder joint.

glossolalia Speaking in tongues; gibberish or jargoning in children; in adults, a psychiatric or religious phenomenon.

glossopharyngeal nerve The ninth cranial nerve; cranial nerve IX is responsible for taste at the back of the tongue, the gag reflex, and palatal elevation on phonation (sound production).

glutamic acid (Glu) A nonessential acid that also acts as a neurotransmitter in the brain; it is a frequent component in a variety of diets that are claimed to improve intelligence; there is no objective support for this claim.

GMFM *See* Gross Motor Function Measure.

GMQ *See* gross-motor quotient.

Goldenhar syndrome Goldenhar-Gorlin syndrome; first and second branchial arch syndrome; facioauriculovertebral dysplasia; a syndrome of extremely variable and asymmetric anomalies of structures embryologically derived from the branchial arches. Its dysmorphology (atypical features) spectrum includes hemifacial microsomia (one half of the face is smaller than the other half), microtia (small ear), hypoplasia (atypical tissue development)/ atresia of the ear canal and preauricular tags (with conductive [involving the middle and outer ear] hearing loss in 30% of cases), macrosomia (an apparent large mouth secondary to lateral clefts), cervical (neck) hemivertebrae, and occasional eye abnormalities. Mental retardation is uncommon (15% of cases). Cosmetic surgery is indicated in all but the mildest cases. Incidence is 1 in 5,000, with a male and a right-sided involvement preference. Recurrence risk is 2%.

Goldman-Fristoe Test of Articulation (G-FTA)   An articulation test for children 2–16 years of age that uses sounds in words, sounds in sentences, and stimulability.

Goldman-Fristoe-Woodcock Auditory Skills Test Battery (GFW–Battery)   Four 15-minute tests of auditory selective attention, diagnostic auditory discrimination, auditory memory, and sound–symbol association for people ages 3 years to adult.

Goldman-Fristoe-Woodcock Test of Auditory Discrimination (GFW)   A test of closed-set word identification in quiet and in noise for people 3 years of age and up.

goniometer   An instrument to measure angles, specifically goniometry (range of motion at a joint).

Goodenough-Harris Drawing Test (Draw-a-Man)   A drawing test for use in children 3 years of age and older; the results simultaneously reflect intelligence, graphomotor and perceptual-motor abilities, emotional state, and sex role identification, and must therefore be interpreted with caution. According to different versions of the test, the child may be asked to draw a person or to draw a man, or to draw a woman, and then to draw him- or herself; the resultant human figure drawings are scored by enumerating specific body parts and details; this score is then converted to a mental-age equivalent and a drawing quotient. The drawings can also be interpreted as projective expressions of the child's emotional state. Children with mental retardation who have often practiced figure drawings may pro-duce drawings that score well above their mental age; certain types of learning disabilities may produce peculiar simplifications or distortions in the resultant figure.

Goodman/Smith reading model   An approach to reading that views reading as a process of deriving meaning directly from print without the intermediary of oral language. Readers make use of syntactic (language structure), semantic (meaning systems), phonological (speech sounds), and morphological (word structure) cues, with errors viewed as a necessary constructive part of learning. This model interprets reading as a process that requires simultaneous processing on a variety of levels and does not advocate the splintering of reading into isolated skills such as drills, exercises, and games that divert children's attention from actually reading. Reading instruction should be meaningful, using a variety of materials to ensure that content is interesting and relevant.

Gordon Diagnostic System   A computerized continuous performance task (CPT) device that administers a 9-minute vigilance task.

Gordon sign   The stimulus of squeezing the calf produces the response of toe dorsiflexion (upgoing movement of the toes); this reflex is a variant of the Babinski sign as an index of pyramidal tract involvement.

Gorlin syndrome   A genetic syndrome with basal cell nevi (skin nodules that tend to become cancerous), mental retardation, broad facies, and rib abnormalities on X ray. Inheritance is autosomal dominant.

GORT–D   *See* Gray Oral Reading Tests–Diagnostic.

GORT–3   *See* Gray Oral Reading Tests–Third Edition.

Gowers sign   Getting up from the floor by climbing up one's own body; a finding characteristic of the muscle weakness typical of muscular dystrophy.

Grace Arthur Performance Scale   A nonverbal IQ test; an adaptation of the Leiter

International Performance Scale for deaf children.

grade-equivalent scores A score derived by determining the average score obtained on a test by children in various grades, expressed in tenths of a grade. For example, if the average raw score for children in fourth grade were 30, that would correspond to a grade equivalent of 4.0. The difference in the raw score between 4.0 and 5.0 is then arbitrarily divided into tenths, with each tenth corresponding to a grade equivalent of 0.1. For instance, if the average raw score for fourth grade were 30 and the average raw score for the fifth grade were 50, then a raw score of 32 would equal a grade equivalent of 4.1; 34 = 4.2; 36 = 4.3; and so forth. Grade equivalents must be interpreted with care. A second-grader who obtains a grade equivalent of 4.1 in arithmetic shares with the average fourth-grader only the numbers right on the test (a score of 32), and should not be assumed to possess other attributes of fourth-grade mathematical ability.

grand mal seizure *See* generalized seizure.

grapheme The written symbol for a phoneme. Graphemes are composed of the letters of the alphabet and their combinations. For example, the graphemes "*t*" and "*sh*" each represent a single phoneme. There are 251 graphemes that represent 44 phonemes (thus, some graphemes represent more than one phoneme). For example, the grapheme "*g*" is used in "gate" to represent the hard "*g*" and in "gem" to represent the soft "*g*."

graphomotor Pertaining to writing or drawing.

grasp reflex An infantile reflex in which the tactile (touch) stimulus to the palm or sole produces the response of tonic (increased muscle tone) flexion of all the digits. Both the palmar (hand) and plantar (foot) grasp reflexes are present at birth. The palmar grasp disappears by around 3 months of age, to be replaced by a voluntary grasp. The plantar grasp persists until 9 or 10 months of age and is one of the last primitive reflexes to disappear before the onset of independent walking. Stages in the development of the voluntary grasp include ulnar rake, radial rake, scissors grasp, and immature and mature pincer; many classification systems describe this evolution.

gravida A pregnant woman. Followed by a Roman numeral, the term refers to the number of pregnancies regardless of duration (gravida III describes a woman who has been pregnant three times). Whereas *gravida* refers to the number of pregnancies, *para* refers to the number of deliveries; thus "gravida 4, para 3" suggests that a mother is currently pregnant with her fourth child.

gravitational insecurity Abnormal anxiety or distress that arises when the gravity receptors of the vestibular (balance) system are stimulated by head position or movement, especially when the child's feet are not on the ground.

gray matter Areas of the central nervous system (CNS) that contain the neurons (nerve cells). The cerebral cortex has a layer of gray matter. Gray matter diseases, such as Tay-Sachs disease, generally damage or destroy the nerve cell itself.

gray matter disease A group of degenerative diseases of the central nervous system (CNS) in which cognitive deterioration, convulsions, and visual (eye) impairment associated with retinal changes occur early in the course of the disorder; motor findings, such as spasticity (increased muscle tone), occur late. (Brain gray matter regulates thought; white matter, motor activity). Most storage diseases (e.g., Tay-Sachs, Fabry, Niemann-Pick) are gray matter diseases.

Gray Oral Reading Tests–Diagnostic (GORT–D) A test for children in kindergarten through grade six who have trouble reading print. The first subtest requires the student to respond to comprehension questions relating to orally read passages. Poor performance on this subtest leads to the administration of remaining subtests: decoding, word identification, word attack, morphemic analysis, contextual analysis, and word ordering.

Gray Oral Reading Tests–Third Edition (GORT-3) A measure of oral reading performance in children 7-0 to 18-11 years of age. Standard scores are reported for Passage Score and Oral Reading Comprehension (with a mean of 10 and a standard deviation of 3), as well as total Oral Reading Comprehension (with a mean of 100 and a standard deviation of 15). The GORT-3 also provides a system for miscue analysis that yields information in four areas: meaning similarity, function similarity, graphic/phonemic similarity, and self-correction. There are two alternate equivalent forms with 13 developmentally sequenced passages, each with five comprehension questions.

Greig syndrome A genetic syndrome with macrocephaly (enlarged head circumference), a high forehead, frontal bossing (swelling), hypertelorism (widely spaced eyes), syndactyly (webbing of the fingers or toes), polydactyly (extra fingers or toes), and occasional mild mental retardation. Inheritance is autosomal dominant. Named after the Scottish surgeon, David Greig (1864–1936)

Grice procedure The use of the tibial (calf bone) bone graft to perform a subtalar arthrodesis (surgical immobilization below the ankle) to treat valgus (outward) foot deformity. Also known as the Grice-Green procedure.

grief Deep and lingering sadness in response to an important loss. Grief, even when intense, can be a normal reaction with predictable stages and behaviors; presentation varies with individuals and different cultures. Failure to grieve after an important loss is more unhealthy than is acute, deep grief. Parents of a child with developmental disabilities experience an initial grief process when first realizing their child has such a disability. Moreover, these parents often face the grief process again with each new developmental stage, such as when their child starts school, adolescence, and at the transition to adulthood. This recurrent grief process, although unique to parents of children with developmental disabilities, is in no way abnormal and should be confronted only when the process gets stuck and prevents the parent from acting in the child's best interest.

Griffiths Mental Development Scale An intelligence test for babies and young children. There are two versions: birth to 2 years and 2–8 years. The tests are based on the Gesell schedules and yield a general quotient and subscores in six domains: locomotor, personal-social, hearing and speech, eye and hand coordination, performance, and (after 3 years of age) practical reasoning.

Gross Motor Function Measure (GMFM) A criterion-referenced motor scale for children with cerebral palsy that assesses motor abilities and progress.

gross-motor quotient (GMQ) Ratio of gross-motor age to age in months of expected motor milestone achievement for chronological age multiplied by 100, where motor age is the normal age of attainment of the most advanced motor milestone. It is important to note that: 1) neither numerator nor denominator is chronological age, and 2) full correction for prematurity is made when estimating the denominator. GMQs below 45 suggest cerebral palsy; GMQs between 45 and 70 suggest apraxia (inability to perform purposeful movements) or clumsiness; GMQs above 70 are compatible with normal motor development.

gross-motor skills Posture and locomotion skills. Early gross-motor skills, such as rolling over, sitting, crawling, walking, and running, seem to be heavily maturational (determined almost exclusively by the preprogrammed myelinization of the central nervous system). Later gross-motor skills, such as swimming, bicycle riding, and certain other athletic abilities, have an increasingly larger environmental or learned component. Gross-motor abilities have little relationship to general intelligence.

group B streptococcal (GBS) infection A severe infection with a specific bacterial strain; in newborns with this infection, there is a 50% mortality rate in the first few days of life; when the onset is after 1 week of age, there is a 25% mortality rate. GBS meningitis (inflammation of the spinal cord and brain membranes) has a high incidence of neurological sequelae, such as severe mental retardation, blindness, deafness, seizures, and spastic cerebral palsy.

group home A residence licensed by the state for persons with mental retardation, other developmental disabilities, and certain mental illnesses. Persons in group homes use the special education, day care, and vocational facilities in the community. Placement in the home may be transitional or permanent. A group home provides its residents with training in independent living skills commensurate with their abilities. The home is supervised by individuals who can live in the home or within close proximity to it. The group home environment serves to foster an approximation of nondisabled living arrangements, encouraging shared responsibility and cooperative social interaction. Group homes must adhere to guidelines established by the Developmental Disabilities Administration of the U.S. Department of Health and Human Services to qualify for federal assistance. The structure may be owned, leased, or part of a larger facility for individuals with disabilities.

growing pains Intermittent mild aches in the leg muscles that occur in approximately 15% of children (girls more frequently than boys); in the presence of headache and stomachache, the possibility of psychosomatic or somaticizing disorder should be considered. A detailed family history can be helpful in the differential diagnosis.

growth Progressive development toward the mature adult; the process includes increasing size, changing proportions, and physiological maturation. Growth rates for individuals and for specific organ systems show variability, accelerations, and plateaus in a complex interactional pattern. Disturbances in either excess or deficiency of growth can reflect either environmental or genetic and metabolic factors; depending on the specific cause of a problem in growth, development may also be involved.

GSR *See* galvanic skin response.

guard Position of upper extremities during walking; the guard position evolves from a high arm position in early walking through a middle to low arm position seen in mature walking.

high

guardian ad litem (GAL) A legal representative to protect the child's interests in legal proceedings and a guardian to protect the child's long-range interests. PL 93-247 (the Child Abuse Prevention and Treatment Act of 1974) mandated GALs for abused and neglected children.

low

guard

guardianship The care and legal responsibility that a mature adult assumes for a person with a disability (e.g., mental retardation, mental illness) with respect to the individual's physical (as in consenting to surgery) and contractual or fiscal affairs. In individual cases, the level of supervision and decision-making responsibility is specified and tailored to be compatible with the needs and abilities of the person with a disability. Thus, guardianship can be limited to only certain aspects of an individual's life, or it may cover all aspects.

gustatory Relating to the sense of taste.

Guthrie test A microbiological inhibition assay (specialized laboratory test) for phenylalanine (an essential amino acid). The amount of phenylalanine present in blood proportionately inhibits the growth of a specific microorganism (virus, bacterium, fungus). This test is the basis for newborn screening for phenylketonuria (PKU), one of a number of causes of hyperphenylalaninemia (increased phenylalanine in the blood).

gyrus A convolution on the surface of the brain. These are numbered, and many are named for their specific functional associations.

H

habilitation The provision of medical, psychological, educational, and family services to children with disabilities, in order to maximize these children's vocational, mental, physical, and social abilities and to allow them to function as independently as possible. Although the term *adult rehabilitation* refers to the recovery of abilities lost, *pediatric habilitation* connotes the development of abilities not previously mastered. The importance of the distinction lies in the differences in instructional techniques and individual motivation dealing with an adult who may remember having achieved a particular goal in the past, compared to a child who has no such experience on which to rely.

habit spasm *See* tic.

habituation Decreased response to a repeated stimulus that is not due to sensory adaptation or fatigue. Increased or decreased habituation may occur in mental retardation and syndromes involving brain damage. Rapidity or failure of habituation is a component of many infant cognitive assessments.

habitus The physical characteristics of a person that are indicative of constitutional tendencies, disposition to (or presence of) disease, or personality traits. Habitus can include facies, somatotype, gait, and other movement patterns. With dysmorphology (atypical features) and physical signs, habitus is one of the major components of visual diagnosis, an approach important in pediatrics because patients often cannot otherwise communicate their concerns.

Haemophilus [also Hemophilus] influenzae (Hib) Also known as "H flu." A common cause of bacterial infections (e.g.,

otitis, pneumonia, meningitis [inflammation of the spinal cord and brain membranes]) in children under 5 years of age.

Haeussermann developmental evaluation An approach to the psychoeducational and developmental evaluation of preschool children that utilizes techniques from an individualized assessment of children with cerebral palsy. Motor and sensory disabilities are bypassed in this nonstandardized clinical assessment; 41 test items tap five areas: physical functioning and sensory status, perceptual functioning, competence in learning for short-term retention, language competence, and cognitive functioning. This method represents a pioneering approach to an assessment for educational intervention purposes.

hair whorl The spiral pattern generated by the hair follicles of the scalp. Variations on the single clockwise posterior (back) hair whorl are minor dysmorphic (atypical appearance) features;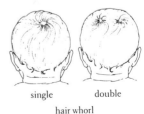

single   double
hair whorl

these include poorly defined, double, and counterclockwise versions.

Haldol *See* haloperidol.

Hall facies The disproportion of forehead to face seen in hydrocephalus (excess fluid in the brain). Marshall Hall (1790–1857) was an English physician who first described this hydrocephalic facies.

Hallermann-Streiff syndrome Hallermann-Streiff-François syndrome; oculomandibulodyscephaly (malformation of the face, especially the lower jawbone and eyes) with hypotrichosis (hair deficiency). A dysmorphic (atypical appearance) syndrome with oculo (eye) findings: microphthalmia (small eyes) and congenital cataracts; mandibulo (jaw) findings: small jaw producing a "double" cutaneous chin with central dimple or cleft and contributing to a parrot nose appearance; dyscephaly: brachycephaly with frontal and parietal bossing (swelling); and hypotrichosis: thin, fine, scant hair. About one in seven cases exhibits mental retardation. Inheritance pattern remains unclear.

hallux   Big toe.

haloperidol   Trade name Haldol; an antipsychotic neuroleptic (major tranquilizer) drug. A butyrophenone, used to treat Gilles de la Tourette syndrome and severe behavior problems in children; it can cause severe extrapyramidal symptoms.

Halstead-Reitan Neuropsychological Test Battery for Older Children   An adaptation of the Halstead-Reitan adult battery to children 9–14 years of age. The battery is composed of 45 subtests grouped under such categories as motor, sensory-perceptual, visual-spatial, alertness and concentration, memory, abstract reasoning and logical analysis, right–left differences, and dysphasia. The simultaneous administration of a Wechsler Intelligence Scale is required to interpret the results and to calculate the Neuropsychological Deficit Scale (NDS) score, a number that estimates the total battery's estimated misclassification of an individual as having brain damage.

hamstrings   The tendons of the calf muscles.

hand regard   A fairly transient behavior observed briefly in children in the first 6 months of life. The infant stares at or through his or her nearly immobile hands. There is little or no touching of the hands and a minimum of movement (mostly slow, stereotyped, and rotatory—

alternating pronation and supination). When prolonged, prominent, or occurring at a later age, this behavior is deviant and may reflect autism, profound deprivation, or mental retardation.

handedness   The tendency to use one hand in preference to the other for activities including writing, eating, and throwing. Predominant use of the left hand is called *sinistrality,* and of the right hand, *dextrality.* A tendency toward a right- or left-handed preference emerges late in the first year but is not usually fully dominant until close to 2 years of age. Strong hand preference prior to 1 year of age suggests motor impairment (e.g., hemiplegia [paralysis of half the body]) of the other side of the body. Failure of handedness to appear by 2 years of age may reflect global cognitive delay (mental retardation), mild motor incoordination, a language disorder, or a learning disability.

handicap   A disadvantage for a given individual resulting from an impairment or disability that limits or prevents the fulfillment of a role that would otherwise be normal for the individual. The term *handicap* is concerned with the value attached to an individual's situation or experience when it departs from the norm. It is characterized by a discordance between the individual's performance or status and his or her personal expectations or the expectations of the group to which he or she belongs. Handicap thus represents the socialization of an impairment or disability and the consequences for an individual. The term *handicap* is often inaccurately used as a synonym for *disability.* People with or without disabilities may have a societal standard or condition imposed upon them. Except when citing laws or regulations, the term *handicap* should not be used to describe a disability.

Handicapped Children's Protection Act of 1986 (PL 99-372)   An amendment to the Education of the Handicapped Act to allow parents who prevail in due process administrative hearings or court actions to be reimbursed for reasonable attorney's fees and other costs of preparing for the proceeding concerning their child's right to a free appropriate public special education and related services.

haptic   Tactile; relating to touch.

Haptic Intelligence Scale for the Adult Blind (HISab)   An adaptation of the Wechsler Adult Intelligence Scale that may be used with adolescents who are blind.

hard neurological sign   A neurological finding that can be interpreted as physiological or pathological, relatively independently of the individual's age. Hard signs contribute to the localization of brain lesions.

hard of hearing   Degrees of hearing loss that may be significantly improved with amplification (hearing aid). Although there is reduced hearing activity and sensitivity of the ears to sound, the ability to communicate orally is generally maintained.

Harrington distraction rod An orthopedic surgery procedure that implants a metal rod into the vertebral column to correct scoliosis (spinal curvature); sometimes combined with a Luque rod.

Harrington distraction rod

Hartford Scale of Clinical Indicators of Cerebral Dysfunction in Child Psychiatric Patients   A 30-item measure of cerebral dysfunction in children 2–17 years of age. The scale is divided into three sections: 1) symptoms and signs related to impulsivity or direct aggression, 2) symptoms and signs related to compensatory adjustments against impulsivity or aggression, and 3) items from the individual's early history. Items are rated present or absent on the basis of clinical interviews with the parents, child, and family, as well as medical or school records. The higher the

score (more than 7 or 8 items present), the greater the likelihood that cerebral dysfunction is present in the child.

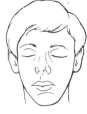

hatchet face   A profile produced by atrophy (wasting) of facial muscles; found in myotonic dystrophy.

hatchet face

Hawaii Early Learning Profile (HELP)   An assessment instrument for birth to 3 years of age that covers six developmental areas encompassing 650 skills: cognitive (with receptive language), expressive language, fine motor, gross motor, social, and self-help. A sequenced checklist can be used to select objectives. The assessment component is keyed to a variety of intervention curricula and approaches.

Hayes-Binet   A dated adaptation of the Stanford-Binet Intelligence Scale for people ages 2 years to adult who are blind.

head lag   Inability of the head to keep up with the trunk when the baby is pulled to sitting; some degree of head lag may be observed up to 4 months of age. A frequent finding in the presence of hypotonia (decreased muscle tone) and motor disorders associated with hypotonia. Most types of cerebral palsy include

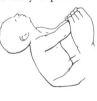

head lag

an early phase of hypotonia, even though they later exhibit hypertonia (increased muscle tone), so head lag may be observed even in children who are later diagnosed with spastic or rigid types of cerebral palsy.

head retraction   A physical sign in infancy that reflects 1) part of a tonic labyrinthine posture (extension of all four extremities [arms or legs]), 2) a respiratory disorder, or 3) part of a transient extensor posture observed in preterm infants.

Head Start   A national program providing enriched early childhood education for children of low-income families. Established in 1965, Head Start's goals include meeting the developmental and educational needs of young children and increasing the likelihood of later school success. The program also provides a range of additional services designed to help meet health, nutrition, and social needs. In 1972, Head Start legislation was amended to include children with disabilities; of the total Head Start enrollment, 10% is reserved for children with disabilities. The inclusion of children with developmental disabilities in Head Start programs emphasizes the need for screening, diagnosis, and individualized program planning. Better grades, fewer grade retentions, limited and more effective use of subsequent special education services, and greater likelihood of completing high school and continuing education are some of the reported positive effects of preschool participation. Most research has examined the impact of early childhood education on children at risk due to economic or educational disadvantage. More recent investigations of early intervention efforts with general populations of parents and young children have shown gains for these children and their families as well.

hearing aid An electronic device that amplifies sound coming to the wearer's ear. The device consists of a microphone, amplifier, and receiver that can route sound for air conduction (to one or both middle ears) or for bone conduction (to the bone of the skull) to augment the amount of sound stimulating the eighth cranial nerve. Hearing aids amplify all sound or only those frequencies (pitches) that are lost (such as in high-frequency hearing loss).

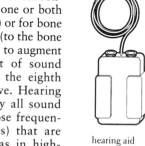

hearing aid

The components of the hearing aid can be placed in a variety of locations to enhance volume, improve directionality of sound, and balance sound between the ears.

hearing impairment Loss of auditory ability ranging in degree from slight to profound. Hearing impairments are generally categorized as conductive (involving the middle and outer ear) or sensorineural (involving the inner ear or the auditory nerve). Hearing impairment can also be classified as congenital (existing at or dating from birth), prelingual (occurring before the development of speech and language skills), and postlingual (occurring after the development of speech and language skills).

hearing impairment degrees The six categories used to identify the level of auditory loss: slight (15–25 decibels [dB]), mild (26–40 dB), moderate (41–55 dB), moderately severe (56–70 dB), severe (71–90 dB), and profound (more than 91 dB). Each category has its own characteristics and indicates the disability most likely to result from such a loss.

hearing loss Any level of auditory impairment ranging from slight difficulty to profound inability to hear. *See also* hearing impairment degrees.

heart disease, cyanotic Heart disease of a type to produce some peripheral cyanosis (blue color) of the fingernails or lips. When such heart disease is not associated with a syndrome that also involves the central nervous system, it does not necessarily affect development. Poor oxygenation leading to cyanosis can, however, slow motor development. In young children, the amount of energy expended combatting hypotonia (decreased muscle tone) can lead to difficulty with breathing, which interferes with the quantity of expressive language. Motor-dependent infant tests tend to underestimate IQ in preoperative cyanotic heart disease.

heart rate response audiometry (HRRA) The use of changes in heart rate on electrocardiogram (EKG) to assess hearing thresholds.

heel cord *See* Achilles tendon.

heel cord lengthening *See* tendo Achilles lengthening (TAL).

HEENT An acronym for head, eyes, ears, nose, and throat; shorthand used in reporting findings on medical examination; an arbitrary grouping.

Helen Keller International An organization founded in 1915 to assist governments and agencies in developing countries with the prevention and treatment of eye disease and with the education and rehabilitation of persons with visual impairment. The organization offers training for teachers and health care workers, with a focus on prevention of eye diseases. Volunteers are also instructed in counseling families of infants who are blind. Helen Keller International collects and compiles data on blindness throughout the world and publishes a newsletter, fact sheets, and other educational materials.

heliotrichous Helical or spiral hair as found in the black populations.

helix The shape of a spiral or coil, such as the ridges of the ear or the molecular structure of the gene.

helix

HELP *See* Hawaii Early Learning Profile.

hematocrit The volume percentage of cells (solids) to whole blood (cells [solids] and plasma [liquid]). A low hematocrit is one indication of anemia.

hemianesthesia Decreased to absent sensation on one side of the body; frequently accompanies hemianopsia (blindness for half the field of vision) and hemiatrophy (decreased growth and development on one side of the body) in hemiplegic cerebral palsy.

hemianopsia Visual field cut; loss of vision for one half of the visual field. In a child with a left hemiplegic cerebral palsy, the motor control centers in the right brain are damaged. If that injury extends to the right occipital region, the child may have a cut in the left visual field and not perceive objects coming from the left side. The measurement of visual field (by perimetry) is difficult in young children, but the possibility of a hemianopsia should be suspected in cases of hemiplegic cerebral palsy with hemiatrophy (decreased growth and development on one side of the body) and hemianesthesia (decreased or absent sensation on one side of the body), especially if the child constantly tilts the head to one side. The degree of visual impairment is rarely significant, but may need to be considered in selecting alternate communication devices such as communication boards.

hemiatrophy Undergrowth of one side of the body. Although this can be associated with several rare syndromes (e.g., Russell-Silver syndrome), it is more typically found on the involved side in a hemiplegic cerebral palsy. The presence of this unilateral growth disturbance also acts as a marker for such associated deficits as hemianopsia (blindness for half the field of vision) and hemianesthesia (decreased or absent sensation on one side of the body).

hemiballismus *See* ballismus.

hemihypertrophy Enlargement of the limbs on one side of the body; can occur in a number of syndromes, such as Russell-Silver, Klippel-Trenaunay-Weber, Beckwith-Wiedemann, chondrodysplasia punctata, and Wilms' tumor (a malignancy of the kidney).

hemiplegia Literally, "half palsy"; a topographical type of spastic cerebral palsy in which one side of the body (the arm more than the leg) is motorically involved, while the other is spared. The prognosis for independent ambulation is excellent. People with hemiplegia frequently have normal intelligence, learning disabilities, seizures, and hemiatrophy (decreased growth and development on one side of the body) and hemianesthesia (decreased or absent sensation on one side of the body) on the involved side. Hemianopsia (blindness for half the field of vision) can be present ipsilaterally to (on the same side as) the motor impairment. Seizure disorders are of such high frequency that they should be closely monitored for the first decade of life. Right hemiplegia is more common than left hemiplegia. *Double hemiplegia* refers to a quadriplegia in which both arms are more involved than both legs.

hemisphere In reference to the brain, one of the two halves (right and left). The left hemisphere is responsible for the comprehension and production of language, whereas the right side controls nonverbal, spatial, and visual tasks. Damage to the left side of the brain may result in aphasia (loss of language skills) or a language problem.

hemisyndrome Any asymmetry of movement, posture, or motor behavior. A hemisyndrome is present in hemiplegic cerebral palsy, but milder asymmetries may be associated with disorders of learning, behavior, and temperament.

hemorrhage Bleeding; loss of blood.

hepatic Relating to the hepar (liver).

hepatolenticular degeneration *See* Wilson disease.

hepatosplenomegaly Pathological enlargement of the liver and the spleen; a common finding in metabolic storage disorders such as mucopolysaccharidoses and Gaucher disease.

heredodegenerative diseases A grouping of diseases that are familial and degenerative in nature. The degeneration is chronic and progressive, resulting in worsening function and often loss of function. These diseases are generally grouped by the area of the brain that is affected and thus determines the functional insult. This can occur in the basal ganglia, for example, causing gait disturbances, tremors, and rigidity without intellectual deterioration such as is found in juvenile paralysis agitans, or juvenile Parkinsonism. In other degenerative disorders, such as Hallervorden-Spatz syndrome, intellectual deterioration occurs with motor findings such as limb stiffness. Another example is Huntington chorea. The pattern of inheritance of these disor-

ders varies. The underlying biochemical abnormalities are under investigation.

heritability A statistical measurement of the degree to which a trait is genetically determined. This is generally used to determine the amount of impact the genes have as compared to environmental factors such as toxins (poisons).

Hermansky-Pudlak syndrome A genetic syndrome with partial albinism (contributing to reduced visual acuity) and a bleeding disorder. Inheritance is autosomal recessive.

hernia Abnormal protrusion of part of an organ.

herniorrhaphy The surgical repair (closing) of a hernia.

herpes simplex virus A DNA (deoxyribonucleic acid) virus group that can produce herpetic skin lesions, meningoencephalitis, and a congenital infection syndrome. One of the sexually transmitted viruses, herpes simplex is to be distinguished from herpes zoster, the virus that causes "cold sores."

hertz A unit of vibration; the frequency of one cycle per second (CPS), named after the German physicist, Heinrich R. Hertz (1857–1894).

heterochromia irides Eyes of two different colors in the same individual; *see also* Waardenburg syndrome.

heterocyclic antidepressants A class of drugs that includes tricyclic antidepressants, trazodone (trade name, Desyrel), and maprotiline (trade name, Ludiomil). These antidepressants are mood normalizers and are not habit forming.

heterodisomy Isodisomy; a condition in which an individual receives two copies of a chromosome from one parent and none from the other. This can result in a loss of the effects of imprinting (the differences in chromosomes from different-sex parents) and can cause genetic disorders such as Prader-Willi syndrome.

heterogeneity The situation in syndromology (the identification of genetic and other syndromes) when multiple genetic causes produce the same effect. The identification of separate genetic causes for the same phenotype (appearance) is the result of a process of "splitting." For instance, the phenotype Marfanoid habitus can be caused by Marfan syndrome, homocystinuria, and several other syndromes. Most malformation patterns, referred to as *sequences*, have multiple pathogenetic etiologies (causes).

heterogeneous grouping In reference to an educational setting, placing students representing a range of characteristics (e.g., ability or age levels) together for instruction.

heterotopia Islands of gray matter in the white matter of the brain. Found commonly with other abnormalities of neuronal (gray matter) migration, such as lissencephaly (smooth, rather than convoluted, brain surface) or micropolygyria (an increased number of smaller ridgings on the brain surface). Most migration abnormalities result in mental retardation, motor findings of spasticity or hypotonia (decreased muscle tone), and seizures. Heterotopia can be found in the brains of children with myelomeningocele (protuberance of both the spinal cord and its lining).

heterotopy Sound displacement during speech, involving transposition and reversal of letters and phonemes; it is a characteristic of cluttered speech: example: "filp" for "flip."

heterozygote An individual with different genes for the same trait.

heuristic Rule or algorithm.

H flu *See* Haemophilus influenzae.

HFV *See* high-frequency ventilation.

HHE syndrome Hemiplegia (paralysis of half the body), hemiconvulsion, and epilepsy syndrome with a characteristic frontotemporal, spike slow wave electroencephalographic (EEG) pattern; a complication of acute hemiplegia with febrile (feverish) illness.

HHHO syndrome *See* Prader-Willi syndrome.

hiatal hernia The protrusion of some part of the stomach above the diaphragm. This contributes to acid reflux and chest pain.

hiatal hernia

Hib *See* Haemophilus influenzae.

HIE *See* hypoxic-ischemic encephalopathy.

high arched palate *See* palate.

high arched palate

high-frequency ventilation (HFV) A type of mechanical ventilation that uses high rates (e.g., more than 900 breaths per minute) with very low tidal volumes. There are several variations of HFV.

hip abduction deformity *See* frog posture.

hip adduction deformity Positioning of the thigh closer to (or across) the midline. This deformity both leads to and results from hip dislocation or subluxation. Bilateral hip adduction deformity produces scissoring; this deformity is common in spastic cerebral palsy.

hip-knee-ankle-foot orthosis (HKAFO) An orthosis that both supports and to some degree limits the entire lower extremity.

hippotherapy Therapeutic horsemanship; the use of horseback riding as a treatment modality to enhance self-esteem and broaden experience in children with disabilities.

hippus Rhythmic dilation (enlargement) and constriction of the pupils.

Hirschberg test Corneal light reflex test; a screening test for strabismus (squint) in which the examiner shines a light and observes its reflection in the child's pupils. If the eyes are both straight, the reflection is at the same o'clock in each eye. An in-turned eye displaces the light laterally, whereas an out-turned eye displaces it medially.

Hirschsprung disease Aganglionic mega-colon, congenital megacolon; functional obstruction of the rectum or colon. A congenital absence of the nerve supply to the lower colon causes an absence of peri-stalsis (wavelike muscular contractions that propel food and waste along the gas-trointestinal tract) that results in a mas-sive enlargement of the colon, constipa-tion, and obstruction. Treatment is in two stages: 1) a temporary colostomy, fol-lowed by 2) colonic resection of the in-volved segment. Infants with Down syn-drome have an above-average (tenfold increased) incidence of Hirschsprung dis-ease. Several other syndromes have an in-creased incidence of the disorder, and it is also associated with a variety of urogeni-tal abnormalities. Named after the Dan-ish pediatrician, Harold Hirschsprung (1830–1916).

hirsutism A nonspecific condition of excessive facial or body hair. The cause may be familial, endocrine, pharmaco-logical (e.g., after prolonged anticonvul-sant usage), or genetic (part of a specific syndrome).

HISab *See* Haptic Intelligence Scale for the Adult Blind.

Hiskey-Nebraska Test of Learning Apti-tudes An intelligence test for deaf chil-dren ages 3–16 years.

histidinemia A disorder of amino acid metabolism with high blood levels of his-tidine; an autosomal recessive condition not associated with any disability. In the past, this disorder was considered an etio-logical factor in language disorders, but this association has been disproven.

HIV-1 *See* human immunodeficiency virus, type 1.

HKAFO *See* hip-knee-ankle-foot orthosis.

HMD Hyaline membrane disease. *See* respiratory distress syndrome.

hockey stick crease A palmar crease variant in which the distal trans-verse crease abruptly exits between the sec-ond and third fingers.

hockey stick crease

Hoffmann sign The stimulus of sudden ex-tension of the middle finger whereby flicking or snapping the nail of that finger produces a flexion re-sponse of the thumb and index finger; a sign of pyramidal tract involvement.

holistic learning An approach to learning in which variables are not broken down into their component parts but are exam-ined in the context in which they occur. Rather than focusing on a specific and of-ten arbitrary sequence of skills aimed at the remediation of impairments, propo-nents of the holistic approach advocate a language-rich environment wherein the fundamental purpose of language (read-ing, writing, speaking, and listening) is the communication of meaning. Teaching and learning are viewed as an interactive process, with the form of language seen as a tool to be refined in order to enhance meaning, rather than as a goal in itself. Proponents suggest that this is particu-larly beneficial to students with learning disabilities, whose cognitive variability often precludes a sequential approach to a task and whose conceptual skills are of-ten far ahead of their mechanical skills. Critics suggest that this approach does not sufficiently stress direct instruction in skills not readily assimilated by students with learning disabilities.

holistic medicine Wholistic medicine; a vague catchword that indiscriminately connotes either or both of two attitudes toward traditional medicine: 1) a critique of scientific medicine as too exclusively focused on the disease, on technology, and on pathology (origin), rather than on the whole person, on health, or pre-vention; or 2) an espousal of a variety of naturopathic, shamanistic, homeopathic, vitamin and health food, and psychic and metaphysical regimens as self-help ap-proaches to health (especially as part of "new age" mysticism). Because of the confusion often deliberately fostered by the term *holistic*, its usage should be abandoned, and whenever used, it should be considered suspect.

holophrastic speech The use by young children of single words to express complete sentences. For example: "Cookie" for "I want a cookie," or "Out" for "Let me out of this stroller."

Holter Pudenz valve A valve that allows unidirectional flow of cerebrospinal fluid in a shunt tube going from the brain to the atrium (heart) or peritoneum (abdomen) in the treatment of hydrocephalus (excess fluid in the brain).

HOME *See* Home Observation for Measurement of the Environment.

home-based programs Intervention that occurs in the child's home that focuses attention on the parent–child relationship and on the natural support systems of the family in order to strengthen family awareness of, and involvement with, the child. Services can be of many types, including those of a medical (physical/occupational therapy), educational (sensory and cognitive stimulation), and preventive (nutritional counseling, visiting nurse consultation) nature. In addition to the prescribed treatment, a goal of in-home intervention is to foster and maximize opportunities within the home to enhance intellectual, social, and emotional development. Home-based intervention is most often used with children from birth to 3 years of age.

home health The provision of supportive medical services in the recipient's own home. Such services may include dressing care, feeding, intravenous (IV) care, physical therapy, respiratory therapy, nursing, dialysis, bathing, and other health-related services.

Home Observation for Measurement of the Environment (HOME) An inventory of the home to quantitate the presence of toys, games, books, language stimulation, the physical environment, nurturance, academic goals, and modeling of social maturity and physical punishment as they relate to infants and preschoolers (one form for birth to 3 years of age, another for 3–6 years of age). The validity of this instrument is limited by the failure to include some measure of the impact of social desirability on the item answer/interpretation.

home school In terms of disabilities, the element of inclusion that requires all students with disabilities to receive their education at the educational facility associated with their residence.

Home Screening Questionnaire (HSQ) A component of the Denver Developmental Screening Test battery. A parent-answered instrument in two forms, blue for birth to 3 years of age, and white for 3–6 years of age.

homebound instruction The provision of educational services for a student in his or her home due to illness, physical injury, or emotional condition. A child is eligible for homebound instruction, to be provided by a visiting or itinerant teacher, when school attendance is made impossible by the preceding conditions. Mandated by PL 101-476, the Individuals with Disabilities Education Act of 1990, homebound instruction is categorized as one of the most restrictive alternatives in a continuum of services, and is to be considered a temporary measure whenever possible.

homemaker services Social or health services to support and help maintain persons with physical or cognitive disabilities in their own homes. Such services may include shopping, budgeting, cleaning, meal planning and preparation, in-home adaptive modifications, and assisting in communication or transportation with other agencies and services. The effort is to provide services in the homes of persons with disabilities, rather than moving them to long-term care facilities.

homeostasis Tendency of biological and other systems to remain internally constant despite interacting with a changing external environment.

homocystinuria A genetic inborn error of metabolism producing increased homocystine in the blood and urine. The habitus (physical appearance) is similar to that seen in Marfan syndrome, with a tall, thin stature, a malar (cheekbone) flush, and arachnodactyly (long, thin fingers and toes), except that the ectopia lentis (lens dislocation) is downward in homocystinuria and upward in Marfan syndrome. Osteoporosis (thinning of the bones), mental retardation (in 50% of cases), and a shuffling ("Charlie Chaplin") gait can be present. Inheritance is autosomal recessive, and the incidence is more common in people of Irish descent. The disorder can be responsive to pyridoxine (vitamin B$_6$) or a special diet.

homolateral limb synkinesis A mutual dependency between the synergies of the affected upper and lower limbs, so that, for example, arm flexion evokes leg flexion.

hospitalism A behavioral syndrome characterized by delays in mental and physical development, apathy, and waxy immobility that occurs when an infant is separated from the mother or primary caregiver. If the situation is prolonged (institutionalization) or includes frequent and recurrent infections, cachexia (general weight loss) and death may occur. To a milder degree, some form of hospitalism is common in infants and young children admitted to the hospital. Although the effects can be ameliorated by parental rooming-in and other techniques, hospitals are not appropriate settings for the cognitive and behavioral development of very young children.

House-Tree-Person Test A projective test that requires children 5 years of age and older to draw and then interpret a house, a tree, and a person (in that order).

HRRA *See* heart rate response audiometry.

HSQ *See* Home Screening Questionnaire.

human immunodeficiency virus, type 1 (HIV-1) The human retrovirus (a class of RNA viruses) that causes acquired immunodeficiency syndrome.

humerus Upper arm bone.

humoral theory/humorism A doctrine of the pathology (origin) and treatment of disease that originated in ancient Greece and influenced medical thinking in the 19th century. The four humors—blood, phlegm, black bile, and yellow bile—correlated with the four elements of ancient cosmology. Many traces of this ancient dogma persist both in language and in scientific popularization and misinterpretation of modern medical ideas about body chemistry, endocrinology, allergy, and immunology.

Hunter syndrome Mucopolysaccharidosis (MPS) II, a genetic syndrome with growth deficiency, coarse facies, stiff joints, and hepatosplenomegaly (enlargement of the liver and spleen). In contrast to Hurler syndrome (MPS IH), MPS II has a more gradual onset with clear corneas. Mental retardation is variable; hearing loss occurs in half the cases. In contrast to all the other types of MPS, Hunter syndrome is X-linked, so there are no affected females. Named after the Canadian physician, Charles Hunter (1873–1955).

Huntington disease Huntington chorea; adult onset hereditary neurodegenerative disease that affects the basal ganglia of the central nervous system and progresses to dementia. There is a rare juvenile onset rigid subtype. Inheritance is autosomal dominant with an incidence of 1 in 18,000. This disorder is one of the classic models for research into the underlying neuropathology of extrapyramidal movement disorders. Named after the American physician, George S. Huntington (1850–1916).

Hurler syndrome Pfaundler-Hurler syndrome; mucopolysaccharidosis (MPS) IH. A genetic syndrome with growth deficiency, coarse facies, stiff joints, hepatosplenomegaly (enlargement of the liver and spleen), mental deficiency, and cloudy corneas. Named after the German pediatrician, Gertrud Hurler (1889–1965).

Hurler-Scheie compound syndrome Mucopolysaccharidosis (MPS) IH/S. A genetic syndrome with symptoms, progression, and severity intermediate between Hurler (MPS IH) and Scheie (MPS IS). Recurrence risk is 25%.

hyaline membrane disease (HMD) *See* respiratory distress syndrome.

hydranencephaly A condition in which the cerebral hemispheres are sacs made of glial (cell and fiber) tissue and filled with cerebrospinal fluid (CSF). Some islands of cortex are preserved, as are the brain stem, midbrain, and diencephalon. Four causes are postulated: 1) gestational insults such as intrauterine infection; 2) genetic abnormality of vessel formation; 3) defects in brain formation (e.g., embryogenesis, cell migration); and 4) the end point of a massive hydrocephalus (excess fluid in the brain) that runs its course in utero. Clinically, babies may have a normal to large head with normal infant reflexes. However, these infantile reflexes persist, and no normal development occurs, leading to a picture of cerebral palsy with spastic quadriparesis (weakness of all four extremities), seizures, and profound mental retardation. Diagnosis can be made by transillumination or imaging studies, such as computed tomography (CT) scan, magnetic resonance imaging (MRI), or ultrasound. There is no treatment.

hydrocephalus "Water on the brain" or, more accurately, "water in the brain." A condition in which there is an enlargement of the ventricular system in the brain due to an increase in the amount of cerebrospinal fluid (CSF) present in the ventricles (fluid-containing spaces) at one time. It may be caused by decreased absorption or increased production of

hydrocephalus (broken line, normal ventriculation space; solid line, enlarged ventricular space)

CSF. Hydrocephalus may be congenital or acquired. Hydrocephalus is divided anatomically into two categories: 1) obstructive, and 2) communicating. Obstructive hydrocephalus is caused by a blockage of the circulation of CSF by a tumor, an anatomical narrowing of the ventricle (e.g., aqueductal stenosis), or a bleeding underneath the dura (the outer layer of the brain). Communicating hydrocephalus occurs when the absorption of CSF from the ventricles is blocked. This occurs in the Arnold-Chiari malformation (commonly associated with myelomeningocele [protuberance of both the spinal cord and its lining]), after an infection such as meningitis (inflammation of the spinal cord and brain membranes) or a hemorrhage (bleeding) in the brain (*see* stroke and intraventricular hemorrhage). Hydrocephalus is commonly manifested by ataxia (unsteady gait) and spasticity affecting the legs more than the arms. Judgment and reasoning are typically affected, and speech is generally preserved. However, children with hydrocephalus tend to have more expressive than receptive language, resulting in a characteristic speech pattern with little content, often called *cocktail party chatter*. Children with hydrocephalus may also experience a decline in mental function, including language use, that may progress with the hydrocephalus. The correlation between intellectual functioning and degree of hydrocephalus is poor, so that many children who have extensive hydrocephalus have normal intelligence. Hydrocephalus ex vacuo presents with the appearance of hydrocephalus (enlarged ventricles) secondary to atrophy (wasting) of brain tissue.

hygroma Chronic subdural hematoma; bleeding into the space between the membranes covering the brain and leading to confusion, weakness, developmental delay, and paralysis.

hyperactivity Spontaneous gross-motor activity that is excessive for age. Motor activity increases as age or mental age decreases and in the presence of a variety of medical (e.g., hyperthyroidism), psychological (e.g., anxiety), interactional (e.g., maternal depression), and neurological (e.g., attention deficit disorder) conditions. Therefore, hyperactivity is not diagnostic of any particular entity but must be correlated with other findings. *See also* attention-deficit/hyperactivity disorder (ADHD).

hyperalimentation Parenteral (intravenous) nutrition; feeding an individual by total parenteral alimentation (TPA) or total parenteral nutrition (TPN).

hyperammonemia, congenital A group of metabolic disorders that present in infancy with vomiting, lethargy, and coma and progress to severe mental retardation or death; dietary treatment is available. There are five enzymatic subtypes: four are autosomal recessive, and one is X-linked. Incidence is 1 in 30,000, with a recurrence risk rate of 25% for the autosomal recessive subtypes and 50% for the X-linked subtype.

hyperbilirubinemia A high level of bilirubin in the blood. Bilirubin is a red pigment produced in the body during the breakdown of hemoglobin (oxygen-carrying red blood cells); an excessive amount of bilirubin results from either too many red blood cells (e.g., polycythemia) or a deficit in hemoglobin breakdown (e.g., liver disease). The clinical presentation of hyperbilirubinemia is jaundice (yellowing of the skin). In infants, hyperbilirubinemia is treated with fluorescent lighting (bililight) and sometimes exchange transfusion to prevent the bile from damaging the basal ganglia of the brain and causing choreoathetoid cerebral palsy.

hyperexplexia, stiff baby syndrome An autosomal dominant syndrome with hypertonia (increased muscle tone) at birth that becomes less pronounced with age. The baby maintains a fetal flexor habitus (appearance) with clenched fists and an anxious expression. The fact that the hypertonicity can be suddenly exaggerated by slight stimuli requires careful discrimination from a seizure disorder. Hyperexplexic babies have a high incidence of hernias and respiratory and gastromotility (movement of food and waste through the gastrointestinal tract) disorders but no cognitive impairment.

hyperkinesis *See* hyperactivity.

hyperkinetic syndrome of childhood A neurobehavioral syndrome with distractibility, short attention span, extreme over-activity, disinhibition, disorganization, occasional underactivity, impulsivity, marked mood fluctuation, and aggression. The preferred term for attention-deficit/hyperactivity (ADHD) disorder in Europe and Great Britain. *See also* attention-deficit/hyperactivity disorder.

hyperlexia Advanced single-word reading skills that exceed grade levels of performance in other areas, as well as levels expected on the basis of intellectual ability. These word-calling skills are high in the presence of poor reading comprehension. The term *hyperlexia* was first used in 1967, although the condition was described in the 1940s. There is no consensus concerning either the etiology (cause) or significance of the condition. Hyperlexia has been reported in populations of children with varying cognitive abilities, including some with severe mental retardation. Intellectual level by itself does not therefore seem to be a definitive factor in the condition. Hyperlexia is considered by some researchers to be a unique type of language disorder and a condition occurring with another reading disability. Others report that children with hyperlexia demonstrate a profile opposite from that shown by children with classic dyslexia on Wechsler performance subtests.

hypermetropia *See* hyperopia.

hypernasality A disorder of resonance secondary to velopharyngeal incompetence (structural or motor incoordination problems with the palate or velum).

hyperopia Farsightedness—sees better at a distance; close vision not as good; also known as hypermetropia; corrected by plus diopter (convex) lenses. Hyperopia has been reported to be more common among children with learning disabilities and reading problems.

hyperplasia An increase in the size of an organ through an increase in the number of cells.

hypertelorism Increased distance between two paired organs. Ocular hypertelorism reflects an increased distance between the eyes (interpupillary distance); the diagnosis of an orbital hypertelorism requires that the measurement be made from a skull X ray. (Hypertelorism is, in practice, often equated with an increased inner canthal distance.) Hypertelorism is common in Down syndrome and in a number of other genetic disorders, but is also a nonspecific dysmorphic (atypical) feature. As an isolated finding, it may be of no significance.

hypertonicity/hypertonia Increased muscle tone; typically found in the spastic or rigid types of cerebral palsy. More generally, a neurological sign of pyramidal tract involvement.

hypertrichosis Excessive hair; this can involve scalp, facial, eyebrow, eyelid, and body hair. Hypertrichosis can be genetic (familial or part of a specific syndrome), endocrinological (hormonal), or drug induced.

hypertrophy An increase in the size of an organ through an increase in the size of the cells that comprise it.

hyperventilation Rapid, deep breathing that mildly changes blood chemistries by decreasing the carbon dioxide (CO_2) level in the blood. Hyperventilation is used clinically to enhance or induce electroencephalogram (EEG) abnormalities, since it is known to precipitate seizures, especially the absence (petit mal) type. Hyperventilation is a routine part of the EEG evaluation in a child old enough to cooperate. Children ages 8–12 years generally show the most dramatic EEG changes to hyperventilation, including diffuse slowing and sometimes abnormal wave complexes such as spike (a sharp pointed deviation) and slow waves (a rounded deviation). Hyperventilation can also be a symptom of a panic disorder or panic attack and can sometimes result in syncope (fainting).

hypocalcemia Low blood calcium levels; acute symptoms include irritability, high-pitched cry, tremors, seizures, and tone abnormalities; chronic symptoms relate to delayed skeletal mineralization and

rickets. Etiologies (causes) include metabolic disorders and deficient calcium or vitamin D intake. Transient hypocalcemia can produce symptoms in newborns with other medical problems.

hypochondriac *See* somatization disorder.

hypoglossal nerve The 12th cranial nerve; cranial nerve XII is responsible for movement of the tongue.

hypoglycemia Low blood sugar; glucose is the principal substrate for brain oxidative metabolism; hypoglycemia may be asymptomatic (without symptoms), or it may produce a range of symptoms that include irritability, seizures, lethargy, fatigue, sweating, high-pitched cry, and coma. Severe prolonged hypoglycemia can produce brain damage leading to mental retardation. The hypothesis that transient, low-grade fluctuations in blood sugar, not documented by glucose tolerance testing, can contribute to disorders of attention and learning and can be treated by dietary intervention has no scientific support.

hypomania Mild form of mania.

hypomelanosis of Ito A genetic syndrome with streaky, patchy or spraylike depigmentation of the skin; seizures; mental retardation; and eye abnormalities.

hyponasality A disorder of resonance that occurs with a stuffy nose, allergies, and enlarged adenoids. Hyponasality can affect speech clarity, as speech will sound muffled.

hyponatremia Salt depletion; marked decrease in the concentration of sodium in the blood. A common cause of hyponatremia in small babies is the ingestion of overly dilute formula; the lowered sodium levels can produce convulsions.

hypospadias A urological malformation in which the urethra opens on the underside of the penis instead of at the distal end. It can be found in different syndromes

hypospadias

and may be associated with other urogenital anomalies (malformation, deformation, disruption, or dysplasia).

hypotelorism Decreased distance between two paired organs. Ocular hypotelorism is a decreased distance between the eyes as reflected by a decreased interpupillary distance and usually a decreased inner canthal distance. It is often part of syndromes with mid-facial hypoplasia (defective tissue development).

hypothalamic midbrain dysregulation syndrome Hypertension (high blood pressure), hyperthermia (fever), hyperventilation (rapid breathing), and decerebration (generalized spasticity) occurring secondary to hypothalamic-mesencephalic dysfunction leading to a diencephalic–brainstem disconnection syndrome or brain-stem release; this can occur during recovery from coma.

hypothyroidism, acquired Decreased production of thyroid hormone after the newborn period with a variety of etiologies (causes), leading to a syndrome displaying many of the following features: decreased height growth, obesity, myxedema (dry swollen skin), goiter (neck swelling), cold intolerance, constipation, thin hair, lethargy, and sluggish deep-tendon reflexes.

hypothyroidism, congenital Cretinism; a clinical syndrome caused by the absence or hypoplasia of the thyroid gland in newborn infants. Findings include prolonged jaundice (yellowing of the skin), feeding difficulties, sluggishness, somnolence (sleepiness), poor cry, and respiratory difficulties exacerbated by a large tongue. Cold mottled extremities (arms or legs), a large abdomen, and an umbilical hernia may also be present. A short thick neck, puffy face, and myxedema (dry swollen skin) develop. Stunting of physical growth and progressive mental retardation occur when diagnosis and treatment are delayed. Newborn thyroid screening is available.

hypotonic cerebral palsy A physiological subtype of cerebral palsy characterized by severe low muscle tone and pronounced motor delay. Many cases of hypotonic cerebral palsy are transient: the early hypotonia eventually resolves into one of the other subtypes of cerebral palsy. Prolonged or permanent severe hypotonia (atonic cerebral palsy) is rare and is often associated with severe diffuse brain damage and profound mental retardation. Flaccid diplegia is an antiquated term for the transient hypotonia that precedes spastic cerebral palsy.

hypotonicity/hypotonia Decreased muscle tone; floppiness, limpness, weakness. This is a frequent, if variable or intermittent, finding in extrapyramidal cerebral palsy. Floppy infant.

hypotrichosis Decreased hair; this can include balding, alopecia (hair loss), and decreased eyelid, eyebrow, or body hair. Hypotrichosis can be genetic (familial or part of a specific syndrome), endocrinological (hormonal), or dermatological (skin) in cause.

hypoxic Describing a low level of oxygen; this state can be due to low ambient oxygen or to respiratory, cardiac, or hematological (pertaining to the blood and blood-forming tissues) disorders.

hypoxic-ischemic encephalopathy (HIE) Nonprogressive brain damage secondary to hypoxia (oxygen deficiency) and ischemia (blood supply deficiency); most perinatal asphyxia (lack of oxygen) occurs in utero.

hypsarhythmia Infantile spasms.

I

IAR I Infantile automated responses I; *see* primitive reflex.

IAR II Infantile automated responses II; *see* postural response.

iatrogenic Resulting from therapy; a cure following an appropriate treatment is most likely iatrogenic. Iatrogenic diseases, however, are often the result of unwanted side effects of therapies. Examples include bronchopulmonary dysplasia from the treatment for respiratory distress syndrome and drugs producing hyperactivity or lethargy. A certain degree of iatrogenic disorder may be implicit in a given treatment approach and does not necessarily negate the value of the therapy or the skill of the therapist. Iatrogenic disease represents a good part of the risk component in the risk–benefit ratio associated with any intervention.

IBIDS syndrome A rare neurocutaneous (of the nervous system and skin) syndrome. The acronym refers to *I*chthyosis (very dry skin), *B*rittle hair (trichothiodystrophy), *I*nfections, *D*ysplastic (atypical) nails, and *S*hort stature. Cataracts, microcephaly (abnormally small head), hypoplasia (less) of subcutaneous (inner) fatty tissue, hypogonadism (small testicles), and mental retardation are also found. Inheritance is probably autosomal recessive.

ICD *See* inner canthal distance.

ICD–9–CM International Classification of Diseases, Ninth Revision, Clinical Modification; a numerical coding system for medical conditions and procedures that is used for billing, research, and statistical purposes.

ICF/MR; ICFMR/DD *See* intermediate care facility for people with mental retardation and developmental disabilities.

ICH *See* intracranial hemorrhage.

ichthyosis Dry scaly skin, much more severe than that seen in atopic dermatitis; it is genetically inherited in a variety of modes. Ichthyosis is an occasional to frequent finding in a number of syndromes, some of which are associated with mental retardation.

ichthyosis-oligophrenia-epilepsy syndrome A genetic syndrome with ichthyosis (very dry skin), mental retardation, epilepsy, and hypogonadism (small testicles) with a eunuchoid habitus (physical appearance). Inheritance remains unclear.

icing The use of a very cold stimulus applied to the skin to facilitate neuromuscular functioning.

ICM *See* integrated classroom model.

ICS *See* Individualized Curriculum Sequencing.

ictal Pertaining to a seizure. Thus, the aura that may precede a seizure is preictal, and the somnolence (sleepiness) that may follow a seizure is postictal.

icterus Jaundice (literally, "yellow").

icterus neonatorum Jaundice of the newborn. Although this can be physiological, hyperbilirubinemia (high levels of bilirubin in the blood) can lead to kernicterus.

IDAM *See* infant of drug-addicted mother.

IDEA *See* Individuals with Disabilities Education Act; *see also* Education of the Handicapped Act Amendments of 1990.

ideational fluency A measure of creativity; the number of new/different ideas that can be generated.

identification A psychological defense mechanism in which a person forms a mental image of another person whom he or she admires and then tries to think, act, and feel the way that person thinks, acts, and feels. Children with developmental disabilities often identify with someone who is very powerful (such as "The Incredible Hulk") as a way of coping with their own feelings of powerlessness. By asking the child whom his or her favorite person or character is, one can get a sense of the emotional impact of the child's disability on self-image and self-esteem.

identified patient (IP) The member of a family or group for whom help is sought. The identified patient may serve as the entry point for services to other family members.

ideographs/ideograms Graphic symbols used in a system of writing to represent an idea or concept rather than a particular object. Ideographs are typically used in conjunction with pictographs (symbols that look like what they represent) as a form of aided augmentative communication that is particularly useful with nonverbal individuals. The symbols are also used in international road signs to eliminate language barriers.

ideomotor apraxia Difficulty in the conscious imitation of gestures and in the conscious carrying out of motor commands with no difficulty in performing these same routine activities automatically.

idiopathic Of unknown origin; from a medical standpoint, a large number of developmental disabilities remain idiopathic.

idiot Obsolete and unacceptable term for a person with mental retardation and an IQ under 25. The original Greek term referred to an uneducated private person or layman who did not involve himself in the political life of the city-state. Its extension to persons who were intellectually deficient on a permanent basis began in the 14th century, but its more exclusively pejorative connotation took several centuries longer to develop.

idiot savant A person with mental retardation or low normal intelligence who can nevertheless perform remarkable intellectual feats in sharply circumscribed areas, most commonly mathematics, music, chess, memory, calendar, or reading (i.e., hyperlexia). These isolated talents require both neurobiological components (nature) and practice (nurture). They are more likely to be noted in the presence of a coexisting developmental disability, such as autism.

IDM *See* infant of a diabetic mother.

IEP *See* individualized education program.

IFSP *See* individualized family service plan.

IHP Individualized habilitation plan; *see* individualized program plan (IPP).

ILBW *See* incredibly low birth weight.

iliac index The sum of the two acetabular angles (the angle at which the hip and the femur meet) and the two iliac angles (the natural angle of the ileum bone) divided by 2; this number is smaller in infants with Down syndrome.

iliac index

ilium The largest of the three bones of the pelvis; the hips.

Illinois Test of Psycholinguistic Abilities (ITPA) A norm-referenced test to delineate strengths and weaknesses in language abilities of children 2⅓ to 10¼ years of age. The 12 subtests include assessments of three language communication processes—receptive (decoding), organizing (association), and expressive (encoding)—with each of these having an auditory and visual-motor subtest; as well as

4 subtests of closure (ability to fill in missing parts in incomplete verbal or visual presentations or to integrate discrete units into wholes); and 2 subtests of sequential memory (auditory and visual). The instrument yields a psycholinguistic age (PLA) in addition to the subscore profile.

illiterate *E* Vision screening test for preschool children 3 years of age and older; administration is similar to the Snellen Test, except that only one letter, *E*, is used; the *E* is placed in different positions and the child is asked to indicate with his fingers or by rotating an *E* card (or a model *E*) which way the legs of the *E* on a given line of the chart are pointing. The test provides an accurate measure of visual acuity in a child who does not know the alphabet.

imbecile Obsolete and unacceptable term for a person with mental retardation and an IQ between 25 and 50; derived from the Latin *imbecillus*, "weak."

imipramine Trade name Tofranil; a tricyclic antidepressant that is also used to treat childhood bedwetting by lessening the depth of sleep. It is also a second-line drug in the treatment of attention-deficit/hyperactivity disorder (ADHD), but may receive stronger consideration when the ADHD is accompanied by depressive symptoms.

imitation Matching the behavior of a model; various types of imitation emerge at different developmental ages: newborns can imitate facial gestures; vowel and consonant sequences can be imitated during the first year of life; echolalia (repetition of what is heard) occurs transiently at around 18 months; toileting is imitated at 3 years; and the imitation of hand gestures has been graded for school-age children.

imitation synkinesis Mirror movements.

immittance audiometry Impedance audiometry; an objective measure of the functioning of the peripheral (noncentral) auditory mechanism.

immunization Preventive medical procedures (usually a vaccination or inoculation) to reduce susceptibility to certain diseases (e.g., smallpox, measles, polio). Such procedures are used prior to exposure to these diseases. Immunizations usually reduce susceptibility by inducing a mild form of the disease against which the body defends itself. Subsequent exposure to these diseases calls upon the already-developed defenses so that the disease itself is averted. Many of these diseases cause severe developmental disabilities if immunizations are not used. Rarely, the immunization itself is sufficient to cause severe disabilities. Such an outcome, however, is considered a minimal risk as opposed to unchecked epidemics in an unimmunized population.

impairment Any temporary or permanent loss or abnormality of psychological, physiological, or anatomical structure or function. Impairment represents exteriorization of a pathological state and, in principle, reflects disturbance at the level of the organ. Examples of an impairment include a birthmark, a brain lesion, and an incomplete or malformed limb.

impartial due process hearing A procedure described in PL 101-476, the Individuals with Disabilities Education Act of 1990, for settling disputes between parents of a child with disabilities and the school system. The hearing is similar to a legal trial in that it includes rules of evidence and other legal procedures, with the decision based on the evidence presented. The decision of the hearing officer is binding. If parents or the school system disagree, an appeal may be made for a state-level review of the hearing, or the appeal may go to state or federal court. Either the parents or the school system can request a due process hearing.

impedance audiometry *See* immittance audiometry.

imperforate anus A congenital malformation in which the bowel ends before exiting through the anus; it is associated with a high incidence of urologic, spinal, and other anomalies, often as part of a specific syndrome (e.g., Down syndrome).

implied consent An assumption of consent or agreement to action based on failure to protest or resist such action. Many young women with developmental disabilities have been surgically sterilized under the guise of implied consent either by the young woman or her parents or guardian. Such abuse of implied consent has led to a legal mandate of informed consent. *See* informed consent.

imprinting A type of animal learning in which a specific environmental stimulus releases a genetically preprogrammed behavior pattern only when the matching of stimulus–response occurs during a critical and sensitive period of development; the resultant behavior is especially resistant to extinction. The phenomenon was first described by Konrad Lorenz in newly hatched greylag goslings. Whether any analogous learning occurs in human beings is debatable.

imprinting, genomic A genetic process whereby a person has two normal chromosomes in a given pair, but both are derived from the same parent. The absence of the chromosome from the other parent causes the failure of an on–off switch in accessing specific genetic information in the chromosome pair. Examples of this genetic accident include Prader-Willi syndrome, secondary to a maternal chromosome 15 disomy, and Angelman syndrome, secondary to a paternal chromosome 15 disomy.

impulsivity A cognitive style characterized by quick responses and acting without thinking. In children with attention-deficit/hyperactivity disorder (ADHD), impulsivity occurs due to neurological dysfunction. It is important to understand the neurological basis of the impulsivity (and to appropriately manage it), rather than to attribute it to a personality or motivational deficit in the child. When properly diagnosed and understood, impulsivity can be managed with minimal resulting trauma to either the child or parents.

IMS *See* infant monitoring system.

inborn error of metabolism A specific enzyme deficiency that is genetic in origin and caused by a deletion or change in a gene. The enzyme may be absent or present in an inactive form and causes a block in normal metabolism. Varying degrees of dysfunction result, most commonly in the central nervous system and liver.

inbreeding *See* consanguinity.

incentive *See* reinforcer.

incest Sexual intercourse between blood relatives, especially father/daughter and brother/sister relationships. Children with developmental disabilities are frequently targeted as incest victims. Children of incestuous relationships may present with apparent developmental disabilities due to the trauma of the incest. When evaluating children with developmental problems, it is important to maintain an index of suspicion for incest or child sexual abuse.

incidence A rate indicating the number of new cases of a disorder occurring in a given population over a specified time period (usually a calendar year). An increasing incidence of a disorder may reflect a genuine total increase (e.g., acquired immunodeficiency syndrome [AIDS], crack babies), a newly recognized condition (e.g., Rett syndrome, fragile X syndrome), or greatly refined diagnostic sensitivity (e.g., attention-deficit/hyperactivity disorder, learning disability). Because of the relative stability and early onset of most developmental disorders, the importance of distinguishing between incidence and prevalence is minimal compared to more acute medical conditions. Because developmental disorders must start in the pediatric age group, their incidence in the adult population should be zero. Furthermore, it is of questionable validity to talk of incidence for a disorder with a prenatal etiology (cause); without accurate data on fetal wastage (spontaneous miscarriage), the prevalence rate at birth is more accurate.

incision Surgical cut.

inclusion *See* inclusive education.

inclusive education An educational model in which students with disabilities receive their education in a general educational setting with collaboration between general and special education teachers. Implementation may be through the total reorganization and redefinition of general and special education roles, or as one option in a continuum of available services.

incompetent Unable to manage one's affairs, make good decisions, or meet one's responsibilities. People with physical and/or cognitive disabilities that prevent informed decision making may need a guardian to oversee their affairs in one or more areas of their lives (e.g., financial, medical). A legal judgment of incompetency must be rendered and a guardian assigned. The judgment of incompetency does not pertain to the person's moral worth; rather, it is a legal means of protecting the person's own best interests. Usually assignment is to a close relative, such as a parent or sibling. *See also* guardianship, conservator.

incontinence Developmentally inappropriate absence or loss of bladder control (i.e., urinary incontinence) or bowel control (i.e., fecal incontinence).

incontinentia pigmenti syndrome Bloch-Sulzberger syndrome; a genetic disorder with depigmented skin lesions, dental abnormalities, alopecia (hair loss), mental retardation, and seizures.

incredibly low birth weight (ILBW) Describing infants who weigh less than 800 grams at birth.

independent living The ability to be self-governing and self-sustaining. For people with developmental disabilities, independent living is often accomplished within a supportive service network that provides protection while maximizing independence for that person. Although this may mean something as simple as home health and adaptive equipment for negotiating the environment, services may also include many life skills supports for people with greater cognitive impairments. These include supports such as transportation, homemakers, budget monitoring, and sheltered or supported work. *See also* support group, group home.

Inderal *See* propranolol.

index case *See* propositus.

index finger exploration A fine-motor milestone that involves poking and feeling objects with the second, or pointer, finger; this tactile (touch) exploration emerges at 10 months and is equivalent to the pincer grasp.

indication A clinical condition or diagnosis for which a given drug is effective. A labeled indication is one that the U.S. Food and Drug Administration allows to be advertised because research data are judged sufficient to support such a claim; an unlabeled indication is one in which the data remain insufficient. Many clinically effective drug therapies remain unlabeled, especially for conditions in the pediatric age group.

indication Suggestion, sign. As reasons for acting, indications can have various degrees of strength. *See* contraindication.

Individualized Curriculum Sequencing (ICS) An instructional model that focuses on skill clusters that cut across content domains in educational programming for children with multiple or severe disabilities.

individualized education program (IEP) A written statement for the education of a child with disabilities that is developed and implemented according to criteria originally presented in PL 94-142, the Education for All Handicapped Children Act of 1975, and now delineated in PL 101-476, the Individuals with Disabilities Education Act of 1990. The education program, based upon the child's individual needs, is to be developed at an IEP meeting, whose members should include a representative of the local school system, the child's teacher, one or both of the child's parents, a professional who participated in or is knowledgeable about the evaluation, the child (when appropriate), and anyone else the parent would like to have involved. The content of the IEP should include 1) a statement of the child's present level of performance; 2) a statement of long-term goals and short-term objectives; 3) a description of services including placement, related services, and the extent to which the child will participate in general programs; 4) a statement regarding the initiation and duration of services; and 5) appropriate objective criteria and evaluation procedures for determining whether goals and objectives are met. The IEP must be reviewed at least once a year. The child's program cannot be changed without another IEP meeting to which parents must be invited.

individualized family service plan (IFSP) A statement of child and family needs, outcomes to be achieved, and a plan of services necessary to meet these needs, including frequency, intensity, location, method of delivery, and payment arrangements. Family-centered services view the family, rather than only the child with developmental disabilities, as the unit of intervention, incorporating concepts that encourage family decision making and empower families to take advantage of the service model. Thus, an IFSP recognizes all family needs and all family members as equally important in devising and implementing an intervention plan. Such an approach was codified in Part H of PL 99-457, the Education of the Handicapped Act Amendments of 1986 (which was reauthorized in 1991 as PL 102-119, the Individuals with Disabilities Education Act Amendments), which required an IFSP that 1) meets the developmental needs of children with special needs, and 2) meets the needs of the family in terms of enhancing the child's development, including communication, social, emotional, adaptive, or developmental needs.

individualized habilitation plan (IHP) *See* individualized program plan.

individualized program plan (IPP) A document containing a statement of present level of functioning for an individual with

a disability, as well as a listing of goals, objectives, and services with stated completion dates, performance criteria, evaluation procedures, and the plan for service delivery to meet these needs and goals. The IPP is analogous to an IEP (*see* individualized education program). An IPP is also referred to as an *individualized habilitation plan.*

individualized service plan (ISP) A document containing a statement concerning the total habilitation needs of the person with developmental disabilities, including education, employment, social, emotional, and placement, combined with a plan for meeting these needs and naming a responsible service coordinator to oversee the plan's enactment.

individualized transition plan (ITP) A written plan specifying the skills to be acquired by a student and the vocational transition services to be received prior to and following completion of formal schooling. The plan should be comprehensive in scope and longitudinal in nature. It should focus on the specific needs of the individual and should identify who is responsible for initiating and following through on each specified activity. The plan should first be developed at least 4 years prior to an individual's graduation and then modified at least once a year until the individual has successfully adjusted to a postschool vocational placement. The informed participation of parents and guardians, as well as interagency cooperation, are critical components of the vocational transition process.

Individuals with Disabilities Education Act (IDEA) of 1990 (PL 101-476) *See* the Education of the Handicapped Act Amendments of 1990.

inductive reasoning *See* bottom up processing.

infancy From the Latin *infans,* "unable to speak"; the period from birth to 1 year. In the antiquated seven ages of man schema, infancy included the first 7 years of life; this usage survives in the United Kingdom, where schoolteachers refer to children between 5 and 7 years of age as "infants."

infant milestones Specific skills that are achieved at ages for which norms have been derived in the first several years of life.

infant monitoring system (IMS) A Gesell-based developmental screening test for children that utilizes parent report forms at 4-month intervals from 4 to 30 months of age and again at 36 months of age, and includes five subtests: communication, gross-motor, fine-motor, adaptive, and personal-social skill areas.

infant of a diabetic mother (IDM) Maternal diabetes is associated with infantile macrosomia (large birth weight and body size) and increased mortality and morbidity secondary to fetal distress, respiratory distress, central nervous system irritability, plethora (elevated hematocrit), and congenital malformations (e.g., cardiac and musculoskeletal abnormalities including caudal regression syndrome). Meticulous control of maternal diabetes reduces the infant mortality and morbidity.

infant of drug-addicted mother (IDAM) Narcotic and non-narcotic drug use during pregnancy tends to produce a premature and/or small-for-gestational-age infant with a withdrawal syndrome (irritability, fever, breathing difficulties, and gastrointestinal disturbances) in the newborn period. Depending on the drugs and their contaminants, there may be an increased risk for congenital malformations. Long-term effects on development are not well defined and may be related in part to a chaotic, neglectful, and abusive prenatal, as well as postnatal, environment. Transient behavioral disturbances are commonly part of a neonatal withdrawal syndrome; long-term problems include hyperactivity, learning disabilities, and behavior disorders.

infant of substance-abusing mother (ISAM) Chronic substance abuse during pregnancy contributes to poor growth of the fetus and a low birth weight or small-for gestational-age newborn. This, in turn, is associated with an increased risk for developmental disabilities. There is concern that exposure in utero to mind-altering substances may have some as yet undetermined long-term influence on the chemical neurotransmitter pathways of the brain and thus affect later mood and behavioral reactivity.

infantile autism *See* autism.

infantile automated responses I (IAR I) *See* primitive reflex.

infantile automated responses II (IAR II) *See* postural response.

infantile spasms Brief symmetrical contractions of the muscles of the neck, trunk, and extremities (arms or legs) resulting in a jackknifing of the body at the waist or only a head bob, depending on the muscles involved. Also known as *salaam seizures* or *infantile myoclonic seizures*, they usually begin between 6 and 8 months of age and rarely after 12 months. The seizures generally occur many times a day and often in clusters. They are frequently accompanied by eye movements (e.g., eye deviation [inward or outward], nystagmus [involuntary eye movements]), and a postspasm cry. The spasms are rarely related to sudden noises or tactile (touch) stimulation and are not precipitated by photic (light) stimulation or feeding. A variety of electroencephalogram (EEG) findings can be associated with infantile spasms, although the most common finding is hypsarhythmia (a continuous disorganized pattern of high-voltage slow waves [rounded curve deviations] and spikes [sharp pointed deviations]). Infantile spasms may be associated with cerebral dysgenesis (e.g., lissencephaly [smooth, rather than convoluted, brain surface]), genetic disorders (e.g., tuberous sclerosis), intrauterine infection, head injury, inborn errors of metabolism (e.g., nonketotic hyperglycinemia), central nervous system (CNS) infections, and intracranial hemorrhage (bleeding). They also may be cryptogenic (with no known etiologic factors). About 85%–90% of infants with infantile spasms have some degree of developmental delay and mental retardation. In general, the outcome is more favorable in children who have no underlying neurological or metabolic abnormality. The triad of infantile spasms, retardation, and hypsarhythmia is called *West syndrome.*

infantilization Treating a person as much younger than his or her age or abilities would dictate. Children with developmental disabilities are often infantilized by family members who, with good intentions, may overprotect and underencourage the child. If allowed to continue unchecked, infantilization can become a second, and even more debilitating, disability.

infection Invasion of the body by microorganisms (viruses, bacteria, fungi) that cause disease.

inferior Below, anatomically.

inflammation A local reaction of the body to insult, injury, or infection that includes redness, heat or warmth, swelling, and pain (the classical rubor, calor, tumor, and dolor).

Information A Wechsler verbal subtest designed to measure the subject's fund of factual information. Included are questions concerning dates, names of objects, geographical and historical facts, and other information. Children are required to know specific facts, not to find relationships or draw inferences from the information. Sequencing and organizing skills, as well as time orientation, are evaluated. The results may also reflect a child's ability to store and retrieve information from long-term memory. The score obtained on the Information subtest partially depends upon a child's experiences and exposure to stimulating situations at home and school. The subtest is discontinued after five consecutive failures. Factitious example: "What does the heart do?"

Information and Referral (I and R) An agency whose sole service is to assess individuals' problems and refer them to the appropriate service or entitlement. Thus, the parent of a child who is newly diagnosed with Down syndrome might be directed to the Social Security Administration for Supplemental Security Income (SSI), the Down Syndrome Association for more specific information and support, the local school district's early intervention program for education, and the local branch of The Arc (formerly, Association for Retarded Citizens of the United States) for socialization and recreational activities.

information processing A broad framework in which intelligence is studied as a process rather than as a definition of abilities. This framework includes an examination of the way in which knowledge is organized and located in the memory system and the mental operations necessary to accomplish intellectual tasks. Cognitive psychologists have used computer simulation and mathematical modeling to discover data patterns that suggest strategies of cognitive processing. Neuropsychological models also include structural brain considerations in the analysis of mental functions.

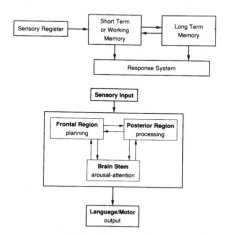

information processing

information processing A theory of human communication processes based on a mechanical model of information processing. Major elements include encoding, decoding, feedback, kinetic loops, and cybernetics. The origins of many family therapy theories can be traced to an information processing theory base.

informative   A term used in the analysis of a genetic condition through use of a pedigree or sophisticated DNA (deoxyribonucleic acid) mapping. An informative family is one that has enough information about a particular disorder to determine its inheritance pattern. For example, a woman who has a son and a brother with muscular dystrophy and sisters and daughters without it carries an X-linked form of muscular dystrophy. This family is informative because the gene can be traced through the family. However, if that same woman had only typical sons and daughters, then it would be uncertain whether she carries the gene, and the family would not be informative.

informed consent   A consent for action based on the assumption of three criteria: 1) adequate information, 2) an ability to understand and process the information, and 3) a lack of coercion in the outcome of the decision-making process. Thus, parents may be asked to sign a statement of informed consent prior to the initiation or termination of a medical procedure on their child. Informed consent becomes a more complex issue when dealing with adults with mental retardation. Current normalization and self-advocacy efforts, as well as empowerment philosophies, offer adults with mental retardation many life-decision opportunities previously denied them. With these opportunities, however, also comes the potential for bad decisions and poor or distasteful outcomes. The question of informed decision making and informed consent becomes inextricably entwined with a person's capacity. *See also* incompetent, guardianship.

inguinal hernia   A weakening of the abdominal wall, leading to a bulging and protrusion of abdominal contents outward in the area of the groin. Because of the high risk of incarceration or strangulation, inguinal hernias are routinely surgically repaired.

inhibition   A condition in which one function or circumstance prevents the expression of another function or behavior; an act or process by which the typical or expected response is restrained despite the presence of the eliciting stimulus.

inion   Occipital prominence; a landmark on the back of the skull.

initial teaching alphabet (i/t/a)   Augmented roman alphabet. A written system for teaching reading phonetically, in which there is a direct symbol for each phoneme. Forty-four characters are used, each representing only one English sound or phoneme; a specific sound is learned for each symbol. Use of the augmented alphabet was originally proposed in the 1960s and 1970s in America and Great Britain to teach beginning reading. It made phoneme–grapheme correspondence more regular and simplified spelling for beginning readers. This alphabet can be used to teach speech and language to individuals with hearing impairments and has been used successfully with children with other disabilities as well. Gifted children (those who have superior intellectual abilities) can also benefit from the i/t/a.

innate   Vague qualifier suggesting a genetic or fixed organic component to a(n) (dis)ability. A cognate of the nature in the nature versus nurture debate.

inner canthal distance (ICD)   A measurement of the distance between the two medial (nasal) canthi. The distance is increased with hypertelorism (widely spaced eyes), telecanthus, and epicanthal folds. Increased ICD is a nonspecific mild dysmorphic (atypical) feature that may be associated with developmental disabilities.

inner canthal distance

insatiable child syndrome   The whining, irritable, and demanding behavior that can accompany attention-deficit/hyperactivity disorder (ADHD) and is interpreted as a biological or learned persistent dissatisfaction.

insensitivity to pain A neurological finding in dysautonomia (hereditary disease of the autonomic nervous system). What is often interpreted as an insensitivity to pain can be a reflection of the difficulty that people with severe developmental disorders have in effectively communicating their awareness of pain.

insidious Not easily detectable evolution of symptoms or disease, due in part to a very gradual onset.

insight In psychology, insight generally refers to the ability to be aware of changes in one's behavior and feeling state—a "psychological mindedness" or self-knowledge that enhances a person's understanding of him- or herself and, to some extent, others. It involves interpreting the significance and purposes of one's behaviors and motives and includes the ability to recognize inappropriateness and irrationality in these behaviors and emotions. An individual's level of insight has implications for the types of treatment approaches that are appropriate and available to that person. In learning theory, insight is a type of knowledge that facilitates the reorganization of the field of experience to create a new idea or discover a solution to a problem. Insight is considered by some to be central to a subtheory of intellectual giftedness. Three distinct, but interdependent, psychological processes collectively constitute insight: 1) selective encoding—recognizing recurrent information in a given context; 2) selective combination—integrating relevant information in a new and productive way; and 3) selective comparison—recognizing how new information is related to old information. Insight plays a more significant role in the learning processes of the gifted compared to those of the nongifted.

instinctive avoiding reaction Hyperextension of the fingers in response to forward-upward elevation of the arm.

institutional care A self-contained facility, usually large in size, that provides temporary custodial supervision, evaluation, training, and treatment for individuals with mental retardation, other developmental disabilities, and certain mental illnesses until appropriate community alternatives are located or become available. In some cases, particularly if the degree of developmental disability is severe to profound or no other form of appropriate placement is available, institutional care can be prolonged and indefinite. Institutional care is also used to generically refer to any residential out-of-home placement that incorporates educational and therapeutic treatment components.

institutionalism A developmental and behavioral profile of motor and language (especially expressive) delay, increased visual interest in adults, rocking, and bland indiscriminate amiability with absence of stranger anxiety in a quiet, sober, noncuddly infant being reared in a nonfamily setting. Institutionalism can be considered a type of maternal deprivation or prolonged hospitalism and can give rise to anaclitic (dependence) depression and failure to thrive. Later impairments in forming emotional ties, controlling impulses, thinking abstractly, and being able to enjoy life can become prominent.

instruction, modality-based Presenting material in a manner aimed at utilizing visual, auditory, or tactile (touch) channels (modalities), according to the channel presumed to be stronger in an individual. Multisensory approaches attempt to combine several modalities (*see* Fernald Word Learning Technique). This is often confused with the psychological process model of educational intervention, in which attempts were made to train auditory and visual-perceptual processes directly in the hope that academic performance would then automatically improve; this approach was not effective. Modality-based instruction does not attempt to train psychological processes but, rather, teaches academic material in a manner designed to circumvent weakness and utilize the learner's strengths. Research has not consistently shown this method to be significantly successful. Critics charge that 1) evidence relating psychological processes to learning failure is correlational rather than causal; 2) tests used to measure psychological processes are inadequate; and 3) processing tests and teaching procedures may be more important in planning for young children rather than adolescents. An alternative approach is that of functional skills training and task analysis, which recommends focusing on academic skills students need to learn rather than on disabilities that impede learning. Each of these theories may be viewed alone as a simplistic approach to a complex problem. The profile of learner strengths and weaknesses must be refined and broadened to capture the relationship of other variables. This more comprehensive theory must also include the interaction of student-centered variables with instructional variables.

instruction, task analysis An approach to teaching in which complex behaviors are broken down into their component parts and taught in an ordered and logical sequence. This theory holds that assessment should be restricted to determining which subskills have been mastered and which have not, and does not acknowledge any ability limitations within the learner other than lack of mastery of specific necessary subskills through lack of practice or experience. Instruction is based on teaching those subskills rather than on tailoring learning to match the learner's processing strengths and weaknesses (*see* instruction, modality-based). Steps to this approach include 1) state objectives to be achieved and skills to be learned; 2) analyze the skill in terms of specific tasks; 3) list tasks in a sequential order; 4) determine which tasks are not known by the student; 5) teach through direct instruction; 6) teach one task at a time, moving to the next when the previous task has been learned; and 7) evaluate the effectiveness of instruction by whether the skill has been learned. Critics of the application of this model to academic tasks have raised several questions, including the following: 1) Can a complex learning task be subdivided into specific measurable and observable skills? Does learning the subskills transfer to what is understood to be, for example, "reading"? 2) Can skills be ordered in a hierarchy? Does an adult determination of a logical sequence

match the way in which a child learns? 3) What does the establishment of a set of skills say about how that skill should be taught? 4) How does this apply to the concept of learning disability? Both task analysis and modality-based instruction, taken individually, are simplistic models for describing a complex process. A comprehensive theory of learning must include a number of student-centered variables in interaction with instructional variables.

insult Injury or that which produces injury to an organ.

integrated classroom model (ICM) A service delivery model for educating students with mild disabilities and students without disabilities in the same classroom, administered jointly by general and special education personnel. The classrooms are highly structured, with clear behavioral and academic expectations.

integration Incorporating individuals with disabilities in the general community through provision of necessary support in educational, vocational, residential, community, and employment settings. In regard to education, integration is the process of educating all children who have needs and interests to which the schools have previously not responded (e.g., students with disabilities, students who are ethnically or culturally different) in a general, rather than segregated, academic setting. *See also* mainstreaming, inclusive education.

intelligence A capacity for knowledge about the world. Intelligence as both an attribute in and of itself and a construct for learning is a vast and controversial field of study. There is little agreement on a precise definition. However, intelligence is generally considered to include the ability to perform more abstract processes, such as understanding and integrating concepts, the capacity to learn and acquire knowledge, and the ability to adapt and deal effectively with new situations. Both biological and environmental factors contribute to the individual expression of intelligence.

intelligence quotient (IQ) A quantitative index of an individual's level of mental development derived from performance on a test designed to measure intelligence. When the concept was originally introduced in the early part of the 20th century, ratio IQs (dividing mental age by chronological age and multiplying the result by 100) were computed. Ratio IQs have been replaced by deviation IQs (test achievement relative to the test performance of a comparable group). Intelligence quotients are limited by the type of skills they are designed to measure, and may not provide a comprehensive description of an individual's abilities. However, IQs are still widely used and generally accepted. IQ ranges vary by instrument, but generally have comparable classifications starting from a mean of 100: 130 and above, very superior; 120–129, superior; 110–119, high average; 90–109, average; 80–89, low average; 70–79, borderline; and less than 70, mentally deficient or mental retardation.

intelligence test Standardized measure used to establish an intelligence level rating, typically an IQ, by measuring an individual's ability to perform a variety of tasks involving information, word meaning, concept formation, and performance on various nonverbal tasks. Intelligence tests are controversial, in part because there is no universally accepted definition of intelligence, making tests to measure it both theoretically and inherently limited and subjectively determined by the test creators' definitions of intelligence. However, intelligence testing is widely practiced and generally accepted when well-standardized and validated tests are used as components of a broadly based assessment process. Valid testing considers cultural and linguistic diversity as well as differences in communication and behavioral factors. The term *intelligent testing* has been coined to serve as a reminder of the hazards of relying solely "on the numbers" and to emphasize the importance of gathering and using all available information and integrating it with clinical acumen and careful reasoning in assessing an individual.

intelligibility threshold *See* speech reception threshold.

intensity The loudness of sound as measured in decibels (dB). To determine a sound's intensity, the sound is compared to the reference level (.0002 dynes/square centimeter), determined to be the faintest sound pressure most humans can detect. Ten decibels is the intensity of a whisper from several feet away, whereas a commercial jet taking off nearby produces a sound intensity of about 120 dB.

interalar distance Width of the nose.

interdisciplinary Describing a team approach to the diagnosis and treatment of developmental disabilities; in such a team, professionals representing two or more disciplines interact so that the final case formulation reflects the conclusions of a staffing conference at which professional disagreements are discussed and resolved in a manner that respects each individual's contribution.

interjacent child Antiquated term for a child with minimal brain dysfunction.

intermediate care facility for people with mental retardation and developmental disabilities (ICF/MR) Also known as ICFMR/DD. A facility that serves people with developmental disabilities (not just those with mental retardation) and that assumes a need for some level of medical or custodial care beyond that required in supported living or group home placements, but less than a full-time intensive medical or custodial need. Although numerous such care arrangements still exist, many have given way to the newer model of supported living arrangements. Funding shifts toward the latter model suggest that this is the preferred model for long-term care in people with mental retardation or developmental disabilities.

intermittent photic stimulation The use of strobe light (flashing lights) during an electroencephalogram (EEG) to stimulate electrical activity. There are three EEG responses to photic stimulation. One is *photic drive,* a normal response of rhythmic activity over the posterior (back) regions of the head. Depression of this response can be seen with destructive brain lesions, whereas increased amplitude is associated with scarring and an epileptogenic focus. The *photomyoclonic* response is a nonspecific response consisting of fluttering of the eyelids, movements of the eye, and sometimes jerking of the face. The *photoconvulsive* (PCR), or *photoparoxysmal*, response is most commonly found in individuals with seizure disorders. It is characterized by a symmetrical spike and wave or multiple spike and wave complexes in response to an intermittent light stimulus. The EEG pattern change may be associated with an impairment of consciousness and brisk jerks of the upper body. The PCR response may be familial and represent a susceptibility to convulsions. It is also present in the EEGs of some degenerative disorders.

intermittent positive-pressure breathing (IPPB) A type of assisted ventilation used in infants and children with respiratory distress.

internal rotation   Turning a limb toward the mid-line of the body.

internal tibial torsion   An orthopedic deformity in which the lower leg is twisted inward so that the feet turn in but the knees face forward. In children without cerebral palsy, this deformity often resolves spontaneously by 3 years of age if weight bearing is normal/typical at this developmental age.

international phonetic alphabet   A system of symbols for writing the speech sounds of all languages.

international standard manual alphabet   A mode of communication in which block letters are stroked with the fingers of the speaker in a prescribed manner on the palm of the listener; this type of fingerspelling is used predominantly in communicating with individuals who are blind and have profound hearing loss.

interpreters for the deaf   Hearing individuals who listen to a spoken message and communicate it in some way to an individual with a hearing impairment. In interpreting a spoken message, it is permissible to depart from the speaker's exact words to paraphrase and explain what the speaker is saying. In this way, interpreting is different from translating, which is a verbatim presentation of another's words. There are various types of interpreters for the deaf, including sign language interpreters who communicate what has been said through some form of sign language or fingerspelling; oral interpreters who mouth (enunciate clearly and more slowly) the speaker's message, allowing the individual with a hearing impairment to speech read; and reverse interpreters who render sign language or difficult-to-understand speech into clearly spoken English. Specialized interpreters familiar with technical language serve in a variety of settings. Educational interpreters are used to facilitate inclusion of students who are deaf. In addition to educational applications, interpreters are mandated to be available as a component of vocational rehabilitation services, and most states require that interpreters be available whenever the civil rights of people with hearing impairments are involved. Before 1964, interpreters were largely friends or relatives of individuals with hearing impairments. In 1964, the National Registry of Interpreters for the Deaf was established to promote training and recruitment, to establish standard competencies, and to maintain a listing of certified interpreters. Training programs are available throughout the United States; many colleges offer degree programs in interpreting.

interpupillary distance   The distance between the two eyes, using the center of each pupil as the landmark for the measurement. Abnormal interpupillary distances occur with hypertelorism (widely spaced eyes), hypotelorism (decreased distance between the eyes), and strabismus (squint); normal distances are present in pseudostrabismus (false squint)

interpupillary distance

and pseudohypertelorism (false impression of widely spaced eyes).

intersensory integration   The use of two sensory modalities in accomplishing a task. For example, listening to a series of numbers and writing them requires auditory-motor integration, whereas seeing a list of numbers and saying them requires visual-verbal integration.

interval sample   Data gathered by monitoring and recording behaviors at predetermined times, rather than continuously. A teacher may set aside three 5-minute intervals during a morning and record a student's behavior only during that time.

intervention   Planned strategies and activities that modify a maladaptive behavior or state of being and facilitate growth and change. *Intervention* is analogous to the medical term *treatment*. Social workers, psychologists, speech-language therapists, and other helping professionals often prefer the term *intervention,* in order to connote a broader range of activities to the individuals they assist. Thus intervention may include such activities as advocacy, psychotherapy, speech-language therapy, obtaining entitlements, obtaining adaptive equipment, modifying the environment, facilitating resource development, and networking, among others.

intracerebral   Within the cerebrum of the brain.

intracranial   Within the skull.

intracranial hemorrhage (ICH)   Bleeding into the substance of the brain.

intrathecal   Within or into the sheath (theca), usually referring to the sheath surrounding the spinal cord.

intrauterine growth retardation (IUGR)   Newborn infant with birth weight low for gestational age. Babies with weight reduction proportional to their other parameters (small head circumference, short body length) are more likely to have underlying genetic, metabolic, toxic, or infectious etiologies (causes) that will adversely influence later development. Disproportionate growth parameters (with head circumference approximating normal percentiles) in newborns allow the possibility of better developmental outcomes, depending on environmental variables.

intraventricular hemorrhage (IVH)   A bleeding into the brain (specifically the subependymal [beneath the innermost layer] area), most common in premature infants because their brain and vascular (blood vessel) structures are more delicate than those of infants born at term. When IVH occurs in a term infant, it can be due to a traumatic delivery or, rarely, to a bleeding disorder. Intraventricular hemorrhages are graded 1–4, with grade 1 being the mildest and involving only the ependymal (innermost) area; grade 2 involving more of the ependymal area than grade 1; grade 3 being hydrocephalus with a grade 2 bleed; and grade 4 bleeding into the brain tissue itself. Complications of IVH include hydrocephalus (excess fluid in the brain), porencephalic cysts, and leukomalacia. The hydrocephalus may be treated with shunts or medication; however, treatment does not ensure typical development. The developmental outcome can include cerebral palsy and mental retardation. The severity of outcome is generally worst in bleeds of grades 3 or 4, although that correlation does not always hold.

intrinsic motivation   Completing a task because of interest and the feeling of personal competence engendered, rather than for an external reward. Theories of intrinsic motivation suggest that some tasks are intrinsically motivating because humans have innate tendencies to develop competencies, to be curious about novel events and activities, and to feel that they are autonomous and engaging in activities by their own volition. An additional assumption is that some children have been socialized to value academic work. Students have been found to be more intrinsically motivated to complete tasks when 1) the tasks are moderately challenging, novel, and relevant to their own lives; 2) the threat of negative external evaluation is not salient; 3) their attention is not focused on extrinsic reasons for completing tasks; and 4) they can take responsibility for their success by having been given some choice in the task.

intubation The placement of a tube through the nose (nasotracheal tube) or through the mouth (orotracheal intubation) into the trachea (windpipe) to provide artificial ventilation (breathing).

intuition Judgment by perception rather than by reason.

in utero In the womb (uterus); that phase of an individual's life cycle preceding birth, the usual duration being 9 months. It is during this time that organogenesis (formation of the baby's organs) occurs, and the developing fetus is therefore susceptible to maternal exposure to harmful substances such as alcohol, drugs, and tobacco. In utero includes the entire prenatal period.

inversion Turning the sole of the foot toward the mid-line of the body; the foot posture utilized in the direct Fog test.

IP *See* identified patient.

IPP *See* individualized program plan.

IPPB *See* intermittent positive-pressure breathing.

ipsilateral On the same side. For example, in hemiplegic cerebral palsy, the ipsilateral arm and leg are involved (the right arm and the right leg in a right hemiplegia and the left arm and left leg in a left hemiplegia). However, because brain control of motor function crosses the mid-line (e.g., the right brain controls movement for the left side of the body), brain injury in a hemiplegia is contralateral (on the opposite side), with a right hemiplegia being secondary to a left brain insult.

IQ *See* intelligence quotient.

Irlen lenses Tinted eyeglasses or lens filters used to treat dyslexia. An intervention devised by Helen Irlen, it first achieved popularity in Australia; the tinted nonrefractive lenses purportedly treat an underlying disorder known as *scotopic sensitivity syndrome*. However, both the treatment and the syndrome remain unproven. An inexpensive variant involves the use of tinted cellophane overlays to be placed on top of material to be read.

iron deficiency anemia Anemia secondary to inadequate dietary iron becomes common from 9 to 24 months of age. Iron deficiency anemia may contribute to apathy, irritability, short attention span, and lowered cognitive performance. It remains uncertain whether iron deficiency in the absence of anemia may produce similar effects.

ISAM *See* infant of substance-abusing mother.

ischemia Decreased blood secondary to decreased blood flow associated with hypovolemia (decreased blood volume or shock) or vasoconstriction (narrowing of blood vessels).

Ishihara test A series of 38 plates used to screen for color blindness. Each plate depicts a large number of colored dots in which a number (or other design) is embedded in colored dots that are visible only to a person with intact color vision. The number and types of errors define the presence and type of color blindness (red–green or total). Overreliance on this test contributed to earlier reports of an increased incidence of color blindness in learning disabilities. In fact, many people with learning disabilities have trouble interpreting these cards because of figure–ground perception problems, rather than color vision problems.

isochromosome An abnormal chromosome with arms of equal length caused by the duplication of one arm and the deletion of the other. Chromosomes normally have a short arm, p, and a long arm, q. For example, instead of a p arm and a q arm, the isochromosome has two p arms. An isochromosome is designated in a chromosome or medical report as an isochromosome number (#), where the number refers to the number of the affected chromosome. This condition may cause anatomical abnormalities as well as developmental disabilities, such as mental retardation.

isodisomy *See* heterodisomy.

isometric power The ability to hold a position against the force of gravity or another resistance.

isotonic power The ability of a muscle to move through its range of motion with resistance applied throughout.

ISP *See* individualized service plan.

i/t/a *See* initial teaching alphabet.

item difficulty The frequency with which any given test item is passed or failed as compared to the other items on the test.

itinerant services In reference to education, support service personnel (e.g., speech and language, learning disability) provide instruction to students in the hospital and home, or travel between schools to supplement instruction provided by the classroom teacher. This differs from a resource room model in that a resource room teacher remains in a specific classroom setting to which students come for instruction.

ITP *See* individualized transition plan.

ITPA *See* Illinois Test of Psycholinguistic Abilities.

IUGR *See* intrauterine growth retardation.

IVH *See* intraventricular hemorrhage.

J

Jacksonian march A progression of a focal motor seizure that follows a particular pattern of spread to other body parts and finally becomes generalized. This is relatively rare and is often associated with an identifiable lesion in the cerebral cortex.

jargon A body of specialized terms used by various subgroups of a society, especially among professionals in a given discipline. Meaningful communication is often hindered by the use of such jargon, particularly when individuals from several disciplines are discussing a given case or topic. This is because some words have different meanings according to the discipline in which they are used. When explaining developmental disabilities to parents, those with disabilities, or others, it is advisable to avoid using jargon entirely. These terms can sound contrived and assume an importance of their own, attributing a higher status to the individual using them. Providing information in a clear, direct, and thoughtful manner facilitates communication and the establishment of a cooperative relationship.

jargoning Vocalization pattern of infants that has the intonation, inflection, and rhythm of conversational speech but is unintelligible; it sounds as though the baby is talking a foreign language. Immature jargoning is completely unintelligible, whereas mature jargoning contains one or more intelligible words mixed in with the gibberish. Jargoning as an expressive language milestone emerges between 14 months (immature) and 18 months (mature).

jaundice A yellow tinge to the skin resulting from hyperbilirubinemia (high levels of bilirubin in the blood) secondary to diseases of the blood or liver. Physiological jaundice occurs in many normal newborns with bilirubin levels up to 9 milligrams/deciliters in the first week of life. Physiological jaundice is due to a transient immaturity of the liver enzymes that help the body to remove bilirubin. In some breast fed babies, this jaundice may be prolonged and somewhat more severe. In older children, jaundice must be distinguished from carotenemia (yellowing of the skin due to excess carotene, rather than bilirubin, in the blood); with carotenemia, the whites of the eyes remain white. In adults, jaundice is most commonly associated with hepatitis.

jaw jerk A sharp tap to the chin (stimulus) produces a reflex closure of the jaw (response).

Jekyll and Hyde personality Dramatic and sudden emotional lability (changeability) in the absence of recognizable cause or precipitating factors; observed in children with attentional disorders and in Gilles de la Tourette syndrome. This term derived from Robert Louis Stevenson's (1850–1894) short story, *The Strange Case of Dr. Jekyll and Mr. Hyde* (1886), has also been used to describe the syndrome of repeated mental and physical deterioration and improvement observed in elderly people.

Jendrassik maneuver An individual is asked to pull as hard as possible against hands hooked together by flexed fingers; this maneuver is utilized to enhance the knee jerk, in part by distracting the person's attention and decreasing anxiety over the examination of the lower extremities.

Jensen controversy Unresolved debate instigated by the educational psychologist Arthur Jensen concerning the degree to which intelligence is hereditary and the implications that such estimates should have for educational programming. In this recent variation on the nature versus nurture controversy, most arguments have depended heavily on philosophical presuppositions or very refined statistical models. Except at the most abstract and theoretical level, this debate contributes nothing to conceptualizations of or approaches to mental retardation or learning disabilities.

Jervell and Lange-Nielsen syndrome A genetic syndrome of profound congenital deafness associated with syncope (fainting) secondary to a heart conduction defect. Distinguishing this specific etiology (cause) for deafness is important, because drug treatment may prevent sudden death during a syncopal episode. Incidence is 1 in 1 million, with an autosomal recessive inheritance pattern.

jitteriness Nonspecific irritability in infants; movements can be tremulous and sometimes jerky with clonus (rhythmic oscillations between flexion and extension); the absence of abnormal gaze or eye movements helps to distinguish jitteriness from neonatal seizures. The most common causes of jittery newborns in the past included asphyxia (lack of oxygen), hypocalcemia (low blood calcium), and hypoglycemia (low blood sugar levels); today the effects of drug withdrawal are rapidly becoming the primary etiology (cause).

Johanson-Blizzard syndrome A genetic syndrome with deafness, hypothyroidism, a peculiar facies, growth deficiency, and frequent mental retardation. Inheritance is autosomal recessive.

Joubert syndrome A genetic syndrome with episodic hyperpnea/apnea (disturbances of respiratory control), opsoclonus (abnormal eye movements), mental retardation, hypotonia (decreased muscle tone), ataxia (an unsteady gait), and dysplasia (defective tissue development) of the cerebellum, resulting in partial or complete absence of the cerebellar vermis (central part of the brain) with other structural abnormalities of the brain. The routine association of this syndrome with severe mental retardation has been questioned; severe visual, motor, and articulation problems contribute to interpretive limitations on cognitive assessment. Inheritance follows an autosomal recessive pattern.

jug-handle ear Protruding auricle. Rather than being a minor dysmorphic (atypical) feature, this type of ear protrusion may reflect the presence of neuromuscular disease.

jug-handle ear

Jukes Fictitious name for a real New York family that included more than 1,000 cases of mental deficiency; used as anecdotal support for the hypothesis that most mental retardation is hereditary. First reported in 1877 by R.L. Dugdale (1841–1883).

K

Kabat *See* proprioceptive neuromuscular facilitation (PNF).

K–ABC *See* Kaufman Assessment Battery for Children.

KAFO Knee-ankle-foot orthosis; *see* orthosis.

Kahn-Lewis Phonological Analysis (KLPA) A measure of articulatory responses for the presence of 15 phonological processes for children ages 2-0 through 5-11 years. The KLPA is designed to be used with the Goldman-Fristoe Test of Articulation (G-FTA).

Kaiser-Permanente (K-P) diet Modification or version of the Feingold diet for hyperactivity; *see also* Feingold diet/hypothesis.

Kallikak Fictional name for a pedigree composed of two distinct lines: 1) kalos (attractive, pleasing)—intelligent, respectable, productive citizens; and 2) kakos (bad, evil)—people with mental retardation and social degenerativeness. In 1912, H.H. Goddard publicized this family as an example documenting the heredity of feeblemindedness. Goddard's conclusions are now considered completely unfounded.

karyotype An individual's chromosomes arranged by size (largest to smallest) from photomicrographs of the actual chromosomes of a cell. The autosomes are paired and then numbered 1–22, with the largest chromosome pair as number 1. The sex chromosomes are the smallest chromosomes and are not numbered. A normal karyotype for a male is 46 XY. The karyotype of a male with Down syndrome is designated 47 XY, extra 21.

Kaufman Assessment Battery for Children (K–ABC) An individually administered test of intelligence and achievement for children 2½–12½ years of age. The K–ABC comprises four global scales, each yielding standard scores (with a mean of 100 and a standard deviation of 15). The intelligence scales consist of subtests (with a mean of 10 and a standard deviation of 3) combined to produce the global scales of sequential processing, simultaneous processing, and the mental processing composite, the latter being a summary score of the sequential and simultaneous scales. The achievement scale comprises a separate set of subtests (with a mean of 100 and a standard deviation of 15). A special nonverbal scale is provided for children ages 4–12½ (with a mean of 100 and a standard deviation of 15). Supplementary percentile ranks that take into account the child's race and sociometric background are provided for the four global scales, the nonverbal scale, and all achievement subtests except expressive vocabulary. Simultaneous processing refers to the mental ability to integrate input simultaneously to solve a problem, and frequently involves spatial, analogic, or organizational abilities as well as the application of visual imagery. Sequential processing emphasizes the arrangement of stimuli in sequential or serial order for problem solving wherein each stimulus is linearly or temporally related to the previous one, creating a form of serial independence. The mental processing subtests were deliberately designed to minimize the role of language and verbal skills. Performance on the achievement scale is viewed as an estimate of success in applying mental processing skills to the acquisition of knowledge. The test items are presented using an easel.

Kaufman factors Three factors that emerge from a factor analysis of the standardization sample of the Wechsler Intelligence

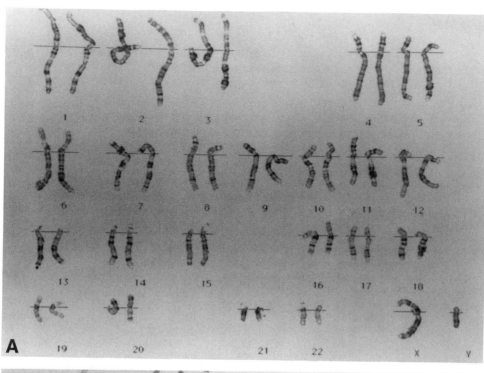

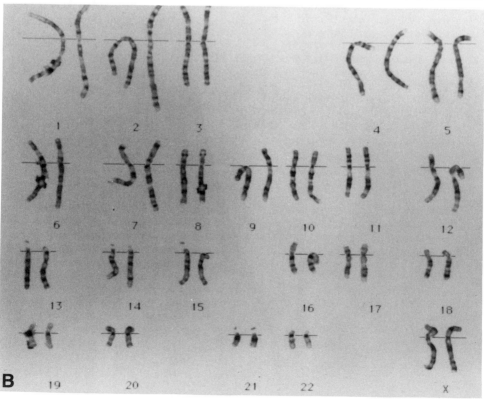

Two karyotypes: A) male, and B) female.

Scale for Children. The factor that appears to measure a variable underlying performance on the vocabulary, information, comprehension, and similarities subtests is labeled verbal comprehension; the factor that is assumed to underlie performance on picture arrangement, block design, object assembly, and picture completion is labeled perceptual organization; and the factor underlying performance on the arithmetic, digit span, and coding subtests is labeled freedom from distractibility.

Kaufman Test of Educational Achievement (K–TEA) An individually administered norm-referenced measure of school achievement for children in grades 1–12. It consists of two separate and nonoverlapping forms: a brief screening form that provides standard scores in the global areas of reading, mathematics, and spelling; and a comprehensive form that provides scores in the specific domains of reading decoding, reading comprehension, mathematics application, mathematic computation, and spelling. The brief form takes approximately 30 minutes to administer, whereas the comprehensive form may require 1–1½ hours to complete. Standard scores (with a mean of 100 and a standard deviation of 15) are available by grade or age for the spring or fall. Percentile ranks, stanines (a scoring system with scores expressed as whole numbers from 1 to 9, with a mean of 5 and a standard deviation of 2), and normal curve equivalents are also available. The comprehensive form produces three composite scores. Three comparisons of standard scores permit the determination of a statistically significant difference (a .05 or .01 level of confidence) between pairs of composites. A systematic method for determining whether there are significant differences in the results among subtests as well as procedures for error analysis are also provided.

Kayser-Fleischer ring Green, yellow, and brown corneal pigmentation in Wilson disease.

kernicterus Nuclear yellowing; in newborn babies with severe hyperbilirubine-mia (high levels of bilirubin in the blood), the basal ganglia and other brain centers are selectively affected to produce a syndrome of choreoathetosis, supraversion gaze palsy (an upward gaze palsy—inability to look up), high-frequency hearing loss, central auditory imperception, and dental abnormalities (green staining of the teeth from the bile pigment biliverdin). The involvement of basal ganglia typically produces a choreoathetoid cerebral palsy.

ketogenic diet A diet used to control seizures. Historically, fasting was found to have some effect on decreasing seizure activity. In 1921, the ketogenic diet was initiated as an attempt to mimic the metabolism (breakdown) of ketone bodies that occurs in the brain during starvation. The diet restricts proteins and carbohydrate consumption by supplying calories through fats. The diet is most effective in children between the ages of 2 and 5 years with minor motor seizures. Poor palatability has a serious negative impact on compliance, however, and failure to provide supplements for fat-soluble vitamins can produce pellagra. The diet is thus reserved for use in children who have multiple drug allergies or are unresponsive to anticonvulsants. A variant of the diet using medium-chain triglycerides (a type of fat) has been effective and may be better tolerated.

KeyMath–Revised A major revision of the KeyMath Diagnostic Arithmetic Test (KMDAT) for children enrolled in first through ninth grades. The test is divided into three dimensions: 1) basic concepts including subtests of numeration, rational numbers, and geometry; 2) operations including addition, subtraction, multiplication, division, and mental computation; and 3) applications including measurement, time and money, estimation, interpreting data, and problem solving. Obtained test data may be treated as norm referenced, domain referenced, or criterion referenced. Norms are provided for fall and spring testing. Standard scores and percentile ranks are the recommended derived scores, but stanines (a scoring system with scores expressed as whole numbers from 1 to 9, with a mean of 5 and a standard deviation of 2), normal curve equivalents, grade equivalents, and age equivalents are also available. There are two alternate forms.

KFD   *See* kinetic family drawing.

Killian/Teschler-Nicola syndrome   Tetrasomy 12p, Pallister mosaic syndrome; a genetic syndrome with profound mental retardation, a changing peculiar facies, contractures, seizures, and deafness.

kinesics/kinesiology   The study of body language, of body posture, movement, and facial expression as communication.

kinesthetic   A sensory modality for acquiring information through receptors in joints, muscles, tendons, and ligaments that are stimulated by bodily movements and tensions. Examples of kinesthetic learning or memory include being able to get a spoon to the mouth, turn on a light in the dark, and walk up or down stairs. Typing is a more complex example. This modality may also be used in conjunction with visual or auditory modalities, when, for example, patterns of movement such as dialing a touch-tone telephone aid in recalling a number. Although the majority of academic learning activities emphasize visual and auditory channels, the kinesthetic modality has been utilized by some educators as a method for teaching children who do not learn easily through traditional modalities. Kinesthetic learning is included in theories about cognitive and learning style. The Fernald Word Learning Technique is a structured method for incorporating the kinesthetic modality.

kinetic family drawing (KFD)   An assessment procedure in which a child is asked to draw a picture of his or her family with every member doing something; interpretation parameters cover inclusion and exclusion, specific activities, interactions, and stylistic indicators similar to the Draw-a-Person Test. This technique is a useful screening indicator for the emotional health of a family.

kleeblattshädel syndrome   *See* cloverleaf skull syndrome.

Klinefelter syndrome   47 XXY; a genetic syndrome in males with hypogonadism (small testes, small penis, inadequate testosterone [male sex hormone] production), tall, slim stature with long legs and a tendency to obesity, and IQs about one standard deviation below expected. Shyness in childhood and personality and behavior disorders in adulthood have been described. Incidence is 1 in 1,000. One fifth of males presenting in infertility clinics have Klinefelter syndrome.

Klonopin   *See* clonazepam.

KLPA   *See* Kahn-Lewis Phonological Analysis.

Klumpke palsy   Paralysis of the forearm due to nerve injury usually received at birth and leading to a "claw hand." This peripheral nervous system injury should not be confused with a central monoplegia; named after August Dejerine Klumpke (1859–1927).

Klumpke palsy

KMDAT   KeyMath Diagnostic Arithmetic Test. *See* KeyMath–Revised.

knee-ankle-foot orthosis   *See* orthosis.

Kniest dysplasia   A genetic syndrome with disproportionate dwarfism (shortened trunk), peculiar flat facies, joint limitation, conductive (involving the middle and outer ear) hearing impairment, and severe myopia (nearsightedness) with other eye defects. Inheritance is probably autosomal dominant.

Knott, Margaret   *See* proprioceptive neuromuscular facilitation (PNF).

Knox Cube Test   A performance task in which the subject taps a series of four cubes in various presented sequences.

Knox Play Scale   A descriptive framework for the analysis of spontaneous play in children from birth to age 6 years; the test is intended to assess the social-emotional maturation of children.

Kohlberg, Lawrence A major theorist of the developmental stages of moral thought and moral reasoning. Kohlberg postulated six stages of moral development: 1) rules are obeyed to avoid punishment, 2) rules are obeyed to obtain rewards, 3) rules are obeyed to avoid being disliked and to enable the person to be seen as "being good," 4) the development of a conscience and an appreciation of society's need for rules, 5) the recognition that there are competing and contradictory (yet equally valid) values requiring judgment, and 6) the appreciation of the presence and validity of universal moral values and a commitment to them. Many children with developmental disabilities and limited ability to think abstractly develop rigid moral codes with fixed ideas of right and wrong; the problem these children have in admitting flexibility in a given situation can lead to difficulties in working with them.

Kohs Block Design Test A performance task in which the subject must reproduce colored designs from 17 test cards using variously colored cubes. It is a subtest on the Grace Arthur Performance Scale.

K-P diet *See* Kaiser-Permanente diet.

K–TEA *See* Kaufman Test of Educational Achievement.

KUB Kidneys, ureters, bladder; an X ray taken to visualize the abdominal contents.

kwashiorkor "Sugar-baby"; severe protein-calorie deprivation leading to failure to thrive (poor growth and weight loss); protein is more deficient than calories (high carbohydrate diet), so weight can be more affected than height, and starvation edema will occur earlier than in marasmus. The Phanaian term *kwashiorkor* refers to the dull brown/reddish-yellow, thin, dry, lifeless hair that can be easily pulled out. This type of malnutrition is common in developing countries; its developmental impact on children may be reversible.

kyphosis An excessive curvature of the vertebral column (upper spine), convex posteriorly, to produce a round-shouldered appearance.

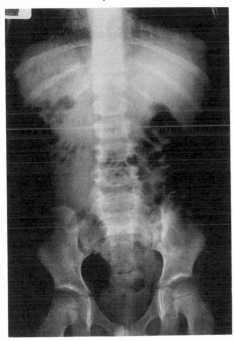

KUB

kyphosis

L

labeling The classification and application of a name to a set of symptoms, characteristics, behaviors, and traits. In medicine, such a process is termed *diagnosis*. Although few challenge the necessity of such "classification" processes for appropriate treatment and planning, many contend that such labels—particularly in the behavioral area—become pejorative, a basis for discrimination, and perhaps even serve as self-fulfilling prophecies. Thus, the description "a mentally retarded adult" has now been discarded in favor of "person with mental retardation," which shifts the focus from "mentally retarded" to "person."

labile unstable, fluctuating.

labyrinth Inner ear; composed of the cochlea (concerned with hearing) and the vestibule and semicircular canals (concerned with balance and equilibrium). The control of balance and equilibrium is complex, and it is inappropriate to automatically attribute problems in these areas to labyrinthine dysfunction in the absence of more specific diagnostic testing.

labyrinthine righting reflex The reflex tendency of the head to move toward an upright vertical position; this reflex can be assessed in a variety of positions from tilted upright supported sitting (head control) to vertical upside-down suspension, as well as many oblique positions.

LAC *See* Lindamood Auditory Conceptualization Test.

laceration Tear.

lacrimal duct stenosis, congenital Dacryostenosis; blockage of the tear duct, which can lead to eye irritation and infection.

LAD *See* language acquisition device.

lallation Sound imitation in infancy; primitive echolalia (repetition of what is heard) not necessarily specific to the sounds heard; describes repetitive vocalizations made between 6 and 9 months of age.

lalopathy Rarely used term for any type of speech disorder.

Landau reflex Precipitation reflex; a postural response that emerges between 2 and 3 months of age, in which an infant held in prone (front) suspension succeeds in raising his or her head to a vertical position with subsequent trunk, hip, and leg extension.

Landau reflex

The Landau is a prerequisite to voluntary rolling over; it is delayed in the presence of hypotonia (decreased muscle tone).

Landau-Kleffner syndrome A rare form of seizure disorder manifested as acquired aphasia (loss of language skills); it may also need to be considered in some presentations of autism. It generally begins with one or more seizures between the ages of 5 and 6 years. First, language comprehension is abruptly lost, followed by a gradual loss in expressive language. The seizures generally do not continue, although the electroencephalogram (EEG) remains abnormal. There may be spontaneous improvement or improvement with anticonvulsant therapy.

Langer-Giedion syndrome A genetic syndrome with mental retardation, growth deficiency, a peculiar facies with a bulbous nose, sparse scalp hair, loose skin, short fingers, and exostoses (tumors/bumps) of the long bones. Inheritance is possibly autosomal dominant, with most cases representing new mutations; a deletion on the long arm of chromosome 8 (8 q deletion) has been observed. Sometimes referred to as trichorhinophalangeal syndrome II. (Trichorhinophalangeal syndrome has the same hair, nose, and finger abnormalities, but tends to lack the exostoses, mental retardation, and short stature.)

language acquisition The process of learning to communicate effectively and appropriately in a transactional context. This includes knowledge of syntax (grammar), semantics (the meaning of words), and pragmatics.

language acquisition device (LAD) The set of linguistic processing skills that enables a child to infer the rules in the speech of others and then use these rules to generate language; LAD is thought to be innate.

language delay Communication skills not developing commensurately with the advance of chronological age. Includes the diagnostic subgroups of language disorder, language and learning disability, mental retardation, and autism.

language disorder A developmental disorder involving disabilities of reception, integration, recall, and/or production of language. Language disorders may be spoken, written, or both.

language experience approach to reading An instructional approach that combines listening, speaking, writing, and reading skills in a single program. This approach assumes that a child learns the following reasoning: What I am thinking about, I can talk about; What I can talk about, I can write (or dictate); What is written, I (and others) can read; and I can read what others have written. Instruction begins with a discussion of what is to be written. The teacher then writes what the student dictates, resulting in an individual story or an experience chart, which then becomes the basic instructional material used for teaching the student to read. Advocates of this approach suggest that the students' level of interest is higher than with other methods because 1) students are reading about something that actually happened, and 2) they tend to learn material based on their personal word patterns faster than those contrived by others. There is some concern that students may practice faulty language patterns and may not receive enough encouragement to learn new words. Perhaps the greatest area of controversy revolves around whether this method includes direct, systematic instruction of skills, particularly phonics. Critics contend that children cannot learn to read if they have not mastered phonics, and all children, especially those at risk, need systematic instruction in phonics. Advocates claim that phonetic instruction does occur, but within a meaningful context. The emphasis on student writing requires students to actually spend more time applying phonics knowledge than is found in a traditional program.

language, expressive A coded system for communication with another person or people. Speaking, writing, and signing are expressive language skills.

Language Processing Test, The (LPT) A language test for 5- to 11-year-olds that assesses associations, categorization, similarities, differences, multiple meanings, and attributes. LPT analysis yields information regarding processing limitations such as word retrieval difficulties, inappropriate word substitutions, nonspecific word usage, inability to correct errors, response avoidance, rehearsing responses, and unusual pauses.

lanugo Primary hair; the fine downy hair that covers the entire fetus from midgestation to term; lanugo is replaced by vellus, or secondary hair, at term.

large for gestational age (LGA) An infant whose birth weight is above the 90th percentile for age. This condition may be constitutional (the baby comes from physically large parents) or related to conditions such as maternal diabetes or Beckwith syndrome. Mechanical birth injuries (injuries secondary to the physical difficulty of delivering a large baby) are more common in LGA babies.

larynx The upper part of the trachea (windpipe); it contains the vocal cords.

larynx

last menstrual period (LMP) A date used in calculating the due date of a pregnancy.

latency A term from behavioral learning theory referring to the time that elapses between an operant behavior and a consequent stimulus event (CSE). The shorter the latency, the easier it is to make an association between the operant and the CSE. For example, if the behavior to be strengthened is "lining up quietly," then children who line up quietly should be recognized (i.e., rewarded) immediately, not at the end of the day.

latency The elementary school–age period from 4-6 to 11-13 years of age. It is named for the latency, or relative inactivity, of the sexual drive between the resolution of the so-called Oedipus complex and the onset of puberty. During latency the sexual drive is sublimated into social learning.

laterality Awareness of and ability to use both sides of the body; the recognition of the existence of both the left and right sides of the mid-line. By 5 years of age, most children discriminate between their left and right. The ability to perform a task involving both sides on demand (touching their right knee with their left hand) appears around 7 years of age, whereas the ability to identify the left and right of another person positioned opposite them usually occurs by 9 years of age. Children with problems involving laterality may have difficulty with certain learning tasks (e.g., reading) and can display other forms of visual-spatial orientation deficits, but laterality training does not necessarily improve reading skills.

Laurence-Moon-Biedl syndrome *See* Bardet-Biedl syndrome (the original cases

reported by Laurence and Moon had spastic diplegia [paralysis on both sides of the body] and lacked polydactyly [extra fingers or toes]).

LBW *See* low birth weight.

L.C.S.W. *See* Licensed Clinical Social Worker.

LD *See* learning disability.

LDA *See* Learning Disabilities Association of America.

lead line On physical examination, a blue line on the gums; on an X ray, a thin line at the growing end of the bone; both lines are indicative of (past) lead poisoning.

lead line

lead poisoning Plumbism. A heavy metal found in old interior paint (made before 1950) and in exhaust from leaded gasoline that is toxic to the nervous system. Lead poisoning is most commonly found in children 1–6 years of age who live in old, deteriorating, inner-city buildings. These children put paint chips, toys, dust, and dirt that often have a high lead content in their mouths (i.e., pica). Remodeling of old buildings with poor ventilation can dramatically increase the airborne lead level, producing toxic levels from inhalation alone. The lead is absorbed through the intestine and into all the tissues in the body. Any level of lead toxicity can probably cause permanent brain damage. The entire range of developmental disorders has been described as symptomatic of lead poisoning, including mental retardation, language disorders, learning disabilities and other school problems, autism, and attention-deficit/hyperactivity disorder (ADHD). Lead levels over 40 micrograms per cubic centimeter have been clearly associated with central nervous system (CNS) impairment and a poor developmental outcome. The effects of low (or subclinical) levels of lead are debated. Lead generally causes anemia by blocking iron binding; anemia also contributes to poor attention span. Treatment involves two goals: 1) prevention through the removal of lead from the environment; and 2) chelation to reduce the lead burden by removing lead from the body and brain, with iron supplementation to treat the anemia.

learned helplessness Failure to respond appropriately to a situation due to previous experience with uncontrollable events in the same or similar situations. The concept combines a behaviorist approach to mastery of the environment with the psychoanalytic concept of inferiority and the humanistic concept of motivation. Learned helplessness is characterized by cognitive and affective disturbances that undermine a person's desire or motivation to respond, distort the ability to perceive success and to learn that responding can work, and result in heightened emotionality due to anxiety and depression. It is not merely the perceived lack of control but (mis)understanding of why one lacks control that encourages learned helplessness. Thus, students with learning disabilities and mental retardation view their failures as being due to their lack of ability despite possessing the skills required to accomplish the task. These children often say, "I can't" or "I'm dumb," or are hesitant to even begin a task for fear of being unable to complete it or do it correctly. Some attributions play a central role in the acquisition and maintenance of learned helplessness. Students must be directly taught to ascribe their learning difficulties to factors they can affect. In addition to classroom intervention, supportive counseling or group therapy can further address issues of self-esteem and depression.

learning disability (LD) A disorder in one or more of the basic psychological processes involved in understanding or using language, spoken or written; the disorder may manifest itself in imperfect ability to listen, think, speak, read, write, spell, or do mathematical calculations. Learning disabilities include such conditions as perceptual disabilities, brain injury, minimal brain dysfunction, dyslexia, and developmental aphasia (loss of language skills). According to PL 94-142/ PL 101-476, the term does not include children who have learning problems that are primarily the result of visual, hearing, or motor disabilities; mental retardation; emotional disturbance; or environmental, cultural, or economic disadvantage. Because many different tests, standards, and criteria have been used to operationalize these definitions, a student may be classified as having a learning disability in one area but not in another. According to a definition of *learning disabilities* developed by the National Joint Council on Learning Disabilities in 1981, these disorders are intrinsic to the individual and are presumed to be due to central nervous system dysfunction. Even though a learning disability may occur concomitantly with other handicapping conditions (e.g., sensory impairment, mental retardation, social and emotional disturbance) or environmental influences (e.g., cultural differences, insufficient/inappropriate instruction, psychogenic factors), it is not the direct result of those conditions or influences.

The definition of *learning disability* subscribed to by the Learning Disabilities Association of America includes the effect of the disability on self-esteem, education, vocation, and daily living activities. The concept of learning disabilities, as it has evolved, reflects a range of neurological dysfunctions that may be manifested in various aspects of life, are innate in the individual, and are lifelong. However, people with learning disabilities can learn to compensate, attend college, and have successful careers.

Learning Disabilities Association of America (LDA) A nonprofit organization formed to advance the education and general welfare of children and adults of normal or potentially normal intelligence who have learning disabilities. The organization was founded by parents of children with learning disabilities in 1964 as the Association of Children with Learning Disabilities (ACLD). The name was subsequently modified to include both "Children and Adults," but the acronym remained the same. In 1990, the name was officially changed to the Learning Disabilities Association of America (LDA).

The LDA holds international and national annual conventions. *Newsbriefs*, the official LDA newsletter, is published six times yearly.

Learning Potential Assessment Device (LPAD) A clinical battery of 14 instruments devised by Reuven Feuerstein. Using adaptations from Raven's Progressive Matrices, Organization of Dots, Plateaux Tests, representational stencil design tests, numerical progressions, positional learning, and verbal and figural analogy tests, the LPAD is a dynamic assessment that focuses on the process rather than the product of learning and on the qualitative rather than quantitative aspects of the individual's thinking.

learning style The manner in which an individual learns most efficiently. In addition to preferred cognitive style, learning style also includes environmental variables, such as lighting, noise level, snacking, time of day, and position.

Learning-Style Inventory (LSI) A brief 12-item questionnaire that characterizes how an individual learns and deals with ideas and day-to-day situations; scores on four learning stages (concrete experience, reflective observation, abstract conceptualization, and active experimentalization) are used to graphically locate the individual's learning style.

least restrictive environment (LRE) Term used in PL 94-142, the Education for All Handicapped Children Act of 1975, to stress the importance of attending school in the most natural and integrated setting possible considering the student's individual needs. The least restrictive environment is one that allows the child to participate in general education programs as much as possible while meeting his or her special needs. The justifications for this include questions regarding the efficacy of special class placement and the idea that children with disabilities would benefit from exposure to typical role models. However, the least restrictive environment may also be used administratively as an excuse to provide minimal special services. Used appropriately, the term stresses the need to find an optimal placement for each child within a continuum of services.

Leber congenital amaurosis A genetic syndrome with progressive blindness (an infant form of retinitis pigmentosa [night blindness and progressively restricted visual field]), mental retardation, and kidney disease. Incidence is 2.5 in 100,000. In most cases, inheritance is autosomal recessive.

legally blind A condition in which an individual has less than 20/200 vision (can see at 20 feet what can typically be seen at 200 feet) in his or her better eye, or a very limited field of vision (20 degrees at its widest point).

leiotrichous Straight hair, as found in the Mongoloid races.

Leiter International Performance Scale (LIPS) Individually administered test of global intelligence. The test requires no language usage for either administration or response. It is suitable for people 2 years of age through adult, although it is used primarily for children with suspected language delays. The tasks range from matching colors and forms to the completion of complex patterns, analogous designs, and classification of objects. The test is especially helpful for people with profound hearing impairment and language impairment and non–English-speaking persons. Differences between the scores achieved by children with language impairments on the Peabody Picture Vocabulary Test–Revised and on the Leiter may help to illuminate the severity of their language impairments. The test takes approximately 40 minutes to administer and provides an intelligence quotient by the ratio method. The Leiter should be used only as a supplementary measure of intelligence, since its norms are outdated and originate from a non-standardized normative group. However, the LIPS is helpful in obtaining a nonverbal measure of ability to compare with results obtained by other measures.

Lennox-Gastaut syndrome Atonic-astatic epilepsy. A syndrome of different types of seizures, including typical absence seizures with myoclonic, clonic, tonic, and atonic seizures present in one individual. It is characterized by frequent seizures, including status epilepticus, that are difficult to control. The electroencephalogram (EEG) generally shows multifocal abnormalities with abnormal background activity and a spike and wave pattern of less than 3 per second. Mental retardation is common, and the syndrome occurs frequently in children who have had previous encephalopathy (brain damage due to lack of oxygen). Lennox-Gastaut can evolve from hypsarhythmia (a continuous disorganized pattern of high-voltage slow waves [a rounded curve deviation] and spikes [a sharp pointed deviation]).

lens Transparent material designed to form an image. Lenses are used to correct vision both in (contact lenses) and outside of (glasses) the eye. The transparent surface that focuses light rays upon the retina (light-sensitive inner back wall) is the eye's lens.

Lenz-Majewski hyperostosis syndrome Craniodiaphyseal dysplasia, Lenz-Majewski type, a syndrome with poor growth, mental retardation, a peculiar facies, atrophic (thin) skin, sparse hair, syndactyly (webbing of the fingers or toes), and dense, thick bones. Etiology (cause) is possibly autosomal dominant; association with advanced paternal age noted.

LEOPARD syndrome *See* multiple lentigines syndrome.

leprechaunism Donohoe syndrome; a genetic syndrome with growth deficiency, marked absence of subcutaneous (inner) fat, an elfin facies, severe failure to thrive, hypoglycemia (low blood sugar level), and early death. Inheritance is autosomal recessive. The name derives from the dwarf cobblers of Irish folklore.

LES *See* lower esophageal sphincter.

Lesch-Nyhan syndrome Lesch-Nyhan disease; a disorder of purine metabolism that causes a progressive syndrome including profound mental retardation, choreoathetosis, and marked self-injurious behavior. Inheritance is X-linked.

lesion Injury; local tissue discontinuity, sometimes with loss of function.

Let's Talk Inventory for Adolescents (LTI–A) An age-normed (in 2-year intervals) language scale for people 9 years to young adulthood that helps identify inadequate or delayed social-verbal communication skills. The LTI–A looks at the ability to formulate speech acts appropriate to pictured situational contexts for the functions of ritualizing, informing, controlling, and feeling. Stimulus pictures present interactions with adolescent peers and with an authority figure.

Let's Talk Inventory for Children (LTI–C) An age-normed language scale for preschool and early elementary–age children with inadequate or delayed social-verbal communication skills; children are asked to formulate speech acts to go with pictured situational contexts.

lever arm dysfunction A group of neuromuscular/orthopedic abnormalities that negatively affect the efficiency of flexible joints.

lethargy State of decreased consciousness in which the individual can be readily aroused, but this aroused state can only be maintained with difficulty.

leukocytosis A transient increase in the white blood count, usually associated with inflammation or infection.

leukodystrophy *See* white matter disease.

leukomalacia Necrosis (tissue death) in the white matter of the brain, generally secondary to an anoxic (oxygen-deficiency) insult. In premature babies, this is most commonly located around the ventricles (fluid-containing spaces) and is termed *periventricular leukomalacia.*

level Any standard, position, or rank in a graded series of values, often as a measure of ability or performance. For example, levels of sensory efficiency, intellectual capacity, or motor development can be determined. Levels are relative and the cutoffs may be arbitrary.

lexicon　Dictionary; a collection of words, their meanings, and associated information.

Lexington Developmental Scales (Short Form)　A developmental screening test for children from birth to 6 years of age. The instrument assesses motor, personal-social, cognitive-preacademic, language, and articulation areas by a variety of measures over an administration time of approximately 35 minutes. Standardization remains limited.

LGA　*See* large for gestational age.

Licensed Clinical Social Worker (L.C.S.W.)　A person legally sanctioned by state statute to practice clinical social work. Licensing implies meeting minimum standards, which may or may not include academic or professional training and competency-based testing. When seeking a fully qualified social worker, the client should inquire about both licensing and Academy of Certified Social Workers certification.

licensing　A state-legislated and state-maintained competency-based sanction for professional practice. License laws restrict those able to perform certain tasks and duties by virtue of both education and tested competency levels. Thus, a medical doctor may not apply for a license to practice medicine without furnishing documentation of specific competencies and educational attainment. Other professions, such as social work, psychology, speech and language specialties, and nursing, must be similarly licensed. When a profession is regulated by licensing, it is illegal to perform those services without a license.

Light Retention Scale　A measure developed by educational psychologist H. Wayne Light; it is used by some school districts to help determine whether a child should be retained in the same grade. Although not a psychometric instrument, the retention scale consists of 19 factors from which a child receives a score cate-

gorizing him or her as being a fair (score of 32–40), good (score of 10–31), or excellent (score of 0–9) candidate for retention. The factors used to make this determination include age, grade, sex, previous retention, intelligence level, and evidence of learning disabilities. On this scale, boys make better retention candidates than girls, as do children who are small for their age and/or young for their grade. A number of the factors used by Light to determine appropriateness for retention are unsupported by research; rather, they are criteria informally established by teachers over the years as a basis for holding back children.

Likert scale　A scaling technique in which the subject indicates his or her degree of (dis)agreement with a variety of attitudinal statements, usually on a 3- or 5-point scale.

limb synergy　A group of muscles acting as a bound unit (all flexing or all extending) in a primitive and stereotyped manner.

limbic system　A group of functionally related brain structures that regulate emotions and primary drives.

Lincoln-Oseretsky Motor Development Scale　A measure of motor dexterity (balance, speed, dexterity, rhythm, and coordination) for children between 6 and 14 years of age.

Lindamood Auditory Conceptualization Test (LAC)　A 10-minute criterion-referenced test for preschool children to adults that measures auditory discrimination and perception of number and order of speech sounds in sequences.

linguistic reader　An instructional model that does not emphasize meaning in beginning reading but, rather, stresses mastery of a limited number of consistent spelling patterns that correspond to syllables heard in oral language. Words are read as wholes, not sounded out letter by letter. Linguistic readers frequently have few pictures to avoid distracting the beginning reader.

linguistics The scientific study of the origin, structure, nature, and function of language.

linkage The coinheritance of two or more traits at a rate greater than one would expect by chance because they are present side by side on the same chromosome. In some families, males are affected with more than one X-linked disorder because the X chromosomes they received had the disease gene for Duchenne muscular dystrophy, chronic granulomatous disease, and retinitis pigmentosa (night blindness and progressively restricted visual field). This linkage helps in the identification of the gene locations for each disorder.

lipidoses A group of progressive neurological disorders characterized by defects in lipid metabolism. Histochemically, the neurons (nerve cells) are filled with lipids (fats). The actual biochemical defects of these disorders are unknown.

lipreading *See* speech reading.

LIPS *See* Leiter International Performance Scale.

lissencephaly Agyria—literally, "smooth brain"; a condition in which there is abnormal migration of neurons (nerve cells) during early fetal life, resulting in lack of gyri (hills). This is often associated with other abnormalities such as heterotopia (displacement of an organ or tissue), pachygyria (broad, flat cerebral convolutions), or micropolygyria (an increased number of smaller ridgings on the brain surface). Clinically, these individuals have severe mental retardation and marked hypotonia (decreased muscle tone). Seizures, including infantile spasms and Lennox-Gastaut syndrome, are common. A small number of children with lissencephaly have an accompanying chromosomal abnormality or a known genetic syndrome (e.g., Miller-Dieker syndrome). Infection with cytomegalovirus (CMV) has also been described. Lissencephaly can be detected on a computed tomography (CT) scan. Both lissencephaly and Miller-Dieker syndrome are associated with deletions on chromosome 17–p13.

lithium An antipsychotic drug that can be used to treat severe behavior disorders in people with developmental disorders. It is believed to normalize receptor site sensitivity in the brain to reduce mood swings. Side effects include drowsiness, tremors, and electrocardiogram (ECG) changes. Blood levels must be carefully monitored for toxicity.

litmus test A test that indicates a solution's degree of acidity or alkalinity. Litmus is a chemical substance (usually in the form of a chemically impregnated paper strip—litmus paper) that turns red in an acid solution and blue in an alkali, or basic, solution. Metaphorically, a litmus test suggests that classification can be successfully achieved using a single parameter—for example, IQ to define mental retardation; such usage often reflects an oversimplification.

Little disease An old term for cerebral palsy in general or spastic diplegia (paralysis on both sides of the body) in particular; eponym after William John Little (1810–1894), who first described cerebral palsy.

Little etiology Old term for perinatal asphyxia (lack of oxygen) as a cause of brain damage leading to later cerebral palsy, mental retardation, or other chronic, central nervous system impairment. Perinatal asphyxia, especially as reflected in low Apgar scores, is no longer considered a significantly frequent cause of cerebral palsy. The contribution of perinatal asphyxia to otherwise unexplained mental retardation continues to be debated.

LMP *See* last menstrual period.

LNNB–CR *See* Luria-Nebraska Neuropsychological Battery–Children's Revision.

loading A statistical term referring to the correlations between factors and tests in factor matrix. Loadings indicate the weight of each factor in determining performance on each; *see also* factor analysis.

locomotion in prone Movement from one point to another with the body horizontal and the chest and abdomen not raised off the ground; movement is accomplished by coordinated and

locomotion in prone

sometimes alternating pulling with the arms and pushing with the legs. Sometimes a synonym for *creeping*.

locomotion in quadruped   Movement from one point to another with the body horizontal and chest and abdomen raised off the floor so the child is supported on elbows/hands and knees/feet; movement is accomplished by coordinated and al-

locomotion in quadruped

ternating actions of all four extremities (arms and legs). Sometimes a synonym for *crawling*. The child who walks before he or she crawls is not necessarily at increased risk for developmental disabilities.

locus of control   A theory explaining a person's view of most causal mechanisms for feelings, successes, failures, or behavioral outcomes. Two loci of control are postulated: external and internal. People tend to base most of their causal explanations on either an external cause (e.g., it was God's will) or an internal cause (e.g., I really did a good job). Many educational and psychological interventions are based on a framework using a person's predominant locus of control attribution.

long leg brace   A brace that extends from the upper thigh to the foot.

long-term care   A coordinated set of health, social, personal, and protective services, usually in an out-of-home place-

long leg brace

ment. The underlying assumption or connotation of this term is long-term, severe, irremediable impairment (physical or cognitive). Some people with developmental disabilities need long-term care of some form (e.g., group homes, sheltered workshops).

long-term memory   The component of conceptual models of memory in which information is stored for later use. In contrast to short-term, or working, memory, long-term memory has a very large capacity, and, although unproven, information stored there may last a lifetime. Often the feeling of not remembering is related to the inability to retrieve the information. This phenomenon is often seen in children with learning disabilities, particularly for specific information on demand. Information retained for 1 or 2 minutes is retained in the same manner as that retained after 1 or 2 days and is assumed to be encoded in long-term memory. Memory theorists have conceptually divided long-term memory into semantic (meaning systems) memory, episodic memory, and procedural memory. *See also* memory.

lorazepam   Trade name Ativan; a drug in the class of benzodiazepines (the most widely known of which is diazepam [Valium]), used to treat seizures. Lorazepam is a rapidly acting drug that is quite successful in the treatment of status epilepticus. The advantage of using lorazepam over diazepam is that it continues to suppress seizure activity for 24–48 hours after administration, and it does not produce as much respiratory depression. Lorazepam also has an antianxiety effect and can be used chronically to decrease anxiety.

lordosis   An excessive curvature of the lower vertebral column (spine), convex anteriorly, to produce a swayback appearance.

Louis-Bar syndrome   *See* ataxia telangiectasia.

low birth weight (LBW)   Describes an infant whose birth weight is less than 2,500 grams, regardless of gestational age (full-term or premature).

low-set ear   *See* pinna.

low-set ear

low vision   Generally refers to a severe visual impairment, not necessarily limited to distance vision. Low vision applies to all individuals who are unable to read the newspaper at a normal viewing distance, even with the aid of corrective lenses.

Lowe syndrome Oculocerebrorenal syndrome; a genetic syndrome with hypotonia (decreased muscle tone), cataracts, kidney disease, and severe mental retardation. Inheritance is X-linked.

lower esophageal sphincter (LES) The pressure difference between the lower part of the esophagus and the stomach; lowering of this gradient can contribute to gastroesophageal reflux.

lower extremity Thigh, leg, and foot.

LPAD *See* Learning Potential Assessment Device.

LPT *See* Language Processing Test.

LRE *See* least restrictive environment.

LSI *See* Learning-Style Inventory.

LTI–A *See* Let's Talk Inventory for Adolescents.

LTI–C *See* Let's Talk Inventory for Children.

lumbar Relating to that part of the back between the ribs and the hips.

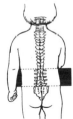

lumbar

lumbar puncture *See* spinal tap.

lumping The tendency to classify together entities that at first do not appear to go together.

Luque rod An orthopedic surgery procedure to treat scoliosis (spinal curvature) by wiring each of the vertebrae to a metal rod; sometimes combined with a Harrington rod.

Luria, Alexander Romanovich (1902–1977) A Russian physician and neuropsychologist whose work with World War II brain injuries laid the foundation for modern neuropsychology and brain localization tests.

Luria-Nebraska Neuropsychological Battery–Children's Revision (LNNB–CR) A neuropsychological battery for children 8–12 years of age.

lymphadenopathy Swelling of the lymph nodes that produces palpable masses and sometimes tenderness; it is often a sign of infection but may be associated with other causes of inflammation. When an infection is localized, the lymph nodes nearest the site of the infection are usually more involved. For example, cervical (neck) lymphadenopathy frequently accompanies tonsillitis or pharyngitis (throat infection/inflammation). Lymph nodes may remain swollen or palpable for some time after an infection has resolved.

M

MA *See* mental age.

MABI *See* Mother's Assessment of the Behavior of her Infant.

MacArthur Communicative Development Inventory: Infants This language assessment tool includes a vocabulary checklist and a parental checklist that assesses first signs of understanding, comprehension of early phrases, and starting to talk. Play, pretending, early gestures, and imitating are also probed.

MacArthur Communicative Development Inventory: Toddlers A parental checklist to assess vocabulary, sentences, and grammar, and different ways of expressing two-word meanings.

Macewen sign A cracked-pot sound elicited on percussion (tapping) of the skull; present with increased intracranial pressure.

macrocephaly Abnormally large head; macrocephaly refers to a head circumference (occipitofrontal circumference) more than 2 standard deviations above the mean for age. It can be familial, associated with a number of dysmorphic (atypical appearance) syndromes, such as Sotos syndrome, fragile X syndrome, and several storage diseases, and is an important marker for hydrocephalus (excess fluid in the brain). In the same way that microcephaly (abnormally small head) is not automatically associated with mental retardation, macrocephaly is not associated with intellectual giftedness. More significant degrees of macrocephaly are likely to indicate the presence of neurodevelopmental disorders.

macrocornea Enlarged cornea, which can occur in glaucoma (increased pressure in the eye, often hereditary) and mucopolysaccharidoses.

macroorchidism Large testicles; this finding can occur in a number of genetic syndromes (e.g., fragile X syndrome) after puberty.

magnetic resonance imaging (MRI) A scan that uses nuclear magnetic resonances (NMR) to visualize parts of the body such as the brain. MR scans do not use radiation, but provide good information about the structural formation of the brain. They are useful for identifying minor brain malformations as well as major ones. MR scans are used to evaluate anomalies of cortical architecture (the rind [outer crust] of the brain) (e.g., lissencephaly [smooth, rather than convoluted, brain surface]) and to evaluate people with refractory seizure disorders for an identifiable focus (location where the seizure activity begins). MRI scans provide information about white and gray matter differences. A not-infrequent finding in children with developmental delay is an immature myelination pattern (a

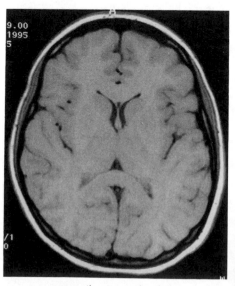

magnetic resonance imaging

186

picture of delayed myelination such as is typical for a younger child). The significance of this pattern is currently under investigation.

MAI *See* Movement Assessment of Infants.

mainstreaming An educational term indicating the placement of children with disabilities in general classrooms. Advocates believe that mainstreaming removes stigma, enhances the social status of exceptional children, facilitates modeling of appropriate behavior, provides a more stimulating and competitive environment, and offers more flexible, cost-efficient service. However, simply placing a child in a general education class does not ensure academic achievement or social acceptance. Appropriate modification of classroom expectations based upon an analysis of the student's strengths and weaknesses is essential for mainstreaming to be effective and to provide successful experiences for the student. *See also* integration.

maladaptive behavior Recurrent, often habitual, behaviors and behavior patterns that prevent an individual, family, or organization from attaining a desired goal or meeting the demands of the environment. Examples of such behaviors include temper tantrums, swearing, and theft. It is not necessarily the behaviors themselves, but the intensity and frequency of the behaviors that render them "maladaptive." Children are placed in classrooms for students with emotional and behavior disorders when school performance problems result in or are exacerbated by persistent or unusual maladaptive behavior. There are four types of maladaptive behavior: verbal and physical aggression, causing interpersonal relationship difficulty; anxious and withdrawn behaviors that hamper interaction and achievement; immaturity or failure to consistently demonstrate age-appropriate behaviors; and socialized aggressive behavior, typically manifested as vandalism or group intimidation and violence. Maladaptive behavior is typically a symptom rather than the problem per se; the origin and etiology (cause) of the feelings and thought processes that result in the behavior should be investi-

gated. Maladaptive behavior can be assessed through behavioral checklists, interviews with teachers and caregivers, and via direct observation of the child's behavior in different settings. Interventions to decrease maladaptive behavior and alleviate its cause include behavior modification, psychotherapy, and medication.

malaise Discomfort; a nonspecific uneasiness; feeling sick or out-of-sorts; malaise is a frequent accompaniment of, and prodrome for, many illnesses.

male-limited Pattern of inheritance that seems to be transmitted only from fathers to their male offspring.

malformation A morphological defect (abnormality of structure or shape) of an organ, part of an organ, or larger body region, resulting from an intrinsically abnormal developmental process. *Intrinsic* implies that the anlage (primordium) was abnormal from the beginning; if the anlage was normal, the morphological defect is referred to as a *disruption*. If the structural abnormality is at the tissue level rather than the organ level, it is referred to as a *dysplasia*. A cumulative number of mild superficial morphological defects (minor atypical features) may be of developmental significance.

malignancy Cancer.

malingering "Enjoying ill health." Malingering has two forms: 1) refusal to engage in pre-illness activities on the basis of "still feeling sick" long after a normal recuperative period and with no obvious signs of continued illness, and 2) faking illness. Whether conscious or unconscious, malingering serves to avoid some undesired obligation or difficult situation through the perceived "legitimate" route of illness when no other "legitimate" route seems feasible. Children with developmental disabilities often malinger when school demands become too stressful.

malleolus The bony prominence on both sides of the ankle.

mandible Jaw; jawbone.

mandibulofacial dysostosis *See* Treacher Collins syndrome.

mania A state of impulsive, excessive, excited, and uncontrolled behavior coupled with accelerated thought and verbal activity, a lessened physiological need for sleep or food, and an excessive, unrealistic feeling of elation. This state is seen in several mental disorders, but is most frequently noted as one phase in bipolar affective disorder. Three additional subcategories of mania are noted: kleptomania (shoplifting), pyromania (firesetting), and nymphomania (sexual intercourse). In these subcategories, the excesses of behavior and activity are limited to a single area of behavioral expression.

manic-depressive illness *See* bipolar illness.

manometry Pressure measurement; a technique that quantifies the force of contraction of the muscular wall of the gut by the use of pressure transducers. Manometry is used in the evaluation of swallowing disorders.

manual English Sign English; a sign system that employs a rapid succession of specific symbols and manual movements, including fingerspelling. Unlike American Sign Language (ASL), manual English employs English syntax (grammar) as its foundation.

MAP *See* Miller Assessment for Preschoolers; *see also* Muma Assessment Program.

maple syrup urine disease (MSUD) An inborn error of metabolism. A familial cerebral degenerative disease in which the breakdown of branched chain amino acids causes the urine to smell sweet, like maple syrup. Babies appear normal at birth, but rapid cerebral deterioration is common. Untreated, this leads to opisthotonos (an arching of the back), spasticity (increased muscle tone), intermittent hypertonia (increased muscle tone), brain damage, and mental retardation. With optimal dietary treatment beginning in the first 2 weeks of life and strict adherence to the diet, IQs are potentially normal. There is an intermediate form with some residual enzyme activity in skin cells. It presents between 6 and 9 months of age with seizures and intermittent ataxia (unsteady gait) and drowsiness. This form nearly always results in mild to moderate mental retardation. Inheritance is autosomal recessive.

marasmus Severe protein-calorie deprivation; infantile atrophy (wasting), athrepsia; malnutrition with a marked weight for height deficit. Marasmus is marked by failure to thrive, progressing to an infant's falling below 75% of expected weight for age; below 65% of expected weight is considered life-threatening. Loss of subcutaneous (inner) fat gives the facies a lined and aged appearance. Skin folds hang loose, the "sucking pads" protrude in the cheeks, and irritability and anxiety may be replaced by apathy. Hypoproteinemia (loss of protein) may lead to peripheral (noncentral) swelling ("starvation edema"). The developmental impact of this malnutrition state tends to be reversible. Also referred to as protein energy malnutrition (PEM).

March of Dimes Foundation An organization founded by President Franklin D. Roosevelt in 1938 as the National Foundation for Infantile Paralysis to combat the nation's polio epidemic. When, in 1938, entertainer Eddie Cantor suggested people send dimes directly to the White House, the organization became known as the March of Dimes Birth Defects Foundation. This name was officially adopted in 1979. With Dr. Jonas Salk's development of a polio vaccine, the foundation refocused its efforts toward the prevention of birth defects and the overall improvement of pregnancy outcomes. The foundation provides research funding, professional education, and volunteer services.

Marcus Gunn jaw winking phenomenon A congenital condition in which unilateral eyelid ptosis (drooping) accompanies ipsilateral (on the same side) jaw movement; when the jaw moves to the opposite side, the involved lid elevates.

Marfan habitus (Marfanoid) A term to describe someone with the physical appearance of Marfan syndrome but who does not necessarily have that syndrome. The habitus (appearance) includes tall stature, long arms and legs, arachnodactyly or spiderlike digits (long, thin fingers and toes), and decreased subcutaneous (inner) fat. This may represent a familial body pattern or another syndrome, such as homocystinuria.

Marfan habitus

Marfan syndrome A genetic syndrome that affects connective tissue to produce a Marfan habitus, hyperextensible joints, subluxation (dislocation) of the lens of the eyes, and serious cardiovascular abnormalities. The tall stature results from extremities (arms or legs) that are disproportionately long compared to the trunk; the head is dolichocephalic (long) with prominent supraorbital ridges (brows) and a long, thin face. Intelligence is normal, but learning disabilities and attention-deficit/hyperactivity disorder have been reported in more than a third of patients. Incidence is 3 in 200,000. Inheritance is autosomal dominant, with a recurrence risk of 50%. Named after the French pediatrician Bernard Marfan (1858–1942).

Marfanoid See Marfan habitus.

Marinesco-Sjögren syndrome A genetic syndrome with cataracts, mental retardation, cerebellar ataxia (unsteady gait), and short stature. Inheritance is autosomal recessive.

Maroteaux-Lamy syndrome Mucopolysaccharidosis (MPS) VI; a genetic syndrome of growth deficiency, coarse facies, stiff joints, cloudy corneas, hepatosplenomegaly (enlargement of the liver and spleen), and normal intelligence.

Marshall syndrome A genetic syndrome with cataracts, sensorineural (involving the inner ear or the auditory nerve) deafness, and a facies with a short depressed nose; mental retardation is an occasional finding. Inheritance is autosomal dominant.

Marshall-Smith syndrome A syndrome with accelerated height, failure to thrive in weight, mild to moderate mental retardation, shallow orbits and prominent eyes, and broad fingers that taper at the ends.

Martin-Bell syndrome See fragile X syndrome.

mass reflex The stimulus of a tap on the suprapubic region (the bony prominence just above the bladder) that produces the response of total body startle or flexion.

Master of Public Health (MPH) A graduate degree in epidemiology of disease and the various factors that influence its prevention, spread, and treatment at a population level.

Master of Social Work (M.S.W.) A degree granted to the student who completes a 2-year graduate program in social work; the M.S.W. curriculum contains both academic and clinical training.

mastoid Postauricular (behind the ear) part of the temporal bone that can become infected concomitant with an otitis media (middle-ear infection). Modern antibiotic therapy of otitis media and mastoiditis has markedly reduced the need for surgical intervention (mastoidectomy).

MAT See Matrix Analogies Test.

MAT–SF See Matrix Analogies Test–Short Form.

Matching Familiar Figures Test (MFF, MFFT) A measure of impulsivity and reflectivity for children 3–6 years of age. Each item consists of an index picture and four to eight similar pictures, only one of which exactly matches the target figure. Time to respond and number of errors are used to place the child in one of four subgroups: impulsives, reflectives, fast accurates, and slow inaccurates. Visual discrimination problems may interfere with this interpretive scheme.

maternal deprivation   Inadequate or absent parenting or nurturance with immediate and potentially long-term consequences on a child's growth and development. Short-term effects can include failure to thrive and developmental and language disorders; sociopathy may be a long-term outcome. This term is actually so poorly defined that, along with its pejorative connotation, it is probably better replaced by a more accurate delineation of underlying mechanisms, such as *abuse, neglect, feeding disorder*, or *disorder of parenting*.

maternal smoking during pregnancy   A risk factor that contributes to fetal distress, low birth weight, and prematurity; it does not have any direct developmental impact.

mathematics disorder   A disorder in which mathematical ability, as measured by individually administered standardized tests, is substantially below that expected, given the person's chronological age, measured intelligence, and age-appropriate education. The disorder significantly interferes with academic achievement and with activities of daily living that require mathematical ability.

Matrix Analogies Test–Short Form (MAT–SF) and Expanded Form (MAT–EF)   An assessment of nonverbal reasoning for students ages 5–17 years that requires the student to correctly select from six options a missing element in an analogical matrix. The MAT–EF is for individual administration; the MAT–SF can be used to screen groups of children. The test items are similar to those used in the Raven Progressive Matrices. Administration time is approximately one half hour.

Matson Evaluation of Social Skills with Youngsters (MESSY)   A rating scale to measure social skills in children 4–8 years

of age; it can be used with children who have mental retardation, visual impairments, or hearing impairments.

maturation   Biological change as a linear function of increasing age. In Gesell's maturational theory, advances in the level of development and behavior are primarily neuroanatomically preprogrammed. Such a theory is not compatible with a large amount of individual variation in the achievement of specific milestones.

maturational theory of development   A theory of human development that attributes achievement of different developmental milestones primarily to the genetically preprogrammed maturation of the central nervous system through myelination of the nerve pathways (insulation through the laying down of a fatty protective layer). Environmental factors play a lesser role, providing these factors remain within certain broadly defined limits (relating to, for example, feeding, clothing, physical contact, and interpersonal interaction). The theory is mostly concerned with development in infancy and early childhood and allows for an increasingly greater impact of environmental and emotional factors in older children.

maxillonasal dysplasia   Binder syndrome; a distinctive facies with flattened nose, hypotelorism (widely spaced eyes), midface hypoplasia (flattening), relative prognathism (a prominent jaw) with reverse overbite, and normal intelligence without other associated anomalies (malformation, deformation, disruption, or dysplasia). Plastic surgery is indicated.

mazes   A supplementary Wechsler scale subtest performance test consisting of one sample problem and nine maze problems. The child is required to draw a line from the center of the maze to the outside without reaching a dead end or crossing any of the lines representing walls. Each maze is presented separately, and all mazes are timed. The subtest measures visual-motor skills, planning, anticipation, and directionality; visual memory, attention, and focusing skills are also involved. Success on the subtest requires visual-motor coordination executed quickly and accurately. Mazes is an optional subtest that is not used in the computation of the IQ when the standard performance subtests are administered. Although not routinely required, mazes can provide much information with children who have language impairments or who are from culturally different backgrounds. Mazes is usually a difficult test for children with visual-spatial problems. The test is discontinued after two consecutive failures.

MBD *See* minimal brain damage/dysfunction; *see also* attention-deficit/hyperactivity disorder (ADHD).

MBP *See* myelin basic protein.

MBTI *See* Myers-Briggs Type Indicator.

McCarthy reflex An infant reflex in which the stimulus of a tap on the supraorbital (just above the eye or brow) area produces an ipsilateral (on the same side) blinking response.

McCarthy Scales of Children's Abilities A test of abilities for children ages 2-6 to 8-6. Abilities are assessed in six areas: verbal, quantitative, perceptual performance, general cognitive, memory, and motor development.

McCarthy Screening Test (MST) An assessment of abilities critical to early school success for children 4 to 6-6 years of age; the test items are derived from six scales of the McCarthy Scales of Children's Abilities. The MST classifies children as "at risk" or "not at risk" for later need of special education services. Administration time is 20 minutes.

McDaniel-Piers Young Children's Self-Concept Scale A 40-item measure for 6- to 9-year-old children that is a downward extension of the Piers-Harris Children's Self-Concept Scale. Items deemed appropriate for younger children were selected from the original instrument, and their wording was simplified. The tester reads the item and the child responds yes or no on an answer sheet. The scale provides a total score and three subscores: feeling self, school self, and behaving self.

mean The arithmetic average of all the scores in a set of scores. To obtain the mean, the sum of all the scores in the set is divided by the total number of scores in the set. Example: $8 + 2 + 6 + 4 = 20/4 = 5$. In the set of scores, 20 (the sum of the scores) divided by 4 (the number of scores) results in a mean of 5. This most commonly used measure is responsive to the exact position of each score in a distribution, but is sensitive to a few relatively extreme scores. *See also* measures of central tendency.

mean length of utterance (MLU) The average number of morphemes in a sentence; a simple measure of early language development.

meaningful Of consequence. In reference to memory, contextual, connected terms are easier to retain than less-meaningful, disjointed, or nonsense terms. Meaningfulness is not synonymous with a word's definition or meaning.

means test Financial criteria that determine eligibility for certain government-funded health or social services. An applicant's current income, assets, debts, dependents, and earning status are weighed against preexisting criteria for eligibility. Failure to meet the criteria implies that the applicant already has sufficient "means" to meet his or her obligations and does not need government subsidy. Programs that apply means tests include Supplemental Security Income (SSI), Medicaid, Food Stamps, Special Health Care Needs, and Aid to Families with Dependent Children (AFDC).

measles *See* rubeola.

measures of central tendency Descriptive statistics that measure the central value in a distribution of scores. The three most commonly used measures are 1) mean (appropriate for interval and ratio scale data); 2) median (appropriate for ordinal, interval, or ratio scale data); and 3) mode (the only measure of central tendency appropriate for nominal scale data).

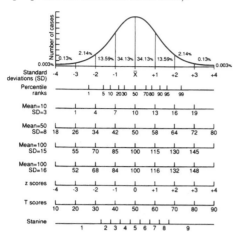

measures of central tendency

Mebaral   *See* methylphenobarbital.

Mecham Verbal Language Developmental Scale (VLDS)   A test of general communication ability for children from birth to 15 years of age; an extension of the communication subscale of the Vineland Social Maturity Scale, the VLDS uses an interview method to yield a language age equivalent.

mechanical ventilation   The use of a respirator (breathing machine) to assist an individual with respiratory distress.

meconium   The newborn baby's first stool.

medial   Toward the mid-line, anatomically.

median   The median is the midpoint, or the point that divides a range of scores in half. When the number of scores is odd, the middle score is the median (example: 10, 8, 6, 4, 1; median = 6). When the number of scores is even, the median is the average of the middle pair of scores (example: 10, 9, 7, 4, 2, 1; median = 7 + 4/2 = 5.5). Because the median divides a set of scores into equal groups, 50% of the scores are below the median; thus, the median is always the 50th percentile. *See also* measures of central tendency.

median cleft palate face syndrome   Frontonasal dysplasia; a nongenetic, congenital defect in mid-facial development producing marked hypertelorism (widely spaced eyes), cleft lip/nose/palate, and a widow's peak anterior (front) hairline. One fifth of cases exhibit mental retardation.

mediastinum   A region of the chest that includes all the contents of the thorax except the lungs.

mediastinum

Medicaid   A federally supplemented state-administered health insurance program for people with financial needs. Medicaid employs a financial means test to determine eligibility. Administration of the program is usually handled through local income–maintenance (welfare) offices.

Medicaid spenddown   Eligibility for Medicaid as a needy individual on the basis of having expended sufficient assets/income on medical expenses.

medical home   Primary medical care that is comprehensive, continuous, and accessible.

Medicare   A federally funded comprehensive health insurance program enacted as a supplemental entitlement under the Social Security Act of 1935. Medicare has two parts: Hospital Insurance (HI) and Supplemental Medical Insurance (SMI). Eligible populations include 1) all persons ages 65 and over who are eligible for the cash benefits of Old Age and Survivors Insurance, commonly called Social Security; 2) all beneficiaries with disabilities, including workers, widows, and widowers 50 years of age and older, and insured workers' adult children 18 years of age and older whose disability originated before the age of 22; and 3) insured workers' family members who need dialysis or a kidney transplant.

megavitamin therapy   The use of extremely high doses of vitamins to treat schizophrenia, autism, and a range of developmental disorders. The expansion of the therapeutic regimen to include minerals and trace elements (orthomolecular therapy) does not alter its essential lack of efficacy. Vitamin deficiency can cause developmental symptoms, and some children's metabolism does require higher vitamin intake; however, outside the fairly narrow range of vitamin deficiency syndromes, (mega)vitamin treatment of developmental disorders is an unacceptable alternative intervention.

Mellaril *See* thioridazine.

Melnick-Fraser syndrome Branchio-otorenal (BOR) syndrome; a genetic syndrome with hearing loss, kidney abnormalities, and branchial arch anomalies (malformation, deformation, disruption, or dysplasia) (e.g., preauricular pits, neck fistulas). Prevalence is 1 in 40,000. Inheritance is autosomal dominant with variable expression.

memory The store of things learned and retained from an organism's activity or experience. Most theoretical models of memory include a sensory register, short-term memory, working memory, and long-term memory. Long-term memory has been conceptually divided into semantic (meaning systems) memory (memory for words), procedural memory (memory for the steps comprising an activity), and episodic memory (memory for one's past history). Other conceptualizations of memory include auditory memory, visual memory, motor memory, and recognition memory. *See also* declarative knowledge, procedural knowledge.

menarche Onset of menstruation in adolescent girls; the average age is 13 years, approximately 3 years after the adolescent growth spurt. It tends to occur earlier in physically larger girls and later in physically smaller girls. There is a strong genetic influence with familial patterns of early or late menarche. Very early (before 8 years of age) menarche may suggest precocious puberty and the need for an endocrinological evaluation. Late menarche is not uncommon in the presence of severe mental retardation, especially when accompanied by short stature; it is also sometimes associated with sex chromosome anomalies (malformation, deformation, disruption, or dysplasia).

meninges The layers of tissue covering the brain and spinal cord. There are three layers labeled from outside to inside: the dura mater, the arachnoid, and the pia mater. The arachnoid is thin and transparent with a space between it and the pia mater, where cerebrospinal fluid (CSF) is found. The pia mater is the closest to the brain and spinal cord. Inflammation or infection of these layers is called *meningitis*.

meningitis An infection of the meninges (covering of the brain and spinal cord). The infection is commonly bacterial but may be viral and termed *aseptic meningitis*. Other causes (e.g., fungal, protozoan) are less common in normal hosts. Bacterial meningitis can be treated with antibiotics; however, damage to the brain may occur from the inflammatory response to the infection. Complications include brain abscess, infarction (stroke), hydrocephalus (excess fluid in the brain), subdural effusions (fluid under one of the meningeal layers), and seizures. Diagnosis is made by examining the cerebrospinal fluid (CSF) obtained by lumbar puncture for white blood cells, bacteria, and chemical abnormalities. Antibiotic treatment is aimed at the causative organism. Long-term sequelae include mental retardation, learning disabilities, attention-deficit/hyperactivity disorder (ADHD), cerebral palsy, seizure disorders, and sensorineural (involving the inner ear or the auditory nerve) hearing loss. Outcome depends on the organism, age of the child (younger children have poorer prognoses), and duration of symptoms prior to treatment.

meningomyelocele *See* myelomeningocele.

Menkes' kinky hair syndrome A genetic syndrome with seizures and a severe neurodegenerative course ending in death; growth deficiency and mental deficiency; and sparse, lightly colored hair that demonstrates structural abnormalities under the microscope. Abnormal copper metabolism has been documented. Inheritance is X-linked recessive.

mental age (MA) Age-equivalent score; a measure of mental development as determined by intelligence and achievement tests, expressed as the age for which that level of performance is the average. Intelligence test tasks are arranged in a progressive order of difficulty so that age levels can be assigned to items. Mental age is determined by the highest age level of the tasks successfully passed. For example, a child with a mental age score of 8 is considered to have the general mental ability of an average 8-year-old, regardless of chronological age. Mental age serves as the numerator in the calculation of a ratio IQ. Although mental age provides a general description of an individual's level of performance, MA units vary throughout the developmental period, and by the early teens the concept of mental age has little meaning. Furthermore, two children with the same mental age may display different skills, strengths, and rates of progress in school, suggesting that additional information is necessary to best describe a child's cognitive abilities.

mental retardation (MR) Substantial limitations in present cognitive functioning. Mental retardation is characterized by significantly subaverage intellectual functioning, existing concurrently with related limitations in two or more of the following applicable adaptive skill areas: communication, self-care, home living, social skills, community use, self-direction, health and safety, functional academics, leisure, and work. Mental retardation manifests before age 18. In the past, mental retardation was qualified by severity of cognitive impairment as mild (IQ between 69 and 50–55), moderate (IQ between 50–55 and 35–40), severe (IQ between 35–40 and 20–25), and profound (IQ below 20–25). In 1992, this categorization was replaced by a more qualitative description of the level of supports necessary for a given person to function. Although *mental retardation* denotes a level of behav-

ioral performance without reference to etiology (cause), in light of current genetic, biochemical, and neuroanatomical knowledge, a functional description of mental retardation mandates a meticulous evaluation for such an etiology.

mental retardation attendant (MRA) Outdated terminology for a one-to-one caregiver for an individual with mental retardation or developmental disabilities. *Behavioral coach* is the current preferred terminology for such a person.

Mental Retardation Facilities and Community Mental Health Centers Construction Act of 1963 (PL 88-164) The federal legislation that created university affiliated facilities (UAFs), now known as university affiliated programs (UAPs), as centers for clinical training and research in mental retardation.

mental status Examination of cognition, memory, and orientation (awareness of one's environment with regard to place, time, and people). Disruption may be relatively permanent (as in mental retardation) or transient (as in diabetic ketoacidosis).

mentum Central point of the chin.

Merrill Language Screening Test (MLST) A brief screening test of receptive and expressive language and articulation for kindergarten and first-grade students. Using a storytelling technique, five areas are assessed: production of complete sentences, utterance length, verb tense agreement, elaboration, and communication competence.

Merrill-Palmer Scale of Mental Tests A battery of infant tests for children 18–71 months of age; the items are predominantly nonverbal and heavily based on perceptual-motor skills. The instrument is rarely used, but isolated subtests are employed in more individualized assessments. The newer Extended Merrill-Palmer Scale exhibits improved standardization but is a more verbal test.

mesomelic   Referring to the central segment of a limb (forearm or leg).

mesomorph   Athletic body type.

MESSY   *See* Matson Evaluation of Social Skills with Youngsters.

meta-analysis   Quantitative research synthesis; statistical methods for integrating data across studies. It is an inductive method that proceeds from particular observations (studies) to general inclusive statements and yields a statistic that represents the magnitude of experimental effects reported in these studies.

metabolite   A chemical by-product or waste produced in the body. The presence of a metabolite of abnormal quantity or quality in the blood or urine suggests the presence of a metabolic disorder. Untreated metabolic disorders often have significant developmental consequences. *Metabolic screening* describes a panel of laboratory tests to search for the presence of atypical metabolites and is a frequent item in the assessment of a child with serious mental retardation of unknown etiology (cause).

metachromatic leukodystrophy (MLD)   A progressive and ultimately fatal disorder of the central nervous system due to an enzyme (arylsulfatase A) deficiency. Hyporeflexia and profound mental retardation are characteristic in MLD. Incidence is 1 in 40,000. Inheritance is autosomal recessive, with a recurrence risk of 25%.

metacognition   Knowledge about one's thought processes and how to regulate strategies for thought or learning. Knowledge about cognition develops during adolescence. Regulation of learning is generally acquired early (in preschool) and includes planning, monitoring one's activities, and checking outcomes. Some students with learning disabilities and many students with attention-deficit/hyperactivity disorder (ADHD) have difficulty with one or more aspects of metacognition.

metatarsus adductus   An orthopedic deformity of infants in which the feet appear to turn inward at mid-foot.

metatarsus adductus

methyl mercury   A chemical fungicide that can affect the developing central nervous system; prenatal exposure has been linked to cerebral palsy, mental retardation, and blindness.

methylmalonic aciduria   A metabolic disorder that, if untreated, leads to episodic vomiting, lethargy, and coma as well as mental retardation. Treatment includes a protein-restricted diet and vitamin B_{12}. Incidence is 1 in 100,000. Inheritance is autosomal recessive, with a recurrence risk of 25%.

methylphenidate (MPH)   Trade name Ritalin; the most commonly used stimulant medication for treatment of attention-deficit/hyperactivity disorder (ADHD) and hyperactivity in children and adults. It is manufactured in multiples of 5 milligrams. The duration of action is 4 hours, although a long-acting (SR, sustained release) formulation is available. Because of its addictive potential, the distribution of Ritalin is regulated as a controlled substance; however, addiction is not a problem in subjects with attentional problems. Side effects include headache, stomachache, anorexia (loss of appetite), poor growth, and sleep problems; these can usually be managed by titrating the dosage.

methylphenobarbital   Trade name Mebaral; a derivative of phenobarbital used in the past instead of phenobarbital because it was thought to have fewer side effects. It has no advantage over phenobarbital in controlling seizures.

metoclopramide   Trade name Reglan; a dopamine antagonist used in the treatment of gastroesophageal reflux.

Metropolitan Readiness Tests–Fifth Edition (MRT)   A skill-based assessment of skills in reading, mathematics, and language development that contribute to early learning success for children in prekindergarten through first grade.

MFF   *See* Matching Familiar Figures Test.

MFFT   *See* Matching Familiar Figures Test.

MFP   *See* Multidisciplinary Feeding Profile.

microcephaly   Abnormally small head; significantly small head sizes are variously considered to be 2.0, 2.5, or 3.0 standard deviations below the mean for age. Small head size automatically implies small brain size, but this in turn does not necessarily indicate mental retardation. Nevertheless, decreasing head size does correlate with an increasing incidence of mental retardation, whereas milder decreases in head size (on the order of 1.5 standard deviations below the mean) have been associated with learning disabilities and language disorders. Proportional microcephaly—a small head size with short stature—is less strongly correlated with mental retardation. Microcephaly can result from intrauterine infection and radiation, as well as numerous genetic syndromes. Familial microcephaly can be a marker for familial mental retardation.

micrognathia   A small jaw; can be a normal variant, a familial trait, a minor malformation, or part of an identifiable syndrome (e.g., Pierre Robin syndrome).

micronutrient   A dietary element necessary only in small quantities.

micropolygyria   A migrational anomaly in cerebral architecture where the gyri (hills) are too small and too numerous. There are also abnormalities in the number of cortical layers and their orientation (columnar rather than laminar, as in the normal brain). Clinically, these people have severe mental retardation and hypotonia (decreased muscle tone) or spasticity (increased muscle tone) depending upon the areas of brain affected. This can be present in syndromes such as Zellweger syndrome (cerebrohepatorenal syndrome, an autosomal recessive disorder); how-

ever, most cases are sporadic. Magnetic resonance imaging (MRI) can visualize this pattern of gyral architecture.

microswitch   An adaptive technology category of electronic devices and mechanisms that simplifies the operation of electrical equipment from toys to computers. These devices reduce the more elaborate operation of many common items to the manipulation of a single control, increasing the accessibility and utility of the items for individuals with severe physical disabilities.

micturition   Urination.

mid-line   Sagittal plane; an imaginary vertical line dividing the body into the left and right sides. The motor acts of skipping and of drawing a line from the right to the left side of the page variously involve crossing the mid-line. Difficulty crossing the mid-line or coordinating both sides of the body can be an indication of a perceptual or neurological problem.

mid-parental height   The arithmetic mean of the heights of both biological parents; used to project a child's adult height and expected height growth percentile.

mid-temporal epilepsy   *See* benign rolandic epilepsy.

Mietens syndrome   A genetic syndrome with mild mental retardation, short stature, corneal clouding (with visual defect), narrow nose, flexion contractures of the elbows, and short forearms. Inheritance is probably autosomal recessive.

Milani-Comparetti Motor Development Screening Test   A motoscopic (visual pattern analysis) evaluation procedure for children in the first 2 years of life that relates postural control and active movement to primitive reflexes, tilting, righting, and parachute reactions. The protocol sheet provides a graphic record of the child's progress.

mild mental retardation   Mental retardation in which the IQ level is between 50 and 70. Adults with mild mental retardation typically achieve functional literacy and are able to live independently (or with minimal assistance) in the community. Sometimes referred to as *educable mental retardation (EMR)*.

MILI *See* Multilevel Informal Language Inventory.

milieu teaching A naturalistic language intervention strategy using everyday instances of social-communicative exchange to teach elaborated language. It incorporates many features of incidental teaching but is broader in focus. This model requires teachers to 1) arrange the environment to facilitate a child's use of language, 2) assess the functioning levels of a child, and 3) discover ways for a child to interact with the environment.

milieu therapy A form of residential treatment that attempts to create and maintain a wholly positive living environment within a residential community by enlisting the efforts of all staff members as providers of therapeutic contact. *See also* residential treatment.

milkmaid grip A grasp that waxes and wanes abruptly; seen in choreoathetosis.

Miller Assessment for Preschoolers (MAP) A comprehensive developmental screening test for identifying children (ages 2-9 to 5-8) who exhibit moderate preacademic problems. Administration time is approximately 20–30 minutes.

Miller-Dieker syndrome Lissencephaly syndrome; a specific pattern malformation including lissencephaly (smooth, rather than convoluted, brain surface), with other central nervous system malformations: small brain stem, heterotopia (tissue displacement), absence of the corpus callosum, and areas of pachygyria (broad, flat cerebral convolutions). Also associated with facial anomalies, microcephaly (abnormally small head), a high forehead with vertical and central furrowing, small nose with anteverted nostrils, and low-set, posteriorly rotated ears. Severe mental retardation with hypotonia (decreased muscle tone), opisthotonos (arching of the back), failure to thrive,

and seizures are the rule. Death usually occurs in the first 2 years of life. Etiology (cause) is a visible deletion on chromosome 17 p 13.

Miller-Yoder Language Comprehension Test (MY) A picture-format test of language comprehension for children between the ages of 4 and 8 years. Comprehension of short sentences with a variety of grammatical structures is assessed.

Milwaukee brace A thoracolumbosacral brace that goes from the chin to the hips and is used to treat scoliosis (spinal curvature).

Milwaukee Project A controlled, intensive early intervention program for 20 disadvantaged children (and their mothers, who have mental retardation) from early in their first year of life to 6 years of age. The dramatically positive results of this study remain controversial.

Milwaukee brace

minimal brain damage/dysfunction (MBD) A loosely organized constellation of symptoms that includes short attention span, distractibility, impulsivity, hyperactivity, emotional lability (changeability), motor incoordination, visual-perceptual motor disturbance, and language disorder. MBD encompasses the current attention-deficit disorder (with and without hyperactivity), learning disability, developmental language disorder, and clumsy child syndrome. The utility of the MBD concept is that it stresses comorbidity—the marked overlap among these diagnostic categories.

Minneapolis Preschool Screening Instrument (MPSI) A brief screening test for 4-year-olds, for the purpose of identifying children who may need special education services.

Minnesota Percepto-Diagnostic Test (MPD) A test of visual-perceptual motor skills with separate age norms for children 5–14 years of age as well as for adults.

The test requires the subject to copy six designs, with the score based on rotations, separations, and distortions. The results assist in the classification of learning disabilities and emotional disorders. The six stimulus cards are rotations of two Bender Gestalt figures.

minor dysmorphic features Mild superficial malformations; singly these dysmorphic characteristics are best considered normal variants or familial traits; the presence of several of these features may contribute to an overall appearance that is part of a specific syndrome. When no syndrome is identified, the presence of more than four minor dysmorphic features on a scale such as the Waldrop scale (developed by Mary Waldrop) is interpreted as suggesting a disturbance occurring during the first trimester of pregnancy and affecting the ectodermal layer of the embryo and contributing to mild abnormalities of ectodermal derivatives—hair, skin, and brain. Increased dysmorphology scores are associated with attention problems, hyperactivity, cognitive impairments, and the entire spectrum of neurodevelopmental disabilities. In the presence of a developmental diagnosis, a high minor malformation score provides support for a prenatal etiology (origin). Common minor dysmorphic features include abnormal hair whorl patterns, microcephaly (abnormally small head), macrocephaly (enlarged head circumference), epicanthal folds, pinna (external ear) anomalies (malformation, deformation, disruption, or dysplasia), high-arched or steeled palate, geographic tongue, clinodactyly (deflection of fingers), palmar crease abnormalities (e.g., simian crease, Sydney line), sandal gap deformity, and syndactyly (webbing of the fingers or toes).

minor motor seizure Lennox-Gastaut syndrome; consists of at least four seizure types: atonic (akinetic), myoclonic, brief tonic, and atypical absence/petit mal. The etiology (cause) of these seizures ranges from infections of the brain (encephalitis and meningitis) to perinatal problems and genetic disorders. Minor motor seizures are generally present throughout the indi-vidual's life span and can be seen with focal and generalized tonic-clonic seizures. Mental development in children with these types of seizures is slow, with 65% having an IQ below 75, reflecting the frequency of seizures as well as the underlying brain disease. Many anticonvulsants are used, but the success rate is poor. Those used include valproic acid (Depakene), clonazepam (Klonopin, formerly Clonopin), ethosuximide (Zarontin), adrenocorticotropic hormone (ACTH), lorazepam (Ativan), primidone (Mysoline), and diazepam (Valium). The ketogenic diet is also prescribed under some circumstances.

minor neurological dysfunction *See* soft neurological sign.

minor tranquilizer Sedatives and antianxiety drugs.

mirror movements Associated or overflow movements on the contralateral (opposite) side of the body, such as those that can be observed when testing fine-finger movements. A soft neurological sign or sign of minor neurological dysfunction.

missing parts test A type of test in which the subject must identify the part missing from a picture.

mitochondrial myopathy A class of disorders affecting peripheral (noncentral) muscles and the central nervous system, often resulting in progressive weakness, seizures, and cognitive deterioration. One such example is MERRF syndrome, in which the muscle tissue has a characteristic pattern described as red ragged fibers. These disorders are inherited through the mitochondria, which are found in the cytoplasm. Because the only cytoplasm in the embryo comes from the egg, these disorders are always inherited from the mother.

mixed cerebral palsy Describes a case of cerebral palsy that has significant features of more than one subtype, usually a combination of a spastic subtype with an extrapyramidal subtype. There are no fixed guidelines for how many individual characteristics of each subtype need to be present to qualify for the descriptor "mixed." This is especially confusing, because the more closely one examines a given case of cerebral palsy, the more likely one is to find signs of more than one subtype: all cases are mixed to some extent. A good rule of thumb is to label the case as mixed only when the presence of each subtype must be recognized because of the risks for associated deficits specific to those subtypes.

MLD *See* metachromatic leukodystrophy.

MLST *See* Merrill Language Screening Test.

MLU *See* mean length of utterance.

MMR Combined live attenuated vaccines against measles, mumps, and rubella; one of the primary routine immunizations (vaccinations) of childhood.

mnemonic Relating to memory, and especially to artificial techniques to improve the memory.

mobility The ability to move with appropriate ease, flexibility, and range. A person with physical or motor disabilities may be impaired in one or more of these respects, requiring assistive devices and environmental modifications to facilitate mobility. Thus, an amputee may require a prosthesis; a person with orthopedic disabilities may require special shoes, braces, canes, or crutches; and a person with cerebral palsy or a stroke may require a wheelchair. In addition, ramps, elevators, widened doors, and car and bus lifts may be necessary environmental modifications to ensure complete mobility. For many people, personal mobility may be compromised by a lack of accessible public transportation to allow linkage with needed health and welfare services. The Americans with Disabilities Act of 1990 (PL 101-336) mandates the removal of architectural barriers from all public buildings and the alteration of facilities and their amenities to ensure physical accessibility to individuals with disabilities as one aspect of widening the experiences of, and opportunities for, Americans with disabilities.

Möbius syndrome Congenital and usually bilateral facial (sixth and seventh cranial nerves) paralysis with an expressionless, masklike facies. This is a fairly nonspecific syndrome with a variety of associated features (e.g., micrognathia [small jaw] and clubfoot) and diverse etiologies (causes), including rare autosomal dominant inheritance. Other cranial nerve involvement (III, IV, V, IX, X, and XII) can lead to ptosis (drooping eyelids) and feeding and articulation problems. The Möbius syndrome may be part of a broader malformation pattern including syndactyly (webbing of the fingers or toes), clubfoot, and limb reduction defects. Only 15% of people with this syndrome have mental retardation, but early appearance of the expressionless face, poor speech, feeding disorder, and other impairments may misleadingly contribute to a misdiagnosis of mental retardation. In older children, the dull, apathetic, Möbius facies can resemble the adenoidal facies. Named after the German neurologist Paul Möbius (1853–1907).

mode The most frequent score in a set of scores (e.g., 3 is the mode for the data 1, 1, 2, 3, 3, 3, 4, 9, 9, 18). When two scores occur more frequently than others with the same frequency, the distribution is bimodal (e.g., 2 and 7 are the modes for the data 1, 2, 2, 2, 3, 6, 7, 7, 7, 10, 12). When the same is true of more than two scores, the distribution is multimodal (e.g., 4, 5, and 10 are the modes for the data 2, 4, 4, 4, 6, 5, 5, 5, 7, 9, 10, 10, 10, 11).

modeling Behavior modification technique that uses imitation. *See also* behavior modeling.

moderate mental retardation Mental retardation in which the IQ level is between 35 and 55. Adults with moderate mental retardation typically have learned to read survival words, have been trained to perform semiskilled labor, and can live in supervised group homes in the community.

Sometimes referred to as *trainable mental retardation (TMR)*.

Mohr syndrome Mohr-Rimoin syndrome; oral-facial-digital syndrome, type II (OFD–II). A genetic syndrome with cleft tongue, a peculiar facies, an abnormality of the big toe, and conductive deafness. Mental retardation is an occasional associated feature. Inheritance is autosomal recessive.

Mongolian spot Bluish discoloration of the skin over the back and buttocks, present at birth, more common in African American babies, and tending to fade with time; not to be confused with bruising secondary to battered child syndrome.

Mongoloid/mongolism/mongolian idiocy An antiquated and unacceptable term to describe people with Down syndrome. Derived originally from John Langdon H. Down's (1828–1896) hypothesis in 1866 of an ethnic atavism (racial throwback) etiology (cause) for this subgroup of individuals with mental retardation, and later fostered by both popular misconceptions and pseudoscientific theories masquerading as physical anthropology. (The term *Mongoloid* still has an accurate, if restricted, usage in anthropology.)

Mongoloid slant An apparently upward (going from the nose laterally) slant to the palpebral fissure (eye slit). A component of the facies in Down syndrome, many other genetic syndromes, a racial and familial characteristic, and a potentially sporadic isolated finding of no clinical significance. The Mongoloid slant

Mongoloid slant

may be more common in conditions with microcephaly (abnormally small head) or with malar (cheekbone) hypoplasia (atypical tissue development).

monitoring ability The capacity to exercise quality control over one's performance. Difficulty with monitoring can result in careless mistakes with no perceptual awareness of their having occurred. Chil-

dren with attention problems often demonstrate poor self-monitoring skills.

monoplegia Literally, "one palsy"; a topographical subtype of spastic cerebral palsy. By the usual mechanisms of brain injury, it is very difficult to localize the resulting impairment to a single extremity (arm or leg); thus, a pure monoplegic cerebral palsy is exceedingly rare. What is thought to be a monoplegia usually turns out, on closer inspection, to be a hemiplegia (paralysis of half the body) with almost undetectable lower extremity involvement, the common Erb palsy, or the rare Klumpke palsy. Because of the mildness of the condition, the associated findings are minimal.

monosomy A condition in which one of a pair of chromosomes is missing, resulting in only 45 chromosomes (as found in Turner syndrome—the absence of one X chromosome). No other complete monosomies are compatible with life. Individuals with a partial monosomy are missing part of one chromosome in a pair. Children with partial monosomies of chromosomes other than the sex chromosomes tend to have major anatomical abnormalities (e.g., heart disease), dysmorphic (atypical) features, and mental retardation.

monotherapy The practice of using a single anticonvulsant in seizure treatment. The selection of the appropriate anticonvulsant is based on the type of seizures and the potential toxicity. Although monotherapy is the ideal treatment, it is not always successful, and in complicated cases polytherapy (more than one medication) may be needed.

monozygotic twins Identical twins; two individuals with the same genetic makeup (same genotype) who came from the same egg and sperm.

Monroe Diagnostic Reading Test A reading readiness test for kindergarten and primary grade children. It profiles reading skills and yields an arithmetic, spelling, and mental age for comparison.

Montessori method Educational approach developed by Italian physician Maria Montessori (1870–1952) that is based on the heavily sensorimotor activity programs developed by two French physicians (Jean Marc Gaspard Itard [1774–1838] and Edouard Seguin [1812–1880]) for their work with people with mental retardation. There are two major divisions in the current application of the Montessori method: the International Montessori, which adheres fairly strictly to the original program; and the American Montessori, which has developed a more eclectic approach.

mood A pervasive and sustained emotion that, if extreme, has a marked impact upon a person's perception of the world. Examples of mood include depression, anxiety, anger, and elation. *See also* emotion.

mood disorder A class of psychiatric disorders in which mood is abnormally depressed or elevated beyond a specific time period and is accompanied by behavior and cognitive changes uncharacteristic of the person's normal level of functioning. Examples of such mood disorders include major depressive disorder, panic states, and manic-depressive illness (bipolar and unipolar types). In children, particularly those with developmental disabilities mood deviance is more commonly present as anhedonia (inability to feel happy) or irritability, rather than active depression or elation. These variations are viewed both in children and adults as diagnostic equivalents to more classic mood deviances. When such modes of expression are presented, other behavior, cognitive, and physiological symptoms may not be so apparent.

Moos Family Environment Scale A 90-item self-report instrument to measure the social and environmental characteristics of all types of families and to generate 10 conceptually based subscales and three factors. Originally normed on 285 families, the reported psychometric properties have recently been challenged by more recent data that have failed to replicate and support the original results. Nonetheless,

the scale remains a frequently used instrument.

Moral Judgement Inventory (forms A and B) A structured interview for elementary school–age children to adults, designed to assess stages of moral development as defined by Lawrence Kohlberg. There are two forms of the interview, each consisting of three stories and accompanying questions addressing various aspects of the moral issue presented. To facilitate scoring, examples are provided to exemplify answers characteristic of Kohlberg's five developmental stages.

morbidity Illness or disease.

morbidity rate A count of the number of diseases per unit of population per unit of time.

Morgan Neonatal Neurobehavioral Examination An assessment of tone and motor patterns, primitive reflexes, and behavioral responses in newborns born at term.

Moro reflex A primitive reflex in which sudden extension of the head at the neck (stimulus) produces extension followed by flexion of all four extremities (arms or legs) (an embrace response). It is present in all newborns and fades in the first several months. Absence, exaggeration, and asymmetry are significant.

moron Obsolete and unacceptable term for an individual with mental retardation and an IQ between 50 and 70. Derived from the Greek word for "stupid," its usage to describe the highest class of feeble-minded was suggested by Henry Herbert Goddard (1866–1957) and adopted by the American Association for the Study of the Feeble-minded in 1910.

morpheme The smallest meaning-bearing unit in a language. For example, the word *dog* is a morpheme; in the plural form *dogs,* the *s* is an added morpheme. In the sentence, *clean the table,* all three words are morphemes because even the two-syllable word *table* cannot be divided without destroying its meaning. The acquisition of grammatical morphemes generally occurs in the same sequence and is probably controlled by a combination of syntactic (language structure) and semantic (meaning systems) complexity.

morphology The study of meaning units in any particular language; the study of morphemes. *See* morpheme.

Morquio syndrome Brailsford syndrome; mucopolysaccharidosis (MPS) IV. A genetic syndrome of growth deficiency, mildly coarse facies with severe kyphosis (curvature of the spine) and knock-knees, cloudy corneas, and hepatomegaly (liver enlargement); intelligence is usually normal. Named after the Uruguayan pediatrician Luis Morquio (1867–1935).

mortality Death.

mortality rate The number of deaths per unit of population per unit of time.

mosaicism A condition in which different cells in an individual have a different genetic makeup. For example, some children with Down syndrome have trisomy 21 in skin cells but not in blood cells. In general, individuals with mosaicism have less severe manifestations of chromosomal abnormalities; however, they do manifest many of the characteristics of disorders.

motherese Baby talk; short, simple, repetitive sentences that adults use with a high-pitched voice when talking with infants and young children.

Mother's Assessment of the Behavior of her Infant (MABI) A modification of the Brazelton Neonatal Behavior Assessment Scale (BNBAS) that can be administered by mothers.

motivation A hypothetical construct devised to make behavior more understandable and predictable. Although some theorists have described motivation as an unconscious trait resulting primarily from early learning experiences, others conceptualize it in terms of conscious beliefs and values and stress the effects of recent success and failure experiences. Individuals are motivated to achieve particular goals.

When individuals attend to one thing and not another, they are motivated with regard to the former and not the latter. The motivational orientations of teachers and students may be incompatible. Students who do not work hard on school tasks may not be unmotivated; instead, they may have different goals. The term *unmotivated* is often used pejoratively, as though the student's lack of success is his or her own fault. This is a simplification of motivational theory. Any motivational change must begin with the question "Why?" and encompass both past and present experiences. Motivation may be classified as external and internal; most efforts to improve students' motivation use an external frame of reference. This is sometimes, but not always, appropriate.

motor disorders A disorder of movement that involves a delay in the achievement of or a limitation in the performance of gross-motor (posture and locomotion) or fine-motor (eye–hand) skills.

Motor-Free Visual Perception Test (MVPT) An individual test for visual perception in children in which the tasks avoid motor involvement. The 36 test items tap spatial relationships, visual discrimination, figure–ground, visual closure, and visual motor; each item is multiple choice and requires only a pointing response. The raw score yields a perceptual age and a perceptual quotient for children whose visual-perceptual abilities are between the levels of a 4-year-old and a 9-year-old.

motor function Functioning of the voluntary muscles of the body and the nerves supplying them. Important features are muscle mass, tone, and strength. Motor dysfunction is found in many forms of cerebral palsy. For example, in a right hemiplegia (paralysis of half the body), muscle mass and strength are decreased on the right side compared to the left, but muscle tone is increased. The pattern of dysfunction is used to determine not only into which diagnostic category a person fits but also the location of the lesion in the nervous system. A knowledge of the level of a lesion in a case of myelomeningocele (protuberance of both the spinal cord and its lining) may allow some prediction of later functional levels in motor skills.

motor impersistence An impaired ability to maintain a motor position for an age-appropriate time period. A number of tests have standardized norms for standing on one foot, but the behavior may be observed spontaneously during the physical examination.

motor memory The ability to recall distinct motor patterns; the capacity to remember letter formations and play piano chords are examples. Children with motor memory limitations may have particular trouble with handwriting. *See also* memory.

motor neuron disease An impairment of voluntary movement by the destruction of nerve cells involved in the motor pathway. In upper motor neuron disease, the motor nerve cells that are destroyed are in the brain; in lower motor neuron disease, they are in the spinal cord.

motor overflow Involuntary movements that are associated with voluntary movements; *see also* associated movements.

motor planning Praxis; the ability to plan new or nonhabitual movements.

mouth breathing A behavior commonly secondary to nasal obstruction (adenoidal facies). When not associated with allergy and nasal obstruction, it is sometimes present in mental retardation.

mouth-opening finger-spreading phenomenon A test of associated movements in which the child's relaxed arms are draped over the examiner's extended forearm and the child is asked to close the eyes, open the mouth, and stick out the tongue. The degrees of extension and spreading of the fingers and spooning (hyperextension) are noted. Excessive response for age suggests nervous system immaturity.

Movement ABC *See* Movement Assessment Battery for Children.

Movement Assessment Battery for Children (Movement ABC) A physical skills assessment and program-planning instrument for children ages 4–12 years; it yields both normative and qualitative measures of manual dexterity, ball skills, and static and dynamic balance, and offers guidelines for management and remediation.

Movement Assessment of Infants (MAI) A test used to evaluate and describe motor skills in infants from birth to 12 months of age; 65 items comprise four subtests of tone, primitive reflexes, automatic reactions, and voluntary movement.

movement disorder A condition characterized by involuntary movements—including chorea, athetosis (involuntary twisting of the upper extremities), tremor, dystonia (impaired muscle tone), and tics—or a decrease or absence of normal movement. Movement disorders may be associated with neurological or developmental problems in the cases of cerebral palsy and Rett syndrome. These can be acute (generally precipitated by an identifiable event such as an infection or head injury) or chronic. Chronic disorders may be isolated, associated with progressive neurological deterioration, or found with a systemic (body) disease. Movement disorders caused by medication generally resolve after the medication is discontinued. Those caused by diffuse brain damage after head injury or lack of oxygen to the brain tend to be resistant to many medications such as haloperidol or anticonvulsants, which are generally used to treat movement disorders. There are many genetic causes of movement disorders: Tourette syndrome, Wilson syndrome, juvenile Huntington disease, and Lesch-Nyhan syndrome. Some movement disorders, such as transient tics, resolve; others, such as the fine tremor of thyrotoxicosis (toxic hyperactivity of the thyroid gland), respond to treatment of the underlying condition; while still others do not respond to medication and may worsen with age.

MPD *See* multiple personality disorder; *see also* Minnesota Percepto-Diagnostic Test.

MPH *See* methylphenidate; also denotes an advanced degree, Master of Public Health.

MPS *See* mucopolysaccharidosis.

MPSI *See* Minneapolis Preschool Screening Instrument.

MR *See* mental retardation.

MR scans *See* magnetic resonance imaging.

MRA *See* mental retardation attendant.

MRI *See* magnetic resonance imaging.

MRT *See* Metropolitan Readiness Tests.

MS *See* multiple sclerosis.

MSBP *See* Münchausen syndrome by proxy.

MSEL *See* Mullen Scales of Early Learning.

MST *See* McCarthy Screening Test.

MSUD *See* maple syrup urine disease.

M.S.W. *See* Master of Social Work; *see also* social work.

Muckle-Wells syndrome A genetic syndrome with urticaria (hives), progressive sensorineural (involving the inner ear or the auditory nerve) deafness, and nephritis (kidney disease) due to a pathological process known as amyloidosis; onset is in adolescence. Inheritance is autosomal dominant with variable expressivity.

mucolipidoses A group of diseases characterized by physical findings similar to the mucopolysaccharidoses (MPS); there is a storage of mucopolysaccharides (complex carbohydrates) and other chemicals in body tissues with normal levels of metabolites in the urine. There are four types —mucopolylipidoses I–V; mucopolylipidosis II is also called I-cell (for inclusion cell) disease. In all of these disorders, an enzyme that enables the breakdown of mucopolysaccharides is not working;

therefore, the levels of mucopolysaccharides build up in the cells and cause damage. The resulting physical features include coarsening of the face, poor growth, enlarged liver and spleen, restricted joint mobility, and progressive mental deterioration. These disorders are generally inherited in an autosomal recessive manner and can be diagnosed by testing for enzyme activity or visualizing deposits of mucopolysaccharides and their products under the microscope. The course of the disorder is dependent upon the type of enzyme deficiency and can range from blindness and mental retardation to death in childhood.

mucopolysaccharidosis (MPS) A group of heterogeneous genetic syndromes in which excess mucopolysaccharide (complex carbohydrate) is stored in various body tissues and organs; depending on the specific enzyme deficit, the severity, the time course, and the organ system involved, a variety of clinical pictures can result. Coarse, thickened facial features, stiff joints leading to a crouched jockey stance, growth deficiency, hepatosplenomegaly (enlargement of the liver and spleen), microcephaly (abnormally small head), corneal clouding, and mental retardation are present in diverse combinations and with varying degrees of severity depending on the specific type and subtype of enzyme deficiency, as follows: IH, Hurler; IS, Scheie; IH/S, Hurler-Scheie compound; II, Hunter; III, Sanfilippo; IV, Morquio; V, former designation for Scheie; VI, Maroteaux-Lamy; and VII, Sly. Hunter syndrome is X-linked; all of the other MPS syndromes are autosomal recessive with a 25% recurrence risk.

Mullen Scales of Early Learning (MSEL) A developmental assessment tool with an information processing orientation; it consists of five subscales that may be employed independently: visual receptive, visual expressive, language receptive, language expressive, and in infants, gross motor. The MSEL is for children 15–69 months of age; the Infant MSEL is for children from birth to 36 months of age. The scales are both screening and diagnostic tests.

multiaxial classification system An approach to diagnosis that utilizes several different dimensions in composing the final formulation, rather than reducing data to a single label or category. A case is characterized in terms of a number of clinically important factors, rather than being assigned to a single diagnostic category. The *Diagnostic and Statistical Manual of Mental Disorders* (4th edition) has five axes: Axis I, the primary classification or diagnosis of a psychiatric syndrome; Axis II, existence and evaluation of an individual's developmental and personality disorders of childhood or adolescence that persist into adulthood; Axis III, determination of possible physical or medical disorders; Axis IV, the severity of psychosocial stressors in the recent past that may have contributed to the current clinical problem or may influence the course of treatment; and Axis V, a global assessment of adaptive functioning, with ratings made for both current functioning and the highest level of functioning during the past year. Although a multiaxial approach to developmental disabilities is desirable, the *Diagnostic and Statistical Manual of Mental Disorders* (4th edition) is not sufficiently refined in the major developmental categories.

multicultural education Teaching toward a pluralistic society. This concept includes both the impact of various cultures and ethnicities on society at large, as well as an awareness of cultural diversities of learning and behavior within the educational system.

multidisciplinary Describing a team approach to the diagnosis and treatment of developmental disabilities; in such a team, the interactions among the professionals representing two or more disciplines are limited to each professional's independent case formulation, focusing on that professional's traditional boundaries; integration of the findings is cumulative, with disagreements being arbitrated by nonprofessional parameters such as discipline hierarchy or bureaucratic policy.

Multidisciplinary Feeding Profile (MFP) A numerical rating scale to describe a variety of feeding-related behaviors in dependent individuals with severe disabilities; the scale takes 30–45 minutes to administer.

multifactorial Descriptive of a disorder caused by the interaction of multiple factors (e.g., genetic, environmental, psychological), with each factor contributing a small, but additive or multiplicative, effect. Contrast with *polygenic.*

multifocal In many places.

Multilevel Informal Language Inventory (MILI) An informal language assessment for children from kindergarten through grade six that uses survey scenes, survey stories, and other probes to assess critical semantic (meaning systems) relations and syntactic (language structure) constructions.

multiple disabilities The coexistence of more than one disability in a single individual. The more severe a single disability, the more likelihood that a second disability may be present. The overall impact of multiple disabilities is greater than the impact of the sum of the individual disabilities.

multiple lentigines syndrome LEOPARD syndrome; a genetic syndrome with *L*entigines (dark freckles), *E*lectrocardiographic (EEG) abnormalities, *O*cular hypertelorism (widely spaced eyes), *P*ulmonic stenosis (a heart valve problem), genital *A*bnormalities, growth *R*etardation, and sensorineural (involving the inner ear or the auditory nerve) *D*eafness. Inheritance is autosomal dominant with variable expressivity.

multiple personality disorder (MPD) A psychiatric disorder characterized by two or more distinct personalities, each with its own identity, characteristics, and memories. The etiology (cause) for such extreme psychological fragmentation is severe physical, sexual, or emotional trauma occurring under conditions that allow for no physical escape—so that the individual can only escape psychologically. The personalities often coexist with no awareness of each other. Thus, multiple personality disorder is a creative psychological solution to a horrifying, inescapable situation. Unfortunately, such an escape route becomes a difficulty in and of itself. Untreated people with multiple personality disorder have severe emotional disabilities.

multiple sclerosis (MS) A progressive disease of the central nervous system with adult onset; not to be confused with childhood onset muscular dystrophy.

Muma Assessment Program (MAP) A nonstandardized criterion-referenced "testing for teaching" assessment of cognitive-linguistic-communication systems for children from preschool through early elementary ages that taps: different learning styles; sensory motor skills; rule- and nonrule-governed learning; and concepts of conservation, quantity, and likeness.

Münchausen syndrome by proxy (MSBP) A condition in which a child is presented for medical care with symptoms that are fabricated or produced by the caregiver. Significant maternal psychopathology is usually the cause. Fictitious developmental disability symptoms have been reported. The syndrome is at one end of the spectrum of child abuse. Münchausen syndrome (typically manufactured by the adult who concocts symptoms to obtain repeated and unnecessary surgical and medical procedures) is named after the 18th-century German raconteur Baron Karl Friedrich Hieronymous Münchausen, whose exploits were exaggerated in Rudolph Eric Raspe's (1737–94) satirical and ludicrous *Adventures of Baron Münchausen.*

murmur A soft sound; usually refers to an unusual heart sound that may be innocent (not indicative of heart disease) or pathological (indicative of heart disease). The presence of a heart murmur does not reflect the severity of any heart disease that may be present. Some childhood heart murmurs resolve spontaneously (are outgrown).

muscular dystrophy A group of genetic disorders leading to progressive muscular atrophy (wasting) and weakness; the different types exhibit varying distribution, severity, and temporal evolution. When the muscles that carry out respiration are involved, the disorder can become fatal.

music therapy A treatment approach that utilizes music and movement in a variety of forms to modify nonmusical behavior and to promote mental health, social development, emotional adjustment, and motor coordination. Used as a therapeutic tool in rehabilitation to meet recreational or educational goals, music therapy includes playing instruments, moving to music, creating music, singing, and listening to music. Music therapy is utilized in a variety of applications in hospitals, schools, institutions, and private settings through both individual and group approaches, often in conjunction with other types of therapy and/or rehabilitation. Both music education and music therapy contribute to special education by promoting learning and self-growth through enjoyable activities.

mutation A change in the gene such that the protein coded for by that gene is manufactured in a nonfunctional form. Commonly, disorders inherited in an autosomal dominant manner (by a single gene) can be caused by a mutation to a single gene.

mutism Inability or refusal to speak. *Deaf-mute* refers to a person who does not speak and has severe hearing impairment; *deaf and dumb* is not acceptable usage.

MVPT *See* Motor-Free Visual Perception Test.

MY *See* Miller-Yoder Language Comprehension Test.

myasthenia gravis An immunological syndrome of muscle weakness and exhaustion that occurs in episodic and reversible attacks.

myelin basic protein (MBP) A biochemical marker of brain injury; increased levels of MBP in the cerebrospinal fluid (CSF) correlate with brain (white matter) damage and degenerative (demyelinating) disorders.

myelination Myelinization; the process of covering the axon (part of the nerve cell) with a sheet of myelin (a fatty insulation material). The rate of development can be slowed by delays or abnormalities in myelination.

myelomeningocele Meningomyelocele, spina bifida; a congenital defect of the spinal column resulting in the protrusion of the spinal cord and its coverings (meninges) from the baby's back. There

myelomeningocele

are varying levels of functional impairment (motor paralysis and sensory loss) depending on the size and level of the sack. The condition is also associated with hydrocephalus (excess fluid in the brain) and a variable degree of cognitive impairment. Long-term considerations include ambulation and bowel/bladder control.

Myers-Briggs Type Indicator (MBTI) A self-administered measure of personality dispositions and preferences; this 20- to 30-minute test has a seventh-grade reading level and places the individual on four Jungian continua: extraversion/introversion, sensing/intuition, thinking/feeling, and judging/perceiving. The Murphy-Meisgeier Type Indicator for children extends the MBTI down to grades two to eight to allow a better delineation of individual learning styles.

myoclonic-astatic *See* Lennox-Gastaut syndrome.

myoclonus Rapid and sudden unpredictable jerks that are involuntary. These are present in some kinds of seizures. They may occur normally when falling asleep or with hiccups (i.e., myoclonus of the diaphragm).

myoclonus, epileptic Synchronous, small, recurring twitches generally occurring in the fingers and hands and associated with chronic seizure disorders such as Lennox-Gastaut syndrome. Myoclonic movements are preceded by abnormalities of the electroencephalogram (EEG). These movements are associated with viral encephalitis (brain inflammation), metabolic disturbances such as uremia (found in kidney disease), and progressive cerebral degenerative diseases.

myoclonus, nonepileptic Myoclonus not associated with seizures, as found in many situations (e.g., in typical people who are going to sleep). A familial form of myoclonus (probably autosomal dominant) called *paramyoclonus multiplex*, or *essential myoclonus*, combines frequent but nonprogressive myoclonus with low-average intelligence. This condition is also associated with an exaggerated startle, hypertonia (increased muscle tone) in infancy, nocturnal leg jerking, and an unsteady gait. It often responds to clonezepam (Klonopin). Myoclonus may originate in the brain stem or the spinal cord and produce myoclonic jerks unresponsive to sensory stimuli that persist in sleep. Response to anticonvulsant medication in this situation is generally poor. Cortically mediated myoclonus is generally precipitated or aggravated by sensory stimuli such as light or noise; these contractions are irregular and disappear in sleep.

myopathy Disease of muscle, such as muscular dystrophy.

myopia Nearsightedness; common in the third and fourth decades of life; corrected by minus diopter (concave) lenses. A child with myopia typically squints and cannot see the blackboard.

myotactic reflex *See* stretch reflex.

myotonic dystrophy *See* Steinert syndrome.

myringotomy The surgical incision of the tympanic membrane (ear drum) to relieve pressure and allow fluid drainage from the middle ear; it is usually accompanied by the insertion of a polyethylene (PE) tube designed to be pressure equalizing (PE) so as to maintain drainage for several months.

myxedema A condition including edema, puffiness, fatigue, weight gain, apathy, and sluggish deep-tendon reflexes resulting from hypothyroidism; the acquired or adult form of congenital cretinism.

myxovirus A ribonucleic (RNA) group of viruses that can produce respiratory disorders but also includes the viruses for measles and mumps.

N

NAD *See* National Association for the Deaf.

NAGC *See* National Association for Gifted Children.

NAPI&FI *See* Neurological Assessment of the Preterm Infant and Full-term Infant.

narcolepsy An uncontrollable desire to sleep or periodic attacks of deep sleep.

nasal bridge The portion of the nose lying directly between the eyes. A low (deep-set) nasal bridge contributes to the appearance of a saddle nose; a high nasal bridge leads to a beaked nose.

nasal bridge/nasion

nasion Root of the nose; where the nose meets the frontal bone or forehead.

nasogastric tube A feeding tube that goes through the nose into the stomach. It is intended for short-term usage; if prolonged tube feeding is antici- pated, a gastros- tomy will be con- sidered.

nasogastric tube

nasopalpebral reflex Nose–eyelid reflex; an infant reflex in which a tap on the bridge of the nose (stimulus) produces bi- lateral blinking (response).

NASW *See* National Association of So- cial Workers.

National Association for the Deaf (NAD) Founded in 1980, the NAD is open to all adults with profound hearing impairment and other interested individuals. The or- ganization is active in legislative advocacy for the protection of civil rights of people with profound hearing impairments in such areas as employment, communica- tion, and citizenship. The NAD maintains a speakers bureau and a legal defense fund and also offers educational, thera- peutic, and vocational services to its members. It provides training in commu- nication and publishes newsletters and educational materials. The NAD is affili- ated with the World Federation of the Deaf.

National Association for Gifted Children (NAGC) Founded in 1954, the NAGC pursues improved education of the gifted (those who have superior general intellec- tual ability) and sponsors programs to en- hance such children's creative potential and capacity for individual thought. The NAGC publishes *Gifted Child Quarterly*.

National Association of Social Workers (NASW) The national professional organization of social workers whose function is to promote the professional development of social work and social workers, establish and maintain profes- sional standards of practice, promulgate and administer professional ethics boards, and certify advanced level practice compe- tency. The Academy of Certified Social Workers (ACSW) is a suborganization within the NASW for social workers who achieve advanced practice competencies. The Diplomate in Clinical Social Work de- notes the highest competency level. The NASW publishes the journal *Social Work*.

National Center for Learning Disabilities (NCLD) Formerly the Foundation for Children with Learning Disabilities, the NCLD promotes public awareness of learning disabilities, neurological disor- ders, and related impairments that can be a barrier to literacy. Founded in 1977, the NCLD provides resources and referrals on a national level to volunteers, parents, and professionals. The NCLD is active in grant making, legislative advocacy, training seminars, and dissemination of information to the public about learning disabilities. The center publishes *Their World*, an annual magazine describing true life stories about ways individuals cope with learning disabilities; a parent list of recommended readings and other resources; and various training materials.

National Down Syndrome Congress (NDSC) A national organization of parents and professionals that disseminates information and assists in referrals with regard to Down syndrome. The group's newsletter, *Down Syndrome News*, is published 10 times yearly; many local Down syndrome family associations are affiliated with this organization.

National Education Association (NEA) The National Education Association is the largest professional organization in the United States for teachers at all levels of education. The primary focus of the organization is the rights and welfare of teachers; it functions predominantly as a teachers' union. Founded in 1857 as the National Teacher Association, the organization changed its name to the National Education Association in 1876. The NEA does advocate for improved education for all people, including those with disabilities, maintains a governmental relations unit and a political action network, and endorses candidates for national office.

National Institute of Mental Health (NIMH) A federal agency—part of the National Institutes of Health—that provides a national focus for federally funded teaching and research efforts to prevent and treat mental illness and promote mental health. It also provides technical assistance to state and local mental health agencies.

National Institutes of Health (NIH) A federal agency that supports and conducts research into the causes and prevalence of diseases and furnishes information to health professionals and to the public. It is composed of 13 research institutes and eight other components. The research institutes include the National Institute of Child Health and Human Development (NICHD), the National Institute on Deafness and Other Communication Disorders (NIDCD), and the National Institute of Neurological Disorders and Stroke (NINDS).

natural fool Term used in the Middle Ages to describe a person with mental retardation. It was recognized that such a person's intellectual capacities had never progressed beyond those of childhood. *Natural fool* was later replaced in common usage by the word *idiot. Contrast with* persona non compos mentis.

natural language Children's attempts to produce adult words. These attempts are not random with respect to approximation or error but seem to follow distinct processes. Innate limitations are hypothesized to prevent the correct production of the adult speech model. These limitations (physical, mental, and experiential) lessen as a child matures and develops increased mental operational abilities. The term *natural language* is also used to describe oral communication in the daily life experiences of a child.

natural proportion The element of full inclusion that requires students with disabilities to be placed in general classrooms at a rate consistent with the incidence rate of the disability within the general population.

NBAS *See* Brazelton Neonatal Behavioral Assessment Scale.

NCLD *See* National Center for Learning Disabilities.

NCV *See* Nerve conduction velocity.

NDA *See* neurodevelopmental assessment.

NDSC *See* National Down Syndrome Congress.

NDT *See* neurodevelopmental therapy.

NEA *See* National Education Association.

NEC *See* necrotizing enterocolitis.

neck extensor hypertonia Increased resistance on repeatedly flexing the head in infants under 6 months of age; this may be an early sign of later motor disability.

neck righting Log rolling; nuchal righting; a primitive reflex in which turning the head to one side (stimulus) causes the body to follow along as though it were a log or all of one piece (response). This pattern must break up into a segmental rolling response before voluntary rolling over can emerge. Persistent neck righting can accompany severe hypertonia (increased muscle tone) and related neuromotor disorders.

necrotizing enterocolitis (NEC) A condition that occurs commonly in preterm infants, in which parts of the bowel become ischemic (blood supply deficiency), potentially leading to paralysis (ileus), perforation, and peritonitis (massive infection). Surgical treatment may include colectomy or colostomy. A history of NEC suggests a complicated neonatal course.

negative practice A form of punishment that requires the individual to perform or engage in a maladaptive behavior so many times that it becomes aversive to him or her. For example, if a child plays with matches, one can have the child light several hundred matches in succession.

negative reinforcement Encouraging a behavior by the removal of an aversive consequence (e.g., not losing recess if classwork is completed).

Nellhaus chart Composite international and interracial head circumference graphs for boys and girls from birth to 18 years of age. The name derives from Gerhard Nellhaus, who pooled data from numerous other studies to produce this chart.

neologism Word substitutions or mispronunciations that may indicate underlying language problems. They may be structural (coptiheler for helicopter), phonological (brad/bread), or semantic (pull on/boots). Structural neologisms usually occur along with other difficulties in organizing semantic relations; semantic neologisms often reflect a problem in understanding perceptual and functional attributes of words; and phonological neologisms occur frequently with auditory misperceptions. Phonological neologisms are not so much an indication of extensive language difficulties as are structural and semantic neologisms.

Neomullsoy *See* chloride-deficient formula.

neonatal Pertaining to the first 28 days of life after birth; that part of the perinatal period after birth.

Neonatal Behavioral Assessment Scale (NBAS) *See* Brazelton Neonatal Behavioral Assessment Scale.

neonatal intensive care unit (NICU) A designation applied to a range of regionalized hospital-based services to diagnose and treat perinatal problems. There are three levels of NICU. Level I provides for resuscitation, observation, and stabilization; relatively uncomplicated deliveries and normal newborns are accommodated at such hospitals. Level III centers have the ability to handle complicated deliveries and the pediatric subspecialty staff to support severely premature babies; teaching and research are usually carried out at such centers. Level II hospitals are intermediate between Levels I and III with regard to the services available.

Neonatal Neurological Examination (NNE) A brief qualitative assessment, developed by Lilly and Victor Dubowitz, of habituation, movement, tone, reflexes, and neurobehavioral items in preterm and full-term newborn infants, with items scored in terms of maturity and normality.

Neonatal Oral-Motor Assessment Scale (NOMAS) A brief 42-item semiquantitative scale that rates tongue and jaw responses during nonnutritive and nutritive sucking in newborns.

neonatal seizures Seizures occurring during the neonatal period (the first 28 days of life). Manifestations of seizures in neonates may be subtle and include lip smacking, eye deviation, or blinking; or they may have more motor involvement, such as pedaling movements ("bicycling") or tonic (increased muscle tone) extension of the extremities (arms or legs) (similar to stretching). Tonic seizures have a poorer prognosis, as they are often associated with intraventricular hemorrhage (bleeding). Neonatal seizures may also be caused by hypoxic-ischemic encephalopathy (brain damage due to lack of oxygen), hypoglycemia (low blood sugar level), hypocalcemia (low blood calcium), infection (e.g., meningitis [inflammation of the spinal cord and brain membranes]), drug withdrawal, or abnormal formation of the brain. The outcome of neonatal seizures is related to the underlying etiology (cause), with reversible problems such as hypocalcemia having a better developmental outcome than meningitis or intraventricular hemorrhage.

neonate Newborn.

nerve block A procedure in which a liquid is injected into a nerve or the muscle surrounding the nerve. This liquid can be an anesthetic agent that causes local or regional anesthesia (numbness) in the area supplied by the nerve. Another use for such an anesthetic agent occurs in the obturator nerve (in the hip) block in a child with cerebral palsy. The function of the obturator nerve is blocked to simulate the effect of an adductor tenotomy and hip flexor release. If too much function is lost, then the surgery may be contraindicated. Another type of nerve block, the phenol block (named for the compound injected into the nerve), produces a temporary reduction in hypertonia (increased muscle tone) and spasticity by damaging the involved nerve. Although nerve regeneration makes this effect temporary, the period of decreased tone can be used to stretch the tendons and thus postpone, or obviate, the need for surgical lengthening.

nerve conduction study A measurement of the velocity of the conduction of a nervous impulse. It is performed by stimulating a nerve in two locations and measuring the difference between the stimulus and time for muscle contraction. Nerve conduction velocities (NCVs) are reduced

in diseases that damage the myelin (fatty insulation material) sheath (e.g., Cockayne syndrome). They are normal in muscular diseases.

nerve conduction velocity (NCV) A neurophysiological measure of the speed with which electrical impulses travel along the path of specific nerves; this measure is used to help distinguish muscle disorders due to peripheral nerve problems from those due to muscle disorders.

nervous breakdown A nonmedical, nonspecific term for a mental disorder. In the family history of children with developmental disabilities, it is not unusual to find a history of "nerves" or "nervous breakdowns" in extended family members often spanning several generations. This anecdotal observation may weakly support the familial transmission of neurological disorders manifesting as both psychological and learning problems.

nervous system The body's communication network. It consists of two divisions (the central nervous system and the peripheral nervous system) that function by responding to the environment outside the body in a coordinated manner.

NESS *See* Neurological Examination of Subtle Signs.

networking The use of formal and informal linkages of people and resources for the purpose of facilitating access to services, skills, contacts, and knowledge.

neural tube The brain and the spinal cord in early fetal development. Neural cells migrate to form folds that fuse together and create the neural tube, leading to development of the brain and spinal cord. Defects in production of the neural tube occur early in gestation and produce a range of neural tube defects (NTDs) such as anencephaly (no brain or absent top of skull) and myelomeningocele (protuberance of both the spinal cord and its lining) in the head-to-tail direction and holoprosencephaly (forebrain deficiency) and craniospinal rachischisis (congenital spinal column fissure) from front to back. These result in various forms of developmental disabilities (e.g., mental retardation, learning disabilities) and medical problems (e.g., neurogenic bladder).

neurodevelopmental assessment (NDA)   A nonstandardized clinical evaluation performed by a developmental pediatrician to diagnose the presence, etiology (cause), and severity of a developmental disability. The assessment battery includes a medical and developmental history, a physical examination (including dysmorphic [atypical] features), an expanded neurological examination (including, for example, primitive reflexes and signs of minor neurological dysfunction), and evaluation of developmental levels. The NDA may be the sole battery conducted in a preschool-age child, but in a school-age child it is almost always supplemented by psychological and educational testing.

neurodevelopmental therapy (NDT)   A system of physical therapy for the treatment of cerebral palsy. Devised by Berta Bobath (a physical therapist) and Karl Bobath (a physician), the approach interprets the abnormal tone, movement, and posture of cerebral palsy as secondary to a failure of primitive reflexes to disappear; postural and balance reactions are facilitated. NDT is the most popular form of physical therapy for cerebral palsy. Training and certification are available to physical and occupational therapists, but the approach can be used by parents, teachers, and anyone who handles and interacts with children with motor impairment. Sometimes referred to as the *Bobath method*.

neurofibromatosis (NF)   von Recklinghausen disease; elephant man disease. A genetic syndrome that includes café au lait spots (more than five coffee-with-milk colored skin patches of at least 1.5 centimeters in diameter), neurofibroma(ta) (tumors of the skin, brain, optic and auditory nerves), and bone lesions. Axillary (armpit) freckling may occur; the number of café au lait spots, neurofibromata, and secondary symptoms all tend to increase with age. Lisch nodules (pigmented

specks) in the iris (the colored part of the eye that surrounds the pupil) on ophthalmological examination can help to clarify the diagnosis. Mental retardation occurs in less than 5% of cases, but seizures are more common (20% of cases), and learning and attention problems may be even more frequent. The orthopedic, visual, and auditory complications of this syndrome suggest that routine follow-up in a multidisciplinary specialty (NF) clinic may be advisable for many people with NF. Incidence is 1 in 3,000. The gene for NF is localized to chromosome 17. Inheritance is autosomal dominant with a high occurrence of spontaneous mutations (50%); recurrence risk is 50%. There are two genetic subtypes: NF1 is classical NF; NF2 is severe bilateral acoustic neurofibromatosis. Named after the German pathologist Friederich von Recklinghausen (1833–1910).

neuroleptic malignant syndrome   An idiosyncratic response to neuroleptic drugs (phenothiazines, butyrophenones, and thioxanthenes) that includes rigidity, fever, sweating, hypertension (high blood pressure), and altered consciousness, with a 20% mortality rate.

neuroleptics   Major tranquilizers; a broad class of antianxiety, antipsychotic, mood-stabilizing drugs that includes phenothiazines, butyrophenones, and thioxanthenes. In people with developmental disabilities, these drugs are often used to treat agitation and depression and may cause tardive dyskinesia (slow, rhythmic, automatic movements), constipation, sedation, and cataracts.

neurolinguistics (NLP)   A communication model of behavior and therapy based on human channels of perceiving and processing information. Neurolinguistic programming assesses the way information is received through the five senses, the organization of the data through verbal and nonverbal linguistic channels, and the output of information and its ultimate impact on communication.

neurological assessment   Examination of the nervous system of the body, including a systematic evaluation of the function of each component of the central and peripheral nervous systems. The following are assessed: 1) cranial nerves, 2) motor function, 3) sensory function, 4) reflexes, 5) cerebellum, and 6) mental status and speech. Abnormalities may indicate an etiology (cause) for a developmental problem and suggest necessary additional testing. A neurological examination can be done by any physician. An evaluation more specific to a child with developmental disabilities should be performed by a developmental pediatrician or a child neurologist. All children with developmental disabilities or suspected developmental disabilities should have neurological assessments.

Neurological Assessment of the Preterm Infant and Full-term Infant (NAPI&FI) A standardized clinical assessment used to document changes in the neurological examination in the newborn period to evaluate the impact of the perinatal environment on the baby.

Neurological Examination of Subtle Signs (NESS) A National Institutes of Health/National Institute of Mental Health (NIH/NIMH) research battery of soft neurological signs that allows comparisons of children at different ages.

neurometrics Computerized mapping and analysis of auditory evoked response potentials that can visually display (using, for example, brain electrical activity mapping [BEAM]) diagnostic brain activity patterns. This research approach to brain localization is being applied to a variety of cognitive and psychiatric disorders.

neuromuscular Pertaining to the joint functioning of muscles and nerves; neuromotor.

neuromuscular reflex therapy *See* patterning.

neuron The nerve cell that comprises a cell body and a "tail" called the axon. Within a nerve cell, the message is passed from the cell body to the axon by a change in electrical potential that stimu-

lates the release of the chemicals (neurotransmitters) responsible for passing the message from neuron to neuron. When killed, nerve cells do not regenerate.

neuron-specific enolase (NSE) A biochemical marker for brain injury; increased levels of NSE in the cerebrospinal fluid (CSF) correlate with neuronal (gray matter) damage.

neuropathy Disease of the peripheral nerves (those outside the brain and spinal cord).

neuropsychological battery A group of tests of distinct brain processes for the purpose of localizing brain damage and dysfunction and discriminating those higher cortical dysfunctions secondary to central nervous system damage from those that are not. The Halstead-Reitan neuropsychological batteries must be administered with the age-appropriate Wechsler intelligence scale and the Wide Range Achievement Test–Revised (WRAT–R); the Luria-Nebraska Neuropsychological Battery does not include these measures. These tests are frequently used with adults and teenagers with acquired brain injury; their ability to localize brain dysfunction in the more plastic brains of younger children with developmental disabilities remains unproven.

neurotransmitter A chemical released by the nerve cell axon that transmits a message from one nerve cell to another. Many substances are clearly neurotransmitters (e.g., dopamine, acetylcholine), and others are thought to be. Neurotransmitters are specific to certain areas of the nervous system (e.g., acetylcholine in the parasympathetic [cholinergic] system regulating breathing and heart rate). They can be inhibitory or excitatory and often work in conjunction with each other to control body movement and function.

nevus flammeus *See* port-wine stain.

nevus sebaceus of Jadassohn A skin lesion, usually on the face or scalp, with linear yellow/orange/tan stripes that become increasingly greasy and verrucous (warty) over time. It is sometimes associated with seizures and mental retardation; *see* Schimmelpenning-Feuerstein-Mims syndrome.

newborn intensive care unit *See* neonatal intensive care unit.

NF *See* neurofibromatosis.

NICU *See* neonatal intensive care unit; newborn intensive care unit.

Niemann-Pick disease A group of disorders characterized by deficiencies in lysosomal enzymes that break down sphingomyelin, a chemical in the body. This results in a buildup or storage of sphingomyelin in the reticuloendothelial system (cells that ingest matter). These disorders, termed *lysosomal storage diseases*, are generally inherited in an autosomal recessive manner. Neurological symptoms including hypotonia (decreased muscle tone), dystonia (impaired muscle tone), developmental arrest, cerebellar ataxia (unsteady gait), or seizures may be seen in types A, C, or D; type B has no neurological symptoms. Treatment with anticancer drugs has been unsuccessful; however, since the buildup is in the reticuloendothelial system, it is thought that bone marrow transplant may prove an effective therapy.

NIH *See* National Institutes of Health.

NIMH *See* National Institute of Mental Health.

Nine Diagnostic Points A clinical checklist devised in Great Britain to define childhood schizophrenia; in this preliminary instrument no distinction was made between autism and schizophrenia. The nine descriptors included impairment of relationships with people, unawareness of one's personal identity, preoccupation with objects, resistance to environmental changes, abnormal perceptual experiences, acute anxiety, delay or absence of speech development, distorted motility (spontaneous movement), and mental retardation. It is only of historical interest.

9p monosomy 9p−; monosomy of the short arm of chromosome 9. A chromosomal disorder with mental retardation, craniosynostosis (premature fusion of skull sutures) with trigonocephaly (triangularly shaped head), a peculiar facies, and congenital heart disease.

NLP *See* neurolinguistics.

NNE *See* Neonatal Neurological Examination.

no The infant's receptive language ability to respond to the verbal command "no" emerges at around 1 year of age; the child's expressive language use of "no" emerges at around 2 years of age and is, from an ego psychology perspective, the child's first word; and, from a behavioral perspective, part of the phase known as the "terrible twos."

nociceptive Relating to the perception of pain.

noise Sound that distorts a signal or message; the level of background, or ambient, noise can affect the ability of a person with (or without) a hearing impairment to successfully discriminate sounds.

NOMAS *See* Neonatal Oral-Motor Assessment Scale.

nondisabled Descriptive term for people without disabilities that is often used in speech or writing. Use of the term *nondisabled* avoids the more subjective term *normal*, which implies that people with disabilities are not "normal" on the basis of their disabilities. The preferred term in the disabilities field, however, is *people without disabilities*.

nondisjunction A failure of two homologous chromosomes (those that are paired with the same number) to separate during meiosis or mitosis. This can result in two chromosomes from one parent and one chromosome from the other parent being passed on to the child, producing a trisomy (an individual with three chromosomes of the same number). This is how Down syndrome commonly occurs.

nondominant The side of the body (usually left) innervated by the contralateral (opposite) brain hemisphere (usually right) that is not specific for language; the nondominant side of the body is usually very slightly weaker, smaller, and less coordinated.

nonexclusionary discipline Those disciplinary practices that do not remove a student from the school environment and thus allow for continued implementation of individualized education program (IEP) goals; nonexclusionary discipline includes loss of recess and other privileges, detention, time-out, and in-school suspension. Because some states and many school districts do not prohibit corporal punishment, the IEP should specify accepted disciplinary procedures as part of the behavior management plan.

nonnutritive sucking Sucking when not feeding.

nonverbal Without oral language.

nonvocal Describes individuals who have not developed functional oral communication skills. Individuals with hearing impairment, mental retardation, autism, tracheostomy tubes, or other severe physical impairments may be nonvocal. The terms *nonvocal* or *nonverbal* are preferred to *mute* or *dumb* because the latter suggest that mental incapacitation accompanies hearing loss or the inability to speak.

Noonan syndrome Turner-like syndrome, Turner phenotype. A syndrome with many features identical to those in Turner syndrome (e.g., short stature, webbed neck, low posterior (back) hairline, shieldlike chest, cubitus valgus [lateral deviation of the forearm], and abnormalities of the pinnae [earlobes]), except that it occurs in both sexes and has normal chromosomes. In Turner syndrome the cardiac defect is left-sided (coarctation of the aorta); in Noonan syndrome it is right-sided (valvular pulmonic stenosis). Mental retardation is rare in Turner syndrome but occurs in over half of people with Noonan syndrome. Menstrual cycles are normal in females with Noonan syndrome. Incidence is 1 in 1,000 severely af-

fected and perhaps as many as 1 in 100 mildly affected. Three quarters of cases are parent-to-child transmission, suggesting autosomal dominance with markedly variable expressivity. The term *male Turner syndrome* reflects incorrect usage. Named after the American pediatrician Jacqueline Noonan (b. 1921).

nootropic A class of psychoactive drugs that are purported to selectively improve the efficiency of higher cortical functions; an example of such a drug is piracetam, which has been claimed to selectively improve reading ability.

normalization The philosophy and principle of making available to all people with developmental disabilities—regardless of the severity of those disabilities—daily experiences and activities that are culturally normative and as close as possible to the prevailing patterns of mainstream society. Wolf Wolfensberger is recognized as an originator and major proponent of the normalization movement in the United States.

norm-referenced test A test in which an examinee's performance is compared with the performance of a specific group. A norm provides a typical performance of the specified group. Raw scores are converted into derived scores, which indicate the examinee's standing relative to the norm group. Most intelligence tests are examples of norm-referenced tests. In contrast, criterion-referenced tests measure levels of mastery compared with established levels, rather than with the performance of other individuals.

Norrie syndrome Oculoacousticocerebral degeneration; a genetic syndrome with visual loss progressing to blindness, progressive mental retardation, and nonprogressive sensorineural (involving the inner ear or the auditory nerve) hearing loss. Inheritance is X-linked recessive. Named after the Danish ophthalmologist Gordon Norrie (1855–1941).

Northwestern Syntax Screening Test (NSST) A language test for children 3–8 years of age: a picture-pointing task measures receptive language and a delayed-imitation task measures expressive language.

nosology Systematic or scientific classification of disease; especially concerned with the criteria to define and distinguish subtypes from one another.

NSE *See* neuron-specific enolase.

NSST *See* Northwestern Syntax Screening Test.

nuchal righting *See* neck righting.

nuchal rigidity Stiff neck; a finding on physical examination that raises the suspicion of meningitis (inflammation of the spinal cord and brain membranes) in young children.

nuclear family A separately housed family unit consisting of parents and their dependent children.

nucleotides The component parts of the nucleic acids that form the genetic material of all living cells.

nursemaid elbow Pulled elbow; dislocation of the proximal radial head (forearm near the elbow) by excessive traction; a common injury in preschool children.

nutritive sucking Sucking during feeding.

nyctalopia Night blindness.

nystagmus A rhythmic back and forth movement of the eyes that consists of at least a slow phase in the horizontal plane. Optokinetic nystagmus, which is elicited in infants by rotating a drum with alternating dark and light stripes, can be used to detect vision in a young child. Nystagmus in far lateral gaze can be a normal variant. Congenital nystagmus can be inherited and may be associated with decreased vision. Occasionally, nystagmus accompanied by a head tilt and titubation (bobbing and nodding) can be indicative of a central nervous system disturbance, such as a tumor or a postinfectious encephalopathy (brain damage due to lack of oxygen). Nystagmus can be induced by drugs like antidepressants, anticonvulsants, or tranquilizers. It can also occur during seizures and in some degenerative disorders or ischemic (blood supply deficiency) disorders. Treatment is specific to the characteristics of the nystagmus and the underlying cause.

O

OAE *See* otoacoustic emission.

obesity State of being markedly overweight for height. Most obesity is exogenous (related to overeating) and familial. Rarely, obesity is related to a specific syndrome. A baby large at birth may have Beckwith-Wiedemann syndrome or Sotos syndrome, or the child's mother may have diabetes; obesity of later onset occurs in Prader-Willi syndrome and Laurence-Moon-Biedl syndrome. Exogenous obesity secondary to a combination of overeating and inactivity is a common occurrence in adolescents with developmental disabilities as they become acutely sensitive to their being "different."

Obetrol Trade name for a mixture of salts of dextroamphetamine and amphetamine that had been used in the treatment of attention-deficit/hyperactivity disorder (ADHD) under the trade name Adderal.

object assembly A Wechsler performance subtest consisting of one sample and four test-item jigsaw puzzles of common objects. The child is asked to assemble the pieces to complete a picture. Items are presented one at a time in a specified pattern. The items are timed, with bonus points awarded for speed; some points are awarded for partially correct responses. Object assembly is a test of synthesis, involving visual organization and visual-motor coordination and attention. Performance is also related to constructive ability, the speed and ease of motor activity, and long-term visual memory. The child's approach to problem solving and work habits can be observed on this subtest. All children receive all items, beginning with the sample and ending with item number four. Example: a seven-piece jigsaw puzzle of a girl.

object permanence The realization that objects continue to exist when they can no longer be perceived; for example, when a toy falls and the child can no longer see it, he or she will look to see where it has gone. This developmental milestone emerges late in the first year of life.

objective Independent of observer bias.

obligatory Compulsory, necessary, not facultative.

Observation of Communicative Interactions (OCI) An observational measure of 10 categories of caregiver responsivity to an infant's communicative cues. Based on a continuum ranging from basic caregiving to more sophisticated efforts to facilitate language and conceptual development, the observational outcomes can be used to plan and guide intervention efforts.

observational learning Learning by observing and remembering how others achieved success.

obsessive-compulsive disorder Obsessive-compulsive neurosis; persistent, unremitting, unrelenting, and irrational thoughts, feelings, or "driven" behaviors (e.g., worries about germ contamination with accompanying excessive hand washing) that are refractory to ordinary coping and change methods. These rare obsessions and compulsions may be viewed as maladaptive coping mechanisms for unconscious conflicts and anxieties. Treatment usually requires a multimodal approach including medication, psychotherapy, and long-term support.

obstipation Intractable constipation that can occur in Hirschsprung disease associated with Down syndrome.

obstructive sleep apnea Cessation of breathing during sleep for greater than 8–10 seconds. The usual cause of obstructive sleep apnea in children is hyperplasia (enlargement) of the tonsils and adenoids, but it may accompany or complicate a variety of genetic syndromes and static encephalopathies (brain damage due to lack of oxygen).

obtained score Raw score.

obtundation State of decreased consciousness in which the individual can be aroused with some difficulty (and without painful stimuli), but the aroused state cannot be maintained.

obturator nerve The nerve that supplies sensation to the inner thigh and movement to adduct the thigh (pull it inward).

obturator neurectomy A surgical procedure in which the obturator nerve is cut. In children with spastic cerebral palsy and scissoring, the adductors (thigh muscles that pull the legs inward) are too strong; this operation relieves the extreme adduction in such cases. It is frequently performed in conjunction with adductor tenotomy.

occipital cortex The posterior (back) area of the brain responsible for the reception and interpretation of visual stimuli.

occipital cortex/lobe

occipital lobe The back part of the brain that contains the visual centers; the part of the cerebrum behind the parietal lobe. The occipital lobe contains the optic radiations that bring messages from the eye; damage to the occipital cortex can produce cortical blindness.

occipitofrontal circumference (OFC) Head circumference.

occiput The back of the head. The occipital cortex of the brain is concerned with vision. A bulging occiput suggests the possibility of Dandy-Walker syndrome.

occult Hidden; not readily observable; such as occult (internal) bleeding.

occupational therapy (OT) The use of adaptive, work, and play activities to increase independent function, enhance development, and prevent disability; the task or the environment may be adapted to achieve maximum independence and to enhance the quality of life.

OCI *See* Observation of Communicative Interactions.

oculoauriculovertebral dysplasia *See* Goldenhar syndrome.

oculogyric crisis A fixed upward gaze that can occur as a side effect of certain antipsychotic drugs.

oculomotor nerve The third cranial nerve. Cranial nerve III is responsible for pupillary constriction, eyelid elevation, and vertical and medial (nasal) gaze.

oculus dexter (O.D.) The right eye.

oculus sinister (O.S.) The left eye.

O.D. *See* oculus dexter.

ODD *See* oppositional defiant disorder.

odor Smell. Odors can suggest specific metabolic diagnoses: maple syrup (maple syrup urine disease [MSUD]); musty, mousey, horsey (phenylketonuria [PKU]); yeast or dried celery (oasthouse urine disease, methionine malabsorption, or Smith-Strang disease); sweaty feet (isovalericacidemia). Strong body odors in children are, most often, a reflection of hygiene and quality of care.

OFC *See* occipitofrontal circumference.

OFD–I syndrome *See* oral-facial-digital syndrome.

off-task Interfering with criterion behavior.

Office of Special Education and Rehabilitative Services (OSERS) One of 13 federal offices within the U.S. Department of Education charged with overseeing education in the United States. OSERS directs, coordinates, and recommends policy for special education programs and services to address the needs of individuals with disabilities. It supports programs to assist children with special needs, provides for the rehabilitation of youth and adults with disabilities, and supports research that addresses quality of life issues for individuals with disabilities. OSERS comprises the Office of Special Education Programs (OSEP), the Rehabilitation Services Administration (RSA), and the National Institute on Disability and Rehabilitation Research (NIDRR). The OSEP administers and oversees all programs related to the free appropriate public education (FAPE) of all children, youth, and adults with disabilities. The RSA funds vocational rehabilitation agencies and programs—with priority given to programs for individuals with severe disabilities—and also provides information about benefits available to individuals with disabilities through the Client Assistance Program. The NIDRR supports a coordinated national and international program of rehabilitation research through a network of training and research centers. The American Printing House for the Blind, the National Technical Institute of the Deaf, and Gallaudet University are administered through the Office of the Assistant Secretary for Special Education and Rehabilitative Services.

OKN *See* optokinetic nystagmus.

OKN drum *See* optokinetic nystagmus.

olfactory Relating to the sense of smell.

olfactory nerve The first cranial nerve; cranial nerve I is responsible for the sense of smell.

oligohydramnios Decreased volume of amniotic fluid during a pregnancy. Oligohydramnios is a risk factor associated with abnormalities of the urinary tract, postmaturity (birth after a prolonged pregnancy), and intrauterine growth retardation.

oligophrenia An antiquated 20th-century term for mental retardation (from the Greek *oligos* ["small"] and *phren* ["mind"]). The term's brief life span was most prominent in references to phenylpyruvic oligophrenia, or phenylketonuria.

OLSAT *See* Otis-Lennon School Ability Test.

omega personality A neurobehavioral syndrome that includes complex problems of memory, reasoning, and judgment, with verbal skills that surpass verbal understanding. Children and adults with this pattern are described as fearless, uncooperative, lazy, amoral, antisocial, and isolated. The omega personality appears to represent a combination of subtle language-processing disorders with attention-deficit/hyperactivity disorder (ADHD) that is especially resistant to routine interventions. Omega personality has been proposed as a specific outcome of fetal alcohol syndrome.

on-task Consistent with criterion behavior.

One-Word Picture Vocabulary Tests Receptive One-Word Picture Vocabulary Test (ROWPVT) for ages 2-0 to 11-11; Receptive One-Word Picture Vocabulary Test–Upper Extension (ROWPVT–UE) for ages 12-0 to 15-11; Expressive One-Word Picture Vocabulary Test–Revised (EOWPVT–R) for ages 2-0 to 11-11; and Expressive One-Word Picture Vocabulary Test–Upper Extension (EOW-PVT–UE) for ages 12-0 to 15-11. These tests provide measures of receptive and expressive vocabulary for children ages 2–15 years. The receptive tests require the examinee to select the picture that matches the word spoken by the examiner thus assessing receptive vocabulary. The expressive tests require the examinee to name the picture presented by the examiner. All four tests allow raw scores to be converted to percentile ranks, standard scores, and age equivalents.

onychotillomania Picking at or pulling out one's nails; a behavior that may be pathognomonic (indicative) for Smith-Magenis syndrome.

OPD–1 syndrome *See* otopalatodigital syndrome.

operant behavior A term from behaviorist learning theory that refers to behaviors that "operate" on or produce an effect on the environment. Walking, talking, hitting, and reading are examples of operants. Operants are different from respondent or reflexive behaviors.

operant conditioning A form of learning first hypothesized by psychologist B.F. Skinner (1904–1990). Operant behavior is shaped (modified or changed) and maintained by its consequences. A *consequent stimulus event* (CSE) always follows an operant and may serve to strengthen, weaken, or maintain the current status of the operant. The condition or conditions upon which a CSE occurs are called the *contingency*. CSEs that strengthen the operants they follow are called *reinforcers*; these may be either positive or negative. The weakening of an operant by withholding a known reinforcer is referred to as *extinction*. CSEs that serve to weaken behaviors are called *punishers* or *aversive stimulus events* (ASE). Operant conditioning is reciprocal (successfully modifying another's behavior results in the successful CSE being used again). Reinforcers and punishers may be primary (unlearned or unconditioned) or secondary (learned or conditioned). Satiation occurs when a reinforcer loses its reinforcing properties over time. Deprivation refers to a state of need in which the reinforcer becomes more powerful—the opposite of what happens in satiation.

operational definition The specific procedures or steps for putting a specific concept into effect. For example, the definition of *learning disability* has been operationalized (made equal to the meeting of itemized objective criteria) in various ways in different states.

ophthalmologist Oculist; eye specialist; a physician who specializes in the diagnosis and treatment of eye disease and performs delicate eye surgery.

ophthalmoscope A medical instrument with lenses and a source of light that is used to look into the eye to visualize the retina (light-sensitive inner back wall).

opisthotonos A posture of the body with markedly increased muscle tone and trunk arching such that the spine is markedly extended and the individual rests on his or her head and heels. This

opisthotonos

posture can be seen in tetanus but occurs intermittently in severe cerebral palsy. These tonic spasms may be misinterpreted as seizures. When they are prominent in choreoathetosis, the term *tension athetosis* may be used. Opisthotonos may be considered the most extreme form of decerebrate posture (stiff and extended extremities and retracted head) or tonic labyrinthine position (extension of all four extremities).

Opitz syndrome Opitz-Frias syndrome; a genetic syndrome with hypertelorism (widely spaced eyes), hypospadias (genital abnormality in males), severe swallowing problems, and mental retardation in two thirds of cases. Inheritance is autosomal dominant.

Oppenheim sign Stimulation down the medial tibia (lower leg) produces dorsal (upward) extension of the big toe; a variant of the Babinski sign as an indication of pyramidal tract involvement.

oppositional defiant disorder (ODD) Pattern of negativistic, hostile, and defiant behavior more pronounced than usually seen in children of similar mental age. ODD includes such symptoms as anger, argumentativeness, resentment, swearing, deliberate rule breaking, and annoying others. It needs to be distinguished from the attention-deficit/hyperactivity disorder (ADHD) that it frequently accompanies; ODD can evolve into a conduct disorder.

optic atrophy A paling of the optic disc (nerve ending) as seen on fundoscopic examination of the retina at the back of the eye. A pale optic disc can be associated with damage secondary to vascular compromise because of trauma, blood clotting problems, or vascular (blood vessel) disorders. Other causes are inflammation of the nerve, demyelinating diseases in which the lipid cover of the nerve cell is destroyed, congenital malformations, diseases of the retina, brain or eye tumors, and glaucoma (increased pressure in the eye, often hereditary). Clinical symptoms can include loss of visual acuity or a visual field defect. Treatment is of the causative agent, and prognosis for vision is related to the extent of injury as well as the causative agent.

optic disc The circular tip of the optic nerve (cranial nerve II) that can be seen on the retina (light-sensitive inner back wall) of the eye through the pupil. Abnormalities of the optic disc can be hereditary, secondary to toxins (poisons) or infection, or vascular (blood vessels). Often the evaluation of the eye and optic disc can reveal the etiology (cause) of some genetic and ocular abnormalities.

optic nerve The second cranial nerve. Cranial nerve II is responsible for vision and is the only nerve in the body that can be seen on direct physical examination (i.e., ophthalmoscopy) via the optic disc on the retina. Damage to the optic disc can result in blindness in that eye.

optician A lens grinder; a professional who fills eye prescriptions; opticians are not qualified to perform eye examinations or prescribe corrective lenses.

optokinetic nystagmus (OKN) Opticokinetic nystagmus. Nystagmus (involuntary eye movements) induced by tracking a kinetic (movement) stimulus. Because the tracking does not need to be voluntary, the response can be used to test vision in infants by rotating a striped OKN drum or passing a tape or tie with broad stripes in front of the infant's eyes. The presence of OKN documents the presence of some degree of visual acuity, but quantification is difficult.

optometric training An intervention for reading disorders based on the observation that children who experience difficulties reading frequently display abnormal saccades (small eye movements) made when tracking print across a page. The coincidence of visual-motor and visual-perceptual disturbances in children with reading problems reinforces this theory, as does the phenomenon of reversals. The training is supervised by an optometrist and consists of the daily practice of visual pursuit and tracking exercises. The intervention is not effective, and the theory confuses an effect of the reading disorder (poor visual tracking) with the cause of the reading disorder.

optometrist A professional who measures visual acuity and prescribes corrective lenses (glasses); the optometrist is not a physician, is not qualified to diagnose or treat eye diseases, and does not perform eye surgery.

OPV *See* oral poliovirus vaccine.

oral-facial-digital syndrome (OFD–I) Léage-Psaume syndrome. A genetic syndrome with multiple frenula (webs) in the mouth; clefts in the tongue, lips, and palate; hypoplasia (undergrowth) of the nasal cartilages; and a variety of digital (finger and toe) abnormalities. Mild mental retardation occurs in about half the cases. Inheritance is autosomal dominant; OFD–I is lethal in males. *See also* Mohr syndrome.

Oral-Motor/Feeding Rating Scale An observational tool for assessing oral-motor and feeding functioning in eight areas: breast feeding, bottle feeding, spoon feeding, cup drinking, biting (soft cookie), biting (hard cookie), chewing, and straw drinking. The scale is applicable to people of all ages, and the assessment results can be used for planning interventions.

oral-motor function All aspects of motor and sensory function of the structures in the oral cavity and pharynx (throat) related to swallowing until food enters the esophagus.

oral poliovirus vaccine (OPV) One of the primary routine immunizations given to children. It is trivalent (effective against all three poliovirus types).

oralism Method of educating people who are deaf (i.e., those who have profound hearing loss) that focuses on verbal communication to the exclusion of manual or unaided augmentative communication.

orchiopexy Surgical treatment of crypt-orchidism (undescended testes).

Ordinal Scales of Infant Psychological Development Uzgiris-Hunt Ordinal Scales of Psychological Development. A group of Piagetian scales used to describe cognitive functioning in infants up to 1 year of age. The scales include descriptions of visual pursuit, object permanence, circular reactions, vocal and gestural imitation, and object relations.

organ of Corti The sensory part of the inner ear that converts sound pressure waves into nerve impulses that are then transmitted to the brain by cranial nerve VIII (the auditory nerve).

organic acids Chemicals found in blood and urine that in increased amounts may indicate an enzyme deficiency. Disorders termed *organic acidurias* are characterized by episodes of vomiting, lethargy, and ketosis (an increase in certain kinds of chemicals, namely ketones). These conditions can be present with striking odors of urine, such as isovalericacidemia, in which an odor resembling that of sweaty socks occurs. Treatment can include a low-protein diet, sometimes supplemented with carnitine. Cognitive functioning can be normal in some disorders (e.g., isovalericacidemia) and poor with profound mental retardation the rule in others (e.g., methylmalonic acidemia).

organic impairments A disability with a physical (organic) etiology (cause) as contrasted to a nonphysical (emotional or social) etiology.

organomegaly Enlargement of an organ; typically used without further specification in reporting negative abdominal examination findings with regard to the size of the liver and spleen. Thus, "no organomegaly" means that neither the liver nor spleen were enlarged. Hepatomegaly (liver enlargement) or splenomegaly (large spleen) can reflect gastrointestinal, cardiac, or hematological (pertaining to blood and blood-forming tissues) disorders. In the area of developmental disorders, hepatosplenomegaly (enlargement of the liver and spleen) may be part of a storage disease.

orientation Neuropsychological awareness of the environment with respect to place, time, and people; developmentally, the locating and turning toward the source of a stimulus (light or sound).

orienting, auditory Turning toward a sound stimulus; localizing at least the general direction of a sound source, if not its exact location, by use of the sense of hearing unsupported by visual cues. Orienting is a receptive language milestone that has cognitive content; failure to orient does not necessarily reflect a hearing deficiency. Orienting is one of the few language milestones readily open to direct observation in the clinical setting. Orienting to mother's voice (at 4 months) precedes orienting to a bell (5 months and later); orienting accurately to a sound source above the horizontal precedes orienting to a sound source below the horizontal.

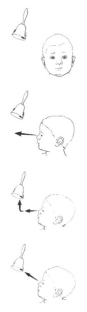

orienting, auditory

ornithine transcarbamylase (OTC) deficiency A hereditary urea cycle disorder leading to hyperammonemia, mental retardation, failure to thrive, headaches, vomiting, and lethargy in cyclic episodes related to protein intake. Inheritance is X-linked.

oromotor dysfunction Difficulty in the motor control and coordination of the lips, tongue, cheeks, and pharynx (throat); oromotor dysfunction can contribute to and be associated with early feeding problems (which can lead to failure to thrive), drooling and choking, and later articulation disorders. The relationship between oral motor reflexes, infantile feeding experiences, and mouth sensation (stimulation) is complex. Some of the most severe oromotor dysfunction occurs in infants with cerebral palsy. Also referred to as *oromotor apraxia* or *oral motor apraxia*.

orotracheal tube A tube going from the mouth to the trachea (windpipe) and used both to clear an airway and to passively assist ventilation (breathing) either through a manually pumped bag or a mechanical ventilator.

orotracheal tube

orthogenetic principle The theory that development proceeds in a directed manner from a lower state of less differentiation to a higher state of greater differentiation, increasing complexity, and hierarchic organization.

orthomolecular treatment Therapy based on a hypothesized vitamin deficiency localized to (a small region of) the brain. After having been disproved to have any efficacy in the treatment of schizophrenia in adults, the therapy continues to be offered as a panacea for all types of developmental disorders in children, where it remains unproven. The vitamin regimen (i.e., megavitamin therapy) is quite varied and often also includes diverse trace elements on the basis of a rationale reminiscent of alchemy and homeopathy.

orthopedist A surgeon who specializes in the treatment of diseases of the bones, joints, and muscles.

orthopsychiatry An interdisciplinary field that emphasizes the development of mental health (rather than illness) from infancy and supports efforts for the prevention of mental illness. *See also* American Orthopsychiatric Association.

orthoptics Eye exercises; optometric training.

orthoroentgenogram An X ray that includes a ruler next to the index limb to accurately measure bone length.

orthosis Orthopedic appliance; any device or appliance used to support, align, prevent, or correct orthopedic deformities or otherwise improve motor functioning; orthoses include braces and splints.

orthotics The science and practice of designing, measuring, fitting, evaluating, and teaching the use of orthoses (corrective appliances); sometimes used as a synonym for "splinting."

Ortolani sign A maneuver to elicit an audible hip click; when present, such a click is indicative of congenital dislocation of the hip. Testing for hip dislocation is a routine component of the pediatric examination in early infancy.

Orton-Gillingham reading method A structured multisensory approach to reading, spelling, and penmanship. The psychologist Anna Gillingham based this remedial methodology on the neurologist Samuel T. Orton's (1879–1948) theories about dyslexia. This method is based on the rationale that children must be taught through the constant use of association of 1) how a letter or word looks, 2) how it sounds, and 3) how the speech organs and the hand feel when producing (writing and tracing) the word. The Orton Society continues to focus on dyslexia.

O.S. *See* oculus sinister.

os calcis Calcaneus, heel bone.

oscillation The absence of a clear trend toward traversing the sequence of Piagetian stages; children with mental retardation may be observed to fluctuate between the various stages.

OSERS *See* Office of Special Education and Rehabilitative Services.

ossicles Small bones; usually refers to the three small bones of the middle ear (incus, malleus, stapes).

ostension Definition by pointing: "That's a(n). . . ." A technique to increase young children's vocabulary.

osteomyelitis Bone infection.

osteotomy An orthopedic surgery procedure that changes the alignment of a bone, usually by removing a wedge-shaped portion of that bone.

OT *See* occupational therapy.

OTC deficiency *See* ornithine transcarbamoylase (OTC) deficiency.

Otis-Lennon School Ability Test (OLSAT) A measure of cognitive ability as related to school success for children in kindergarten through grade 12; there are seven levels of the test for the different grades, with clusters of 10–15 items in the five areas of verbal comprehension, verbal reasoning, pictorial reasoning, figural reasoning, and quantitative reasoning.

otitis externa "Swimmer's ear"; inflammation of the external auditory canal.

otitis media Middle-ear infection; inflammation of the middle ear. There are three subtypes: serous (with an accumulation of fluid in the middle ear); secretory (with an accumulation of thick fluid—"glue ear"), and suppurative (pus accumulation). Associated ear pain, fever, and hearing loss are variable.

otoacoustic emission (OAE) Experimental hearing screening test for children based on the principle underlying sonar.

otolaryngology A surgical specialty of the ears, nose, and throat.

otology The science or study of the ear and its functions. Physicians who specialize in otology are otolaryngologists, or ENT (ear-nose-throat) doctors.

otopalatodigital syndrome (OPD–1 syndrome) A genetic syndrome with moderate conductive (involving the middle and outer ear) hearing loss; cleft palate; irregular digits with short, broad terminations; mild mental deficiency; a variety of skeletal abnormalities, and a characteristic pugilistic facies. Inheritance is X-linked.

ototoxic Damaging to the eighth cranial nerve; drugs that cause nerve deafness are ototoxic.

OTR *See* registered occupational therapist.

outer canthal distance A measurement of the distance between the two lateral (outside) canthi of the eyes. It is not a very sensitive indicator of dysmorphology because it is variably influenced by the angle of the palpebral fissures (eye slits):

outer canthal distance

Large angles will relatively decrease the significance of variations in this measurement.

outer directedness A personality characteristic of people with mental retardation that includes both their imitativeness and their reliance on external (especially adult) cues to guide their behavior.

overcorrection A mildly aversive behavior modification technique. In restitutional overcorrection, the person being treated is made to restore the environment to a better condition than before the inappropriate behavior (washing all the desks in the classroom as punishment for writing on one). Positive practice overcorrection requires the overpractice of acceptable behaviors incompatible with the behavior to be eliminated or the repeated performance of a behavior until it becomes learned (writing a missed spelling word 100 times).

overdetermined Having multiple causes, with the implication that one cause would suffice. In psychiatry, an overdetermined symptom would reflect a confluence of defenses, needs, and unconscious drives. In developmental disabilities, a disability is often overdetermined by a combination of genetic, environmental, familial, social, and learning etiologic (causal) factors.

overflow movements *See* associated movements.

overprotection A style of parenting characterized by 1) an encouragement of dependency by the child on the parent or family, and 2) an exclusion by the parent of family or outside influences on the child. In an attempt to protect the child from any perceived danger, the parent constantly intrudes on and controls the child's world. The result is a child with lessened opportunities to learn from experience, diminished capacity to cope with new situations, and a mistrust of his or her own capacities. Thus, the child develops socialization difficulties, anxiety, depression, and sometimes retributive aggression. In the long term, the child functions at suboptimal levels of independence. Furthermore, both child and family become trapped in a system in which individual autonomy is compromised. Parents of children with developmental disabilities are especially vulnerable to the trap of overprotection in an effort to protect everyone from hurt and rejection. Overprotection can contribute to developmental, emotional, and family problems.

oxybutynin Trade name Ditropan; a spasmolytic drug that increases bladder capacity and decreases the urgency to void; used in the treatment of neurogenic bladder.

oxycephaly Turricephaly. A small "tower"-shaped skull produced by craniosynostosis (premature fusion of skull sutures) involving all sutures. There is a high vertical index (height of skull divided by length of skull).

oxycephaly

P

p— The short arm of a chromosome. Cri-du-chat syndrome is 5p— (a deletion on the short arm of chromosome 5).

PA *See* posteroanterior view.

P&A *See* protection and advocacy.

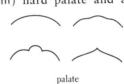

p

pachygyria (macrogyria) A condition in which there are few broad gyri (hills) with shallow sulci (valleys and ridges). This anomaly is more common than lissencephaly (smooth, rather than convoluted, brain structure), and the insult producing it can occur later in gestation. The clinical picture includes severe to profound mental retardation with seizures; many people with pachygyria also have spasticity (increased muscle tone). Most cases are sporadic; however, when found with lissencephaly, pachygyria can be familial. Pachygyria can be visualized on a magnetic resonance imaging (MRI) scan.

pachymeningitis hemorrhagica interna Antiquated name for chronic subdural hematoma.

PAIP *See* Preverbal Assessment Intervention Profile.

paired associate learning (PAL) A learning task used to measure attention; the subject is presented with a series of pairs (of words, letters, symbols, or combinations of these) and is then asked to provide the other item when one of the pair is presented. Numerous standardized and nonstandardized test procedures employ this task.

pairing Associating one stimulus with another; presenting pairs and requiring the subject to learn to give one pair member as the response to the other stimulus pair member.

PAL *See* paired associate learning.

palate Roof of the mouth, composed of an anterior (front) hard palate and a posterior (back) soft palate. Deviations in the shape of the palatal arch, variously described as high-arched, elevated, or steepled, are counted as minor dysmorphic (atypical) features, and can be components in a variety of syndromes; they are independently associated with both microcephaly (abnormally small head) and mid-facial hypoplasia (atypical tissue development).

palate

palilalia The tendency to repeat one's own words (as opposed to *echolalia*, the tendency to parrot or repeat the words of others); this has been described in Tourette syndrome.

Pallister mosaic syndrome *See* Killian/Teschler-Nicola syndrome.

palmar grasp Reflex closure on or voluntary prehension of an object or stimulus with the hand.

palmomental reflex An infant oral-motor reflex in which the stimulus of stroking the palm of the hand produces the response of a wrinkling of the ipsilateral (on the same side) mentalis muscle (an elevation of the angle of the mouth). An intact palmomental reflex in infants reflects normal facial nerve (CN VII) function; an easily elicited palmomental reflex in older chil-

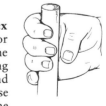

palmar grasp

227

dren is associated with postencephalitic syndrome or degenerative disorders.

palpation Examination by means of the hands; to feel the size, shape, and consistency of various body organs.

palpebral fissure Eye slit; the opening between the upper and lower eyelids. The corners of the palpebral fissures are canthi; the distance between them is the palpebral fissure length (PFL). The most common syndrome with decreased PFL is fetal alcohol syndrome (FAS). Upslanting eyes (palpebral fissures that rise going outward from the nasal side) are associated with Down syndrome and many other genetic syndromes; downslanting (from the nose laterally) palpebral fissures are also associated with a number of genetic syndromes. PFL is normally 80%–90% of the inner canthal distance (ICD) measurement; PFL values below 80% of ICD represent shortened PFLs. As with other dysmorphic (atypical) features, isolated findings may be of no significance.

PALS *See* Program for the Acquisition of Language with the Severely Impaired.

palsy Paralysis or weakness.

pandemic An epidemiological term indicating an epidemic of global magnitude. In actual usage, the term has come to mean physical or mental disorders that affect multiple and often unrelated, although not necessarily global, populations. Thus, acquired immunodeficiency syndrome (AIDS) is a pandemic of an infectious agent; babies exposed to cocaine in utero constitute a pandemic of a lifestyle agent.

papillary ridges Fingerprints; the three basic patterns of papillary ridges are the loop, the whorl, and the arch. In addition to providing a quantitative means of identifying each individual, gross deviations from the normal patterns of loops, whorls, and arches are often part of specific genetic syndromes. *See also* dermatoglyphics.

papilledema A swelling of the head of the optic nerve called the *optic disc*. This can be seen on visualization of the optic fundus (the back of the eye or retina) and may be an indication of acute brain swelling (increased intracranial pressure), such as in head trauma or a vascular (blood vessel) etiology (cause) such as hypertension (high blood pressure) or leukemia. Toxic levels of certain drugs (tetracycline, dexamethasone, or chloramphenicol) or vitamins (e.g., vitamin A) can also produce papilledema. There often is a history of intermittent blurring of vision. Treatment is specific to the cause, and the optic discs are generally not permanently damaged.

para Refers to the number of pregnancies carried and delivered; thus, para III describes a woman who has delivered three pregnancies (not necessarily three children, because twins and triplets only represent one pregnancy each). A common, but extremely variable, usage summarizes a woman's pregnancy history with a four-digit number: T—term pregnancies delivered; P—premature pregnancies delivered; A—abortions/miscarriages; and L—living children. Sometimes a fifth digit is placed at the beginning of the number to sum the first three; thus, 6-3-2-1-5 describes a woman who has been pregnant six times, delivered three term and two premature infants, had one miscarriage, and currently has five living children. Occasionally, the brief two-digit coding of gravida/ para (where the first number does reflect current pregnancy status) is expanded to a three-digit code: G—gravida; P—para; and A—abortions and miscarriages. Local variations in the usage of these numerical shorthands require clarification before they can be interpreted.

parachute Anterior parachute response; a postural response (EAR-II) in which the stimulus of being suddenly thrown forward toward the floor from a position of horizontal suspension produces the response of rapid protective extension of both upper extremities. This is one of the last postural responses to emerge before the onset of independent walking.

parachute

There is also a downward parachute in which the baby is moved suddenly toward the floor in a position of vertical suspension; the response involves a transition from sitting in air to extension of both lower extremities. The downward parachute emerges by 3 months of age with receding flexor habitus (appearance).

paradigm The constellation of beliefs, values, standards, and techniques shared by members of a scientific community. The many professions and disciplines concerned with developmental disabilities do not share a common paradigm and have actually contested whether such a paradigm exists. Developmental pediatrics takes cerebral palsy as the paradigmatic disorder for the entire spectrum of developmental disabilities (i.e., brain damage, often congenital, represents the key explanation for a variety of cognitive, perceptual, and motor disabilities).

paradoxical directive A set of psychotherapeutic strategies. Although these strategies have a number of forms, the unifying theme revolves around the therapist overtly advocating the retention of a symptom or dysfunctional behavior with the covert intention that the opposite will occur. Thus, the paradox is that the therapist advocates for no change with the outcome a change in the direction of health.

paragraphia Insertion of wrong and unintended words in what one writes.

paraldehyde An anticonvulsant drug given intramuscularly or by rectum as an adjunct to phenobarbital or a benzodiazepine to treat refractory status epilepticus.

paralexia A disturbance of reading in which letters, words, or syllables are substituted or transposed.

paralinguistics Nonverbal communication through, for example, intonation and gestures.

parallel play Playing independently beside but not with other children.

paralysis Loss or impairment of voluntary movement; a neurological impairment.

paraphasia A disorder of verbal output that includes transposition of letters in a spoken word and, in semantic paraphasia, the substitution of one word for another while the two words remain in the same class. Semantic paraphasia occurs in Wernicke aphasia.

paraplegia A topographical subtype of spastic cerebral palsy in which only the lower extremities are involved. Theoretically, a pure paraplegia must be secondary to a spinal cord injury, transection, or tumor and would not therefore be a "cerebral" palsy; it would also lack any associated dysfunction secondary to brain involvement. In fact, many childhood nontraumatic cases of paraplegia represent cases of spastic diplegia (paralysis on both sides of the body) in which lower extremity involvement is more noticeable and upper extremity involvement is very mild. In such mild cases of spastic diplegia, delay in walking and a clumsy gait are observed in the first several years of life, but the upper-extremity fine-motor difficulties associated with handwriting do not become apparent until school age.

paraprofessional An aide or associate-level staff person who has not completed the educational requirements for licensure or certification as an independent practitioner; different disciplines have different formal educational requirements for paraprofessional status. This nomenclature is falling out of favor in the developmental disabilities field in deference to a team-based approach to service provision.

parasympathetic nervous system The division of the autonomic nervous system that unconsciously controls life-sustaining processes when the individual is not under stress. The vagus nerve is one of the major components of this cholinergic system. Also characterized as *craniosacral* or *anabolic*.

Parent–Infant Interaction Scale An assessment of parents' interaction with their infants who have developmental delays; the scale addresses caregiver interaction behaviors, caregiver and child social referencing, reciprocity, and caregiver affect.

Parent Perception Inventory (PPI) A questionnaire that provides a comprehensive measure of a family's coping with the presence of chronic illness or disability in a child.

Parent Stress Index A 120-item self-report questionnaire designed to assess stress in the parent–child relationship as it emanates from three sources: characteristics of the child, characteristics of the parent, and situational or life-stress. The instrument has been normed in a number of subgroups with means, standard deviations, percentiles, and profiles developed for the various subgroups.

parental child Usually an older child who assumes responsibility for and functions as a parent for younger children. Situations such as these can be adaptive in large or single-parent families when supported by clear rules and power boundaries. These circumstances are maladaptive when resulting from an abdication of parental responsibility. In families with a parent with mental retardation, the child frequently assumes parenting functions not only for the other children but also for the parent. In families whose firstborn child has a disability, another child frequently assumes a parental-child role in relation to the child with a developmental disability.

parenteral Describes nutrition administered via an intravenous route.

parietal lobe The area of the cerebrum between the frontal and occipital lobes. This area contains the somesthetic (sensory) or parietal cortex, which receives messages (intake) from all sensory neurons except those involved with vision and hearing. Damage in this area can produce impairment in sensation or paresthesias (numbness, tingling, or heightened sensitivity).

parietal lobe

parity The status of a woman with regard to childbearing; see also para.

Parkinsonism A motor syndrome similar to Parkinson disease of older adults (with resting tremors) that can complicate the use of antipsychotic drugs often used to treat severe maladaptive behavior in people with developmental disorders.

parotid duct transposition/ligation Surgical procedures that redirect or eliminate salivary flow from the parotid gland as treatment for drooling.

partial seizures Seizures that arise from a specific location on the cortex. These may be manifested by a convulsive movement of part of the body or even disorders of thought or sensation. Partial seizures may be simple or complex.

partial trisomy 10q Partial trisomy of the long arm of chromosome 10; a chromosomal disorder with growth deficiency, severe mental retardation, microcephaly (abnormally small head), a peculiar facies, camptodactyly (permanent flexion of the fingers or toes), and heart and kidney malformations.

parturition The birth process.

PAT *See* Photo Articulation Test.

Patau syndrome *See* trisomy 13 syndrome.

patella Kneecap.

patent ductus arteriosus (PDA) A cardiac defect common in premature babies where a fetal structure (the ductus arteriosus [DA]) continues to function after birth. The DA in the fetus shunts blood from the pulmonic (right) side of the heart to the systemic (left) side, bypassing the lungs. In the typical newborn, the ductus closes around the time of birth. In many premature and some full-term babies, the ductus remains open and must be closed medically with a drug (indomethacin) or

patent ductus arteriosus

surgically. The relationship between neurological damage due to hemorrhage (bleeding) and a PDA in premature babies is unclear.

paternal age Chronological age of the father; age of the biological father at the time of conception of a child. Although advanced maternal age is associated with the incidence of Down syndrome, advanced paternal age is associated with nonchromosomal dominant mutations, such as achondroplasia, Apert syndrome, and Marfan syndrome.

pathognomonic A sign, symptom, or behavior that is highly characteristic, almost uniquely so, of a given diagnosis. A truly pathognomic individual sign or symptom is rare; most signs and symptoms must be interpreted in context, especially the context of other signs and symptoms. Until one gets to the level of certain laboratory signs, most clinical findings can be imitated or produced by other conditions. A pathognomonic test has a high positive predictive value (true positives/all positives) rate.

patrician foot The second toe longer than the first—in contrast to the plebian foot, in which each successively numbered toe is shorter.

patterning Neurological reorganization; a system of physical therapy for the treatment of

patrician foot

cerebral palsy. Derived by the neurosurgeon Temple Fay from the phylogenetic principle that ontogeny (the development of the individual) recapitulates phylogeny (the evolution of the species), this approach involves exercises in which the child imitates the movement patterns of fishes, amphibians, and reptiles before assuming an anthropoid (upright) posture. The concept that proficiency at each evolutionary level must be achieved before proceeding to the next level is the source of the myth that it is pathological to walk before one crawls. In an expanded form such as the Doman-Delacato approach (with elements such as fluid restriction, fa-

cilitation of cerebral hemispheric dominance, and CO_2 rebreathing), this approach has made controversial claims to be effective treatment for a wide variety of developmental disorders.

PCA *See* postconceptional age.

PDA *See* patent ductus arteriosus.

PDD *See* pervasive developmental disorder.

PDMS *See* Peabody Developmental Motor Scales.

Peabody Developmental Motor Scales (PDMS) and Activity Cards A standardized norm-referenced test that assesses fine- and gross-motor skills in children from birth to 83 months of age. The 170 gross-motor items yield subscores in the following areas: reflexes, balance, nonlocomotor, locomotor, and receipt/propulsion of objects. The 112 fine-motor items yield scores in the following areas: grasping, hand use, eye–hand coordination, and manual dexterity. These scores can then be used to generate a specific instructional program for children with motor delays and disabilities. Administration takes less than 1 hour.

Peabody Individual Achievement Test–Revised (PIAT–R) A 1989 revision of an individually administered measure of school performance for children 5–18 years of age. Six subtests assess five dimensions: knowledge, reading, mathematics, spelling, and language.

Peabody Picture Vocabulary Test–Revised (PPVT–R) A 1981 revision of a 1959 edition test of receptive language for subjects from 2-6 to 40-11 years of age. The child or adult must identify the one picture (on each page of four pictures) that best illustrates the target word from a graded list of increasingly difficult words. The content has been revised to include a broad sample of women and ethnic groups engaged in a variety of activities. The PPVT–R is individually administered and untimed, usually taking 8–16 minutes. Two forms, *L* and *M*, are provided. The total number of correct responses can be converted to standard scores (with a mean of 100 and a standard deviation of 15), national percentile ranks, and age equivalents. The PPVT–R is sensitive to only one aspect of language (receptive one-word vocabulary) and should not be used as an indicator of global language skills; neither is it interchangeable with general intelligence scores. Although PPVT–R performance correlates well with verbal IQ for children under age 10, the more abstract nature of the items above the 10-year level produces stronger correlations with performance IQ.

pectus　Chest; pectus carinatum is keel chest, pigeon breast, or chicken breast, in which the sternum projects forward; pectus excavatum is funnel breast, in which the sternum appears caved into the chest. Although these anterior (front) chest wall deformities may be cosmetically problematical, it is rare for cardiac or pulmonary functioning to be impaired to a degree sufficient to indicate surgery. Occasionally, these unusual chest shapes are components of a larger malformation syndrome.

pectus carinatum

pectus excavatum

PEDI　*See* Pediatric Evaluation of Disability Inventory.

Pediatric Early Elementary Examination (PEEX)　*See* Pediatric Neurodevelopmental Examinations.

Pediatric Evaluation of Disability Inventory (PEDI)　A functional assessment parent report instrument for evaluation of chronically ill children and children with disabilities between 6 months and 7 years of age. Functional status and functional change are measured in the areas of skill level, caregiver assistance, and adaptive equipment modification.

Pediatric Examination for Educational Readiness (PEER)　*See* Pediatric Neurodevelopmental Examinations.

Pediatric Examination of Educational Readiness at Middle Childhood (PEERAMID)　*See* Pediatric Neurodevelopmental Examinations.

Pediatric Extended Examination at Three (PEET)　*See* Pediatric Neurodevelopmental Examinations.

Pediatric Neurodevelopmental Examinations　A series of neurodevelopmental examinations intended to generate narrative descriptions of relative strengths, weaknesses, and preferred styles in children with learning disabilities. Four separate examinations cover specific age groups: Pediatric Extended Examination at Three (PEET)—age 3; Pediatric Examination for Educational Readiness (PEER)—ages 4–7; Pediatric Early Elementary Examination (PEEX)—ages 7–9; Pediatric Examination of Educational Readiness at Middle Childhood (PEERAMID)—ages 9–15. Each examination includes a physical and neurological assessment, an evaluation of the maturation of the nervous system (minor neurological indicators), tasks tapping specific areas of development, and systematic behavioral observations. The developmental functions evaluated on these examinations include fine- and gross-motor functions, memory, language, visual/spatial processing, temporal sequential organization, and selective attention. These tests produce neither an overall score nor specific subtest scores; rather, they utilize a descriptive approach in evaluating and managing developmental dysfunctions. They take about 1 hour to administer.

pedigree　An organized system presenting the genealogic history of a family. The pedigree depicts both individuals and generations in a manner that is easily analyzed. The diagram showing a family pedigree is called a *genogram*.

pedography　An old and simple approach to gait analysis that measures footprints made on a strip of paper. One of the earliest uses of this methodology was recorded in William Osler's *Cerebral Palsies of Children* (1889).

PEEP *See* positive end expiratory pressure.

PEER Pediatric Examination for Educational Readiness. *See* Pediatric Neurodevelopmental Examinations.

PEERAMID Pediatric Examination of Educational Readiness at Middle Childhood. *See* Pediatric Neurodevelopmental Examinations.

peer tutoring The practice of students assisting other students who need supplemental instruction. Although the practice may be beneficial to both tutor and tutee, some studies indicate that it is the tutors who learn more and are more satisfied with the experience. This suggests that students should have experience as both tutors and tutees.

peering *See* hemianopsia.

peers Social equals; in developmental terms, people who are similar in characteristics such as age or developmental level. Peers form *peer groups*, or close associations, with each other, often in the form of play groups at school or in the neighborhood. Children with developmental disabilities are often described as "immature" and as "having poor social skills," making it difficult for them to associate with their peer groups by age or grade. Often younger children or others with developmental disabilities comprise these children's peer groups, since they are more closely equal on a developmental level. Peer groups are important to all children in forming models for identification, because they are relatively free of adult definitions and authority.

PEET Pediatric Extended Examination at Three. *See* Pediatric Neurodevelopmental Examinations.

PEEX Pediatric Early Elementary Examination. *See* Pediatric Neurodevelopmental Examinations.

PEG percutaneous endoscopic gastrostomy.

pegboard An item in many infant tests to measure both fine-motor coordination and nonverbal problem-solving ability. Successful completion of pegboards typically occurs in the second half of the second year of life. The most commonly used pegboards are the Wallin A (six round pegs evenly spaced in a straight line along the board) and the Wallin B (six square pegs evenly spaced in a straight line along the board).

pellagra A syndrome due to nicotinic acid (niacin, vitamin B) deficiency that includes dermatitis, diarrhea, and dementia (diffuse brain involvement), sometimes progressing to death. These characteristics are known as *the four Ds*. Pellagra can occur with the ketogenic diet when supplementary vitamins are not given. In dogs, "black tongue."

pelvic obliquity The up and down movement of the pelvis in the coronal plane, which divides the body into the front and back; a certain degree of pelvic obliquity is normal during walking and is measured as a component of gait analysis.

pelvic rotation Movement of the pelvis in the transverse plane, which divides the body into top and bottom; a component of gait analysis. The purpose of pelvic rotation is to swing the leg forward and elongate step length.

pelvic tilt A slanting of the pelvis away from the horizontal in the sagittal (median) plane; a certain degree of pelvic tilt is normal during walking and is measured as a component of gait analysis. The term *pelvic tilt* is sometimes used generically to include pelvic obliquity (up and down movement in the coronal plane).

pelvis The lower end of the trunk formed by a ring of bones including the hips and tailbone; the pelvic inlet is the bony canal through which babies pass to be born.

pemoline Trade name Cylert; a long-acting stimulant medication used in the treatment of attention-deficit/hyperactivity disorder (ADHD) in children and adults. It is manufactured in multiples of

18.75 milligrams (18.75 mg, 37.5 mg, and 75 mg). Side effects include headache, stomachache, anorexia (loss of appetite), poor growth, sleep problems, and liver function disturbance; these can usually be managed by titrating the dosage. In contrast to other psychostimulants, abuse potential is quite limited.

Pendred syndrome A genetic syndrome that associates congenital sensorineural (involving the inner ear or the auditory nerve) hearing loss with goiter (swelling). This syndrome accounts for approximately 5% of sensorineural hearing loss in children. Inheritance is autosomal recessive.

penetrance The degree of expression of a gene or trait. A trait that is expressed in a frequency of less than 100% has reduced, or incomplete, penetrance. A nonpenetrant gene is one that could produce an abnormal phenotype (appearance) but clinically does not.

penicillamine A drug given by mouth to treat lead poisoning and Wilson disease.

People to People Committee for the Handicapped A self-help, mutual aid organization that provides information and referral regarding entitlements, services, and organizations for people with disabilities. A periodically published resource manual is available through the organization.

PEP *See* Psychoeducational Profile.

percentile Percentile rank. A score reflecting an individual's position relative to others taking the same test. It is obtained by converting an individual score to the percentage of observations falling below that score (or, technically, to the percentage of observations falling below that score plus half of the observations obtaining that score). A score falling at the 35th percentile reflects a score that is higher than that of 34% of others taking the test (*see* median). A score at the 100th percentile cannot be achieved, since it is impossible to be higher than 100% of people taking the test.

perception Awareness of an object or event through the sense organs. Perception is a pattern of responses to stimuli. Selection, organization, and interpretation of specific stimuli are partially determined by prior learning, experiences, and interests.

perceptual disorder An impairment in one of the modalities used for assimilating information (usually visual or auditory). This is not a disorder of acuity. Hearing and vision are normal; the disorder involves a difference in the way the information is processed or perceived. A child with a visual-perceptual limitation has difficulty making sense of things he or she sees; a child with an auditory-perceptual (more often termed *auditory processing*) impairment has difficulty making sense of information he or she hears.

perceptual-motor The integration of the modalities used for processing information (usually visual or auditory) with a nonverbal response. For example, auditory-motor integration is required for listening and taking notes, whereas visual-motor integration is required for copying forms or words. In practice, perceptual-motor often seems to be used synonymously with visual-motor, although this is not accurate usage. A perceptual-motor model represents one of the earlier (1950s–1960s) attempts to define learning disabilities. This model hypothesized perceptual skills as underlying academic skills (i.e., a learning disability resulted when perceptual skills were disordered). Programs were devised to train perceptual-motor skills. They were not, however, successful in improving academic skills. Although vestiges of these programs remain, they are not accepted.

perceptual organization factor *See* Kaufman factors.

percussion Tapping; determining the density or solidity of a body part by tapping on its surface as one taps a barrel to decide if it is full.

percutaneous endoscopic gastrostomy (PEG) An endoscopic rather than intra-abdominal approach to the placement of a gastrostomy tube that can be performed under local anesthesia.

Perez reflex A primitive reflex in which pressure applied to the spine (vertebral column) in a cephalad direction (from tail to head) causes the infant to flex its arms and legs, elevate its head, and urinate/defecate.

performance test A set of tasks in which the role of language is minimized. Overt demonstrations of various motor skills, rather than verbal responses, are required. The Leiter International Performance Scale is an example of a performance test; on the Wechsler Intelligence Scales, performance subtests include picture completion, picture arrangement, block design, object assembly, and coding.

perimetry A test procedure to determine the extent of the visual fields; this can range from confrontation with a flicking finger at the periphery of the individual's line of sight to the use of complex instrumentation to map visual fields. Visual field cuts occur in many cases of hemiplegic cerebral palsy.

perinatal Pertaining to the period just before, during, and just after birth. Perinatal etiologies (causes) have been equated with obstetrically preventable conditions. However, the majority of perinatal difficulties actually reflect the presence of unsuspected prenatal conditions. The most common perinatal risk factor for developmental disabilities is asphyxia (lack of oxygen). Perinatal death rates are reported for all fetuses or for fetuses above a specified length of gestation (from 20 to 28 weeks), and up to 7–28 days of age.

perineum The diaper area.

periodicity Regularly recurrent or intermittent cycle, often related to the presence of a biological clock. Premenstrual syndrome (PMS) is the most commonly recognized behavioral example; however, many children with developmental disabilities exhibit marked behavioral fluctuations in cycles of varying length.

peripheral vision Sight that utilizes retinal cells outside the macula. Because the macula picks up light stimulation from what one is looking at, the rest of the retina (light-sensitive inner back wall) is, to varying degrees, sensitive to visual stimuli outside one's primary focus of attention—the periphery.

periventricular leukomalacia (PVL) A lesion of the white matter near the lateral (outside) ventricles (fluid-containing spaces) of the brain caused by necrosis (tissue death). This is most commonly found in premature and low birth weight infants and is thought to be related to an asphyxial (lack of oxygen) insult. In premature infants, the brain vasculature (blood vessels) is thought to be immature and fragile and thus more sensitive to changes in blood pressure and oxygen levels, resulting in damage without other complications. In full-term babies, PVL and asphyxial damage are more often associated with other complications, such as heart disease or infection. There is a range of developmental outcomes for babies with PVL, including mental retardation and cerebral palsy. PVL can be diagnosed by ultrasound, computed tomography (CT) scan, or magnetic resonance imaging (MRI).

Perkins-Binet Tests of Intelligence for the Blind An intelligence test adapted from the Stanford-Binet Intelligence Scale for people with severe visual impairments. There are two versions of the test: Form U, for children with usable vision, and Form N, for children with nonusable vision.

perseveration The continuation or repetition of an action or thought after it has become inappropriate. Such fixation may reflect an associated, but opposite, disorder to a short attention span or focus. When a child has difficulty understanding or executing a given direction, he or she may, like a broken record, repeat an earlier correct, but now inappropriate, response. At other times, when a child is asked to do something once, he or she will do it (or some component of it) several times. As a major component of Strauss (minimal brain dysfunction) syndrome, perseveration is considered a key finding in brain damage. More striking examples of perseveration occur in autistic spectrum disorders.

persistent vegetative state (PVS) A condition in which people with severe brain damage exhibit no recognizable mental function, although they may have periods of wakefulness when their eyes open and move.

person-in-environment A view of human behavior that sees both behavior and personality development as a function of environmental variables as well as innate psychological and physiological processes. This perspective encompasses the interactive relationships among an individual, relevant others, and the physical, cultural, and social environment. Thus, for a person with a physical disability, a pervasive sense of helplessness and isolation must be assessed to determine whether this is a personality quality or if, in fact, the environment denies physical and social access, making isolation and helplessness the only possible reality.

persona non compos mentis Term used in the Middle Ages to describe individuals with no apparent mental disability at birth, but who displayed deviant behavior later in life. By the 15th century, the term *lunatic* replaced the phrase. *Non compos mentis*, the Latin term for "not of sound mind," is still used to describe those who, due to mental incapacity, are not legally responsible for their actions.

pervasive developmental disorder (PDD) A poorly defined category of disability that involves problems in social interaction and verbal and nonverbal communication. PDD includes autism as its major diagnostic entity; *PDD not otherwise specified* refers to children who have autistic features but do not formally qualify for that diagnosis. In the past, the major differential point between the two diagnoses was age of onset, so that autism referred to early infantile autism (before 30 months), whereas PDD had a childhood onset (after 30 months of age). PDD is a pattern of atypical development that can coexist with mental retardation.

pes planus Flat foot.

PET *See* positron emission tomography.

petit mal A nonspecific term applied historically to absence seizures, but which has been used for other epileptic events as well. Literally it means "small illness" as opposed to grand mal ("big illness"), used historically to describe generalized tonic-clonic seizures. Sometimes petit mal refers to simple absence seizures with a diagnostic electroencephalogram (EEG) pattern consisting of a 3-per-second spike (a sharp pointed deviation) and wave. The term *petit mal* is falling out of favor because of its lack of specificity.

Peto A system of physical therapy to treat cerebral palsy. Originated by Andras Peto, a Hungarian, it focuses on the conscious rhythmic practice of activities of daily living (ADL); it is also referred to as conductive education.

Pfeiffer syndrome Acrocephalosyndactyly (peaked head and webbed fingers and toes). A genetic syndrome with craniosynostosis (premature fusion of skull sutures) leading to turribrachycephaly (an odd-shaped skull), broad thumbs, big toes, and syndactyly (webbing of the fingers or toes). Neurodevelopmental complications are rare. Inheritance is autosomal dominant.

phacomatoses A group of hereditary neurocutaneous syndromes—disorders with abnormalities involving the skin and the central nervous system. Phacomatoses include neurofibromatosis, tuberous sclerosis, Sturge-Weber syndrome, and ataxia-telangiectasia.

phalanges The small bones in the fingers and toes.

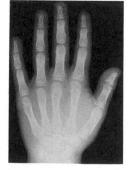

phalanges

pharyngitis Throat infection that may include sore throat, fever, tender cervical (neck) lymphadenopathy (disease of the lymph nodes), erythema (redness) of the pharynx, and sometimes exudate (white patches). Most pharyngitis is viral in etiology (origin) and unresponsive to antibiotics; a rapid streptococcus screen or a throat culture is the only reliable way to diagnose streptococcal pharyngitis, which should be treated with antibiotics to prevent rheumatic fever.

pharynx The throat; this irregular space is capable of considerable change in size and is divided into the nasopharynx (top), oropharynx (middle, behind the mouth), and laryngopharynx (bottom). It is involved in breathing and swallowing, and acts as the principal resonating organ in speech.

phasic bite reflex The stimulus of pressure on the gums produces the response of rhythmic closing and opening of the jaws. This oral reflex is innervated by cranial nerve V; it is present by 1 month of gestation and disappears by 1 year of age.

phasic reactions Movement reflexes that coordinate muscles of the limbs in patterns of either total flexion or total extension.

Phelps A system of physical therapy for the treatment of cerebral palsy; devised by the orthopedic surgeon Winthrop M. Phelps, this all-encompassing program uses Pavlovian conditioning for muscle education, deep massage, bracing, and multisensory (auditory, visual, kinesthetic, and rhyming) stimuli.

phencyclidine "Angel dust"; a veterinary anesthetic agent used as a street drug; maternal use can produce neurological depression at birth followed by an infant withdrawal syndrome.

phenobarbital An anticonvulsant that is a member of the barbiturate family; it can be used to control generalized tonic-clonic or simple partial (focal) seizures. Phenobarbital (sometimes familiarly called *phenobarb*) is generally given twice a day and may initially take 2 or 3 weeks to reach a steady level. Significant side effects include sedation, hyperactivity, a decrease

in attention span, and cognitive impairment with a lowering of IQ by about 5–10 points. Phenobarbital can also increase serum levels of liver enzymes. This is not caused by damage to the liver but by an increased production of enzymes. As the impairment of cognition with phenobarbital has been better documented, its use has tended to decrease somewhat.

phenothiazine A class of antipsychotic drugs that have a calming, antidepressant activity. Side effects include sedation and tardive dyskinesia (slow, rhythmic, automatic movements).

phenotype The physical characteristics of an individual including morphology, biochemistry, and physiology, as determined by the interaction of genes with the environment. For example, a person who is a carrier for a recessive disorder such as cystic fibrosis has one disease gene and one normal gene. He or she, however, is clinically indistinguishable from a noncarrier (one with two typical genes) in terms of lung and intestinal physiology. Thus, the phenotype is the same as an individual without the cystic fibrosis gene.

phenylketonuria (PKU) An inborn error of metabolism in which the enzyme phenylalanine hydroxylase is absent or nonfunctional, resulting in an increase in the level of phenylalanine, an essential amino acid, in the blood. Treatment involves a diet low in phenylalanine. Untreated PKU is associated with mental retardation, microcephaly (abnormally small head), seizures, athetosis (involuntary twisting of the upper extremities), hand posturing, and behavioral stereotypies. Poor hair pigmentation has also been noted. The earlier dietary treatment is initiated, the better the developmental outcome. When the diet is started at under 3 weeks of age, there are no discernible defects. When started between 3 and 6 weeks of age, there are mild impairments. Treatment shows little positive effect if begun after about 6 months of age. Infants with PKU appear normal at birth except possibly for some irritability and vomiting. Delayed development is often not noted until 4–9 months of age. Because of the insidious presentation and the importance of early treatment on developmental outcome, PKU is routinely tested for in the newborn nursery using the Guthrie test. In the past, a low phenylalanine diet was used only until 5 years of age. However, recent studies have shown a decrease in IQ scores after beginning a normal protein diet. Recommendations are now being made to liberalize the diet but to continue to restrict the amount of protein intake. Pregnant women with untreated PKU are at risk for having children with mental retardation, microcephaly, and heart disease. These children do not have PKU; rather, their mental retardation is caused by exposure to high phenylalanine levels in utero and is preventable by diet control during pregnancy. Generally, PKU is inherited in an autosomal dominant manner and is most common in people of northern European descent (Scandinavian, German, and English). Children with PKU are frequently blue-eyed, blonde, and fair-skinned with a tendency toward eczema (skin rash).

phenytoin   Trade name Dilantin; an anticonvulsant that can be used for a number of seizure types: tonic-clonic (grand mal), complex partial (psychomotor), and simple partial (focal). Phenytoin shows the best drug-activity-to-drug-concentration relationship of all the anticonvulsants. Clinically effective levels range from 10 to 20 micrograms per milliliter. Levels greater than 20 micrograms per milliliter produce side effects but no added seizure control. Neurotoxicity (brain symptoms) includes nystagmus (involuntary eye movements), ataxia (unsteady gait), and aggravation of the seizures, but not drowsiness in lower doses. Permanent damage to brain cells in the cerebellum has occurred with acute or chronic high dosages. Other side effects include allergic responses, gingival (gum) hyperplasia (excessive tissue growth), hirsutism (excessive hair growth), and various nutritional deficiencies such as folate deficiency, biotin deficiency, and vitamin D deficiency. An idiosyncratic encephalopathy (brain damage due to lack of oxygen) has been seen in people with mental retardation with therapeutic phenytoin lev-

els. Another reaction occurring in 2%–5% of people beginning phenytoin therapy consists of a morbilliform (measles-like) rash, fever, and enlarged lymph nodes (glands). This reaction disappears when the phenytoin is discontinued. Phenytoin continues to be used judiciously in clinical practice. It is rarely used in infants because of side effects. It is one of the few medications in which the bioavailability (amount of drug the body receives) varies significantly among different preparations.

philtrum   An infranasal upper-lip depression; the groove in the mid-line of the upper lips. The philtrum may be shortened, elongated, or flattened to contribute to various facies characteristic of diverse syndromes. A long philtrum indicates a short nose, and a short philtrum indicates a long nose.

philtrum

phobia   An exaggerated and debilitating fear of an object or situation that is based neither on an actual danger nor on an actual threat. Common phobias include claustrophobia (fear of closed places) and nyctophobia (fear of darkness). Phobias can become extremely problematic if the person with the phobia attempts to avoid the feared object or situation. For example, if one cannot ride an elevator due to a phobia, many situations become unavailable. Often phobias impose severe strains on the phobic person's interpersonal relationships. In addition, phobias are particularly refractory (resistant) to psychotherapeutic intervention.

phocomelia   The congenital absence of the proximal segment of a limb. The hand or foot will sometimes be attached almost directly to the trunk like a flipper. This condition is rare in isolation and can occur as part of another genetic syndrome. Historically there was an international outbreak of tetraphocomelia (limb abnormalities in all four extremities) after the widespread use of the drug thalidomide as a sleeping pill during the first trimester of pregnancy in the early 1960s. *See also* thalidomide embryopathy.

phonation   Voicing; the voluntary production of sound by moving air through the vocal tract. It is a function of the vocal cords in the larynx (windpipe).

phoneme   The smallest unit of sound in any particular language. Various languages use phonemes that are not utilized in any other language. The English language designates 44 different phonemes.

phonemic synthesis   *See* sound blending.

phonetics   A study of the perception and production of all of the speech sounds in language. Phonetics has been applied to the teaching of reading. *See also* phonic analysis.

phonic analysis (phonics)   A word-attack skill involving the sound of letters, the division of words into syllables, and the blending of sounds together to form words. Some phonics programs are synthetic, in that letters and sounds are blended to form words. Others are analytic, in that they depend on the analysis of previously learned words. The functional use of phonic skills also includes checking the derived pronunciation in the context from which the word was taken. The word-attack subtest of the Woodcock Reading Mastery Test–Revised requires the generalization of phonics rules to nonsense words, thus testing only applications of phonics skills without relying on or checking against pronunciation of known words. The "back to basics" movement sometimes views phonics as the best approach to reading, almost an end in itself, rather than one of a variety of tools for extracting meaning from print. Students with auditory processing problems often have difficulty mastering phonics, especially synthetic approaches.

phonology   The study of the linguistic system of speech sounds in a particular language.

phoria   A latent tendency for the eyes to deviate from their normal fusion. In the presence of esophoria (convergence of visual lines) or exophoria (divergence of visual lines), optometric tests that stress the eyes' ability to maintain fusion produce esotropia or exotropia.

photic drive   *See* intermittent photic stimulation.

Photo Articulation Test (PAT)   A test of pronounciation that uses color photographs to test the articulation of all consonants, vowels, and dipthongs. Six articulation age overlays (AAOs) allow comparison of test results with norms.

photoconvulsive response   *See* intermittent photic stimulation.

photomyoclonic response   *See* intermittent photic stimulation.

photoparoxysmal response   *See* intermittent photic stimulation.

photophobia   Extreme sensitivity to light; can be associated with a variety of acute and chronic conditions, such as conjunctivitis (eye inflammation), measles, albinism, meningitis (inflammation of the spinal cord and brain membranes), and encephalitis (brain inflammation).

photosensory seizure   A convulsion induced by visual stimuli, typically flickering light such as a stroboscope, or a television screen. Thus, photic stimulation is one of the techniques used when administering an electroencephalogram (EEG).

phototherapy   The use of "bililights" (special fluorescent light to decrease the degree of jaundice) to lower the level of bilirubin in a newborn baby. The baby's eyes are protected with eye patches or goggles; the brightness of the lights would at the very least be extremely uncomfortable if not painful for the baby. This is a fairly common treatment for babies with mild elevations in their bilirubin levels, and its use in the newborn period has, by itself, no long-term developmental implications.

phrenic nerve   A cervical (neck) nerve that innervates the diaphragm, one of the principal respiratory muscles.

phrenology The pseudoscience of diagnosing personality and other traits by palpating the bumps on a person's head. Phrenology was the historical ancestor of the science of cortical localization, with which the latter is often unfairly equated.

physiatry *See* physical medicine and rehabilitation (PM&R).

physical disabilities A broad category of disabilities that is distinguished from mental or emotional disabilities. Physical disabilities typically involve the motor system and place some limitation on the person's ability to move (about). However, such disabilities can include diseases of any organ system that has significant impact on functional ability. Physical disabilities may overlap with mental disabilities.

physical medicine and rehabilitation (PM&R) A medical specialty concerned with the management of chronic diseases, especially those that are neuromuscular (e.g., stroke, head injury, arthritis). Diagnostic techniques in PM&R include electromyography and nerve conduction studies. Treatment modalities include heat, ice, physical and occupational therapy, traction, and orthoses (corrective appliances). PM&R specialists are also referred to as *physiatrists*.

physical therapy (PT) A discipline that deals with the assessment of gross-motor skills and disorders of movement and posture, and their treatment through a variety of modalities. These modalities include handling and relaxation techniques; a range of exercises (e.g., strengthening, balancing, and increasing or maintaining range of motion to prevent contractures); and adaptive equipment and orthoses (corrective appliances)—all to maximize the motor substrate of development and independent functioning.

physiognomy An antiquated system of interpreting human character by means of specific facial features. Of ancient origin, it was popularized by Johann Caspar Lavater (1741–1801). In its expanded form, physiognomy can involve the study not only of the face but also of the bumps on the head (i.e., phrenology), the markings on the hands (i.e., palmistry or dermatoglyphics), gait, gestures, and even handwriting (i.e., graphology). In a restricted sense, it can be considered a forerunner of certain aspects of medical visual diagnosis as found in modern syndromology (the identification of genetic and other syndromes) and genetics.

physiological classification In reference to cerebral palsy, describes the disorder of tone or movement that characterizes each subtype of cerebral palsy, often with an implication of specific brain area involvement. Spastic and extrapyramidal are the two main subgroups in physiological classification. Also known as *neuroanatomical classification*.

Piaget, Jean (1896–1980) A Swiss psychologist renowned for his explorations of the cognitive development of children. Concepts integral to his theories include structures (organized patterns for dealing with the environment), adaptation, stages of development, conservation, equilibration, and egocentrism. Piaget was educated at the university in Neuchatel, Switzerland, was director of the Jean Jacques Rousseau Institute in Geneva, and professor at the University of Geneva. In 1955, he established the International Center of Genetic Epistemology in Geneva. In the United States, the Jean Piaget Society publishes a newsletter, the *Genetic Epistemologist*, and annual conference proceedings. *See also* stage.

PIAT–R *See* Peabody Individual Achievement Test–Revised.

PIBIDS syndrome IBIDS syndrome plus *P*hotosensitivity (sensitivity to light). *See* IBIDS syndrome.

pica Eating dirt or other nonfood objects. Plumbism (lead poisoning) is a major concern. Pica is seen more frequently in children with autism and mental retardation. When a child pulls out his or her hair and eats it (i.e., trichotillomania), a trichobezoar (hair ball) can form in the stomach. In a developmentally typical child, the latter behavior should lead to a child psychiatry referral. A reported association between pica and iron deficiency anemia may be coincidental and secondary to both problems being more common in children of lower socioeconomic background. However, pica may disappear with iron treatment. Worm infestation should also be considered as a possible complication.

Pickwickian syndrome Reversible cardiopulmonary obesity; hypoventilation syndrome with extreme obesity; this syndrome identifies a tendency to sleepiness in people with cardiac and respiratory problems secondary to being severely overweight. It is named after the behavior that Charles Dickens (1812–70) ascribed to "Fat Boy Joe" in *The Posthumous Papers of the Pickwick Club* (1837).

picsysms A picture symbol system based on easily recognized line drawing of familiar objects.

pictogram/pictograph A picture of an item; graphic symbols that resemble the objects they represent. Pictograms have been employed in some of the earliest systems of written language. Pictograms along with ideographs (symbols representing ideas) constitute a form of aided augmentative communication used by individuals who are unable to communicate verbally in all situations.

Pictorial Tests of Intelligence (PTI) A battery of instruments to measure intellectual ability in 3- to 8-year-old children with multiple disabilities with motor and speech involvement; its six subtests require intact receptive language skills: picture vocabulary, information and comprehension, form discrimination, similarities, size and number, and immediate recall. The examiner presents picture cards that depict four possible answers and asks questions regarding them. The tests require no verbal response and minimal physical responses. Typically the child is asked to point to the answer. However, the cards are designed so the examiner may determine a response from the observation of the eye movements of a child with a physical disability. Testing time is

approximately 45 minutes. The test produces standard scores (with a mean of 100 and a standard deviation of 16) and has an excellent norm group and acceptable reliability and validity. The PTI is a useful supplementary nonverbal measure of learning aptitude for young children with speech and motor disabilities.

picture arrangement A 12-item Wechsler Intelligence Scale for Children–Third Edition (WISC–III) performance subtest in which the child places a series of pictures in logical sequence. The 12 series of pictures are similar to comic strips. Individual cards are placed in a specific out-of-order sequence; the child is then asked to rearrange the pictures to tell a story that makes sense. The number of picture cards per set varies from three to five; time limits for the series vary as well. Nonverbal reasoning, visual sequencing, planning ability, and problem-solving strategies are measured. Anticipation (identifying antecedents and their consequences), visual organization, and temporal sequencing are also involved. Trial and error experimentation is occasionally used, though appreciation of the gestalt depicted by the cards is necessary for success on the subtest. Picture arrangement is timed, which can be a source of anxiety. However, bonus points are awarded for speed on later items. The subtest is discontinued after three consecutive failures.

picture completion A Wechsler Intelligence Scale for Children–Third Edition (WISC–III) performance subtest consisting of 26 pictures of common objects that are each missing an important element. The child is asked to identify and name or point to the missing component within a 20-second time limit. The subtest evaluates visual discrimination and understanding of part-to-whole relationships. Success depends upon the child's word-finding skills and long-term memory. Attention and visual perception are also required, which may serve either to mask or accentuate visual retrieval problems. Perception, cognition, judgment, and the extent and quality of a child's experiences may also influence performance. The time limit places an additional demand on the child. Delayed correct responses may suggest slow processing style or depression, whereas quick but incorrect responses can reflect impulsivity. The subtest is discontinued after four consecutive failures. *Example:* picture of a dog without a tail.

Picture Story Language Test (PSLT) A writing test used in the differential diagnosis of learning disabilities, mental retardation, emotional disturbance, reading disability, and dyslexia. Children ages 7–17 years of age are asked to write the best story possible about a picture. Five scores are derived: total words, total sentences, words per sentence, syntax (grammar), and abstract-concrete meaning.

piebaldness Depigmentation pattern of skin similar to a pinto horse; can be inherited as autosomal dominant or recessive and may be associated with sensorineural (involving the inner ear or the auditory nerve) deafness.

Pierre Robin sequence/syndrome A combination of mandibular hypoplasia (micrognathia [small jaw]), soft palate cleft, and glossoptosis (forward displacement of tongue) to produce a "shrew" facies. The major medical problem with this syndrome is upper airway obstruction and early failure to thrive. It occurs in otherwise normal individuals but may also be part of Stickler syndrome or trisomy 18. Inheritance is polygenic-multifactorial. Recurrence risk is 5%.

Piers-Harris Children's Self Concept Scale (The Way I Feel About Myself) A self-report instrument for children fourth through twelfth grade to quantitate self-attitude. Eighty statements are scored yes or no; the raw scores yield percentile and stanine norms and six factor scores. The scale can be administered individually or to groups of children in 20 minutes.

PIMRA *See* Psychopathology Instrument for Mentally Retarded Adults.

pincer grasp A fine-motor milestone in the evolution of infant pre-

pincer grasp

hension; this stage is characterized by the ability to grasp overhand a small object (e.g., pellet, raisin) between the tips of the first two (thumb and index [pointer]) fingers. This mature pincer typically occurs at 10 months of age; an immature pincer or tripod grasp can be observed a month or two earlier.

pinna External ear. Pinnal abnormalities are examples of minor dysmorphic (atypical) features that can be normal variants, familial traits, or components of genetic syndromes. Significant ear malformations include folded ("lop-eared"), protuberant

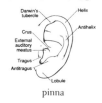

pinna

("jug-handle"), posteriorly rotated, low set, and excessively rounded.

pitch The quality of sound that depends on the frequency of the vibrations producing it. The greater the frequency, the higher or more acute the pitch; the lower the frequency, the lower the pitch and more grave the tone.

PKU *See* phenylketonuria.

PL Abbreviation for Public Law; *see specific PL entries.*

placement An out-of-home living situation for people with long-term care needs due to physical, cognitive, emotional, or social disabilities. Thus, a young adult with mental retardation may be "placed" in a group home to provide a protected, yet semi-independent (according to the person's maximum capabilities), long-term living situation. The person is encouraged to live as typical and independent a life as possible under the protection and support of one of a variety of living arrangement options. May also refer to the educational setting in which a student is "placed" (*see* least restrictive environment [LRE]).

placenta The afterbirth; an organ that exists during pregnancy and links the mother and the fetus. The placenta assumes many of the functions of the lungs, kidneys, liver, and endocrine system in place of the undeveloped fetal organs. Chronic placental dysfunction can contribute to undergrowth of the fetus and low birth weight infants.

placenta previa A placenta that is implanted low in the uterus so that it partially covers the cervical opening; during labor, such a placenta tends to separate and cause bleeding that, if excessive, can threaten the lives of the mother and the baby.

placental abruption *See* abruptio placenta.

placing A primitive reflex in which tactile (touch) stimulation of the dorsum (top) of foot and/or hand or the anterior (front) aspect of the relevant extremity (arm or leg) results in a complex response of flexion and extension ("placing" of the extremity on top of the stimulus). Lower-extremity placing is present at birth, but upper-extremity placing does not emerge until 3 months of age. Absence or asymmetry of the response is significant.

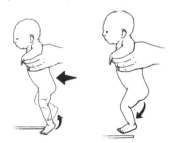

placing—lower extremity

placing—upper extremity

plagiocephaly A deformation of the skull characterized by obliquity with one side more developed anteriorly (toward the front) and the other side more de-

plagiocephaly

veloped posteriorly (toward the back). This asymmetry can be produced by prolonged lying of the head turned to one side. Also known as *asynclitism of the skull.*

PLAI *See* Preschool Language Assessment Instrument.

plantar grasp *See* grasp reflex.

plantar grasp

plantigrade Normal standing/walking posture of the foot with weight-bearing evenly distributed across the sole and feet in a flat position against a surface with ankles flexed at 90 degrees. Human gait is bipedal plantigrade progression.

plateau A level or leveling off; a period of relative stability and decreased change following a period of normal to increased change. The implications of this latter developmental acceleration can be positive (e.g., a recovery spurt after injury) or negative (e.g., a deterioration associated with degenerative disease).

play Voluntary activity engaged in for pleasure (not work) that nevertheless serves other social, emotional, and learning functions. Different theories of play generate diverse stages (with overlapping ages) depending on whether the focus is on the type of social interaction, the toys or games played with, or the level of imagination and degree of creativity involved. Despite the absence of any agreement on the definition and stages of play activities in infants and children, the observation of play can be very informative. An experienced childlife worker or preschool teacher can accurately discriminate the steps in the evolution from solitary, parallel, and mirror play to cooperative play and can reach both quantitatively and qualitatively valid conclusions regarding the child's development.

play audiometry *See* behavioral observation audiometry.

play therapy A method of examination and treatment used with children. The child is observed as he or she plays freely with a selection of toys designed to help him or her address emotional concerns and traumatic past experiences. Play therapy is often used with children who have been abused and with those who have language disorders. In psychotherapy or speech-language therapy, the strategy is based on the premise that play is the child's natural medium of self-expression, allowing him or her to more easily and directly convey thoughts, feelings, and experiences than would be possible through strictly verbal methods.

pleiotropy The situation in syndromology (the identification of genetic and other syndromes) when one genetic cause produces multiple effects; the identification of the full syndrome is the result of a process of "lumping." The process of syndrome identification pulls together the diverse pleiotropic effects of a single genetic disorder.

pleuritis Pleurisy; inflammation or infection of the pleura (linings of the lung and chest); symptoms include chest pain, fever, and cough. Treatment is of the underlying cause and is symptomatic.

PLS–3 *See* Preschool Language Scale–3.

plumbism *See* lead poisoning.

PMA *See* postmenstrual age.

PMH Profound mental handicap; *see* profound mental retardation.

PM&R *See* physical medicine and rehabilitation.

PMR *See* profound mental retardation.

pneumonia Lung infection; symptoms include fever, cough, tachypnea (rapid breathing) and dyspnea (difficult breathing). The infection can (and usually is) localized to one side or to one lobe (part) of the respiratory system. "Double pneumonia" is a vague lay term that probably means there is some involvement of both lungs. Recurrent right middle lobe pneumonia is often associated with swallowing problems and aspiration.

PNF *See* proprioceptive neuromuscular facilitation.

Pohl A system of physical therapy for the treatment of cerebral palsy; this approach focuses on one joint or muscle action at a time.

pointing A gesture that can be used to indicate wants (expressive) and identification (receptive). As receptive language milestones, pointing to pictures and body parts typically begins to emerge at 18 months of age.

Poland anomaly A unilateral defect of the pectoralis muscle (upper anterior [front] chest wall) and the ipsilateral (on the same side) hand (i.e., syndactyly). There are no associated developmental disabilities.

poliomyelitis Polio; infantile paralysis. A viral infection of the central nervous system that can produce a permanent paralysis usually affecting the lower extremities more. The most common source of contagion is respiratory droplets, and most cases are extremely mild. Treatment is supportive and preventive; immunization (vaccination) of all infants with trivalent oral polio vaccine (TOPOV) is recommended. Localized recurrence of muscle weakness can occur decades after initial involvement and is referred to as post-polio weakness.

poliosis Localized depigmentation of hair seen in a variety of syndromes such as tuberous sclerosis. The white forelock of Waardenburg syndrome is the most famous example of this phenomenon.

polydactyly Extra fingers and/or toes (more than five per extremity [arm or leg]); this can be an isolated finding, a familial trait, or a component of a genetic syndrome.

polydipsia Excessive consumption of fluids. It can be due to diabetes insipidus (nonsugar diabetes), kidney disease, or an acquired habit (i.e., psychogenic water drinking).

polygenic A disorder or trait determined by many genes on different chromosomes or on different parts of the same chromosome. Each gene has a small additive effect. Polygenic disorders are not caused by environmental factors.

polyhydramnios Hydramnios; an excessive amount of amniotic fluid (more than 2 liters) during a pregnancy. This is associated with a high incidence of fetal abnormalities, especially in relation to the central nervous system (e.g., anencephaly [no brain or absent top of skull]) and high alimentary tract obstruction (e.g., esophageal atresia).

polyribosyl ribitol phosphate (PRP–D) Haemophilus influenzae type B and diphtheria toxoid conjugate vaccine. The PRP (polyribosyl ribitol phosphate) vaccine is meant to reduce the incidence of Haemophilus influenzae infections, especially bacterial meningitis (inflammation of the spinal cord and brain membrane). Sometimes referred to as *Hib* (Haemophilus influenzae type B) vaccine. Other Hib vaccines include Hboc and PRP-OMP.

polysemy Condition when a single word has two or more meanings.

polysomy Presence of more than two chromosomes of the same kind. A trisomy (three chromosomes of the same number) is a polysomy. Polysomies of chromosomes other than the sex chromosomes are generally lethal or cause multiple congenital malformations and mental retardation. Children with polysomy or multiple X chromosomes may have milder problems, such as language delays and poor social development. The sex chromosome abnormalities, including abnormal numbers of X or Y chromosomes, are associated with a variety of developmental abnormalities, ranging from mild specific cognitive deficits, such as language disorders, to more severe global cognitive problems with mental retardation.

polytherapy The use of more than one therapy (usually drugs). This is generally used in reference to seizure treatment that involves two or more anticonvulsant agents. The rationale behind polytherapy is better seizure control; however, it has some disadvantages and is not the preferred treatment for an uncomplicated

seizure disorder. Chronic toxicity of anticonvulsants is greater with multiple drug therapy, and polytherapy can sometimes aggravate seizures. The cumulative effect of multiple agents often includes an impairment of the sensorium (wakefulness) and decreased cognitive performance. Thus, polytherapy is avoided where possible.

POMR *See* problem-oriented medical record.

population A group of people with similar characteristics. Most references to *population* indicate a specific group, such as those with learning disabilities or those with Down syndrome. Research generally studies the characteristics of a particular group as compared to the general population, which is a larger, more heterogeneous group. Often the effect of an intervention on a particular population is studied. It is important to clearly define the characteristics of a group in a research protocol in order to make the research results generalizable to others in that population.

porencephalic cyst A cavity in the brain caused by focal damage and repair to brain tissue. Porencephalic cysts may be caused by vascular (blood vessel) abnormalities such as hemorrhage (bleeding) or infectious insults. The injury may occur prenatally or postnatally. The cyst can mimic a brain tumor and cause hydrocephalus. Neurological impairments are generally asymmetrical and contralateral (opposite). Normal development can occur even with large porencephalic cysts. Porencephaly must be differentiated from schizencephaly, in which the brain formation is abnormal. Porencephalic cysts are common in premature infants following a parenchymal intraventricular hemorrhage (grade 4 IVH).

port-wine stain Purple, sometimes raised, and irregular skin lesion; can be a component of Sturge-Weber syndrome. Also known as *nevus flammeus*.

Portage Project/Portage Early Education Program A home-based early education program with a focus on parental involvement for preschool children with disabilities; it has its own assessment instrument (i.e., Developmental Sequence Checklist), which is used to generate an individual curriculum by selecting one of four to seven ways to teach each of the 580 skills contained in the assessment. It is named for Portage, Wisconsin, the site of the original program.

Porteus Maze Test   An intelligence test for children 3 years of age to adult; it is composed entirely of paper-and-pencil mazes and has been used as a measure of attention as well as of visual-perceptual motor ability. There are two additional versions, the Maze Test Extension and the Extension Supplement, to control for practice effects.

positive end expiratory pressure (PEEP)   A type of assisted ventilation used in children with respiratory distress.

positive reinforcement   *See* consequent stimulus event (CSE).

positive support   A complex postural response in which pressure on the feet produces varying degrees of lower-extremity extension and body support.

positron emission tomography (PET)   A technique used to look at brain function with radioactively labeled compounds. PET scans can localize areas of abnormal functioning such as in focal seizure disorders. Although PET is primarily a research procedure, it has demonstrated potential in evaluating brain function in children with developmental disabilities.

postconceptional age (PCA)   Chronological age (CA) plus gestational age according to obstetrical history of mother's last menstrual period (LMP); thus, a 4-week-old (CA) infant born at 28 weeks' gestation has a PCA of 32 weeks. PCA (dependent on maternal history) is more accurate than postmenstrual age (PMA) (dependent on physical examination) in extremely premature infants.

postconcussion syndrome   Headache, dizziness, irritability, nervousness, poor concentration, and behavioral and cognitive impairment may follow a brain injury with transient loss of consciousness. Parents may report that a child's personality changed or that hyperactivity and an attention disorder began after a specific head injury. Most of the minor head injuries experienced by toddlers learning to walk have no such neurodevelopmental sequelae.

posteroanterior view (PA)   Descriptive of an X ray taken so that the beam goes from the back of the body to the front.

postictal   Occurring after a seizure, including behavior such as somnolence (sleepiness), confusion, ataxia (unsteady gait), and poor coordination. Often there are mild abnormalities in a neurological examination. Occasionally, temporary blindness, aphasia (loss of language skills), or paralysis (i.e., Todd paralysis) may be seen. The postictal period generally lasts several hours.

postmaturity   When a pregnancy continues longer than 40 weeks, placental insufficiency contributes to the baby's looking thin and wasted, with dry, peeling skin, and meconium staining of the skin and nails; length and head circumference may be increased.

postmenstrual age (PMA)   Chronological age (CA) plus gestational age according to a clinical examination scale; thus, an 8-week-old (CA) infant born at 28 weeks' gestation has a PMA of 36 weeks.

postnatal   Occurring after birth; pertaining to the individual's life cycle after the conclusion of the perinatal period. Etiologies (causes) that are postnatal are typically acquired.

postprandial   After eating.

posttraumatic amnesia   Memory loss for the period of "clouded consciousness" that follows a closed head injury; it ends when the individual remembers waking. Also referred to as *anterograde amnesia*.

posttraumatic stress disorder (PTSD) A psychological syndrome that follows an extraordinary stress or trauma such as rape, incest, or cult abuse. Symptoms of this disorder may include sudden, intrusive vivid visual or auditory memory flashbacks, hyperalertness, difficulty concentrating, feelings of numbness, and inability to participate in intimate relations. Children with PTSD may appear to have developmental delays and often first present for diagnosis in such a clinic. Long-term psychotherapy is the indicated treatment.

postural drainage A variety of techniques used to help clear mucus from the respiratory tract. It is employed in people with chronic respiratory problems (e.g., asthma, cystic fibrosis, cerebral palsy with limited mobility that increases vulnerability to recurrent respiratory infections). Postural drainage can be performed or supervised by a physical therapist.

postural-ocular movement disorder *See* vestibular-bilateral disorder.

postural response Early automated responses III (EAR–III); previously IAR II (Infantile Automated Responses II). A group of reflex patterns that appear after birth, become prominent after 6 months of age, and facilitate the development of voluntary movement. They include the Landau, righting, equilibrium, and propping reactions.

poverty A chronic low standard of living that undermines the health, morale, and self-respect of an individual or group of individuals. The term is relative to the general standard of living in a society, the distribution of wealth, and social expectations. Although developmental disabilities occur in individuals of all economic strata, they are more common in the lower economic levels of society, where their impact is intensified by family educational level and limited access to resources.

PPD *See* purified protein derivative.

PPI *See* Parent Perception Inventory.

PPVT–R *See* Peabody Picture Vocabulary Test–Revised.

practice effect An improved performance or score on a test as a result of repeated exposure to the test items, either from practice or drill on such tasks or, more frequently, from the recent administration of the same version of the test. Most test manuals indicate the period of time needed to elapse to minimize practice effects on readministering the test; other tests provide alternate versions to be used when frequent administration of the same instrument is desirable.

Prader-Willi syndrome (PWS) Prader-Labhart-Willi syndrome; a genetic syndrome with three phases: 1) infancy with hypotonia (decreased muscle tone) and failure to thrive; 2) childhood with almond-shaped eyes, decreased palpebral fissure (eye slits) length, hypogonadism (small testicles), hypoplastic (short to absent) scrotum, hyperphagia (ravenous appetite) with central obesity but small hands and feet, cognitive impairments (two thirds of the cases with mental retardation, one third with learning disabilities and language impairments); and 3) young adulthood with increased severity of childhood symptoms coupled with severe behavior and emotional symptomatology and, occasionally, thought disorders. This syndrome may reflect a hypothalamic dysfunction secondary to a deletion of the long arm of chromosome 15 (q11–q13) on the paternal contribution to the chromosome 15 pair (*see also* Angelman syndrome). Without adequate dietary management, life expectancy is limited by heart failure and Pickwickian symptoms secondary to obesity. Sometimes referred to as *HHHO syndrome* (Hypotonia-Hypogonadism-Hypomentia-Obesity syndrome).

pragmatics The effective use of language appropriate to a given context. For children to achieve communicative competence, they must acquire a repertoire of socially acceptable strategies for controlling or influencing the behavior of their listeners, including informing, requesting information, taking turns in conversations, adjusting what they are saying to their listener's linguistic ability, and responding to requests for clarification. Pragmatics may be described as one more level of rules after phonology (speech sound), syntax (grammar), and semantics (the meaning of words). However, a broader interpretation includes the integration of structural, conversational, and social rules. Thus, a different set of pragmatic strategies would be necessary in the classroom than at home. Assessment is often done informally and may need to be repeated in various settings. Two formal instruments designed to assess pragmatics are the Test of Pragmatic Skills and the Communicative Activities of Daily Living (CADL).

praxis Skill in planning nonhabitual purposive movements; apraxia is the absence of such skill. Praxis is a final common pathway for a variety of brain functions.

preauricular pit A small indentation near the front of the ear; 1 in 200 children with preauricular pits will have a profound hearing loss. See Melnick-Fraser syndrome.

preeclampsia The preconvulsive stage of toxemia of pregnancy.

prehension Physical grasp; the manner in which the hand takes an object (e.g., pincer grasp, radial rake).

prelinguistic vocalizations The guttural sounds, cooing, and babbling that an infant uses before words. Despite a lack of verbal content, such prelinguistic vocalizations exhibit an orderliness and sequentiality that allow them to be used to monitor early expressive language development. A decrease in such vocalizations—the "quiet baby"—suggests the presence of a developmental disorder.

Premack principle If a high-frequency behavior is made contingent upon a low-frequency behavior, the low-frequency behavior will increase in frequency. Also known as Grandma's rule: "You can't have dessert unless you finish eating your broccoli." In a classroom setting, an ex-ample of the Premack principle is allowing a child to color after his mathematics is finished. A broader application of this principle structures a student's academic day so that a difficult task is followed by an easier or more enjoyable one.

prenatal Preceding birth; pertaining to the gestational period from conception to the beginning of the perinatal period.

prenatal diagnosis Identification of a fetal problem before birth. Techniques such as ultrasound and amniocentesis are used to look at the structure of the fetus, the fetal chromosomes, and any fetal or genetic syndrome or disorder that can be identified by a biochemical test (e.g., Tay-Sachs disease).

preoperational stage A Piagetian stage of cognitive development in which the child begins to internalize and manipulate symbols and images in an egocentric fashion. This stage is prominent from 2 to 6 years of age.

presbyopia Farsightedness with advancing age; it often corrects or improves the myopia (nearsightedness) of the preceding years.

Preschool Language Assessment Instrument (PLAI) A nonstandardized test used to assess a variety of language skills: labeling objects and actions, role playing, responding to conversational interactions, describing object functions, solving problems, and defining.

Preschool Language Scale–3 (PLS–3) A language test for chilren from birth to age 6–11 that yields total language, auditory comprehension, and expressive communication scores. Administration time is 30 minutes. A normed Spanish-language version is available.

Preschool Screening System A screening test for children between 2½ and 5½ years of age. Subtests include gross- and fine-motor, vocabulary, and speech and language skills. Administration time is approximately 20 minutes.

presentation   That which characterizes the part of the baby that comes out first during delivery. There are three main types of presentation: vertex (head first), face (chin first), and breech (sacrum first). A transverse presentation usually involves the shoulder coming out first. The most common vertex presentation is left occiput anterior (LOA).

presentation   The chief complaint, signs, and symptoms present when an individual first comes to a physician's attention.

preservation of sameness   Resisting change; a nonspecific sign of mental retardation or brain damage. In its mildest forms, it is similar to a typical child's bedtime ritual; in its more severe forms, the child may throw prolonged tantrums if a book's shelf space is altered. Its frequent occurrence in autism tends to be out of proportion to the degree of associated mental retardation.

Pre-Speech Assessment Scale (PSAS)   A nonstandardized rating scale for pre-speech behaviors (e.g., feeding, oral motor, respiratory-phonatory items) in children from birth to 2 years of age.

prevalence   A rate reflecting the number of cases of a disorder existing in a given population at a specific time (also known as *point prevalence*) or over a defined period of time (also known as *period prevalence*). Prevalence rates are affected by both the rate of occurrence of the disorder as well as the duration of the condition. Whereas an increasing prevalence rate might reflect an actual increase in the rate of occurrence of the condition, it might also reflect improved medical treatment with longer survival. For example, the availability of better medical care and healthier living conditions should increase the total number of people with mental retardation in the population at any given time—an increased prevalence rate. Period prevalence represents the sum of the point prevalence at the beginning of the time period and the incidence during that time period.

prevention   Measures that decrease the incidence or limit the progression of a disease or its sequelae. There are varying classifications of the different levels of prevention; because these were originally developed as part of the epidemiology of acute infectious diseases, they do not always translate smoothly to such chronic neurological disorders as developmental disabilities. The earliest level of prevention for developmental disorders is premarital genetic counseling for members of families or groups considered at risk. Maternal immunization (vaccination) status, nutrition, and other prenatal care will be paralleled by infant immunization, nutrition, and pediatric care. Genetic and metabolic screening can be accomplished prenatally or postnatally. Dietary, pharmacological, surgical, and other therapies can minimize the occurrence or impact of associated impairments; psychological and educational interventions facilitate optimal development and decrease secondary emotional disabilities.

Preverbal Assessment Intervention Profile (PAIP)   A standardized Piagetian assessment of sensory-motor prelinguistic (occurring before the development of speech and language skills) behavior that can be used with individuals of all ages with severe, profound, and multiple disabilities.

primary auditory cortex (A1)   Brodmann areas 41 and 42; Heschl's gyrus. This area is responsible for the reception of sound; although input from the contralateral (opposite) ear is predominant, the temporal lobe of each hemisphere receives input from both ears.

primary process   A psychoanalytic term referring to primitive, irrational, wishful thinking or thought dominated by unconscious emotions and instinctual drives. When counseling parents of children with developmental disabilities, too much focus is often placed on the cognitive content (secondary process) of the information communicated, to the exclusion of the emotional impact (primary process).

primary visual cortex (V1)   Brodmann area 17; the occipital pole and the calcarine fissure; the striate cortex in each hemisphere receives input from the contralateral (opposite) visual field of both eyes.

primidone   Trade name Mysoline; an anticonvulsant used in tonic-clonic seizures. The drug is generally helpful in people with identifiable organic brain disease. Primidone is broken down into phenobarbital in the body. Both primidone and phenobarbital blood levels can be obtained; however, they are useful only for compliance, as they do not always correspond to either seizure control or toxic side effects. Primidone should be started at a low dose, because marked sedation can occur with high initial doses.

primigravida   A woman pregnant for the first time. First pregnancies may need closer observation than later pregnancies and may be associated with slightly increased risks for both mother and child.

primipara   A woman who has delivered one live child.

primitive reflex   Early automated responses I (EAR–I). A group of reflex patterns present at birth that tend to be suppressed or integrated into more functional voluntary movement patterns. These patterns originate in the brain stem and may persist in the presence of cortical or other brain damage that interferes with the evolution of voluntary movements; they may also reappear in older children and adults after severe brain injury. They play an obvious clinical role in the examination of infants under 6 months of age. Most of the patterns involve the overriding impact of head position and movement on the tone, movement, and posture of the four extremities (arms or legs). EAR–I includes the Moro, Galant, asymmetrical tonic neck, symmetrical tonic neck, tonic labyrinthine (extension of all four extremities), stepping, crossed extension, and placing reflexes.

p.r.n.   *See* pro re nata.

proband   *See* propositus.

probe   A test for generalization in operant language training.

problem-oriented medical record (POMR)   An approach to record keeping with a focus on a defined list of problems. Notes are written in a SOAP structure: S—subjective data; O—objective data; A—assessment; and P—plan.

problem solving   Often used to refer to nonverbal cognitive abilities in infants and young children; this stream of development is measured by visual-perceptual-motor items (e.g., playing with toys) on infant tests.

procedure   Surgical operation.

procedural knowledge   A construct of the way in which certain information is represented in memory. Procedural knowledge is composed of productions and represents knowing "how" to do something. A student may be able to tell you that he or she lives at 472 Wilson Street, but may not know "how" to get there. Procedural knowledge is dynamic in that it results not simply in recall but in a transformation of information. For example, the result of doing a mathematics problem ($2 \times 10 = 20$) produces an output (20) that is different from the input (2×10). Once well learned, procedural knowledge operates in a fast, automatic fashion (for example, print is decoded by skilled readers with little awareness of the process). The two main types of procedural knowledge are pattern-recognition and action-sequence; although learned differently, both types are intimately related in performance.

prodrome   An early symptom of a disease, usually before the specific disease shows sufficient other symptoms to allow it to be diagnosed; *prodrome* can refer to a grouping of symptoms that collectively represents the first stage of a disease before the full-blown syndrome shows itself.

profound mental handicap (PMH)   *See* profound mental retardation.

profound mental retardation (PMR)   Mental retardation in which the IQ level is below 25. Adults with PMR often need assistance in adaptive skills and may reside in intermediate care facilities.

progeria Hutchinson-Gilford syndrome; a rare condition with premature aging and shortened life expectancy; cognition remains unaffected.

progestin A hormone used to treat women with developmental disabilities when they exhibit behavior disorders associated with menstrual irregularities or premenstrual syndrome (PMS); long-acting injections of progestin (Depo-Provera) are also used for contraception.

prognathia A protuberant jaw; can be a normal variant, a familial trait, a minor malformation, or part of an identifiable syndrome.

prognosis Prediction; description of the probable course and outcome of a given disease or therapy. More accurate prognoses provide the principal rationale for increased diagnostic refinement.

Program for the Acquisition of Language with the Severely Impaired (PALS) A language assessment instrument that uses caregiver interviews and environmental observations first to identify communication partners, communication content, and communication behaviors. The Diagnostic Interview Survey is then used with nonspeaking or minimally verbal clients. The Developmental Assessment Tool is the more formal third step in this individualized evaluation program.

programmed learning A self-instructional method that presents subject content in a predetermined sequence that allows students to check their progress, determine what part of the sequence they may not have effectively learned, go back in the sequence as necessary, and proceed at their own pace. Programmed learning is presented in the form of workbooks or computer programs.

progressive encephalopathy Degenerative disease; "progressive," in this context, refers to progressive deterioration or a progressively downhill course.

projective test A technique that uses vague, ambiguous stimuli to elicit the subject's characteristic mode of perceiving the world; the individual projects his or her feelings into the unstructured test item. Examples include the Rorschach test and the Thematic Apperception Test (TAT).

prompt An action that increases the probability of a target behavior by reducing the amount the subject has to do to complete it; prompts can range from verbal cues to physically guiding the subject through the motions of the desired response.

pronation Forearm movement that turns the palm downward.

pronation of hand

prone Anatomical position in which the person is lying face downward on his or her abdomen (opposite of supine).

pronominal reversal Confusion between first- and second-person pronouns (and not the genders of third-person pronouns); probably related in part to echolalia (repetition of what is heard), in part to the phenomenon of referring to self by name or by third-person pronouns, and in part to egocentrism. Mixing up the case of pronouns—"I, me; he, him; she, her; and they, them"—does not count as pronominal reversal. Pronominal reversal occurs in autism and other language disorders.

prophylaxis Prevention.

propositus The index case, or proband. The person in a family who first comes to the attention of professionals with an identified trait, possibly leading to identification of that trait or others within a family. For example, the child with mental retardation who is diagnosed with tuberous sclerosis, leading to an evaluation of the family for tuberous sclerosis, is the propositus.

propping *See* protective extension.

propranolol Trade name Inderal; a beta-adrenergic blocker drug with many cardiovascular applications. It has investigational uses in the treatment of behavior disorders, such as aggression and self-injurious behaviors, in people with severe developmental disabilities.

proprietary name   Trade name.

proprioception   Position sense. This sensory function is evaluated during neurological examinations by having individuals close their eyes, lift their toes up and down, and identify the direction in which the toes have moved.

proprioceptive facilitation   Therapeutic activities that treat neuromuscular dysfunctioning by stimulating the proprioceptive system; proprioceptive facilitation techniques include heavy joint compression, stretch, resistance, tapping, and vibration.

proprioceptive neuromuscular facilitation (PNF)   A system of physical therapy for the treatment of cerebral palsy, devised by a physician (Herman Kabat) and two physical therapists (Margaret Knott and Dorothy Voss). The approach uses spiral and diagonal mass movement patterns and heavy resistance isotonic exercises.

pro re nata (p.r.n.)   As needed; whenever necessary; as the occasion arises.

prosody   Voicing patterns of speech determined by rate, inflection, and rhythm. Prosodic variations include shouting, rising versus falling pitch, angry voice, and wheedling tone. The babbling of babies reflects the prosody of the parent language before actual words are uttered. Until 8–9 months of age, the babble-jargon of babies around the world sounds relatively the same. In the typical 9-month-old, the prosody of the parent language becomes apparent. For example, Chinese babies begin to include the rhythmically rising and falling pattern of the Chinese language, whereas Hispanic babies show the rhythm patterns of spoken Spanish.

prosthesis   Artificial body part (e.g., artificial leg, glass eye).

protection and advocacy (P&A)   A system of state agencies established through federal legislation (Section 113, Developmental Disabilities Assistance and Bill of Rights Act of 1975 [PL 94-103]) to protect and advocate for the rights of people with developmental disabilities. P&A agencies are independent of other governmental agencies or units to ensure that they are able to freely serve the interests of their clientele. Duties and activities of the P&A staff may include negotiation, administrative or legal intervention on behalf of individuals seeking services, or securing and protecting people's rights and privileges as citizens. Public dissemination of information concerning the rights of individuals with developmental disabilities through publications, presentations, and workshops is a further responsibility of P&A systems. Education, employment, transportation, housing, recreation, facility accessibility, and the entitlement of people with developmental disabilities to these services are of interest to the protection and advocacy system. The specific name of agencies varies from state to state.

protective extension   Propping reactions; a subgroup of upper-extremity postural responses (EAR–II) concerned with maintaining an upright position. This group of reflexes includes anterior (front), lateral (outside),

anterior parachute

and posterior (back) propping, and the anterior parachute response.

protective services   Provision of services ranging from mandated monitoring to alternative placement for people in danger of harm from others or themselves, or who are no longer physically or cognitively able to care for themselves. Thus, children who are in danger of abuse or neglect, or who have mental retardation or other disabilities, may receive protective services.

protocol   A list of rules; research and treatment protocols detailing how research or therapy is to be conducted (i.e., the research/treatment methodology).

protopathic   Relating to the indistinct peripheral (noncentral) sensation of pain and temperature.

proximal   Closest to the center.

proximal transverse palmar crease   A flexion crease on the palm of the hand; the "head line" of palmistry.

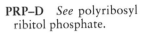

proximal transverse palmar crease

PRP–D   *See* polyribosyl ribitol phosphate.

pruritus   Itching.

PSAS   *See* Pre-Speech Assessment Scale.

pseudarthrosis   False joint; this can occur as a complication of surgery after a fracture fails to heal properly or secondary to some other underlying disease (e.g., neurofibromatosis).

pseudobulbar palsy   Impaired swallowing, talking, and chewing secondary to brain damage. The oral motor control (cranial nerves X and XII) of the lips, tongue, mouth, larynx (windpipe), and pharynx (throat) typically resides in the medulla oblongata (part of the brain stem). Damage to these centers produces a bulbar palsy; when a similar pattern of dysfunction occurs as a result of more diffuse brain involvement, it is referred to as *pseudobulbar palsy* and is sometimes associated with the more severe degrees of cerebral palsy. More accurately, suprabulbar paresis.

pseudohypertelorism   The misleading appearance of (ocular) hypertelorism (widely spaced eyes) when it is not really present. Epicanthal folds and an increased inner canthal distance can contribute to this illusion, but a normal interpupillary distance corrects this impression.

pseudohypoparathyroidism   Albright hereditary osteodystrophy; a genetic syndrome with short stature, short extremities (arms or legs), short hands and feet, obesity, mental retardation, and seizures.

pseudostrabismus   An appearance of strabismus (squint) when it is not really present. A normal interpupillary distance misleadingly looks short because of an increased inner canthal distance, telecanthus, or epicanthal folds.

pseudostupidity   Interpretation (i.e., by professionals) at a more complex level than required.

PSLT   *See* Picture Story Language Test.

psychiatric disorders   Disorders of five separate classes: behavior, affect, cognitive, interpersonal, and somatic. Current diagnostic schemas (e.g., *Diagnostic and Statistical Manual of Mental Disorders* [4th edition] [DSM-IV]) approach diagnosis by classifying disorders on the dimension most symptomatically affected. Current classification schemas by symptom groups avoid the issue of etiology (cause), thus giving little guidance to appropriate treatment.

psychoanalysis   A system for diagnosing and treating mental disorders based on the pioneering work of the Viennese neurologist Sigmund Freud (1856–1939). The approach relies heavily on the use of free association and dream interpretation to reveal and resolve unconscious conflicts between repressed instincts and defense mechanisms. There are no significant psychoanalytical contributions to the understanding of developmental disabilities.

Psychoeducational Profile (PEP)   A norm-referenced instrument used to plan individualized educational intervention for children with autism; seven developmental and five pathological areas are investigated.

psychogenic   Disorders or conditions that are nonorganic in origin, stemming instead from an individual's mind or psyche.

psychogenic pain   Recurrent severe pain with no known organic origin; often in response to external stressors.

psychogenic water drinking   Excessive fluid intake (usually water) that does not result from kidney or other medical disorders but is a behavioral reflection of extreme emotional need. The inadequate nurturance that characterizes deprived children in foster care is a typical setting for this behavioral symptom.

psychometry Psychological testing; the science and practice of testing and quantifying a variety of psychological parameters; often restricted to IQ testing.

psychomotor Pertaining to voluntary (psychically determined) movement; refers to the relationship between the brain and the muscles. The term *psychomotor retardation* is used (sometimes with contradictory meanings) in describing various emotional and/or physical states.

psychomotor retardation *See* psychomotor.

psychopathology Behavioral, emotional, or personality dysfunction within an individual.

Psychopathology Instrument for Mentally Retarded Adults (PIMRA) A 56-item inventory to assess symptoms of psychopathology in adults with mental retardation. Both self-report and informant versions (divided into eight subscales of seven items each) are available for purposes of diagnosing schizophrenia, anxiety, somatization, personality disorders, adjustment disorders, depression, psychosexual disorders, and poor mental adjustment.

psychosocial deprivation syndrome Reversible hyposomatotropinism (condition of inadequate secretion of pituitary growth hormone). A severe disorder of parenting that produces bizarre behavior in the child along with short stature that is secondary to deficient pituitary growth hormone. Abnormal behaviors include drinking from toilet bowls, eating from garbage cans, polydipsia (consuming liquids to excess), polyphagia (eating to excess) alternating with food refusal and food hoarding, insensitivity to pain, encopresis (fecal incontinence), and an unusual wake–sleep cycle. All the behaviors are readily corrected when the child is placed in a nurturant environment, but it may take months for the growth hormone levels to return to normal. Transient developmental delay is the rule.

psychosomatic Describes functional disorders with no detectable organic cause but due, rather, to emotional conflict or stress. The three most common psychosomatic symptoms in children are headaches, stomachaches, and leg pains. They can be precipitated by problems at home or in school but also typically have strong family histories to model or imitate. The female predominance seen in somatization disorder is less striking in young children. In the presence of similar degrees of stress at school, psychosomatic complaints do not seem to be as frequent in children with mental retardation or language-based learning disabilities. Psychosomatic disorders are not imaginary.

psychostimulant *See* stimulant.

psychotropic Describes drugs for modifying the intensity of feelings or modifying behavior or experience.

P 300 A late component of the auditory evoked response (AER) that may be absent or reduced in patients with autism; the consistency and specificity of this finding remain unclear.

PT *See* physical therapy.

PTI *See* Pictorial Tests of Intelligence.

ptosis A falling of any organ so that it is located below its normal position. Without further specification, ptosis often refers to a drooping eyelid. Ptosis can be a congenital minor malformation or acquired and is often due either to a problem with the muscle of the eyelid or the oculomotor nerve (cranial nerve III). Ptosis is commonly found in a number of syndromes such as fetal alcohol syndrome, neurofibromatosis, and Sturge-Weber syndrome.

PTSD *See* posttraumatic stress disorder.

puberty The age period during which secondary sexual characteristics and the ability to reproduce mature (11–15 years, with girls developing earlier than boys); the onset of physical changes that are part of the broader phenomenon of adolescence. Puberty is sometimes early, but more often late, in people with significant mental retardation, but this varies with the specific etiology (cause).

pubis *See* symphysis pubis.

PL 88-164 *See* Mental Retardation Facilities and Community Mental Health Centers Construction Act of 1963.

PL 89-10 *See* Elementary and Secondary Education Act (ESEA) of 1965.

PL 89-313 *See* Elementary and Secondary Education Act Amendments of 1965.

PL 89-750 *See* Elementary and Secondary Education Act Amendments of 1966.

PL 90-247 *See* Elementary and Secondary Education Act Amendments of 1968.

PL 91-230 *See* Education of the Handicapped Act of 1970.

PL 91-517 *See* Developmental Disabilities Services and Facilities Construction Act of 1970.

PL 93-112 *See* Rehabilitation Act of 1973.

PL 93-380 *See* Education Amendments of 1974.

PL 94-103 *See* Developmental Disabilities Assistance and Bill of Rights Act of 1975.

PL 94-142 *See* Education for All Handicapped Children Act of 1975.

PL 95-56 *See* Elementary and Secondary Education Act Amendments of 1978.

PL 95-602 *See* Rehabilitation, Comprehensive Services, and Developmental Disabilities Amendments of 1978.

PL 98-199 *See* Education of the Handicapped Act Amendments of 1983.

PL 98-211 *See* Chapter 1 of the Education Consolidation and Improvement Act of 1981.

PL 98-221 *See* Rehabilitation Act Amendments of 1983.

PL 99-372 *See* Handicapped Children's Protection Act of 1986.

PL 99-457 *See* Education of the Handicapped Act Amendments of 1986.

PL 99-506 *See* Rehabilitation Act Amendments of 1986.

PL 100-146 *See* Developmental Disabilities and Bill of Rights Act Amendments of 1987.

PL 100-407 *See* Technology-Related Assistance for Individuals with Disabilities Act of 1988.

PL 101-336 *See* American with Disabilities Act (ADA) of 1990.

PL 101-392 *See* Carl D. Perkins Vocational and Applied Technology Act of 1990.

PL 101-476 *See* Individuals with Disabilities Education Act (IDEA) of 1990.

PL 101-496 *See* Developmental Disabilities Assistance and Bill of Rights Act of 1990.

PL 102-569 *See* Rehabilitation Act Amendments of 1992.

PL 103-218 *See* Technology-Related Assistance for Individuals with Disabilities Amendments of 1994.

pulses A numerical system to monitor treatment efficacy in cerebral palsy: P = general conditions; U = upper limbs; L = lower limbs; S = special senses/speech; E = excretory functions; and S = cerebration. Each item/letter is scored from 1 (no disorder) to 4 (needs maximum help); higher scores indicate greater dependency.

punishment In behavioral terms, reducing an operant behavior by following it with something negative—an aversive stimulus event (ASE), or punisher. Punishment may be divided into five types: reprimand, cost contingency, negative practice, overcorrection, and corporal punishment. Punishment is often considered first as a way to eliminate undesirable behavior. However, there are pitfalls to this approach. Punishment can lead to avoidance behavior such as sneaking, cheating, or lying. In addition, children pay attention to what is done rather than what is said (e.g., spanking a child for hitting is not likely to teach that hitting is wrong). Punishment has a short-term, rather than a long-term, effect when appropriate behaviors are not taught or reinforced at the same time. If punishment occurs frequently and across enough school settings, the student will come to view the whole school experience as aversive, a situation unconducive to learning. In addition, children with learning disabilities or attention-deficit/hyperactivity disorder (ADHD) may not clearly link cause and effect. For example, the impulsive child who hits another child simply to gain attention with no malice intended does not perceive this as a punishable event. Because he or she intended no harm, punishment is confusing and is unlikely to prevent another incident. In addition, the child with a learning disability who finds that his or her best efforts do not allow completion of work and is therefore consistently kept in from recess eventually learns not to try. Thus, punishment may effectively teach the wrong lesson.

Pupil Rating Scale–Revised A teacher questionnaire used to screen for learning disabilities with students ages 5–14 years of age. A five-point scale is applied to items in five separate areas: auditory comprehension and memory, spoken language, orientation, motor coordination, and personal social behavior. Administration time is 10 minutes.

Purdue pegboard A 50-hole pegboard in which pins and pin-collar-washer assemblies are to be placed; the number correctly placed in a fixed time period is a measure of fine-motor coordination.

Purdue Perceptual Motor Survey An instrument used to assess the perceptual-motor skills required for academic learning in children 6–10 years of age.

pure tone audiometry A method of assessing hearing using a machine that generates pure-tone stimuli, calibrated in decibels, to earphones; it can be used to screen for significant hearing loss and to diagnose the degree of hearing loss to either ear for both bone and air conduction.

purified protein derivative (PPD) A skin test for tuberculosis that involves the subcutaneous (inner) injection of tubercular material that is then observed for an inflammatory response 2–3 days after injection.

PVL See periventricular leukomalacia; see also leukomalacia.

PVS See persistent vegetative state.

PWS See Prader-Willi syndrome.

pyknic body type Round, fat, short.

pyknodysostosis A genetic syndrome with dwarfism, increased bone density, abnormalities of the terminal digits, and a dolichocephalic skull (long front-to-back diameter) with a peculiar facies. About one fifth of cases exhibit mental retardation. Inheritance is autosomal recessive. The artist Henri Toulouse-Lautrec (1864–1901) is believed to have had pyknodysostosis.

pyrexia Fever. Aspirin is an antipyretic.

pyridoxine (vitamin B$_6$) deficiency Symptoms include seizures and hyperirritability in newborns with a familial pyridoxine dependency.

Q

q− The long arm of a chromosome; a designation "4q−" means a deletion on the long arm of chromosome 4.

q

QT *See* Quick Test.

quadriceps Quadriceps femoris; a group of four muscles located on the front of the thigh; it flexes the leg at the hip and extends the knee.

quadriplegia Literally, "four palsy"; a topographical (which parts of the body are involved) subtype of spastic cerebral palsy in which all four extremities (arms or legs) are severely involved. Asymmetries are frequently present but not in such a way as to qualify for another topographic classification. Severe mental retardation is the rule. An inexperienced examiner may easily mistake rigidity for quadriplegia.

quadriceps

quadruped On "all fours"; prone (front) on elbows/knees or hands/feet.

quantifier An adjective that expresses amount, either specific (one, two, three, etc.) or nonspecific (all, some, none, most, more, each, etc.).

quantitative research synthesis *See* meta-analysis.

Quick Test (QT) Ammons Quick Test; a brief (approximately 15-minute administration time) cognitive screening test for children ages 2 years and older. A picture receptive vocabulary test with questionable validity.

quickening The earliest maternal perception of fetal movement, typically in the fourth or fifth month of pregnancy. Deviations in the time of occurrence of quickening may suggest either problems with the fetus or error in the estimated duration of pregnancy. If the baby is felt to be moving earlier than the fourth month, then the pregnancy may be farther along than initially estimated; if the baby is not felt to be moving after the fifth month, then the pregnancy may be less far along or the baby may be experiencing difficulties due to placental or embryological abnormalities.

R

radial rake   A stage in the evolution of voluntary grasp in which the hand approaches the object from the radial (thumb and forefinger) side; prominent from 6 to 9 months of age.

radius   The thicker of the two bones of the forearm (*see also* ulna); dislocation of the radial head (near the elbow) is a common childhood

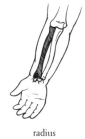

radius

injury that results from the child being pulled by the forearm (also known as *nursemaid elbow*).

railroad track ear   A finding in fetal alcohol syndrome in which the pattern displayed by the inner markings of the ear resembles the parallel lines of railroad tracks.

rake   A stage in the development of reaching and grasping in which the infant scoops an object with the entire hand; in the ulnar rake, which is prominent around 6 months of age, the hand approaches the object with its pinky side; in the radial rake, which becomes prominent after 6 months of age, the hand approaches the object with its thumb and forefinger side.

range of motion (ROM)   A component of the neuromuscular examination that measures the extent (angle in degrees) of movement at a joint; ROM also refers to active and passive exercise designed to maintain or increase the amount of movement at a joint. ROM exercises may prevent or treat contractures in a variety of neuromuscular disorders.

ranitidine   Trade name Zantac; a drug that can be used in the treatment of gastroesophageal reflux. This is an H_2-recep-

tor antagonist that suppresses gastric acid production.

rapid eye movement (REM)   A phase of sleep that coincides with dreaming.

rapport   The relationship established between individuals that allows them to work together in a therapeutic fashion. Ideally, a professional gathering information attempts to create a warm and comfortable atmosphere to facilitate free information exchange and positive regard. With respect to psychological and developmental testing, rapport is an integral part of the testing process; it is required to enhance the likelihood of achieving a valid estimate of the testee's abilities. Establishing and maintaining rapport becomes especially difficult when the therapist or tester has unrealistic expectations of the testee's abilities or is ignorant of the impact of an organic diagnosis on performance. Examples of problem areas include the level of cognitive deficiency, the confusion of attention-deficit/hyperactivity disorder (ADHD) symptomatology with willful maliciousness, and the misdiagnosis of hyperactivity for a language disorder.

RAS   *See* reticular activating system.

Rasch analysis   A statistical technique to group items in clusters according to level of difficulty.

ratio   A numerical value obtained by dividing one number into another to indicate their relative proportion. Some intelligence and developmental quotients are ratios of mental age (MA) or developmental age to chronological age (CA).

ratio IQ   An intelligence score derived by dividing an individual's mental age (MA) by his or her chronological age (CA) and multiplying the quotient by 100 to eliminate the decimal. Thus, ratio IQ = MA/CA × 100. Because the standard deviation of the ratio IQ distribution does not remain constant with age, IQs for different ages are not comparable; the same IQ at different ages has different meanings. By transforming the raw score (a number representing actual test performance) to a standard score with a given mean and standard deviation (deviation IQ), this problem is eliminated. For this reason, the use of the deviation IQ has replaced the use of the ratio IQ in most instances.

Raven Progressive Matrices A test of nonverbal intelligence for people 6 years of age to adult; there are three versions of the test: Standard Progressive Matrices (ages 6 and older), Colored Progressive Matrices (5–11 years of age), and Advanced Progressive Matrices (ages 11 and older). Each version presents a series of progressively more complex, incomplete designs that the subject must complete by choosing from a number of fragments presented. The results are scored as percentiles. The test is completely nonverbal and allows children with language-based learning disabilities to demonstrate their abstract reasoning ability more effectively than in other tests. Although Raven scores correlate well with performance IQ in children younger than 10 years of age, for older children, the correlation becomes stronger with verbal IQ scores, owing to the increasingly sequential character of the more advanced patterns.

raw score The record of test performance expressed in original test units; the actual number of items "passed," correct answers given, or tasks successfully completed.

razzing The raspberry, or "Bronx cheer"; a spluttering sound produced by blowing through vibrating lips. An expressive language milestone of infancy that typically emerges around 5 months of age.

RCBF *See* regional cerebral blood flow.

RDLS–R *See* Reynell Developmental Language Scales–Revised.

RDS *See* respiratory distress syndrome of newborn.

reactive attachment disorder of infancy A behavioral syndrome with an onset before 8 months of age in which poor maternal bonding leads to a lack of social responsiveness, apathy, growth failure (failure to thrive), depressive affect, and developmental delay in an infant.

readiness A condition or state in which it is possible for a person to engage in a given learning activity.

readiness skills In education, those skills that are prerequisite to success in a formal classroom setting. Traditionally they include oral language (speaking in complete sentences, using words adequately to describe), listening (remembering what is heard), perceptual-motor development (development of large and small muscles, knowledge of body parts and direction, balance), visual-perceptual development (eye–hand coordination, knowledge of size, shape, spatial concepts), reading readiness (letter recognition, sound–symbol association), social-emotional development (understanding self and others, interaction with peers, accepting responsibilities), and number readiness (counting, number values, concepts such as more and less).

reading epilepsy A convulsive disorder in adolescents with reading disorders in which reading precipitates complex partial seizures; this condition is extremely rare and seems to result from or correlate with, but not cause, the reading disorder.

rebound In medical terminology, a dramatic increase in the severity of symptoms of a disorder being treated when medication is withdrawn.

rebus A graphic puzzle representing a word, phrase, or sentence. Letters, numbers, and pictures of objects with names that sound similar to the words or syllables they represent are used. A rebus is a form of aided augmentative communication used as an alternative method for teaching reading.

rebus

Receptive-Expressive Emergent Language Scale–Second Edition (REEL–2) A test of perceived language development for children from birth to 3 years of age using the child's mother as an informant; the REEL–2 has an interview format that groups the questions to produce separate receptive and expressive language ages. Chronological age is compared to a receptive language age and an expressive language age. In some cases, a depressed expressive language age may help to provide differential diagnostic information regarding environmental influences on language acquisition. Such results can be used as a guide when counseling parents regarding speech and language stimulation in the home. The REEL–2 shares limitations common to all caregiver report scales; however, in most clinical settings, an interview format remains the only reasonable approach.

Receptive One-Word Picture Vocabulary Test (ROWPVT) *See* One-Word Picture Vocabulary Tests.

Receptive One-Word Picture Vocabulary Test–Upper Extension (ROWPVT–UE) *See* One-Word Picture Vocabulary Tests.

Recipe for Reading A multisensory reading method with a strong phonetic component. The content and sequence of each lesson are as follows: 1) teacher flashes phonic sound cards for previously learned letters and student gives sound; 2) teacher gives sounds and student names and writes letters; 3) if a child is ready, teacher teaches new sound; child learns sound and traces and copies letter; 4) teacher dictates words using new letter; student repeats word, spells it orally, and says each letter while writing it; 5) teacher presents the previous words on flashcards and student reads the words he or she has

spelled; 6) if time permits, teacher dictates one or more sentences, student repeats sentences, tries to remember them, and spells words out loud as they are written; 7) teacher presents sentences on flashcards and student reads; 8) student reads book at appropriate level; 9) lesson ends with game using skills in which student is proficient.

reciprocal questioning A program in which students learn to lead story discussions, first by seeing appropriate question-answering strategies modeled by the teacher, then by having the role of questioner gradually transferred to the student.

recognition memory The realization that some stimuli have been previously encountered. Multiple-choice testing may allow for the use of primarily recognition skills. *See* memory.

record (residential intake record) An intake protocol for developmental disabilities residential agencies. Detailed checklists are provided for a variety of domains, including personal history; family history; intellectual and adaptive behavior; educational, vocational, and medical needs; dual diagnosis; and support services.

rectum The last 6 inches of the large intestine.

red herring A misleading clue. The term is used often in medicine to describe a sign or symptom that can be associated with a particular disease unrelated to the diagnosis.

red reflex A physical finding produced by shining a bright light at the eye and looking for its reflection from the retina (light-sensitive inner back wall), which is red. This red reflex is blocked if there is an abnormality in the cornea (e.g., cloudy cornea found in mucopolysaccharidoses), the lens (e.g., cataract or lens opacity), or the retina itself (e.g., tumor such as retinoblastoma). The red reflex is the cause of red eyes seen in some photographic pictures taken with flash cameras.

REEL–2 *See* Receptive-Expressive Emergent Language Scales–Second Edition.

reflex hypoxic crisis *See* breathholding spell.

reflex seizure Seizures precipitated by a number of specific sensory stimuli. These include music, sound, light, reading, and somatosensory stimuli such as tapping or teeth-brushing.

reflex standing The ability of a child with severely hypertonic cerebral palsy to stiffen all extensor muscles so as to support weight when balance is maintained from outside. Such children are usually unable to sit, and thus reflex standing should not be interpreted as a prelude to walking; it is a pathological rigidity that will actually inhibit mature voluntary movement patterns.

reflexes (deep tendon) Normal reflexes that indicate the motor system is functional. Reflexes are graded according to response, as follows: 4+—hyperactive and brisk, often indicative of disease and associated with clonus (rhythmic oscillations between flexion and extension); 3+—brisker than average, but not always associated with disease; 2+—normal; 1+—slightly decreased; and 0—no response. Each reflex is associated with one or more spinal nerve roots. The following reflexes are paired with their spinal nerve roots: biceps, C5C6; triceps, C7C8; brachioradialia, C5C6; abdominal, upper, T8, T9, T10; abdominal, lower, T10, T11, T12; cremasteric L1, L2; knee, L2, L3, L4; ankle, S1, S2; Babinski, L4, L5, S1, S2.

reflux *See* gastroesophageal reflux (GER).

refractory Unresponsive to treatment. Often used to describe seizures that cannot be controlled with standard anticonvulsants.

Refsum syndrome Hereditary Motor and Sensory Neuropathy Type IV (HMSN–IV), heredopathia atactica polyneuritiformis, phytanic acid storage disease. A rare genetic syndrome with retinitis pigmentosa (night blindness and progressively restricted visual fields), cerebellar ataxia (unsteady gait), and progressive sensorineural (involving the inner ear or the auditory nerve) hearing impairment (50%). Inheritance follows an autosomal recessive pattern with a recurrence risk of 25%. The syndrome is currently detected by manifest clinical symptoms usually within the first 20 years of life. Dietary restriction of phytanic acid precursors may slow the progression of symptoms.

regard Look at, pay attention to; *see also* hand regard.

regional cerebral blood flow (RCBF) A neuroanatomical research procedure used to localize brain abnormalities in developmental disorders such as dyslexia and attention deficits.

registered occupational therapist (OTR) A professional with a baccalaureate degree in occupational therapy and an additional 6 months of fieldwork who has passed the American Occupational Therapy Association's (AOTA) certifying examination. *See also* occupational therapy.

Reglan *See* metoclopramide.

regression The loss of previously acquired developmental milestones that occurs with a degenerative disease of the central nervous system or sometimes with serious emotional disorders. Such a loss of skills can be associated with a decline in measured IQ.

regression toward the mean A statistical phenomenon in which people who achieve very high or very low scores on a given test are more likely to score closer to the mean on a retest. In population genetics, traits controlled by multiple genes may also exhibit this same phenomenon; in each succeeding generation it becomes less likely that this exact same combination of multiple genes will come together to produce extreme variations from the mean expression of that trait.

regular education initiative (REI) A movement to restructure education that would require general and special education programs to work more closely together. Proponents maintain that dual systems of education, separate professional organizations, separate personnel preparation programs, and separate funding patterns inhibit integration of students with disabilities and reduce the effectiveness of education. Some have advocated the merger of special and general education; others, although questioning the "second system" approach, do not advocate the elimination of separate special education services. Opponents fear that many of the gains made in the education of students with disabilities would be lost. Advocates of children with behavior disorders or severe emotional disturbances are among the groups most vocal in their concern that this would result in reduction of services for a group they view as already underserved.

rehabilitation *See* habilitation.

Rehabilitation Act of 1973 (PL 93-112) A federal law with a civil rights component that prohibited denial of participation in federally funded programs or activities to individuals with disabilities who were otherwise qualified. The intent of this law was to implement a national policy of integrating people with disabilities into society by providing and expanding employment opportunities in public and private sectors. Major components of the law included 1) Title IV, which defined an individual with a "handicapping condition" as anyone who had a physical or mental impairment that substantially limited participation in one or more major life activities, who had a record of such impairment, or who was regarded as such at the time; and 2) Title V, which established civil rights protection. Section 503 provides for affirmative action with federal contractors, and Section 504 outlines the civil rights aspects. This law permits parents to file complaints with the U.S. Department of Education's Office of Civil Rights if a qualified handicapped student is being denied access to an appropriate education. Students with disabilities not listed in PL 94-142 (the Education for All Handicapped Children Act of 1975), such as attention-deficit/hyperactivity disorder, have been found

to be eligible for services under Section 504.

Rehabilitation Act Amendments of 1983 (PL 98-221) Federal legislation that authorized several demonstration projects related to transition services from school to work for youths with disabilities.

Rehabilitation Act Amendments of 1986 (PL 99-506) A federal law that reauthorized PL 93-112, the Rehabilitation Act of 1973, and established discretionary programs for supportive employment services for individuals with disabilities. Supportive employment services include job coaching for people with severe disabilities (including learning disabilities) that affect employability.

Rehabilitation Act Amendments of 1992 (PL 102-569) A federal law that revised and extended the programs of the Rehabilitation Act of 1973 (PL 93-112). These amendments incorporate the philosophy of the Americans with Disabilities Act of 1990 (PL 101-336), including provisions to ensure that the individual's issues and concerns are considered during the process of developing the individualized written rehabilitation plan (IWRP) and throughout its implementation. The law also clarifies what services constitute components of vocational rehabilitation, including personal assistance, transition, and supported employment. Individuals with severe and profound disabilities are eligible for vocational rehabilitation, and intensive services are to be provided based on a maximum amount possible, as well as on the person's particular strengths, resources, interests, and concerns.

Rehabilitation, Comprehensive Services, and Developmental Disabilities Amendments of 1978 (PL 95-602) A federal law that enacted a "functional," rather than categorical, definition of developmental disability. This new definition required substantial functional limitations in at least three of the following major life activities: self-care, receptive and expressive language, learning, mobility, self-direction, capacity for independent living, and economic self-sufficiency. This law also shifted the emphasis from planning to priority in use of state grants.

Rehabilitation Services Administration (RSA)   One of the three program areas of the federal Office of Special Education and Rehabilitative Services (OSERS). The Rehabilitative Services Administration allocates grants to state vocational rehabilitation agencies to help people with mental and physical disabilities obtain job training, employment, medical and psychological assistance, and other individualized services. Priority attention is given to individuals with severe disabilities. The RSA also funds training programs for rehabilitation professionals, and programs that enrich and enhance the lives of individuals with disabilities within their communities. The RSA operates the Client Assistance Program, which informs people with disabilities about the benefits available under the Rehabilitation Act of 1973, as amended, and assists them to receive those for which they are eligible. The two other program areas of OSERS are the Office of Special Education Programs (OSEP) and the National Institute on Disability and Rehabilitation Research (NIDRR). The OSEP administers programs relating to the free appropriate public education of children, youth, and adults with disabilities, whereas NIDRR develops and implements a coordinated program of national and international rehabilitation research. *See also* Office of Special Education and Rehabilitative Services (OSERS).

REI   *See* regular education initiative.

reinforcer   Anything that occurs after a behavior and causes an increase in the frequency of that behavior. Primary reinforcers are physiologically or biologically pleasurable stimuli; secondary reinforcers become pleasurable from being paired with primary reinforcers. Food is an example of a primary reinforcer; socialization and attention are examples of secondary reinforcers.

Reiss Scales for Dual Diagnosis in Children   A 60-item problem rating scale for use in people 4–21 years of age with mental re-

tardation; the instrument yields 10 sub-scale scores for anger, anxiety disorder, attention deficit, autism, conduct disorder, depression, poor self-image, psychosis, somatization, and withdrawn behavior. Other significant behaviors are also measured.

Reitan-Indiana Neuropsychological Test Battery for Children   A neuropsychological battery for children 5–8 years of age. The battery was developed as a downward extension from the adult version, with many of the adult tests simply shortened or eliminated for this version. Administration requires extensive training both for administration and interpretation. Reliability and validity are below that of the adult tests.

related services   As originally defined in PL 94-142, the Education for All Handicapped Children Act of 1975, related services are "transportation, and such developmental, corrective, and other supportive services . . . as may be required to assist a handicapped child to benefit from special education." Among services specifically included are speech pathology and audiology, psychological services, medical services (for diagnostic and evaluation purposes only), physical therapy, occupational therapy, recreation, and counseling. The reference to "other supportive services . . . as may be required" has caused the precise definition of related services to remain a subject of debate.

relaxation   Psychotherapeutic approaches to reduce muscle tone in young children with cerebral palsy. These approaches may include slow rocking, rhythmic rotation, and gentle shaking.

REM   *See* rapid eye movement.

remedial (compensatory) education   Specialized or additional instruction in deficient academic areas when the deficiencies are assumed to be a result of environmental factors. The expectation is that the student will master the general curriculum through regular channels. *Contrast with adaptive education.*

remission The lessening or cessation of disease symptoms.

renal Relating to the kidneys.

Renpenning syndrome X-linked mental retardation, otherwise undifferentiated. The clinical manifestations are variable; the most common findings include small head, small testes, and short stature. Although the mental retardation is detectable at an early age, unless a family pedigree of known risk is available, specific diagnosis of Renpenning-type mental retardation may be delayed until adolescence.

residential intake record *See* record.

Residential Services Indicator (RSI) A standardized protocol to collect a variety of data to be used in selecting residential and support services for people with developmental disabilities.

residential treatment A treatment modality in which the child lives away from home in a facility where he or she receives education, psychotherapy, nurturance, structure, safety, and extracurricular and peer interaction opportunities. The need for this intensive, coordinated treatment can be related to significant family pathology (origin) in addition to the child's problems, which not only renders the family unable to cooperate in necessary treatment but also often causes them to undermine the efficacy of existing treatment resources. There is no specific developmental or psychiatric diagnosis in which this level of treatment is indicated per se; it is, rather, the cumulative effect of several factors that lead to the recommendation and utilization of such a milieu.

resonance The tonal quality imparted to voice sounds by the resonance-chamber action of mouth and pharynx (throat) configurations, and, in some cases, also of the nostrils. The eventual outflow of sound waves that are recognized as the human voice is the result of filtering of that sound by the resonance system. The source of the voice is the larnyx (windpipe); impairment of vocal resonance can be any condition in which there is an abnormal acoustical signal due to inappropriate modification of the laryngeal tone. Clinically, hypernasality (excessive nasal resonance) and nasal emission (escape of air through the nose during the production of pressure consonants) are the most frequently seen vocal resonance problems. Hyponasality (insufficient nasal resonance) is also a disorder of resonance. Hypertrophic (thin) tonsils and adenoids, nasal deformities, cleft lip/palate, congenital palatopharyngeal incompetencey (CPI), and craniofacial malformation syndromes can result in disturbances of normal vocal resonance. There are therapeutic, behavioral, and surgical approaches to improve or correct disorders of resonance.

resource services One set of services in a continuum of educational placement alternatives. Assistance is provided to the student for some portion of the school day in a resource room; the rest of the day is spent in the general classroom. The resource services provided are listed in terms of goals and objectives in the student's individualized education program (IEP). The ways in which these goals are met varies among schools and teachers. The resource room teacher may act as a consultant to the general education teacher in planning for an individual child or certain children. The success of this interaction varies across situations and personnel.

respiratory distress syndrome (RDS) of newborn A condition of newborn infants that includes dyspnea (difficult breathing) and cyanosis (blue color). It is most common in premature infants and infants of diabetic mothers (IDM). RDS can present with hyaline membrane disease (HMD) or idiopathic (unknown) respiratory distress syndrome (IRDS). Long-term effects can include chronic lung disease (bronchopulmonary dysplasia—BPD) and adverse neurological and developmental outcomes related to poor cerebral blood flow and bleeding into the head that occur during the acute management of RDS.

respondent behaviors A term from behavioral learning theory that refers to reflexive behaviors controlled by the autonomic nervous system and involuntary muscles. The eye-blink reflex, knee-jerk reflex, and salivation are examples. Respondent behaviors are elicited or caused by a prior stimulus. Pavlov's classical conditioning experiments are examples of eliciting respondent behaviors.

response cost *See* cost contingency.

response cost procedure A behavior modification technique that involves the withdrawal of a reward/reinforcer when an undesirable behavior occurs; it is often employed in the treatment of maladaptive behaviors in people with mental retardation.

retention Holding back; requiring a child to repeat a grade in school. Although retention is one of the most commonly employed interventions, research has documented that in the long run it is ineffective. Its major impact appears to be that of delaying the preparation of a diagnostic workup that could more effectively describe the reasons for this child's failure and how to address it.

reticular activating system (RAS) An area of the brain stem involved in the control of attention, wakefulness, and sleep.

retina The light-sensitive inner layer of the eyeball; it can be examined by looking through the pupil with an ophthalmoscope; it is the only part of the central nervous system available for routine direct visualization.

retina

retinitis pigmentosa A disease of the eye producing nyctalopia (night blindness) and progressive visual loss; it can be associated with a variety of conditions: lipidoses (e.g., Gaucher disease), spinocerebellar degenerations (e.g., as in Friedrich ataxia), hearing loss (e.g., Usher syndrome), mucopolysaccharidoses, myotonic dystrophy, Lawrence-Moon-Biedl syndrome, and syndromes with renal (kidney) disease or external ophthalmoplegia (ocular muscle paralysis).

retinopathy of prematurity (ROP) Also known as Terry disease; an eye disease that is a major cause of blindness. It occurs predominantly in premature infants and is more severe with decreasing birth weight. The cause remains unknown, but high levels of oxygen have an exacerbating effect. Both the active (proliferation) and cicatricial (scarring) stages are scored 1–4, with the higher numbers reflecting more severe involvement.

retrograde amnesia A specific impairment of memory for events experienced immediately before a closed brain injury; the period of time included in the amnesia varies with the severity of the head injury as reflected in the duration of unconsciousness.

retrolental fibroplasia (RLF) *See* retinopathy of prematurity.

Rett syndrome A degenerative condition that occurs in girls who develop typically early in life and then between 6 and 18 months of age undergo a rapid regression in motor, cognitive, and social skills that subsequently stabilizes at a level that leaves the individual with mental retardation. After the regression stabilizes, affected individuals exhibit autistic features and hand stereotypies: wringing, clapping, tapping, washing, and mouthing. Seizures and scoliosis (spinal curvature) are common medical complications requiring care. Treatment is symptomatic and supportive; prognosis is poor. Deceleration of head growth is prominent. Etiology (cause) remains unknown.

return to clinic (RTC) An acronym for return to clinic, typically followed by a time interval; thus, "RTC 3 months" indicates that the individual's next appointment should be in 3 months.

reversals Letters or numbers written backward (e.g., *b*/*d*, *p*/*q*, *was*/*saw*); often erroneously considered a pathognomonic (indicative) sign of dyslexia. Younger children frequently reverse the direction of letters and numbers; some degree of reversals persists in the early elementary grades and should not be considered pathological until 8 years of age or third grade. Marked use of reversals (and mirror writing) can be considered suspicious for learning disabilities in earlier grades when accompanied by other findings suggestive of academic difficulties. Rotations or inversions of letters or numbers across an axis other than the vertical should probably be considered more serious than the common right-left reversals.

reversals frequency test   A three-part instrument that measures the frequency of letter and number reversals in three situations: execution (writing), recognition (reading), and matching (same/different comparison). This test, devised by Richard Gardner, purports to differentiate children with minimal brain dysfunction from typical children when used as a screening instrument.

reverse genetics   A laboratory procedure using gene mapping (identifying the location of a gene on a chromosome) to make copies of a gene found in a particular disease where the biochemical problem is not known. The goal is to identify the protein that is made from the gene and perhaps learn more about the process of that particular disease. Although identifying the abnormal protein, such as locating the gene that makes an abnormal dystrophin in Duchenne muscular dystrophy, helps explain what goes wrong in muscular dystrophy, it does not imply that a cure is readily possible.

reversed tailor   A sitting posture associated with hypotonia (decreased muscle tone) or hip instability; sometimes referred to as *mermaid sitting*, after the statue of the Little Mermaid in Copenhagen.

reversed tailor

reversible hyposomatotropinism   *See* psychosocial deprivation syndrome.

reversible obstructive airway disease (ROAD)   *See* asthma.

Revised Prescreening Developmental Questionnaire (R–PDQ)   A brief parent/caregiver survey to decide on the need to administer the full Denver Developmental Screening Test to children 3 months to 6 years of age; 10 questions are asked at selected ages. Despite extensive development, both the prescreening instrument and the Denver Developmental Screening Test lack adequate sensitivity and specificity.

Revised Problem Behavior Checklist (RPBC)   A 1987 revision of the original Behavior Problem Checklist (BPC; Quay and Peterson), for children from kindergarten through grade 12. Items are organized into four major subscales: conduct disorder (22 items), socialized aggression (17 items), attention problem—immaturity (16 items), and anxiety—withdrawal (11 items). Two minor subscales are also included: psychotic behavior (6 items) and motor tension—excess (5 items). Using a 3-point rating scale, respondents (parents, teachers, or other professionals associated with the child to be rated) score the degree to which each item characterizes the child's behavior. Items from the subscales are scattered throughout the test. Templates are provided for adding circled numbers (1, 2, and 3) to yield a raw score for each subtest. Twelve rated items are not scored. Raw scores for each subscale are then converted to normalized T scores with a mean of 50 and a standard deviation of 10. The tables have some potentially confusing features, and the user is advised to read the headings carefully. The authors suggest that local norms be developed.

revisualization   A memory task in which the person must recall the configuration (shape of a letter or word) in the absence of visual clues; phonetic spelling errors are common in children with revisualization deficits.

Reye syndrome   An acute, life-threatening, postinfectious (following flu or chickenpox) encephalopathy (brain damage due to lack of oxygen) with hepatitis. Salicylate (aspirin) has been implicated in the etiology (cause); this risk has markedly reduced the usage of aspirin in children.

Mortality is 30%. Morbidity can include the entire spectrum of neurodevelopmental disorders of varying severity.

Reynell Developmental Language Scales–Revised (RDLS–R) A test that provides separate measures of expressive language and verbal comprehension for children 1–17 years of age. The RDLS was normed and is most commonly used in the United Kingdom.

Reynell-Zinkin Developmental Scale for Visually Impaired Young Children An assessment instrument for infants and preschoolers with visual impairments who are from birth to 5 years of age, with separate age norms for children who are totally blind, partially sighted, and sighted.

Rh factor A genetically determined blood antigen, the presence or absence of which is important in the compatibility of blood for transfusion purposes. Repeated maternal–fetal Rh incompatibility with the mother not having the factor (Rh−) and the baby having the factor (Rh+) can lead to the mother producing antibodies against the baby's red blood cells with increasingly severe responses with each successive incompatible pregnancy. Treatment with RhoGAM prevents this sequence.

rhinitis An inflamed or runny nose.

rhinorrhea Runny nose.

rhizomelic Referring to the proximal segment of a limb (e.g., the upper arm or thigh).

rhizotomy Cutting a nerve root; *see also* selective posterior rhizotomy.

Rhode Island Test of Language Structure (RITLS) A test of language structure designed for use with children with hearing impairments ages 3–20 years; it can also be used with children ages 3–6 years who have mental retardation or learning disabilities or who are bilingual.

rib hump An elevation of one side of the thorax (chest) when an individual bends forward 90 degrees at the hips in the presence of scoliosis (spinal curvature). A rib hump indicates rotation of the thoracic vertebrae to the convex side of a scoliosis.

Richards-Rundel syndrome A genetic syndrome with progressive severe mental retardation, nystagmus (involuntary eye movements), ataxia (unsteady gait), muscle wasting, absent secondary sexual characteristics, and sensorineural (involving the inner ear or the auditory nerve) deafness. Inheritance follows an autosomal recessive pattern.

rickets Stunting of growth and bone deformities secondary to a failure of normal calcification of bone; this condition can be nutritional or based on a variety of metabolic disorders.

RIDES *See* Rockford Infant Developmental Evaluation Scales.

Rieger syndrome A genetic syndrome or anomaly (malformation, deformation, disruption, or dysplasia) with abnormalities of the anterior (front) part of the eye (i.e., iris), glaucoma (increased pressure in the eye, often hereditary), hypodontia (decreased number of teeth), and mental retardation. Inheritance follows an autosomal dominant pattern. The syndrome is detected in the neonatal period or later, depending on the presence of structural eye defects. Treatment is restorative for the hypodontia, with ongoing ophthalmological care for the eye complications.

righting reaction One of a subgroup of postural reactions (EAR–II) concerned with maintaining the position of the head in space.

rigidity A physiological type of extrapyramidal cerebral palsy with consistently increased tone ("lead pipe" or "cogwheel" variety), such that there is resistance to

righting reaction

passively moving an extremity (arm or leg) throughout the entire range of motion. In many ways, this stiffness or inflexibility is similar to the most severe forms of spastic quadriplegia (paralysis of all four extremities) and is usually associated with severe to profound mental retardation.

rigidity A lack of flexibility or sluggishness in the thought processes of people with mental retardation (as interpreted by the Lewin-Kounin model).

Riley-Day syndrome Familial dysautonomia, hereditary sensory and autonomic neuropathy, type III (HSAN III); a genetic syndrome of insensitivity to pain, lack of tearing contributing to corneal ulceration, dysarticulation, poor motor coordination, increased sweating, cutis marmorata (blotching or marbling of the skin), smooth tongue, and normal intelligence. The primary defect is one of the autonomic nervous system, with death often occurring before the age of 20 from respiratory complications. Incidence rates are 1 in 10,000 in Ashkenazic Jews. Inheritance patterns follow an autosomal recessive mode. Although the disease is often suspected at birth, confirmation usually is delayed until the child is older. Antibiotic treatment for recurrent respiratory infections is indicated.

Riley Preschool Developmental Screening Test A 15-minute screening test that includes six graphomotor tests of visual perceptual and fine-motor skills in children 3–6 years of age. Standardization and validity are limited.

ring chromosome A structural abnormality in a chromosome, in which both ends of the chromosome are deleted and the broken ("sticky") ends join to form a ring. The clinical picture varies with the amount of genetic material that is missing and the chromosome involved.

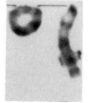

ring chromosome

ringworm *See* tinea.

RIPA *See* Ross Information Processing Assessment.

Ritalin Trade name methylphenidate.

RITLS *See* Rhode Island Test of Language Structure.

ritodrine hydrochloride Trade name Ritodrine; a beta-sympathomimetic drug used to treat preterm labor and prevent premature birth.

RLF *See* retrolental fibroplasia, retinopathy of prematurity (ROP).

R/O *See* rule out.

ROAD Reversible obstructive airway disease; *see* asthma.

Roberts–SC phocomelia syndrome *See* tetraphocomelia—cleft palate syndrome.

Robin syndrome *See* Pierre Robin sequence/syndrome.

Robinow syndrome *See* fetal face syndrome.

rocker bottom foot *See* congenital vertical talus.

Rockford Infant Developmental Evaluation Scales (RIDES) A developmental behavior checklist for children from birth to 4 years of age.

roentgenogram X ray, radiograph; named after Wilhelm Conrad Roentgen (1845–1923), discoverer of the medical usefulness of X rays.

role taking The ability to put oneself in another's place; to experience his or her perspective; egocentricity describes immaturity or deficiency of role taking.

rolfing Structural integration; manipulation of body tissue via deep massage. A form of body-centered psychotherapy that has been applied to treatment of cerebral palsy, with no proven efficacy; after Ida Rolf (1897–1979).

roll over Gross-motor milestone of infancy; typically children roll from prone (front) to supine (back) (P→S) at 4 months of age and from supine to prone (S→P) at 5 months of age. Markedly delayed rolling over is considered a sensitive early indicator of cerebral palsy. Rolling S→P before P→S suggests the possibility of significant hypertonia (increased muscle tone).

rollator Walker with wheels; an assistive device to aid ambulation.

ROM *See* range of motion.

Rood A system of physical therapy for treatment of cerebral palsy. Developed by Margaret Rood, a physical and occupational therapist, this approach uses exaggerated sensory input in the form of stroking, brushing, icing, heating, pounding, squeezing, and pressure to facilitate an awareness of normal movement patterns.

rooting reflex A primitive oral motor reflex found in infants from 32 weeks' gestation to 6 months of age; a tactile (touch) stimulus to the lips or cheeks causes the infant to respond by turning the head in the direction of the stimulus and reaching the mouth toward the stimulus. Because there are four possible directions (up, down, right, left), the reflex is also referred to as the four cardinal points reflex. The reflex persists longer and actually becomes stronger in breastfed infants. This reflex is innervated by cranial nerves V, VII, XI, and XII.

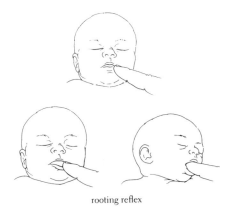

rooting reflex

ROP *See* retinopathy of prematurity.

Rorschach inkblots A projective technique developed by the Swiss psychiatrist Hermann Rorschach (1884–1922). The test consists of 10 symmetrical inkblot cards, half colored and half black and white, with the various nuances of shading. The test is administered by showing the cards one at a time in a definite order and asking the individual what he or she sees in them. After the person has responded to the inkblots in an unstructured manner (i.e., free association or performance proper period), the examiner asks questions about particular responses (i.e., inquiry period) to clarify ambiguous answers and to elicit latent repressed content. A third period (i.e., testing of limits) may be employed to further clarify any responses that remain confusing. The first step in interpreting the Rorschach record is the numerical tabulation of formal scoring categories and percentages. Records are scored for area or location, determinants, content, and popularity of responses. This composite Rorschach picture is based on the reciprocal relationship between formal structure and dynamic content. The administration and scoring of the Rorschach requires specific training and considerable practice. There are many scoring systems. In assessment batteries, the Rorschach may provide information regarding the individual's reality contact, organizational ability, affect, defenses, areas of conflict, and richness of resources. In addition, comparison of performance on more structured measures with the Rorschach may demonstrate how ambiguity affects the individual. It is important to note that most of the Rorschach data on children were derived from typical children, many of whom were above average with respect to intelligence and socioeconomic level. Rorschach responses of children tend to be brief and unelaborated. Records from children with emotional disturbances can help define problems of thought and affect and also aid in identifying specific conflict areas. When viewed from the developmental perspective of a continuum of various degrees of normality and disturbance, the task is to determine whether a long chart record represents a consolidation or a disruption of psychological and emotional growth.

roseola Exanthem subitum; a viral illness in preschool children in which 3–4 days of very high fever are followed by a transient (i.e., subitum) rose pink rash. It has no developmental sequelae.

Ross Information Processing Assessment (RIPA) A test instrument that assesses cognitive-linguistic impairments following acquired brain injuries in adolescents and adults. It quantitates cognitive impairments, establishes severity ratings, and develops rehabilitation goals and objectives with profiles in 10 areas: immediate memory, recent memory, temporal orientation (recent memory), temporal orientation (remote memory), spatial orientation, orientation to environment, recall of general information, problem solving and abstract reasoning, organization, and auditory processing and retention.

Rosseti Infant-Toddler Language Scale A criterion-referenced assessment scale for infants and toddlers, birth to 3 years of age, that probes multiple developmental areas: interaction and attachment, gestures, pragmatics, play, language comprehension, and language expression.

rotated ear *See* pinna.

rotator cuff of shoulder A bandlike arrangement of muscle, cartilage, and bone that holds the shoulder joint together.

ROWPVT Receptive One-Word Picture Vocabulary Test; *see* One-Word Picture Vocabulary Tests.

rotator cuff of shoulder

ROWPVT–UE Receptive One-Word Picture Vocabulary Test–Upper Extension; *see* One-Word Picture Vocabulary Tests.

RPBC *See* Revised Problem Behavior Checklist.

R–PDQ *See* Revised Prescreening Developmental Questionnaire.

RSA *See* Rehabilitation Services Administration.

RSI *See* Residential Services Indicator.

RTC *See* return to clinic.

rubella (German measles) An acute infectious disease with low-grade fever, exanthem (rash), coryza (nasal inflammation), lymphadenopathy (swelling of the lymph nodes), and arthritis. The importance of prevention through immunization (vaccination) with live virus stems from the teratogenic (causing malformation) effects of the rubella virus (i.e., fetal rubella syndrome). Rubella is also known as "3-day" measles in reference to the typical duration of the rash.

rubella embryopathy *See* fetal rubella syndrome.

rubeola Measles; a highly contagious viral exanthem (rash) with fever, cough, coryza (nasal inflammation), conjunctivitis (eye inflammation), an enanthem (Koplik spots), and photophobia (extreme sensitivity to light). It is also known as "7-day" measles, based on the duration of the rash. Unlike German measles (i.e., rubella), rubeola is not teratogenic (causing malformation). It is, however, a much more severe illness with a 0.1% incidence of encephalitis (brain inflammation) and a 1 in 100,000 risk of subacute sclerosing panencephalitis (SSPE) (a generally fatal hardening in the brain).

Rubinstein-Taybi syndrome A dysmorphic (atypical appearance) syndrome that includes broad thumbs and toes, a characteristic facies (downslanting palpebral fissures [eyeslits], maxillary hypoplasia [atypical midfacial development], and a beaked nose), and mental retardation. The etiology (cause) is unknown.

rule out (R/O) An abbreviation prefixed to a diagnosis or condition and indicating that tests must be or were done to assess the presence of that diagnosis. "R/O appendicitis" as an admission diagnosis suggests that the physician was concerned over that possible diagnosis. "R/O appendicitis" as a discharge diagnosis suggests that the diagnosis was not confirmed.

rumination The regurgitation (spitting up after meals) of food or liquid that is either allowed to run out of the mouth or is rechewed and reswallowed. Originally considered a bizarre psychosomatic disorder of infancy, it is more common in people with significant mental retardation; its frequent occurrence in institutional and deprivational settings suggests that it may be a self-stimulatory behavior. Behavior modification techniques represent the most effective intervention approach. The behavior can be fatal due to chronic malnutrition.

Russell-Silver syndrome A dysmorphic (atypical appearance) syndrome with short stature of prenatal onset, skeletal asymmetry, clinodactyly (deflection of fingers), café au lait spots, and a small triangular facies that contributes to a misleading impression of hydrocephalus (excess fluid in the brain) (i.e., pseudohydrocephalus). Cognition is usually normal. Etiology (cause) is unknown.

Ruvalcaba syndrome A dysmorphic (atypical appearance) syndrome with mental retardation, "jovial" personality, peculiar facies with small mouth, short fingers, and other bone abnormalities. Etiology (cause) and inheritance are unclear.

S

sacral agenesis A congenital malformation including absence of the sacrum and coccyx (tailbone). If the sacral nerves are involved in the bony abnormality, a neurogenic bladder will result; toilet training and gait disorders are the most commonly associated disabilities. Cognitive functioning is usually normal unless associated with a congenital malformation causing mental retardation. Children with sacral agenesis often have recurrent urinary tract infections leading to hydronephrosis (urine collection due to obstructed flow) and chronic pyelonephritis (kidney inflammation). Sacral agenesis occurs in 1% of infants of mothers with insulin-dependent diabetes. This term is often used synonymously with *caudal regression syndrome*.

sacrum Tailbone; triangular bone at the base of the spine deriving from the fusion of the last five vertebrae.

sacrum

Saethre-Chotzen syndrome Acrocephalo-syndactyly type III. A genetic syndrome with craniosynostosis (premature fusion of skull sutures) leading to brachycephaly (irregular, flat head shape), maxillary hypoplasia (underdevelopment of jaw), prominent crus (an ear landmark), facial asymmetry, and syndactyly (webbing of the fingers or toes). Mild mental retardation and hearing loss are occasional findings. Early closure of cranial sutures may lead to optic nerve atrophy (wasting). The syndrome is detectable at birth, although mild cases may not be identified until later. Inheritance is autosomal dominant with variable expressivity. Treatment is primarily for correction of cranial-facial abnormalities.

sagittal plane An anatomical plane that divides the body into a right half and left half.

sagittal plane

salaam seizures *See* infantile spasms.

salicylate *See* aspirin sensitivity.

salmon patch Small, flat reddish pink, irregularly bordered birthmarks sometimes found on the back of the neck (commonly called "stork bite" or Unna's mark), over the eyes, and on the forehead (commonly called "angel's kiss") of newborns. These marks tend to fade with time as subcutaneous (inner) tissue increases in thickness, and are of no diagnostic significance.

SAMI *See* Sequential Assessment of Mathematics Inventories—Standardized Inventory.

sandal gap deformity An increased space (more than a quarter of an inch) between the first two toes. This is a minor dysmorphic (atypical) feature that may occur with developmental disabilities either as part of a syndrome or nonspecifically.

sandal gap deformity

Sandifer syndrome The combination of reflux of gastric contents into the mouth accompanied by abnormal head cocking and neck extension/flexion movements, with esophagitis (inflammation of the esophagus) and anemia. Often misinterpreted as disordered parenting or an emotional disorder, the syndrome is secondary to a hiatal hernia

273

and resolves upon surgical correction of the hernia.

Sanfilippo syndrome Mucopolysaccharidosis III. A genetic syndrome with mild physical features of mucopolysaccharidosis but severe mental retardation and significant behavior management problems. Synophrys (condition in which the eyebrows grow together) is present. There are four enzymatic subtypes (*A, B, C, D*); type *A* is the most common. Inheritance is autosomal recessive. The syndrome is detectable prenatally by enzyme assay of the chorionic villi. No curative treatment is currently available; therefore, affected individuals are expected to have significantly shortened life spans.

Santmyer swallow A primitive reflex in which the stimulus of a puff of air blown into an infant's face produces the response of a swallow; this reflex is present in premature infants and disappears by 2 years of age.

SBFE *See* Stanford-Binet Intelligence Scale: Fourth Edition.

SCA *See* sex chromosome abnormalities.

scaled score A score on a test resulting from the conversion of the raw score to a number or position on a standard reference scale. For example, the college achievement tests are typically reported on a scale of 200–800; using this scale, a score of 600 is intended to indicate the same level of ability from year to year regardless of the form of the test used or the composition of the candidate group at a particular administration.

SCAN *See* Screening Test for Auditory Processing Disorders.

scanning speech Speech that is slow, with pauses between each syllable.

scanogram An X ray that includes a ruler on the film so that accurate bone measurements can be made; especially useful for leg length discrepancies.

scapegoat A family member who is held responsible for all family conflict and who takes the blame for all family distress. Over time, this member is targeted by other family members as the sole cause of all that is wrong with the family. Thus, marital conflicts, sibling rivalry, and even financial problems are described in terms of the scapegoated member's culpability for the problem. Scapegoats evolve when at least two people in a family (usually the parents) cannot openly deal with their own issues. Often the weakest member of the family is selected as the scapegoat. Therefore, a child with developmental disabilities is a likely target for becoming the family scapegoat.

scaphocephaly A narrow skull (low cephalic index) often with a ridge along the prematurely closed sagittal suture (i.e., craniosynostosis); linked with dolichocephaly (prominent forehead), this is a common, but transient, skull shape in premature infants.

scaphocephaly

scapula Shoulder blade.

scarf sign A technique to evaluate tone in the newborn; the baby's hand and arm are drawn across the front of the neck as if they were a scarf. In a full-term baby with normal tone, the elbow will not pass the chin and the hand will not pass the shoulder; in a premature or hypotonic (decreased muscle tone) infant, these landmarks will be passed.

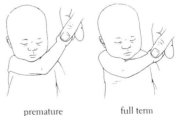

premature   full term
scarf sign

Schaltenbrandt reaction Landau 2; a postural reaction usually included in the description of the Landau reaction. It is the phase in which head flexion produces a loss of all the extensor tone that comprises the Landau 1.

Scheie syndrome Mucopolysaccharidosis (MPS) I-S (MPS I-S); "mild Hurler (MPS IH)." A genetic syndrome with cloudy corneas that can lead to blindness, mild growth impairment, and joint contractures, but normal intelligence; frequently, psychotic episodes are present. The disorder is detectable at 10 weeks' gestation by enzymatic assay of chorionic villi. There is no curative treatment yet available, although surgery for joint contractures may be indicated. Formerly termed MPS type V.

schema Theoretical abstract knowledge structures that organize familiar experiences and provide a framework for making inferences. A schema is a hierarchically organized description of classes of concepts and their interrelations. At the top of the hierarchy is a general schema that incorporates all aspects of the concept class, including both an abstraction and a conceptual frame of reference for all events within this area. For example, in a schema for going to a restaurant, the highest and most abstract level is a stereotype that encompasses everything known about restaurants. Embedded in this highest level are more specific schemata. The restaurant schema, for instance, may organize information about gourmet restaurants, cafés, and fast-food chains. As one moves down the hierarchy, the number of embedded schemata increases at each level, each becoming narrower in scope. At the lowest level are specific perceptual events such as yesterday's lunch at the hot dog stand. Because a schema includes the relations among its component parts, elements are understood in context. Thus, the idea of escargot, for example, would be sufficient to rule out the possibility of a fast-food chain. According to this theory, thinking, reasoning, and problem solving do not occur in a fixed sequence from top to bottom or bottom to top in the hierarchy. Rather, top-down and bottom-up processes are interactive; when there are gaps at one level, information can frequently be supplied from another. In a narrower Piagetian sense, schema are the sensorimotor equivalents of concepts.

Schema Theory Reading Model A construct that envisions the process of reading as requiring the simultaneous coordination of schema at all levels. Bottom-up processes (visual features) may lead to higher-level schemata (letters) and then to even higher-level schemata (words), and the process continues upward. At the same time, higher-level schemata are evoked by information from the print. These higher-level schemata structure readers' expectations and enable them to fill in gaps in specific information in a top-down manner. Reading, like other forms of thinking, does not occur in a fixed sequence. The interaction of top-down and bottom-up processes enables children who have difficulty with decoding to use higher-level knowledge to compensate and make guesses about unknown words on the basis of their prior knowledge and context clues.

Scheuthauer-Marie syndrome *See* cleidocranial dysostosis.

Schilder Arm Extension Test The child stands at attention, eyes closed, feet together with arms stretched out in front for 20 seconds. Spooning, choreiform (involuntary twitching) movements, swaying, or drifting of the arms is noted. The head may be passively turned to one side of the trunk to further assess balance.

Schimmelpenning-Feuerstein-Mims syndrome The association of mid-facial linear nevus sebaceus of Jadassohn with epilepsy and mental retardation. Diagnosis is made at birth. Inheritance patterns are unclear, but evidence suggests an autosomal dominant pattern. Treatment is cosmetic for the nevus, with pharmacological management for the seizures.

Schinzel-Giedion syndrome A genetic syndrome with growth deficiency, profound mental retardation, seizures (hypsarhythmia [a continuous disorganized pattern of high-voltage slow waves and spikes]), spasticity (increased muscle tone), a peculiar facies, vision and hearing impairments, and kidney disorders. Inheritance is thought to be autosomal recessive. Death usually occurs in the first 2 years of life.

schizencephaly An anomaly in cortical architecture (the rind [or outer crust] of the brain) characterized by clefts in the brain tissue that run from the surface of the brain to the ventricle. The tissue around the clefts is hypoplastic (underdeveloped) and arranged in a symmetrical fashion. Schizencephaly may be mistaken for porencephaly, which is damage to the brain with cavity formation replacing brain tissue. Unlike the clefts in schizencephaly, a porencephalic cyst may or may not abut the ventricular system. Depending on the location of the clefts, children with schizencephaly may show a variety of neurological abnormalities including cerebral palsy, mental retardation, hypotonia (decreased muscle tone), spasticity (increased muscle tone), hemiparesis (one-sided paralysis), tetraparesis (paralysis of all four extremities [arms or legs]), microcephaly (abnormally small head), or seizures. Schizencephaly does not produce hydrocephalus (excess fluid in the brain).

school phobia Fear of school. The child who exhibits school phobia is usually not afraid of school, but rather of what might happen at home while the child is away at school. (For example, a parent might leave and not come back or a depressed parent might commit suicide.) The child wants to stay home to prevent these occurrences, although the basis of the fear is not always conscious. There is no specific term to describe the anxiety and fear related to school that occurs in a child who is being bullied or is failing academically. Biological psychiatry successfully treats these cases with antidepressants.

scissoring A posture of the legs in which the legs tend to assume a crossed position with extension at the knees. This is typically a sign of increased tone in the lower extremities or tight adductor muscles. It is common in spastic cerebral palsy, espe-

scissoring

cially diplegia (paralysis on both sides of the body). An increasing tendency to scissor will make an ambulatory child trip more frequently over his or her own feet and contribute to hip instability. An adductor tenotomy (with or without an obturator neurectomy) is an orthopedic surgical procedure that will help correct the scissoring. Also called *Forster sign*.

sclera The white of the eye. The sclera will become yellow in the presence of jaundice (yellowing of the skin), remain white with carotenemia (yellowing of the skin due to excess carotene, rather than bilirubin, in the blood), and develop a bluish tinge in a variety of systemic diseases.

scoliosis An abnormal lateral (side to side) curvature of the spine (vertebral column). Curves may be C-shaped or S-shaped. The etiology (cause) of scoliosis may be idiopathic (with strong genetic or familial influences), congenital (defective formation of the vertebrae, possibly associated with other anomalies (malformation, deformation, disruption, or dysplasia) or a recognizable genetic syndrome), or neuromuscular disorders. Scoliosis on a neuromuscular basis worsens even after growth is complete; this puts these people at increasing risk for respiratory infection and cardiopulmonary compromise.

scoliosis

scooting Locomotion in sitting; a rare pattern of locomotion that may reflect motor disability, mental retardation, severe psychopathology, or some combination of these.

scotopic sensitivity syndrome A group of visual distortions relating to light sensitivity, resolution, attention, and perseverance grouped together on the basis of two arbitrary principles: 1) being distinct from visual-perceptual processing and peripheral/central visual field problems, and 2) being susceptible to remediation by the use of tinted lenses or filters. The syndrome remains a hypothetical entity, unproven and highly controversial; ophthalmology does not accept it even as a theoretical possibility. *See also* Irlen lenses.

SCPNT *See* Southern California Postrotary Nystagmus Test.

SCREEN *See* Screening Children for Related Early Educational Needs.

screening The presumptive identification of unrecognized disease or defects by the application of tests, examinations, or other procedures that can be applied rapidly, inexpensively, and often by personnel with a lower level of training than that required to make a definitive diagnosis. A first step in diagnosis, screening is a form of secondary prevention. Screening requires diagnosis prior to the initiation of therapy or other intervention. Screening is applied only to asymptomatic (without symptoms) populations. Thus, when a parent has concern about a child's development, the child is not asymptomatic and should not be screened but assessed. If a screening test or procedure is used for this assessment, it is not being used as a screening test.

Screening Children for Related Early Educational Needs (SCREEN) An educational screening test for current or potential school problems in children 3–7 years of age. The four subtests take approximately one-half hour to administer.

Screening Kit of Language Development (SKOLD) A screening assessment of preschool language development for 2- to 5-year-old children in six areas: vocabulary, comprehension, story completion, individual and paired sentence repetition without pictures, and comprehension of commands. Administration time is 15 minutes. The test is norm referenced both for children who speak black English and for those who speak standard English.

screening test An instrument that distinguishes apparently well people who probably do not have a specific disease or condition from those who probably do have the condition. The validity of a screening test is measured by its sensitivity, specificity, false positive, and false negative rates. Bayesian analysis suggests that the prevalence of the disorder screened for in the population under consideration has a significant impact on a screening test's validity. An example of a medical screening test is the tuberculin skin test for tuberculosis. The difficulties of achieving definitive developmental diagnoses in infants and young children are multiplied in developmental screening. The dividing line between diagnostic and screening tests is not fixed; a test used as a screening instrument in one context may be diagnostic in another context.

Screening Test for Auditory Processing Disorders (SCAN) A test of auditory processing in children ages 3–11 years. The SCAN yields three subscores: filtered words, auditory figure–ground, and competing words. The SCAN is administered with a portable stereo-cassette player.

Screening Tests for Young Children and Retardates (STYCAR) Block letters, miniature toys, and graded balls are used to screen vision; noisemakers, toys, and pictures are used to screen hearing in children as young as 6 months of age. These clinical procedures were developed by Mary Sheridan, an English pediatrician, as especially appropriate for usage with children who have physical and cognitive limitations. These vision and hearing tests are part of a more comprehensive approach to screening referred to as the STYCAR sequences, which describe children's developmental progress from birth to 5 years.

SD *See* standard deviation.

SDCT for Children and Adults *See* Slosson Drawing Coordination Test for Children and Adults.

SDRT *See* Stanford Diagnostic Reading Test, Third Edition.

Seckel syndrome Bird-headed dwarfism. A genetic syndrome with short stature, microcephaly (abnormally small head), mental retardation, and a "bird" facies (e.g., protuberant beaked nose, thin face, sloping forehead, and prominent eyes). Inheritance is autosomal recessive. Detectable at birth, the syndrome has been picked up prenatally by serial ultrasound. There is currently no available treatment.

second signaling system One of two phylogenetic lines used by Ivan Pavlov (1849–1936) to describe brain function: 1) the first signaling system, which is the animal part of the brain that uses direct sensory perceptions; and 2) the second signaling system, which is the human division that uses intellect with an emphasis on language. These levels are somewhat analogous to Sigmund Freud's (1856–1939) primary and secondary process thinking.

secondary gain The advantages experienced through being ill, such as being pampered and cared for, and getting out of school or other work responsibilities.

secondary process A psychoanalytic term that refers to logical, controlled thinking with minimal affective components; conscious intellectualization. Secondary process thinking is also characterized by delay or postponement, unlike the immediate discharge or gratification seen in primary process thinking. The second signaling system identifies language as the principal component of rational control; *see also* second signaling system.

SED *See* seriously emotionally disturbed.

sedative A calming agent; a drug that allays nervous excitement.

SEE₁ *See* Seeing Essential English.

SEE₂ *See* Signing Exact English.

Seeing Essential English (SEE₁) A manual sign language modification of American Sign Language (ASL) to resemble English; signs stand for English prefixes, roots, suffixes, and verb tenses. English syntax (grammar) is emphasized; words are represented by the American sign word plus affixes (suffixes or prefixes) as needed.

segmental rolling The mature phase of derotative righting in which the infant rolls over with one body segment preceding another or in a "corkscrew" fashion.

Seguin Formboard A puzzle that requires the correct placement of 10 distinct geometric shapes in the matching hole in the test surface. One of a variety of different formboards designed for training and later used for testing purposes, the Seguin Formboard has been used frequently to assess the presence of higher-level visuomotor problem-solving skills in young children with autism. Many such children between 3 and 6 years of age exhibit superior timed performances on this specific type of puzzle; this usually represents a splinter skill common in autism. The Seguin Formboard can also be administered with the subject blindfolded as a measure of tactile (touch) form recognition, memory for shapes, and spatial location. Sometimes referred to as the *Seguin-Goddard Formboard*.

seizure A convulsion or epileptic attack. Epilepsy is a form of recurrent chronic seizures. A seizure is characterized by a paroxysmal burst of electrical activity in the brain that is clinically manifested by unconsciousness or impaired consciousness usually with rhythmic movements of the extremities (arms or legs) and/or other atypical behaviors. The etiology (cause) of seizures may be identified as idiopathic (unknown). Seizures of known organic etiology are more likely to be associated with abnormalities and specific genetic conditions. Seizures are classified as partial, generalized, and unclassified based on the seizure type. Combinations of seizure types that commonly occur together are termed *epileptic syndromes*. Diagnosis and treatment typically require a clinical history of the event and a corresponding abnormal electroencephalogram (EEG). Treatment with anticonvulsant medication is based on age and seizure type.

selective posterior rhizotomy A neurosurgical ablative procedure to eliminate spasticity (increased muscle tone) in spastic cerebral palsy by destroying the reflex arc at the level of the dorsal root of the spinal cord. The operation is characterized as selective because only nerve rootlets that demonstrate an exaggerated electromyographic response on stimulation are cut. This operation is relatively new and is still controversial.

self-concept   An evaluation an individual makes and strives to maintain with regard to him- or herself. Self-concept includes the thoughts, attitudes, characteristics, feelings, and behaviors a person considers vital to who he or she is. Self-concept is a fundamental issue for everyone, but it is especially important for people with disabilities. There are two issues that must be considered: 1) How the person views him- or herself (i.e., how the person integrates his or her particular disability and the "disabled" concept into the total self-concept); and 2) how the person feels that his or her disability is regarded by others on personal, social, and cultural levels.

self-esteem   An individual's perception and valuation of him- or herself when compared with a particular reference group. Having a "disability," requiring "special education," and experiencing "failure" in "typical" situations can negatively affect a child's self-esteem. Self-esteem can be enhanced by the experience of success in any of a range of areas. Realistic awareness of specific strengths and limitations, positive relationships, and the use of an appropriate reference group to whom the individual can fairly and accurately compare him- or herself can promote positive self-esteem.

self-help group   *See* support group.

self-injurious behavior (SIB)   Self-inflicted repetitious and chronic behaviors that can cause physical harm and tissue damage to the person performing these behaviors. The behaviors, which appear dysfunctional and devoid of desirable consequences, can include face slapping, head banging, biting, pinching, scratching, gouging of the self, rumination, pica, and coprophagia (eating feces). The behaviors are stereotyped, self-stimulatory, and most common in individuals with severe mental retardation. They occur more frequently in specific syndromes (e.g.,

Lesch-Nyhan), but they are also common in the absence of meaningful ways for an individual to communicate. Behavior modification, drugs, and protective devices (e.g., helmets) are the mainstays of therapy. Significant acquired brain injury is rare, but permanent eye damage can occur.

self-monitoring   Recording one's own behavior in order to effect change. The process of self-monitoring first involves recognition of the need to regulate or change a specific behavior (e.g., negative comments, time off task, talking out). The behavior to be changed must be measured against a standard, often defined by determining a baseline (data collected on a behavior before any intervention occurs). This phase may require another person to collect the data. The individual then keeps a record of the occurrence of the targeted behavior. Self-monitoring may be combined with self- or external reinforcement; however, in some cases, the act of record keeping alone has been effective. Studies regarding the long-term effects of this change have been inconclusive.

self-stimulatory   behavior   Persistent, highly repetitive, invariant motor actions, mannerisms, or sequences that have no recognizable purpose and are not injurious to the individual. They include such stereotypies as hand flapping and rocking; if they become harmful to the subject, they are reclassified as self-injurious behavior.

semantic memory   Conceptualized by memory theorists as the memory component containing the most knowledge of the world (word definitions, names of presidents, etc.). The most obvious fact about this memory component is that it is highly organized, as shown by the ability to quickly recall one relevant bit of information from the millions stored. The form of this organization is not clear, but a network model with concepts and categories playing key roles seems likely. For example, terriers and spaniels are both members of the dog category, which is a member of the mammal category. Information may be initially encoded in episodic memory ("The dog I saw yesterday at the beach was a spaniel") before becoming part of the semantic network. The organizational structure of semantic memory is similar to that described in the construct of declarative information.

semantics The study of the history and meaning of words. Knowledge of semantics involves understanding the way in which meaning is associated with words as well as how meaning is conveyed through sentences. Knowledge of vocabulary refers to a part of semantics that relates to the ability to understand and use the meaning of the independent word. For example, to use the word *ball* in a coherent sentence requires particular semantic knowledge. "The ball threw the boy" is syntactically correct but semantically impossible. Semantics also extends to broader contexts. For example, the meaning of "The fan is loud" is conveyed by previous reference to a spectator at a ball game or to a mechanical device. Some aspects of semantics have been associated with simultaneous processing.

semiotics The signs and gestures that accompany verbal language. The signs and gestures may clarify or disqualify the verbal communication.

sensation The most fundamental level of receptive behavior. Sensation refers solely to the activation of sensory-neural structures. Impairments at this level include deafness, blindness, and other peripheral (noncentral) nervous system impairments. Sensation contrasts with perception, which is the interpretation or processing of sensory information. Mild disorders in sensation can often be compensated for by the perception operations of the brain.

sensitive period A period of time in the organism's development when conditions are optimal for the emergence of a specific function. Missing this temporal window of opportunity does not preclude the later evolution of this function, but renders it more difficult. It would seem almost impossible to distinguish whether the difficulty in later achieving a missed milestone is due to having passed the sen-

sitive period or whether it reflects, instead, the continued or long-term impact of those very factors (organismic or environmental) that caused the milestone to be missed in the first place. The sensitive period is to be contrasted with *critical period*.

sensitivity An epidemiological term denoting a true positive rate. Sensitivity is a statistic that describes the ability of a screening test to successfully identify those tested who actually have the condition for which they are being screened. Sensitivity is the ratio of true positive (positive test result, condition present) to all positive test results (whether the condition is present or true positives plus false positives). The closer this ratio is to 1.0, the better the screening test.

sensorimotor Relating to the use of sensory information (including visual, auditory, tactile [touch], olfactory [smell], proprioceptive, and kinesthetic) to produce an adapted (purposeful, goal-directed) motor response.

sensorimotor The earliest Piagetian stage of cognitive development; six substages during the first 2 years of life demonstrate increasing structuring of motor responses to immediately perceived objects.

sensorineural hearing impairment (SNHI) Also termed *sensorineural deafness*; a hearing impairment in which the abnormality is located along the auditory nerve (cranial nerve VIII) from the inner ear to the brain stem. This can be caused by a congenital abnormality in the nerve, by damage to the nerve (e.g., from certain antibiotics such as gentamicin [brand name, Garamycin]), or by diseases such as Friedreich ataxia. Many syndromes can be associated with a sensorineural hearing loss that may be static or progressive. Frequent monitoring of hearing acuity is necessary in individuals with progressive hearing loss to keep their hearing aids functioning effectively.

sensory function Neurological screening tests of sensation. These include a pinprick to test for pain sensation, light touch, temperature, position sense, vibration, stereognosis (solid form recognition by touch), graphesthesia (recognition of items written on the skin), and two-point discrimination. Sensation requires that both the central and the peripheral nervous systems be intact. Riley-Day, or familial dysautonomia (hereditary disease of the autonomic nervous system), is a condition in which affected members cannot feel pain. Asymmetric brain lesions may result in the loss of sensation on one side only.

sensory integration The neurological process that organizes sensation from one's own body and from the environment and enables one to use the body effectively within the environment. The spatial and temporal aspects of inputs from different sensory modalities are interpreted, associated, and unified. The brain selects, enhances, inhibits, compares, and associates sensory information in a flexible, constantly changing pattern.

Sensory Integration and Praxis Tests (SIPT) A battery of 17 performance (nonverbal) tests to assess the relationships among tactile (touch) processing, vestibular-proprioceptive processing, visual perception, visual-motor coordination, practic ability, and bilateral integration and sequencing in children 4–8 years of age with moderate learning, behavior, or developmental irregularities. Administration time is 1.5 hours, with computer scoring to compare patterns in six different cluster groups: deficit in bilateral integration and sequencing, visuo- and somatodyspraxia, dyspraxia on verbal command, generalized sensory integrative dysfunction, low-average sensory integration and praxis, and high-average sensory integration and praxis. This is a 1989 revision of the 1972 Southern California Sensory Integration Tests.

sensory integration theory A theory of brain behavior relationships that attempts to explain deficits in interpreting sensory information from the body and the environment, and deficits in academic or neuromotor learning in people with learning disabilities or clumsiness. The theory has a specific battery of assessment instruments and a menu of intervention techniques for a wide variety of developmental disorders. The founder of sensory integration theory was A. Jean Ayres (1920–1988).

sensory register A construct hypothesized by memory theorists to store information from the sensory receptors (rod and cone sensitivity to light, middle-ear bone sensitivity to sound, proprioceptor cells sensitivity to touch, etc.) in the central nervous system. It is usually assumed that there are as many sensory registers as there are sense modalities, each being modality specific. Most stored information fades quickly, with the temporal duration of auditory information (approximately 2 seconds) generally lasting longer than that for visual information (about 0.5 seconds). From the immediate representation of sensory information, a small fraction is kept for continued representation in short-term memory, while the rest is lost from the system. Although the sensory register is the first stage of the hypothetical construct, it is not often tested or considered outside of laboratory settings.

sentence completion technique (Rotter) A projective measure that is an extension of the word association test. The subject is presented with incomplete sentences and is asked to complete them. Examples include: "I worry about. . . ." or "I am happy when. . . ." The sentences are typically analyzed in terms of the attitudes, concerns, and motivations expressed in the responses. Caution must be exercised when analyzing responses from people with developmental disabilities. The length and quality of responses can be significantly affected by language impairment, processing problems, and attention deficits.

separation anxiety Childhood anxiety caused by actual or threatened separation from mother; a positive sign of the presence of attachment or bonding. It becomes prominent late in the first year of life around the same time as stranger anxiety, from which it is distinct. Although separation anxiety may recur briefly on the first day of school, it is distinct from the more pathological school phobia.

sepsis workup A battery of tests (microbiological, hematological [pertaining to the blood and blood-forming tissues], chemical, and others) to identify the presence and nature of an infection (i.e., sepsis); the particular battery of tests varies with the age of the child and the nature of the presenting signs and symptoms. Infections in premature babies and young infants can be nonspecific and so quickly life-threatening that sepsis workups are more frequent in this pediatric age group and are often performed simultaneously with the initiation of antibiotic treatment for a yet-undiagnosed infection. If cultures and other test results are negative after several days, therapy may be discontinued. The child suspected of having an infection is referred to as "septic" or "ill-looking"; this does not require fever but may include lethargy and anorexia (loss of appetite).

septo-optic dysplasia De Morsier syndrome. A syndrome including abnormal development (i.e., agenesis [absence of formation]) of the septum pellucidum (a membrane separating the anterior [front] portions of the lateral [outside] ventricles [fluid-containing spaces] of the brain), optic nerve hypoplasia (underdevelopment) resulting in severe visual impairment, and growth hormone deficiency with short stature and sometimes other hypothalamic pituitary endocrine dysfunction. Many people with this syndrome have no associated limitations, but a wide spectrum of neurodevelopmental disabilities can be present. Endocrine follow-up with replacement hormone therapy can be beneficial.

sequela, pl. sequelae A morbid condition that follows as a consequence of another disease or condition; the original condition is a cause of the sequelae, which are effects. For example, mental retardation, deafness, and cardiac disease are possible sequelae to prenatal rubella.

sequence anomolad A pattern of multiple anomalies (malformation, deformation,

disruption, or dysplasia) derived from a single prior anomaly or mechanical factor. The term *sequence* implies greater understanding of the impact of the initial event or subsequent formation than a syndrome.

Sequenced Inventory of Communication Development–Revised (SICD–R) A scale of expressive and receptive language milestones for children 4 months to 4 years of age. The instrument, which is part parent interview and part child performance, evaluates receptive items of awareness, discrimination, and understanding and expressive items of imitation, initiating, responsiveness, and verbal output. It is grossly scored in 4-month increments; however, standardization figures are available.

Sequential Assessment of Mathematics Inventories–Standardized Inventory (SAMI) An individual test of mathematics achievement for children from kindergarten through eighth grade. The 243 items assess eight curriculum strands: mathematical language, measurement, ordinality, geometric concepts, number and notation, mathematical applications, computation, and word problems.

sequential processing The manipulation or processing of stimuli one at a time, with each idea linearly and temporally related to the preceding stimulus. Both verbal and nonverbal information may be processed sequentially when the order of the stimuli is necessary for extracting meaning or problem solving. Sequential processing is related to a variety of school-oriented tasks including memorization of number facts, applying stepwise mathematical procedures, phonics, spelling, grammatical relationships and rules, chronology of historical events, and following directions. The Kaufman Assessment Battery for Children (K–ABC) is based on the concept of sequential versus simultaneous information processing.

serial casting A sequence of casts used to progressively correct a deformity; each successive cast positions the body part closer to the desired norm.

seriously emotionally disturbed (SED) An educational condition including impaired learning, unsatisfactory interpersonal relationships, inappropriate behaviors, depression, and physical symptoms related to school.

serous otitis media Otitis media with effusion (OME), catarrhal otitis, secretory otitis media, nonsuppurative otitis media, mucoid ear, glue ear. A middle-ear effusion (fluid collection) as evidenced by visual and tympanometric findings and without the signs and symptoms of acute otitis media (e.g., fever, pain).

service coordination Term previously referred to as *case management*. PL 101-476, the Individuals with Disabilities Education Act (IDEA) of 1990, renamed this service provided to people with disabilities and their families. *See* case management.

Serum Multichannel Analysis (SMA) A battery of blood tests performed on one specimen. SMA is followed by a number indicating the number of electrolytes and other blood chemicals being measured.

SES *See* socioeconomic status.

setting sun sign Deviation of the eyes below the horizontal so that the white of the sclera is visible above the cornea. This finding can be a sign of progressive hydrocephalus (excess fluid in the brain).

setting sun sign

severe mental retardation (SMR) Mental retardation in which the IQ level is between 20 and 40. Adults with SMR are typically independent in self-help skills and can live in supervised group home settings in the community.

severe and profound mental retardation (SPMR) A grouping of people with severe mental retardation (IQ level between 20–25 and 35–40) and people with profound mental retardation (IQ level below 20 or 25) for purposes of education and habilitation. One can also see references

grouping people without mental retardation but with severe to profound handicaps (SPH) together with people with mental retardation as SPH/SPMR.

sex chromosome The chromosomes responsible for the determination of sex (XX in females, XY in males).

sex chromosome abnormalities (SCA) A group of chromosomal disorders involving abnormal numbers of X and Y chromosomes (i.e., the sex chromosomes). This group includes both monosomies (e.g., Turner syndrome [XO]), with only one X chromosome instead of the normal two [XX], and polysomies (e.g., Klinefelter syndrome [XXY]), which have an extra X or Y chromosome. Other variations are multiple X chromosomes (e.g., trisomy X [XXX or XXXY]), tetrasomy X (XXXX or XXXXY), and multiple Y chromosomes (XYY). In general, abnormal numbers of sex chromosomes are associated with milder cognitive and behavioral effects than with other chromosomal abnormalities. Nonetheless, the trend is that individuals with greater numbers of chromosomes have lower cognitive functioning.

sex-influenced A trait that, although not X-linked in its inheritance, is nonetheless expressed differently (either in the extent or frequency of expression) in males and females.

sex-limited A trait that is expressed in only one sex, even though the gene may be present in the other sex. Sex-limited genes are not necessarily X-linked.

S–FRIT *See* Slosson Full-Range Intelligence Test.

SGA *See* small for gestational age.

shagreen patch A skin lesion found in tuberous sclerosis; a patch of thickened, raised, green/gray/brown skin in the lumbosacral region (lower back).

shaken baby syndrome Caffey syndrome, Caffey-Kempe syndrome. A type of child maltreatment with intracranial injury and long bone fractures that represents an important masked presentation of child abuse. When an infant is violently shaken, flailing of the limbs causes metaphyseal lesions (X-ray irregularities at the growing ends of long bones), and shaking of the head causes subdural bleeding and retinal (eye) hemorrhages (bleeding).

shaping A term from behavioral learning theory referring to the process of gradually changing a person's behavior by reinforcing progressively closer approximations of the desired behavior. For example, a student who is seldom in his seat more than 3 minutes at a time might be reinforced for progressively closer approximations of the target behavior of staying in his or her seat for 20 minutes. First, the student would be reinforced for staying in his or her seat for 3 minutes, then 4, then 5, and so on until the student reaches the target of 20 minutes.

sheltered employment A protected, monitored work environment for people with developmental disabilities (and other cognitive or physical impairments). Work programs are based on an individual's capacity to produce rather than an external production standard. Thus, one worker may produce 5 units per hour and another 25 units per hour, yet each is producing at his or her maximum capacity.

sheltered workshop A specialized work setting for people with developmental disabilities. Workshops provide employment based on the person's ability to produce, rather than on a competitive employment model. Levels of performance are measured against a competitive productivity standard. However, a person whose productivity is maximized at 10% of such a standard is rewarded for producing at his or her maximum, and is not penalized for inability to meet normative production standards.

short bowel syndrome Any malabsorption condition that results from loss or resection of significant lengths of small intestine; symptoms can include diarrhea, poor growth and nutrition, and fatty stools.

short leg brace A brace extending from just below the knee to the foot.

short leg brace

short-term memory A hypothesized component of memory with the function to receive information from a sensory register. This information corresponds roughly to awareness. It is also called *working memory*. The term *short-term memory* emphasizes the duration of information, whereas the term *working memory* emphasizes the function. Two key characteristics usually associated with short-term memory are the fragility of storage and an extremely limited capacity. Unless it is rehearsed, information passes out of short-term memory in about 10 seconds. A slight distraction will cause the information to be lost sooner. Approximately seven chunks of information can be held in short-term memory at one time. A chunk may be described as the highest-level integration of stimulus material available to an individual. For example, 346 represents one chunk while 3-4-6 represents three. In students with learning problems, it may be difficult to discriminate between deficits in attention and deficits in short-term memory, as either can appear as a lack of ability to accurately retain information for immediate recall. The normally limited capacity also plays a part in reading and mathematics disabilities. If decoding skills or mathematics facts are not learned automatically, they "take up space" in working memory that would otherwise be utilized for comprehension or problem solving. Thus, providing an aid to working memory (e.g., a number chart, number line) can allow some students to utilize their intact conceptual skills. *See also* memory.

Shprintzen syndrome A genetic syndrome including cleft palate, congenital heart disease, and a peculiar facies (long face, prominent nose, and micrognathia [small jaw]) leading to the synonym *velo-cardio-facial syndrome*. Mental retardation is uncommon, but the syndrome exhibits a striking learning disability and personality profile. Inheritance is autosomal dominant with a recurrence risk of 50%. Treatment is special education for language and cognitive impairments.

shunt A surgical anastomosis or artificial passage. *See also* ventriculoperitoneal (VP) shunt.

SI *See* social intelligence.

sialorrhea Excessive drooling; unintentional loss of saliva and other oral contents from the mouth. Some normal drooling can persist until 18 months of age.

SIB *See* self-injurious behavior.

sibling A brother or sister. One of two or more children with the same mother or father. When a family includes a child with a disability, siblings often feel left out owing to the attention and "special treatment" the child with a disability requires and receives. Research suggests that parents of children with developmental disabilities often place increased demands on their other children. Siblings may be expected to help care for the child with a disability and to subordinate their needs and feelings to those of their sibling. These children may feel guilty over their lack of a disability and pressured to excel and to be "perfect" in order to compensate for their sibling with a disability. Other possible reactions include behavioral acting out and single-handedly "solving" problems. Young siblings of children with disabilities may mistakenly think they are at risk of developing the same disability. Sibling support groups to address many of these issues are available for selected disorders.

sibling rivalry Competition among children of the same generation in a family for parental attention, approval, recognition, and affection. The quality of sibling relationships helps to determine the degree to which individuals will have successful interpersonal relationships later in life. A weakness, special need, or disability can complicate and alter this typical developmental process, making the competition one-sided, cruel, unfulfilling, or

ineffective, and can create negative feelings (e.g., guilt, shame, anger) that hinder growth. Siblings of children with developmental disabilities have a unique perspective on and experience of themselves as well as their families. This perspective must be identified and addressed to facilitate optimal individual development and family functioning. Groups and organizations for siblings exist for these purposes.

sibship A group including all of the brothers and sisters (siblings) in a family. This is an important grouping for determining the mechanism of transmission of a genetic disorder. For example, a disorder in a family with normal parents but two affected siblings is probably recessive.

sicca cell therapy Implantation by injection of fetal sheep brain cells to promote brain growth and improve intelligence; an unproven and hazardous intervention in Down syndrome and mental retardation.

SICD–R *See* Sequenced Inventory of Communication Development–Revised.

sickle cell anemia An autosomal recessive disorder that is common in African American and Mediterranean populations. It is caused by a gene base-pair substitution that produces a type of hemoglobin (oxygen-carrying red blood cells) that does not bind oxygen well. In the disease, the red blood cells assume a sickle shape that can cause a stroke by blocking blood flow through the vessels. Such brain damage can produce loss of function in the form of hemiparesis (one-sided paralysis), aphasia (loss of language skills), or even mental retardation. The sickling can also cause pain (called a *sickle crisis*) and swelling of the hands or feet. Children with sickle cell anemia are prone to infections.

sidelying A posture in which a person lies on the right or left side with the legs slightly bent; a variety of cushions or pads are sometimes used to help maintain this posture.

sight word Recognition of a whole word based on the memory of the whole word.

This is in contrast to the phonetic (representing sounds) sequential analysis of a word.

sign An objective, atypical, physical marker or symptom of a condition or disease; a finding that is objectively measurable or localizable (e.g., fever can be a sign of infection or other disease). Signs are usually detected on the physical examination of the individual, but some signs are found on laboratory or radiological examination.

signed English Siglish, pidgin sign English. A sign system that shares some of the characteristics of American Sign Language and some of English, effectively reducing the grammar employed from each.

Signing Exact English (SEE₂) A sign language system in which signs represent words instead of word roots, as in SEE₁. Prefixes and suffixes are added when necessary.

sign systems Manual communication systems used by people with severe and profound hearing loss. A sign system may have its own structure and syntax (grammar), or may use that of another language. Signs can be either phonetic (representing sounds), idiographic (representing ideas), or pictographic (representing objects). Sign systems in use include American Sign Language, manual English, signed English, SEE₁, and SEE₂.

Silver syndrome *See* Russell-Silver syndrome.

Silverskiold test An orthopedic examination to differentiate whether limited dorsiflexion (upgoing movement of the toes) at the ankle is due to gastrocnemius (muscle in the lower leg) contracture or to gastrocnemius and soleus (muscle in the calf) contractures. If foot dorsiflexion is greater with the knee flexed than with the knee extended, the gastrocnemius is the main site of the contracture. In the latter condition, orthopedic surgical treatment of equinus (an involuntary foot extension) deformity of the foot involves a transplantation of the heads of the gastrocnemius muscle; if the equinus deformity persists regardless of the position of the knee, then a tendon lengthening is in order.

simian crease A single transverse palmar crease instead of the more common pattern of two incomplete palmar creases. This is a minor dysmorphic (atypical) feature that occurs (at least unilaterally) in approximately 50%–55% of people with Down syndrome, in approximately 0.4%–10% of people without disabilities, and with variable frequency in a variety of other syndromes and throughout the spectrum of neurodevelopmental disorders.

simian crease

similar sequence hypothesis A theory that people with mental retardation and those without mental retardation traverse the same stages of cognitive development but at different rates and with final attainment of different stages.

similar structure hypothesis A theory that, when matched for mental age, people with mental retardation and those without mental retardation solve problems in the same way (with regard to the underlying formal cognitive structures).

similarities A Wechsler intelligence scale–verbal subtest consisting of 14–20 pairs of words for which the child must explain how the items in each pair are alike. The subtest measures verbal concept formation that can be an effortful process or can also reflect well-automatized verbal conventions. Categorizing and capturing an abstract concept in a couple of words that form a category require simultaneous processing recall skills and language facility. The subtest is discontinued after three consecutive failures. Example: "How are oil and electricity alike?" Reliability and validity coefficients are contained in the WISC–III manual.

simple partial seizure A seizure type with unilateral hemispheric involvement resulting in focal or localized symptoms, including motor, sensation, or psychic characteristics. Consciousness is unimpaired during a simple partial seizure. Simple partial seizures may evolve into generalized seizures or complex partial seizures. Partial seizures arise from a specific locus (area) in the brain, and the symptoms manifested are related to that location. For example, abnormal electrical seizure activity in the motor cortex around the arm produces a twitching of that arm. Treatment includes use of one of the following anticonvulsants: carbamazepine (Tegretol), phenobarbital, valproic acid (Depakene), phenytoin (Dilantin), or primidone (Mysoline).

simultaneous processing The manipulating or processing of many stimuli or aspects of stimuli at the same time in a holistic fashion. Both verbal and nonverbal stimuli may be processed simultaneously when the meaning or solution requires the input to be integrated and synthesized at once, rather than one step at a time. Simultaneous problem-solving skills are related to a variety of academic skills including deriving meaning from pictures and other visual stimuli, number shapes, basic arithmetic concepts, and more complex mathematical principles, shapes of letters, configuration of words, understanding main ideas, diagrams, flow charts, and creative problem solving. The Kaufman Assessment Battery for Children (K–ABC) is based on the concept of simultaneous versus sequential information processing.

single gene disorder A disorder produced by a single mutant (changed) gene with a large effect on phenotype (appearance).

single photon emission computed tomography (SPECT) A procedure using gamma-ray emission isotopes to measure regional blood flow in an area of the brain.

single umbilical artery The umbilical cord typically has two arteries and one vein (three vessels); when there are only two vessels (and one umbilical artery), there is a significant association with a variety of major organ malformations. The presence of three vessels is ascertained when the cord is cut.

sinus A recess, cavity, or channel; often used synonymously with a collection of skull cavities (paranasal sinuses: frontal, ethmoidal, sphenoidal, and maxillary) that are subject to allergic inflammation and secondary infection (i.e., sinusitis) and contribute to sinus headaches.

SIPT *See* Sensory Integration and Praxis Tests.

sit Gross-motor milestone of infancy; there are three distinct phases in the achievement of sitting: 1) *tripod sitting* with anterior (front) propping at 5 months, 2) *sitting unsupported* with lateral (outside) propping at 7 months, and 3) *mature sitting* with posterior (back) propping at 9 months.

tripod sitting

Failure to achieve sitting by 1 year of age suggests the presence of cerebral palsy or other motor disability; failure to achieve sitting by 2 years of age suggests that the child will never walk independently.

unsupported sitting with lateral propping

Long sitting is sitting with the legs straight out in front. *Cross-legged sitting* is sitting with the knees flexed and the legs crossed in front. *Side sitting* is sitting with the legs and thighs flexed to the same side. *Between-heel sitting* is the reversed tailor position.

mature sitting with posterior propping

SIT–R *See* Slosson Intelligence Test–Revised.

sitting in air A descriptive phrase applied to the posture assumed by a very young infant attempting to elicit a positive support response.

sitting in air

Sjogren Hand Test   A vision screening test for children 3 years and older. A variant of the illiterate E test that uses a hand rather than an E as the directional stimulus. *See also* illiterate E.

Sjogren-Larsson syndrome   A genetic syndrome with ichthyosis (very dry skin), short stature, spasticity (increased muscle tone), and mental retardation. Chorioretinal lesions are noted in approximately 50% of affected individuals. The syndrome is usually detected in the neonatal period. Treatment is symptomatic for the skin lesions, with special education modifications for the cognitive limitations. Inheritance follows an autosomal recessive pattern.

Skeels and Dye study   A follow-up study (1939) of 25 infants who had exhibited variable developmental delay in an institutional setting; those children who received mothering from women with mental retardation while living in institutions made dramatic cognitive gains, they qualified for adoption, and they continued to exhibit significantly better outcomes about 30 (1966) years later. These results seem more descriptive of the severely deprivational impact of institutional settings in the 1930s than of the qualifications of adults with mental retardation to parent.

skiascopy   Measurement of the refractive error of an eye by focusing on the retina (light-sensitive inner back wall).

skinfold thickness   Calipers are used to measure the compressed double fold of fat plus skin at normed sites of the body to estimate the size of subcutaneous (inner) fat stores.

Skinner, Burrhus F. (B.F.) (1904–1990)   A psychologist who distinguished between two types of behavior—respondent and operant—and clarified how various reinforcement contingencies could control or modify behavior. His theories indicate that speculation on any intervening process between stimulus and response is superfluous. In *The Behavior of Organisms* (1938), Skinner described the results of years of research using white rats in an operant conditioning chamber, and in *Beyond Freedom and Dignity* (1971), he applied behaviorist principles to the concepts of freedom, value, and dignity. His novel, *Walden Two* (1948), is a utopian blueprint based on behavioral principles.

SKOLD   *See* Screening Kit of Language Development.

skull fracture   A break in one of the bones of the head; a history of head trauma including a skull fracture diagnosed by X ray is unlikely to adequately explain the presence of a significant developmental disability. A depressed skull fracture with neurological impairments, seizures, and coma may, however, contribute to a later developmental disorder.

SLES   *See* Speech and Language Evaluation Scale.

Slingerland Multisensory Approach   An approach to reading and writing that teaches patterns for the automatic association of the auditory, visual, and kinesthetic modalities. The letters of the alphabet are taught first. Strategies are then taught for thinking through what is not simply memorized. It is an integrated language arts approach that incorporates the teaching of reading, spelling, handwriting, and oral and written expression.

Slingerland Screening Tests for Identifying Children with Specific Language Disability   A group-administered test designed to identify children with specific language disabilities. This instrument actually tests perceptual-motor functions thought to affect receptive and expressive language skills. The basic tasks required for all grades are the same, differing mainly in vocabulary difficulty. Subtests in each form include: copying from a sample; visual perception and memory of words, letters, and numbers; visual discrimination to perceive similarities and differences; visual perception and memory linked with kinesthetic-motor performance; brief exploration of groups of words, phrases, letters, and numbers; auditory perception and memory linked with visual-kinesthetic-motor association—groups of letters, numbers, and words are to be written; auditory-visual-kinesthetic linkage, adding the requirement of making auditory discrimination of single sounds within whole words; auditory-visual linkage without the kinesthetic-motor requirement of writing from dictation—a word, letter, or number is located from a group; echolalia (repetition of what is heard) test (individually administered to selected pupils) permits more careful evaluation of auditory perception and memory than can be made from verbal responses alone. These tests would seem to give more information regarding learning or cognitive style than language functioning. Forms include: A—grade 1 and beginning grade 2; B—grade 2 and beginning grade 3; C—grade 3 and grade 4; and D—grade 5 and grade 6.

Slosson Drawing Coordination Test (SDCT) for Children and Adults   A figure-copying test for children 1–12 years of age; accuracy scores below 85 warrant further evaluation. Age norms for accuracy are reported in the manual.

Slosson Full-Range Intelligence Test (S–FRIT)   A brief verbal, performance, and memory screen for the purpose of tentative diagnosis of intellectual strengths and weaknesses in subjects 5-0 through 21-11. The instrument yields standard scores (with a mean of 100 and a standard deviation of 16) for general cognitive measures of Full-Range Intelligence Quotient (FRIQ), Rapid Cognitive Index (RCI), and Best g Index (BgI). Standard scores (with a mean of 50 and a standard deviation of 8) are provided for cognitive subdomains by a Verbal Index (VI), Abstract Index (AI), Quantitative Index (QI), Memory Index (MI), and a combined abstract and quantitative Performance Index (PI).

Slosson Intelligence Test–Revised (SIT–R) An individually administered screening test to measure general verbal intelligence in subjects 4 years old to adult. The SIT–R generates a mental age equivalent (MAE) that can be converted to a total standard score (TSS) with a mean of 100 and a standard deviation of 16.

Slosson Oral Reading Test (SORT) for Children and Adults   A reading screening test for children from first grade through high school. The test stimuli are 10 lists of 20 single words of graded difficulty. The test yields a grade score; reliability and validity coefficients are contained in the manual.

slow learner   An imprecise educational term used to refer sometimes to children with borderline intellectual functioning (IQ 70–85), or to children with mental retardation (IQ 50–70), or both.

Sly syndrome   Mucopolysaccharidosis (MPS), type VII. A genetic syndrome of growth deficiency, coarse facies, cloudy corneas, and mental retardation. Affected individuals often have dislocated hips and are subject to frequent respiratory illness. Inheritance patterns are autosomal recessive; detection at 10 weeks' gestation is possible through chorionic villi sampling. Treatment is symptomatic.

SMA   See Serum Multichannel Analysis.

small for gestational age (SGA)   Small for date; dysmature; a low birth weight (less than 2,500 grams) infant whose weight is also below the 10th percentile for gestational age. Thus, there are SGA term and SGA premature infants.

SMH   severely mentally handicapped; see severe mental retardation.

Smith-Johnson Nonverbal Performance Scale   A performance intelligence test for children 2–4 years of age; instructions are in pantomime, and hearing impairment norms are provided.

Smith-Lemli-Opitz syndrome   A genetic syndrome with poor growth, anteverted nostrils, eyelid ptosis (drooping), syndactyly (webbing of the fingers or toes) of second and third toes, genital abnormalities in boys (e.g., hypospadias [lower urethral opening], cryptorchidism [undescended testes]), and moderate to severe mental retardation. Inheritance is autosomal recessive. The disorder is detectable at birth; it has occasionally been prenatally picked up by ultrasound findings.

Smith-Magenis syndrome (SMS) A genetic syndrome with mental retardation, characteristic facies (brachycephaly [irregular, flat head shape], midface hypoplasia [defective tissue development], and prognathism [a prominent jaw]), short stature, sleep disturbances, orifice stuffing, and onychotillomania (pulling out one's nails). The last behavior is pathognomonic (indicative) for this syndrome, which is due to a deletion on the short arm of chromosome 17. The syndrome is detectable in the neonatal period. Treatment involves supportive care.

Smith syndrome Fetal alcohol syndrome phenotype (appearance) without a known history of prenatal alcohol exposure. This is also used as a nonculpatory synonym for fetal alcohol syndrome.

SMR *See* severe mental retardation.

SMS *See* Smith-Magenis syndrome.

Snellen Chart/Letters An "eye chart"; a chart with lines of letters of graded sizes to allow translation of successful letter discrimination and/or identification into standardized distance visual acuity designations based on administration at 20 feet. Normal vision is described as 20/20 (in feet) or 6/6 (in meters), meaning that the subject can accurately discriminate at 20 feet (or 6 meters) what an individual without visual impairments can discriminate at 20 feet (or 6 meters). A diagnosed visual acuity of 20/200 indicates that what the subject can discriminate at 20 feet can be discriminated by a person without visual impairments at 200 feet. This test can be used with children 5–6 years of age and older (as soon as they know the alphabet). Other measures of visual acuity need to be used with children who do not know or cannot consistently discriminate alphabet letters because of age or nonvisual impairments, such as mental retardation or learning disabilities.

SNHI *See* sensorineural hearing impairment.

Snijders-Oomen Nonverbal Intelligence Scale–Revised A Dutch instrument to measure nonverbal intelligence in children 5½–17 years of age and children with hearing and/or speech-language impairments.

snout reflex An infant reflex in which the stimulus of percussing (tapping) the upper or lower lip produces blinking and lip protrusion. The snout reflex is innervated by the facial nerve (cranial nerve VII); its prominence suggests the presence of a degenerative process.

SOAP *See* problem-oriented medical record (POMR).

social desirability A frequent source of test bias in which the test taker responds to questions with answers perceived as socially desirable rather than with responses that truly reflect the test taker's thoughts, feelings, and attitudes.

social history A multidimensional, in-depth social work description and evaluation of a client's biological, psychological, and social history along with current functioning. The social history serves as the basis for service planning by many professionals including social workers, physicians, lawyers, teachers, and judges.

social intelligence (SI) The ability to understand and deal effectively with social and interpersonal events.

Social Maturity Scale for Blind Preschool Children (Maxfield-Buchholz) An adaptation of the Vineland Social Maturity Scale for preschool children (ages birth to 5) with visual impairment. Seven categories of social development are assessed: personal-social growth, dressing, eating, communication, socialization, and occupation. The instrument is normed against children who are legally blind and partially sighted. Validity and reliability coefficients are lacking.

social promotion Passing a child to a higher grade despite the fact that he or she does not appear to have successfully mastered the prerequisite skills in the current grade; social promotion is based on the reasoning that it would do more harm to socially separate the child from his or her peers, that his or her self-image would be damaged by the failure, that he or she is growing physically too large to repeat a grade, or some combination of these. Research has shown that social promotion does not succeed, but merely delays more appropriate intervention based on a diagnostic assessment that uncovers the treatable reasons for failure.

social reinforcer   The reward of positive interpersonal contact.

Social Security   A group of federally funded social insurance programs to provide a minimum income for people in their old age, for workers with disabilities, and for worker survivors in case of death. The following programs are included in Social Security: Old Age Survivors Insurance (OASI), part of the original Social Security Act of 1935 for the aged; Survivors Social Security, added in 1939; Disability Insurance, amendments added in 1956 providing cash for workers with disabilities and their families; and Medicare, added in 1965.

social services   The range of professional activities and social programs enacted to help people in need. People in need may include troubled families, families that have lost the ability to produce their own income, families with members who have disabilities, children whose families are no longer able to care for them, people with mental illnesses, and others. Social services include the helping relationships provided by social workers and other professionals and the linkage of those services with other direct services and entitlements such as Aid to Families with Dependent Children (AFDC) and Supplemental Security Income (SSI).

social skills training   Specific training in the skills necessary for successful peer interaction. Learning and attention disorders may hinder the development of social as well as academic skills. These limitations are being addressed in learning disability textbooks and through the development of commercially available social skills curricula.

social smile   A milestone in early infant development; the baby's smile should be in response to a social interaction such as being talked to and not a spontaneous behavior associated with, for example, burping. The social smile characteristically emerges at 6 weeks of age, but will not be noted until later in babies born prematurely. It is more frequently considered a language milestone than a milestone in the other streams of development. Sometimes referred to as a *communicative smile*.

social welfare   A nation's system of laws, programs, benefits, and services in the areas of health, education, and economic, social, and basic human needs. In the United States, there are both federal (nationally mandated and supported) social welfare programs (e.g., Social Security) and state-determined programs (e.g., Medicaid). In state programs, those who are eligible, the range of entitlements, and the level of benefits may vary by state. Some states have superb social welfare programs, whereas others work to avoid expending funds for such programs.

social work   According to the National Association of Social Workers, social work is the professional activity of helping individuals, groups, or communities enhance or restore their capacity for social functioning and creating societal conditions favorable to this goal. Social workers provide clinical services (counseling and psychotherapy), information, and referral, and when necessary, facilitate access to services that individuals may be unable to obtain alone.

socioeconomic status (SES)   A measure of one's relative standing in society by a hierarchical grouping of people on a scale of prestige and privilege. Status is determined by such factors as type and amount of income, nature of occupation, location and type of residence, and level of education. SES has implications for educational and economic opportunities, range of experiences and activities, and expectations regarding future achievement.

sociogram   A visual representation or map of social relationships among members of a group. Symbols representing each group member are connected by lines indicating either real or preferred relationships. From this mapping, one can determine leadership, "in" versus "out" groups, cliques, and isolates.

sociopathy Antisocial personality disorder; a possible outcome for inadequately treated conduct disorder, attention-deficit/hyperactivity disorder (ADHD), and learning disability.

soft neurological sign A neurological finding that cannot be interpreted as physiological or pathological without taking into account the individual's age. All "abnormal" soft neurological findings are normal at some (usually younger) age. Soft signs do not contribute to the localization of central nervous system lesions but, rather, reflect a more generalized immaturity of the brain such as occurs in learning disabilities and mental retardation.

soft spot Fontanel.

somatization disorder Recurrent multiple psychosomatic complaints of several years' duration, of sufficient severity for medical consultation to be sought, not due to any underlying physical disorder. Anxiety and depression are frequently seen; females are more likely to be diagnosed with this disorder than are men.

somatodyspraxia An impairment in learning new motor responses that results in motor clumsiness (dyspraxia); somatodyspraxia is hypothesized in sensory integration theory to be caused by impaired tactile (touch) discrimination and proprioceptive processing.

somatotopy A homunculus (dwarf) projection; the mapping of a human figure on a section of the brain, reflecting either motor or sensory distortions.

somatotopy

somatotype A body type that implies the presence of a specific personality type or trait. A constitutional theory of personality

popularized by W.H. Sheldon in the first part of the 20th century included thin, fragile ectomorphs (worrisome, rigid, and inhibited temperament), obese endomorphs (socially outgoing temperament), and thick, muscular mesomorphs (assertive and competitive temperament). To a limited degree, somatotyping does contribute to the visual diagnosis of selected medical conditions such as genetic syndromes and endocrinological (hormonal) disorders, but its relevance outside of this restricted range is questionable. It appears to be a modern variant of physiognomy, another system with a similar grain of truth sufficient to maintain some research interest.

SORT for Children and Adults *See* Slosson Oral Reading Test for Children and Adults.

Sotos syndrome Cerebral gigantism; a syndrome in which the child has a large body size (birth weight over 8½ pounds), large hands and feet, poor coordination, and variable mental retardation. The rapid growth slows down by middle childhood. Because of their large size and motor clumsiness, children with Sotos syndrome often appear slower or to have more severe retardation than is actually the case. They also tend to have macrocephaly (abnormally large head), dolichocephaly (prominent forehead), prognathism (prominent jaw), and an advanced bone age. Etiology (cause) is sporadic; several families with parent-to-child transmission suggest the possibility of autosomal dominance, with the majority of cases representing fresh mutations. Sotos syndrome is usually detected in the neonatal or early childhood period. Treatment involves endocrine management and special education.

sound blending (phonemic synthesis) Synthesizing the individual sound components (i.e., phonemes) of a word, leading to recognition of the word as a whole. This synthesis is an important aspect of developing word attack skills in reading. However, by presenting sounds in isolation, several forms of distortion are introduced into the speech signal, presenting a considerable challenge to individuals with auditory processing problems.

sound–symbol association The knowledge that specific sounds go with specific visual symbols. This knowledge is important for learning to read, particularly when a synthetic phonics (*see* phonic analysis [phonics]) approach is used.

Souques finger phenomenon Automatic extension of the fingers when the shoulder is flexed; this phenomenon is common in hemiplegia (paralysis of half the body).

Southern California Postrotary Nystagmus Test (SCPNT) A test in which the person being tested is spun around 10 times in 20 seconds on a special "nystagmus board," and the duration of the resulting nystagmus (involuntary eye movements) is measured with a stopwatch. This is repeated in the opposite direction. Longer than normal durations of nystagmus are interpreted as compatible with learning disabilities.

s.p. Status post; indicates that the person had a previous condition (disease or operation) that may be relevant to the current situation. For example, "s.p. appendectomy" indicates that the person no longer has an appendix; "s.p. encephalitis" indicates that the person had encephalitis (brain inflammation) in the past. There is no automatic suggestion of recency, relevance, or sequelae. Thus, most adults are "s.p. chickenpox."

Spache Diagnostic Reading Scales *See* Diagnostic Reading Scales (revised edition).

Spasmus nutans Head rolling or nodding associated with nystagmus (involuntary eye movements) in preschool children who may otherwise be typically developing. Malnutrition, neglect, and mental retardation may result in a slightly higher frequency of this benign, self-limited condition. Onset is usually before 1 year of age, and it disappears by 3 years. Unlike bobble-head doll syndrome, the bobbing is usually dysrhythmic, intermittent, and inconstant.

spastic cerebral palsy The most common physiological subtype of cerebral palsy. Spasticity refers to an increase in muscle tone that is not the same throughout passive range of motion; rather, the extremity (arm or leg) exhibits a sudden "give" or loss of passive resistance or what is called "clasp-knife" hypertonicity. Strabismus (squint), contractures, and seizures are common associated deficits in spastic cerebral palsy. This type of cerebral palsy is further broken down according to a topographical classification into monoplegia, hemiplegia (paralysis of half the body), triplegia, diplegia (paralysis on both sides of the body), quadriplegia (paralysis of all four extremities), and paraplegia. Cerebral palsy that is not spastic is categorized as extrapyramidal because spasticity is considered a major finding in pyramidal tract involvement (hypertonicity, increased deep-tendon reflexes, and upgoing Babinski reflexes).

spasticity "Clasp-knife" hypertonicity; velocity-dependent increase in resistance to passive movement, resulting in increased muscle tone with exaggerated deep-tendon reflexes, clonus, and upgoing Babinski reflexes. The adjective *spastic* describes tone or a type of cerebral palsy and should never be used to characterize a person.

spatial orientation The perception of the position and configuration of objects in space from the observer's viewpoint; it is said to involve imagining movement of the entire stimulus without movement of its parts. Orientation enters into tasks requiring a geographic sense of direction, such as map reading and piloting a plane through three-dimensional space.

spatial relationships Above/below, right/left, right side up/upside down, inside/outside, near/far, before/behind. This factor has emerged as significant in research comparing differences in spatial ability of males and females (*see also* spatial visualization).

spatial visualization Spatial visualization involves the ability to mentally manipulate a stimulus configuration and the movements of parts within the configuration. The ability enters into the abstract reasoning required in solving math problems. This factor has emerged in research comparing differences in spatial ability of males and females (see also spatial orientation).

special Uncommon or unique. Describes what is different about any person. The term *special* should not be used to categorically describe or specifically characterize people with disabilities; the term can have the patronizing ring of a false compliment or can be interpreted as a euphemism for a more accurate description of a person's needs, limitations, or abilities. Terms like *special, handicapable,* and *physically challenged* are generally considered condescending. They reinforce the idea that disabilities cannot be addressed directly and honestly. The word *special* is acceptable, however, in reference to the citation of laws and regulations regarding services, rights, and provisions for people with disabilities.

special education Education designed to meet the individual needs of children with disabilities. Originally designated in PL 94-142, the Education for All Handicapped Children Act of 1975, children with disabilities are those evaluated as having mental retardation, deafness, serious emotional disturbances, orthopedic impairments, hearing impairments, visual impairments, learning disabilities, speech impairments, deaf-blind multiple disabilities, or other health impairments, and who, because of these impairments, need special education and related services.

special education service delivery model—alternative Criticism of the traditional "pull-out" service delivery model (see also special education service delivery model—traditional) has led to the development of several models emphasizing the integration of people with milder disabilities. Some of these newer models include Class Within a Class (CWC), Adaptive Learning Environment Model (ALEM), Integrated Classroom Model (ICM), and full inclusion with all individualized education program (IEP) goals being met in the general classroom.

special education service delivery model—traditional In order to place students in the least restrictive environment (LRE), school districts are required to provide a continuum of services. These may include 1) general class with consultative assistance from special education personnel, 2) general class and consultation plus special materials from special education, 3) general class plus special education itinerant teaching services, 4) general class plus assistance from special education teachers in a resource room, 5) special class in a general school, 6) special class in a special (separate) day school, 7) home or hospital programs (usually temporary), and 8) residential schools.

specialist A professional who has taken further training in a specific area of professional competence. A physician (M.D. or D.O.) will take further training (usually at least 3 years after internship) in a specific area of medical practice such as pediatrics, surgery, psychiatry, or neurology. In addition to their state-regulated license to practice medicine, most physician specialists are further nationally certified in their speciality area by a national accrediting board.

specific developmental disorder A subclass of developmental disorders that is characterized by inadequate development of specific academic, language, speech, and motor skills not due to other diagnosed disorders or deficient educational opportunities.

specificity The true negative rate; conegativity. A statistic that describes a screening test's ability to successfully identify those tested who do not have the condition for which they are being tested. Specificity is the ratio of true negatives (negative test result, absent condition) to all negative test results (whether the condition is present). The closer this ratio is to 1.0, the better the screening test.

SPECT *See* single photon emission computed tomography.

spectrum concept The possibility that several differently classified disorders may be the result of the same general genetic pattern. These disorders are then considered to be genetically related (e.g., attention-deficit/hyperactivity disorder [ADHD], alcoholism, and antisocial personality disorder).

spectrum of developmental disabilities An approach to classifying neurodevelopmental disorders that focuses on the major category of impairment: cognitive (e.g., mental retardation), motor (e.g., cerebral palsy), and central processing (e.g., learning disability, language disorder). Complementary to the continuum of developmental disabilities.

speech Oral communication using a system of vocal symbols.

Speech and Language Evaluation Scale (SLES) A teacher rating scale for screening speech and language abilities in the areas of articulation, voice, fluency, form, content, and pragmatics. The scale can be used by the classroom teacher for screening, referral, and follow-up assessment. Administration time is approximately 20 minutes.

speech disorder *See* articulation disorder.

speech-language pathologist An individual with a degree and/or certification in communication disorders who is qualified to make diagnoses, prescribe therapy, and employ therapeutic measures for the remediation and amelioration of speech and language problems.

speech-language pathology The study of communication disorders for the purposes of diagnosis and treatment. Communication disorders include disorders of speech, language, and voice.

speech reception threshold (SRT) Intelligibility threshold; the faintest intensity (decibel level) at which an individual identifies and repeats 50% of the simple spoken words presented.

speechreading A form of aural rehabilitation (educational methods for people with hearing impairments) that utilizes visual cues to determine what is being said.

People with hearing impairment "read" speech through interpretation of the speaker's lips, facial movements, hand and body expressions, and gestures. Formerly known as lipreading.

spend down The required reduction of all assets to a minimal level before meeting financial eligibility for federal and state entitlements.

SPH Severe to profound mental handicap; *see* severe and profound mental retardation.

sphingolipidosis A group of hereditary disorders with abnormal metabolism of chemicals called *sphingolipids* present in the brain. Whereas each disorder presents with its own clinical picture, the disorders share the symptoms of progressive loss of vision and mental retardation. With the exception of the type *E* variant, all other affected individuals have a significantly shortened life span. Prenatal diagnosis is available for types *A* and *B* in high-risk populations. Type *A* is more commonly found in persons of Ashkenazic Jewish descent. Once diagnosed, treatment is supportive care for patients and their families.

Spica cast A cast that immobilizes an extremity (arm or leg) by incorporating part of the body near that extremity.

spike wave complex Spike and slow-wave complex; an electroencephalographic (EEG) finding in which a spike (a sharp pointed deviation) is followed by a slow wave (a rounded curve deviation). At the rate of 3 per second, this pattern complex is associated with absence (petit mal) seizures. At the slower  rate of 1–2.5 per second, this pattern complex is associated with severe and intractable epilepsy referred to as *Lennox-Gastaut syndrome*.

spike wave

spina bifida Neural tube defect (NTD); a constellation of malformations of the central nervous system that presents with a failure of fusion of the bones in the vertebral column (upper spine) and with an accompanying herniation (protuberance) of neural components, including meningocele (protuberance of the lining of the spinal cord) and myelomeningocele (protuberance of both the spinal cord and its lining). In addition, there is generally abnormal cellular migration in the brain leading to an Arnold-Chiari malformation and hydrocephalus (excess fluid in the brain). Syringomyelia (cavitation in the spinal cord) can also be found. Vertebral abnormalities (e.g., misshapen and partial vertebrae) can lead to scoliosis and kyphosis (curvatures of the spine). Deformities of the lower extremities (most commonly clubfeet and rocker-bottom feet) may also be present. Other anomalies (malformation, deformation, disruption, or dysplasia) such as heart defects, kidney agenesis (absence of formation), and congenital intestinal obstructions (e.g., duodenal atresia, pyloric stenosis) are present in a greater than normal incidence. Clinically, the peripheral (noncentral) neurological problems depend on the level of the lesion. Low sacral lesions cause bladder and sphincter paralysis, but no motor impairment. Lesions in the lumbar region generally result in some degree of flaccid paraplegia with poor function of the anal and bladder sphincters. Higher lesions can result in hypertonic bladders with normal rectal sphincter tone. Treatment of myelomeningocele requires the expertise of pediatric surgical subspecialties, including orthopedics for lower extremity and back problems; neurosurgery for initial closure (fusion or ossification), shunt placement, and monitoring; and urology for management of incontinence, infection, and reflux of urine into the kidneys causing hydronephrosis (kidney enlargement due to obstructed flow). Care should also address managing bowel incontinence, as this contributes to a significant social disability. About 40% of children with myelomeningocele will have some degree of mental retardation; however, many children have normal overall cognitive abilities with accompanying learning disabilities. Inheritance is multifactorial.

spina bifida occulta A failure of fusion of the posterior (back) part of the vertebra without any protuberance of nerve tissue or meninges (covering of brain and spinal cord). Although the skin over the spine is generally intact, there may be associated dermal sinuses (tunnels in the skin), nevi (moles), dimples, or a hirsute (hairy) patch. A relatively common occurrence (10% of the general pediatric population), spina bifida occulta may be associated with abnormalities in the formation of the spinal cord, especially in the presence of neurological impairments. Lesions may be present at more than one level of the spinal cord. Surgical repair is indicated in the presence of infection (meningitis [inflammation of the spinal cord and brain membranes] or deep abscess in a dermal sinus) or with progressive loss of neurological function.

spinal accessory nerve The 11th cranial nerve; cranial nerve XI involvement causes the shoulder to sag and the tongue to deviate to the affected side.

spinal tap A procedure in which a needle with a bore is inserted between the vertebrae of the spinal column into the cerebral spinal fluid (CSF) that surrounds the spinal cord of the lower back. The CSF can be removed and tested for evidence of infection (i.e., meningitis [inflammation of the spinal cord and brain membranes]) or a bleed (i.e., hemorrhage); the pressure of the fluid in the CSF system can also be measured. This procedure is performed with the individual in either a lateral reclined position (lying on one side) or a sitting position.

SPLATT *See* split anterior tibial tendon transfer.

splint A flexible or rigid appliance for the immobilization of broken bones or dislocated joints.

split anterior tibial tendon transfer (SPLATT) An orthopedic surgery procedure to treat varus (inward) foot deformity in children with spastic cerebral palsy.

splitting The tendency to classify as separate entities items that at first appear to go together; *see also* heterogeneity.

SPMR *See* severe and profound mental retardation.

spooning A hand posture of curved hyperextension. Spooning can be present in a variety of neuromuscular disorders, but is most often a sign of minor neurological dysfunction. It is one component of athetoid posturing of the hand in cerebral palsy, and it tends to be exaggerated under stress.

spooning

Sprengel deformity Asymmetry of the scapula, with one shoulder blade being higher than the other, accompanied by some limitation in abducting (turning outward) and elevating the shoulder with the higher scapula.

Sprengel deformity

squint *See* strabismus.

SRT *See* speech reception threshold.

SSI *See* Supplemental Security Income.

SSPE *See* subacute sclerosing panencephalitis.

stability Maintenance of equilibrium with resistance to sudden change of position, achieved through co-contraction of muscle groups so that a joint remains fixed while allowing other muscles to move.

stadiometer One of a number of instruments to accurately measure height; usually composed of a measuring strip fixed to a wall and a vertically sliding headboard.

staffing An interdisciplinary team meeting in which members of the team utilize their respective expertise to assist in diagnosing and evaluating a disease or disability. Team members representing several disciplines make recommendations with regard to educational programming, psychological or family intervention, medication, and various ancillary (assistive) therapies. The staffing may include the professionals who performed specific components of the evaluation, teachers, parents/guardians, and other involved professionals. The collaborative effort helps promote a comprehensive and multifaceted view of the individual being evaluated and recognizes the need to consider the condition from several different, but related, perspectives.

stage A hierarchical level of development, with each level characterized by structural and qualitative changes. There is an implicit, but unproven, assumption that such stages are invariant and universal. The concept remains heuristic and controversial. (*See* the table on p. 297.)

staggering Reflex foot movements to maintain upright posture when the body is externally displaced.

stance phase That part of the gait cycle when the index foot is in contact with the ground (from heel strike to toe-off); double stance is that part of the gait cycle when both feet are in contact with the ground. Stance phase represents 60% of the gait cycle.

standard deviation (SD) A statistic that equals the square root of the variance. It is a commonly used measure of the extent to which individual scores differ from the mean. A small standard deviation indicates that the group under study is homogeneous with respect to the characteristic in question; a large standard deviation indicates the opposite. Approximately 68% of children fall within one standard deviation of the mean. The different Wechsler intelligence scales have a standard deviation of 15 around a mean of 100 for IQ scores and a standard deviation of 3 around a mean of 10 for subtest scores. Thus, approximately 68% of the children will achieve IQ scores between 85 and 115 and subtest scores between 7 and 13.

standard error of measurement *See* error of measurement.

standard score A score that is adjusted to indicate how many standard deviations a score is above or below a given mean. Commonly used types of standard scores include *z*-scores, *t*-scores, deviation IQs,

Stage theories of development

Age (years)	Sexual (Freud)	Social (Erikson)	Cognitive (Piaget)	Moral (Kohlberg)
0–1	Oral-sensory	Basic trust/ mistrust	Sensorimotor primary circular reaction (1–4.5 months) secondary circular reaction (4.5–9 months) coordination of secondary schemata (9–12 months)	
1–2	Anal-muscular		tertiary circular reaction (12–18 months) invention of new means	
2–3		Autonomy/ shame/doubt	Preoperational preconceptual (2–4 years)	
3–4	Genital-locomotor	Initiative/guilt		
4–7			intuitive (4–7 years)	Preconventional punishment reward
7–12	Latency	Industry/ inferiority	Concrete operations (7–11 years)	Conventional social approval respect for authority ("law and order")
12–	Adolescence/ puberty	Identity/role confusion	Formal operations (11 years–)	Autonomous social contract personal ethics

and stanines. Standard scores allow the comparison of the performance on one test to a performance on another.

standardization sample Norm group; the group of subjects whose performance on a specific test becomes the basis of comparison for future individual performances on the same test. The standardization of well-normed tests is based on the performance of a large, representative group of subjects. Norms are scores (percentile ranks, stanines, standard scores, mean, standard deviation) obtained by comparing the subjects' performance to the standardization sample. The norm group should be relevant to the examinee. For example, the performance of a 12-year-old African American female cannot be accurately judged when compared to norms obtained from a sample of 8-year-old Caucasian males. The Kaufman Assessment Battery for Children (K–ABC) is one of the few tests normed on a sample that included proportional representation of exceptional children.

standardized test A test with a consistent and uniform procedure for administering, scoring, and interpreting results such that each examinee is assessed in the same manner as was done in the standardization sample or norm group. Deviations from procedure may change the meaning of the resulting test score. The Wechsler Intelligence Scale for Children–III (WISC–III) and the Woodcock-Johnson Psychoeducational Battery–Revised are examples of tests that are uniform in administration, scoring, and the wording to be used by the examiner.

standing height The height in the standing position is typically 1–2 centimeters shorter than height (length) in the recumbent, or lying down, position.

Stanford-Binet Intelligence Scale: Fourth Edition (SBFE) A battery of 15 subtests measuring intelligence over an age range of 2–23 years. The original Stanford-Binet scale was published in 1916 and introduced the concept of the ratio IQ. The test was revised in 1937 and again in

1960; in 1973 updated norms were published. Some continuity is maintained between the SBFE and prior editions. Item types common across editions include vocabulary, comprehension, picture absurdities, paper folding and cutting, copying, repeating digits, memory for sentences, reproducing a bead chain from memory, similarities, formboard items, and quantitative items. The SBFE has new items in these areas as well as some new item types. Not all 15 subtests are administered to all subjects. In addition to six subtests that are always administered (vocabulary, comprehension, pattern analysis, quantitative, bead memory, and memory for sentences), age of the subject determines the use of the other subtests (absurdities, verbal relations, copying, matrices, paper folding and cutting, number series, equation building, memory for digits, and memory for objects). Approximate administration time is 1 hour.

Stanford Diagnostic Reading Test, Third Edition (SDRT) A diagnostic reading test with four levels (red, green, brown, and blue) to measure specific strengths and needs in reading.

stanine A single-digit scoring system with a mean of 5 and a standard deviation of 2. All stanines except 1 and 9 are one half of a standard deviation in width. They differ from standard scores, such as z-scores, t-scores, and deviation IQs, in that stanine scores are normalized or forced to fit the normal curve as closely as possible.

STARCH A variant of the acronym TORCH, amended to include acquired immunodeficiency syndrome (AIDS). *See* STORCH, TORCH.

staring spells *See* absence seizure.

startle response In the newborn, the startle response is very similar to the Moro reflex with extension of the extremities (arms or legs) followed by flexion; as the Moro fades between 2 and 6 months of age, the initial component of the startle is a protective flexion of the upper extremities. The startle can be part of the alerting response to sound in the first weeks of life.

state A key variable in Prechtl's neurological examination of infants; the depth of sleep, degree of alertness, and presence of crying are scored; the infant's state influences neurological findings and behavioral repertoire.

station The position or posture assumed in standing (or sitting).

status epilepticus A continuous seizure or multiple seizures occurring over a short period of time. Practically, status epilepticus is a seizure lasting 30 minutes or longer. Status epilepticus does not refer to the type of seizure, but only to its continuous and prolonged nature. Thus, one may have tonic-clonic status epilepticus, absence status epilepticus, complex partial (psychomotor) status epilepticus, and so forth. Status epilepticus is a medical emergency that requires treatment to stop the seizure and prevent brain damage that can occur secondary to such a prolonged seizure. Initial management includes the basic principles of cardiopulmonary resuscitation (CPR), maintaining the airway, breathing, and cardiac function. The remainder of the evaluation and treatment is aimed at determining the cause of the seizure activity and using an appropriate anticonvulsant medication to stop it. The outcome of status epilepticus depends on the cause and duration of the seizures. Prolonged status epilepticus often leads to brain damage manifested by a decrease in cognitive functioning, motor impairment (hemiplegia [paralysis of half the body], diplegia [paralysis on both sides of the body]), movement disorders, or cerebellar dysfunction. Rapid diagnosis and treatment have been shown to decrease the morbidity and mortality of status epilepticus.

status marmoratus Hypoxic-ischemic encephalopathy (brain damage due to lack of oxygen) that involves the basal ganglia and produces extrapyramidal cerebral palsy. The name derives from the marbled (i.e., marmoratus) appearance of the basal ganglia at autopsy.

steadiness tester A mechanical device to measure attention deficits, motor impersistence, hyperactivity, resting tremors, and choreiform (involuntary twitching) movements by having the child hold a stylus (pointer) in a hole (sometimes of varying sizes) without touching the sides. "Touch time" decreases with age and neurological maturation.

Steinert syndrome (myotonic dystrophy) An extremely variable genetic syndrome that represents a type of muscular dystrophy with mild motor symptoms and cataracts. Apathetic facies, a "hatchet face," or "lugubrious" appearance have been described in addition to dysarthria (difficulty pronouncing words). Mental retardation is rare, but learning disabilities are common. Inheritance occurs through an autosomal dominant gene located on the long arm of chromosome 19. When the syndrome is suspected, prenatal diagnosis is possible but is extremely complicated. Incidence is on the order of 1 in 10,000. Treatment is normally unnecessary, owing to the mildness of the disorder.

step length The distance covered in one step.

stepping A primitive reflex in which a newborn baby held in supported standing appears to "walk." Such newborn walking is readily elicited in the first 6 weeks of life, but then rapidly fades. Head extension facilitates the reflex.

stereognosis Form perception; the ability to identify objects by feel or touch. A component of the neurological assessment; problems with stereognosis are attributed to parietal lobe dysfunction.

stereotactic neurosurgery A group of procedures in which brain nuclei (control centers) are destroyed in order to improve movement. Thalamotomy to treat Parkinson disease in adults provided the paradigm; success in applying this type of procedure to cases of severe cerebral palsy has been limited to those of extrapyramidal type.

stereotypy Constantly repeated meaningless gestures or movements such as hand flapping. Stereotypy is common in autism and in self-stimulatory behaviors seen in individuals with severe mental retardation.

sternum The breastbone.

Stickler syndrome Hereditary progressive arthro-ophthalmopathy. A genetic syndrome with flat facies, progressive myopia (nearsightedness), and arthritis. Infants may present with the Pierre-Robin sequence, and a marfanoid habitus (appearance) may be noted later; up to half of Pierre-Robin anomalies (malformation, deformation, disruption, or dysplasia) may represent cases of Stickler syndrome. Total retinal (eye) detachment has been noted in over half the reported cases. Inheritance is autosomal dominant with a recurrence risk of 50%. Ophthalmological care for prevention and care of eye problems is indicated.

stiff baby syndrome *See* hyperexplexia.

stigmata Signs of a diagnosis or condition, usually physical.

stimulant Psychostimulant medication; a class of drugs used to treat attention deficit disorders and hyperactivity in children and adults. These drugs include dextroamphetamine (Dexedrine, DA), methylphenidate (Ritalin, MPH), and pemoline (Cylert). They are less effective in preschool children and people with mental retardation. The side effects of all these drugs are similar, with anorexia (loss of appetite) or appetite suppression primary.

stimulus Any object, action, or factor that causes an organism to act or that elicits a response; the input to a stimulus–response arc.

stoma Mouthlike opening; especially a surgically created drainage opening (e.g., colostomy, ureterostomy).

storage disease A subgroup of inborn errors of metabolism that tend to present late in infancy. These disorders are usually genetic in etiology (cause) and are characterized by the inability to break down certain compounds in the body, which then build up in the cells and cause damage and poor function of the involved organ system(s). The central nervous system is often involved, with a presentation of the loss of developmental milestones or developmental regression. Other organs that can be involved include the liver and the reticuloendothelial system (the organs that make and clear blood cells). Mucopolysaccharidoses are examples of storage diseases.

STORCH An acronym for the more common congenital or perinatal (around birth) infections that have many clinical similarities among them and can often be differentiated only by laboratory diagnosis. These include *Syphilis, Toxoplasmosis, Other* infections, *Rubella, Cytomegalovirus,* and *Herpes simplex virus.* Their common symptomology includes intrauterine growth retardation (stunting), jaundice (yellowing of the skin) or hepatitis (inflammation of the liver), hepatosplenomegaly (enlargement of the liver and spleen), cataracts or retinal (eye) involvement, microcephaly (abnormally small head), encephalitis (brain inflammation), and hearing defects. Hepatosplenomegaly and a skin rash are prominent in congenital syphilis; retinopathy and brain calcifications are common with toxoplasmosis; cataracts and heart disease with rubella; microcephaly, hearing loss, hepatitis, and a bleeding tendency with cytomegalovirus; skin rash, retinopathy, and encephalitis with herpes. They all can contribute to the occurrence of mental retardation.

stork bite *See* salmon patch.

strabismus Crossed eye, squint. A condition in which each eye looks at a different object, rather than the norm in which both eyes look at the same object. The causes of strabismus are muscle weakness, central nervous system disease (i.e., stroke, hemiplegia [paralysis of half the body]), or amblyopia (poorer vision in one eye). The eye deviation may be out-

strabismus

ward (i.e., exotropia), inward (i.e., esotropia), upward (i.e., hypertropia), or downward (i.e., hypotropia). Strabismus is treated by an ophthalmologist (a medical doctor trained in eye diseases) using glasses, patching, or occasionally surgery. Some forms of strabismus are inherited in an autosomal dominant manner. Strabismus is common in spastic cerebral palsy and myelomeningocele (protuberance of both the spinal cord and its lining).

stranger anxiety Childhood anxiety in the presence of unfamiliar people; also known as *8-month anxiety* or *organic bashfulness.* Severity may be muted in households with multiple caregivers. Age-inappropriate lack of wariness of strangers may reflect either cognitive limitations or emotional pathology (origin).

Stransky reflex The stimulus of suddenly releasing the abducted (turned outward) fifth (little) toe produces the response of dorsiflexion (upgoing movement of the toes) of the first (big) toe. A sign of pyramidal tract dysfunction.

Strauss syndrome Brain-damaged child syndrome; the neurobehavioral constellation of distractibility, perseveration, conceptual rigidity, emotional lability (changeability), and difficulty with figure–ground perception that was first reported in children with both mental retardation and cerebral palsy and was then extended to children without obvious evidence of brain pathology (origin). These symptoms became known as *minimal brain damage* (a term now outdated) and later were subsumed under the term *attention-deficit/hyperactivity disorder (ADHD).*

straw drinking A developmental feeding milestone with a wide range for age of first achievement: 12 to 36 months.

Straw Peter syndrome A literary reference describing the hyperactive child syndrome. The term comes from *Struwwelpeter* (1845), a 19th-century German children's book written by pediatrician Heinrich Hoffman (1809–1894). The title character's name has been variously translated as Straw Peter or Slovenly Peter, but is more accurately Shaggy-headed Peter, a possible reference to the minor dysmorphic (atypical) feature of electric hair often found in children with hyperactivity. Peter's friends, Cruel Fred and Fidgety Phil, personify other aspects of the syndrome. *See* attention-deficit/hyperactivity disorder (ADHD).

strephosymbolia Twisted symbols, letter reversals; an individual sign of learning and reading disorders that was stressed as fundamental by Samuel Orton (1879–1948).

stretch reflex The reflex contraction of a muscle when passively stretched; the resistance of the muscle to being longitudinally stretched.

stride length The distance covered in two steps, or one complete gait cycle.

stridor A harsh, high-pitched, shrill sound during inspiration associated with upper airway obstruction. Congenital laryngeal stridor is often associated with weakness in the walls of the windpipe. Such stridor may reflect an isolated airway abnormality that will resolve over time or a congenital defect that is part of a wider syndrome.

stroke A cerebrovascular accident (CVA). Damage to the brain caused by either a tear in a blood vessel with bleeding (i.e., hemorrhage) in the brain or a blockage in the vessel, reducing blood flow and oxygen to the tissue. Strokes can occur at or before birth and at any time during childhood. They are commonly associated with certain medical conditions such as sickle cell anemia, leukemia, or problems with the heart valves. They can also occur with malformations of the vessels in the brain such as a berry aneurysm. The damage from a stroke is usually to one side of the brain and thus presents with one-sided neurological findings. Resolution of the stroke with healing usually results in an improvement, but not always a complete disappearance of the impairments. Motor function is affected on the opposite side of the body from the brain damage, whereas cognitive function is affected on the same side.

Stroop test A neuropsychological measure of ease in shifting perceptual set and suppressing habitual responses in order to conform to changing demands. For example, in one version of the test, the subject must name the color ink in which nonmatching color names are printed; any resulting decrease in color-naming speed is referred to as the "color-word interference effect" and can be interpreted as suggesting left frontal lobe damage.

structural analysis A word attack skill involving the recognition of prefixes and suffixes that may be added to a root word in order to compound words or to change the meaning in a predictable fashion. Examples are prefixes—*un*happy, *pre*mature; suffixes—runn*ing*, hopp*ed*; compound words—raincoat, football.

structural theory The psychoanalytic division of mental function into the id, the ego, and the superego.

stupor A state of decreased consciousness in which the individual can only be aroused by painful stimuli.

Sturge-Weber syndrome Encephalofacial angiomatosis; a disorder with unilateral vascular malformations (birthmarks) on the face and eyes and ipsilateral (on the same side) involvement of the meninges (covering of the brain and spinal cord). The vascular (blood vessel) abnormalities are nonraised hemangiomas (similar to a port-wine stain) that can be seen on the face, generally in the distribution of the fifth cranial nerve. The hemangiomas of the meninges are involved, with cerebral calcifications ("railroad track" lines on skull X ray). Seizures are present in 56% of cases, and 30% will exhibit hemiplegia (paralysis of half the body). Many, but not all, of these children have mental retardation. Seizure control is often difficult. Etiology (cause) is unknown, but the clinical picture is consistent with a defect in the cephalic (head) neural crest that migrates to the meninges, the choroid of the eye, and the skin above the eye. Diagnosis can be made in the neonatal period. Treatment involves seizure management and special education.

stuttering A disorder in the rhythm of speech that includes sound, syllable, and word repetitions, prolongations, pauses, and hesitations often accompanied by anxious, tense, and avoidant behaviors. Stuttering is more common in males with a familial susceptibility but no clearly defined genetic transmission pattern. Stuttering is not indicative of occult (internal) developmental disorders.

STYCAR *See* Screening Tests for Young Children and Retardates.

subacute sclerosing panencephalitis (SSPE) A degenerative disease of the central nervous system associated with a persistent measles virus infection of the brain. The insidious course of this slow virus infection includes mental deterioration, myoclonic seizures, visual impairment, and a variety of movement disorders progressing to opisthotonus (an arching of the back) and decorticate rigidity. The electroencephalogram (EEG) shows suppression bursts.

subarachnoid hemorrhage Bleeding into the subarachnoid space in the head; usually seen in hypoxic (lowered oxygen to the brain) premature infants; it has a good prognosis for recovery, although hydrocephalus (excess fluid in the brain) may occur.

subcutaneous Under the skin.

subluxation Incomplete or partial dislocation of a bone at its joint.

submucous cleft A palpable defect in the hard palate that is not immediately visible because it is covered with normal oral mucosa; it can be suspected in the presence of a bifid (cleft) uvula and a white line running down the middle of the roof of the mouth. Submucous clefts can contribute to severe articulation disorders.

subspecialist A physician (M.D. or D.O.) who has completed a fellowship training program (at least 2 years beyond the requirements for specialty certification) in a restricted area of a specialty. Examples include pediatric surgery (under the area of surgery), neonatal-perinatal medicine (under pediatrics), and nephrology (under internal medicine). A Certificate of Special Qualifications nationally certifies most subspecialty practitioners.

substance abuse The use of a substance (either legal or illegal) that deviates from accepted social, medical, or legal patterns.

substance dependence The psychological and/or physiological dependence on a drug, either legal or illegal.

subtest scatter The degree of variability of an individual's scores on specific components of a test. The highs and lows comprise a profile that indicates strengths and weaknesses in particular areas as defined in specific subtests. The term is most commonly used with intellectual assessment, though it may be applied to any multiple subtest battery of basic skills, adaptive behavior, or academic achievement. The precise role that this scatter has in diagnosing and differentiating among populations and conditions has not been definitively determined. Scatter occurs frequently in the general population, so care must be taken when determining if scatter is rare or different from that of the general population before associating it with significant deviance or abnormality. However, characteristic scatter has been reported consistently for specific groups. For example, low scores on arithmetic, comprehension, information, and digit span subtests of the Wechsler Intelligence Scale for Children–Revised (WISC–R) have been shown to characterize the performance of several groups of children with learning disabilities. Yet such categories and score performance profiles of the WISC–R often have no clinical significance when subjected to meta-analysis (a quantitative method for integrating data across studies). Thus, learning disabilities are more likely to be indicated by individual differences than by set profiles. Scatter has been associated with behavior, emotional, and organic problems, as well as with learning disabilities. Analysis of subtest scatter, although not recommended by itself as a diagnostic standard, is helpful in the diagnostic process and in educational intervention planning.

subthalamic syndrome Hemichorea and hemiballismus; a syndrome of chorea and/or ballismus on one side of the body secondary to a lesion in the contralateral (opposite) subthalamic nucleus (corpus Luysii).

subtraction The most common source of error that occurs during calculation of test scores and subscores (especially in relation to determining a child's age).

subtrainable An older term lumping together severe and profound mental retardation; now considered pejorative.

sucking Propulsion of food into the mouth by creating negative pressure in the oral cavity by a complex interaction of the lips, tongue, and cheeks. This phase of oral feeding follows suckling between 6 and 9 months of age and is characterized by vertical (up and down) tongue movements and jaw opening/closing.

suckling An early infantile version of sucking. Suckling is an oral motor reflex that represents the earliest intake phase for liquids with a definite backward (more pronounced)-forward, horizontal (in-out) tongue movement in a rhythmic licking action. Suckling begins in the second to third trimester of gestation and may persist to 12 months of age. It is innervated by cranial nerves V, VII, IX, and XII.

sulcus A groove or furrow, especially one separating the gyri (hills) on the surface of the brain.

sunset sign *See* setting sun sign.

supernumerary An excess number (e.g., a sixth finger on a hand, a third nipple on the chest).

supersensitivity A hypothetical mechanism of recovery after brain damage in which surviving neurons in the damaged system become increasingly sensitive to neurotransmitter molecules, thus allowing them to function in a deprived state.

supination Forearm movement that turns the palm upward.

supine An anatomical position in which the individual is lying face upward on the back (opposite of prone).

Supplemental Security Income (SSI) A federally funded income maintenance program that provides people with developmental disabilities a minimum monthly income. Although administered through the Social Security Administration, SSI funds are separate from social insurance funds that support Social Security income to retired elderly people without disabilities. In practice, SSI may be partially supplemented or supplanted by other entitlement programs; however, the goal for the individual is to maintain a minimum monthly income. Established in 1972, SSI consolidated previous programs for people who are blind and those with hearing impairments into one program. Eligibility to receive SSI requires evidence of both disability and low income.

support group Self-help group; voluntary small groups formed for mutual help and to accomplish a specific purpose. Although support groups may employ professional facilitators, they are typically composed of peers who have joined together to help and support each other in satisfying a common need, coping with a common problem, or targeting and seeking a desired social change. Such groups employ face-to-face interactions and assume personal responsibility by group members. Many parents of children with developmental disabilities find support group input a vital tool for education and emotional support in meeting the demands of their children and families. Active support groups include the Down Syndrome Association, Prader-Willi Syndrome Association, Williams Syndrome Association, and the Rett Syndrome Association.

supported employment On-the-job coaching that supports the worker with mental retardation (or other developmental disabilities) in a competitive employment situation. The term *supported employment* embraces the processes of job placement, job coaching, and continuous support in and on the job.

supported living A coordinated system of supports clustering around the individual with disabilities and designed to facilitate that person's choices to live, work, learn, and actively participate with people without disabilities in the community. Supported living is based on the philosophy that people with developmental disabilities have a right to make responsible decisions consistent with the choices afforded people without disabilities. The system includes life skills and vocational training, protective oversight, environmental adaptations, and physical assistance. The aim is to normalize the individual with developmental disabilities into the mainstream society by bringing services to him or her, rather than placing the individual in a segregated facility that provides such services.

suppression burst activity An electroencephalographic (EEG) pattern with a depressed or flat background accompanied by high-voltage bursts of slow waves with intermingled spikes. This pattern is frequent in comatose people.

suprabulbar paresis *See* pseudobulbar palsy.

surfactant A phospholipid (chemical) that contributes to the elasticity of pulmonary tissue (the lungs). Preterm babies have less surfactant, so that it is harder for their lungs to breathe. Artificial surfactant is now being used in the treatment of respiratory distress syndrome (RDS) in such babies.

surfactant replacement therapy A treatment for respiratory distress syndrome (RDS) that increases the survival rate of very premature infants with less of an effect on the incidence of disabilities in the survivors.

surrender posture *See* tonic labyrinthine response.

swallowing The neuromuscular process in which liquids and solids move from the mouth into the stomach via the esophagus (throat). Swallowing is both voluntary and involuntary; in newborn infants swallowing follows automatically on sucking; later it will be dissociated from sucking. This oral motor reflex is innervated by cranial nerves V, VII, IX, X, and XII.

swing phase The part of the gait cycle when the index foot is not in contact with the ground, from toe-off to heel strike; swing phase represents 40% of the gait cycle.

Sydenham chorea One of five major manifestations of rheumatic fever (arthritis, carditis, subcutaneous [inner] nodules, and rash being the other four) after streptococcal infection. The grimacing, wriggling, and writhing can briefly be brought under voluntary control, but are exaggerated by excitement. Like most extrapyramidal symptoms, the chorea disappears during sleep. This disorder is transient, more frequent in girls, and can include emotional lability (changeability), handwriting deterioration, "making faces," "society smile," variable hand grip, and sustained knee-jerks. Thomas Sydenham (1624–1689), the "English Hippocrates," first described this condition in 1686.

Sydney line A palmar crease pattern in which the proximal crease runs completely across the palm. This variant was first identified in rubella embryopathy in Sydney, Australia. It is a minor dysmorphic (atypical) feature that may be found as part of other neurodevelopmental disorders.

Sydney line

Sylvian epilepsy *See* benign rolandic epilepsy.

symmetric tonic neck reflex "Cat reflex" or "cat posture." A primitive reflex in which neck extension produces upper extremity extension and lower extremity flexion ("cat looking up"), and neck flexion produces upper extremity flexion and lower extremity extension ("cat eating"). This reflex pattern is

symmetric tonic neck reflex

both transient (occurring at around 2 months of age) and faint in typically developing infants; exaggeration or persistance of this pattern strongly suggests serious neuromotor impairment such as cerebral palsy.

sympathetic nervous system Adrenergic system; that division of the autonomic nervous system that responds to threats or danger by a "fight or flight" reaction; this reaction is mediated by a burst or rush of adrenalin. Also characterized as *thoracolumbar* or *catabolic.*

symphysis pubis The most anterior (front) bone of the pelvis just above the genital area.

symptom A subjective concern of a person; the individual's (or parent's) report of pain, discomfort, morbid appearance, or dysfunction; a component of the history. The chief complaint is the symptom that precipitates a diagnostic assessment. Symptoms are subjective; signs are objective. Signs indicate a past or present disease process; symptoms indicate an illness that may or may not reflect an underlying disease process.

symptom complex Syndrome.

symptomatology A collection of symptoms; the study of such collections. Some groupings of symptoms suggest specific diagnoses; other groupings do not at first point to a diagnosis but are only coincidentally present in one individual.

syndactyly Webbing or fusion of fingers or toes; a physical feature found in a number of syndromes. In its mild form, it is a common nonspecific minor dysmorphic (atypical) feature.

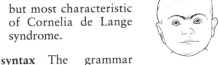

syndactyly

syndrome Literally, "a running together." The term is used to denote a concurrence of signs and symptoms associated with, and together comprising, the clinical presentation of a disease or disorder. Syndromes can be genetic, dysmorphic (atypical appearance), behavioral, or complaint oriented. Older syndromes were eponymous—named after the person who first described the association—such as Down syndrome. There is a tendency to replace eponyms with etiologies (causes); thus, Down syndrome has become trisomy 21. But etiology has receding layers, so there are translocation and other trisomies. In dysmorphology, a syndrome reflects a greater understanding of pathogenesis (origin) than an association, but less understanding than a sequence. Some syndromes are named by a listing of involved organs (e.g., oto-palato-digital or ear-palate-finger syndrome) or by acronyms (e.g., OPD). Loosely, the term *syndrome* can refer to any patterned association; thus, there are, for example, literary and artistic syndromes.

syndromic Pertaining to a syndrome; suggestive of the presence of a specific syndrome or a nonspecific syndrome, the latter because of the presence of dysmorphic (atypical appearance) features. *Synonyms:* dysmorphic.

synergistic movement pattern Simultaneous flexion (or extension) at all joints in an extremity such as hip/knee/ankle.

synergy Cooperation between muscles to perform an action or to pathologically lock the individual into an abnormal pattern of flexion/extension.

synkinesia Associated or overflow movements on the ipsilateral (same) side of the body; synkinesia suggests central nervous system immaturity.

synophrys Eyebrows that meet in the middle; an abnormality of facial hair distribution found in a number of conditions but most characteristic of Cornelia de Lange syndrome.

synophrys

syntax The grammar system of a language by which words are arranged in order into phrases and sentences according to specific rules. These rules may vary with languages. Imperfect understanding of these rules may lead to the misunderstanding of meaning. Misuse of syntax has been related to sequential processing impairments.

syringoma   A small skin-colored or slightly yellow, firm papule (raised skin lesion) that appears in crops in the periorbital (around the eye) area. These benign lesions are common in persons with Down syndrome after puberty.

syringomelia   A tubular-shaped area in the brain stem or spinal cord. Also termed *hydrosyringomyelia*, this is often found associated with an Arnold-Chiari malformation or a spinal cord tumor, or as a posttraumatic occurrence. The initial symptoms of loss of pain and temperature sensation generally do not occur until adult life. As the syrinx (tube) enlarges, symptoms progress to include spasticity (increased muscle tone), hyperreflexia (increased reflexes), loss of position and vibratory sense, and rapidly progressing scoliosis (spinal curvature). Diagnosis is made by magnetic resonance imaging (MRI) scan. Treatment includes surgical decompression of the spinal cord.

systemic   Relating to the entire organism; widespread. The opposite of local or localized.

T

tache cérébrale Gently stroking the skin with a fingernail to produce a red streak bounded by pale margins (in contrast to dermatographia, in which a pale streak is bounded by red margins); this sign is present in meningitis (inflammation of the spinal cord and brain membranes), hydrocephalus (excess fluid in the brain), and a variety of febrile (feverish) illnesses.

tachyphylaxis A term typically employed when describing a rapid onset of resistance to the therapeutic effect of medication. For example, when the antihistamine diphenhydramine (Benadryl) is used to help get a child to sleep at night, the effect wears off in several weeks.

tachypnea Rapid breathing with an increased respiratory rate; one of the signs of respiratory distress for a variety of reasons, including pneumonia.

TACL–R *See* Test for Auditory Comprehension of Language–Revised.

tactile Relating to the sense of touch. People who are blind utilize the tactile sensory modality when learning to read braille. Educators have used this modality as an adjunct to the more traditional visual and auditory modalities with preschoolers and with students experiencing difficulty learning to read. This may include tracing sandpaper letters or drawing shapes in clay. The Fernald Word Learning Technique is a structured method for incorporating both tactile and kinesthetic modalities with auditory and visual modalities in learning to read.

tactile defensiveness Tactile hypersensitivity; a sensory integrative dysfunction characterized by observable aversive or negative behavioral responses to certain types of tactile (touch) stimuli that most people would find non-noxious (not painful). Strong emotional reactions, hyperactivity, and other behavior problems may occur. Sensory integration theory hypothesizes that this affective misinterpretation of tactile experience is the effect of a disorder in the modulation or regulation of tactile sensory input.

Tactile Test of Basic Concepts An adaptation of the Boehm Test of Basic Concepts that substitutes raised figures for pictures to predict success in kindergarten and first grade.

Tagamet *See* cimetidine.

TAL *See* tendo Achilles lengthening.

talipes equinovarus Clubfoot; a (usually congenital) deformity of the foot. The term derives from talus (heel/ankle), pes (foot), equinus (an involuntary foot extension), and varus (inversion/supination of the foot so that only the outer sole touches the ground). This deformity has a polygenic mode of inheritance with a threshold effect; the greater its rate of occurrence in a family, the greater the risk of its recurrence with an increasing severity. Clubfoot is also found in cerebral palsy, spina bifida, arthrogryposis (fixation of joints), and a variety of genetic syndromes. Orthopedic treatment should take into account etiology (cause). The presence of any otherwise unexplained congenital orthopedic deformity in a newborn should lead to the consideration of a possible neurodevelopmental diagnosis.

talus Ankle bone.

tandem walking Toe–heel gait; walking in a straight line with the toes of one foot and the heel of the other being in contact at the end of every step. A sensitive indicator of problems with balance.

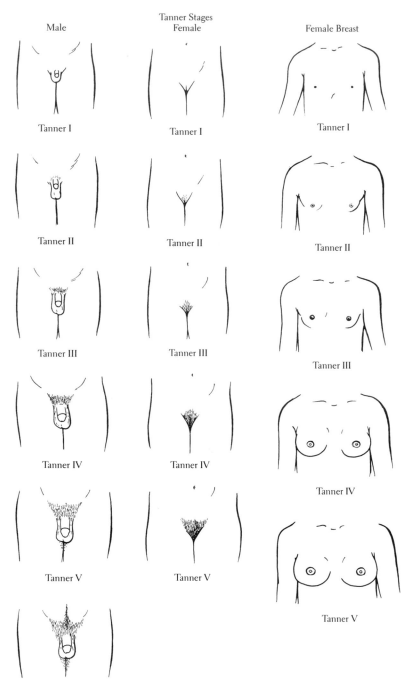

Tanner stages A scoring system for rating sexual maturation of male genetalia, female pubic hair, and female breast development that is especially useful in the physical examination of adolescents. There is no stage 0; preadolescent/early childhood sexual maturity ratings are all Tanner I. Tanner V/VI represents the mature adult stage.

TAPS *See* Test of Auditory-Perceptual Skills.

tardive dyskinesia Choreiform (involuntary twitching) movements that can result from the use of neuroleptic (major tranquilizer) medications. These movements occur late (i.e., *tardive*) in the course of therapy and tend to be limited to stereotypic face/tongue/mouth activities, such as chewing and lip smacking, facial grimacing, blinking, tongue thrusting, and writhing movements of the fingers, hands, and toes. The overall incidence is on the order of 1%, and in children the tardive dyskinesia tends to resolve when the drugs are discontinued.

tarsus The instep of the foot. Tarsi palpebrarum are the edges of the eyelid.

TASH *See* The Association for Persons with Severe Handicaps.

TAT *See* Thematic Apperception Test.

TAWF *See* Test of Adolescent/Adult Word Finding.

Tay Sachs disease A lipid storage disease characterized by typical development until 4–6 months of age, when progressive loss of motor and other developmental milestones occurs. Classic features include psychomotor retardation, hypotonia (decreased muscle tone), loss of interest in surroundings, poor head control, and apathy. Visual acuity decreases, and the retina (light-sensitive inner back wall) shows a characteristic cherry red spot on the macula. Seizures may occur, as can macrocephaly (abnormally large head) in the final stages. The biochemical defect is a lack of breakdown of a chemical in the brain called a *ganglioside* by the enzyme hexosaminidase *A*. The course is one of progressive intellectual and neurological deterioration leading to death in middle childhood. Diagnosis is made by clinical history and measuring the level of the defective enzyme hexosaminidase *A* in serum. Tay Sachs disease is found most commonly in Jewish families from Eastern Europe. Although there is currently a prenatal screening test available, there is to date no known treatment. Inheritance follows an autosomal recessive pattern.

Tay syndrome *See* IBIDS syndrome.

TCA *See* tricyclic antidepressant.

TDD *See* Telecommunicating Devices for the Deaf.

TEACCH *See* Treatment and Education of Autistic and Communications handicapped CHildren.

Technology-Related Assistance for Individuals with Disabilities Act of 1988 (PL 100-407) Federal legislation designed to assist states in developing comprehensive and consumer-responsive programs involving technology-related assistance and in expanding the availability of such technology to individuals with disabilities and their families. To give states considerable flexibility in developing and implementing their programs, "assistive technology device" is broadly defined as "any item, piece of equipment, or product system, whether acquired off the shelf, modified or customized, that is used to maintain or improve functional capabilities of individuals with disabilities." Under this law, assistive technology services encompass eight activities related to developing services that are responsive to the consumer. In addition to the efforts made by the states, the federal government is authorized to assist states in a variety of ways to help them develop their service delivery systems.

Technology-Related Assistance for Individuals with Disabilities Amendments of 1994 (PL 103-218) Federal legislation that refunded the original legislation, PL 100-407, allowed its extension to states that had not previously enrolled, and strengthened the advocacy and systems change components of the act.

teething Eruption of teeth through the gums, often associated with drooling, mouthing, irritability, and low-grade fever.

TEF *See* tracheoesophageal fistula.

TELD–2 *See* Test of Early Language Development–Second Edition.

telecanthus Lateral displacement of the inner canthi (angle of the eyelid slits) giving rise to an increased inner canthal distance can contribute to both pseudostrabismus (false squint or crossed eyes) and pseudohypertelorism (false impression of widely spaced eyes).

Telecommunicating Devices for the Deaf (TDD) Communication apparatuses that allow individuals with hearing impairments to receive and send messages via telephone. The sender types in a message that is transmitted via telephone lines to a visual receiver (either a display screen or a receiving typing machine that types the message). TDDs are becoming increasingly available and are routinely used by police and fire departments as well as other public service agencies including libraries, airlines, utility companies, and schools.

telegraphic speech Highly condensed noun–verb utterances with few to no adjectives, adverbs, prepositions, conjunctions, articles, and auxiliary verbs. Transiently observed in early language development, the presence of telegraphic speech in older children suggests language disorders.

TEMA–2 *See* Test of Early Mathematics Ability–2.

temperature A measurement of body heat; often used colloquially as an inaccurate synonym for fever (e.g., "he has a temperature," meaning elliptically, "he has an elevated temperature").

temporal cortex The area of the brain responsible for the reception and interpretation of sound, including speech; damage to this area of the dominant (usually left) hemisphere can contribute to a wide variety of aphasias (loss of language skills) (e.g., Wernicke aphasia) and other language disorders. *See also* primary auditory cortex (A1).

temporal cortex/lobe

temporal lobe The part of the cerebrum located underneath the frontal and parietal lobes. This part of the brain appears to be related to memory and a variety of autonomic (automatic), motor, and sensory responses.

temporomandibular joint (TMJ) The hinge at which the lower jaw connects to the skull. In addition to causing local pain or tenderness, TMJ problems have been implicated in nonspecific symptoms such as dizziness, headache, backache, and chronic fatigue. No convincing evidence supports a role for TMJ in the etiology (cause) of developmental disabilities.

tendo Achilles lengthening (TAL) Any one of a variety of orthopedic surgery procedures used to lengthen a short, tight, or spastic heel cord. The procedure may be a Z lengthening or a sliding lengthening.

tendon Connective tissue structure that attaches a muscle to a bone.

tendon reflex *See* deep-tendon reflex (DTR).

tendon transfer An orthopedic surgery procedure that realigns abnormal forces at a joint. The procedure corrects posture and improves movement by reinserting a tendon so as to give the contraction of the treated muscle a different impact on posture and movement. The treated muscle need not initially contribute to the original deformity or disorder.

tenotomy A surgical operation in which a tendon is cut; most tenotomies are orthopedic in nature; however, some eye muscle surgeries also involve tenotomy.

TERA–2 *See* Test of Early Reading Ability–2.

teratogen A chemical or physical agent that causes or increases the incidence of congenital malformations. Teratogens are intrauterine toxins (poisons) to the fetus and generally have the biggest impact early in pregnancy. Human teratogens that produce known syndromes include alcohol, hydantoin (Dilantin), trimethadione, thalidomide, valproic acid (Depakene), diethylstilbestrol (DES), warfarin (Coumadin), aminopterin, and isotretinoin (Accutane).

terbutaline A beta-sympathomimetic drug used to treat preterm labor and prevent premature birth.

test A historical fact, physical sign, or laboratory value that has diagnostic value.

Test for Auditory Comprehension of Language–Revised (TACL–R) A language test for children from 3-0 through 9-11 years of age that can also be administered to adults. The TACL–R yields scores for word classes and relations, grammatical morphemes, and elaborated sentences.

Test of Adolescent/Adult Word Finding (TAWF) A standardized test of word-finding skills for persons aged 12-0 to 80. Naming tasks are organized into five sections: picture naming (nouns), picture naming (verbs), sentence completion naming, description naming, and category naming.

Test of Adolescent Language–2 (TOAL–2) A language test for children ages 12-0 through 18-5. It yields an adolescent language quotient (ALQ) and 10 composite subscores in listening, speaking, reading, writing, spoken language, written language, vocabulary, grammar, receptive language, and expressive language. Each subtest and an overall composite yields a standard score with a mean of 100 and a standard deviation of 15.

Test of Auditory-Perceptual Skills (TAPS) A 15-minute battery of auditory-perceptual tasks for children 4–12 years of age. Subtests include auditory number memory, auditory sentence memory, auditory word memory, and auditory interpretation of directions.

Test of Early Language Development– Second Edition (TELD–2) A norm-referenced measure of spoken language abilities for children ages 2-0 through 7-11 that yields an overall language score and an expanded diagnostic profile. Receptive and expressive language is assessed by 38 items in a variety of semantic (meaning systems)/(language structure) and syntactic tasks. Administration time is 20 minutes.

Test of Early Mathematics Ability–2 (TEMA–2) A norm-referenced measure of early mathematics performance for children ages 3-0 through 8-11. This 15-minute test is used to determine specific strengths and weaknesses in a child's mathematics knowledge.

Test of Early Reading Ability–2 (TERA–2) A measure of reading ability for children from 3-0 to 9-11 years of age. Items measure knowledge of contextual meaning, alphabet, and conventions. Two equivalent forms allow test–retest comparisons.

Test of Early Written Language (TEWL) A measure of the emerging written language skills of young children ages 3–7. Test items cover transcription, conventions of print, communication, creative expression, and record keeping.

Test of Language Competence–Expanded Edition (TLC–Expanded) An instrument to identify language and communication impairments in children ages 5–19. TLC–Expanded includes the following subtests: ambiguous sentences, listening comprehension, oral expression, figurative language, and remembering word pairs.

Test of Language Development–2 (TOLD–2) Tests measuring several components of spoken language. The primary-level edition is designed for ages 4-0 to 8-11; seven subtests measure different components of spoken language: picture vocabulary, oral vocabulary, grammatical understanding, sentence imitation, grammatical completion, word articulation, and word discrimination. The intermediate edition, for ages 8-6 to 12-11, has six subtests: general, malapropisms, vocabulary, sentence combining, word ordering, and grammatical comprehension. Both editions combine subtests to provide composites of listening (receptive language), speaking (expressive language), semantics (the meaning of words), and syntax (grammar). The TOLD–2 primary edition also includes a phonology (speech sound) composite.

Test of Mathematical Abilities (TOMA) An instrument designed to identify students significantly above or below their peers in 1) attitude toward mathematics, 2) vocabulary, 3) computation, 4) general information, and 5) story problems. Normative tables are provided for ages 8-6 through 18-11.

Test of Nonverbal Intelligence–2 (TONI–2) A language-free measure of intelligence, aptitude, and reasoning that requires no reading, writing, speaking, or listening on the part of the subject. The test includes two equivalent forms for people ages 5-0 through 85-11 (including individuals with severe speech impairments, brain injury, and deafness or hearing loss). Each item presents a set of figures in which one or more components is missing. The individual must identify one or more problem-solving rules that define the relationship among the figures and then select a correct response. The test is typically administered individually but can be given to small groups of as many as five individuals by an experienced examiner. Administration usually takes 10–15 minutes. The TONI–2 yields standard scores (with a mean of 100 and a standard deviation of 15) and percentiles.

Test of Practical Knowledge (TPK) A reading level of ninth grade or beyond is required for this test, which assesses knowledge believed to be necessary for daily functioning. The three areas assessed are 1) personal knowledge relating to day-to-day independent living, 2) social knowledge relating to understanding of social interaction and community ser-

vice, and 3) occupational knowledge assessing knowledge relating to job situations. The TPK can be administered individually or in groups via a silent-reading multiple-choice format. The test is not suitable for students with severe disabilities, non–English-speaking students, or students who lack motivation.

Test of Pragmatic Language (TOPL) An individually administered, norm-referenced test for children 5-0 to 13-11 years of age that measures ability to use pragmatic language (i.e., language used socially to achieve goals and emphasizing not only what is said but why and for what purpose it is said). Administration time is 45 minutes; the test can be used as a criterion-referenced assessment for older individuals.

Test of Pragmatic Skills–Revised Edition (TOPS–R) A test to assess the use of language by children ages 3-0 to 8-11 to signify conversational intent through four guided play interactions. The test probes the conversational intentions of requesting information, requesting action, rejection/denial, norming/labeling, answering/responding, informing, reasoning, summoning/calling, greeting, and closing conversation. This is a standardized assessment instrument, but is typically administered on the floor in order to create a "nontesting" environment for the child.

Test of Reading Comprehension–Revised (TORC–R) A test of silent-reading comprehension for students ages 7–17 years. Four subtests are combined to determine a basic comprehension score that is expressed as a reading comprehension quotient. These subtests include general vocabulary (the ability to identify words that are related to a common concept), syntactic (language structure) similarities (the understanding of meaningfully similar but syntactically different sentences), paragraph reading (the ability to answer questions related to paragraphs), and sentence sequencing (the ability to build plausible relationships among sentences). Supplementary subtests measure reading the vocabularies of mathematics, science, and social studies; reading directions; and sequencing sentences.

Test of Variables of Attention (TOVA) Formerly, Minnesota Computer Assessment (MCA). An objective, standardized, visual continuous performance task used in the diagnosis and medication management of children and adults with attentional disorders. This is a non–language-based, 23-minute, fixed-interval computerized test with negligible practice effects.

Test of Visual-Motor Skills (TVMS) A 26-item design copying test for children ages 2–13 years. The TVMS was developed to measure how well the child translates with his or her hand what is visually perceived.

Test of Visual-Perceptual Skills (TVPS) A nonmotor multiple choice (by pointing) response measure of the following visual skills: discrimination, memory, spatial relationships, form constancy, sequential memory, figure–ground, and closure; the 16 items in each subtest yield perceptual ages, perceptual quotients, and percentile ranks.

Test of Word Knowledge (TOWK) An assessment of receptive and expressive vocabulary for children 5–17 years of age with an administration time of under 1 hour.

Test of Written Language–Second Edition (TOWL–2) A test of language components, including conventional (punctuation, capitalization, and spelling), linguistic (word usage and vocabulary), and conceptual (maturity and effectiveness) for children ages 7-6 through 17-11 using both contrived and spontaneous formats. Five subtests are provided in the contrived format: 1) vocabulary—a stimulus word is read by the student and is then used in a composed written sentence; 2) spelling, 3) style—the student writes dictated sentences, with each sentence scored for each subtest; 4) logical sentences—sentences are read and rewritten to eliminate the illogical element; and 5) sentence combining—several sentences are read

and combined into one written sentence. The spontaneous format requires the student to view a picture and write a story that is then scored for thematic maturity, conceptual vocabulary, syntatic (language structure) maturity, contextual spelling, and contextual style.

Test of Written Spelling–2 (TWS–2) An assessment of spelling that may be administered individually or to groups in grades 1–12. The TWS–2 assesses the student's spelling of words whose spellings are readily predictable in sound–letter patterns; words with spellings that are less predictable; and both types together. Administration time is 20 minutes; the TWS–2 yields a spelling quotient.

testing of limits Modification or deviation from standard test administration procedures to gain additional information about a child's abilities. Testing of limits techniques include providing additional information, presenting or accepting information in an alternate form, encouraging the child's own problem-solving strategies, eliminating time limits, and asking probing questions. These techniques should only be used after the entire test has been administered in its standardized form. Successes obtained through testing of limits are not added to the child's score, although the information obtained from testing of limits procedures can often be helpful in clinical and psychoeducational settings. Such testing can validate or threaten future test results if retesting is likely to occur within a short time period.

Tests of General Educational Development (GED) A measure for determining whether an individual meets requirements for a certificate of high school equivalency. A successfully completed GED is generally accepted as the equivalent of a high school diploma.

tethered cord A dysraphic condition like myelomeningocele (protuberance of both the spinal cord and its lining) in which the spinal cord's natural movement upward during the growth of the bony spinal column is impeded. This can occur because of a tumor, scar tissue, or catching the spinal cord on a bony spur, resulting in traction on the cord and damage to the nerve cells. A tethered cord is suspected when there is loss of motor skills, sensation, or sphincter function. Diagnosis is made by computed tomography (CT) scan or magnetic resonance imaging (MRI). Treatment is generally surgical in nature with the goal being to loosen the traction on the cord and to restore neurological function.

tetraphocomelia Cleft palate syndrome. Roberts–SC phocomelia syndrome, SC syndrome, pseudothalidomide syndrome, hypomelia-hypotrichosis-facial hemangioma syndrome; a genetic syndrome with hypomelia (shortness) of all four extremities (arms or legs), cleft lip and palate, and mental retardation. Inheritance follows an autosomal recessive pattern.

tetraplegia An old term for quadriplegia (paralysis of all four extremities [arms or legs]).

tetrasomy 12p *See* Killian/Teschler-Nicola syndrome.

TEWL *See* Test of Early Written Language.

texture A qualitative gradation of food used in assessing and treating feeding and its disorders; texture involves both viscosity (thickness or thinness) and consistency (smoothness or coarseness).

TFC *See* three-finger crease.

thalamotomy A neurosurgical procedure (brain operation) sometimes used in treating dystonia (impaired muscle tone) and cerebral palsy.

thalidomide embryopathy Fetal thalidomide syndrome. Reduction deformities of the limbs with a shortening or absence of several to all bones in the extremities (arms or legs) sometimes leading to phocomelia. Many other organ systems can be involved. Etiology (cause) is maternal ingestion of thalidomide during the first 1–1½ months of pregnancy.

The Arc Formerly Association for Retarded Citizens of the United States

(ARC–US). The Arc is a national network of state and locally based parent–professional cooperatives that provide a range of services to individuals with mental retardation. The association defines its mission as that of conducting programs that promote the general welfare of people with mental retardation. Services provided by each local unit are dependent upon local financing. The acronym usually begins with a regional designation such as SLARC (St. Louis Association for Retarded Citizens) or MARC (Missouri Association for Retarded Citizens). In 1991, the national association changed its name to The Arc.

The Association for Persons with Severe Handicaps (TASH) An organization of professionals in partnership with people with disabilities, their families, and others involved in education, research, and advocacy on behalf of individuals with severe cognitive impairments and their families. The association publishes a newsletter and a quarterly journal.

The Association for Retarded Citizens of the United States *See* The Arc.

thelarche The onset of breast development in adolescent females.

Thematic Apperception Test (TAT) A commonly used projective technique originally published in 1943 by Henry Murray. The test utilizes over 24 picture cards, some depicting everyday life experiences and others that are more bizarre and ambiguous in form. Different combinations of cards, selected for age and sex, are used with male and female adults and boys and girls. The subject is asked to tell a story about the picture, indicating what is currently happening, how the story ends, and what the characters are thinking and feeling.

thenar (radial) longitudinal crease A crease on the palm of the hand; the "lifeline" of palmistry. (*Thenar* refers to the fleshy mass over the ball of the thumb.)

thenar crease

therapeutic handling Optimal techniques for transporting, positioning, and physically interacting with children and adults with motor disorders or hypersensitivity to such handling; goals include both relaxation and maximizing the individual's independence.

therapeutic range A term usually used in reference to treatment with a drug, the therapeutic range is the upper and lower blood levels (concentrations generally expressed in micrograms of drug per milliliter of serum [the blood without the cells]) within which a desired effect is achieved without undesirable side effects. These ranges are specific to each drug and are commonly used with anticonvulsants, antibiotics, antidepressants, and asthma medications. In certain cases, levels above the therapeutic range will be more effective without undue side effects. Many medications do not have reliable therapeutic ranges, and therefore levels are not routinely determined.

thermoregulation The body's ability to control its temperature, a function of the autonomic nervous system. Severe damage to the brain centers involved can produce episodic hyperpyrexia (fever) or poikilothermic behavior (fluctuation of body temperature in response to environmental temperature). Thermoregulatory disorders are common in babies born severely prematurely and in people with profound mental retardation.

thioridazine Trade name Mellaril; a phenothiazine used to treat hyperactivity and severe behavior disorders in people with mental retardation; it has an appetite-increasing effect and at therapeutic levels adversely affects (lowers) IQ.

third-degree relative A first cousin; someone who has one eighth of his or her genes in common with the index case (identified patient).

13q- Deletion of part of the long arm of chromosome 13; a chromosomal disorder with mental retardation, microcephaly (abnormally small head), a peculiar facies, eye abnormalities, and hypoplastic (short to absent) thumbs.

thoracic Relating to the thorax (chest); the curve of the thoracic spine is concave forward; when exaggerated, it produces kyphosis ("round shoulders").

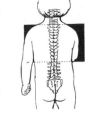

thoracic spine

thoracolumbar sacral orthosis (TLSO) A brace to treat scoliosis (spinal curvature).

three-finger crease (TFC) The distal transverse palmar crease.

three jaw chuck draw A phase describing a primitive form of grasp similar to the manner in which a drill head holds its bits.

tibia Shinbone; the larger of the two leg bones; *see also* fibula.

tibial torsion, internal Toeing in, due to a leg problem and not a foot problem.

tic Repetitive twitching, often in the face or upper trunk. Examples include eye blinking, grimacing, and shrugging. There are also vocal tics such as sniffing, coughing, or clearing of the throat. Gilles de La Tourette syndrome is a disorder expressed by severe motor and vocal tics.

TIE *See* Touch Inventory for Elementary School-Aged Children.

time-out (TO) A behavioral procedure in which the subject is temporarily (usually only for minutes) removed from the environment where the environmental stimuli are precipitating undesirable behaviors.

tine test A screening skin test for tuberculosis that involves four small pinpricks that are then observed for a local reaction 2–3 days later. The tine is one of the four prongs used to administer the test.

tinea Ringworm; a fungal infection.

Title I of the Elementary and Secondary Education Act of 1965 The federal government's first effort to provide compensatory education services for educationally disadvantaged and low-income students; *see*

Chapter 1 of the Education Consolidation and Improvement Act of 1980.

Title I Program *See* Chapter 1 of the Education Consolidation and Improvement Act of 1980.

Title V of the Social Security Act of 1935 Federal legislation that established the Crippled Children's Service (CCS), the first categorical health care program for children, and the Maternal and Child Health Bureau. PL 99-272, passed in 1985, changed the CCS to the Program for Children with Special Health Care Needs.

Title XIX of the Social Security Act of 1935, as amended in 1965 Medicaid. A federally supervised, state-administered medical assistance program. This entitlement has financial (income) qualifications for eligibility.

titubation Head bobbing with a to-and-fro movement of the body that is often due to cerebellar damage or disease in the vermis (central part of the cerebellum).

TLC–Expanded *See* Test of Language Competence–Expanded Edition.

TLSO *See* thoracolumbar sacral orthosis.

TMH Trainable mentally handicapped; *see* trainable mental retardation.

TMJ *See* temporomandibular joint.

TMR *See* trainable mental retardation.

TO *See* time-out.

TOAL–2 *See* Test of Adolescent Language–2.

tobacco *See* maternal smoking during pregnancy.

tocolytic Any pharmacological agent used to postpone the process of labor.

Todd paralysis The transient paralysis of a body part involved in a focal seizure; it may continue for several (always less than 24) hours after the seizure is complete.

toe walking Equinus gait; walking on the balls of the feet with the heels not touching the ground. When associated with spasticity (increased muscle tone), tight calf muscles, shortened heel cords, and brisk deep-tendon reflexes, toe walking is a sign of spastic cerebral palsy, most commonly diple-

toe walking

gia (paralysis on both sides of the body). Toe walking is also frequently seen in children with autism. A motor or other developmental disorder should be suspected when toe walking persists for longer than 3 months. As a normal variant, toe walking should raise the examiner's index of suspicion for developmental disorders of language.

Tofranil *See* imipramine.

token A term in behavioral psychology meaning an object that can be later exchanged for another reinforcer/reward.

token economy A comprehensive behavior modification program involving the use of tokens, such as points, ships, stars, play money, and so on. The tokens are earned for prespecified behaviors and may be turned in at a later time for tangible items such as food or favored activities.

token test A screening test for receptive language in children from 3-0 to 12-5 years of age. The technique of using tokens of different shapes, sizes, and colors to assess receptive language abilities was derived from work with adults who have aphasia (loss of language skills).

TOLD–2 *See* Test of Language Development–2.

toluene embryopathy A teratogenic (causing malformation) syndrome that includes low birth weight, microcephaly (abnormally small head), developmental delay, and facial features similar to those of fetal alcohol syndrome. Etiology (cause) is maternal substance abuse with the solvent methylbenzene (found in spray paint) during pregnancy.

TOMA *See* Test of Mathematical Abilities.

tone reducing ankle foot orthosis (TRAFO) A brace used to treat equinus deformity or posture in spasticity (increased muscle tone).

tone/tonus The degree of involuntary muscle contraction or passive resistance that persists during voluntary relaxation. Tone can be described as normal, hypertonic (increased), hypotonic (decreased), or atonic (absent).

tongue protrusion reflex An oral-motor reflex innervated by cranial nerve XII, in which a tactile (touch) stimulus to the anterior (front) tongue produces the response of tongue protrusion between birth and 6 months of age. Diminution of this reflex permits the introduction of solids.

tongue thrust Forceful, intermittent protrusion of the tongue, often associated with a generalized increase in extensor tone. It is of concern because it can interfere with feeding and speech.

tongue-tie Hypertrophic lingual frenulum, ankyloglossia; a short lingual frenulum that restricts the movement of the tongue, especially at the tip. This is a common finding in children, and, except in extreme cases, rarely affects speech. Once a common office procedure, clipping the frenulum is no longer routinely recommended.

TONI-2 *See* Test of Nonverbal Intelligence-2.

tonic bite An exaggerated version of the bite reflex in which the jaw clamps shut with minimal oral stimulation.

tonic-clonic seizure *See* generalized seizure.

tonic labyrinthine response A primitive reflex in which neck extension (stimulus) produces shoulder

tonic labyrinthine response

retraction ("surrender posture" or hands above shoulders/in air posture) and lower extremity extension. Persistence or exaggeration of this reflex reflects serious underlying neuromotor disability.

tonic seizure A seizure type classified under minor motor seizures or Lennox-Gastaut syndrome. This is characterized by brief spells of muscle tightening. These generally occur during sleep and are resistant to anticonvulsant therapy.

tonic spasms Sudden extension of the entire body, often on the basis of an overactive labyrinthine reflex; this postural extensor thrust is not a true seizure.

tonsillectomy The surgical removal of the tonsils; often an adenoidectomy (surgical removal of the adenoids) is accomplished at the same time—a T&A. Indications for T&A have tended to become more restrictive or conservative. Recurrent otitis (ear infection) or some degree of cardiac or respiratory compromise are considered necessary to justify the risk of severe postoperative bleeding. The fact that tonsillar tissue normally begins to involute (spontaneously grow smaller) by early in the second decade of life should also be taken into account prior to deciding on surgery.

tonsillitis An infection/inflammation of the tonsils (masses of lymphoid tissue in the throat/oropharynx). Tonsillitis is distinct from (although often associated with) pharyngitis (throat infection/inflammation). The presence of a runny nose (rhinitis) can suggest a viral etiology (cause) to a throat infection that will not benefit from antibiotics.

tooth grinding Bruxism.

top-down processing (conceptually driven) A term found in cognitive psychological theory referring to processing that is affected by what an individual brings to a stimulus situation. For example, when a word is unclear or unknown in a sentence, the reader utilizes expectations based on context and past experience (top-down), rather than relying on a detailed analysis of the word (*see* bottom-up processing). In most circumstances, perception involves the interaction of bottom-up and top-down processing.

TOPL *See* Test of Pragmatic Language.

topographical classification of cerebral palsy Describes which of the four extremities are significantly involved in cerebral palsy; such a classification is typically used only with spastic cerebral palsy because most extrapyramidal cerebral palsy involves all four extremities fairly equally. Topographical subtypes include monoplegia, hemiplegia (paralysis of half the body), triplegia, diplegia (paralysis on both sides of the body), quadriplegia (paralysis of all four extremities), and paraplegia.

topography In psychoanalysis, the division of mental function into three regions: the conscious, the unconscious, and the preconscious.

TOPS–R *See* Test of Pragmatic Skills–Revised Edition.

TORCH *See* STORCH.

TORC-R *See* Test of Reading Comprehension–Revised.

torsion dystonia *See* dystonia muscularum deformans.

torticollis Stiff neck, wryneck; a spasm or tightening of neck muscles leading to the head being turned to one side.

torus palatinus A benign donut-shaped bony swelling over the posterior (back) portion of the hard palate; this represents a normal anatomical variant without any developmental significance.

torus palatinus

total communication An educational approach employed with individuals with hearing impairments in which all communication methods available to the individual are utilized. Finger spelling, oral and written language, speech reading, and sign language are among the techniques incorporated to enhance receptive and expressive communication. Synthesizing all sensory modalities and communicative abilities facilitates both the acquisition of language and social development, particularly with children who have congenital or prelingual (occurring before the development of speech and language skills) hearing loss.

total parenteral alimentation (TPA) *See* total parenteral nutrition.

total parenteral nutrition (TPN) Total parenteral alimentation (TPA), hyperalimentation; parenteral refers to feeding not through the alimentary canal, typically by the intravenous route. TPN would provide all the nutritional requirements to build and maintain body tissue and expend energy through an intravenous catheter in cases where the intestine's ability to absorb food has been acutely or chronically compromised.

Touch Inventory for Elementary School-Aged Children (TIE) A brief 10-minute, 26-question inventory to assess tactile (touch) defensiveness. It can be administered alone or as part of a comprehensive sensory integration assessment.

Tourette syndrome *See* Gilles de La Tourette syndrome.

TOVA *See* Test of Variables of Attention.

tower A visual-perceptual motor milestone in infancy and early childhood in which the child is requested to imitate stacking blocks; a tower of 2 blocks can usually be completed by 15 months of age, and a tower of 10 blocks by 3 years. The qualitative aspects of the motor grasp and release can also be evaluated during this task. Tower-building block tasks are commonly included components in many infant tests.

TOWK *See* Test of Word Knowledge.

TOWL–2 *See* Test of Written Language–2.

toxemia of pregnancy EPH (*E*dema, *Pro*teinuria, and *H*ypertension) complex that, untreated, will progress to seizures; this preeclampsia–eclampsia syndrome occurs in the last trimester of pregnancy and is associated with high fetal and maternal morbidity and mortality.

TPA Total parenteral alimentation; *see* total parenteral nutrition.

TPBA *See* transdisciplinary play-based assessment.

TPK *See* Test of Practical Knowledge.

TPN *See* total parenteral nutrition.

trachea Windpipe.

tracheoesophageal fistula (TEF) A congenital malformation in which the esophagus opens into the trachea (windpipe) and leads to aspiration. TEF is part of the VATER association, Down syndrome, and other malformation syndromes.

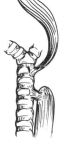
tracheoesophageal fistula

tracking Grouping students on the basis of ability. Being assigned to specific classes at the secondary level based on academic ability also influences student friendships, extracurricular activities, and attitudes.

traction response A test for tone that can be elicited in premature infants at 33 weeks' gestation; the stimulus involves grasping the infant by both hands and pulling to sit. The response includes flexion at the neck, elbows, knees, and ankles. Hypotonia (decreased muscle tone) is suggested by head lag and lack of limb flexion.

trade name Brand name, proprietary name; the particular formulation of a drug that is copyrighted or patented by a pharmaceutical manufacturer.

TRAFO *See* tone reducing ankle foot orthosis.

train A visual-perceptual motor milestone that requires the child to imitate the construction of a four-block (at 24 months of age) or five-block (at 30 months) structure.

train

trainable *See* moderate mental retardation.

trainable mental retardation (TMR) An outdated term to describe people with moderate mental retardation whose IQ scores fall below 50 and above 34.

trainable mentally handicapped (TMH) *See* trainable mental retardation.

trait An inherited or acquired characteristic that is consistent, persistent, and stable.

tranquilizer An antianxiety drug; there are two groupings: major tranquilizers, which include the antipsychotic neuroleptics; and minor tranquilizers, which include the anxiolytic (antianxiety) drugs such as diazepam (Valium), chlordiazepoxide (Librium), and meprobamate (Miltown).

transdisciplinary Describing a team approach to the diagnosis and treatment of developmental disabilities. Such a team goes beyond the interdisciplinary model, in that one or more of the professionals on the team cross the traditional discipline boundaries. For example, both the pediatrician and the occupational therapist may assess and comment on a child's cognitive level. Thus, with the transdisciplinary approach, an individual professional can incorporate parts of the interdisciplinary team interaction.

transdisciplinary play-based assessment (TPBA) A set of criterion-referenced informal assessment scales for children functioning developmentally between the ages of 6 months and 6 years. A videotaped play interaction session is scored by multiple professionals to observe four domains: cognitive, social-emotional, communication and language, and sensorimotor. The outcome focuses on intervention planning.

transduction Reasoning by association. In psychology, reasoning from the particular to the particular, with co-occurrence being taken for a causal relationship.

transfer A visual-perceptual motor milestone in which the infant can get both hands to the mid-line and pass a grasped object from one hand to the other; it is typically present by 5 months of age.

transfer The modification that occurs in one behavior, resulting in changes in a similar behavior (i.e., transfer of learning), or a behavior reinforced in the presence of one stimulus event occurring in the presence of a different one (i.e., transfer of training).

transient tachypnea of the newborn (TTN) Wet lung; a self-limited breathing disorder in newborns that typically has no long-term developmental sequelae.

transillumination A method of examining the head of a newborn or young infant; a light source (either a cuffed flashlight or a high-intensity "Chun Gun") is placed against the baby's head in a darkened room and the amount of surrounding lucency (light transmission) is observed. A marked increase in craniolucency suggests underlying impairments such as hydrocephalus (excess fluid in the brain), subdural effusion (fluid under one of the meningeal layers), porencephaly, cerebral atrophy (wasting), or hydranencephaly (excess water on the brain due to an absence of cerebral hemispheres).

transitional feeding A stage of infant feeding when breast milk and/or infant formula no longer adequately meets the child's nutritional needs and must be supplemented by the introduction of smooth or semisolid food.

transitional object An object that is transitional between mother and child, such as a security blanket or thumbsucking.

transverse plane An anatomical plane that divides the body into an upper and a lower half.

transverse tongue reflex An oral motor reflex innervated by cranial nerve XII, in which a tactile (touch) stimulus to the lateral (outside) surface of the tongue produces the response of tongue movement toward the side of the stimulus. This reflex is present by 7 months of gestation and disappears by 9 months of age.

trauma A wound or injury.

trazodone Trade name Desyrel; an antidepressant that can be used in the treatment of aggressive behavior.

Treacher Collins syndrome Mandibular dysostosis, Franceschetti-Zwahlen-Klein syndrome. An extremely variable genetic syndrome involving anomalies (malformation, deformation, disruption, or dysplasia) of structures embryologically derived from the first branchial arch. The dysmorphology (atypical features) spectrum includes malar hypoplasia (undergrowth of the midface with cheekbones flat or depressed), downslanting palpebral fissures (antimongoloid slant), lower-lid defects (e.g., absent lower eyelashes), a large fishlike mouth, a receding chin, and malformations of the external pinna (ear). Mental retardation is present in only 5% of cases, but learning disabilities occur in almost 50%; these latter may be due in part to chronic obstructive apnea (temporary cessation of breathing) in childhood. Neurocognitive impairments are more common in the presence of microcephaly (abnormally small head). Plastic surgery is usually indicated. Named after the British ophthalmologist Edward Treacher Collins (1862–1932). Inheritance follows an autosomal dominant pattern with 100% penetrance; 60% of cases are fresh mutations.

Treatment and Education of Autistic and Communications handicapped CHildren (TEACCH) A North Carolina network of autism-related services that has published much research in autism.

tremor Shaking, trembling; an extrapyramidal type of cerebral palsy whose chief characteristic is involuntary motor oscillations. This is exceedingly rare as an isolated finding and is most often part of a mixed cerebral palsy picture with rigidity.

Trendelenburg gait   Gluteus medius gait; a lurching gait associated with hip abnormalities and weaknesses of the abductor muscles on the involved side.

Trendelenburg sign   When a child stands on one leg, the opposite side of the pelvis should rise; when it falls, congenital hip dislocation or muscular weakness on the opposite side should be suspected.

triangular facies   A facial appearance associated with a number of different syndromes (e.g., Russell-Silver syndrome); the appearance results from disproportionate rates of growth of the calvarium (upper skull) and facial bones. Hydrocephalus (excess fluid in the brain) can contribute to a triangular facial appearance.

triangular facies

trichoglyphics   Patterning of hair follicles; usually expressed as hair whorl patterns. Abnormal trichoglyphics are associated with underlying abnormalities of brain development.

trichorrhexis nodosa   Poorly pigmented brittle hair found in some metabolic disorders.

trichosis   An abnormality of hair. *See also* hypertrichosis, hypotrichosis.

trichothiodystrophy   Brittle hair and sulfur deficiency seen in BIDS, IBIDS, and PIBIDS syndromes.

tricyclic antidepressant (TCA)   Drugs that block the re-uptake of the neurotransmitters norepinephrine and serotonin in the brain, and thus alleviate depression in people without organic brain damage. Major side effects include sedation, heart problems, and tardive dyskinesia (slow, rhythmic automatic movements). These antidepressants can serve as second- and third-level drugs in the treatment of attention-deficit/hyperactivity disorder.

trigeminal nerve   The fifth cranial nerve; cranial nerve V provides sensation to the face and movement to the jaw for chewing.

trigonocephaly   A triangular-shaped skull with one of the apexes (extremities) of the triangle being the mid-forehead. It results from the premature fusion of the metopic suture (mid-forehead) and can contribute to the appearance of hypotelorism (decreased distance between the eyes). A cosmetic deformity, it rarely exhibits any developmental consequences. In the presence of a more generalized craniosynostosis (premature fusion of skull sutures) or microcephaly (abnormally small head), the risk of developmental disability would be increased.

trimester   A time period of 3 months. The term *trimester* is usually used when describing the thirds of a pregnancy. Common features and certain predictive pathologies (conditions) in the developing fetus are noted by their occurrence in the first, the second, or the third trimester of a pregnancy.

trimester bleeding   Maternal bleeding during pregnancy, indicating a potential problem with the pregnancy. First trimester bleeding (during the first 3 months of the pregnancy) is related more to problems with the baby (e.g., congenital defects leading to a threatened miscarriage), whereas third trimester bleeding (during the last 3 months of the pregnancy) suggests a problem with the placenta (e.g., previa or abruptio).

triplegia   Literally, "three paralysis"; a topographical subtype of spastic cerebral palsy in which three extremities (arms or legs) are seriously involved and one extremity is relatively spared. Most cases of triplegia represent the overlapping occurrence of a diplegia (paralysis on both sides of the body) with a hemiplegia (paralysis of half the body).

triploidy   The state of having three times the haploid number of chromosomes. *See* Karyotype on page 322.

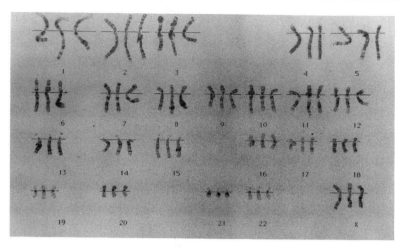

triploidy

trisomy The state of having three of a given chromosome instead of the usual pair. Trisomy 21, usually called Down syndrome, is an example.

trisomy 4p A trisomy for all or most of the short arm of chromosome 4. A chromosomal disorder with growth deficiency, severe mental retardation, a peculiar facies, and seizures. Inheritance patterns are unclear; however, when the disorder is suspected, prenatal diagnosis can be made through chorionic villi sampling, amniocentesis, or percutaneous umbilical blood. Treatment is symptomatic for congenital defects and includes special education.

trisomy 8 mosaicism A chromosomal disorder with a peculiar facies (thick lips, deep-set eyes, and jug-handle ears), mental retardation, and camptodactyly (permanent flexion of the fingers or toes). Inheritance patterns are unclear; however, when the disorder is suspected, prenatal screening from amniotic fluid in the second trimester is available. Treatment aims at correcting anatomical deformities and special education.

trisomy 9 mosaicism A chromosomal disorder with severe mental retardation, growth deficiency, a peculiar facies, joint contractures, and congenital heart disease. Inheritance patterns are unclear; however, when the disorder is suspected, prenatal screening from amniotic fluid is available. Treatment aims at correcting anatomical deformities and includes special education.

trisomy 9p A trisomy for all or part of the short arm of chromosome 9. A chromosomal disorder with mental retardation, growth deficiency, a peculiar facies, and short fingers and/or toes. Although rare, if a parent is a carrier of a balanced translocation, recurrence risks are high. When de novo (new) cases occur, there is no apparent recurrence risk. Treatment is symptomatic and includes special education.

trisomy 13 syndrome Patau syndrome, D_1 trisomy syndrome. A chromosomal disorder secondary to the presence of an extra chromosome 13 (D group). Findings include microcephaly (abnormally small head), incomplete development of the forebrain, severe mental retardation, clefting, hyperconvex nails, and polydactyly (extra fingers or toes). Less than one child in five with this syndrome survives the first year of life. Advanced maternal age is a contributing factor in the occurrence of this syndrome. Incidence is estimated at 1 in 8,000. Although inheritance patterns are unclear, when the syndrome is suspected, prenatal diagnosis can be made through chorionic villi sampling or amniocentesis. Occasionally, ultrasound indications of a decreased ratio of head to trunk circumferences indicate the need for prenatal screening. Treatment is symptomatic.

trisomy 18 syndrome Edwards syndrome, E trisomy. A chromosomal syndrome secondary to the presence of an extra chromosome 18 (E group). Findings include clenched hands with overlapping fingers, rocker-bottom feet, short sternum, heart disease, severe mental retardation, and failure to thrive (poor growth). Only 10% of children with this syndrome survive the first year of life. Incidence is noted as 1 in 3,000 births. Although inheritance patterns are unclear, when the syndrome is suspected, prenatal diagnosis can be made through amniocentesis by the second trimester. Occasionally, ultrasound indicates the need for prenatal screening. Advanced maternal age is a contributory factor in the occurrence of this syndrome. There is no treatment available.

trisomy 21 *See* Down syndrome (DS).

trochlear nerve The fourth cranial nerve. Cranial nerve IV innervates one of the muscles of the eye; damage will produce mild convergent strabismus (squint), diplopia (double vision) or downward gaze, and a compensatory head tilt.

truancy Unjustifiable absence from school without parental knowledge or consent. Unjustifiable absence with parental consent can lead to charges of educational neglect. Truancy and other forms of sociopathic behavior are common outcomes for children with attention-deficit/hyperactivity disorder (ADHD) or learning disabilities that are inadequately treated.

true negative rate Specificity.

true positive rate Sensitivity.

T-score A standard score based on a distribution with a mean of 50 and a standard deviation of 10. The differential aptitude tests use this scale.

TTN *See* transient tachypnea of the newborn.

tuberous sclerosis syndrome Adenoma sebaceum, Bourneville disease, epiloia; a genetic neurocutaneous (of the nervous system and skin) syndrome of multiple raised skin lesions that may vary in color from white to yellow to brown (predominantly on the face), café au lait spots, renal (kidney) cysts, tooth enamel defects, mental retardation, and seizures resulting from growths in the cortex and white matter of the brain. Occasionally, malignant brain tumors occur. Incidence is estimated at between 1 in 10,000 to 1 in 50,000. Inheritance is autosomal dominant, with most cases (85%) representing de novo (new) mutations. Treatment includes anticonvulsants for seizures and surgery/plastic surgery for dermatological (skin) involvement.

Turner syndrome XO syndrome; a genetic syndrome in girls with one X chromosome missing. It is characterized by short stature; pterygium colli (a webbed neck) with a low posterior (back) hairline; widely spaced nipples on a shield-shaped chest; congenital lymphedema with residual puffiness on the tops of the fingers and toes; and ovarian dysgenesis (failure of the ovaries to develop normally) leading to sexual infantilism with amenorrhea (lack of periods), infertility (sterility), and absent secondary sexual characteristics (e.g., lack of breast development). There is also cubitus valgus (an increased carrying angle at the elbows) and occasional other skeletal (50%), cardiac (35%), and renal (kidney) abnormalities (60%). Frequent abnormalities of the pinnae (earlobes) are associated with the presence of a progressive sensorineural (involving the inner ear or the auditory nerve) hearing loss that often does not begin until the second decade of life. There is an increased incidence of otitis (ear infections) contributing to decreased speech and language abilities; however, overall, girls with Turner syndrome have a low prevalence of speech-language disorders compared to the rate in other sex chromosome anomalies (malformation, deformation, disruption, or dysplasia). Mental retardation is rare (less than 10%), attention-deficit/hyperactivity disorder (ADHD) occurs, and there is a strikingly distinctive neuropsychological profile with disordered spatial function, poor right–left directionality, impaired shape copying, dysgraphia (impaired writing), dyscalculia (impaired mathematical skills), and lowered performance IQ scores. The brain localization for this pattern remains the subject of much debate. Most (95%) XO nondisjunctions are lethal early in gestation; many (40%) XO phenotypes (appearances) are mosaics. Turner syndrome is the only sex chromosome abnormality identifiable at birth. It was named after the American endocrinologist Henry Turner (1892–1970). Incidence occurs on the order of 1 in 5,000 births, or 1 in 2,500 phenotypic females; it is sporadic, with minimal recurrence risk. Prenatal diagnosis is available. Treatment is symptomatic, with recent focus on both growth hormone and cyclic estrogen replacement therapy to more completely normalize psychobiology for affected individuals. *See also* Noonan syndrome.

turribrachycephaly *See* acrocephaly.

TVMS *See* Test of Visual-Motor Skills.

TVPS *See* Test of Visual-Perceptual Skills.

twin Either of two offspring produced from one pregnancy. Two separate, abnormal conception processes can produce twins. Monozygotic twinning (*mono* meaning one) results from a single fertilized egg that duplicates itself. Although this duplication process occurs in all pregnancies, typically only one of the duplicates survives. The children resulting from this type of process are called *identical twins*. The second type of twinning process, *dizygotic twinning* (*di* meaning two), results from the production and fertilization of two separate eggs during the conception process. Both fertilized eggs are nurtured during a single pregnancy, resulting in *fraternal twins*. Fraternal twins can be either the same or opposite sex. Although most twin births produce typical children, twinning is nonetheless an atypical process in that the uterus of the human female is built for one fetus. Thus, many twin pregnancies are complicated by prematurity, infants smaller than expected for the length of the pregnancy, and

a greatly increased number of birth complications including premature rupture of membranes, preeclampsia, toxicity, hypertension (high blood pressure), and fetal distress. In addition, one twin is usually smaller in utero and postnatally is much slower to grow. Twin pregnancies, therefore, are at greater risk for pre- and perinatal birth trauma leading to developmental disabilities.

two group approach In the study of mental retardation, the careful separation of organic brain damage from cultural–familial retardation; the former group fits into a difference approach and the latter into a developmental approach. With the increasing identification of medical etiologies (causes) for people with mild mental retardation, this theory may receive increasing support, although with a significant reapportionment between the two groups.

two-point discrimination A component of the neurological assessment of sensation; difficulty in discriminating whether the skin has been touched at one or two close points is interpreted as a sign of parietal lobe dysfunction.

TWS–2 *See* Test of Written Spelling–2.

tympanic membrane The ear drum; a pearly gray glistening membrane with a triangular area of reflected light; the tympanic membrane is examined visually with an otoscope for signs of otitis media (middle-ear infection).

tympanic neurectomy A surgical procedure that disrupts parasympathetic innervation to the parotid gland as a treatment for drooling. It is usually performed bilaterally and is combined with a chorda-tympani section.

tyrosinemia An inborn error of metabolism in which the defect is in the metabolism of tyrosine. There are two types: 1) type 1, affecting liver, kidneys, and growth; and 2) type 2, or oculocutaneous tyrosinemia, causing mental retardation, microcephaly (abnormally small head), and corneal clouding.

U

UA *See* urinalysis.

UAF University affiliated facility. *See* university affiliated program.

UAP *See* university affiliated program.

UCBL Shoe-insert-type orthosis (corrective appliance); named for the original brand, University of California Biomechanics Laboratory.

UCP *See* United Cerebral Palsy.

ulna The thinner of the two bones of the forearm (*see also* radius).

ulna

ulnar grasp Simian grasp; an immature grasp pattern in which the object is apprehended from the side of the hand farthest from the thumb.

ulnar grasp

umbilical hernia A weakening of the abdominal wall leading to a bulging and a protrusion of the abdominal contents outward at the site of the umbilicus. The hernia remains well covered with skin, causes no discomfort, does not become incarcerated or strangulated, and usually closes off spontaneously by 2 years of age.

umbilicus Navel; belly button.

uncinate fit Olfactory (related to the sense of smell) hallucinations associated with temporal lobe tumors or seizures. These are described as the perception of unpleasant but usually unidentifiable odors.

unconditioned reflex Inborn, biological, permanent reactions of organisms to environmental stimuli, mediated by the nervous system.

unfisted A tendency of infants' hands to remain open at rest for more than half of the time; in contrast to the earlier fisting, this becomes the preferred hand posture after 3 months of age.

unidisciplinary An approach to the diagnosis and treatment of developmental disabilities that focuses almost exclusively on the contribution by a single professional discipline or specialty; not a team approach.

unilateral Pertaining to one side of the body.

United Cerebral Palsy (UCP) A national voluntary association of state and local affiliates along with the national organization, United Cerebral Palsy Associations (UCPA), that provides and coordinates direct services and formulates national policies for providing services for children and adults with cerebral palsy. Standards, advocacy, research, and training represent additional goals and activities. Founded in 1948.

university affiliated program (UAP) A national network of programs affiliated with universities and teaching hospitals that provides interdisciplinary training for professionals and paraprofessionals in the field of developmental disabilities and offers programs and services for children with disabilities and their families. Some UAPs provide direct services, whereas individual UAPs have staffs with expertise in a variety of areas and can furnish information, technical assistance, and inservice training to community agencies, service providers, parent groups and others. UAPs that received building construction monies were originally referred to as UAFs (university affiliated facilities).

untoward reaction   Harmful side effect.

upper extremity   Arm; forearm and hand.

upper/lower segment ratio   Distance from the top of the head to the pubic bone divided by the distance from the pubic bone to the sole of the foot. This ratio is 1.7 at birth; 1.0 at 10 years of age; and just below 1.0 in adults. The changes in this ratio are useful in the diagnosis of both endocrine and genetic growth disorders.

urea cycle defect   A group of genetic metabolic diseases, each representing a failure in one of the steps in the conversion of ammonia to urea. Symptoms associated with the resulting hyperammonemia include recurrent episodes of lethargy, vomiting, seizures, and mental retardation. Four of the five enzyme deficits are inherited in an autosomal recessive pattern. Dialysis is used in the acute stage to reduce the hyperammonenia; drugs, low-protein diets, and amino acid supplements can then be used to regulate the ammonia level depending on the type and severity of the disorder.

Urecholine   *See* bethanechol.

urinalysis (UA)   A group of visual, physical, and chemical tests performed on urine specimens. As a routine screening test, urinalysis is rarely successful in detecting asymptomatic (without symptoms) kidney or other disease.

urinary tract infection (UTI)   A bladder infection; symptoms include urinary frequency and urgency, dysuria (pain and discomfort on urination), fever, and malaise. Recurrent UTIs in children with disability syndromes should raise the suspicion of either an underlying genitourinary malformation or sexual abuse. UTIs during pregnancy have a nonspecific association with an increased incidence of mental retardation in the baby.

Usher syndrome   A genetic syndrome with congenital nonprogressive sensorineural (involving the inner ear or the auditory nerve) hearing loss of variable severity, retinitis pigmentosa (night blindness and progressively restricted visual field), and loss of olfactory (sense of smell) and vestibular (balance) functions. Neuropsychiatric difficulties occur in 25% of cases. Inheritance is autosomal recessive (rarely, X-linked) with an incidence of 3 in 100,000. The syndrome accounts for approximately 5% of children with severe hearing loss and half of all adults with deafness and blindness. Named for the Scottish ophthalmologist Charles Usher (1865–1942).

Utah Test of Language Development– Third Edition (UTLD–3)   A language test for typical children and children with disabilities ages 3-0 to 10-11; it yields subtest standard scores for language comprehension and language expression as well as a language quotient. Administration time is 30–45 minutes.

UTI   *See* urinary tract infection.

UTLD-3   *See* Utah Test of Language Development–Third Edition.

Uzgiris-Hunt Scales   *See* Ordinal Scales of Infant Psychological Development.

V

VAB *See* Vulpe Assessment Battery.

VADS *See* Visual Aural Digit Span Test.

vagus nerve The 10th cranial nerve; cranial nerve X provides the motor and sensory innervation to the pharynx (throat) and the larynx (windpipe) (including the vocal cords), as well as parasympathetic innervation to the thoracic (heart and lungs) and abdominal viscera (gastrointestinal tract).

VAKT Acronym for *V*isual, *A*uditory, *K*inesthetic, *T*actile; *see* Fernald Word Learning Technique.

valgus Bent outward, away from the midline.

validation The process of determining a test's validity—its ability to measure what it claims to measure.

validity The degree to which an instrument measures what it purports to measure. Face validity is a subjective impression that the test strongly appears to measure what it claims to measure. Content validity requires that the test adequately sample the range of target behaviors (e.g., that a test that claims to measure mathematical ability actually includes all types of mathematics problems). Concurrent validity correlates performance on the test with performance on another test recognized as a valid measure of the same domain. Construct validity refers to the ability to explain scores on the test in accordance with a theoretical model of behavior. Predictive validity is a measure of how well test scores hold up over time and predict future behavior including later performance on the test itself.

Valium Trade name for diazepam.

Valproate *See* valproic acid.

valproic acid Trade names Valproate and Depakene; an anticonvulsant drug used for absence seizures (both isolated and when other seizure types are present), generalized tonic-clonic seizures, and partial seizures. Valproic acid is rarely used in infants, as they are more likely to develop liver damage. It can also produce nausea, weight gain, reversible hair loss, drowsiness, and tremors. Rarely, it can affect blood cells. Usage in pregnancy has been associated with an increased incidence of neural tube defects, as well as a risk of fetal antiepileptic drug syndrome. Valproic acid produces only minimal cognitive impairment; when used concurrently with phenobarbital, it can increase the blood level of that drug and cause sedation (sleepiness). It can also increase the side effects of other anticonvulsants such as carbamazepine (Tegretol) or phenytoin (Dilantin) used concomitantly. Valproic acid has successfully treated hypomanic states in people with severe mental retardation.

van Buchem syndrome Hyperostosis corticalis generalisata; a genetic syndrome with generalized bone overgrowth that can compress cranial nerves to produce facial palsy and vision and hearing loss. Inheritance is autosomal recessive. (There does exist an autosomal dominant variant.)

van der Woude syndrome Lip pit syndrome; a genetic syndrome that includes lower lip pits, cleft lip with or without cleft palate, and hypodontia (decreased number of teeth). Conductive (involving the middle and outer ear) hearing loss problems are common. Incidence is 1 in 100,000; inheritance is autosomal dominant with variable penetrance.

varicella Chickenpox; an exanthem (rash) produced by the human herpes virus, varicella-zoster virus (VZV). The disease has a 2-week incubation period and is highly contagious with airborne spread via respiratory secretions from several days prior to the onset of the rash through the first week of the rash. The individual pockmarks are similar to those found in variola (smallpox), but have a different temporal course. An acute cerebellar syndrome with ataxia (unsteady gait), nystagmus (involuntary eye movements), vertigo (dizziness), tremor, slurred speech, and vomiting may persist for several weeks after the rash. A live attenuated (weakened) VZV vaccine was approved for usage in the United States by the Food and Drug Administration in 1995.

variola Smallpox; *variolation* refers to smallpox inoculation that leaves a scar at the vaccination site.

varus Bent inward, toward the mid-line.

VA shunt *See* ventriculoatrial shunt.

VATERS Acronym for an association of congenital malformations: *V* for vertebral anomalies (malformation, deformation, disruption, or dysplasia) and ventricular septal defect (heart disease), *A* for anal atresia, *TE* for tracheoesophageal fistula with esophageal atresia, *R* for radial and renal (kidney) dysplasia, and *S* for single umbilical artery. When not part of a broader genetic syndrome, such as trisomy 18, this condition is compatible with normal cognitive functioning.

VC *See* verbal comprehension.

velo-cardio-facial syndrome *See* Shprintzen syndrome.

velum Soft palate.

venipuncture The drawing of blood through a vein for a laboratory test.

ventral The front; the anterior or belly surface; opposite of dorsal.

ventricle A cavity or chamber, usually of the heart or brain.

ventricular Pertaining to a ventricle.

ventricular septal defect (VSD) A relatively common congenital heart defect in which there is an opening between the two ventricles (large lower chambers) of the heart, sometimes accompanied by a murmur (abnormal heart sound on physical examination), cyanosis (blue color), and other symptoms of heart failure. VSD can be one of a number of organ system malformations included in genetic syndromes associated with mental retardation and other developmental disabilities. It is possible to outgrow the effect of a small VSD.

ventriculoatrial (VA) shunt A neurosurgical treatment for hydrocephalus (excess fluid in the brain). This procedure connects the ventricle of the brain with the right atrium of the heart by means of a tube with a pressure-regulated one-way flow valve. The VA shunt is more prone to infection but less likely to become obstructed than the ventriculoperitoneal (VP) shunt.

ventriculogram/ventriculography A radiographic procedure to visualize (with or without contrast material) the ventricles (fluid-containing spaces) of the brain.

ventriculomegaly Enlargement of the ventricles (fluid-containing spaces) of the brain. Large ventricles seen on computed tomography (CT) scan or ultrasound can be due to hydrocephalus (excess fluid in the brain) or to brain atrophy (wasting).

ventriculoperitoneal (VP) shunt A mechanical pump with a pressure-regulated one-way valve connecting the ventricle of the brain with the peritoneal (abdominal) cavity so that the excess fluid (and pressure) in the brain in hydrocephalus is relieved; also, sometimes, the neurosurgical procedure to place such a shunt.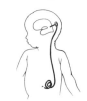

ventriculoperitoneal shunt

Complications of shunts include infection and meningitis (inflammation of the spinal cord and brain membranes), blockage, disconnection of the shunt tubing from the shunt, and relative shortening of the tubing caused by the child's growth. Shunt infections may contribute to brain injury and a decrease in cognitive functioning. The VP shunt is more prone to obstruction but less likely to get infected than the ventriculoatrial (VA) shunt.

VEP *See* visual-evoked potential.

VER Visual-evoked response; *see* visual-evoked potential.

verbal comprehension (VC) One of the three Wechsler Intelligence Scale for Children–Revised (WISC–R) factor scores; these are sometimes referred to as the Kaufman factors. VC is a measure of verbal knowledge and comprehension learned through formal education and other life experiences. This factor score is obtained by summing the scaled scores for the information, similarities, vocabulary, and comprehension subtests. VC seems to measure a common component of the verbal scale subtests by addressing both item content (verbal) and the related mental process (comprehension). Perceptual organization (PO) and freedom from distractibility (FFD) are the other two WISC–R factor scores. Factor scores are used to generate additional information and also support the interpretation of the child's WISC–R subtest pattern of strengths and weaknesses. On the Wechsler Intelligence Scale–Third Edition (WISC–III), VC has become the verbal comprehension index (VCI).

versive seizure One of the more common presentations of a focal seizure, in which the movement of the eyes, head, and extremities (arms or legs) is away from the side of the lesion. Seizure disorders with versive movements and no loss of consciousness often have a frontal lobe focus, whereas those with automatisms (robotic behaviors) and staring have a temporal IWS lobe focus. Electroencephalographic (EEG) abnormalities are found anterior (front) to the rolandic gyrus in either the frontal or temporal lobes and may not be present between seizures. The etiology

(cause) of these seizures ranges from underlying structural lesions (e.g., heterotopias [tissue displacement]) to idiopathic (unknown). Treatment is similar to that for other focal seizures.

vertigo Loss of balance usually accompanied by a sense of dizziness, often attributed to vestibular (balance) dysfunction, as in Ménière disease.

very low birth weight (VLBW) Description of infants with birth weights below 1,500 grams.

vestibular-bilateral disorder A sensory integrative dysfunction characterized by shortened duration of postrotary nystagmus (involuntary eye movements), poor integration of the two sides of the body and brain, and difficulty in learning to read or calculate.

vestibular dysfunction A hypothetical etiology (cause) for learning disabilities derived from 1) an analogy with the perceptual distortions induced by Ménière disease, and 2) the interpretation of mild motor dysfunction as labyrinthine rather than cortical in origin. Two treatments rely on this hypothesis: 1) the Ayres sensory integration approach, and 2) the use of antimotion sickness drugs (e.g., meclizine) to treat dyslexia.

VF *See* videofluoroscopy.

vibrotactile hearing aid A device used to assist individuals with severe hearing impairments to detect sound by converting the sound into vibrations felt by the skin on the chest or arm; the vibrations are spread out in a regional manner with high frequencies at one end and successive frequencies decreasing at the other end. A vibrotactile hearing aid is often used to supplement an augmentative hearing aid.

vicariation A hypothetical process of recovery after brain damage that involves the takeover by other parts of the nervous system of functions lost when part of the brain is damaged. The degree of vicariation depends on age; it is more likely to occur in early development.

videofluoroscopy (VF) A radiographic technique that allows a visual diagnosis of swallowing disorders and helps identify specific feeding adaptations to manage such disorders.

Vineland Adaptive Behavior Scales A structured interview to measure adaptive behavior in four separate domains: communication (receptive, expressive, and written subdomains), daily living skills (personal, domestic, and community subdomains), socialization (interpersonal relationships, play and leisure time, and coping skills subdomains), and motor skills (gross- and fine-motor subdomains). The domains and the adaptive behavior composite can be expressed in a variety of derived scores including age equivalents and adaptive levels. The survey form (297 items) and the expanded form (577 items) are used to assess adaptive behavior in children from birth to 18-9 years of age and in adults with low functioning; the classroom edition (244 items) is for school children from 3 to 12-9 years of age. This test is the 1984–1985 revision of Edgar A. Doll's (1889–1968) Vineland Social Maturity Scale (1935, 1965). Extensive standardization, reliability, and validity data are provided in the manuals for the different editions. Deficits in adaptive behavior as measured by this type of instrument are a necessary component in the diagnosis of mental retardation.

virus A noncellular infectious agent consisting of either DNA (deoxyribonucleic acid) or RNA (ribonucleic acid) surrounded by a protein coat. Viral infections do not respond to antibiotics and are treated preventively by active immunization (vaccination) when available.

viscera (s., **viscus**) Internal organs of the body. The abdominal viscera include the liver, stomach, and intestines.

viscosity The persistence of traces of earlier structures of thinking into later, more mature levels; for example, children with mental retardation will remain in a state of transition between two Piagetian (or other) stages for a longer time period than children without mental retardation.

visual acuity Vision, a measure of how well one sees. Most vision screening generates a distance that one eye can see in relation to the distance most people can see. For example, 20/100 vision means that the eye with impaired vision can see at 20 feet what the normal eye can see at 100 feet. More severe visual disturbance is reflected by the inability to detect movement or light. Lack of visual acuity is blindness. Corrective lenses (glasses or contact lenses) attempt to correct vision as closely as possible to 20/20. Legal blindness is defined as a visual acuity that can only be corrected to 20/200 or by contraction of peripheral (noncentral) visual fields in the better eye. Monocular (one eye) poor vision is often asymptomatic (without symptoms), but can result in a strabismus (squint). Visual acuity screening for children is routinely performed in most doctors' offices and schools.

Visual Aural Digit Span Test (VADS) A refinement of digit span (the repetition of increasingly longer sequences of digits as a test of auditory sequential memory) to assess learning style in children from 5-5 to 12-9 years of age. The number sequences are presented both aurally (spoken) and visually (on printed cards), and the responses are both oral and written. These four subtest results are combined to generate six further subscores for aural input, visual input, oral expression, written expression, intrasensory integration, and intersensory integration. The test is brief and nonthreatening, and provides a useful screening or confirmation of more extensive learning disability evaluations. Reliability and validity data have been published. VADS was devised by Elizabeth Koppitz, whose scoring system for the Bender Gestalt test is widely used.

visual-evoked potential (VEP); visual-evoked response (VER) A quantitative measure of the response of the occipital lobes of the brain on the electroencephalogram (EEG) to a light stimulus. The VEP provides information about visual activity as well as the integrity of the nerves in the visual system. It is used in the diagnosis of leukodystrophies, lipidoses, demyelinating diseases, and the optic neuritis found in Friedreich ataxia. Values will be abnormal in cortical blindness (loss of sight due to a brain lesion located in the specific occipital or visual area of the cerebral cortex), but normal with visual-perceptual problems.

visual fields The area that the eye can see. There is an overlap between the visual fields of the two eyes, but they do not overlap completely. Damage to the brain or optic nerve can cause a "visual field cut" or deficit. This results in a partial loss of vision in each eye. If the damage is to the right side of the brain, then the vision loss will be to the left side of each eye (i.e., the temporal side of the left eye and the nasal side of the right eye). Visual field cuts are sometimes discovered when the individual neglects or ignores the side of the task that cannot be seen. These are often difficult to diagnose in children, but should be suspected in the presence of a hemiplegia (paralysis of half the body).

visual impairment Visual acuity worse than 20/70 in the better eye after correction.

visual memory The ability to retain information presented through visual sensory and perceptual pathways. Visual memory is the capacity to revisualize or retrieve specific images as needed and the ability to recognize previously viewed information on demand. The ability to recognize a face or recall the configuration of a previously viewed word as such are examples of visual memory.

visual motor *See* perceptual-motor.

visual perception The ability to interpret information provided to the brain by the eyes. Determination and discrimination of spatial information (e.g., position in space and relative object size and location) are components of visual perception. Visual perception is not directly related to visual acuity or eye movements.

visual-perceptual motor (VPM) function The ability to interpret and integrate information obtained through the eyes in such a way that a motor act can be performed based upon that information. VPM ability can be tested by having the child copy geometric forms and designs. Tests such as the Beery Developmental Test of Visual Motor Integration (DTVMI) and the Bender Gestalt test are commonly used to assess VPM ability.

visual threat Blinking in response to a hand moving suddenly toward the eyes; such a response becomes consistent in infants after 2 months of age.

visual tracking Perceptual-motor milestones observed in early infancy; at 1 month of age, the infant can consistently follow objects moving in a horizontal direction; by 2 months, in a vertical direction; and by 3 months, in a circle. Subtle limitations in visual tracking in older children have been implicated in reading disorders, but this association probably confuses cause and effect.

visual training *See* optometric training.

vitiligo Depigmentation of the skin, producing white patches; it is acquired and often erratically progressive; a localized albinism. Vitiligo is seen in syndromes (e.g., Waardenburg syndrome), can be an isolated dermatological (skin) disorder, and may be associated genetically with sensorineural (involving the inner ear or the auditory nerve) hearing loss.

VLBW *See* very low birth weight.

VLDS *See* Mecham Verbal Language Development Scale.

vocabulary A lexicon; the number of words that a person understands (i.e., receptive) and can use (i.e., expressive). Vocabulary generally increases with age, so that tests that estimate vocabulary size are employed as measures of language function and as components of more generalized cognitive and educational assessments.

vocabulary A verbal subtest on the Wechsler tests consisting of words presented in increasing order of difficulty. The child is asked to orally define each word, as a measure of the child's intellectual (general mental) ability. This test of word knowledge taps a variety of factors including expressive (spoken) language skills, word-finding skills, exposure to and involvement with the environment, simultaneous or gestalt information processing ability, and long-term memory. Information regarding the child's fund of information, richness of ideas, and concept formation can also be obtained. Vocabulary is relatively resistant to neurological deficits and psychological disturbances. The subtest is difficult to score, as subjective judgments about the quality of responses are part of the scoring procedure, and the examples provided do not exhaust the spectrum of possible answers. The subtest is discontinued after five consecutive failures.

Vocabulary Comprehension Test A criterion-referenced checklist of 95 vocabulary words and phrases for use with children through kindergarten.

Vocational Rehabilitation The state agency that provides medical, therapeutic, counseling, education, training, assessment, and other services needed to prepare people with disabilities for work.

Vojta A system of physical therapy to treat cerebral palsy. Developed by the Czech neurologist Vaslav Vojta, it focuses on reflex creeping patterns.

von Economo encephalitis Encephalitis lethargica; an encephalitis (brain inflammation) that was epidemic between 1915 and 1926 and provided examples of postencephalitic brain injury that contributed to the evolution of the concept of minimal brain damage.

von Recklinghausen disease *See* neurofibromatosis.

VP shunt *See* ventriculoperitoneal shunt.

VPM function *See* visual-perceptual motor function.

VSD *See* ventricular septal defect.

vulnerable child syndrome A behavioral syndrome observed in parents in reaction to the earlier threatened loss of their child. A mother may continue to express and act on (usually in the form of overprotection) unrealistic fears over the health and survival of, for example, a child who had been premature but was now a healthy preschooler. Illness in the first several months of life is especially liable to engender a continuing parental misperception of childhood vulnerability and deserves firm and caring supportive counseling. Separation (anxiety), infantilization, and hypochondriacal (excessive and unjustified worry about health) concerns are common. Vulnerable child syndrome can be observed in children with developmental disabilities when these latter were secondary to an early life-threatening event. The vulnerable child syndrome can also occur in a child who has always been healthy but whose sibling has died.

Vulpe Assessment Battery (VAB) A comprehensive developmental instrument for use with children from birth through 6 years of age.

W

Waardenburg syndrome A genetic syndrome that includes pigmentary disturbances (poliosis [white forelock], heterochromia iridis [different colored eyes], vitiligo [white patches on the skin]), sensorineural (involving the inner ear or the auditory nerve) hearing loss, and lateral displacement of the inner canthi (widely spaced eyes, observed in Type I, but absent in Type II). Severe congenital bilateral hearing loss is present in 25% (Type I) – 50% (Type II) of cases; it accounts for 1.4% of all children with congenital deafness. Inheritance is autosomal dominant, with an incidence of 1 in 40,000. A similar association between albinism and deafness has been reported in cats. Named after the Dutch ophthalmologist Petrus Waardenburg (1886–1979).

Wachs Analysis of Cognitive Structures A nonverbal Piagetian scale for preschool children from 3 to 6 years of age.

Wada test A neurodiagnostic procedure in which a strong sedative (amobarbital sodium) is injected directly into a neck artery (the carotid) to discover how rapidly a loss of verbal skills follows, to compare the responses on both sides, and thus help document the lateralization of cerebral dominance. This is a serious procedure that is employed only when it is critical to document such lateralization, such as prior to ablative brain surgery.

WAIS–R *See* Wechsler Adult Intelligence Scale–Revised.

walking Ambulation.

Wallin A six-hole pegboard used in a variety of infant tests. The Wallin *A* has round pegs and holes; the Wallin *B* has square pegs and holes. The ability to successfully complete both pegboards emerges between 18 and 24 months of age. Named for John Wallin (1876–1969).

Warburg syndrome An association of congenital hydrocephalus (excess fluid in the brain) (sometimes with microcephaly [abnormally small head]), lissencephaly (smooth, rather than convoluted, brain surface), and ocular abnormalities contributing to blindness and early death. Recurrence risk for siblings is over 50%, but the genetics of this association remain unclear.

ward A legal term indicating that a person has been judged unable to care for or make decisions for him- or herself in one or more areas of his or her life. This may occur due to age (e.g., abandoned children), disability (e.g., mental retardation), or health (e.g., stroke). After legal determination of this inability has been made, a guardian is assigned, and the person is then declared a *ward*.

Washer Visual Acuity Screening Technique (WVAST) A screening test for near and far visual acuity in people with severe disabilities and low functioning. Intended for people with a mental age of 2–6 years and above, the test can be used to screen down to the 18-month level with conditioning.

water on the brain Lay term for *hydrocephalus*. The "water" is actually the clear, straw-colored cerebrospinal fluid that circulates through and bathes the brain and spinal cord; an excess or buildup of this liquid under pressure inside the head to enlarge and the brain tissue to stretch and thin out. Radiologic examination will show marked dilation (enlargement) of the ventricles (fluid-containing spaces) in the brain.

watershed phenomenon   An analogy to explain the susceptibility of the parasagittal cortex of the brain to injury when blood perfusion (circulation) is reduced in full-term infants; such parasagittal injury leads to hemiplegia (paralysis of half the body), quadriplegia (paralysis of all four extremities), and mental retardation.

WCST–R   *See* Wisconsin Card Sorting Test–Revised.

Weaver syndrome   A rare syndrome with macrosomia (large body size) from birth through adulthood, camptodactyly (permanent flexion of fingers and toes), a peculiar facies, developmental delay, and a variety of orthopedic deformities. Etiology (cause) remains unknown.

Wechsler Adult Intelligence Scale–Revised (WAIS–R)   An individually administered 11-subtest measure of an adult's capacity for intelligent behavior. The WAIS–R extends and completes the line of test development that began with the publication of the Wechsler-Bellevue Intelligence Scale in 1939 and was followed by its revision, the WAIS, in 1955. The WAIS–R has both a verbal scale and a performance scale. Verbal subtests include information, digit span, vocabulary, arithmetic, comprehension, and similarities. Performance subtests include picture completion, picture arrangement, block design, object assembly, and digit symbol. The test provides subtest standard scores (with a mean of 10 and a standard deviation of 3), and deviation IQs (with a mean of 100 and a standard deviation of 15) for the verbal, performance, and full scales. The test is used with individuals 16–74 years of age. WAIS–R norms, reliability, and validation are excellent. The test takes approximately 1 hour to administer. The verbal scale can be used alone with individuals who have visual or motor impairments, and the performance scale can be used alone with individuals who cannot adequately understand or produce spoken language.

Wechsler Individual Achievement Test (WIAT)   An individually administered battery to assess educational achievement in eight areas: basic reading, mathematics reasoning, spelling, reading comprehension, numerical operations, listening comprehension, and oral and written expression. There is a WIAT Screener that assesses the first three of these areas. The WIAT was standardized with the Wechsler Intelligence Scale for Children–Third Edition (WISC–III).

Wechsler Intelligence Scale for Children–Revised (WISC–R)   A 12-subtest measure of intelligence for children 6-0 to 16-11 years of age. The WISC–R generates three IQ scores: full scale, verbal, and performance. IQs are obtained by comparing the child's scores to those earned by a representative sample of age peers. IQ scores have a mean of 100 and a standard deviation of 15; each of the 12 subtests has a mean of 10 and a standard deviation of 3. The verbal scale measures the ability to use language in cognitive processes through six subtests: information, similarities, arithmetic, vocabulary, comprehension, and digit span. The performance scale evaluates motor abilities and visual spatial processing through six subtests: picture completion, picture arrangement, block design, object assembly, coding, and mazes. In addition to IQ scores, the WISC–R also provides three factor scores (Kaufman factors) that identify meaningful dimensions of psychological processing and can be helpful in evaluating a child's strengths and weaknesses. They are obtained by summing scaled scores of specific subtests. Three factors have been identified. The verbal comprehension (VC) factor score measures verbal knowledge and reflects the application of language skills to new situations. The perceptual organization (PO) factor reflects the ability to organize and to interpret visually presented material within a prescribed amount of time. The freedom from distractibility (FFD) factor score measures the ability to attend and concentrate, but may also include a partial measure of numerical ability and short-term memory. The WISC–R was published in 1974, 25 years after David Wechsler's original scale (the WISC) had been developed as a downward extension of the Wechsler-Bellevue Intelligence Scale for Adults. The WISC–R has good validity, high reliability, and excellent standardization. Its limitations include a restricted range of possible full-scale IQs (40–160) and the limited applicability of norms for ages 6-0 to 6-3 and 16-7 to 16-11 years of age. It was one of the most widely used and accepted intelligence tests for children. Certain physical abilities are required in order for a child to respond to WISC–R subtests. Children must be able to hear to take most verbal subtests, although vision may sometimes be used as an alternative administration modality. Arm and hand use is a prerequisite for almost all performance subtests, although some adaptations are possible. Allowances for alternative adaptative administration and the existence of two separate scales facilitate the testing of children with such disabilities.

Wechsler Intelligence Scale for Children–Third Edition (WISC–III) An individually administered intelligence test for children 60–16-9 years of age. The WISC–III yields a verbal IQ, performance IQ, and a full-scale IQ. The verbal subtests include information, similarities, arithmetic, vocabulary, comprehension, and digit span. The performance subtests include picture completion, coding, picture arrangement, block design, object assembly, symbol search, and mazes. Four factor-based index scores can also be calculated: verbal comprehension index (VCI) from information, similarities, vocabulary, and comprehension; perceptual organization index (POI) from picture completion, picture arrangement, block design, and object assembly; freedom from distractibility index (FDI) from arithmetic and digit span; and processing speed index (PSI) from coding and symbol search. The subtest standard scores each have a mean of 10 and a standard deviation of 3; the deviation IQs and the factor indices each have a mean of 100 and a standard deviation of 15. This 1991 revision is better validated for clinical groups of children with learning disabilities and other developmental disabilities.

Wechsler Preschool and Primary Scale of Intelligence–Revised (WPPSI–R) A 12-subtest standardized measure of intellectual abilities in young children 3–7 years of age. WPPSI–R verbal subtests include information, comprehension, arithmetic, vocabulary, similarities, and sentences. WPPSI–R performance subtests include geometric design, block design, mazes, picture completion, animal pegs, and (the one new addition over the original WPPSI) object assembly. The WPPSI–R overlaps 1 year with the WISC–R: 9 of the 12 subtests are downward extensions and adaptations of their WISC–R analogues; the 3 novel subtests include animal pegs, sentences, and geometric design. Animal pegs and sentences are optional and are not used to calculate IQ. Norms, reliability, and validity are excellent. In keeping with the WISC–R and WAIS–R, WPPSI–R scores have a mean of 100 and a standard deviation of 15. Administration time is approximately 1 hour and 15 minutes.

Wechsler tests A family of tests developed by David Wechsler (1896–1981) to measure intelligence in adults and children. These tests currently include the Wechsler Adult Intelligence Scale–Revised (WAIS–R), the Wechsler Intelligence Scale for Children–Third Edition (WISC–III), and the Wechsler Preschool and Primary Scale of Intelligence–Revised (WPPSI–R). Because Wechsler believed that intelligence is an aggregate of multiple abilities and should be measured as such, his tests are composed of numerous subtests that measure both verbal and nonverbal (performance) aspects of intelligence.

WeeFIM *See* Functional Independence Measure for Children.

weighting Mathematically assigning to any given test item that proportion of the total score it will determine.

Wender sign Wender foot sign; unilateral or bilateral foot tapping or crossed-knee foot jiggle as a sign of adult attention-deficit/hyperactivity disorder (ADHD) or alcoholism.

Wender Utah Rating Scale (WURS) A 61-item checklist to aid in the diagnosis of attention-deficit/hyperactivity disorder (ADHD) (active or residual) in adults. Such a diagnosis in adults requires a childhood history of ADHD in addition to current symptomology. The WURS checklist rates a variety of childhood behaviors on a 5-point scale (from 0 for not at all to 4 for very much).

Wepman Auditory Discrimination Test A test of auditory discrimination in which 40 pairs of words (10 identical and 30 differing by only a single phoneme or sound) are read to the child, who then responds as to whether they are the same or different. Although this test is supposed to measure auditory processing, the results are influenced by hearing acuity, short-term memory, and attention; very hyperactive children tend to score quite low on this test.

Werdnig-Hoffmann syndrome Spinal muscular atrophy; a genetic neurological disorder that leads to severe muscle weakness in infancy and early childhood with fatal respiratory compromise. Inheritance is autosomal dominant.

Wernicke aphasia The loss of the ability to find the correct word (i.e., anomia) secondary to damage to a specific area of the temporal lobe (Brodmann area 39, the angular gyrus, Wernicke area, posterior [back] speech cortex). Paraphrasia (using circumlocutions or talking around the word that cannot be found) is a common sign of Wernicke aphasia.

West syndrome Blitz-Nick-Salaam Krämpfe. The triad of infantile spasms, hypsarrhythmia (a continuous disorganized pattern of high-voltage slow waves and spikes), and mental retardation. Onset is usually between 4 and 7 months of age; boys are more commonly affected than girls. West syndrome can be separated into a symptomatic group (in which a specific cause is identified or other evidence of brain damage is present) and an idiopathic (unknown) group (in which no evidence of brain damage or other cause is found). Etiological (casual) conditions include phenylketonuria, maple syrup urine disease, leucine-sensitive hypoglycemia (low blood sugar level), porencephaly (a large piece of brain missing), rubella, Sturge-Weber syndrome, and tuberous sclerosis. Signs of brain damage include preexisting developmental delay, atypical neurological findings, other types of seizures, and atypical radiographic findings (e.g., on computed tomography [CT] scan). The prognosis for infants with West syndrome is poor, but is better for those without any known etiology (idiopathic or cryptogenic [with no known etiological factors] cause). Dr. J. West wrote a letter to the *Lancet* in 1841 with the first case description of infantile spasms in his son.

Wharton duct relocation A surgical procedure that reduces the salivary flow from the submandibular gland as a treatment for drooling.

wheelchair bound An inaccurate phrase used to refer to an individual in a wheelchair. It is objectionable because it creates a false impression; without the wheelchair, the individual would be bound (confined) to a bed or chair. The preferable wording is "uses a wheelchair." This phrasing emphasizes function and ability; the wheelchair and other aides are employed by individuals to enhance their quality of life by enabling mobility, not by restricting it.

whistling face syndrome Freeman-Sheldon syndrome; craniocarpotarsal dysplasia. A genetic syndrome with a peculiar facies (a masklike face with a small mouth giving the impression of puckering to whistle), small narrow nostrils, club feet, and flexion contractures of the fingers. Mental retardation is an occasional finding. Inheritance is autosomal dominant (rarely, autosomal recessive).

white matter Areas of the brain that contain the myelinated nerve axons. These are the units that transfer messages from one brain area to another. White matter diseases affect the cells that manufacture the myelin (a fatty insulation material) sheaths (coverings).

white matter disease Leukodystrophy. A group of degenerative diseases of the central nervous system in which motor signs of pyramidal tract involvement occur early, whereas cognitive deterioration and seizures occur late in the course of the disorder. (Brain white matter controls motor functions; gray cells are involved in thinking.)

white pupil Leukocoria; a physical finding that suggests the possibility of cataract, coloboma (an eye lesion), retinoblastoma (a tumor), or retinal (eye) detachment.

whorl A spiral pattern that occurs in nature; variations from expected whorl patterns in fingerprints and hair can contribute to a dysmorphology (atypical appearance) diagnosis; the depigmented skin lesions of incontinentia pigmenti may also occur in a whorl pattern.

WIAT *See* Wechsler Individual Achievement Test.

Wide Range Achievement Test–Third Edition (WRAT–3) A measure of reading, spelling, and arithmetic. There are two equivalent test forms (blue and tan) normed by age that can be used for pre- and postintervention assessment of people 5–75 years of age and that provide standard scores, percentiles, and grade equivalents for each of the three areas of learning.

Wide Range Assessment of Memory and Learning (WRAML) An individually administered test of memory for children 5–17 years of age, with nine subtests and a general memory index; administration time is about 1 hour.

widow's peak A downward V-shaped extension of the frontal hairline; a minor variation from normal that can be a component of certain syndromes (e.g., Waardenburg syndrome).

widow's peak

Wiedemann-Rautenstrauch syndrome Congenital pseudohydrocephalic syndrome; a genetic syndrome that presents at birth with pseudohydrocephalus, a senile triangular facies, congenital teeth, an extensive deficiency of subcutaneous (inner) fat, and, usually, mental retardation. Inheritance is probably autosomal recessive.

Wiig CRIL *See* Wiig Criterion-Referenced Inventory of Language.

Wiig Criterion-Referenced Inventory of Language (Wiig CRIL) A criterion-referenced assessment of language for children 4–15 years of age; it complements norm-referenced testing and helps plan intervention in the areas of semantics (the meaning of words), morphology (word structure), syntax (grammar), and pragmatics.

Wildervanck syndrome A genetic syndrome including the Klippel-Feil syndrome, the Duane syndrome (a sixth nerve palsy limiting the outward movement of the eye), and a congenital hearing impairment. Inheritance is X-linked dominant, or polygenic-multifactorial limited to females.

Wildervanck-Smith syndrome *See* Treacher Collins syndrome.

Williams syndrome Elfin facies syndrome; Williams-Beuren syndrome; Fanconi-Schlesinger syndrome. A dysmorphic (with an unusual facies [especially full lips]) syndrome, mild to moderate mental retardation, a hoarse or metallic voice, and congenital heart disease (i.e., supravalvular aortic stenosis). Affected individuals may also exhibit "cocktail party chatter" syndrome with an outgoing loquaciousness that makes them appear more intelligent due to an inflation of verbal rote skills compared to other cognitive abilities. Etiology (cause) remains unknown, although abnormalities in calcium metabolism and connective tissue have been suspected.

Wilson disease Hepatolenticular degeneration. An inborn error of copper metabolism, Wilson disease clinically involves primarily liver and brain (especially the basal ganglia) with neurological presentations (dystonia [impaired muscle tone], drooling, and other bulbar symptoms, gait disturbances, and mild intellectual impairment) occurring between 10 and 20 years of age. Learning disabilities and emotional disturbances are occasionally prominent. Physical findings include liver enlargement, Kayser-Fleischer ring (a pigmented ring around the outside of the cornea), and motor dysfunction in the absence of sensory and reflex abnormalities. Diagnosis can be confirmed by a serum ceruloplasmin (a copper-binding protein) level and an ophthalmological examination for the eye findings. Chelation treatment involves the administration of a copper-binding chemical, such as penicillamine. Neurological prognosis is variable. Inheritance is autosomal recessive Named after the British neurologist Samuel A.K. Wilson (1878–1937).

windswept hip deformity   Both hips and knees are flexed, but one hip is abducted and externally rotated and the other is adducted (pulled inward) and inter-
nally rotated (and often subluxed [dis-
located] also); this

windswept hip deformity

deformity pattern occurs in people with severe cerebral palsy and gives a misleading impression of leg-length discrepancy.

Wisconsin Card Sorting Test–Revised (WCST–R)   An individually administered neuropsychological test used to assess the ability of children and adults to form abstract concepts and to both shift and maintain the set. The subject is asked to categorize 64 or 128 cards as belonging to one of four stimulus card groupings; each card has one to four examples of one to four different shapes in one to four different colors (e.g., two red triangles or three blue squares). Perseveration errors are interpreted as indicative of dorsolateral frontal lobe damage and sometimes chronic alcoholism. Norms are available for ages 6-5–89.

WISC–R   *See* Wechsler Intelligence Scale for Children–Revised.

WISC–III   *See* Wechsler Intelligence Scale for Children–Third Edition.

withdrawal syndrome, neonatal   Infants of drug-addicted mothers (IDAMs) may exhibit the following acronymic "withdrawal" syndrome: wakefulness, irritability, tremulousness, tachypnea (rapid breathing), hyperactivity, high-pitched cry, hyperreflexia (increased reflexes), diaphoresis (sweating), diarrhea, respiratory distress, rhinorrhea (runny nose), apnea (temporary cessation of breathing), autonomic nervous system dysfunction (poor temperature control), weight loss, respiratory alkalosis (alteration of the body's acid–base balance due to a loss of acid from the rapid breathing), lacrimation (excess tears), and seizures.

WJ–R   *See* Woodcock-Johnson Psycho-Educational Battery–Revised.

Woodcock-Johnson Psycho-Educational Battery–Revised (WJ–R)   A wide-ranging set of individually administered tests designed to measure cognitive abilities, scholastic aptitude, and academic achievement in people 2–95 years of age. There are two forms for the achievement tests, and for both the achievement and cognitive tests there are standard and supplemental batteries. The cognitive tests are based on the Horn-Cattell theory, an extension of the fluid/crystallized model of intelligence. Seven broad cognitive factors are included: 1) long-term retrieval, 2) short-term memory, 3) processing speed, 4) auditory processing, 5) visual processing, 6) comprehension-knowledge, and 7) fluid reasoning. Each of the tests in this standard battery measures one of the cognitive factors. The supplemental battery consists of 14 subtests: The first 7 subtests correspond to the 7 cognitive factors in the standard battery; the other 7 subtests are used selectively to probe specific cognitive areas. The 21 WJ–R subtests may be combined in various ways to form several clusters: broad cognitive ability (extended), long-term retrieval, short-term memory, processing speed, auditory processing, visual processing, comprehension-knowledge, fluid reasoning, reading aptitude, mathematics aptitude, written-language aptitude, knowledge aptitude, oral language, and oral-language aptitude. All seven tests from the standard battery can be combined for a broad cognitive ability score. An early developmental scale can be used with children as young as 2 years of age. The nine subtests on the achievement standard battery can be combined to form clusters of broad reading, broad mathematics, broad written language, broad knowledge, and skills, with the latter two being applicable to younger children. The five supplemental subtests, in combination with the standard battery, yield cluster scores for basic reading skills, reading comprehension, basic mathematics skills, mathematics reasoning, basic writing skills, and written expression. Six subtests from the standard achievement battery can be used with children as young as 2 years of age as measures of early development. Raw scores may be converted to percentile ranks, standard scores (with a mean of 100 and a standard deviation of 15), and relative mastery index (the percentage of material the examinee has mastered, of which members of a reference group have mastered 90%). Norms may be based on either age or grade. If both achievement and cognitive batteries are administered, it is possible to calculate aptitude/ achievement discrepancies in the areas of oral language, reading, mathematics, written language, and knowledge, which are expressed by both percentile ranks and the standard deviation differences. There are also procedures to determine intraachievement and intracognitive discrepancies that provide a profile of relative strengths and weaknesses. Scoring is tedious.

Woodcock Language Proficiency Battery
This battery measures language in three areas: oral language (picture vocabulary, antonyms and synonyms, analogies), reading (letter–word identification, word attack, passage comprehension), and written language (dictation, proofing,

punctuation and capitalization, spelling, usage). There are English and Spanish forms of the test.

Woodcock Reading Mastery Test–Revised (WRMT–R) A test of reading ability that is used for children from kindergarten to college seniors and adults to 75 years of age. The organization of the WRMT–R is hierarchical and includes five levels: total reading, clusters (readiness, basic skills, reading comprehension), tests, subtests (and vocabulary), and item error. Across the first three levels, a full array of norm-referenced scores can be obtained (grade and age equivalents, percentile ranks, standard scores with a mean of 100 and a standard deviation of 15, normal curve equivalents with a mean of 50 and a standard deviation of 21.06, T scores with a mean of 50 and a standard deviation of 10, stanines with a mean of 5 and a standard deviation of 2, relative performance index, and instructional range) for as many as 10 dimensions. Readiness is assessed by reading passages made up of newly learned rebus symbol–word associations and by naming upper- and lower-case letters in a variety of type styles. Reading is assessed by reading written words on sight; applying phonic and structural analysis skills to pronounce unfamiliar words; reading a stem aloud and orally providing an antonym or synonym or completing an analogy; and by providing a key word missing from a silently read passage. Scoring is tedious, but a computer scoring program is available. Care should be taken when interpreting basic skills and comprehension scores in kindergarteners who are at or below average for the group as a whole, since a raw score of zero can result in an above-average percentile score.

Wooster-Drought syndrome *See* pseudobulbar palsy.

word association test A projective technique in which the individual is presented with a list of words one at a time and asked to respond with the first word or idea that comes to mind. The examiner is most interested in the length of time required to respond and the degree of uniqueness or peculiarity of the associations the subject makes. When used as part of an assessment for developmental disabilities, the examiner must be sensitive to the effects of language impairments, processing problems, attention deficits, and other neurological impairments on the individual's response style and the quality of the answers produced.

word attack Techniques that enable a child to decode an unknown word to pronounce it and to understand it in context. These techniques include phonic analysis (phonics), structural analysis, contextual clues, and dictionary skills.

word blindness, congenital Antiquated term originally coined by Adolf Kussmaul (1822–1902) in 1877 to describe a case of acquired dyslexia. The term was adopted and used by J. Hinshelwood in his classic 1917 monograph by that title.

Word Test A norm-referenced test of semantic (meaning systems) knowledge for children ages 7–11 years with six subtests: associations, synonyms, antonyms, definitions, semantic absurdities, and multiple definitions.

Word Test–Adolescent A norm-referenced test of semantic (meaning systems) knowledge for children ages 12–17 years of age that uses four tasks: brand names, synonyms, signs of the times, and definitions.

working memory *See* short-term memory.

WPPSI–R *See* Wechsler Preschool and Primary Scale of Intelligence–Revised.

WRAML *See* Wide Range Assessment of Memory and Learning.

WRAT–3 *See* Wide Range Achievement Test–Third Edition.

WRMT–R *See* Woodcock Reading Mastery Test–Revised.

wryneck *See* torticollis.

WURS *See* Wender Utah Rating Scale.

WVAST *See* Washer Visual Acuity Screening Technique.

X

xeroderma pigmentosum A genetic syndrome with extreme sensitivity to sunlight leading to progressive disfigurement and skin cancer. There are eight subgroups, some of which exhibit progressive neurological deterioration, both motor and cognitive. Inheritance is autosomal recessive with an incidence of 1 in 100,000. *See also* de Sanctis-Cacchione syndrome.

X-linkage Sex-linkage; characteristics, traits, or disorders carried on genes on the X chromosome. Males are more often affected, as they have only one X chromosome. These traits are never transmitted from father to son.

X-linked hydrocephalus syndrome A genetic syndrome with hydrocephalus (excess fluid in the brain), short flexed (cortical) thumbs, spasticity (usually diplegia [paralysis on both sides of the body]), and mental retardation. Inheritance is X-linked recessive. Ultrasound may be used to attempt prenatal diagnosis in families considered at risk.

XLMR X-linked mental retardation.

XO syndrome *See* Turner syndrome.

XYY syndrome Additional Y chromosomes contribute to tall stature and mild mental retardation. Severe acne, psychosexual problems, and aberrant behavior are also reported. Originally this syndrome was thought to be associated with a genetic predisposition to criminal behavior, but later studies showed that subjects were not more aggressive or criminally inclined but simply more liable to get caught and go to prison (where the genetic studies were being performed) than more intelligent criminals. Incidence is 1 in 840 with a recurrence risk of 1%.

Y

Yale Children's Inventory (YCI) A 63-item parent questionnaire that assesses attention, behavior, and cognitive problems in children. The YCI is part of the Yale Neuropsychological Assessment Scales (YNPAS), which also includes a Child's Personal Data Inventory (CPDI) and a Teacher's Behavior Rating Scale (TBRS).

YCI *See* Yale Children's Inventory.

yeast *See Candida albicans.*

Z

Z score A standard score with a mean of zero and a standard deviation of 1. If a test had a mean of 63 and a standard deviation of 9, a raw score of 72 would be equivalent to a Z score of 1. The Z score is the number of standard deviations a given value is from the test mean.

Zantac *See* ranitidine.

zebra A rare disease or condition. A term used in medicine to describe a diagnosis that is extremely rare. The aphorism "Uncommon presentations of common diseases are more common than common presentations of uncommon diseases" is an anti-zebra statement. It suggests that more time, effort, and energy should be expended pursuing statistically more probable conditions before pursuing more expensive explorations of possible zebras.

Zellweger syndrome Cerebrohepatorenal syndrome; a syndrome caused by the absence of a peroxisomal enzyme and manifested by atypical brain structures, hypotonia (decreased muscle tone), enlarged liver, large fontanels (soft spots), heart disease, and kidney cysts. Most babies with this syndrome are born breech and live only a few months. The hypotonia and atypical brain structures are associated with severe developmental delay. Inheritance is autosomal recessive. Decreased enzyme and increased fatty acid levels in amniotic fluid cells allow prenatal diagnosis.

zero reject The element of full inclusion that requires special education services for all students with disabilities to be provided in the general classroom.

Z-plasty A tendon-lengthening procedure that involves sectioning half of the tendon (e.g., tibialis posterior) lower down and the contralateral (opposite) half of the tendon higher up and then suturing the overlapped ends with the extremity (e.g., foot) in neutral.

zygomatic bone Zygoma; cheekbone.

Bibliography

Aase, J.M. (1990). *Diagnostic dysmorphology*. New York: Plenum Medical Book Company.

Accardo, P.J., Blondis, T.A., & Whitman, B.Y. (Eds.). (1991). *Attention deficit disorders and hyperactivity in children*. New York: Marcel Dekker.

American Psychiatric Association. (1987). *Diagnostic and statistical manual of mental disorders* (3rd ed.—Rev.) (DSM-III-R). Washington, DC: Author.

American Psychiatric Association. (1994). *Diagnostic and statistical manual of mental disorders* (4th ed.) (DSM-IV). Washington, DC: Author.

Barker, R. (1991). *Social work dictionary*. Silver Spring, MD: National Association of Social Workers Press.

Barness, L.A. (1981). *Manual of pediatric physical diagnosis*. Chicago: Yearbook Medical Publishers.

Batshaw, M.L., & Perret, Y.M. (1986). *Children with handicaps: A medical primer* (2nd ed.). Baltimore: Paul H. Brookes Publishing Co.

Batshaw, M.L., & Perrett, Y.M. (1992). *Children with disabilities: A medical primer* (3rd ed.). Baltimore: Paul H. Brookes Publishing Co.

Beighton, P., & Beighton, G. (1986). *The man behind the syndrome*. New York: Springer-Verlag.

Bergsma, D. (Ed.). (1979). *Birth defects compendium*. New York: Alan R. Liss.

Blauvelt, C.T., & Nelson, F.R. (1990). *A manual of orthopedic terminology*. Saint Louis: C.V. Mosby.

Bry, A. (1975). *A primer of behavioral psychology*. New York: New American Library.

Buros, O.K. (Ed.). (1965). *The sixth mental measurement yearbook*. Highland Park, NJ: Gryphon Press.

Buros, O.K. (Ed.). (1972). *The seventh mental measurement yearbook*. Highland Park, NJ: Gryphon Press.

Buros, O.K. (Ed.). (1978). *The eighth mental measurement yearbook*. Highland Park, NJ: Gryphon Press.

Bush, C.L., & Andrews, R.C. (1980). *Dictionary of reading and learning disability*. Los Angeles: Western Psychological Services.

Capute, A.J., & Accardo, P.J. (Eds.). (1991). *Developmental disabilities in infancy and childhood*. Baltimore: Paul H. Brookes Publishing Co.

Capute, A.J., & Accardo, P.J. (1996a). *Developmental disabilities in infancy and childhood* (2nd ed.). *Vol. I: Neurodevelopmental diagnosis and treatment*. Baltimore: Paul H. Brookes Publishing Co.

Capute, A.J., & Accardo, P.J. (1996b). *Developmental disabilities in infancy and childhood* (2nd ed.). *Vol. II: The spectrum of developmental disabilities*. Baltimore: Paul H. Brookes Publishing Co.

Capute, A.J., & Accardo, P.J. (in preparation). *The infant neurodevelopmental assessment: A clinical interpretative manual for the first two years of life*.

Carter, C.H. (1975). *Handbook of mental retardation syndromes*. Springfield, IL: Charles C Thomas.

Chaplin, J.P. (1968). *Dictionary of psychology*. New York: Dell.

Cooke, R.E. (Ed.). (1968). *The biological basis of pediatric practice*. New York: McGraw-Hill.

Dorland's illustrated medical dictionary. (1981). Philadelphia: W.B. Saunders.

Firkin, B.G., & Whitworth, J.A. (1987). *Dictionary of medical eponyms*. Park Ridge, NJ: Parthenon.

Frankenburg, W.K., & Camp, B.W. (Eds.). (1975). *Pediatric screening tests*. Springfield, IL: Charles C Thomas.

Fraser, B.A., Hensinger, R.N., & Phelps, J.A. (1990). *Physical management of multiple handicaps* (2nd ed.). Baltimore: Paul H. Brookes Publishing Co.

Fritsch, M.H., & Sommer, A. (1991). *Handbook of congenital and early onset hearing loss*. New York: IGAKU-SHOIN.

Gellis, S.A., Feingold, M., & Rutman, J.V. (1968). *Atlas of mental retardation syndromes: Visual diagnosis of facies and physical findings*. Washington, DC: U.S. Government Printing Office.

Goldenson, R.M. (Ed.). (1970). *The encyclopedia of human behavior: Psychology, psychiatry and mental health* (Vols. I–II). New York: Doubleday.

Goldenson, R.M. (Ed.). (1978). *Disability and rehabilitation handbook*. New York: McGraw-Hill.

Gorlin, R.J., Cohen, M.M., & Levin, L.S. (1990). *Syndromes of the head and neck* (Oxford monographs on medical genetics No. 19). New York: Oxford University Press.

Grossman, H.J. (Ed.). (1983). *Classification in mental retardation*. Washington, DC: American Association on Mental Deficiency.

Gurman, A.S., & Kniskern, D.P. (Eds.). (1981). *Handbook of family therapy*. New York: Brunner/Mazel.

Hall, J.G., Froster-Iskenius, U.G., & Allanson, J.E. (1989). *Handbook of normal physical measurements*. Oxford, England: Oxford University Press.

Harrel, R., & Lamb, R. (Eds.). (1986). *The dictionary of ethology and animal learning*. Cambridge, MA: MIT Press.

Harrel, R., & Lamb, R. (Eds.). (1988). *The encyclopedic dictionary of psychology*. Cambridge, MA: MIT Press.

Hopkins, H.L., & Smith, H.D. (Eds.). (1988). *Willard and Spackman's occupational therapy*. Philadelphia: W.B. Saunders.

Jones, K.L. (1988). *Smith's recognizable patterns of human malformation*. Philadelphia: W.B. Saunders.

Jung, J.H. (1989). *Genetic syndromes in communication disorders*. Boston: College-Hill.

Kaplan, H.T., & Sadock, B.J. (1991). *Comprehensive glossary of psychiatry and psychology*. Baltimore: Williams & Wilkins.

King, R.C., & Stansfield, W.D. (1990). *A dictionary of genetics*. New York: Oxford University Press.

Konigsmark, B.W., & Gorlin, R.J. (1976). *Genetic and metabolic deafness*. Philadelphia: W.B. Saunders.

Kuper, A., & Kuper, J. (Eds.). (1985). *The social science encyclopedia*. London: Routledge and Kegan Paul.

Landau, S.I. (Ed.). (1986). *International dictionary of medicine and biology* (Vols. I–II). New York: John Wiley & Sons.

Luckasson, R., Coulter, D.L., Polloway, E.A., Reiss, S., Schalock, R.L., Snell, M.E., Spitalnik, D.M., & Stark, J.A. (1992). *Mental retardation: Definition, classification, and system supports* (9th ed.). Washington, DC: American Association on Mental Retardation.

McKusick, V.A. (1988). *Mendelian inheritance in man: Catalogs of autosomal dominant, autosomal recessive, and sex-*

linked phenotypes (8th ed.). Baltimore: The Johns Hopkins University Press.

Menkes, J.H. (1990). *Textbook of child neurology.* Philadelphia: Lea & Febiger.

Merin, S. (1984). *Inherited eye diseases.* New York: Marcel Dekker.

Mervyn, L. (1984). *The dictionary of vitamins.* New York: Thorsons.

Miller, B.F., & Keane, C.B. (1987). *Encyclopedia and dictionary of medicine, nursing, and allied health.* Philadelphia: W.B. Saunders.

Millington, T.A., & Millington, W. (1971). *Dictionary of mathematics.* New York: Barnes & Noble.

Moore, B.E., & Fine, B.D. (Eds.). (1968). *A glossary of psychoanalytic terms and concepts.* New York: American Psychoanalytic Association.

Mussen, P.H. (Ed). (1983). *Handbook of child psychology* (Vols. I–IV). New York: John Wiley & Sons.

Nelson, L.B., Brown, G.C., & Arentsen, J.J. (1985). *Recognizing patterns of ocular childhood disease.* Thorofare, NJ: Charles B. Slack.

Nicolosi, L., Harryman, E., & Kresheck, J. (1989). *Terminology of communication disorders: Speech-language-hearing* (3rd ed.). Baltimore: Williams & Wilkins.

Noshpitz, J.D. (Ed.). (1979–1987). *Basic handbook of child psychiatry* (Vols. I–V). New York: Basic Books.

Oski, F.A., DeAngelis, C.D., Feigin, R.D., & Warshaw, J.B. (Eds.). (1989). *Principles and practice of pediatrics.* Philadelphia: J.B. Lippincott.

Pinney, E.L., Jr., & Slipp, S. (1982). *Glossary of group and family therapy.* New York: Brunner/Mazel.

Reynolds, C.R., & Mann, L. (Eds.). (1987). *Encyclopedia of special education* (Vols. I–III). New York: John Wiley & Sons.

Sapira, J.D. (1990). *The art and science of bedside diagnosis.* Baltimore: Urban & Schwarzenberg.

Smith, D.W. (1981). *Recognizable patterns of human deformation: Identification and management of mechanical effects on morphogenesis.* Philadelphia: W.B. Saunders.

Smith, S.D. (Ed.). (1986). *Genetics and learning disabilities.* San Diego: College-Hill.

Spreen, O., & Strauss, E. (1991). *Compendium of neuropsychological tests.* New York: Oxford University Press.

Stanaszek, M.J., Stanaszek, W.F., Carlstedt, B.C., & Strauss, S. (1991). *The inverted medical dictionary.* Lancaster, PA: TECHNOMIC.

Stedman's medical dictionary (25th ed.). (1990). Baltimore: Williams & Wilkins.

Subcommittee of the Committee on Public Information. (1975). *A psychiatric glossary.* Washington, DC: American Psychiatric Association.

Taybi, H., & Lachman, R.S. (1990). *Radiology of syndromes, metabolic disorders, and skeletal dysplasias.* Chicago: Yearbook Medical Publishers.

Tecklin, J.A. (1989). *Pediatric physical therapy.* Philadelphia: J.B. Lippincott.

The compact edition of the Oxford English Dictionary (Vols. I–III). (1971–1987). Oxford, England: Oxford University Press.

Tymchuk, A.J. (1980). *The mental retardation dictionary.* Los Angeles: Western Psychological Services.

Walker, B. (1978). *Encyclopedia of metaphysical medicine.* London: Routledge and Kegan Paul.

Wallach, J. (1983). *Interpretation of pediatric tests: A handbook synopsis of pediatric, fetal, and obstetrical laboratory medicine.* Boston: Little, Brown.

Warkany, J. (1971). *Congenital malfor-mations*. Chicago: Yearbook Medical Publishers.

Warkany, J., Lemire, R.J., & Cohen, M.M., Jr. (1981). *Mental retardation and con-genital malformations of the central nervous system*. Chicago: Yearbook Med-ical Publishers.

Wiedemann, H.R., Grosse, K.R., & Dib-bern, H. (1985). *Characteristic syn-dromes: A visual aid to diagnosis* (M.F. Passage, Trans.). Chicago: Yearbook Medical Publishers.

Wolman, B.B. (1978). *Dictionary of behav-ioral sciences*. New York: Vannostrand Reinhold.

Wolman, B.B. (Ed.). (1982). *Handbook of developmental psychology*. Englewood Cliffs, NJ: Prentice Hall.